BEHAVIORAL ECOLOGY *and the* TRANSITION *to* AGRICULTURE

ORIGINS OF HUMAN BEHAVIOR AND CULTURE

Edited by Monique Borgerhoff Mulder and Joe Henrich

BEHAVIORAL ECOLOGY *and the* TRANSITION *to* AGRICULTURE

Edited by Douglas J. Kennett and Bruce Winterhalder

UNIVERSITY OF CALIFORNIA PRESS
Berkeley   Los Angeles   London

University of California Press
Berkeley and Los Angeles, California

University of California Press, Ltd.
London, England

© 2006 by
The Regents of the University of California

Library of Congress Cataloging-in-Publication Data

Behavioral ecology and the transition to agriculture / edited by Douglas
J. Kennett, Bruce Winterhalder.
    p. cm.
  Includes bibliographical references and index.
  ISBN 0-520-24647-0 (cloth : alk. paper)
1. Agriculture—Origin. 2. Agriculture, Prehistoric. 3. Human behavior.
4. Human ecology. 5. Human evolution. I. Kennett, Douglas J.
II. Winterhalder, Bruce.
  GN799.A4B39 2006
  306.3′64—dc22

                            2005011959

Manufactured in Canada
15 14 13 12 11 10 09 08 07 06
10 9 8 7 6 5 4 3 2 1

The paper used in this publication meets the minimum requirements
of ANSI/NISO Z39.48-1992(R1997) (*Permanence of Paper*).

FOR OUR ACADEMIC AND SOCIAL FAMILIES

CONTENTS

CONTRIBUTORS

MARK ALDENDERFER
Department of Anthropology
The University of Arizona
Tucson

ATHOLL ANDERSON
Research School of Pacific and Asian Studies
Division of Archaeology and Natural History
The Australian National University
Canberra, Australia

K. RENEE BARLOW
Utah Museum of Natural History
University of Utah
Salt Lake City

HUW BARTON
School of Archaeology and Ancient History
University of Leicester,
England

C. MICHAEL BARTON
Department of Anthropology
Arizona State University
Tempe

ROBERT L. BETTINGER
Department of Anthropology
University of California
Davis

TIM DENHAM
School of Geography and Environmental Science
Monash University
Victoria, Australia

MICHAEL W. DIEHL
Desert Archaeology, Inc.
Tucson

KRISTEN J. GREMILLION
Department of Anthropology
The Ohio State University
Columbus

MICHAEL JOCHIM
Department of Anthropology
University of California
Santa Barbara

WILLIAM F. KEEGAN
Florida Museum of Natural History
University of Florida
Gainesville

DOUGLAS J. KENNETT
Department of Anthropology
University of Oregon
Eugene

DEAN MARTORANA
Environmental Science Associates
San Francisco

SARAH B. McCLURE
Department of Anthropology
University of Oregon
Eugene

JOY McCORRISTON
Department of Anthropology
The Ohio State University
Columbus

DOLORES R. PIPERNO
Smithsonian Tropical Research Institute,
    Panama
and Department of Anthropology
National Museum of Natural History
Washington, DC

BRUCE D. SMITH
Archaeobiology Program
National Museum of Natural History
Washington, DC

BRAM TUCKER
Department of Anthropology
University of Georgia
Athens

BARBARA VOORHIES
Department of Anthropology
University of California
Santa Barbara

JENNIFER A. WATERS
Desert Archaeology, Inc.
Tucson

BRUCE WINTERHALDER
Department of Anthropology
University of California
Davis

FOREWORD

William F. Keegan

The evolution of human subsistence economies has always been a major topic of anthropological interest. Within this domain the transition from foraging to farming and the emergence of horti-cultural/agricultural economies has occupied a central place. One of the most intriguing issues concerns the relative simultaneity with which different crops were first cultivated around the world; a situation that produced the view that the adoption of agriculture was a revolution. So significant was this "Neolithic Revolution" that it came to embody the foundations of civilization.

On closer examination, it has become clear that this revolution did not happen quickly, and that centuries passed before the transition from foraging to farming was complete. Research in the Midwestern United States illustrates this point. In many parts of the world the original domesticates eventually became staples (e.g., wheat, rice, maize, potatoes), but in the American heartland the first plants cultivated were so inauspicious that scholars had a hard time believing that they really were cultigens. Moreover, after other crop plants were imported from outside the region (e.g., maize), the initial set was relegated to secondary status and never became true staples.

The lesson from the Midwestern United States is important, and I share Tom Riley's sentiments regarding the adoption of cultigens. Riley understood that cultigens were added gradually to the diet and that the initial system of cultivation is better termed horticulture and not agriculture: "the connotation of horticulture is one that puts emphasis on the plant (Latin *hortus*), while that of agriculture is on the land (Latin *ager*)" (Riley 1987, 297). This may appear to be simply a semantic difference. However, in the same way that foraging theory tends to focus on the capture of individual food items, the initial view of farming will do well to focus on the capture of individual plants. From this perspective *farming* is *gathering* in a human-managed context.

Years ago I was inspired by Winterhalder and Smith (1981), and recognized that human behavioral ecology (HBE) provided an elegant set of formal models that could be used to examine subsistence behavior in horticultural societies (Keegan 1986). The models provided new and useful perspectives. Moreover, because the models can be used to study foragers and horticulturalists, they provide an important framework for evaluating the transition between them.

HBE focuses on decision making. It attempts to define the coordinates between humans and their subsistence resources as these coevolved through time. The main issue is not what people ate, but how and why they chose to exploit particular resources. In this regard the goal of HBE is to demonstrate how subsistence needs (practical reason) were expressed in social and cultural contexts. The papers in the book use this perspective to break important new ground that promises to redirect our efforts and explanatory potential in addressing the transition from foraging to farming.

PREFACE

For twenty-five years human behavioral ecology (HBE) has provided a general conceptual framework for the analysis and interpretation of hunter-gatherer subsistence behavior in living and prehistoric societies. Similar micro-economic models have received preliminary application in the study of pastoral and agroecological adaptations. This volume is the first collection to consistently apply this framework to one of the most fundamental economic shifts in human history—the evolutionary transition from foraging to farming through processes of plant and animal domestication and the emergence of agriculture. The chapter authors use a variety of geographically dispersed case studies and analytical approaches, including subsistence choice optimization, central place foraging, discounting, risk minimization, and costly signaling theory. Their contributions are novel in presenting regionally comprehensive case studies that address the transition to agriculture from a consistent conceptual framework informed by neo-Darwinian theory.

The volume is presented as fourteen chapters, organized by their setting in the New and Old Worlds, respectively. Following an introductory chapter by Winterhalder and Kennett, Tucker presents an ethnographic analysis of Mikea foraging and farming. The rest of the papers are archaeological and cover cases located in: Eastern Kentucky (Gremillion), southeastern Arizona (Diehl and Waters), the Fremont (Barlow), the Pacific coast of southern Mexico (Kennett, Voorhies, and Martorana), the neotropics (Piperno), the Andean Highlands (Aldenderfer), Valencia, Spain (McClure, Jochim, and Barton), Southern Arabia (McCorriston), New Guinea (Denham and Barton), and Oceania (Kennett, Anderson, Winterhalder). The last two chapters, by Smith and Bettinger, contain general commentaries on the application of HBE to the question of agricultural origins. In keeping with the exploratory nature of the volume, these chapters are eclectic in structure, part essay and part commentary, mixing discussion of relevant problems, approaches or applications not covered in the papers themselves, with the occasional dose of speculation. All of the papers of the volume are directed toward explaining the origin, spread and persistence of domesticates and food production, evolutionary gifts from our foraging ancestors.

We wish to thank the contributors to this volume for their perseverance through several editorial rounds. Blake Edgar, Scott Norton, Joanne Bowser, and the staff at the University of California Press have produced this book efficiently and effectively. The production of this volume also benefited greatly from the substantial and time-consuming copy editing by Sheryl Gerety—thank you.

DOUGLAS KENNETT
AND BRUCE WINTERHALDER

June 12, 2005

Behavioral Ecology and the Transition from Hunting and Gathering to Agriculture

Bruce Winterhalder and Douglas J. Kennett

THE VOLUME BEFORE YOU is the first systematic, comparative attempt to use the concepts and models of behavioral ecology to address the evolutionary transition from societies relying predominantly on hunting and gathering to those dependent on food production through plant cultivation, animal husbandry, and the use of domesticated species embedded in systems of agriculture. Human behavioral ecology (HBE; Winterhalder and Smith 2000) is not new to prehistoric analysis; there is a two-decade tradition of applying models and concepts from HBE to research on prehistoric hunter-gatherer societies (Bird and O'Connell 2003). Behavioral ecology models also have been applied in the study of adaptation among agricultural (Goland 1993b; Keegan 1986) and pastoral (Mace 1993a) populations. We review below a small literature on the use of these models to think generally about the transition from foraging to farming, while the papers collected here expand on these efforts by taking up the theory in the context of ethnographic or archaeological case studies from eleven sites around the globe.

THE SIGNIFICANCE OF THE TRANSITION

There are older transformations of comparable magnitude in hominid history; bipedalism, encephalization, early stone tool manufacture, and the origins of language come to mind (see Klein 1999). The evolution of food production is on a par with these, and somewhat more accessible because it occurred in near prehistory, the last eight thousand to thirteen thousand years; agriculture also is inescapable for its immense impact on the human and non-human worlds (Dincauze 2000; Redman 1999). Most problems of population and environmental degradation are rooted in agricultural origins. The future of humankind depends on making the agricultural "revolution" sustainable by preserving cultigen diversity and mitigating the environmental impacts of farming. Simple population densities tell much of the story. Hunter-gatherers live at roughly $0.1/km^2$; rice agriculturists in Java at $1,000/km^2$, a ten-thousand-fold difference. There were an estimated ten million humans in the world on the eve of food production (Price and Feinman 2001: 194); now over six billion people live on this planet, an increase of 600% in only ten millennia. Agriculture is the precursor, arguably the *necessary* precursor, for the development of widespread social stratification, state-level societies, market economies, and industrial production (Diamond 1997; Zeder 1991). Social theory (e.g., Trigger 1998) maintains that present-day notions of property, equality and inequality, human relationships to nature, etc., are shaped, at least in part, by the social organization, technology, or food surpluses entailed in our dependence on agriculture.

Domestication today is a self-conscious enterprise of advanced science and global-scale effort, an applied research endeavor comprised of thousands of highly trained and well-supported international specialists. Major research centers like the International Potato Center in Lima, Peru (www.cipotato.org/) support ongoing efforts to further the domestication of useful species; seed banks have been established in many countries to insure the future diversity of the world's key domesticated plants (www.nal.usda.gov/pgdic/germplasm/germplasm.html). The prehistoric beginnings of agriculture though were quite different. The modern world that funds and depends on this continuing process of domestication is, in fact, a creation of the first early humans that pursued, consumed and, in doing so, modified the wild ancestors of the staples that we consider to be important today—wheat, millet, sweet potato, rice, and domesticated animals such as camelids, pigs, sheep, goats, and cows—to name a few. At present it appears as if at least six independent regions of the world were the primary loci of domestication and emergent agriculture: the Near East; sub-Saharan Africa; China/Southeast Asia; Eastern North America; Mesoamerica; and South America (Smith 1998), roughly in the time period from thirteen thousand to eight thousand years ago (Binford 1971; Diamond 2002; Flannery 1973; Henry 1989). The archaeological record suggests that this transformation took place in societies that look much like modern day hunter-gatherers (Kelly 1995; Lee and Daly 1999). Many of the early domesticates

were transmitted broadly through preexisting exchange networks (Hastorf 1999), stimulating the migration of agriculturalists into the territories of hunter-gatherers, who were in turn ultimately replaced or subsumed into agricultural economies (Cavalli-Sforza 1996; Diamond and Bellwood 2003).

Foraging peoples initiated domestication. They did so through the mundane and necessary daily tasks of locating, harvesting, processing, and consuming foodstuffs. The Mass from the 1928 Book of Common Prayer (Protestant Episcopal Church 1945, 81) speaks eloquently of "these thy gifts and creatures of bread and wine..." In less poetic non-ecclesiastical terms, but with no less awe at the high importance and, well, the simple gastronomic pleasure of domesticates in our lives, this volume attempts to advance our understanding of why and how this happened. In particular, we hope to demonstrate the utility of a branch of evolutionary ecology, human behavioral ecology.

DEFINITIONS

Clear, standardized terms for the biological and cultural processes involved in the origins of agriculture worldwide remain elusive, despite considerable efforts to define them (Flannery 1973; Ford 1985; Harris 1989; Harris 1996a and b; Higgs 1972; Piperno and Pearsall 1998; Rindos 1984; Smith 1998; Smith 2001a; Zvelebil 1993; Zvelebil 1995; Zvelebil 1996). The reasons for inconsistencies in the treatment of terminology are several and tenacious because they are ultimately rooted in the nature of the problem itself. These include, but are not necessarily limited to the following: (1) research on domestication and agricultural origins is inherently a multidisciplinary activity, and as such, a wide-ranging set of specialists have worked on the problem, each emphasizing definitions that are somewhat parochial; (2) historical change in each research tradition of archaeology, botany, and genetics has resulted in a range of definitions that may have been suitable at the time they were conceived but now add to the confusion; (3) rapidly expanding empirical knowledge and the characterization of local developmental sequences results in specialized language that does not transfer well to other regions where similar transformations occurred; (4) agricultural origins are an inherently evolutionary qu[...] with mod[...] [dis]tinctions [...] unevenly [...] boundarie[...] ture have [...] human so[...] cial, and i[...] featured in [...].

[handwritten note: H-G: daily sustence of wild foods]

Like earlier attempts, our definitions reflect limitations of our knowledge and approach. *Hunting and gathering* entails obtaining daily sustenance through the collection or pursuit of wild foods; wild foods in turn being species whose reproduction and subsistence are not directly managed by humans. Data from around the world indicate that prior to approximately thirteen thousand years ago, all people known archaeologically relied upon hunting and gathering wild foods. Hunting and gathering populations expanded into a broad range of habitats during the Terminal Pleistocene and Early Holocene when foraging strategies diversified (Stiner 2001), in part due to the extinction of previously targeted, large-game species, but also because of the broad array of resource alternatives afforded by warmer Holocene climates (Richerson et al. 2001). Hunting and gathering societies have persisted in various parts of the world (Lee and Daly 1999), but starting after about 13,000 BP (before the present) most foragers evolved into or were subsumed or replaced by groups practicing mixed foraging and cultivation strategies and, ultimately, agriculture (Diamond and Bellwood 2003).

On the other end of a mixed spectrum of subsistence strategies is agriculture. We define *agriculture* as the near total reliance upon domesticated plants or animals; domesticates being varieties or species whose phenotype is a product of artificial selection by humans, and whose reproduction and subsistence are managed directly by people. For plants, such management almost always involves an investment in seed selection; clearing, systematic soil tillage, terracing to prepare fields, crop maintenance, weeding, fertilization, and other crop maintenance; and, development of infrastructure and facilities from irrigation canals to processing facilities and storage bins. Parallel efforts are entailed in animal husbandry. Even societies practicing the most intensive forms of agriculture may engage in incidental hunting and gathering of wild foods, depending upon their availability or desirability (e.g., deer, blackberries). Dense populations and centralized state-level societies like our own depend upon increasingly complex systems of agriculture (B[...]; Zeder 1991) inv[...] [t]exture, struc[...] [...] some-times result[...] [de]grada-tion[...] Stock[...] day (Stock[...]

Our [...]izes *domestic[...]tes are new[...] or species created f[...] wild species through incidental or active selection by humans (Smith 1998). Typically selection leads to biological characteristics that are advantageous to humans; larger seeds, thinner seed coats, greater docility, smaller size animals. Because humans intervene in the natural lifecycle of these plants and animals, many domesticates loose their ability to survive without human management. This outcome is not surprising since it is well known that foragers alter the landscape that they inhabit by burning, transferring plants and animals between habitats, and occasionally interjecting themselves into other species' lifecycles (Hastorf 1999; Smith 1998).

[handwritten note: confirms FFLH's def of domestic + leads to species dependency on humans for survival]

Some plant species were better suited to domestication than others due to their ability to do well in the artificial environments created by humans (Smith 1998). In some instances, the biological changes may have begun incidentally as a co-evolutionary by-product of human exploitation

(Rindos 1984). In other cases domestication may have occurred under conditions of repeated cultivation and harvest (Harlan 1992c; Harris 1989; Ford 1985; Piperno and Pearsall 1998). *Cultivation* is the tending of plants, wild or domesticated; *husbandry* is the parallel term for animal species. Use of the term cultivation specifically acknowledges the possibility that humans tended wild plants for significant time periods before we would classify them as domesticates based on observable genetic alterations (Keeley 1995; Piperno and Pearsall 1998). We reserve the term *cultigen* for domesticated plants under these same conditions.

A variety of stable subsistence economies, extant, historic, and prehistoric, draw upon elements of hunter-gatherer *and* agricultural modes of production. These are difficult to characterize ... strategies except as "mixed" ... what Smith ... *food production* ... on hunting ... es using ... animals. *Horticulture* ... nting of domesticated ... gardens or the use of swidden ... combined with routine hunting and gathering of wild foods for a significant part of the diet, would be considered a form of low-level food production. Contemporary casual farming by the Mikea hunter-gatherers of Madagascar would be an example of this practice (Tucker 2001; Chapter 2, this volume).

The boundary between low-level food production systems and agriculture is inherently fuzzy. We believe the term agriculture is merited when foraging recedes to an episodic, infrequent or recreational activity, regular provisioning using domesticates takes over daily subsistence, while agricultural work and animal husbandry come to dominate the activity schedules of adults. Although numeric boundaries are somewhat arbitrary and unsatisfactory, agriculture implies that approximately 75% of foodstuffs are acquired from domesticated sources. Although few contemporary societies engage in low-level food production, the archaeological record suggests that mixed foraging and cultivation/husbandry strategies were common and often stable, in the sense that they were practiced by people for thousands of years before they developed a full commitment and reliance upon agriculture (Smith 2001a).

RESEARCH TRADITIONS IN AGRICULTURAL ORIGINS

Speculation about the origins of food production is probably as old as the first encounter between peoples who recognized that they differed appreciably in their dependence upon domesticated plants or animals. Longstanding traditions in western thought have seen foragers as scarcely removed from animal nature, thus, as societies, simple and primitive, living without the many accoutrements and means of control over nature that we associate with agriculture and industrial culture (Darwin 1874, 643; Powell 1885). Agriculture as an advance was instantly understandable. Hobbes's famous sentiment that hunting and gathering was a life "solitary, poor, nasty, brutish, and short" (Hobbes 1952, 85) is widely cited, but his views were generally shared in the nineteenth century, for instance by the novelist Charles Dickens (Dickens 1853). We today dismiss this kind of progressive evolutionism as simple-minded ethnocentrism. Foragers may not be the "original affluent society" claimed by Sahlins (1972; Hawkes and O'Connell 1981), but most foraging societies elude the generalizations implied in each of Hobbes's five famous adjectives. We cannot so easily dismiss questioning just what distinguishes foragers from food producers and how humans evolve, in either direction, from one to the other of these subsistence forms or maintain a mixture of the two for long periods of time.

European scholarly tradition, informed by increasingly reliable ethnography and archaeology, has a long engagement with agricultural origins (see Gebauer and Price 1992b; Redding 1988; Smith 1998). We highlight three of the most popular forces employed by archaeologists to explain the origins of agriculture: demographic pressure, environmental change, and socioeconomic competition. Demographic pressure and environmental change are exogenous forces and socioeconomic competition is endogenous. None in and of itself satisfactorily explains the origins of agriculture; each was probably an important element of the process, whatever the strength of its causal role. One of the virtues of HBE is its ability to integrate multiple variables like these, with an emphasis on behavioral responses to changing socio-ecological conditions.

DEMOGRAPHIC PRESSURE

Population-resource imbalance caused by demographic pressure is one of several univariate explanations for the origins of agriculture (Cohen 1977). Using this model, Smith and Young (1972) examined the population of the southern Levant and argued that demographic stress explained why hunter-gatherers in different locations independently turned to agriculture at the end of the Pleistocene. The argument was based on the premise that the adoption of agriculture resulted in a net increase in workload and a decrease in food diversity and sufficiency, and therefore an overall reduction in the quality of life, a situation that any rationally minded hunter-gatherer would not enter into freely. Cohen argued that as hunter-gatherers exceeded environmental carrying capacity, food shortages pushed them to experiment with plants and animals and, ultimately, with agriculture. Hunter-gatherers over-filled salubrious habitats worldwide and were compelled to augment their subsistence with food production.

Critics of this position were quick to point out that the archaeological record does not support the idea that environments worldwide were saturated with hunter-gatherer populations on the eve of agricultural development (Bronson 1977; Reed 1977; Rindos 1984). Even localized populations in the primary centers of early domestication appear to be relatively small (Piperno and Pearsall 1998). Others have emphasized the difficulties of measuring population levels in the archaeological record or determining the overall population levels that could be sustained without significant amounts of environmental degradation and pressure for change (Glassow 1978). There have been attempts to better contextualize demographic change by melding it with ecological models, usually in relation to variations in climate (Bar-Yosef and Meadow 1995; Binford 1971; Flannery 1971; Flannery 1973; Hassan 1977; Henry 1989; Hesse 1982b). These models sometimes lack specificity about the form or degree of demographic pressure required to provoke subsistence change, and they seldom explain why hunter-gatherer populations grew more rapidly and stimulated domestication and agricultural development in certain parts of the world and not others (Keeley 1995).

One response to the early overemphasis on demography has been to heavily discount its importance in the process of domestication and agricultural development (Hayden 1990; Hayden 1995a). This is unfortunate because foragers clearly have dynamic relationships with their local environments, including their population dynamics and the distribution and availability of harvested plant and animal species (Smith 1995). Sometimes this results in decreased availability or resource depression; in other instances, it may result in increased resource abundance. The effects that hunter-gatherers have on the density, distribution, and productivity of resources is well documented in California (e.g., Kumayeey; Shipek 1989) and Australia (Gidjingali; Jones and Meehan 1989). Environmental change independent of humans is ubiquitous and can also affect the distribution and availability of important species. Economic decisions by prehistoric foragers to experiment with and ultimately manage certain species of plants and animals occurred within this dynamic context of demographic change and varying plant and animal densities.

ENVIRONMENTAL CHANGE

V. Gordon Childe was one of the first, and certainly the most notable, archaeologists to explicitly hypothesize that changes in climate at the end of the Pleistocene stimulated the transition to agriculture (e.g., his Oasis or Propinquity Theory; Childe 1928; Ch... according to Childe, agricul... ...ence the term N... ...as syn- ch... ...s that clin... ...Near East... ...ive, huma... ...en- trated ... ...ns like oases an... ...eir close inter- actions na... ...domestication and ulti- mately agr...ture. The discovery of sickle blades and grinding stones in the Carmel Caves of coastal Palestine suggested that hunter-gatherers collected wild cereals during the Natufian Period (13,000 BP–10,000 BP), evidence used by Childe in support of this idea (Henry 1989, 6). Although propinquity is overly simplistic (Redding 1988), subsequent paleoenvironmental and archaeological work suggests that regionally specific climatic and biotic changes did occur at the end of the Pleistocene. These surely played a role in shaping spatially local cultural developments, including the domestication of plants and animals and ultimately the adoption of agricultural practices (Henry 1989; Wright, Jr. 1968; Wright, Jr. 1993).

Unfortunately, the overly deterministic nature of the Oasis Theory also provoked a backlash in the broader archaeological community against the importance of changing environmental conditions during the Late Pleistocene and Early Holocene (e.g., Braidwood and Howe 1960; Wagner 1977). For many years the role of climate change was simply ignored or deemphasized relative to other mechanisms perceived to have greater explanatory value. With several noteworthy exceptions (Harris 1996a; McCorriston and Hole 1991; Piperno and Pearsall 1998; Watson 1995; Wright, Jr. 1993), this continues today, even with the development of sophisticated paleoenvironmental techniques (e.g., Piperno 1998) and the aggressive advance of earth system science and high resolution climate records (Hodell et al. 1995;

Hostetler and Mix 1999; Kennett and Kennett 2000; Rittenour et al. 2000; Whitlock 1992; Woodhouse and Overpeck 1998).

These records show that the domestication of key cultigens in the Old and New Worlds occurred during an interval marked by significant fluctuations in global climate (13,000–8,000 BP; Richerson et al. 2001; Piperno and Pearsall 1998). Environmental change at the end of the Pleistocene was most pronounced at higher latitudes as ambient air temperature increased, glaciers receded, sea-levels rose, and forests replaced periglacial tundra (Roberts 1998). Dramatic fluctuations in high latitude environmental conditions parallel substantial changes in temperature and rainfall regimes at lower latitudes (Henry 1989). These changes instigated regional biotic shifts in resource abundance and density. Some regions witnessed the extinction of several large animals, a likely product of environmental change and intensified human predation at the end of the Pleistocene (Lister and Sher 1995; Piperno and Pearsall 1998; cf. Grayson and Meltzer 2003). Others experienced the expansion of wild plant species that were intensively harvested by foragers and, through selective manipulation, became important cultigens (e.g., barley and emmer wheat; Henry 1989, 32). It is under these dynamically changing environmental conditions that foragers altered their subsistence regimes and made dietary choices that led to plant and animal domestication, low-level food production, and ultimately agriculture.

SOCIOECONOMIC COMPETITION

Endogenous social change, particularly the development of prestige economies via socioeconomic competition, has recently become a popular explanation for the transition to agriculture (Bender 1978; Blake et al. 1992a; Hayden 1990; Hayden 1995a; Price 1995b; Smalley and Blake 2003). The mechanism for change in these models is status-seeking individuals, usually men, who encouraged and controlled the growth of potential domesticates to create surpluses for social purposes such as competitive feasting, alliance formation, and extortion, rather than as primary sources of food. Hayden (1995a, 289) has been the most outspoken advocate of this idea as a general explanation for the transition to agriculture worldwide—from the earliest plant and animal domestication through the development of more intensive forms of food production.

Hayden's model is based on five testable hypotheses (Hayden 1990; see Keeley 1995: 244): (1) domestication and agriculture will emerge in resource-rich, not resource-poor, zones; (2) it will first develop in ranked societies that have marked status inequalities; (3) individuals within these societies will hold competitive feasts; (4) the first plants and animals domesticated will be intoxicants, delicacies, or prestige goods rather than bulk or mundane food items; and (5) evidence for resource stress and malnutrition caused by population pressure or climate change will be absent. In archaeological terms Hayden's scenario implies correlation between plant and animal domestication and agricultural development, and the emergence of socioeconomic complexity, marked archaeologically by a high degree of sedentism (typically large sites with substantial architecture), at least two-tiered settlement hierarchies, intensified production agriculturally or otherwise, storage, specialized production of prestige items or status markers, intensified exchange, acquisition of exotic items by elites, and differential distribution of prestige items in households and burials.

There are several fundamental flaws with the socioeconomic competition model; there are also some intriguing and potentially important insights. As a stand-alone model for agricultural origins, socioeconomic competition fails on two levels. First, it lacks a unifying explanation for why agriculture developed in several independent regions at approximately the same time—other than suggesting it was a historical accident (Piperno and Pearsall 1998, 14). Second, although there is evidence that agriculture often developed in resource-rich habitats (Price and Gebauer 1995b, 8), the initial domestication of most plants and animals occurs well

before conditions promoted socioeconomic competition, at least in Asia, Africa, and the Americas (Piperno and Pearsall 1998, 14; Smith 1998, 209). It appears that many domesticates in Mesoamerica, the Near East, and eastern North America were used by hunter-gatherers at a low level for thousands of years prior to their intensified use (Smith 2001a, 19). This hints that socioeconomic competition is more likely to be significant in the later stages of the transition.

The social significance of food is patent. That some plant species might initially have been grown to brew beer is intriguing; the social aspects of drinking intoxicating liquids are difficult to refute (Blake et al. 1992a; Hayden 1990; Smalley and Blake 2003). However, plants used to brew intoxicating liquids can also serve as valuable food items whether they are fermented or not. This means that multiple currencies must be considered when resource value is assessed by archaeologists. The ability to store surplus food must also be analyzed for its social significance. Individuals who successfully grow, store, and defend food items can use these stores to their social advantage, gaining prestige and influence. Use of surplus food to improve social advantage, at least under certain enviro_____ ____ _____ ____ions, should __ ____ ____ ____ ____ ____ying HBE m____

horticulture as informer

HBE RE_____ __ _____
ORIGIN

There is ____ ____ HBE _____ __ _____ral origins. Keegan (1986, 92) made an early and prescient argument that foraging models could be extended to the study of horticultural production. He highlighted horticulture because it represents a mixed subsistence system, transitional between the economies of hunter-gatherers and agriculturalists. Using data from the Machiguenga of Peru, Keegan argued that the key variables of the diet breadth and patch-use models have direct analogs in food production, facilitating the use of these cost-benefit models in analysis of this system and the evolutionary transitions that gave rise to it. His calculations showed that the Machiguenga generally were stocking their gardens with optimal combinations of cultigens and, with allowance for seasonal and nutritional constraints, making efficient trade-offs among fishing, forest hunting, and gardening.

In a 1991 paper, Layton et al. (1991) described a "complete break" from the standard, evolutionary progression theories of agricultural origins. They proposed instead an approach that sees hunting, gathering, herding, and cultivation as alternative strategies of subsistence that may be taken up alone or in various, stable combinations, depending on socio-ecological circumstances, and without any implication of irreversible directionality to transitions among them. For instance, there is nothing to prevent food producers from evolving into foragers. Various conceptual elements from foraging theory, such as the ranking of resources by pursuit and handling costs, cost-benefit analysis of subsistence trade-offs, boundary defense, and risk minimization are found throughout their argument. In support of their interpretation they summarized numerous ethnographic cases in which these strategies are mixed in shifting and sometimes stable balances, reminiscent of Smith's (2001a) concept of low-level food production.

Layton et al. stimulated two follow-up papers, both of them making more explicit use of foraging theory to critique or amend specific predictions from their article. Hawkes and O'-Connell (1992; cf. Layton and Foley 1992) used a sharper distinction between search, and pursuit, and handling times—the central conceptual distinction of the diet breadth model—to argue that high-ranking resources will *not* drop out of a forager's diet in response to exploitation and depletion. However rare, they will always be pursued when encountered. Hawkes et al. expand discussion of the circumstances likely to promote subsistence innovation, and argue that "increases in diet breadth result from reduced foraging return rates and so lead to *declines* in population growth rates" (Hawkes and O'Connell 1992, 64). They also draw attention to HBE arguments for a gendered division of labor (Hawkes 1991) that might have been important in the evolutionary processes underlying subsistence transitions.

In a second follow-up paper, Winterhalder and Goland (1993) addressed the population growth prediction by Hawkes and O'Connell, cited just above. They used a dynamic, population ecology variant of the diet breadth model to show that declining foraging efficiency associated with expanding diet breadth may result in a decrease *or* an increase in forager population density. The deciding factors are the density and reproductive potential—together, the sustainable yield—of the low-ranking resources that happen to come into the diet.

Subsequently, Winterhalder and Goland (1997) expanded on these arguments for using a HBE form of analysis in agricultural origins research. They cited three advantages that distinguish HBE from other research traditions: (1) it engages selectionist explanations (Smith and Winterhalder 1992b) that are more powerful than the more commonly used functionalist ones; (2) it has tools for non-normative analysis of unpredictable variation in environmental features and the risk-minimizing adaptive tactics they elicit; and (3) it focuses on localized and immediate resource decisions and their consequences for people "on the ground." HBE thus engages the behaviors most likely to be causal to evolutionary change: "The changes we summarize under broad concepts such as *domestication* and the *Neolithic revolution* have their origin and form in the ecologically situated choices and actions of individuals" (Winterhalder and Goland 1997, 126; italic in original). Winterhalder and Goland used the diet breadth model to show how foragers might initially come to exploit the organisms that became domesticates, and to speculate on the adaptive consequences of this co-evolutionary engagement. Among the effects examined were the consequences for resource depletion, human population density, and risk management tactics, using evidence from eastern North America to exemplify their arguments.

Working on the prehistoric development of agriculture in eastern North America, Gremillion (1996a) used diet-breadth and risk-minimization models along with opportunity-cost arguments to generate and evaluate predictions about the circumstances in which new cultigens will be adopted by groups already practicing some agriculture, and whether they will replace existing plant resources, as did maize following a significant delay from its first appearance, or become a supplement, as in the case of peaches. In a second study, Gremillion (1998) analyzed macrobotanical data from the Cold Oak rock shelter in eastern Kentucky to show that increased dependence on cultivation of seed crops around 1000 BC was accompanied by greater anthropogenic disturbance of habitats and a shift in mast resources from acorns to hickory nuts. She developed several HBE hypotheses to address this situation, finding greatest credence for the idea that an increase in the overall abundance of mast resources led to specialization on the most profitable species, in this instance hickory, at the expense of the less highly ranked oak. Alternatively, increases in the ranking of profitability of seed crops such as maygrass, chenopod, and knotweed may have displaced acorns from the diet due to their high processing costs. In each of these applications Gremillion argued that HBE is a fertile source of new and archaeologically testable hypotheses about the subsistence and economic changes associated with the origins of agriculture.

The most thorough existing application of HBE to the question of agricultural origins is Piperno and Peasall's (1998) monograph, *The Origins of Agriculture in the Lowland Neotropics*. Over half the crop plants domesticated in the Americas are thought to have wild progenitors native to neotropical lowland habitats. Among them are New World staples such as manioc, yams, achira, sweet potato, peanut, gourds, squashes, beans, and perhaps maize. These plants likely were first used by foragers, who cultivated, domesticated, and subsequently incorporated into specialized agricultural production systems, in seasonal, low elevation forested habitats of the neotropics.

Piperno and Pearsall focus their analysis on the climate and vegetation changes occurring at 11,000 to 10,000 radiocarbon years BP and their likely effects on Neotropical foragers. The first inhabitants of the neotropics encountered a salubrious, open-grassland foraging environment that persisted for only a short time. At around 10,500 BP, the transition to a wetter Holocene climate began to produce a seasonal, deciduous forest cover in the lowland tropics. Piperno and Pearsall hypothesize that due to this habitat shift, and perhaps also to human exploitation (1998, 181), the abundance of the high ranking, "open habitat," plant and animals species decreased, along with foraging efficiency. While the new seasonal forests remained relatively hospitable to mobile hunter-gatherers at low population density (1998, 71), the diets of early Holocene foragers expanded to encompass a broader array of dry-forest plants, species that previously had been ignored. For instance, comparative studies of the efficiency of harvesting tubers suggest they likely were outside of the optimal diet in the late Pleistocene (1998: 85), but moved into that diet as a low-ranked but critical resource once early Holocene habitats became more forested.

The low-ranking, newly important species found in seasonally dry forests were subject to human interest and manipulation, either intentional or inadvertent, routed into cultivation and eventually domesticated (1998; 27, 82). Because they were sparsely distributed over the landscape, hence relatively unattractive to human foragers, there arose an immediate advantage for those who manipulated through burning or harvested species from these habitats so as to increase their density and yield of useful energy or materials.

Piperno and Pearsall cite three rationales for using the diet breadth model in this analysis (1998, 236): (1) the archaeological evidence shows that early hunter-gatherer/horticultural residents of the neotropics had an expanding diet breadth followed by increasing subsistence commitment to low-ranked species; (2) the prehistoric changes of concern are evident enough that short-term precision in the use of the model isn't necessary (cf. Smith, this volume); and finally (3) evidence from ethnographic tests shows that this model and an energy currency are commonly successful in predicting the economic response of foragers to changing environmental circumstances. They conclude, "[b]ehavioral ecology seems to us to be the most appropriate way to explain the transition from human foraging to food production" (1998, 16).

Many of the dozen or so early HBE papers on domestication and agricultural origins are fairly general and conjectural. They ask, without too much attention to specific cases or the empirical record of prehistoric findings on this topic, how might the ideas of HBE be used to address the question of agricultural origins? By and large, their authors are ethnographers whose experience is with extant hunter-gatherer societies. And, they generally have been written by people who already placed themselves within the research tradition of HBE. By contrast, most of the papers in this volume are based on empirical case studies, and they are written largely by archaeologists. Most are authored by individuals for whom behavioral ecology is a new analytic tool.

We do not claim that the HBE research tradition is a complete replacement for the other approaches that we have identified and briefly described. We view it rather as a sometimes complementary and sometimes competing form of explanation. It is complementary in two respects: (1) HBE takes up issues rarely or never addressed in these approaches; search and pursuit trade-offs in the harvest of low-ranking resource species; risk-sensitive adaptive tactics; and, (2) it frames these issues in quite a different manner than other, sometimes older, anthropological and archaeological research traditions by focusing on the costs and benefits associated with individual-level subsistence decisions in localized ecological settings. This framing difference is determined largely by the analytical

effort of modeling and hypothesis testing within an explicitly selectionist, neo-Darwinian theoretical framework (Smith and Winterhalder 1992b; Winterhalder and Smith 1992). In both respects, HBE provides tools that complement or make other traditions more complete. At the very least, HBE provides a theoretically well-grounded set of tools to begin exploring the transition to agriculture in a variety of environmental and social contexts.

For instance, although Hayden (Hayden 1990; Hayden 2001) presents his competitive feasting model as a sufficient social explanation for the origins of agriculture, in effect as an alternative to models drawing on materialist or ecological explanations, we would prefer a more cooperative form of analytic engagement. We might assume that social stratification and competitive feasting increase the demand for resources and then ask how this source of ecological change would be represented in terms of foraging models—those extant, adapted, or developed specifically for this purpose—and with what consequences for predictions about subsistence choices and the co-evolution of humans and their resources. Taking this a step further, HBE might help us to identify the socio-ecological circumstances and evolutionary processes that combine to generate a competitive social hierarchy like that expressed in feasting (Boone 1992). A signal strength of HBE is its ability to carry into hypothesis generation a wide variety of postulated sources of causation—global climate change to the aggrandizement of dominant individuals.

Nonetheless, to the extent that HBE is successful in addressing the question of agricultural origins, it will raise doubts about or contradict elements of other research traditions. In the process it will help us sort out, appraise and discard faulty elements of these approaches. Thus, for reasons of parsimony as well as theory, those working in the HBE tradition are skeptical of the adequacy of explanations couched at the level of global prime movers such as climate change. Likewise we doubt the efficacy of explanations made in terms of universal, directional pressures, such as Childe's postulated trend of increasing energy capture (Childe 1965) or ecosystem approaches premised on cybernetic properties such as homeostasis (Flannery 1968).

HUMAN BEHAVIORAL ECOLOGY

HBE has been used to analyze hunter-gatherer economies with favorable results for over two decades. This work is both ethnographic (Hill and Hurtado 1996; Smith 1991) and archaeological (Bettinger 1991b). Because the basics of this approach are well-described elsewhere (Smith and Winterhalder 1992a), we offer here only minimal coverage of assumptions, fundamental concepts, analytic tools, and models and hypotheses, with an emphasis on the models employed by the contributors to this volume and concepts and tools that may be of future use to scholars interested in exploring the problem of agricultural origins.

THE OPTIMIZATION ASSUMPTION

Behavioral ecology begins with an optimization premise. As a result of natural and cultural evolutionary processes, behavior will tend toward constrained optimization (Foley 1985). This assumption makes operational the long-standing view of anthropologists that hunter-gatherers tend to be skilled and effective in the food quest (Winterhalder 2001). Efficiency, say in capturing food energy, is important even if food is not in short supply because it affords hunter-gatherers the time and resources to engage fully in other essential or fitness-enhancing activities (Smith 1979). We state this premise as *constrained* optimization because we do not expect behavior to be fully optimal. Temporal lags in adaptation and compromises among conflicting adaptive goals impede this outcome. Optimization likewise must be determined within the cognitive capacities, beliefs and goals of the organism under study. We adopt the assumption of constrained optimization rather than "satisficing" because the latter—while it may lead to superficially similar predictions—is an empirical concept and is therefore not able to

generate theoretically robust predictions (Elster 1986). Constrained optimization is an analytically powerful starting point that does not entail the belief that behavior is routinely optimal, only that there be a tendency towards optimal forms of behavior.

FUNDAMENTAL CONCEPTS

Behavioral ecology likewise is grounded in the observation, now well confirmed by non-human as well as anthropological studies, that some fundamental economic concepts transcend their scholarly origins in microeconomic attempts to explain the functioning of market-oriented economies. They are useful for studying adaptive decision making whether the questions concern the behavior of capitalists and workers, or the subsistence choices of hunter-gatherers, horticulturalists, and agriculturalists, not to say juncos (Caraco et al. 1980) and bats (Wilkinson 1990). At a minimum this list would include marginal valuation, opportunity costs, discounting, and risk sensitivity.

MARGINAL VALUE. For most tasks we pursue and things we consume, immediate value changes with quantity, be it duration of the activity or the amount of a good obtained or ingested. The first breakfast sausage is more satisfying than the sixth or seventh; an hour-long bath is a delight, but four hours in the tub makes even insipid alternatives attractive. This would be trivial except for the additional observation that the decision to suspend consuming something like sausage or doing something like taking a bath is based on its marginal rather than initial, average or total value. Because of marginal valuation we move from doing one thing to another even though the intrinsic qualities of the options themselves may be unchanging. The formulation of marginal analysis was fundamental to microeconomics (Rhoads 2002), and the careful reader will find marginal trade-offs in each of the foraging models we discuss below.

OPPORTUNITY COSTS. The idea of opportunity costs is closely related: the decision to switch from one behavior—a kind of consumption; a work activity—to another depends not only on its marginal value, but on the return to be gained from the available alternatives. Thus, one ceases to consume sausage when it becomes more attractive to sip orange juice; one stops bathing when preparing a ceremony is more compelling. More to the point of our subject, one ceases to forage for mussels when the opportunity and benefits of doing something else take precedence. In each case we assess the current activity, be it consumption or purchase against what we might be doing instead. In technical terms, the opportunity cost of an activity refers to the value of the opportunity that is foregone or displaced by continuing it. For instance, the diet breadth model (see below) sets the decision to pursue a particular resource against the opportunity cost of ignoring it in favor of searching for a more profitable resource to pursue.

Much of microeconomics is a logical and mathematical elaboration on the workings of marginal valuation and opportunity costs, as they are manifested in the environment of a market economy. Using these ideas, economists ask how a wage earner's consumption patterns change in response to an increase in her income. By contrast, the behavioral ecologist analyzes how these two concepts play out as an organism interacts with a natural environment of physical processes and other organisms in the roles of predators, competitors, food resources, potential mates, and offspring. She asks, how might the resource choices of a forager shift as a consequence of a decline in the density of a highly valued resource, or an improvement in the technology used to harvest a particular species?

Marginal value and opportunity costs and benefits are at the heart of behavioral ecology models. The most basic claim of the papers in this volume is that these same ideas can be adapted to an understanding of decisions faced by humans during the evolutionary transition between foraging and agriculture.

DISCOUNTING. Discounting refers to the situation in which we assign a future reward less value than if it were available immediately and with certainty. For instance, we would pay less at planting time for a corn crop which might after all fail, than for that same crop at harvest time when the yield is certain. We discount in this manner when the cost of an activity such as planting occurs immediately but the reward, the harvest, is delayed and, perhaps because of that delay, uncertain. Delay alone can be important because the opportunity to benefit, even from a completely assured harvest in the most extreme case might diminish or pass, were the cultivator to die in the meantime. Delay also offers opportunities for hailstorms, locust plagues and other unforeseen events to reduce the value of the reward itself. For both reasons, effective behavior will hedge, finding it economical to discount delayed rewards. Use of this concept is fairly recent in behavioral ecology theory (Tucker 2001). Because the shift from hunting and gathering to agriculture represents a shift from immediate- to delayed-reward activities (the original terms are those of Woodburn 1982) this basic concept likely will be quite important in economic analyses of the transition from foraging to farming.

RISK-SENSITIVE BEHAVIOR. Basic (or deterministic) behavioral ecology models assume that all environmental variables are constants and that a forager pursuing an optimal set of resources gets the expected (average) reward at all times. By contrast, risk-sensitive models aim to be more realistic by introducing a stochastic element to the relevant environmental variables. All hunters recognize the large role of chance in the discovery and successful capture of game. In a risk-sensitive model the acquisition rate experienced by the forager is expressed by a statistical distribution; outcomes can be assigned probabilities but the actual rate at any time is unpredictable. Therefore, the optimization problem must take into account both the long-term average and the inevitable periods of shortfall. Risk-sensitive models do this. They are generally more realistic and more complicated than deterministic models, sometimes generate like predictions and, given the heuristic nature of the modeling effort, may not always be the preferred option for analysis (Winter-halder 1986).

There is a well-developed literature regarding the risk-sensitive behavior of foragers and food-producers, taken separately (Cashdan 1990; Halstead and O'Shea 1989; Winterhalder et al. 1999), but little has been written about risk-sensitive adaptation during the transition from one of these subsistence systems to the other (Winterhalder and Goland 1997).

MODEL FEATURES

The concepts just reviewed—marginal valuation, opportunity cost, discounting, and risk-sensitive analysis—signal that behavioral ecology is an attempt to assess the costs and benefits of alternative courses of action under a range of environmental conditions. In operational terms, we accomplish this task with models that have in common four features: an alternative set, constraints, some form of currency, and a goal.

Within a particular model, the range of possible behavioral actions is known as the *alternative set*. For instance, the diet breadth model specifies an alternative set of ranked combinations of potential resources (see below). In the marginal value theorem, the alternative set refers to patch residence times. The alternative set is the dependent variable in the analysis; a particular socioenvironmental factor constitutes the independent variable. The model itself does not specify what might cause the independent variable to take on a certain value, or to change. It thus leaves open the opportunity for exploring how diverse influences such as habitat or climate change, seasonal variations in population density, over exploitation, competition from another predator or pressure to extract a surplus might affect a behavior like resource selection.

The specifics of the organism's capabilities and the environmental features that structure resource selection opportunities are *constraints*. In the diet breadth model constraints include things like the size of the forager, the hunting and gathering technology used, and the distribution and caloric value of the targeted resources. Constraints are all of the elements of the situa-tion that are taken for granted (more formally, treated with a *ceteris paribus* assumption; see Boyer 1995), in order to focus analysis on one set of effects.

The measure we use to assess costs and benefits is known as the *currency*. While the currency might be any feature of a resource that gives it value, foraging theorists typically assume that food energy is the most important attribute. After oxygen and water, mammals require metabolic energy in large amounts on a nearly continuous basis. The omnivorous diet of most hunter-gatherers makes it likely that meeting one's need for energy entails meeting the needs for other nutrients. This may be more problematic with agriculturalists. The kcal currency is expressed as an efficiency, the net acquisition rate (NAR) of energy. Where energy is not limiting or is less limiting than some other factor—e.g., protein—then that can be used as the currency. For instance, we know that some forms of energy, especially those from large or dangerous game animals, are more prestigious than others (tubers, for instance; Hawkes and Bliege Bird 2002), suggesting that not all kilocalories are equal. Prestige might enter into currency in some cases. Behavioral ecologists generally emphasize secondary currencies like kcals or mating success because they are more tractable than the primary neo-Darwinian measure of reproductive fitness (Shennan 2002, 108–11).

The final feature of models is the *goal*. A deterministic foraging model likely would have the goal of maximizing energy capture while foraging. A risk-sensitive model would emphasize the goal of avoiding harmful shortfalls of energy. Behavioral ecology models of food transfers in a social group might stress the evolutionarily stable equilibrium of distribution tactics. The polygyny threshold model for mating tactics would emphasize the goal of reproductive success. Different goals usually imply different methods: simple optimization analysis for energy maximization; stochastic models for risk minimization; game theory for frequency dependent behaviors, like intragroup transfers, that result in evolutionarily stable strategies. The optimization assumption ties together constraints, currency, goal, and the costs and benefits of the alternative set. For instance, given constraints of resource densities and values, and their associated costs and benefits, we predict that organisms will select the alternative that provides them the highest available net acquisition rate of energy. As noted earlier, even when there is no particular shortage of foodstuffs, efficient foraging frees time for alternative activities and lessens exposure to risks associated with foraging. While we don't expect the organism always to engage in the optimal behavior, models based on this assumption have proven to be robust when compared to ethnographic and archaeological datasets (Broughton 1999; Smith 1991).

FORAGING MODELS

Foraging models typically come with a long list of assumptions, awareness of which is critical to their successful use. The models are most often expressed precisely in mathematical formulas or graphs (Stephens and Krebs 1986). In this chapter we provide qualitative and verbal summaries only; explications of greater detail can be found in individual chapters. We trust that the reader wishing to apply the models and understand them more thoroughly and critically will study the references we give for each model.

DIET BREADTH (RESOURCE SELECTION)

The diet breadth or resource selection model (DBM) is one of the oldest and most commonly used (MacArthur and Pianka 1966; Schoener 1974; Winterhalder 1987), particularly by archaeologists (e.g., Broughton 1999; Butler 2000). It is sometimes called the encounter-contingent model because it focuses on the decision to pursue or not to pursue, to harvest or not harvest, a resource once it is encountered. The decision entails an immediate opportunity cost comparison: (a) pursue the encountered resource, or (b) continue searching with the

expectation of locating more valuable resources to pursue. If the net return to (b) is greater than (a), even after allowing for additional search time, then the optimizing forager will elect to pass by the encountered resource, and will continue to do so no matter how frequently this type of resource is encountered.

The general solution to this trade-off is devised as follows: each of k potential resources is ranked in descending order by its net return rate for the post-encounter work to obtain it. This represents a resource's net profitability with respect to pursuit, harvest, and handling costs. The alternative set then is made up of diet breadths from 1 to k, in the form db = 1, db = 1 + 2, db = 1 + 2 + 3, up to db = 1 + ... + k). The derivation of the best-choice diet begins with the most profitable resource (1), and, stepwise, adds resource types, continuing until the first resource ($n + 1$) with a profitability less than the overall foraging efficiency of the diet that does not include it (diet breadth = n). Resources ranked ($n + 1 ... k$) are excluded because to pursue them would impose an unacceptable opportunity cost: a lower return rate for time spent pursuing them relative to the expected benefits from ignoring them in favor of both searching for and pursuing more profitable types. Think of picking up change in tall grass: if there are enough silver dollars and quarters the income-minded gleaner will ignore the dimes, nickles, and pennies, no matter how frequently they are encountered. Notice that the DBM also entails a marginal decision: It asks, is the profitability of the next ranked item above or below the marginal value of foraging for all resources ranked above it?

Creative use of this or any foraging model entails thought experiments of the form: how will an optimizing forager respond to a change in independent variable x. Predicted responses are confined to options with the alternative set, but the independent variable x might be any change in the environment or the behavioral capacities of the forager that affects the primary model variables: resource encounter rates and profitability. For instance, resource depression, environmental change, and other factors which diminish encounter rates with highly ranked resources will increase search costs, lower overall foraging efficiency, and as a result, may cause the diet breadth of a forager to expand to include items of lower rank. One or more items that previously ranked below that boundary may now lie above it, making these resources worth pursing when encountered. The converse is also true. Sufficiently large increases in the density of highly ranked resources should lead to exclusion from the diet of low ranked items. A seasonal elevation of fat content, or adoption of a technology that makes its pursuit, harvest or processing more efficient or any factor that raises the profitability of a particular resource will elevate its ranking, perhaps enough to move into the best-choice diet. It may, in fact, displace resource items previously consumed. Winterhalder and Goland (1997, Fig. 7.4) provide an extended list of factors that might operate through encounter rate and pursuit and handling costs to change resource selectivity.

The diet breadth model also implies that, under a given set of conditions, resources within the optimal diet are always pursued when encountered; those outside the optimal diet will always be ignored. There are no "partial preferences," such as "take this organism 50% of the time it is encountered." Likewise, the decision to include a lower-ranked item is not based on its abundance, but on the abundances of resources of higher rank. Think of the small change mentioned earlier.

PATCH CHOICE

In the diet breadth model, we envision a resource that is harvested as a unit with a fixed value (e.g., a steenbok). By contrast, a patch is a resource or set of resources which is harvested at a diminishing rate, either because it is depleted in such a way that makes continued harvesting more difficult; the densest and ripest berries are picked first, or because the continuing presence of the forager disperses or increases the wariness of remaining resource opportunities as in the second or third shot at

a dispersing flock of grouse. Patches can be ranked like resources, by their profitability upon encounter. As a first approximation, the same predictions apply. However, predictions are somewhat less clear for the selection of patches than for resources, because a definitive prediction about patch choice is interdependent with a decision about patch residence time, the focus of the next model.

PATCH RESIDENCE TIME (THE MARGINAL VALUE THEOREM)

If a resource patch—which we envision as a small area of relatively homogeneous resource opportunities, separated by some travel distance from other such locales—is harvested at a diminishing rate of return, it is obvious to ask when the forager should abandon its efforts and attempt to find a fresh opportunity. By moving on, he or she will incur the cost of finding a new patch, but upon locating it, will be rewarded with a higher rate of return, at least for a while. The optimizing solution to this foraging decision is given by the marginal value theorem (Charnov 1976; Charnov et al. 1976; Stephens and Krebs 1986). The marginal value theorem postulates a decline in return rates for time spent in the patch, usually approximated by a negative exponential curve. The optimizing solution specifies that the forager will leave the present patch when the rate of return there has dropped to the average foraging rate. The average foraging rate encompasses the full set of patches being harvested *and* the travel costs associated with movement among them. To stay longer incurs unfavorable opportunity costs because higher returns were available elsewhere. To stay a shorter duration is also sub-optimal, because rates of return are, on average, higher when compared to the costs of moving on to another resource patch.

In this model, short travel times are associated with short patch residence (take the highest return opportunities and move on quickly); long travel times with longer residence times. The forager optimizing his or her patch residence time rarely will completely deplete a patch;

the resources left behind are significant for the recovery of the patch. Finally, the value of harvested patches, upon departure, is the same.

The inter-dependence between the two patch-related models should now be more apparent. Predictions about patch residence time depend on patch choice; reciprocally, predictions about patch choice depend on residence time. Use of one of these models must assume the other; Stephens and Krebs (1986, 32–34) give a more detailed discussion of this model.

HABITAT SELECTION (THE IDEAL FREE DISTRIBUTION)

The ideal free distribution is a model of habitat choice (Fretwell 1970; Sutherland 1996). The distinction between patches and habitats is one of scale: patches are isolated areas of homogenous resource opportunities on a scale such that a forager may encounter several to several dozen in a daily foraging expedition. Habitats are similarly defined by their aggregate resource base, but at a regional scale. As suggested by their greater relative size, habitats also invoke somewhat different questions, such as where to establish and when to move settlements, and when to relocate by migration. Generally, we ask how populations will distribute themselves with respect to major landscape features like habitats.

In the ideal free distribution, the quality of a habitat depends on resource abundance and the density of the population inhabiting and using it. The model assumes that the initial settlers pick the best habitat, say "A." Further immigration and population growth in habitat A reduce the availability of resources and the quality of the habitat drops for everyone. Crowding, depletion of resources, and competition are possible reasons for this. The marginal quality of habitat A eventually will drop to that of the second-ranked, but yet unsettled, habitat B. If each individual in the population seeks the best habitat opportunity, further growth or immigration will be apportioned between habitats A and B such that their marginal value to residents is equalized. Lower ranked habitats will be occupied in a similar manner. This model predicts

that habitats will be occupied in their rank order, that human densities at equilibrium will be proportional to the natural quality of their resources, and that the suitability of all occupied habitats will be the same at equilibrium.

In the IFD the creative element resides in imaging how various socioenvironmental settings might affect the shape of the curves representing the impact of settlement density on habitat quality. For instance, it is possible that settlement at low densities actually *increases* the suitability of a habitat. Forest clearing by the newcomers leading to secondary growth might increase the density of game available to them and to emigrants. This is known as the Allee effect. Likewise, some habitats (e.g., small islands; see Kennett et al., this volume) may be quickly affected by settlement, generating a sharply declining curve of suitability as population densities increase, whereas others may be much more resilient. If immigrants to a habitat successfully defend a territory there, then newly arriving individuals will more quickly be displaced to lower ranked habitats, a variant known as the ideal despotic distribution (IDD; see Sutherland 1996).

CENTRAL PLACE FORAGING

Many foragers, human and nonhuman, locate at a dry rock shelter, potable water, or a valuable or dense food source or other particularly critical resource—e.g., an attractive habitation site, or perhaps at a location central to a dispersed array of required resources—and then forage in a radial pattern from that site. Central place foraging models (Orians and Pearson 1979) address this circumstance. They assume that a forager leaving such a home base must travel a certain distance through unproductive habitat to reach productive foraging zones. The goal—optimizing delivery of foodstuffs or other valuables to the central place—must take account of the round trip travel costs between the central place and the foraging site, in addition to the standard considerations about resource selection. The basic prediction of this model is the following: as travel costs out and back increase with a load on the return trip, the forager should become more and more selective about what is harvested. At long travel distances only the most valuable loads justify the effort.

This model has been adapted in an intriguing way by archaeologists who have used it to address the question of field processing (Bettinger et al. 1997; Metcalfe and Barlow 1992). Field processing entails removing parts of a resource with little or no value, in order to carry more of the valued portions back to the central place. Shelling marine bivalves or removing pinyon nuts from their cones are examples. With data on parameters such as distance, feasible bulk and weight of loads, and the costs and benefits of field processing a particular resource (e.g., Barlow et al. 1993), it is possible to predict rather precisely the travel distance at which the forager will process in the field rather than carry the unprocessed resource back to the central place. Field processing of course improves the efficiency of transportation, but it also commits to processing field time that could have been used to locate, harvest and transport more of the unprocessed resource. This model predicts that field processing will become more likely as travel distance increases.

We cite this adaptation of the central place foraging model in part because it makes the important point that foraging theory is not a closed, off-the-shelf set of tools (Kelly 2000). Rather, it must be, and it has considerable potential to be, adapted to the particular circumstances of human subsistence, whether foragers, farmers, or populations that mix these sources of production.

SETTLEMENT (RE)LOCATION

Settlement models attempt to predict when foragers will relocate their central places, due to localized depletion of resources (Kelly 1992), seasonal or other shifts in the relative values and availability of local and distant resource opportunities (Zeanah 2000). Zeanah's model, for instance, imagines a foraging group whose two most important resources, say lake margin lacustrine species (A) and mountain sheep or pinyon nuts (B), are found in geographically separated habitats. They also change in their relative seasonal importance. We would expect the forager to locate adjacent to the more dominant of the two food sources (say, A), especially if the resource targeted is difficult to transport, and to harvest the less dominant (B) or easier to transport item through logistic foraging expeditions. Zeanah's model specifies in quantitative terms what shifts in yield and transport costs will lead to the decision to switch the pattern of settlement and logistic procurement, residing adjacent to B, while harvesting A logistically.

Although settlement models have not, to our knowledge, been applied in studies of domestication and agricultural origins, the likelihood that the better foraging and farming sites have non-overlapping distributions, and the implied changes in mobility and sedentism during a transition from foraging, to a mixed foraging & farming, to farming, or back to foraging, offers fertile ground for exploration.

CURRENT DEVELOPMENTS IN FORAGING THEORY

A list of established models might give the sense that behavioral ecology, however useful to interpretation, is a static or completed field. In fact, it is in a rapid state of expansion and development both in ethnography and archaeology. In this section we note several of the more important developments. The trends described here also make it evident why the more encompassing term, behavioral ecology, often is more apt than foraging theory.

BEYOND KCALS

Early applications of foraging models, especially the diet breadth model, adopted a straightforward energy currency to measure the costs and benefits of options in the alternative set. The value of a moose was the weight of its edible tissue represented as kcals. This is consistent with a prime methodological predilection of behavioral ecologists (Winterhalder 2002a): begin simply. Once you understand how the simple model works and have appraised its relevance to the empirical problem, it is appropriate to relax restrictive and sometimes unrealistic assumptions. Thus, in foraging theory, studies of resource selection led naturally to examination of intra-group resource transfers. This move from issues of economic production to those of distribution drew attention to a different metric: marginal value. After a filling meal or two, the marginal value of the balance of a moose carcass to the forager who obtained it may drop rapidly relative to the kcals it represents. This observation—that medium to large food packets are subject to marginal valuation—is at the heart of behavioral ecology models of food transfers through tolerated theft and reciprocity-based sharing (Blurton Jones 1987; Gurven 2004; Winterhalder 1996; Winterhalder 1997). Of equal importance, there may be some cases in which the marginal value of a resource is the appropriate valuation of its profitability for purposes of the original diet breadth model.

A more radical variation on currency is evident in models devised to help explain an anomaly in early field studies of foraging behavior: although each sex often could do better by harvesting the same set of resources, men sometimes specialize on large game and women on plants and small animals (Hill et al. 1987), each at a cost to their potential foraging efficiency. The show-off (Hawkes and Bliege Bird 2002) and costly signaling (Smith et al. 2003) models assume that resource values—and hence their patterns of acquisition and distribution—will sometimes be predicated on the prestige associated with their use or on the information their capture conveys about the prowess of the hunter. With these models foraging theory has carried us beyond "the gastric" (Zeanah and Simms 1999) and into the realm of social theory (Bliege Bird and Smith 2005), making plausible our earlier claim that foraging theory offers broad grounds for complementing other research traditions in the field of agricultural origins (e.g. Hayden 1995a). Social valuation moves the modeling effort of HBE from the narrow question of resource selection to broader anthropological issues—the roles of gender, prestige, and power in structuring economic activity (e.g., Broughton and Bayham 2003; Elston and Zeanah 2002; Hildebrandt and McGuire 2002; Hildebrandt and McGuire 2003).

BEYOND DETERMINISTIC APPROACHES

Risk-sensitive and discounting models are another set of variations on early foraging theory efforts. In the original models for diet breadth, patch choice, and patch residence time, all input values were taken to be averages unaffected by stochastic variation. Thus the average search time to locate the next resource was treated as a constant, making foraging a more predictable enterprise than is the case. These models focused on a goal of maximizing acquisition rate during foraging. Risk-sensitive models allow for stochastic variation in the factors influencing foraging decisions, such as encounter rate or pursuit time. They assume that the forager has the goal of risk minimization (Winterhalder et al. 1999). For instance, Stephens and Charnov (1982) modified the marginal value theorem to show that a risk-minimizing forager, in positive energy balance and facing a normal distribution of unpredictable inter-patch travel times, would stay somewhat longer in a patch than a rate maximizing forager whose travel times were a constant.

In general, risk-sensitive models predict that optimizing foragers who are not meeting their average requirements will be risk prone. They will elect the higher variance options from the alternative set because those offer their greatest chance of a survival-enhancing windfall. Foragers in positive energy balance will be risk averse, electing the low variance options that minimize the chance of a threatening shortfall. The implications of these generalities for specific types of decisions must be worked out individually.

A variation on risk-sensitive models is discounting (Benson and Stephens 1996). If the forager has reason to discount, and faces a choice between a small reward at present or a larger one at some point in the future, he or she may do best by taking the less valuable but immediate option. Tucker (Ch. 2, below; see also Alvard and Kuznar 2001) argues that discounting is likely to be especially important in the transition from foraging to food production.

BEYOND DERIVED AND GRAPHICAL SOLUTIONS

The basic foraging models described above are products of mathematical derivation, often represented graphically. A desire for more realistic variants is associated with new analytic methodologies, such as simulation and agent-based modeling. For instance, Winterhalder and students (Winterhalder et al. 1988) simulated the population ecology of a foraging population interacting with multiple resource species. In this dynamic model, the human population grows or contracts in density as a function of foraging efficiency. It harvests species identified by the diet breadth model, in amounts required to meet its food needs. And, to complete the dynamic circuit, the densities of the resource species themselves expand or contract according to their degree of exploitation and their logistic potential to recover from being harvested. The result is a more realistic application of the diet breadth model: exploitation actually changes prey densities and thus encounter rates in a plausible manner, generating new hypotheses relevant both to agricultural origins (Winterhalder et al. 1988) and conservation biology (Winterhalder and Lu 1997).

Agent-based modeling is another new technique of great promise. Agent-based analyses rely on computer simulations to represent a population of agents interacting with an environment and among themselves. These models iterate a cycle in which the agent collects information from the environment, and then acts in some fashion that changes the agent and environment. The agent-based approach, "emphasizes dynamics rather than equilibria, distributed processes rather than systems-level phenomena, and patterns of relationships

among agents rather than relationships among variables" (Kohler 2000, 2). Agent-based models have the added advantage that they can incorporate basic processes of learning or evolution, for instance by allowing the agent to adjust its behavior according to its monitoring of performance criteria. Because of this property, they are thereby especially useful for simulating adaptive or co-evolutionary processes (see examples in Brantingham 2003; Kohler and Gumerman 2000). Although there are at present no agent-based models of domestication or agricultural origins, behavioral ecology adaptations of the agent-based approach appear an especially promising avenue for research.

BEYOND ETHNOGRAPHY

The specific claim of this volume—that behavioral ecology theory is an essential tool in the analysis of the transition from hunting-and-gathering to agriculture—is set within a broader assertion: that behavioral ecology can be used to understand prehistory in general (Bird and O'-Connell 2003; O'Connell 1995). Although archaeologists have been enthusiastic consumers and occasionally developers of foraging theory, the models themselves and the bulk of their testing are the province of biologists and anthropologists working with living species and peoples. As a consequence, the models typically make predictions at the level of individual behavior over very short time scales—minutes to days or perhaps weeks. In contrast, archaeological data on subsistence production, food distribution, mobility, settlement, and the other topics of behavioral ecology represents the aggregate consequences of many individual actions over decades, centuries or longer. Much archaeological data conflate individual, temporal and perhaps spatial variability. This disparity of scale and resolution raises thorny problems regarding how HBE models are to be verified, applied and interpreted in archaeological contexts (e.g., Smith, this volume). How do we get from a chronological sequence of faunal samples, each of which represents perhaps dozens of foraging expeditions by different individuals over decades or centuries of time, to the seasonally and habitat specific foraging choices of a particular hunter?

This problem is serious but may not be as daunting as appears on first consideration. For instance, careful investigation does occasionally reveal the individual and momentary in prehistory. Enloe and Davis (1992) and Waguespack (2002) both have shown that by analyzing the "refitting" of bones scattered among the different hearths of a campsite it is possible to reliably infer patterns of prehistoric food sharing. In broader terms, Grayson and Delpech (1998; Grayson et al. 2001), Lyman (2003), Broughton (2002) and Gremillion (2002) are exploring how well and under what circumstances various archaeological measures of floral and faunal residues are able to capture foraging behavior changes in diet breadth. A series of reports analyzing broad spectrum type diet breadth changes in late prehistory have made creative use of changing ratios of large, presumably, highly ranked, to small prey (Broughton 1999; Broughton 2001; Butler 2000; Lindström 1996; Nagaoka 2001, 2002) in order to document declining foraging efficiencies and expanding diets. Through a combination of archaeological investigation and population ecology simulation, Stiner and colleagues (Stiner et al. 2000; Stiner 2001; Stiner and Munro 2002) have shown that small prey may be especially sensitive indicators of human resource selection and the impacts of exploitation. We expect these efforts to find archaeologically viable means of using foraging theory to continue.

BEYOND HUNTER-GATHERERS AND FORAGING

The research tradition represented in this volume originated as foraging theory focused on the study of food production in hunter-gatherer populations (Winterhalder and Smith 1981). In both biology and anthropology the approach since has adopted the broader name—human behavioral ecology—as it has expanded its topical focus to encompass resource distribution, group size and structure, mating and reproductive tactics, and life history evolution, while—in the anthropological case—simultaneously moving into the analyses of societies engaged in other modes of production (reviews in Borgerhoff Mulder 1991; Cronk 1991; Smith 1992a; Smith 1992b; Smith and Winterhalder 1992a; Winterhalder and Smith 2000). The impetus for this expansion has at least four sources: (1) the early empirical success of field studies using the approach; (2) the generality of the neo-Darwinian theory that inspired it; (3) the generality of the underlying concepts of marginal valuation, opportunity cost appraisal, risk-sensitivity, discounting; and, (4) the flexibility of individual models, which often have been readily adapted to problems or settings not foreseen by their original authors. The present volume continues this trend by carrying behavioral ecology theory and models into analyses of domestication and agricultural origins.

The transfer and extension of ideas and concepts in order to bring new topics under the compass of existing theory has obvious scientific merit (Kuhn 1977; McMullin 1983). It also has pitfalls. The failings of early "evolutionist" models of social evolution and their archaeological adaptations, as well as social Darwinist interpretations, are well-rehearsed subjects in anthropology. Contemporary anxieties about the use of neo-Darwinian theory in anthropology are more narrowly and analytically focused, and sometimes not so easy to set aside. A recent example would be debate over the claim by Rindos (1984) that his co-evolutionary account of plant domestication had successfully banished human intent from an explanatory role in this process (Rindos 1985).

In the present volume we take for granted the relevance to agricultural origins of neo-Darwinian and behavioral ecology theory. We reject without explicit argument the substantivist claim of economic anthropology that none of the tools of formalist, microeconomics has any purchase outside of modern capitalist economies (e.g., Sahlins 1972). To the contrary, we believe it evident that the basic concepts of HBE (see above) are fundamental to the analysis of *any* economy. Close attention to their use in HBE we believe will stimulate new applications and models specifically designed to analyze mixed economies and food production.

We are more receptive to the argument that specific foraging models, developed as they were for foragers, may be only partially appropriate to the analysis of emergent food producers. For instance, the diet breadth model assumes random encounter with resources, a condition increasingly likely to be violated as foragers become involved in the manipulation of individual species. In as much as all models simplify reality and thus violate at least some conditions of their application, the unavoidable judgment is this: does the failure to fit this particular assumption completely vitiate the heuristic or analytical value of the model? With the specific cautions cited in individual papers, we believe the combined weight of the case studies developed in this volume add up to a strong presumption in favor of the utility of foraging theory, even as the foragers being analyzed direct more and more of their effort toward agricultural activities.

We envision three levels where HBE might be applied to the question of agricultural origins. (1) Extant models, although designed for the analysis of foraging, might be applied in the analysis of agricultural origins with little or no alteration in their structure and assumptions. This is the procedure of most authors in this volume. (2) Extant models might be modified so to more directly address questions or situations specific to non-foraging aspects of economy, including cultivation and agricultural production. The modification of central place foraging models to analyze the question of field processing is an especially good example of this. (3) Finally, entirely new models, inspired directly by the problem of explaining human subsistence transitions, might be devised using fundamental behavioral ecology concepts such as opportunity cost or discounting. We think of these options as adopt, adapt, or invent, respectively. While options (2) and (3) hold great potential for novel and perhaps quite interesting analyses, it appears from the papers assembled here that there is much to be accomplished with the simple adoption of existing models.

2

A Future Discounting Explanation for the Persistence of a Mixed Foraging-Horticulture Strategy among the Mikea of Madagascar

Bram Tucker

This chapter pursues dual goals. The first goal is to argue in favor of the use of future-discounting concepts when modeling choices among subsistence activities with dissimilar delay to reward, such as the choice to practice foraging versus farming. While foraging theory makes the value of all options commensurate by expressing them as a rate of gain per unit time, people may subjectively devalue options with long waiting times, such as agricultural harvests. A literature review and guide to discount rates are presented for readers unfamiliar with these concepts. The second goal is to demonstrate the applicability of future discounting models by presenting a simple dynamic model explaining why Mikea of Madagascar prefer labor-extensive cultivation despite the high risk and low mean payoff, and despite their familiarity with the techniques and benefits of intensive farming. Mikea cultivate because the rewards are high compared with foraging, but they refrain from intensification because immediate needs limit their capacity for future investment.

Low-investment extensive horticulture, the planting of cultigens with minimal labor invest-

ment in patches of wilderness that remain more-or-less untended until harvest time, seems a curious strategy. Payoffs tend to be low on average, for the cultigens compete with wild plants for soil and solar resources. Returns are also highly variable, for the crop is left vulnerable to pests, predators, and unpredictable climatic conditions. Extensive horticulturalists compensate for low and variable harvests by hunting and gathering wild foods, which constitute the bulk of the diet in some years. Given this heavy reliance on foraging, one may well ask why plant cultigens at all? Conversely, why refrain from intensifying agricultural inputs to produce a more dependable and satisfying agricultural payoff?

As curious as the foraging/low investment horticulture strategy may appear, archaeological evidence suggests this was a persistent strategy for millennia in many parts of the world. Some of the first cultigens may have been domesticated rather rapidly, in the span of 20 or so plant generations (Hillman and Davies 1990a, b; Hillman and Davies 1992). There followed a long period of time in which people continued to rely primarily on foraging while horticulture played an ancillary role. According to Bruce Smith (2001a), this middle ground between plant domestication and intensive farming lasted 3000 years in the Near East, 4000 years in some parts of North America and Europe, and 5500 years in central Mexico (see also Piperno and Pearsall 1998; Doolittle 2000).

Archaeologists interested in subsistence decisions have as a guide the behavior of living peoples, observed and documented with ethnographic and experimental methods and informed by evolutionary theories of human behavior (O'Connell 1995). This chapter describes Mikea of southwestern Madagascar, a contemporary ethnographic population who combine low-investment maize and manioc horticulture with foraging for wild tubers, honey, and small game.

The most important subsistence and cash crop for Mikea was, until recently, maize grown in slash-and-burn fields called *hatsake* (the "ethnographic present" for this chapter is before the government effectively banned hatsake cultivation in 2002). Mikea invest little labor and no other inputs into their maize fields. New fields are cleared by felling and burning trees. Old fields are reused for several years and then abandoned. They are usually cleared of weeds and saplings before planting, although some farmers reduce labor costs even further by planting among the weeds. After planting, no additional labor is invested until harvest time. The fields are exposed to severe sunlight, unpredictable rainfall, poor soil nutrition, weedy competition, and predation by grasshoppers and unsupervised herds of cattle and goats. Mikea are aware of a variety of intensification techniques that could increase maize yields and reduce risk of failure, such as tillage, irrigation, manure fertilizers, weeding, enclosure, and field guarding, but they rarely practice these. Instead, they return to their fields three months after planting and harvest whatever happens to be there.

Most Mikea households in the study area also grow manioc in permanent fields in the savanna, alongside their Masikoro agropastoral neighbors. Masikoro cultivate manioc semi-intensively on a 12-to 15-month schedule. Some farmers plant in plowed furrows or mounds, and dig drainage ditches to avert flood damage; and they weed their fields three to four times a year. Fields are enclosed with fences and guarded with talismans to protect them from animal, human, and supernatural predators. Forest-dwelling Mikea rarely practice these techniques. Because they only check their fields during periodic visits, they often neglect to drain or weed in a timely fashion, if at all. Loss to livestock and thieves is common. Even when alerted that their field was being plundered by thieves in the night, two brothers in 1998 refused to save their crop, insisting that the wild tubers and honey in the forest were sufficiently plentiful.

Are Mikea cultivation decisions irrational? As foragers, Mikea are viewed as primitives who have yet to discover the intensive farming techniques of their more "advanced" Masikoro neighbors. Their horticulture would appear to be a transitional stage between foraging and farming. But such unilinear-evolutionary assertions are contradicted by Mikea ethnohistory and oral history, which indicate that Mikea and Masikoro are historically the same people. Mikea are descended from Masikoro who sought refuge in the forest to escape the slave raids and tribute demands of the Andrevola kings, and during the French colonial era, to avoid mandatory resettlement and taxation (Yount et al. 2001; Tucker 2003). Foraging is not just an occupation; it is symbolically significant to Mikea identity as refugees from Andrevola hegemony. Mikea have probably always planted some cultigens in combination with foraging. Fanony (1986, 139) reported Mikea cultivating crops in the late 1970s. Twenty years earlier, Molet (1958) documented maize and butter beans in swidden patches deep in the Mikea Forest. Mikea oral histories from the nineteenth century are replete with references to forest fields of maize, manioc, sweet potatoes, rice, sorghum, and taro (Tucker 2003). Shipwrecked sailor Robert Drury, circa

1710, observed that foragers of southern Madagascar "content themselves with small plantations" in addition to "the products of nature" (Drury 1826 [1729], 139). Mikea are active participants in Masikoro society, and indeed, all Mikea self-identify as being either Masikoro or Vezo in addition to Mikea. Mikea and Masikoro belong to the same clans, intermarry freely, and participate in the same family ceremonies. Mikea often labor in their neighbors' fields for wage payments. So Mikea and Masikoro share the same knowledge of agricultural intensification techniques. Masikoro choose to intensify; Mikea do not. Nor do Mikea choose to specialize on foraging. For centuries many have chosen a middle path.

Which is most profitable: foraging or cultivation? This depends on how one defines "profitable." Agricultural profitability is usually measured as yield per unit of land. But because mobile foragers' harvest is not land-limited, it makes little sense to quantify wild tuber production as kilograms per hectare.

Alternatively, we can compare foraging and farming with the logic of foraging theory. Foraging theory calculates rewards as a net rate of energy gain, or net acquisition rate (Pyke et al. 1977; Stephens and Krebs 1986, 9). When digging wild *ovy* tubers (*Dioscorea acuminata*), Mikea children average 500 net kcal/hr, while adults gain 1200–2700 kcal/hr (Tucker and Young 2005). If cultivated rewards are calculated in the same manner, then foraging is clearly an inferior choice. The most extensive form of Mikea cultivation is planting maize in an unweeded hatsake field, for which the only required investment is 11 person-hours of planting labor per hectare. The net acquisition rate is approximately 165,215 kcal/hr.[1] In a survey of 247 hatsake in 1998 and 1999, only 6.5% of fields were cultivated in this manner. In the majority (57%) people cleared weeds before planting, adding an extra 24.7 person-hours of labor investment to the venture. This increases average yield from 500 kg/ha to 910 kg/ha. But the net acquisition rate is actually lower: 92,469 kcal/hr.[2] Net acquisition rate does not

adequately describe the value of foraging and farming, nor does it explain the costs and benefits of intensification.

I argue that the best way to model the choice between foraging versus cultivation is with a future-discounting model. When offered a choice between a small reward available now versus a larger reward after a delay, decision-makers often prefer immediate gratification, indicating that they subjectively devalue rewards for which they must wait (Samuelson 1937; Mazur 1984, 1987; Rachlin et al. 1991; Myerson and Green 1995; Green and Myerson 1996; Frederick et al. 2002). To borrow Woodburn's (1980) terms, foraging is an "immediate return" economic system while farming is a "delayed return" economic system. The reward for a few hours' foraging is a certain catch of food: small in comparison to an agricultural harvest, but available for immediate consumption. A day spent cultivating is rewarded with sweat, blisters, and an empty stomach, along with the promise of a large quantity of food some time in the future. Exogenous factors such as high risk of crop loss may make agriculture an empty promise. Factors endogenous to the household, such as food supply adequacy, may limit a household's ability to survive on promises alone. Mikea cultivate because the rewards are high compared with foraging, but they refrain from intensification because immediate needs limit their capacity for future investment.

This chapter has two goals. The first is to present a theoretic argument for the use of a future discounting framework when modeling the choice to forage or to farm. I begin with a critical evaluation of the way foraging theory deals with time. Then I present a brief review of descriptive models, methods, and explanations from future discounting studies in economics, psychology, and anthropology. I follow with a guide for modelers to choosing discount rates. The second goal of this chapter is to illustrate the applicability of future discounting to modeling subsistence decisions. To this end I return to the Mikea example provided above, and present a future-discounting model to explain why Mikea practice a mixed foraging-horticulture strategy.

TIME AND FORAGING MODELS

Foraging theory was developed in the 1960s and 1970s to explain predatory behavior (MacArthur and Pianka 1966; Schoener 1974; Charnov 1976; Pyke et al. 1977; Stephens and Krebs 1986), and was soon after applied to the decisions of human foragers in ethnographic contexts (Winterhalder and Smith 1981; Hawkes et al. 1982). Models from foraging theory such as the encounter-contingent prey choice model (MacArthur and Pianka 1966; Schoener 1974) and the patch use model (Charnov 1976) make specific predictions about the selection and exploitation of food resources. Options such as prey and patch types are evaluated according to their gross energy payoff (the number of calories gained by consuming the resource) minus the energy and time costs involved in locating the resource and its "handling" (pursuit, harvest, transport, processing, etc.). Foraging theory models assume that decision-makers evaluate time and energy information together as a rate; they maximize average net rate of energy gain (Pyke at al. 1977; Stephens and Krebs 1986, 9). This maximization assumption has proven sufficiently general to explain a wide range of subsistence behavior (Pyke et al. 1977; Smith 1983), including choices under risk (Stephens and Charnov 1982; Winterhalder 1986; Weissburg 1991).

Average rate maximization may be insufficient when options differ significantly by delay-to-reward (see discussion in Stephens and Krebs 1986, 147–150). Average rate maximization asserts that one rabbit worth 1000 net kcals caught in one hour is equivalent in value to one deer worth 100,000 net kcals caught in 100 hours, or one giraffe worth 1,000,000 net kcals caught in 1000 hours; all have a net acquisition rate of 1000 kcal/hr. But from a forager's perspective there may be a significant difference between dedicating oneself to a one-hour rabbit

chase versus a 1000-hour giraffe hunt. The latter requires the forager to defer consumption for a longer period of time (he would have to pack a lunch). Since time spent foraging cannot be allocated to alternative tasks—longer foraging time has greater opportunity cost—the giraffe hunter would have to make arrangements to manage his nonforaging activities during his absence (he would have to hire a babysitter). Also, there is more uncertainty associated with a longer hunt. The forager has less information in a Bayesian sense about the outcome. And from a statistical perspective, one failed giraffe hunt is devastating, while the consequences of a failed rabbit hunt are comparatively minor.

Experimental studies suggest that decision-makers evaluate time and energy information separately, rather than together as a rate (Reboreda and Kacelnik 1991; Bateson and Kacelnik 1995). Captive starlings were offered a series of choices that varied in reward amount and reward delay. The average rate was held constant for all choices, so that if the birds evaluate options in terms of energy-per-time rates, they should be indifferent among all options. Interestingly, subjects indicated little preference (positive or negative) for variability in amount. This supports the use of average rate maximization in stochastic foraging models (for example, Stephens and Charnov 1982; Winterhalder 1986; Weissburg 1991). But the birds preferentially chose options with variable delays. Time, manifested in delay to reward, affects perception of value in a subjective manner that is not captured by rate maximization alone.

Foraging models have provided a useful starting point for explaining the inclusion of low-ranking plants into an ecological relationship favorable to domestication (Winterhalder and Goland 1997) and the adoption of cultivated foods into a foraging economy (Gremillion 1996a). Because agriculture involves lengthy delays from when cultivation decisions are made to when fields are harvested, agricultural options should be discounted in value when compared with the immediate rewards of foraging. The

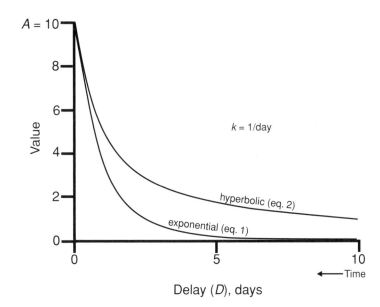

$A = 10$

$k = 1/\text{day}$

hyperbolic (eq. 2)

exponential (eq. 1)

Value

Time

Delay (D), days

FIGURE 2.1. Demonstration of the exponential and hyperbolic discounting functions, using arbitrary values. Note that time passes from right to left, as delay to reward counts down to zero at the origin.

simplest way to model this is to modify the value of the delayed option by a discount rate.

FUTURE DISCOUNTING: A REVIEW

DESCRIPTIVE MODELS

Behavioral researchers have long been interested in the effect of time on value, a phenomenon known alternatively as intertemporal choice (Loewenstein and Prelec 1992), time preference (Rogers 1994; Becker and Mulligan 1997), temporal discounting (Green et al. 1994a; Myerson and Green 1995; Green and Myerson 1996), patience (Godoy et al. 2004), or impulsiveness/self control (Green et al. 1981; Logue et al. 1987, 1988). Economists have, since the eighteenth century, discussed time in the context of savings behavior and differences in individual and national wealth (Böhm-Bawerk 1970 [1889]; Fisher 1930; Loewenstein 1992; Frederick et al. 2002). Psychologists have empirically explored impulse control using choice experiments with animal and human subjects (Green et al. 1981; Mazur 1984, 1987; Rachlin et al. 1991; Green et al. 1994b; Kirby and Hernnstein 1995; Myerson and Green 1995; Green and Myerson 1996). Anthropologists have long recognized the applicability of intertemporal choice to such topics as

life history tradeoffs (Hill 1993, 81–82), reciprocal exchanges (Hawkes 1992, 285–287), and resource conservation and inheritance (Rogers 1991, 1994; Alvard and Kuznar 2001), but so far there has only been one major ethnographic investigation of time preference (Godoy et al. 2001, 2004; Kirby et al. 2002).

Following Samuelson (1937), most descriptive models of intertemporal choice have been discounted utility models. Imagine a decision maker faced with the choice between a smaller reward available now versus a larger reward available after a delay. The decision maker may prefer the immediate reward, implying that the value of the delayed option is subjectively discounted. Despite being of greater quantity, the delayed reward offers less utility in the present than the immediate option due to disutility associated with waiting. As time passes the delayed option is perceived to have increasing value.

Samuelson (1937) described discounted utility with an exponential function:

$$V = Ae^{-kD} \tag{1}$$

Where V is the discounted subjective value at time D (the D stands for delay, so $D = 0$ on

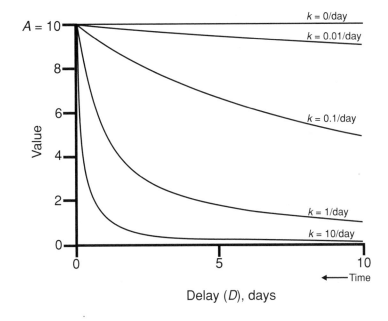

FIGURE 2.2. Hyperbolic discounting for a range of discount rates (k).

harvest day); A is the final reward value when D = 0; e is the exponential constant 2.71828; and k is the discount rate. While the exponential discounting function has enjoyed considerable use among development economists (for example, Pender 1996), many economists and psychologist alike prefer a hyperbolic model such as that offered by Mazur (1984, 1987):

$$V = A/(1 + kD) \qquad (2)$$

Both the exponential and hyperbolic functions are graphed in Figure 2.1 using arbitrary values: a reward of 10 units available after 10 days discounted at k = 1/day.

The k variable is a measure of preference; it determines the extent to which a future reward is discounted. Figure 2.2 demonstrates hyperbolic discounting for a range of k values. A k value of 0/day indicates no discounting at all; the reward has the same value (equal to A) regardless of delay. As k increases, future rewards have decreasing value from a present perspective.

The hyperbolic model has several demonstrated advantages over its exponential counterpart. First, the exponential model assumes a constant rate of temporal discounting; a deci-

sion-maker devalues a future harvest at the same rate 50 days before harvest as he does one day before harvest. The hyperbolic function simulates increasing confidence in a delayed reward as harvest time draws nearer (Green and Myerson 1996, 497; Frederick et al. 2002, 366).

Second, the hyperbolic model accounts for a well-documented anomaly in intertemporal choice behavior: preference switching (Figure 2.3a). Imagine a decision maker faced with the choice between two delayed options, a smaller reward available sooner versus a larger reward available later. If the delay to both rewards is sufficiently long, the decision maker is likely to ignore time altogether and base judgment on quantity alone, thus preferring the larger, later option. But as time elapses, the smaller, sooner reward increases in value until it surpasses the alternative and preference switches (Green et al. 1981; Green et al. 1994b; Kirby and Hernnstein 1995).

Third, when the exponential and hyperbolic models are used in regression analysis to describe responses from choice experiments, the hyperbolic model consistently describes data better, with greater R^2 values (Mazur 1987; Rachlin et al. 1991; Myerson and Green 1995;

Green and Myerson 1996). Mazur (1987) and Rachlin et al. (1991) show that the hyperbolic model can achieve even greater accuracy if the denominator is raised to a power s.

It should be noted, however, that both exponential and hyperbolic models describe data quite adequately ($R^2 > 0.90$), and in the same general accelerating manner. Neither model is derived from explanatory theory. There remains a gulf between these descriptive models and possible explanatory variables. How might environmental, personal, or societal factors influence the rate at which individuals discount the future? What explains individual differences in discounting behavior?

EXPLANATION: WHY DO DECISION-MAKERS DISCOUNT THE FUTURE?

In 1834, economist John Rae, seeking to explain differences in wealth among nations, posited four determinants of ability to accumulate wealth by deferring consumption. The first two promote patience and frugality: (1) the desire to pass resources to future generations, and (2) the capacity for self-restraint. The latter two set limits on future investment: (3) the uncertainty and hazards of life, and (4) the pleasures of immediate gratification (Loewenstein 1992, 6–7; Frederick et al. 2002, 352–353). Recent theories have expounded upon these determinants.

(1). Conserving resources for the benefit of future generations requires limiting benefits in the present generation. Rogers (1991, 1994) has developed a theory of the evolution of time preference based on the intergenerational fitness costs and benefits of conserving resources. An individual may rationally choose to conserve resources if he stands to gain more fitness through the reproduction of his grandchildren than from his own children. An important constraint is the probability that someone other than the conserver's genetic descendants will benefit from the saved resources. If time preferences are at an evolutionary equilibrium, then the rate at which individuals trade off current versus future reproductive benefits will be equal to the rate at which they make intertemporal production and con-

sumption tradeoffs. Demographic data from Utah, Lybia, and Taiwan suggest that the real biological discounting rate is 2% per year, which is similar to the 3% long-term real interest rate for the economy, 1727–1900.

(2). Economists since Bentham and Jevons have theorized capacity for self-restraint with the concept of anticipated value; a decision-maker is able to wait when the pleasures of expectation are greater than pleasures of consumption (Loewenstein 1992, 10; see also Loewenstein 1987). Becker and Mulligan (1997) offer a theory in which anticipated value takes the form of "future oriented capital": resources spent imagining the future. Imagine you have just found out that you will move to a new city in three months' time. It is tempting to spend your time and other resources imagining the move and all its associated arrangements. The more you plan—research real estate values, investigate schools, etc.—the greater the benefits once the move occurs; but planning occurs at the cost of the work already on your desk. Given a limited budget of resources, people must strategically allocate this capital between present needs and future plans.

Becker and Mulligan assert that time preference is a function of wealth, for the wealthy have more resources to spend on planning. Age is also a significant predictor. Children learn to imagine the future as they grow older, and the elderly make fewer plans during their waning years. Social and cultural institutions affect the value of future-oriented capital by making the future more or less "vivid" (their term). Schooling, good health (and therefore long life expectancy), visits to the elderly, and a belief in an afterlife make the future more vivid and thus worth investing in. The immediate satisfaction of drug use reduces the vividness of future opportunities.

(3). Several authors have noted that there is an implicit risk associated with delayed outcomes (Rachlin et al. 1991; Green and Myerson 1996). Longer delays mean less information about the outcome, as well as greater exposure to hazards that could avert the anticipated outcome. The decision-maker may decide to consume what he assuredly has today rather than to hazard the investment failing in the future. Long-term investments are also higher-stake gambles, more eggs in fewer baskets.

(4). The "pleasures" of immediate gratification may be related to the immediacy of resource requirements. A starving person who needs to consume 1000 kcals within the next hour to avoid death will prefer a one-hour rabbit hunt, while the larger giraffe offers zero effective value. Animal behavior studies suggest that decision-makers may follow simple cognitive "rules of thumb" relative to their energetic needs. Caraco et al. (1980) argue for an "expected energy budget rule" for choices under risk, in which decision-makers choose probabilistic rewards when in energetic deficit. Snyderman (1983) has found evidence for a similar decision rule with delayed rewards. He offered captive pigeons the choice of two feeding options, represented by red or green illuminated keys that blinked asynchronously. Pecking the red key yielded six seconds of grain access after a ten-second delay. Pecking the green key yielded two seconds of grain after the same ten-second delay. Thus it was always more profitable to peck the red key, especially since the delay to the green key's reward represents an opportunity cost. Pigeons at 95% free-feeding body weight showed a strong preference for the larger reward. Pigeons at 80% free-feeding body weight would peck at any illuminated key without regarding its color. The decision-rule appears to be, when need is dire, take whatever you can get (seek risk, be impulsive).

These explanations are difficult to test comparatively for several reasons. First, they explain different phenomena: Roger's (1991, 1994) model explains the evolution of our species-wide time preferences, but does not explain interindividual differences in time preference, except to predict that young people will discount the future more than older people. Becker and Mulligan's (1997) future-oriented capital theory explains individual variation, but it does so without an evolutionary explanation for the benefits of valuing future-oriented capital. Uncertainty and hunger could be

incorporated into Becker and Mulligan's model, for both reduce the vividness of future plans. However, Becker and Mulligan have, by their own admission, changed the order of causality normally associated with risk and time preferences. Neoclassical game theory assumes that preferences determine behavior (von Neumann and Morgenstern 1944). In Becker and Mulligan's model, behavior (schooling, beliefs, wealth, etc.) determines time preferences.

Clearly more work is required to evaluate these explanations. I take from this discussion a list of candidate factors for determining an individual's discount rates: wealth, income, health, age, education, drug use, uncertainty, risk, and hunger. There is mixed support for the effects of many of these factors. Godoy and colleagues (Godoy et al. 2004; Kirby et al. 2002), in their ethnographic study of time preference among Tsimane' forager-horticulturalists of Bolivia, found that discount rates increase with age and education, while nutritional status, wealth, and moderate drug use have insignificant effects. In rural India, Pender (1996) found that wealthier individuals discount the future at lower rates, which he relates to their differential access to credit and their role as creditors themselves. In studies of Western subjects, Kirby and Hernnstein (1995) found a clear trend of decreasing discounting with increasing age. Kirby and Marakovic (1996) found a significant difference by sex, a factor not predicted by any of the explanations presented here.

METHOD AND EMPIRICAL RESULTS

Neoclassical economic theory posits that the equivalency of any two dissimilar options can be measured by examining the rate at which an individual is indifferent between bundles (quantities) of both, called the marginal rate of substitution. Fisher (1930), following the theoretic work of Böhm-Bawerk (1970 [1889]), formalized time preference as the marginal rate of substitution between present and future consumption (Loewenstein 1992, 16). Choice experiments reveal time preference by presenting an individual with a series of choices between immediate and delayed options in which either the quantities or delays are adjusted, until the subject cannot perceive one to be worth more than the other. The hyperbolic model predicts that the indifference values (v_i) are related to delay in a linear fashion, at slope k:

$$v_i = A(1 + kD) \qquad (3)$$

Thus, a single indifference value is sufficient to determine an individual's discount rate k.

I have made preliminary attempts to measure Mikea discount rates using two simple choice experiments. The methods, results, and interpretations are presented in detail elsewhere (Tucker in prep; Tucker and Steck in prep), but I summarize them here to illustrate how choice experiments work. The purpose of the first experiment was to test whether there are significant differences in time preferences among Mikea who primarily forage versus those who emphasize cultivation in their diversified portfolios. The reward amounts and delays were scaled to mimic the actual decision whether to forage or farm as closely as possible. Rewards were expressed as 100 kg gunnysacks of maize, which for logistical reasons were hypothetical rewards. The use of hypothetical rewards permitted repeated questions (see methodological discussions in Camerer and Hogarth 1999; Hertwig and Ortmann 2001).

The first question asked the participant to choose between one sack available now versus 12 sacks after six-months. If the participant preferred the one sack now, this indicates that his indifference value is greater than 12 sacks, for it would take some quantity greater than 12 sacks to make a six-month delay worthwhile. The next question is, which do you prefer, one sack now or 24 sacks after six months? If the participant prefers the 24 sacks, then his indifference value is greater than 12 and less than 24. A third question narrows the range. Which is better, one sack now or 18 sacks after six months? A choice of one sack now indicates the participant's indifference value is between 18 and 24 sacks. I record the indifference value as the midpoint of

this range, 21 sacks. A second trial repeated these questions with a delay of one month, and the third trial offered a delay of one year. As is typical in temporal choice experiments, results are expressed as the median k value because median is a more appropriate measure of central tendency than the mean in skewed and truncated distributions. Results suggest a median k value for the population as a whole of 2.00/month (N = 27). Median k value for those who primarily forage is 3.90/month, while those who emphasize farming discount at 1.40/month. This difference is statistically significant.

In the second experiment I offered a one-shot choice between a quarter-liter cup of cooking oil available now versus three cups after a delay of several days. This experiment offered real rewards, meaning that I actually gave the participant the cups of oil they chose after the promised delay. Cooking oil served well as a reward currency because it represents food value (cash is often spent on tobacco, which has its own unique utility curve); cooking oil is also easily storable and transportable, and highly desired. To limit potential jealousy related to unequal distribution of rewards, I offered the same choice to all participants in a given village and changed the delay to receive the three-cup option at each village visited. The three-cup option was delayed by two weeks at the first village, one week at the next site, and three days at the final location. A median indifference value was estimated for the population as a whole at 0.3–0.7/day (N = 49).

The only long-term ethnographic investigation of time preference among non-Western peoples was conducted by a team of researchers working among Tsimane' forager-horticulturalists of Bolivia (Kirby et al. 2002; Godoy et al. 2004). Their experiment consisted of eight choices between small, immediate rewards and larger delayed rewards, representing eight values for k as calculated by the hyperbolic discounting model. They repeated the experiment with the same 154 participants during five consecutive seasons, both to habituate participants to the procedure (the first season was considered a training period and the data were not used) and to test for seasonal variation, although individuals' preferences remained remarkably stable over time. They estimate median k values of 0.12/day for cash and 0.14/day for candy (Kirby et al. 2002, 302).

Pender (1996) conducted one of the few temporal choice experiments among peasants, rice cultivators in Andhra Pradesh, India. In his first experiment, he offered 96 participants the choice between eight pairs of options. The first option was an immediate reward of 10 kg rice, while the second was X kg rice after a delay of seven months, where X increased from 9 to 20 kg over the questions. Subsequent experiments used different amounts and delays. Pender calculates a median discount rate of 0.26–1.19/year, although it should be noted that unlike the other studies discussed here, he uses the exponential equation rather than the hyperbolic model.

A MODELER'S GUIDE TO DISCOUNT RATES

USING EMPIRICALLY REVEALED k VALUES

I argue that modelers concerned with subsistence choice should modify the value of delayed rewards by a discount rate. But as Figure 2.3 demonstrates, modelers can basically tell any story they wish about the comparative value of immediate versus delayed rewards depending on the k value that is used. Since archaeologists and other modelers of prehistoric decisions cannot conduct choice experiments with their subjects, this section provides a rough guide to choosing reasonable discount rates, based on two lines of argumentation.

The first line of thought is empirical and comparative, based on the results of the choice experiments described above, and summarized in Table 2.1 (see also Tucker in prep). Modelers may choose reasonable k values in the range of those revealed in previous experiments. The key is that k must be expressed in the proper time units. Notice that the rates reported in the first Mikea experiment are expressed per month, while the

second Mikea experiment and the Tsimane' experiment report rates per day, and Pender's rate is per year. Table 2.1 converts discount rates across a range of time units. This reveals a problem with cross-study comparison: the value of k is highly sensitive to the scale of reward amount and delay length. Discount rates for small rewards over small time units predict unreasonably high discount rates over larger time units, and vice-versa, suggesting that decision-makers discount large rewards at lower rates than small rewards (Kirby and Marakovic 1996). The best way to counteract this is to choose k values from experiments with similarly scaled rewards and delays.

For example, if we wanted to compare results from different experiments, it would be inappropriate to compare the Tsimane' results with the Indian peasant results, even when k is converted into the same time units. Because the second Mikea experiment and the Tsimane' experiment use small rewards with delays spanning several days, we can justifiably compare them and conclude that both populations of forager-horticulturalists discount at similar rates.

EXOGENOUS FACTORS

The second line of argumentation is a theoretical speculation about the probable influence of our list of candidate determinants on an individual's discount rates for a particular activity. I divide these candidate determinants into categories: exogenous factors relate to the activity itself, while endogenous factors pertain to the decision-making individual.

The two exogenous factors are the rate and manner in which objective value appreciates over time; and production risk, or the probability that an activity will fail before the rewards are received. Generally speaking, faster accumulation of marginal value, low risk, and the ability to harvest early if necessary should decrease discount rates, while a contrary set of conditions should increase discount rates.

The longer the herder defers slaughtering his animals, the more their value appreciates through growth and reproduction (although disease, theft, etc. could lead to a negative

a.

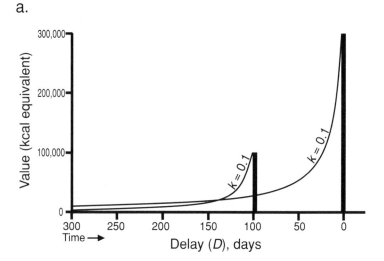

b.

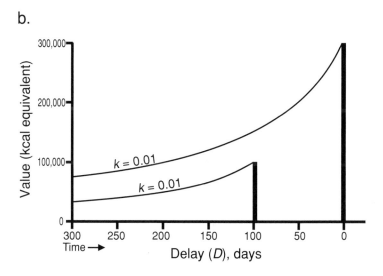

c.

FIGURE 2.3. Given a choice between a smaller reward after a shorter delay versus a larger reward after a longer delay, a subject's preference depends entirely on discount rates. Figure 2.3a demonstrates "preference switching," at long delay, the larger reward is preferred, but preferences switches to the smaller reward when it becomes more immediately available. In Figure 2.3b, the larger reward is always preferred. In 2.3c, the smaller reward is always preferred. Intertemporal choice models depend entirely on which discount rate values are used.

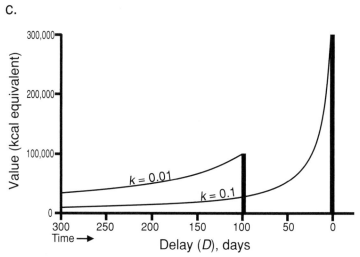

TABLE 2.1
Discount Rates Revealed in Experiments with Nonwestern Peoples, Converted Across Time Units (Original Units in Bold)

POPULATION AND STUDY	N	REWARD CURRENCY	k/DAY	k/MONTH	k/YEAR
Mikea (Tucker in prep)	49	Real cups of cooking oil	**0.30–0.70**	9.13–21.32	109.65–255.85
Mikea (Tucker & Steck in prep)		Hypothetical 100 kg sacks of maize			
– all	27		0.07	**2.00**	24.00
– primarily foragers	10		0.13	**3.90**	46.80
– primarily farmers	17		0.05	**1.40**	16.80
Tsimané, Bolivié (Kirby et al. 2002)	154	Cash	**0.12**	3.66	43.86
		Candy	**0.14**	4.26	51.17
Indian peasants (Pender 1996)	96	Real kg rice	0.00	0.10	**1.19**

interest rate). Animals with rapid growth and reproduction such as sheep and goats should be discounted less than slow reproducers such as cattle and camels. But, as Mace and Houston model (1989), smallstock may reproduce rapidly, but they are more likely to die during droughts than are slow-reproducing cattle and camels. This risk should increase the discount rate for small stock.

With regards to plant foods, there may be a significant difference between plants with edible leaves, stems, roots, and tubers versus plants with edible fruit, seeds, and flowers. The former provide a small amount of objective value shortly after germination, followed by a long period of time during which they gradually increase in size or number. Eventually, appreciation diminishes asymptotically as leaves reach a maximum size and stems, roots, and tubers become increasingly fibrous. With these plants the decision-maker always has the option of early harvest ("cashing-in"), so they should be discounted less than the second category. The second category, plants with edible fruit, seeds, and flowers, provide no objective food value until several months after planting and germination, at which point they must be promptly harvested or the food value will degrade. The long delay to food value coupled with the shorter harvesting window suggests that these rewards should be discounted more highly. To the degree that risk-minimizing strategies such as sharing (Winterhalder 1986, 1990; Hames 1990) and field scattering (Winterhalder 1990; Goland 1993a, b) can effectively reduce the variance, they may also decrease k accordingly.

As an example, consider the effect of exogenous variables on the discounted value of the two most significant cultivated plants for Mikea: maize and manioc. A maize field offers zero objective food value until very late in the delay. The earliest a farmer can "cash in" on his investment is to consume immature green corn, which is mealy, difficult to digest, and 20% less calorie-rich than mature maize grains (Morrison 1954, 569). O'Shea (1989, 61) has suggested that green corn consumption, which was common among pre-contact Native Americans, was a strategy to minimize risk. Farmers accept a 20% loss to offset the probability of crop loss before the maize is properly ripened. Mikea do not harvest green corn, but they do harvest a portion of their crop to eat as corn-on-the-cob.

In maize *hatsake*, risk is greatest shortly after planting. If rainfall is insufficient, the seed will fail to germinate. Mikea commonly say that the best strategy is to plant the day *before* the first heavy rainfall (a strategy called *katray* or *soima*), but this is obviously difficult to predict. It is not uncommon for hatsake farmers to replant a field a second or third time if the previous planting failed to result in germination. Once the maize has sprouted, risk increases steadily as the plant becomes a larger and more tempting target for grasshopper swarms. Because hatsake are not guarded or enclosed, mature maize stalks are frequently lost to livestock and thieves. Stories of farmers losing entire crops a day or two before harvest are common. Because maize is a long-term investment that yields little food value until the end of the delay, and because the field is likely to fail up until the last moment before harvest, hatsake are likely to be highly discounted compared to other activities.

Manioc differs significantly from maize in that the plants have objective food value a month or two after planting, in the form of growing tubers (as well as leaves). The farmer is free to harvest the crop at any time, but the longer she defers harvest, the larger and more valuable the tubers become. Manioc tubers grow fastest during the rainy season, but this is also the time of greatest risk of crop loss due to rot and flooding. Mikea and their neighbors typically practice three strategies. The first strategy is to plant and harvest manioc continually. They harvest what they need to eat each day, then replant the stems immediately to harvest them again four months later. The tubers tend to be small, bitter, and require high processing labor per unit food, but manioc grown in this fashion resembles an immediate-return investment. This method is mostly practiced by Mikea in lakebed gardens. The most common strategy among Masikoro is to let manioc grow for 12 months before harvest. The field is planted before the first rains (November or December) to take advantage of the rapid tuber growth in the wet soil. It is then harvested and replanted just before the next rainy season, thus maximizing maturation time while obviating the risk of a second rainy season. A third strategy, called *aritse*, requires leaving manioc to mature for 16 to 24 months, thus enduring two rainy seasons. Because manioc can potentially be harvested at any time, future manioc harvests should be discounted less than maize. A farmer can often pre-emptively harvest ahead of floodwaters or thieving neighbors. However, delays to large harvests are typically much longer than for maize.

ENDOGENOUS FACTORS

Endogenous factors include age, sex, education, drug use, health, wealth, income, and hunger. Generally speaking, greater age (at least until advanced years), education, wealth, health, and income should lower discounting rates, while greater use of drugs and hunger should increase discounting. Archaeologists may not be able to distinguish individual age and sex differences, and drug abuse and formal education may have less meaning in prehistoric contexts. I suggest that immediate food supply may be the endogenous factor with the greatest tractability and causal salience. Individuals with low health status, wealth, or income may discount the future because they are hungry. As hunger changes over relatively short spans of time, discount rates may also experience fluctuation.

FUTURE DISCOUNTING AND THE MIKEA ECONOMY

A FORMAL MODEL OF FORAGING AND FARMING

Here I demonstrate the application of future discounting to subsistence choice by providing a possible explanation for the persistence of the mixed foraging-horticulture strategy among Mikea and other populations occupying Bruce Smith's middle ground.

I propose that Mikea cultivate because the potential rewards from agriculture are very high compared with daily foraging gains, even when the value of the future harvest is discounted in the present. But because agricultural labor yields no immediate food value, every day spent farming increases the households' hunger. Increasing hunger, as an important endogenous factor, increases the rate at which agricultural rewards are discounted, until farming is valued less than foraging, leading to a switch in preference to immediate gratification. Foraging solves immediate food needs, reducing the discount rate again. But time spent foraging robs anticipated labor from agriculture, thus reducing the expected value of future harvests. The result is a downward spiral of expectations. Despite a clear motivation to farm, and although more labor investment would provide a greater reward, immediate needs cyclically limit the household's capacity to invest "future oriented capital."

I formalize this explanation as a simple dynamic model below, then discuss its basic behavior using values from Mikea research (which I have operationalized in a spreadsheet). Like all simple models, this one requires a certain relaxation of "real world" accuracy in favor of increased generality. Modelers commonly make this tradeoff when offering a new hypothetical set of interactions; the number of interacting variables are kept to a minimum so that the effect of each can be easily understood (Starfield and Bleloch 1986). The important simplifying assumptions of this model are that every day must be spent either foraging or farming (no resting or engaging in other activities). A day spent doing either activity provides a constant gain, either in the present (foraging) or in the future (farming).

The first element of the model is the anticipated outcome of agriculture. The household imagines that working a field will yield a quantity $\hat{A}$ when $D = 0$ (time is measured as delay D, a countdown to harvest). The variable A_D is a cumulative measure of value invested in the field up to delay D. A_D starts at zero and increases by a each day the household spends doing agricultural labor. Meanwhile, if important agricultural labor is neglected, expectations are lowered and $\hat{A}$ decreases. Eventually, $\hat{A}$ (the expectation) and A_D (the reality) will converge. The value of agriculture on any given day before this convergence is the discounted value of $\hat{A}$.

$$\hat{A}/(1 + kD) \qquad (4a)$$

After the convergence, the decision to spend the day farming means that more labor will be

invested into the field than was originally anticipated. The value of farming becomes:

$$(\hat{A} + a)/(1 + kD) \qquad (4b)$$

In contrast, a day spent foraging will yield a certain immediate gain of food value g, which is not discounted. The gains from foraging are in addition to the value the household has confidently invested in its field up to this point. A day spent foraging has the value:

$$g + [A_D/(1 + kD)] \qquad (5)$$

If (4) is greater than (5), the household will spend the day working in the fields, contributing $+a$ to A_D (as well as to $\hat{A}$ after the convergence). But spending the day cultivating also carries an opportunity cost. By choosing not to forage, the household has failed to gain any more immediate food value. The increased threat of hunger contributes a penalty h to the discount rate k.

If (5) is greater than (4), the household will spend the day foraging. Because a day spent foraging produces immediate food value, hunger is satisfied, and k is reduced by h. For current purposes I set the condition that k can never diminish below its initial value. Before the convergence of $\hat{A}$ and A_D, there is an opportunity cost to foraging. Because the anticipated value of the field is based on an implicit prediction of labor investment, a day spent foraging cannot be used to achieve $\hat{A}$. Thus, $\hat{A}$ is reduced by a.

If h is sufficiently large, cyclical changes in k, $\hat{A}$, and A_D cause preference switches between foraging and farming producing the result that households spend less labor on agriculture than they originally anticipate. The household must forage to meet immediate needs, limiting their capacity to invest in future harvests.

WILD OVY TUBERS VERSUS MAIZE

To illustrate this model, let us consider the hypothetical case of a Mikea household of six individuals (two children, two adolescents, and two adults of both sexes) who plant a three-hectare

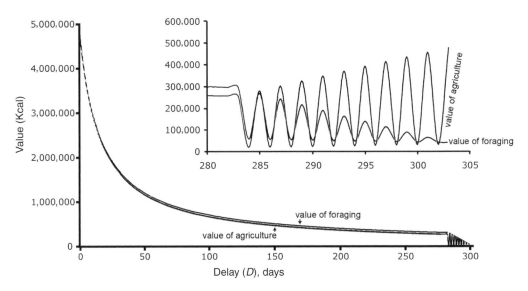

FIGURE 2.4. Results of dynamic simulation of foraging/framing preference model using reasonable values from Mikea research (see text).

hatsake. Consistent with time allocation data, all six household members forage while only the adolescents and adults contribute agricultural labor (Tucker and Young 2005). The simulation begins in the month of July, which is typically the time of year when Mikea decide whether and to what extent they should cultivate maize in the coming year; D begins 303 days before the maize harvest. The household imagines a three-hectare cleared hatsake. The anticipated value of this field is 930 kg/ha times 3640 kcal/kg times three hectares: $\hat{A}$ begins at approximately 10,000,000 kcal. The daily gain from foraging is provided by mean age and sex-specific net acquisition rates reported in Tucker and Young (2005) times the average duration of tuber foraging trip, 300 minutes; $g = 39,400$ kcal/day spent foraging.

I assume that Mikea discount future agricultural rewards at the average rates revealed experimentally. Because this simulation involves large rewards and long-scale delays, the appropriate discount rates are those revealed in the sacks of maize experiment: $k = 2.00$/month (Tucker and Steck in prep). I convert this into the daily rate of $k = 0.066$/day.

To begin with, let us assume that a day's agricultural labor contributes $a = 500,000$ kcals to the final harvest. At this rate, the household will have to work 20.3 days to achieve an $\hat{A}$ of 10,000,000 kcals. Let us further assume the hunger penalty is $0.5k$ (0.033/day). The results of this simulation are presented in Figure 2.4. The inset demonstrates oscillating values before the convergence point. The convergence point occurs on day 19. Up to this point, the household spends alternating days foraging and farming. They only contribute half the labor (ten days) to farming that they originally anticipated, and the final harvest is 5,000,000 kcal.

What happens if the discount rate is increased? Recall that preliminary experiments revealed that Mikea who primarily forage discount future sacks of maize at 3.9/month (0.13/day). Changing k by this magnitude has little effect on the model's predictions, except that one day fewer is spent farming, and the final reward is 4,500,000 kcal. At $k = 0.4$/day, only six of the anticipated 20 days of agricultural labor are invested, producing a final reward of only 3,000,000 kcal.

What happens if the discount rate is decreased? As k approaches zero, more days are spent farming. If we use the midpoint of Pender's (1996) value for Indian peasants, converted to days (0.0016/day), the household

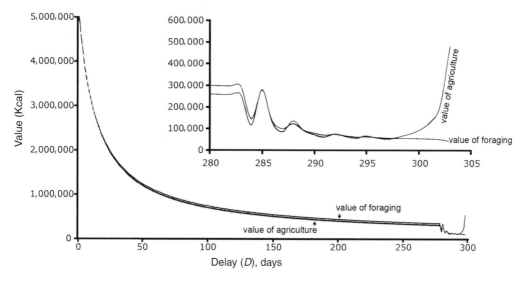

FIGURE 2.5. Results of dynamic simulation of foraging/farming preference model when the hunger penalty is reduced by an order of magnitude (see text).

accomplishes 13 days of agricultural labor. Because h is a fraction of k, the small h means value does not oscillate, and the 13 days are spent consecutively. The final harvest is 6,500,000 kcal. If $k = 0$, there is no discounting, and every day is spent farming.

What happens if the hunger penalty is decreased? Resetting k at 0.066/day, h is then reduced by an order of magnitude (0.0033/day). Results are displayed in Figure 2.5. The number of days spent farming remains at ten, but preference switches between foraging and farming at a different frequency. Six days of farming occur before the household is hungry enough to be forced into foraging; two days of foraging are required before the household can farm again. An artifact of the simplifying assumptions of this model is that increasing h beyond 0.5k has no effect on the model, for no matter how grave the effect of hunger after a day spent farming, a day of foraging resets k to its initial value.

ELABORATIONS

The realism of this model is constrained by its simplifying assumptions. To better approach "real life," this model could be modified in a number of ways. First, a household is unlikely to spend every day working. A day of rest would

still have subsistence value, for the household can enjoy the anticipated rewards of the labor they have already invested in their maturing fields. The value of a day of rest would be simply the discounted value of A_D. In order for rest to ever be worth more than foraging, the model would have to track the energetic costs of days spent farming, foraging, and resting. Resting is a cheaper way to spend the day. Alternatively, need for rest could affect k in a similar way as hunger.

Another limiting assumption is that any day spent foraging will produce the same amount of food, and any day spent farming will contribute equal marginal benefit to the eventual harvest. The variables g and a should really be nonlinear functions of D. The benefits of foraging and farming labor change over the course of time. Among Mikea, tuber foraging efficiency decreases over the dry season, as travel times to unharvested patches increases. Agricultural labor is of course highly seasonal, with regards to labor tasks and marginal benefits, and generally exhibits diminishing marginal returns to labor.

The model's insensitivity to increasing the value of the hunger penalty h suggests that this is probably not a constant value. It may take more than one day to accrue and pay off hunger debts. Future research should explore the affect of hunger and other immediate needs on time preference.

IMPLICATIONS FOR THE EVOLUTION OF INTENSIVE CULTIVATION

If immediate food needs doom would-be cultivators to chronic under-investment of labor, how does intensive agriculture evolve? The model suggests two possible answers. First, exogenous factors could affect reward amounts and discount rates. If agriculture becomes more profitable or less risky (given the same level of labor investment), or if foraging becomes less profitable or more risky, the household will increase its allocation of labor to agriculture. This prediction is consistent with Price and Gebauer's (1995b) assertion that agriculture is adopted most readily in areas of resource abundance, in contrast to the traditional view that agriculture is a desperate invention to deal with food scarcity (Childe 1965; Cohen 1977). Second, endogenous factors could affect an individual's time preferences. Alternative sources for immediate food needs could eliminate the effects of hunger altogether.

Neighbors to Mikea are Masikoro intensive cultivators. Savanna farmers have access to better soils and more dependable and predictable rainfall, as well as surface water sources that can be used for irrigation. Cheap pesticides and herbicides have been made available in recent years. Masikoro farmers experience higher rewards with less risk, and so discount future harvests to a lesser degree.

Masikoro farmers have at least two sources to meet their immediate food needs that detract little from their farming labor: storage, and the market economy. Stored agricultural foodstuffs provide a constant source of immediate food value. Farmers subsist off these stores while waiting for the next harvest. They can also sell their surplus, or their surplus labor, to earn cash. Cash retains its value over time, and can be used to obtain food whenever the household is in need. Masikoro farmers use their cash to purchase foraged products from the Mikea,

thus gaining the same immediate gratification that Mikea gain from foraging.

Storage of large surpluses would be an effective way to limit preference switches between immediate and delayed rewards, favoring investment of future-oriented capital. Caches of seeds found in Archaic-period rockshelter sites in Kentucky and Arkansas suggest that storage predates intensive cultivation by millennia (Gremillion 1997b; Fritz 1997). These stores probably represent buffers of predictable, seasonal food stress. How could enough food be stored to support a household during the proceeding agricultural cycle? Surplus on this order of magnitude can only be produced by intensifying labor input, and intensification is impossible without stored foods from the previous year.

One possibility has been suggested by Flannery's (1986a) study of the emergence of agriculture at Guila Naquitz in Oaxaca, Mexico. In a computer simulation of foraging and incipient cultivation, Reynolds (1986) predicted that people would be more likely to practice experimental food producing strategies in wet years, and conservative strategies during dry years. Flannery (1986b, 503) suggests that adaptation moves fastest when the two states alternate; new strategies are introduced in wet years and then rigorously selected in dry years. This may be the case here. Surplus for storage is produced during an extremely good year, and then in the bad year that follows, large stores lead to more intensive labor investment.

Trade represents another source of immediate food value. Foragers and farmers may develop symbiotic relationships. Foragers assure immediate food needs so that farmers can invest intensively in higher-yielding agricultural pursuits Farmers provide the majority of calories in the diet. The classic example is the relationship between the foraging Mbuti and Efe and their farming neighbors in the Congolese rainforest (Turnbull 1965). Relationships of this sort may have occurred at the origins of settled agriculture in the Levant, where foragers and farmers co-existed (Bar-Yosef and Meadow 1995). The need to exchange immediate and delayed-return foods may help to explain the origins of the market economy.

CONCLUSIONS

This chapter has pursued dual goals: first, to review the future discounting literature and establish its applicability and appropriateness to studies of human subsistence decision-making, and second, to illustrate the potential of future discounting models by offering an explanation for the persistence of a mixed foraging-horticultural strategy among Mikea of Madagascar, and by ethnoarchaeological extension, to other populations in the middle ground between foraging and intensive cultivation. The main conclusions are as follows.[3]

1. The average rate maximization assumption of foraging theory is inappropriate when modeling choice among options with dissimilar delays to reward, such as the choice between foraging and farming.

2. Descriptive models of the effects of waiting time on value have usually taken the form of discounted utility models. While there are certain reasons for preferring the hyperbolic model, neither is derived from theory nor parameterized in terms of exogenous or endogenous factors.

3. Possible explanations for why people discount the future include the value of intergenerational inheritance, the value of anticipation, the risk and uncertainty of delayed outcomes, and the priority of immediate needs. Future research is required to better evaluate these theories.

4. When using empirically revealed discount rates in subsistence models, it is important to use rates from experiments with similarly scaled rewards and delays. Time preference is sensitive to scalar issues, so that preferences for small rewards over short delays may not adequately predict preferences for large rewards after long delays.

5. While a modeler interested in prehistoric decisions cannot conduct choice experiments, discount rates may vary predictably according to certain exogenous and endogenous factors, such as the rate objective value appreciates, risk, and immediate food supply.

6. One explanation for why many subsistence populations practice a mix of foraging and low-investment horticulture is that farming provides higher rewards even when discounted, but investment in future profits is limited by immediate needs.

7. A simple model demonstrates cyclical switches in preference between foraging and farming labor. The value of agriculture on a given day is the discounted value of the anticipated harvest; this expectation diminishes when agricultural labor is neglected. The value of foraging is a nondiscounted constant, added to the discounted value of labor invested in the field up to that point, which increases with every day spent farming. The discount rate oscillates as farming increases hunger without yielding immediately-available food.

8. This model predicts agricultural intensification when harvests increase in size or decrease in risk, consistent with Price and Gebauer's (1995b) assertion that agriculture is adopted under conditions of food abundance. Labor may also be intensified if immediate food needs are met somehow other than foraging (or another work activity), such as by storage or trade.

NOTES

1. I calculate the net acquisition rate for an uncleared hatsake as follows. Focal follow data suggest planting costs of 11 hrs/ha at 4 kcal/min. A survey of 16 fields in 1998–1999 (including fields with total crop loss) revealed a mean yield of 500 kg dry grain/ha. According to Wu Leung (1968), 1 kg maize = 3640 kcal. The gross gain is thus (500 kg * 3640 kcal/kg) = 1,820,000 kcal/ha. Divided by 11 labor hrs/ha = 165,455 kcal/hr. Minus labor costs of 240 kcal/hr = 165,215 kcal/hr.

2. I calculate the net acquisition rate for weeded hatsake in the same manner. Focal follow data estimate clearing costs of 24.7 hrs/ha at 5.8 kcal/min, and a survey of 141 fields including those with total crop loss revealed a mean yield of 910 kg/ha. The gross gain is 910 kg * 3640 kcal/kg = 3,312,400 kcal/ha, divided by 35.7 labor hrs/ha = 92,784 kcal/hr; minus labor costs of 315 kcal/hr = 92,469 kcal/hr.

3. Acknowledgments. Many of the ideas in this paper evolved during conversations with Bruce Winterhalder and Mitch Renkow. Bruce the ecologist encouraged me to think about how objective value changes through time, while Mitch the economist urged me to consider the subjective value of deferring gratification. Insightful comments and encouragement were also provided by Doug Kennett, Daniel Steck, Robert Kelly, Kris Gremillion, Alyson Young, Richard Yerkes, Ivy Pike, Christopher Rodning, Amber VanDerwarker, Gregory Wilson, and James Yount. Fieldwork in Madagascar was funded by a Fulbright grant and a National Science Foundation Dissertation Improvement Grant. Fieldwork was facilitated by the hard work and cooperation of Tsiazonera, Jaovola Tombo, Tsimitamby, Gervais (Veve) Tantely, and our friends in the Mikea Forest.

3

Central Place Foraging and Food Production on the Cumberland Plateau, Eastern Kentucky

Kristen J. Gremillion

Forager-farmers of the eastern Kentucky uplands had to decide where to locate their garden plots relative to the cliff shelters in which food was stored for winter use. This decision often involved a tradeoff between distant, but fertile, alluvial soils and nearby erosion-prone hillsides of relatively low fertility. The key role of travel and transportation costs in this case makes it well suited to analysis using central place foraging theory. The classical model of central place foraging developed within behavioral ecology assumes that animals that transport food to a secure area before consuming it tend to maximize the rate of delivery of energy to this central place; energy acquired after accounting for the costs of round-trip travel and transport. Central place foraging theory is used to structure a quantitative simulation of subsistence options available to a prehistoric group that used the Courthouse Rock shelter as a storage location. This simulation estimates the economic outcomes expected from alternative choices of crop species (Iva annua vs. Chenopodium berlandieri), ecological status (uncultivated vs. domesticated), and habitat (floodplain vs. upland) in a specific environmental setting. Results indicate that the floodplain habitat offers superior return rates for both plants when harvested seeds are transported to Courthouse Rock, despite the costs of travel. Iva annua (sumpweed) collected in the floodplain habitat is more profitable than chenopod at this distance, irrespective of whether the plants harvested are domesticated or wild. Greater distances favor a switch to hillside cultivation of chenopod, but not of sumpweed, which loses much of its competitive edge when it is grown in upland settings. These results suggest it is unlikely that either floodplain or hillside farming was consistently superior economically, and that in some situations, cultivation had no significant advantage over harvesting wild stands.

Between 4000 and 3000 radiocarbon years ago (cal 2600 to 1300 BC) prehistoric human foragers living on the Cumberland Escarpment of eastern Kentucky began cultivating seed crops (Cowan 1985b; Cowan et al. 1981; Gremillion 1993c, 1994, 1996b, 1998; Smith and Cowan 1987). People of this region frequently stored their seed harvests, as well as other foods, in dry rock shelters situated on the high cliffs above stream valleys. The occurrence of hearths and other cultural features in these shelters, along with the density of habitation refuse, indicate that they were also used as habitation sites (Cowan 1985a; Gremillion 1995). People camped not only beneath these sheltered overhangs, but also on the alluvial terraces that are separated from the cliffs by steep slopes (Cowan 1985a). Given the long-established function of rock shelters as storage places, plant cultivation necessarily involved a decision of potentially great economic importance: whether to grow seed crops in close proximity to their destined storage spots, or to cultivate the highly fertile, but more distant, alluvial soils.

This tradeoff, which entails some sacrifice of habitat quality in favor of low travel costs, or vice versa, has essentially the same structure as certain foraging models that assume that food is acquired some distance away from the place where it is consumed. Modeling, foraging theory in particular, has proven useful for furthering explanation of subsistence changes observed archaeologically (Barlow and Metcalfe 1996; Bettinger et al. 1997; Bird 2002; Bird and Bliege-Bird 1997; Bird 1997; Bird and Bliege-Bird 2000; Broughton 1997, 2002; Gardner 1992; Grayson and Delpech 1998; Grayson and Cannon 1999; Gremillion 2002; Madsen 1993; Madsen and Schmitt 1998; Metcalfe and Barlow 1992; Piperno and Pearsall 1998; Reidhead 1976; Reidhead 1980; Simms 1987; Winterhalder and Goland 1997). By reducing decisions to their most essential variables, those most likely to affect the adaptedness of the individual, models simplify real-world complexity. This process allows us to unpack the jumble of interrelated economic components of any subsistence choice in order to better understand the relative utility of the options available to prehistoric people. Some of the hypotheses generated to explain actual behavior fare better than others under this kind of scrutiny, and point to potentially fruitful programs of analysis.

Foraging theory—microeconomic analysis embedded within a Darwinian explanatory framework and an ecological context—can in principle be applied to any fitness-enhancing behavior, not food acquisition exclusively. The flexibility of foraging models also holds when we turn our attention from food *collecting* in the strict sense to food *production,* in which the decision-making individual has a significant influence on the distribution and density of resources. Recognition of the relevance of foraging models to food production has prompted archaeologists to explore the development of agricultural systems within an evolutionary ecology framework (Barlow 2002; Gardner 1992; Gremillion 1996a, 1998; Keegan 1986; Piperno and Pearsall 1998; Reidhead 1976).

I use a model of central place foraging to investigate the economic consequences of different garden plot settings for human groups using rock shelters as storage locations. The goal of this exercise is neither to test the predictions of central place foraging theory against the archaeological record, nor to assess the validity of the models themselves. The theoretical model is used to provide a framework for analysis and to identify variables relevant to decision making when the costs of round-trip travel have a significant effect on the efficiency of gathering and gardening. Interrelationships between these variables are incorporated into a simulation that predicts the return rates of various strategies in a specific environmental setting. The simulation illustrates in quantitative terms how the constraints of central place foraging might affect the value, in the currency of energetic efficiency, of cultivation strategies that vary by habitat, the distance between cultivated plots and a central storage location, and crop characteristics. The results of this analysis are used to frame a number of new hypotheses and chart directions for future research.

CENTRAL PLACE FORAGING

Several candidate models exist for the analysis of food choice, each of which operates under a different mix of decisions and constraints. The most familiar is the diet breadth or prey choice model, which predicts the "menu" of food items that yields the best average energy return rate under specified conditions of resource density (Kaplan and Hill 1992; Pyke et al. 1977; Stephens and Krebs 1986). Other models of diet choice examine related problems such as habitat selection or time allocation where the decision to be made is which resource patches to visit and how long to exploit them (Charnov 1976; MacArthur and Pianka 1966; Wiens 1976) or central place foraging examined here (Bettinger et al. 1997; Bird and Bliege-Bird 1997; Bird 1997; Orians and Pearson 1979; Rands et al. 2000). The constraints of central place foraging broadly affect optimal diet choice. I have used a formal model to isolate key relationships between round-trip travel distance, load size, and prey choice. This body of theory is a promising one for archaeologists because humans deposit accumulations of refuse at their central places, including traces of food-related activity. In this paper, I apply central place foraging theory, hereafter refered to as CPF, to an archaeological issue: the location of cultivated plots relative to habitation sites. More specifically, CPF provides the tools for a comparison of the economic utility of different strategies of garden location available to a small, mobile group producing crops primarily for storage.

PREDICTIONS OF THE CENTRAL PLACE FORAGING MODEL

The central place foraging model considers the effects of travel costs on the decisions analyzed by theories of patch choice; where to forage, and prey choice; what resources to pursue while foraging within a patch. For a central place forager, *efficiency while feeding* does not necessarily translate into increased fitness; success is more appropriately measured by the *rate of delivery* to the central place (Orians and Pearson 1979). Central place foraging therefore changes the costs and benefits of decisions foragers must make regarding which resources and patches to exploit; how much to transport on each trip; op-

timal load size; and where to locate the central place with respect to resource patches (Orians and Pearson 1979).

Round-trip transport has several important implications for resource choice. Returning to a central place, as opposed to on-the-spot consumption, constrains the optimal resource set to items that yield sufficient energy to offset the costs of round-trip travel. The greater the distance between central place and patch, the larger the minimum acceptable prey size; the minimum load offsets handling costs. This relationship is illustrated graphically in Figure 3.1. The horizontal axis represents time, with time spent acquiring food increasing to the right of the origin and time spent traveling to its left. The horizontal axis represents energy acquired. The solid curve plots the relationship between time spent in the patch and energy acquired, the within-patch return rate. A line drawn tangent to the returns curve from a point T_1 on the horizontal axis to the left of the origin (T_1ret) represents the rate of return the forager can expect by spending that amount of time traveling to the patch, then returning with its prey to a central place. As travel time increases from T_1 to T_2, 1) the slope of T_2ret is lower than that of T_1ret, indicating a drop in return rates as travel costs go up, so that 2) the forager must acquire more energy in order to offset these added costs, thus increasing the minimum acceptable load size. For human foragers longer trips should produce larger, more energy-rich loads than shorter trips.

ARCHAEOLOGICAL APPLICATIONS OF THE CENTRAL PLACE FORAGING MODEL

Jones and Madsen (1989) observed that there is an upper limit on net energy capture per trip that is set by the size of the load a human forager can carry. In the Great Basin, for example, grasshoppers occur in large drifts and can be collected and consumed with minimal effort, providing extraordinarily high return rates. However, when transported in basketloads over long distances, a load of grasshoppers results in

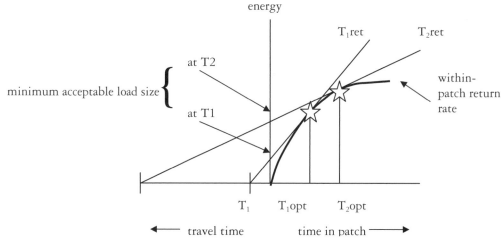

FIGURE 3.1. Graphical version of the central place foraging model. The horizontal axis represents time, with travel time increasing to the left of the origin and time spent foraging increasing to its right. The vertical axis measures energy acquired. The curved line shows the returns curve expected while foraging within the patch. The two straight lines T_1ret and T_2ret are drawn tangent to the returns curve from points representing different amounts of travel time (T_1 and T_2) on the horizontal axis. The slope of each line indicates the rate of return expected from the patch at that distance when round-trip travel to and from a central place is considered. Optimal amounts of time to spend foraging within the patch (T_1opt and T_2opt) are found at the intersections of the line drawn from these points of tangency (marked by stars) and perpendicular to the horizontal axis. The minimal acceptable load size for each travel distance is found where the straight lines from T_1 and T_2 cross the vertical axis.

a net loss of energy because their ratio of energy per unit volume is so low. Jones and Madsen calculated the maximum transport distance, MTD, for a number of important Great Basin resources using burden baskets from ethnographic collections to estimate load size. Although they do not refer to CPF, Jones and Madsen elaborated on the CPF model by showing how some resources fail to provide the minimal acceptable "prey size" for a relatively distant patch even though they offer high return rates if they are consumed immediately. Rhode (1990) critiqued this model, arguing that Jones and Madsen's MTDs were never reached in actuality because of the availability of less costly alternative resources located nearer to forager camps.

Ecologists and archaeologists have both observed that central place foraging creates a tradeoff between the costs of field processing and the costs of transporting the inedible portions of a resource packet. Field processing adds to overall handling time per trip but at the same time increases the energy content of each load. Removal of waste such as bones, mollusc shell, or nutshell in the field pays off when the time thus spent is offset by the resulting reduction in costs of transport. A threshold is most likely to appear when substantial travel distances are involved and waste materials that can be removed and discarded are bulky, heavy, or both. Partial processing optimizes food acquisition at intermediate distances (Bettinger et al. 1997; Bird 1997; Metcalfe and Barlow 1992; Rands et al. 2000).

CENTRAL PLACE FORAGING AND GARDEN LOCATION IN EASTERN KENTUCKY

THE CUMBERLAND ESCARPMENT LANDSCAPE AND ITS RESOURCES

The western edge of the Cumberland Escarpment in eastern Kentucky contains extensive

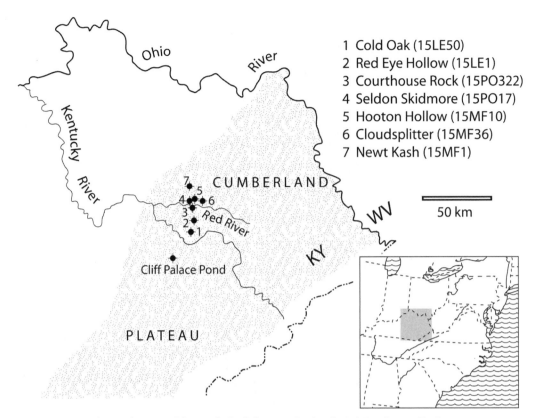

1 Cold Oak (15LE50)
2 Red Eye Hollow (15LE1)
3 Courthouse Rock (15PO322)
4 Seldon Skidmore (15PO17)
5 Hooton Hollow (15MF10)
6 Cloudsplitter (15MF36)
7 Newt Kash (15MF1)

FIGURE 3.2. Map showing locations of the Cumberland Plateau and archaeological sites discussed in the text.

sandstone cliffs that tower above the valleys of the Kentucky River and its tributaries (Figure 3.2). Differential erosion of these cliffs has formed numerous rock shelters, shallow overhangs that were frequently occupied by prehistoric people (Figure 3.3). In some cases, human groups remained in these shelters long enough, or visited them frequently enough, to leave substantial refuse deposits. The Red River, a major tributary of the Kentucky, flows through a deep gorge near its headwaters, traversing larger expanses of alluvium as it continues downstream. Approximately 20 km south of the main channel of the Red River, Big Sinking Creek meets the Kentucky River. Rock shelters located within the drainages of the North Fork of the Red River and Big Sinking Creek contain some of the best-preserved collections of prehistoric plant remains in the Eastern Woodlands.

These materials owe their survival to the unusual microclimates found within the sandy, nitrate-rich, dry sediments of rock shelters. Shelters that were often favored by human groups are extremely dry due to the protection of sandstone cliffs. Aridity and the nitrate-rich deposits within the shelters inhibit the activity of many biotic agents of decay, creating ideal conditions for the preservation of organic remains. At the same time, anthropogenic ash accumulation counteracts the potentially damaging effects of the naturally acidic sandstone (Mickelson 2002). Having some of the attributes of a giant dessicator filled with preservatives, the shelters are well suited to both food

FIGURE 3.3. Photograph of Courthouse Rock shelter during excavation.

storage and living quarters for small groups of people.

The landscape surrounding the shelters is dominated by steep slopes; level land is restricted to valley bottoms and some of the ridgetops that divide drainages (McGrain and Currens 1978). Considerable topographic diversity exists within relatively small areas due to locally high relief, which may exceed 122 m (McGrain and Currens 1978, 63). The highest elevations are approximately 440 m and are found above the sandstone caprock. Spatial relationships between upland and lowland landforms are illustrated schematically in Figure 3.4. Ridgetops support pine oak forests with an understory that includes *Vaccinium* sp. (blueberries), *Gaylussacia* sp. (huckleberries), and *Hamamelis virginiana* (witch hazel). Beneath the ridgetops lie the sandstone cliffs in which rock shelters form. Steep slopes below the cliff zone become less rugged, as they approach the valley bottoms, which may be narrow benches or broader floodplains, such as that of the Red River, with alluvial terraces. The upper slopes just above and below the cliffs are dominated by

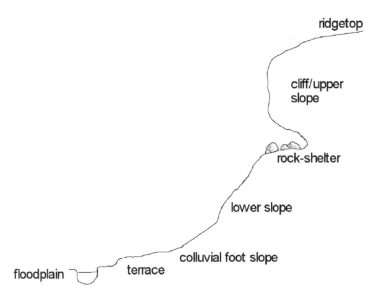

ridgetop

cliff/upper
slope

rock-shelter

lower slope

colluvial foot slope

floodplain   terrace

FIGURE 3.4. Schematic cross-section of a transect from ridgetop to valley bottom along the North Fork of the Red River, showing landforms and characteristic vegetation.

Quercus sp. (oaks), *Carya* spp. (hickories), *Pinus* sp. (pines), and/or *Castanea dentate* (chestnut) (Braun 1950; Higgins 1970). On lower slopes and along stream banks the diversity of woody species increases, exemplifying the Mixed Mesophytic forest type described by Braun (1950). These diverse forests vary in species composition according to degree of slope, slope aspect, soil moisture, and disturbance. Paleoecological evidence indicates widespread forest clearance and increased frequency of fires along the Cumberland Escarpment after about 1200 cal yrs BC (Delcourt et al. 1998).

The dendritic drainage pattern that divides the ridges of the Plateau distributes water throughout the landscape, with water levels varying seasonally. Drinking water can be collected in rock shelters as runoff from the ridgetops, while some shelters contain natural springs. Raw material for tool manufacture is available locally in streambeds and as chert outcrops (Graham 1990). The fruits of oak, chestnut, and hickory were staple food resources for prehistoric foragers in the Red River Gorge area, as were game animals, especially *Odocoileus virginiana* (white-tailed deer), *Meleagris gallopavo* (turkey), *Procyon lotor* (raccoon), and *Didelphis virginiana* (opossum) (Cowan 1985a; Gremillion 1995, 1999; Gremillion and Mickelson 1996).

THE ARCHAEOLOGICAL RECORD OF PREHISTORIC FARMING ON THE CUMBERLAND ESCARPMENT

Archaeological research has established the presence of domesticated forms of weedy annual plants at several rock shelter sites on the Cumberland Escarpment. Seeds of *Chenopodium berlandieri* (chenopod) from the Cloudsplitter rock shelter on the Red River exhibit the distinctive thin outer seed coat characteristic of domesticated forms of this species. Some of these specimens have been directly dated to 3450 +/− 150 BP (Smith and Cowan 1987). *Iva annua* (domesticated sumpweed) and *Cucurbita* (gourd) are also present in deposits dating to between cal 1800 and 1200 BC at both Cloudsplitter and the Cold Oak shelter (located in the Big Sinking Creek drainage (see Figure 3.2 for site locations; Cowan 1985a, b; Cowan et al. 1981; Gremillion 1993c, 1995). After cal 1200 BC, and perhaps somewhat earlier at the Courthouse Rock shelter on the Red River, the seeds of these plants, along with those of other cultivated plants such as *Phalaris caroliniana* (maygrass) and *Polygonum* spp. (knotweed) appear in dense concentrations in rock-shelter middens (Gremillion 1999).

Survey data suggest that shelter use increased in frequency and/or duration after cal

1200 BC, as seed crops became more prevalent (Cowan 1975, 1976, 1985b). People also spent time on ridgetops and in alluvial valleys, where they camped on stream terraces and colluvial slopes. Less is known about these open-air occupations, although test excavations have been carried out at some of them (Cowan 1975, 1976, 1985a; Cowan and Wilson 1977). Most archaeological effort in the region has focused instead on sheltered sites because of their paleoethnobotanical significance and losses to vandals.

ROCK SHELTERS AS CENTRAL PLACES

Although other kinds of food storage or habitation existed, rock-shelters offered advantages as central places that are unique in this landscape: shelter from precipitation and wind, sediments with preservative characteristics, and easy access to ridgetops where game and nut resources were abundant. Archaeological evidence indicates that shelters served as both seasonal or year-round habitations and as storage facilities.

Most of the rock-shelters on the Cumberland Escarpment investigated archaeologically show substantial accumulations of refuse such as broken pottery, lithic artifacts and debitage, faunal remains, and plant remains. Early reports of rockshelter excavations in Lee, Powell, and Menifee Counties of eastern Kentucky describe thick "ash beds" and numerous features, including human burials (Funkhouser and Webb 1929, 1930; Webb and Funkhouser 1936). More recent work at both Cloudsplitter and Cold Oak revealed pit features and hearth remnants that suggest long stays of weeks or months between cal 1800 and 500 BC (Cowan 1985a, b; Cowan et al. 1981; Gremillion 1993c, 1995). Repeated occupation of these rock-shelters is indicated by the presence of site furniture (such as bedrock mortars) and food and artifact caches.

The storage and consumption of crop seeds by forager-farmers of the Cumberland Plateau is demonstrated by their co-occurrence with seasonally specific plant macroremains in paleofeces from the Hooton Hollow and Newt Kash shelters (Gremillion 1996b). *Fragaria vir-*

giniana (strawberry), for example, is considered a reliable seasonal indicator because of the high likelihood that it was eaten fresh rather than dried for storage (Yarnell 1974a, b). Paleofeces that contain strawberry were most likely deposited in spring, whereas most of the crops represented in the same specimen were likely harvested in the late summer or early fall. Somewhat farther afield, in the Green River drainage of west-central Kentucky, pollen and macrobotanical data indicate that prehistoric cavers of the mid–first millennium BC also ate stored crops including sunflower, sumpweed, and chenopod (Gremillion and Sobolik 1996).

Storage pits appear in the archaeological record of the Cumberland Plateau prior to cal 1200 BC, but in most cases any food remains indicative of their original use were replaced by hearth sweepings and other refuse. One notable exception is Feature 8 at the Hooton Hollow rock shelter on the North Fork of the Red River (15Mf10), which contained several hundred whole hickory nuts (still in the shell but minus the leathery involucre that encases the nut). Red Eye Hollow shelter (15Le1) in the Big Sinking drainage contained a fiber bag filled with "shelled chinkapins" (W. S. Webb Museum of Anthropology catalog entry; the chinkapin is *Castanea pumila*, a close relative of the American chestnut, *C. dentata*). There were also several pits at Red Eye lined with pine bark, and oak and sassafrass leaves, all of which contain bioactive chemicals likely to have inhibited seed predation, including antibacterial, antifungal, and antipermeability agents (Duke 2002). However, the earliest direct evidence of seed crop storage comes from several pits excavated at the Cold Oak shelter. All of these features postdate cal 1200 BC (Gremillion 1995).

EARLY PLANT CULTIVATION AND LAND USE ON THE CUMBERLAND PLATEAU

The incorporation of plant cultivation into dietary regimes required some reallocation of time and space to the new resource. Along the Cumberland Escarpment, alluvial soils are generally lim-

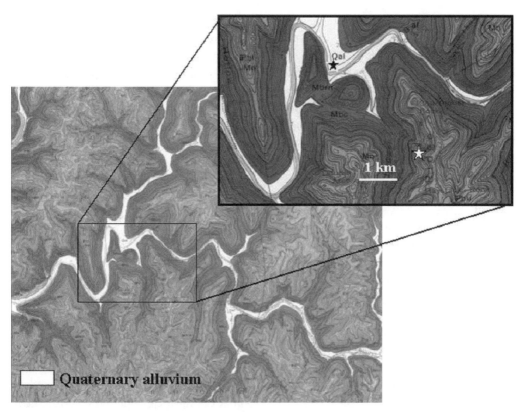

FIGURE 3.5. A section of the North Fork of the Red River showing local relief and expanses of alluvium (represented by the lightest shading on the map). Reproduced from Weir and Richards (1974). The white star marks the location of Courthouse Rock shelter; the black star, that of the Seldon Skidmore site.

ited to the banks of the Red River and parts of its major tributaries (Figure 3.5). Alluvial soils are ideal for cultivation because they retain their fertility due to the annual deposition of organic matter from floodwaters. Flooding can also create sandy natural levees that are easy to cultivate using relatively simple tools such as hoes and digging sticks (B. Smith 1985, 1986). However, if rock-shelters continued in use for storage in eastern Kentucky, cultivation of bottomlands would have introduced significant travel costs. Even short distances between river and cliff might require people carrying burdens to traverse steep slopes.

In contrast, hillside farming would have minimized travel costs between cultivated plots and the rock shelters. Ison (1991) has argued, based on ecological grounds, for the economic superiority of hillside farming. Factors that seem to favor this option include a temperature inversions

effect that can make hillsides at higher elevations warmer than the valleys below them, the difficulty of clearing stands of *Arundinaria gigantean* (giant cane) that often choke small floodplains to this day, and the greater potential sun exposure on slopes in constrast to heavily shaded streambanks. Cultivation of slopes entails costs that the floodplain option avoids, such as the risk of damaging erosion and relatively low soil fertility (see discussion below).

Other factors being equal, the obvious least-cost option would be to locate the garden "patch" as near as possible to the central place, as CPF would predict. There is good reason to believe, however, that other variables were not equal: particularly the return rates obtainable from the two habitat types. Exploitation of the more productive patch entailed some sacrifice in the form of increased travel costs. This tradeoff forms the core of the analysis described below.

MODEL APPLICATION

GOALS

The CPF model is used to estimate the optimal location of a central place with respect to an array of resource patches (Horn 1968). A slight shift of perspective shows that the CPF model provides an estimate of the economic consequences of varying the location of a garden "patch" when the location of the central place is held constant. The variables that determine the economic efficiency of alternative solutions to the garden location problem, such as patch quality, travel distance, and load size, are those identified by the CPF model. Plots distant from the rock-shelter base will need to provide a high-quality "package" in the form of a load of seeds to offset travel costs; as distance decreases, less productive but nearby hillside plots will offer the more efficient alternative.

In the absence of direct evidence for garden location in the study area, the CPF model plays an important heuristic role. The relationships between variables as drawn from the model is used to simulate behavior, such as the management of cultivated plots, that cannot be observed or reliably reconstructed from material evidence. Quantitative simulation yields reasonably realistic estimates of the magnitude of gain or loss in net energy that prehistoric populations would have faced while experimenting with the tradeoff between travel distance and patch quality in the context of CPF. This analysis should increase understanding of the origins of food production by (1) framing questions about causality in terms of intensive, that is, measurable and behaviorally relevant variables (Winterhalder and Goland 1997); (2) supplementing the incomplete archaeological and paleoenvironmental records with empirically derived estimates of the economic consequences of alternative subsistence strategies in a given ecological context; and (3) identifying testable hypotheses that link regional historical developments to the evolutionary logic of human decision making.

THE CASE STUDY

I have chosen an archaeological locality known as the Courthouse Rock shelter (15PO322) as a source of data for the simulation. The shelter itself consists of a sandstone shelf that forms a protected niche in the line of cliffs above the Red River in Powell County, Kentucky. Prehistoric activity there resulted in the accumulation of ash, charcoal, and organic refuse to a depth of approximately one meter. This deposit includes a mixture of seeds and fruits of cultivated plants and weed crops, including goosefoot, sumpweed, *Cucurbita pepo*, *Lagenaria siceraria* (bottle gourd), and *Ambrosia trifida* (giant ragweed). Associated charcoal has been dated to 3080 +/− 80 BP (cal 2-sigma range 1520–1100 BC), earlier than other large accumulations of crop seeds from area shelters. Additional radiocarbon dates from Courthouse Rock fall between 250 and 910 cal BC (combined 2-sigma ranges; Gremillion 1999). The shelter is directly across the river from an alluvial terrace on which the Seldon Skidmore site (15PO17) is located. Skidmore has produced a series of dates and diagnostic projectile points that span the latter part of the Late Archaic period, from about 5000 to 3000 radiocarbon years BP (Cowan 1976, 1985a). Analysis of flotation samples and phytoliths is still ongoing at this writing, but the presence of seeds of *Hordeum pusillum* (little barley) and *Chenopodium berlandieri* (chenopod) indicate involvement of the site's occupants with plant cultivation. The parsimonious explanation for the presence of these seeds at Skidmore is that they were the products of nearby alluvial garden plots.

MODEL CONSTRUCTION

HABITAT CHARACTERISTICS. Potential garden sites are limited to slopes and ridgetops within one kilometer of Courthouse Rock; the characteristics of these topographic situations are reviewed below. Because some degree of forest opening would have been required to allow populations of weedy plants to persist, it is assumed that exposure to solar radiation was nearly constant across all combinations of domestication status and topographic setting. This assumption is reasonable because the simulation does not take into account the effects of aspect on plant growth. Similarly, I assume exposure to rainfall and temperature extremes to be nearly constant because of the relatively small area being considered.

SLOPE. Slopes near Courthouse Rock are considered too steep for cultivation today because of the risk of erosion (Hayes 1993). Some of the constraints of slope may pertain to the use of mechanized methods irrelevant to the prehistoric situation. However, erosion on slopes in the Red River Gorge area quickly depletes topsoil once the forest vegetation is removed. Although fertility (see discussion below) may not have strictly ruled out hillside cultivation, growing crops in any one location is unlikely to have been a sustainable strategy. Sustainability is not considered in the present model.

SOIL CHARACTERISTICS. Modern soil surveys were used in this study as a source of soil data (Hayes 1993). Erosion and colluvial deposition may have affected soil fertility during the last 3000 years. Contemporary figures may well be too low for soils on steep slopes with high erosion potential. However, in the absence of a reliable correction for this possible bias, I make the assumption that these data provide an adequate surrogate for actual prehistoric conditions.

The Grigsby silt loams of the terrace are frequently flooded, have high natural fertility and moderate organic content, and are considered prime farmland. Their suitability as cropland today is limited only by their susceptibility to flooding. Floods on the North Fork of the Red River typically occur several times per year, and although they are often both broad and deep, floodwaters usually recede quickly. Flooding is most common in the spring, but winter and summer floods have been recorded. Average corn yields on Grigsby silt loams under modern conditions of cultivation are 272 bu/ha (2772 kg/ha).

The Helechewa soil occupies the hillsides just below the sandstone cliffs in which Court-house Rock shelter is located. This soil is characterized by low natural fertility and moderate to high organic content. The 35–55% slopes on which it occurs create a severe erosion hazard. Primarily because of the steep slope, the Helechewa soil is today considered unsuited to cultivation and ranks as poor habitat for grains and legumes grown as wildlife forage. No crop yield figures are available for the Helechewa soil. To create a basis for comparison of the productivity of these two soil types, the Grigsby silt loam was compared instead to the Gilpin silt loam which occurs on 12–25% slopes and is the lowest-quality soil within two kilometers for which crop yield figures are available. Corn yields on Gilpin silt loam are approximately 64% and wheat yields 86% of those reported for the Grigsby silt loam. Because the Helechewa soil has low natural fertility, as opposed to the medium fertility of the Gilpin silt loam on steep slopes, I expect an even greater difference in yields between Grigsby and Helechewa. Accordingly, I estimate that hillside yields will be 50% of those obtainable from floodplains near Courthouse Rock.

RESOURCE CHARACTERISTICS

CROP SPECIES

Because patch quality is a function not only of soil fertility but of human management, the simulation also incorporates the effects of choice of crop and the process of domestication on return rates. Yields were estimated for two different cultigens: *Iva annua* and *Chenopodium berlandieri*. These taxa were chosen in order to provide a small sample of the variability in yield and nutritional content available to prehistoric farmers for planting. The presence of seeds or fruits of these plants in midden deposits at Courthouse Rock indicates that they were cultivated and brought back to the shelter for consumption and possibly for storage. Another key reason for selecting these plants is that they have both been subjected to harvesting experiments that provide detailed data on yields in different habitats (Smith 1987a, 1992).

CHENOPODIUM BERLANDIERI

Smith (Smith 1987a) has investigated the natural habitat and yield potential of *Chenopodium berlandieri* Moq., a morphologically distinctive form of which is present in archaeological deposits in eastern Kentucky as early as ca. 3500 radiocarbon years BP (Smith 1984; Smith and Cowan 1987). It is both frequent and abundant in rockshelter middens of the Red River Gorge area, sometimes in contexts suggesting storage, and has been recovered from human paleofeces (Gremillion 1993a, b, c, 1994, 1996b). Chenopod seeds are present in deposits at the Seldon Skidmore site (see discussion above).

Smith's harvest yield data reflect a broad range of growth conditions for *Chenopodium*, which allowed the model input to be finely tuned to reflect as closely as possible actual prehistoric conditions in the vicinity of Courthouse Rock. Smith notes that *Chenopodium* is usually found on sandy soils in gardens or fields, although it does occur in upland disturbed settings. Much of the variability in yields seems to be attributable to varying amounts of sunlight. Plants growing in shade produce diffuse fruiting heads and low seed counts per unit area, characteristics that keep yields per unit area low, making harvesting more time consuming. The effects of sunlight on seed production mimic those that occur under domestication and are discussed below.

To estimate wild *Chenopodium* yields, I considered the range of yields in kg/ha obtained by Smith from wild populations. Because the river terrace below Courthouse Rock appears to be prime habitat for this plant, I presume that prehistoric yields were comparable to the highest obtained in Smith's harvesting experiment. Since about 28% of collected material consists of the "chaff"—everything collected that is not part of the fruit, including flower remnants (the perianth) that adhere to the fruit—the 1500 kg/ha of cleaned seed reported by Smith has been converted to 2083 kg/ha of uncleaned seed. For hillside plantings, this quantity was halved using the rationale given above.

I assume that no processing of the harvest took place in the field. This is a reasonable assumption given the relatively short travel distances involved at this site (see below). Studies that have demonstrated a strong biasing effect of field processing on central place archaeological assemblages involve longer travel distances (Metcalfe and Barlow 1992), or waste products that are more costly to transport, such as mollusc shell (Bird 2002). Minimal field processing is also observed in botanical collections from rock shelters that sometimes include items such as entire sunflower inflorescences, maygrass inflorescences, and tobacco capsules from the Newt Kash shelter in the Licking River drainage (Jones 1936). Although *Chenopodium* and *Iva* leaves and stems were not recognized during analysis of midden refuse from rock shelters in the area, they are highly fragmented after hand stripping and may simply not have been recognizable without higher magnification than is now routinely used for sorting (10–40 X).

IVA ANNUA

A comparable harvesting experiment was carried out with *Iva annua* (Smith 1992). This species, a relative of *Helicanthus* (sunflower), shows a clear trend of increasing seed size in prehistoric eastern North America (Yarnell 1972) beginning as early as 4000 radiocarbon years BP in west-central Illinois (Asch and Asch 1985). Today, *Iva* is often found on disturbed soils where flooding occurs. Although it may colonize drier upland sites, the lack of floodwaters to disperse the seeds prevents such populations from becoming permanently established (Smith 1992). Because it is a poor competitor, *Iva* only forms large stands in the wild where there is very low relief and poor drainage (Smith 1992, 194). Based on his experimental data, Smith estimates a range of 350–850 kg/ha of winnowed achenes; whole fruits composed of seed surrounded by dry husk, or pericarp for the crop form of *Iva*. The upper limit of 850 kg/ha can be converted to 1735 kg/ha including chaff, which makes up about 51% of the weight originally collected. Half of this quantity is 425 kg/ha of cleaned achenes, which converts to 867 kg/ha unwinnowed for a hillside plot.

DOMESTICATION

Domestication of seed crops affects fruiting structures, which are the parts harvested for human use and subsequently replanted. This management regime selects for: (1) simultaneous ripening of seeds because the product of a single harvest produces the next generation of plants, (2) reduced germination dormancy in the form of chemical or physical barriers (such as thick seed coats), (3) increased number of seeds per plant (creating dense, compact clusters), and/or (4) larger seeds as an outcome of seedbed competition (and eventually of intentional selection) (Donald and Hamblin 1983; Harlan et al. 1973; Smith 1984, 1987b).

In *Chenopodium berlandieri*, morphological changes under domestication include the reduction or loss of the seed coat and terminalization and compaction of infructescences or fruit clusters (Smith 1984; Wilson 1981). Seed coat reduction improves the quality of a load of the seeds because it reduces the quantity of indigestible material that must be transported since the seed coat cannot be separated from the nutritive tissue it surrounds and must be ingested, although it consists largely of fiber. In wild populations, approximately 30% of the cleaned seed consists of indigestible seed coat; the thinner seed coats of domesticated forms are estimated to account for only 10% of total seed weight (see below, "Load characteristics"). Terminalization and compaction would have affected the efficiency of harvest (see discussion below), but there is no reason to think that this change would have been accompanied by an increase in the number of seeds per plant. Harvest yields of a domesticated form of a related species of *Chenopodium, C. quinoa*, are comparable to those obtained by Smith experimentally (Smith 1987a). Therefore, the same harvest yield estimates were used for both domesticated and wild forms of *Chenopodium*.

For *Iva annua*, the most recognizable difference between modern wild and prehistoric domesticated samples is the larger size of domesticated achenes and the seeds contained in them. The length of achenes increased under domestication from around 3 mm in wild specimens to an average of 7 mm in the largest domesticated examples (Asch and Asch 1978; Smith 1992; Yarnell 1972, 1978). *Iva* achenes from Courthouse Rock average around 5 mm in length, yielding an estimated increase in size of 67%. Although such a projected boost for yields of domesticated *Iva* might be expected under the optimal growth conditions of the floodplain, on upland sites competition with other weedy plants probably interfered with phenotypic expression of traits associated with domestication. Taking this factor into account, the yield increase for domesticated *Iva* on hillsides has been reduced by half (from 67% to 33%).

LOAD CHARACTERISTICS

Central place foraging requires that goods be delivered in discrete packages that may vary in size depending on the physical constraints imposed by the individual's body size and strength. Prehistoric people in the Red River Gorge area probably transported seeds in the baskets or bags of a well-developed textile industry (Funkhouser and Webb 1929, 1930; Gremillion et al. 2001; Jones 1936). Some curated textile fragments from the area resemble bags, but they retain no evidence of their functions. In the absence of an appropriate artifactual analog from eastern Kentucky, it was necessary to determine a maximum load weight. Using standard safety guidelines for backpacking which recommend that an individual carry no more than 15% of his or her body weight (American Occupational Therapy Association 2002), a 50-kg (110-lb) woman could have carried a 7.5 kg load. This is probably too low to set as an upper limit considering that, for example, conical burden baskets used in the Great Basin with an average capacity of 64 liters could hold anywhere from 7.7 to 47.7 kg depending on their contents, although the heavier of these hypothetical loads is acknowledged to be possibly too massive to carry (Jones and Madsen 1989). As a compromise between modern recommendations based on health concerns and values suggested by ethnographic data, I consider the maximum possible load to weigh 15 kg. My upper limit is still conservative compared to Gardner's estimate of 18.2 kg for prehistoric forager-farmers in southwestern Virginia (Gardner 1992). The volume of a carrying bag or basket is to be 50 liters, somewhat less than the maximum burden basket volume measured by Jones and Madsen for their study of Great Basin transport costs (Jones and Madsen 1989). Load weights of *Chenopodium* and *Iva* calculated using this capacity fall within the 15-kg maximum (Table 3.1).

The total energy content of each load was calculated on the basis of weight-to-volume ratios of harvested, unprocessed plant material. A value of .117 kg per liter derived from *Chenopodium berlandieri* collected by Bruce Smith during his collecting trips in 1984 and 1985 (BDS 112) was used in this simulation (Smith 1987a). This material is curated at Ohio State University; weight and volume were measured by the author. The value of .23 kg/l for *Iva* was obtained from a sample curated at OSU and collected by C. Wesley Cowan in 1979 in Butler County, Kentucky using the same procedure.

Energy content of wild chenopod seeds was taken from Asch and Asch (1978). The energy content of the seeds has been adjusted slightly to reflect possible effects of domestication on nutritional quality. The South American *Chenopodium quinoa* contains 3740 kcal/kg (United States Department of Agriculture 2000), whereas Asch and Asch (1978) report 3200 kcal/kg for wild *C. berlandieri*. The intermediate value of 3470 kcal/kg was selected as a conservative estimate for the varieties of *C. berlandieri* used prehistorically in eastern Kentucky because *C. quinoa* has a much longer history of selection under human management. For *Iva*, I have used the same value of 5350 kcal/kg for all populations (Asch and Asch

1978) because no data exist for the now-extinct domesticated variety.

COSTS

AGRICULTURAL COSTS

The costs of agricultural labor were estimated for domesticated plants on the basis of ethnographic data. Most of the data on costs for non-mechanized, traditional agricultural systems come from observations of Central American maize farming. This is probably the most appropriate of available analogs on the basis of technological similarity. However, in contrast to these modern analogs, the earliest systems of plant cultivation in eastern North America fit the criteria for "low-level food production" as described by Smith (2001a); that is, they were characterized by limited dietary dependence on crops as well as fluctuating and frequently low levels of time and labor investment in cultivation. Therefore, the simulation included no costs for maintenance tasks such as weeding and mulching. Field investments in Mexican and Guatemalan maize farming presented by Barlow (2002) range between 124 and 208 hr/ha/year, including clearing, burning, planting, weeding, and harvesting. To subtract time spent weeding, which is assumed to be zero, and harvesting, which is calculated separately (see below), I used the breakdown of time allocation to various tasks cited by Gardner (1992) for Belizan maize farmers. Subtracting 27% of total time spent for harvesting, and 19% for weeding from Barlow's lowest figure of 124 hr/ha/yr yields an estimate for prehistoric Kentucky farmers of 57 hr/ha/yr. This has been increased to 100 hr/ha/yr in recognition of uncertainty about maintenance activities, and to ensure that agricultural costs are not underestimated.

Energy expenditure for collecting, which was probably relatively low and unlikely to affect the outcome of the model, was not calculated. However, some of the agricultural activities, such as clearing land, were probably arduous, at least during the initial preparation of a plot. Costs of such activities were estimated

TABLE 3.1
Estimated Values for Variables Included in the Simulation

	CHENOPOD						SUMPWEED					
	FLOODPLAIN				HILLSIDE		FLOODPLAIN				HILLSIDE	
	Wild		Domesticated		Wild	Domesticated	Wild		Domesticated		Wild	Domesticated
	ACTUAL DISTANCE	INCREASED DISTANCE	ACTUAL DISTANCE	INCREASED DISTANCE	ACTUAL DISTANCE	ACTUAL DISTANCE	ACTUAL DISTANCE	INCREASED DISTANCE	ACTUAL DISTANCE	INCREASED DISTANCE	ACTUAL DISTANCE	ACTUAL DISTANCE
resource characteristics[a]												
yield, unprocessed (kg/ha)	2083	2083	2083	2083	1042	1042	1735	1735	2949	2949	867	1154
% waste (chaff)	28	28	28	28	28	28	51	51	51	51	51	51
yield after winnowing (kg/ha)	1500	1500	1500	1500	750	750	850	850	1445	1445	425	565
kcal/kg	3200	3200	3470	3470	3200	3470	5350	5350	5350	5350	5350	5350
load characteristics[b]												
wt. per liter	0.12	0.12	0.12	0.12	0.12	0.12	0.23	0.23	0.23	0.23	0.23	0.23
wt. per load	5.85	5.85	5.85	5.85	5.85	5.85	11.50	11.50	11.50	11.50	11.50	11.50
% waste (seed or fruit coat)	30	30	10	10	30	10	27	27	27	27	27	27
food wt. per basketload	2.95	2.95	3.79	3.79	2.95	3.79	4.11	4.11	4.11	4.11	4.11	4.11
kcal/basketload	9435	9435	13154	13154	9435	13154	22007	22007	22007	22007	22007	22007
time costs[c]												
travel time												
travel distance (km)	5.60	20.00	5.60	20.00	0.25	0.25	5.60	20.00	5.60	20.00	0.25	0.25
travel, hr/load	2.52	9.00	2.52	9.00	0.11	0.11	2.52	9.00	2.52	9.00	0.11	0.11
collect time												
collect time, hr/kg	0.73	0.73	0.53	0.53	1.47	1.07	0.59	0.59	0.21	0.21	1.18	0.88
collect time, hr/load	4.29	4.29	3.12	3.12	8.58	6.24	6.76	6.76	2.39	2.39	13.53	10.17

(continued)

TABLE 3.1 (continued)
Estimated Values for Variables Included in the Simulation

	CHENOPOD						SUMPWEED					
	FLOODPLAIN				HILLSIDE		FLOODPLAIN				HILLSIDE	
	Wild		Domesticated		Wild	Domesticated	Wild		Domesticated		Wild	Domesticated
	ACTUAL DISTANCE	INCREASED DISTANCE	ACTUAL DISTANCE	INCREASED DISTANCE	ACTUAL DISTANCE	ACTUAL DISTANCE	ACTUAL DISTANCE	INCREASED DISTANCE	ACTUAL DISTANCE	INCREASED DISTANCE	ACTUAL DISTANCE	ACTUAL DISTANCE
preparation time												
soil preparation, hr/ha/year	0	0	100	100	0	100	0	0	100	100	0	100
soil preparation, hr/kg	0.00	0.00	0.14	0.14	0.00	0.10	0.00	0.00	0.03	0.05	0.00	0.07
soil preparation, hr/load	0.00	0.00	0.30	0.30	0.00	0.61	0.00	0.00	0.67	0.67	0.00	0.77
Total time costs per load	6.81	13.29	5.94	12.42	8.69	6.96	9.28	15.76	5.58	12.06	13.64	11.05
energy costs[d]												
kcal expended (per load)	1618	5780	1686	5874	1618	208	72	5780	1713	5874	72	314
RETURN RATES												
return rate kcal/hr	1148	275	1937	589	1077	1872	2196	1029	3831	1370	1608	1923

[a]Asch and Asch 1978; Smith 1987a, 1992; USDA 2002.
[b]AOTA 2002.
[c]Barlow 2002; Smith 1987a, 1992; Winterhalder and Goland 1997.
[d]Ainslie 2002.
Note: All data for the Courthouse Rock case (5.6 km round-trip distance) are included. In addition, values for the 20 km round-trip hypothetical case are given to illustrate the effects of increased travel distance on related variables and overall return rates. See text for additional data sources.

from the database of the University of Vermont Department of Nutrition and Food Sciences. Energy expenditure by a 100-lb (45.4 kg) person while clearing land and hauling branches, chopping wood, and digging, spading, and filling a garden averages 242 kcal/hr. These costs reflect use of modern metal tools; actual energy expenditures using stone or wooden tools were probably somewhat higher.

COLLECTION COSTS

The time spent harvesting chenopod seeds depends both on the method of collection and patch characteristics such as the density and spatial distribution of plants. The simulation assumes that both *Chenopodium* and *Iva* were harvested by hand-stripping. There is some archaeological evidence for uprooting of whole plants and storage of *Iva* as "sheaves" (Jones 1936). In upland situations, chenopod plants tend to occur as small clusters within larger stands dominated by the related *C. missouriense* (Smith 1987a). Although upland stands may be quite dense, they are small and widely separated. Floodplain stands may also be widely scattered, although density is highly variable. I assume that cultivated plots were planted so as to minimize travel time between plants. To represent harvest times for wild stands, the average rate for ten scattered plants in Smith's collection number 94 (6.7 min/m², or 1100 hr/ha) was used. Converted values for the same stand if the plants were located at the center of adjacent one-m² units (4.6 min/m², or 800 hr/ha) were used for domesticated stands.

Harvest rates for *Iva* were also based on Smith's (1992) harvesting experiments. The size and density of stands is highly dependent upon soil moisture since *Iva* can only outcompete other floodplain weeds under relatively hydric conditions. Therefore, it is likely that floodplain populations were more efficient to harvest than upland stands. Domestication has the potential to further reduce travel time between plants. Accordingly, to estimate harvest rates for domesticated sumpweed on the terrace near Skidmore, the highest-density stands harvested by

Smith were used, after discounting samples that had suffered major loss of achenes by the time of collection. Smith obtained a rate of 300 hr/ha for his sample 60, located on an inundated terrace. For wild floodplain stands, an average of six samples was used, eliminating those with substantial achene loss: 0.05 hr/m² or 500 hr/ha. The density of stands on the hillsides was assumed to be lower due to competition from upland specimens sharing the same habitat. Both cultivated and wild stands in upland settings were likely subject to this constraint, assuming that no culling was carried out. In the absence of a reliable method of more precisely estimating the effects of upland location on density, it was assumed that all upland plots of *Iva* were harvestable at rates similar to those estimated for floodplain wild stands (500 hr/ha).

TRAVEL COSTS

To create a baseline case, travel distance between Courthouse Rock and a hypothetical floodplain garden was set at the actual minimum round-trip distance between the shelter and the Seldon Skidmore site (5.6 km). For purposes of comparison, the average round-trip distance from Courthouse to a hypothetical hillside plot was set at .5 km. It was necessary to incorporate some measure of terrain variability, e.g., in slope and obstacles, into estimates of time and energy costs. In addition, the assumption that Courthouse Rock shelter functioned as the relevant central place implies that, in the case of alluvial garden plots, travel to the collection locale was largely downhill without a significant load, whereas the return trip would have been uphill carrying a burden such as a basket filled with seeds. It would be possible to create a highly realistic model of costs. However, I opted for a more general-purpose estimate for two reasons. One, actual slope and distribution of obstacles has almost certainly changed somewhat since prehistory, possibly to a degree that would significantly influence resulting estimates of cost, making a high degree of precision not only unproductive but potentially misleading. Two, I wanted to compare the

Courthouse-Skidmore return rates to hypothetical larger and smaller travel distances in order to assess the effects that travel costs would have had on decisions regarding garden location. For this purpose, a more general estimate of costs was appropriate.

Travel time was based on a rate of 2.5 km/hr (Winterhalder and Goland 1997) without a load and estimated at 2 km/hr with a load, and for the most part traveling uphill. Total travel time in each case was then calculated based on these rates and actual or hypothesized distances. The same procedure was followed for hillside and floodplain plots; although the assumptions about slope variation on outbound vs. return trips may not be met in this case, any error introduced by this procedure should be small because of the short distances involved.

Estimates of the energetic costs of travel were based on a study of energy expenditure over 12 km of variable terrain (between 100 and 902 m elevation) in which each participant (11 male and 2 female) carried a 9.5 kg backpack load (Ainslie et al. 2002). These characteristics are assumed to capture a similar magnitude and degree of variability of energy expenditure to that experienced by prehistoric forager-farmers living along the Red River. This seems a reasonable assumption given the topographic relief present in Powell County and the variation in load weight for the two crop species considered in the simulation (5.85 kg and 11.5 kg for *Chenopodium* and *Iva*, respectively). The mean energy expenditure measured in the experimental sample was 14.5 Mjoules or 3466 kcal, for an average of 289 kcal per km.

PROCESSING COSTS

The costs associated with processing crops are not included in the model, thereby making the assumption that harvested seed was transported as collected, with associated inedible parts (see discussion of resource characteristics above). This is a reasonable assumption both on theoretical and empirical grounds. Experimental studies show that field processing is likely to be efficient only when large travel distances are involved, due to the tradeoff between improving the quality of each load by removing parts with little or no utility and reducing overall travel costs by limiting time spent at the collection site. If travel costs are not significantly reduced by processing at the collection site, it is more efficient to return the material to the central place, where the costs may be assumed by someone other than the forager (Barlow and Metcalfe 1996; Bird and Bliege-Bird 1997; Bird 1997; Metcalfe and Barlow 1992). Archaeobotanical assemblages from eastern Kentucky indicate that, at least in some cases, waste products were returned to the shelters along with edible seeds. Such waste products include the fruiting heads, minus the grains, of maygrass, sunflower receptacles and bracts, and sumpweed achene coats (Gremillion 1993c, 1995, 1997b; Jones 1936). *Chenopodium* perianth parts are not reported from such sites, but if fragmentary they might well be difficult to recognize after threshing.

RESULTS

The time and energy estimates described above were used to calculate return rates for chenopod and sumpweed under the environmental conditions and constraints that confronted prehistoric occupants of the Courthouse Rock shelter (Table 3.1). Return rates r were calculated according to the formula:

$$r = \frac{e_{obt} - e_{exp}}{t_h}$$

where r = return rate (kcal per hour); e_{obt} = energy obtained per basketload (kcal); e_{exp} = energy expended in agricultural activities and travel per basketload (kcal); and t_h = time cost of travel, harvest, and agricultural activities per basketload (h).

Results were calculated for domesticated and wild versions of each crop species in each of two habitats; floodplain/terrace and hillside. In addition to Courthouse Rock, I calculated the return rates expected for an identical floodplain

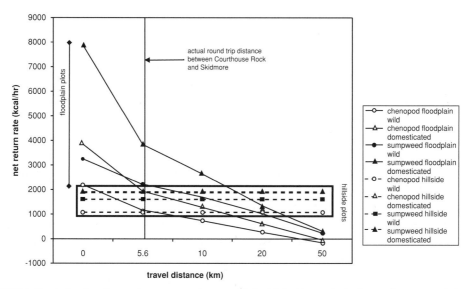

FIGURE 3.6. Graph showing changes in return rates (measured in kcal/hr) with round-trip distance from a central place for scenarios assuming different combinations of crop species, domestication status, and habitat. Distances are plotted as categorical, not continuous, variables on the horizontal axis. Dashed lines represent hillside plots and solid lines show changes in return rates as distance between the central place and alluvial soil increases.

plot located at varying distances from the central place (Figure 3.6). This was done to provide a graphic illustration of the effects of increasing travel distance on return rates. For comparison, the ranking of resource options was also calculated with travel costs set to zero.

INTERACTIONS BETWEEN KEY VARIABLES: DOMESTICATION STATUS, CROP SPECIES, AND HABITAT

For the case in which wild stands of both species are harvested for storage at Courthouse Rock, *Iva* is more profitable, has higher *r*, than *Chenopodium* in both habitats: 2196 vs. 1148 kcal/hr in the floodplain, and 1608 vs. 1077 kcal/hr on hillsides (Figure 3.6; Table 3.1). *Iva* kernels are higher in energy per unit weight than *Chenopodium*; 5350 kcal/kg vs. 3200 kcal/kg, respectively (Table 3.1). A basketload of *Iva* represents 22,007 kcal as compared to 9435 kcal for a basketload of *Chenopodium*, after correcting for the presence of waste. Thus, *Iva* kernels are of higher quality, representing over twice the number of calories. Nutrient content therefore more than compensates for the high proportion of

chaff attached to harvested *Iva* seeds; 51% as compared to only 28% for chenopod.

Domesticated versions of the two species also differ considerably in the floodplain habitat, but not in the upland setting. Whereas sumpweed is clearly superior in the floodplain, yielding 3831 kcal/hr to chenopod's 1937 kcal/hr at a round trip travel distance of 5.6 km, it does only slightly better than chenopod on hillside plots; 1923 kcal/hr vs. 1872 kcal/hr for chenopod. The simulation incorporates the assumption that *Iva* seed production, seed size, and stand density on hillsides are limited by competition. Thus, although *Iva* domestication improves yields within the upland environment by making seeds larger, the change is less dramatic than it is in the floodplain, and harvest rates do not improve over the wild condition, because plant density is assumed to remain the same. In contrast, domesticated *Chenopodium* contains more energy than the wild form, 3470 kcal/kg as compared to 3200 kcal/kg; has a thinner seed coat, reducing the amount of waste that must be transported and ingested; and can be harvested more efficiently. This differential response to habitat accounts for the narrowing of the gap separating the two species when cultivation is shifted from floodplain to upland. This result suggests that the success of low-level food production can be highly dependent on the choice of crop combination and habitat, particularly in the absence of management activities, such as weeding, that remove competing vegetation.

EFFECTS OF TRAVEL DISTANCE ON RETURN RATES

Projecting return rates beyond the actual distance that separates Courthouse Rock and the terrace at the Skidmore site illustrates the mathematical logic of the CPF model. Figure 3.6 represents in graphic form the decline and convergence of return rates as round-trip distance from the central place increases (Figure 3.6). Simulation results also highlight an important caveat with regard to resource rankings; namely that they may be somewhat misleading when based on return rates while foraging, as in the diet breadth and patch choice models, rather than the rate of delivery to a central place, as in the CPF model. When travel costs are set at zero, rankings sort out first by habitat, second by domestication status, and finally by species. That is, floodplain options must be exhausted before any hillside options rise to the top-ranked position; within habitats, domesticated resources always outrank wild ones; within ecological status categories, *Iva* always outranks *Chenopodium*. The introduction of travel costs disrupts this pattern by eroding the benefits of high yields available from floodplain soils, creating a more diverse set of top-ranking options that includes both habitats. CPF also modifies rankings by taking into account the effects of the quality of the harvested package on return rates. A basketload of domesticated *Chenopodium* outranks a basketload of *Iva* only until they are both carried back to a central place; the added cost of transporting the seeds reverses this ranking in favor of energy-rich *Iva*.

The travel costs associated with the Courthouse-Skidmore case reduce the *r* of cultivating *Iva* in the floodplain from 7890 kcal/hr, for the unrealistic scenario in which the seeds are consumed at the collection site to 3831 kcal/hr. However, this option remains superior to hillside farming of the same crop, 1923 kcal/hr. The gap between floodplain and hillside cultivation options narrows considerably as travel becomes more costly. At 5.6 km, cultivation of *Chenopodium* in the floodplain, and of *Iva* in an upland plot, offer approximately equal returns, 1937 kcal/hr and 1923 kcal/hr, respectively (Figure 3.6), but both are inferior to *Iva* harvested from a floodplain stand (2196 kcal/hr). At 20 km, the three most highly ranked options involve hillside cultivation. At 50 km, floodplain stands of *Chenopodium* result in a net energy loss, and the remaining floodplain options yield only a small gain. Soil fertility and its effects on plant growth make floodplain settings preferable for growing crops, as they even produce a better wild harvest than a cultivated slope can manage, at least until travel costs become high enough to cancel out these benefits. This threshold is reached more quickly for *Chenopodium*; between 5.6 and 10 km round-trip distance, than for *Iva* which is more profitable to cultivate in the floodplain until travel distance exceeds 10 km. These results suggest it is unlikely that either floodplain or hillside farming was consistently superior economically, and that in some situations, cultivation would have had no significant advantage over harvesting wild stands.

DISCUSSION

This application of foraging theory differs somewhat from approaches pioneered by other archaeological researchers. One of these is to first identify patterning in some element of the archaeological record, such as a faunal assemblage, and then use foraging theory to explain the behavioral correlates of these archaeological patterns in terms of adaptation (Grayson 2001; Grayson and Delpech 1998; Grayson and Cannon 1999). From this perspective, a model such as the diet breadth model is taken to adequately represent complex subsistence alternatives as a simpler system of interacting variables: resource abundance, procurement costs, and energy capture. Such studies rely on quantitative analysis of archaeological data, which are then compared with the model's predictions. Many researchers have enlisted aspects of foraging models informally and nonquantitatively to develop explanations for long-term subsistence shifts, such as a growing dependence on agricultural production or the adoption of novel crops (Gremillion 1996a, 1998; Piperno and Pearsall 1998; Winterhalder and Goland 1997). This practice accepts, at least implicitly, the explanatory power of foraging theory and uses its predictions to construct a framework for discussion and hypothesis development (Winterhalder et al. 1999). A particularly promising line of investigation employs CPF coupled with ethnoarchaeological research to assess the effects of field processing on accumulations of midden refuse (Bird 1997, 2002; Bird and Bliege-Bird 1997). This approach has great potential for improving the accuracy of inferences about behavior based on the archaeological record. Other studies of field processing create detailed predictions of costs and benefits of different levels of processing (Barlow 2002; Barlow and Metcalfe 1996; Metcalfe and Barlow 1992).

The approach taken in the present study most closely resembles this last category methodologically, although without considering the issue of removing low-utility parts before transport back to the central place. Instead, I am concerned with the problem of developing a system of low-level food production in an environment characterized by naturally occurring central places, rock shelters, high travel costs due to rugged terrain, and spatial separation of highly productive soils and cache locations. This problem set emerged from a tandem consideration of environmental and archaeological data and the similarity of the decisions faced by prehistoric people in the Cumberland Escarpment environment to those that inspired initial formulations of CPF theory. By combining theory and data to create a simulation, it was possible to compare alternative solutions to the problem of garden location in this setting in

terms of economic efficiency. Although, unlike archaeological data, simulations cannot be used to infer what prehistoric people actually did, the scenarios played out within the simulation offer an empirical basis for a detailed analysis of the strategies available to them. This approach sometimes raises new questions that might not have emerged from a less rigorous analysis.

For example, the superiority of domesticated *Iva* as a crop implied by the results of the simulation raises the question of why *Chenopodium* was cultivated at all. This prediction appears to be at odds with archaeological evidence indicating that both crops, as well as several others, were stored, consumed, and planted by the people who occupied local rock shelters. Assuming that the estimates of yield and nutrient content are reasonably accurate, alternatives to *Iva* were likely economically viable under conditions not envisioned within the framework of the model. For example, if floodplain soils were a fairly small proportion of the local landscape, access to them was probably contested as populations grew larger. Forced into a reliance on cultivating hillsides, farmers might expect similar return rates from *Chenopodium* and *Iva*. Whereas both habitats are likely to have come into play as garden sites, this flexible land-use strategy was probably more efficient if accompanied by habitat-specific planting strategies.

Creation of several hypothetical scenarios involving round-trip transport distances of 10, 20, and 50 km shows that a positive energy balance could have been maintained only by farming floodplains less than 25 km from a rock shelter base (Figure 3.6). At that distance (which entails a 50 km round trip), more energy is expended than obtained by producing, or harvesting, and transporting *Chenopodium* from the floodplain; *Iva* still offers a positive return rate, although it is lower than that estimated for hillside farming. However, the alternative of hillside cultivation emerges as the most efficient option well before the point at which floodplain farming results in a net loss. Even harvesting of wild stands on hillsides would have offered better return rates than *Iva* growing in a floodplain 25 km from the central place.

This observation raises an important point with regard to the calculation of maximum transport distance (MTD) (Jones and Madsen 1989). Rhode (1990) expressed concern that the high MTDs estimated by Jones and Madsen were misleading because they were seldom approached in actuality; he argued instead that a switch to alternative resources probably occurred well before the MTD was reached. Thus, although the MTD marks a threshold beyond which a net energy loss would occur, the actual distance people are willing to travel for a given resource is probably more accurately predicted as a function not only of the energy and time expenditure associated with it, its resource costs, but also of costs entailed by alternative activities that are foregone in its favor, opportunity costs.

CONCLUSIONS

The case study presented here identifies potentially fruitful lines of investigation regarding the functions and implementation of low-level food production. For example, the observations about return rates for the two crops in different habitats suggest that rather than trying to characterize prehistoric farming systems in eastern Kentucky as either floodplain- or upland-oriented, it might make more sense to acknowledge that both habitats could have played a role in food production. Attention might then be turned to acquiring a better understanding of the environmental circumstances under which one, the other, or a mixed strategy might prevail. One of the implications of the model—that *Chenopodium* is more likely than *Iva* to be a hillside crop—is amenable

to testing using archaeological data. Although all crops, wherever cultivated, should be represented in rock-shelter deposits, floodplain sites should be dominated by *Iva* assuming that some of the harvest was consumed locally. It might also be expected that the relative abundance of chenopod seeds in archaeobotanical assemblages from rock-shelters should be positively correlated with distance from alluvial soils.

The simulation explored in this chapter advances understanding despite the fact that no test of the validity of CPF theory itself was either intended or implied (Winterhalder et al. 1999). Estimation of environmental parameters in order to illustrate the interplay of variables identified by the CPF model allows comparison of the actual benefits and costs of subsistence decisions available to prehistoric people, such as which crops to plant, where to plant them, and indeed whether to cultivate at all. Although the model's results are not a substitute for archaeological and paleoecological evidence, they assess the plausibility of different behavioral scenarios given the assumption that economic efficiency guided subsistence decisions. This assessment is a potentially powerful source of insight into the causes of subsistence change, particularly when the incompleteness and ambiguity of the archaeological record make empirical testing difficult. However, I prefer to end this chapter on a more optimistic note by emphasizing foraging theory as a powerful source of hypotheses that can be, and will be, eventually tested against archaeological evidence. These hypotheses owe their existence not to inductive reasoning from a body of archaeological data, but rather to the creative synergy between empirical knowledge and established evolutionary theory.

4

Aspects of Optimization and Risk During the Early Agricultural Period in Southeastern Arizona

Michael W. Diehl and Jennifer A. Waters

Recent excavations of Early Agricultural period (1700 BC–AD 150) sites in southeastern Arizona show that the adoption of agriculture was a complicated and prolonged process. The application of a diet breadth model from optimal foraging theory suggests that the use of domesticated plants and irrigation to increase crop yields did not instigate an immediate decline in taxonomic diversity. Instead, cultigens were one component in a diverse foraging economy in which low-ranked plant and animal resources continued to be extensively used. This emerging model of the adoption of agriculture defies previous expectations. In comparison with Early Ceramic period (AD 150–650) and Hohokam Pioneer, Colonial, and Sedentary periods (AD 650–1150), the Early Agricultural period subsistence economy is best described as a mixed foraging and cultivation economy. Changes in the subsistence economy with increased dependence on maize were delayed until the Early Ceramic period, when the advent of high-quality ceramic containers reduced yield losses in storage, resulting in higher return rates and reduced risk from agricultural production. The fact that the mixed foraging and farming economy endured for at least 1350 years challenges the idea that the period of initial agriculture constitutes a "transitional" episode "from foraging to farming."

The adoption of crops in the American Southwest is a subject of perennial interest in southwestern U.S. archaeology and of general interest among scholars who study the spread of cultigens worldwide. In this paper we summarize the osteofaunal and paleobotanical remains from San Pedro phase (1200–800 BC), Early Cienega phase (800–400 BC) and Late Cienega phase (400 BC–AD 150) sites in southern Arizona. These intervals collectively make up the last two-thirds of the Early Agricultural period (1700 BC–AD 150). We are interested in assessing the accuracy of claims that the Early Agricultural period subsistence economy was primarily dependent upon and structured around maize cultivation. Towards this end we compare the Early Agricultural period information with evidence from the subsequent Early Ceramic (AD 150–650), Hohokam Pioneer (AD 650–750), Colonial (AD 750–950) and Sedentary (AD

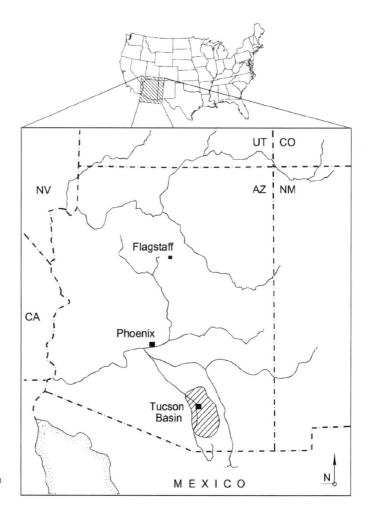

FIGURE 4.1. The Tucson Basin in southern Arizona.

950–1150) periods (see Figure 4.1 and Table 4.1). Our research applies a diet breadth model from optimal foraging theory to assess whether or not the Early Agricultural period economy was substantively similar to the economies of subsequent prehistoric Hohokam irrigation farming economies.

We find that there are marked economic differences between Early Agricultural period forager-farmers and subsequent Early Ceramic period and Hohokam farmers. The differences indicate that a stable, mixed foraging and farming economy prevailed in southern Arizona during the Early Agricultural period—an interval of at least 1350 years. Smith (2001a) has referred to the general phenomenon that we envision for this period as "low level food produc-tion." This economy differed substantially from more recent economies, in that diet breadths were greater, and primary reliance on agriculture was delayed at least until the Early Ceramic period. Although many questions remain, suffi-cient data have been analyzed to identify changes in land use through time, and to pro-pose hypotheses that relate increased maize de-pendence and narrowing diet breadths to the introduction of high-quality storage vessels. We suspect that Early Agricultural period diet breadths were greater because maize agricul-ture was a riskier strategy prior to AD 150. The primary risk was the loss of nutritive quality and high rates of seed infertility due to inferior storage technologies during the Early Agricul-tural period.

TABLE 4.1

Chronology of Southern Arizona Archaeology

PERIODS	PHASES	DATE RANGES
Historic	Arizona Statehood period	AD 1912–present
	American Territorial period	AD 1854–1912
	Spanish-Mexican period	AD 1690–1856
Protohistoric		AD 1450–1690
Hohokam Classic	Tucson	AD 1300–1450?
	Tanque Verde	AD 1150–1300
Hohokam Sedentary	Late Rincon	AD 1100–1150
	Middle Rincon	AD 1000–1100
	Early Rincon	AD 950–1000
Hohokam Colonial	Rillito	AD 850–950
	Cañada del Oro	AD 750–850
Hohokam Pioneer	Snaketown	AD 700–750
	Sweetwater	AD 675–700
	Estrella	AD 650–675
Early Ceramic	Tortolita	AD 550–650
	Agua Caliente	AD 150–550
Early Agricultural	Late Cienega	400 BC–AD 150
	Early Cienega	800–400 BC
	San Pedro	1200–800 BC
	Unnamed	1700–1200 BC
Archaic	Chiricahua	3000–1700 BC
	(Occupation gap?)	6000–3000 BC
	Sulphur Springs-Ventana	8500–6000 BC
Paleoindian		10,000?–8500 BC

We begin by providing a background discussion of the contributions of prior Southwestern archaeologists, upon which this study builds. We also discuss the sources of data, including site names, designations and occupation dates. In the second section we demonstrate that the southern Arizona Early Agricultural period sites meet the basic assumptions for applying optimal foraging models to their subsistence practices. The discussion includes details about energy return rates from Tucson Basin plants. We realize, however, that more work is required to increase the accuracy and precision of our estimates of resource return rates. In the third section we discuss long-term trends in plant and animal use. We document changes in diet breadth that occurred from 1200 BC through AD 1150. Detailed investigations of the kinds of plants included in the diet and, eventually, dropped from the diet, provide further evidence for the increasing importance of cultivation after AD 150, contrary to B. Huckell's (1995) claim that Early Agricultural period subsistence economies were produced by sedentary, maize-dependent intensive farmers. In the fourth section we discuss, as a triggering event, the introduction or *in situ* invention of high-quality pottery vessels, that initiated an increase in the dependence on cultigens and a narrowing of diet breadths to exclude many wild foods. In our conclusion, we suggest that the lexicon used to discuss farming and foraging, and many of the ethnographic case studies upon which the lexicon is built, may be inadequate as analogies for discussing nascent, prehistoric instances of the adoption of agriculture. It should further be noted that the use of behavioral ecology, a theoretical approach that does not require the use of ill-fitting ethnographic analogies, frees us from what Wobst (1978) called the "tyranny of the ethnographic record."

BACKGROUND

The initial use of cultigens in southern Arizona occurred around 1700 BC, during the Early Agricultural period (Cordell 1997; B. Huckell 1990)—formerly called the Late Archaic period (Cordell 1984; Lipe 1983). Early Agricultural period sites share a suite of common attributes and are known primarily from the San Pedro (1200–800 BC), Early Cienega (800–400 BC), and Late Cienega (400 BC–AD 150) phases. There is an unnamed interval mentioned in Table 4.1 (1700–1200 BC), from which no open-air sites and no residential sites have been excavated. Little is known about that period except that maize was present in samples recovered from caves and from a few test pits excavated in exposed riverine cut-banks. Here it is included with the Early Agricultural period on the basis of the presence of maize, but little is known of this interval in the prehistory of southern Arizona.

San Pedro and Cienega phase residential sites are usually found in floodplains along the margins of extinct channels of rivers. Many of them have been observed along ancient watercourses of the Santa Cruz River in Tucson, Arizona; these tend to be found near locations where underlying bedrock would have forced underground stream flows to the surface, even in very arid years. These residential sites are quite large and are comprised of hundreds of house depressions. Storage pits are numerous

and are sometimes densely packed. More is known about the Cienega phase dwellings because many more of these have been excavated (see Figure 4.2 and Figure 4.3). Despite the high feature density, it is apparent that some sites were intermittently occupied by as few as the occupants of two houses, and by as many as 16 (Gregory and Diehl 2002). We are probably studying hamlet populations that in any given year ranged from 10 to 80 persons.

Early Agricultural period clay objects included crude pinch-pots and figurines made with untempered, possibly unfired clay (Heidke 1999; Heidke and Habicht-Mauche 1998, 75). High-quality ceramic vessels suitable for storing water or seeds, or cooking or serving food are absent. Maize is usually found in most features (Diehl 1997). Other cultigens may have been present as well, but extant evidence does not conclusively support that finding; a cotyledon fragment was recovered from a deep pit at the Las Capas site (AZ AA:12:111) and identified by Diehl as "cf. *Phaseolus* sp." It was not conclusively a cultigen although it was probably a bean of some kind, and it did not resemble other desert legumes. Ground stone tools include a wide variety of handstones and lapstones. Among milling tools, the largest implements are elliptical-cylindrical pestles, simple mortars, small, round manos, and basin metates (Adams 2001; Lipe 1983). Other commonly observed ground stone tools include chipped-and-ground cruciforms, conical or cylindrical pipes, and spheres. Formal projectile points are of three types, including one type used for arrows (Sliva 1999). Bone tools include awls, pendants, pipe-stems, and tubes.

The primary residential structures were small, shallow depressions with thatched walls and roofs. They varied considerably in space and time, but were built of wattle and thatch, generally using flimsy materials. The least complex ones were elliptical with few posts and shallow, basin-like floor pits. The most complex ones were round, with posts regularly and closely spaced around the circumference, and they often had large bell-shaped floor pits.

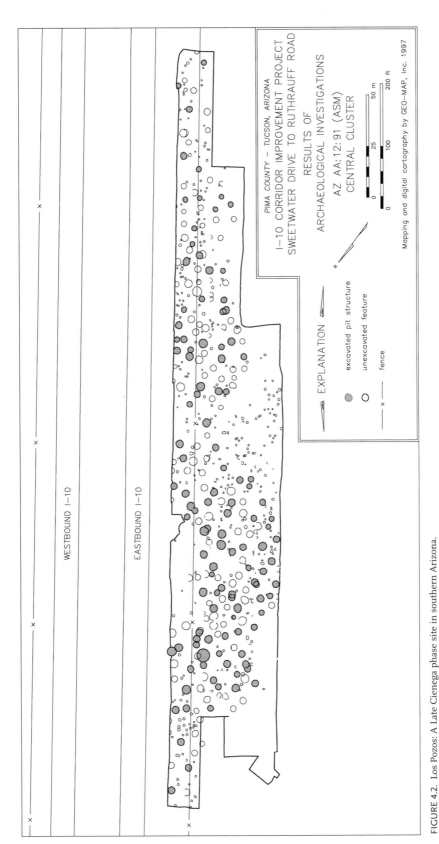

FIGURE 4.2. Los Pozos: A Late Cienega phase site in southern Arizona.

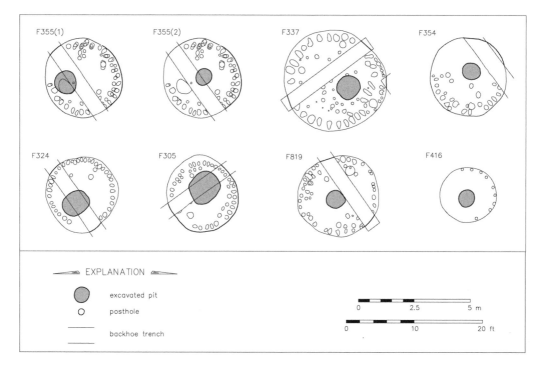

FIGURE 4.3. Examples of early agricultural period houses from Los Pozos.

Interior hearths were, in some cases, obvious and deep floor depressions. At other times the presence of an interior on-floor hearth was obvious only because of a hardened, oxidized patch of floor. Exterior storage pits are always found, and they sometimes occur in high densities (Gregory 2001). At Los Pozos, for example, 183 pits and residential features were exposed in a surface area of 4108 m². Since the distribution is not homogeneous, feature density is as great as one per 5 m² in some areas of the site.

FORAGING VERSUS FARMING: DEBATES ABOUT SUBSISTENCE STRATEGIES

Limited investigations at the Donaldson, Milagro, and Los Ojitos sites produced evidence that did not meet the predictions of extant models of crop use during the Late Archaic period (B. Huckell 1995; B. Huckell et al. 1994). Prior to B. Huckell's (1995) efforts, it had been assumed that early Southwestern maize farmers of the Early Agricultural period were residentially mobile and that maize was relatively unimportant

in the diet (Haury 1962, 114; Martin and Plog 1973, 69–80, Minnis 1985, 54–56; see Cordell 1997, 137–147 for a review). In contrast, the evidence from Donaldson, Los Ojitos, and Milagro excavated in the early 1990s seemed to indicate that the earliest maize farmers in the Southwest were relatively sedentary and heavily dependent on crops (B. Huckell 1995, 127). Beginning in 1994, major excavations at several very large Early Agricultural period sites from the San Pedro (1200–800 BC), and Early (800–400 BC) and Late Cienega (400 BC–AD 150) phases were undertaken along the Santa Cruz River floodplain in metropolitan Tucson, Arizona. On first examination, these sites (Clearwater, Las Capas, Los Pozos, Santa Cruz Bend, and Stone Pipe) seemed to generally support B. Huckell's (1995) characterization of the occupants as classically sedentary, intensive farmers.

The claim that the Early Agricultural period subsistence regime was substantively the same as subsequent Hohokam systems (B. Huckell 1995, 127) was challenged, however, in a review of the paleobotanical evidence from southern

Arizona sites (Diehl 1997), and it was demonstrated that Early Agricultural period farmers used a much broader range of resources than did more recent Early Ceramic period and Hohokam farmers. That review cast doubt on the equivalence between Early Agricultural period and Hohokam subsistence economies. Maize is abundant at Early Agricultural sites, but the high representation of wild plant foods casts doubt on the primacy of maize in subsistence efforts. In this paper we build on the earlier study by including more paleobotanical data from more sites, by including osteofaunal data for the first time, and by developing the foraging models in greater detail.

There is no general consensus about the most suitable model of subsistence strategies among researchers who work with materials from San Pedro and Cienega phase sites. Some feel that the best documented Early Agricultural period sites possess all of the attributes that one would expect of fully sedentary and agriculturally dependent people (B. Huckell 1995; Mabry 1998, 767–768). If the traits discussed by Rafferty (1985) are used as a laundry list of indicators of sedentism, then the presence of cultigens, discrete trash areas, heavy stone tools, irrigation ditches, storage pits, and structures might lead one to infer that these people were sedentary. Others (contributors to Diehl, ed. 1996; Diehl 1997; Gregory and Diehl 2002; Roth 1992, 1995; Wills 1995) find evidence for greater residential or logistical mobility than classically sedentary subsistence regimes allow.

DATA USED IN THIS STUDY

The primary goal of our research is to assess the utility of the aforementioned descriptions of Early Agricultural period subsistence strategies. We avoid the use of either the term "farmer" or "forager" here as a classificatory device for a wide variety of reasons (see Gregory and Diehl 2002). It is clear that throughout the prehistory of the Southwest, crop growers also hunted and used wild plants (Cordell 1997). Moreover, one cannot describe a group as "maize dependent farmers" on the basis of a high maize ubiquity if the same plant assemblage also has high ubiquities among many wild plant taxa. Instead, our approach compares assemblages from different prehistoric intervals, using the concepts of behavioral ecology as guidelines for evaluating changes in the organization of subsistence. Our ultimate goal is to resolve debates about the degree of foraging versus farming. We assume that prehistoric subsistence practices differed to the extent that the diet breadths were different, and to the extent that the kinds of resources that were used were different with respect to their phenology in space and time.

Inferences about diet breadth, and the nature of land use, are based on the analyses of macrobotanical and osteofaunal data from a wide range of archaeological sites from southern Arizona, and one site in northern Chihuahua. Data from many site-components were compiled. By "site-component," we mean temporally discrete components from the same site. These were treated as separate observations. The sites with osteofaunal or macrobotanical assemblages that contributed information to this study are listed in endnote one.

APPLICATION OF BEHAVIORAL ECOLOGY TO EARLY AGRICULTURAL PERIOD SITES

Behavioral ecologists study the relationship between the behavioral consequences of natural selection and circumstances that tend towards optimization. This type of analysis focuses on choices among suites of behaviors that have predictable outcomes, and the results of those behaviors in conferring a selective advantage at some desirable goal (for example, reproduction; Boone and Smith 1998; Foley 1985). Most applications of behavioral ecology have been concerned with resource selection and the degree of optimization or the tendency for selection to promote behaviors that enhance fitness through the optimization of resource use (for example: Barlow 1997; Beck 1999; Broughton and O'Connell 1999; Hemphill and Larsen 1999; Kelly 1995; Simms 1987). There has also been moderate success in applying behavioral ecology to human social organization in archaeological cases (Diehl 2000; Hegmon 1991; Storey 2000)—a logical outgrowth of success in primate, broadly construed here to include humans, behavioral studies that focus on resource selection or aspects of social organization (Berkovitch 1991; Boehm 1992; Boehm 2000; Boone 2000; Hawkes 2000; Krebs and Davies 1991; Winterhalder 1993; Winterhalder et al. 1988; Winterhalder and Smith 2000).

A tendency towards the optimization of resource use should occur when one or more of the following conditions is met (Kelly 1995, 54–57): (1) there is a threat of starvation, (2) specific nutrients (calories in most studies) are in short supply, (3) constraints limit the amount of time available for obtaining food, (4) subsistence activities expose people to risk, or (5) surplus food or time may be used to enhance reproductive fitness. When optimization occurs one expects rational decision-making to favor the use of the most efficient food acquisition systems. It is not necessary to assume, a priori, that this was likely to be the case. It is sufficient to show that resources were used commensurate with their ranking based on their energy returns, and that diet breadths changed through time in ways consistent with optimization models.

To apply this behavioral ecology model to prehistoric southern Arizona, or to any other archaeological case, two problems must be solved. First, it needs to be demonstrated that at least one of the aforementioned five conditions existed during or prior to the prehistoric period under consideration. Second, a model for the return rates of different resources must be derived. Both tasks are quite difficult.

Could prehistoric southern Arizonans have benefited from optimization? While there is no basis for assessing the *intensity* of the selective pressure in favor of optimization, it is probably the case that optimization would have conferred selective benefits. Analyses of human skeletal remains suggest that Early Agricultural Period forager-farmers suffered episodes of impaired health, either as a result of infectious disease,

injury, or malnutrition (Minturn et al. 1998). Enamel hypoplasia—which is attributable to early weaning among agriculturists, early onset of infections, or infant malnutrition—has also been observed (Guthrie and Lincoln-Babb 1997, 142–143). Interestingly, Minturn et al. (1998, 754–755) found that Early Agricultural Period burials exhibited osteological development (related to musculature) that was more consistent with a foraging or mixed foraging and farming pattern than with a highly agricultural one; that observation contravenes the proposition that the hypoplasias may be attributed to early weaning. That leaves infection and malnutrition as potential causes of observed human osteopathologies. In general, good nutrition promotes greater disease resistance and longer life spans, as well as increasing human fertility.

It is more difficult to rank the returns of prehistoric resources because so little is known about the precise ways that each resource was acquired and used. In addition, little is known about the frequency with which the resources occurred on the prehistoric landscape. Studies of the yields of various wild plant taxa, even economically important ones such as rangeland grasses, are rather rare. To construct a rank order of the energy returns from resources requires detailed knowledge of the performance characteristics of plants and animals and detailed knowledge of the ways that they were used. One must rely on return rates of plants and animals that are estimated from studies in agricultural science and range management, by analogy to other resources whose return rates have been studied, or by experimentation. It is understood that further research on the phenology, circumstances of availability, concentration, duration and timing on the landscape, of these resources may result in subsequent changes to our model. The rank orders of six indicator plants or plant groups, each of which represents a different land use strategy (Diehl 2001) are presented in Table 4.2. These ranks were determined on the basis of energetic returns per unit of time, after accounting for gross yields, harvesting, processing and transport costs. The assumptions used

TABLE 4.2

Ranks and Ubiquities of Selected Food Plants during the Early Agricultural Period

TAXON	RATE (Cal/hr)	EXPECTED RANK	REVISED EXPECTED RANK	CLEARWATER	DONALDSON	LAS CAPAS	LOS POZOS	MILAGRO	SANTA CRUZ BEND	STONE PIPE	VALLEY FARMS	WETLANDS
Zea mays[2]	2341	1	1	.93	1.0	.84	.78	.95	.87	.88	.87	.73
Carnegiea gigantea (all)[3]	2253	–	–	–	–	–	–	–	–	–	–	–
Prosopis juliflora[4]	2079	2	2	.14	.67	.30	.43	.09	.16	.40	.26	.09
Carnegiea gigantea (fruit)[3]	1553	–	–	–	–	–	–	–	–	–	–	–
Carnegiea gigantea (seeds)[3]	700	3	–	.57	0.0	.12	.54	.14	.39	.36	.22	.18
Cheno-ams[5]	386	4	3	.78	.77	.94	.84	.55	.48	.56	.83	.75
Descurainia pinnata[6]	370	5	4	.64	0.0	.50	.43	.18	.52	.44	.13	0.0
Gramineae[7]	304	6	5	.15	.44	.05	.11	.27	.32	.32	.05	.27

Note. No saguaro (Carnegiea gigantea) fruit tissue has been recovered.

to construct this model are discussed extensively in the endnotes.

Interestingly, the rank order model predicts the ubiquities of the taxa as they occur in archaeological sites. It appears that Early Agricultural Period forager-farmers tended to optimize plant use. The ranks in Table 4.2 were compared with a rank order, by ubiquity, of the same taxa from nine southern Arizona sites that were occupied during the Early Agricultural period. The selected sites were Clearwater (Early Cienega phase), Donaldson (Early Cienega phase), Las Capas (San Pedro phase), Los Pozos (Late Cienega phase), Milagro (early San Pedro phase), Santa Cruz Bend (Late Cienega phase), Stone Pipe (Late Cienega phase), Valley Farm (late San Pedro phase), and Wetlands (Early Cienega phase). They were chosen because they all produced large numbers of flotation samples with good recovery rates, and all were portions of residential sites.

With 54 observations, the Spearman rank-order correlation[8] was moderate and statistically significant ($R_s = -.41$; $p < .00$). There are, however, compelling reasons to omit saguaro cactus from the comparison. It preserves poorly in archaeological deposits (Miksicek 1987), and the window of its availability was very brief (Crosswhite 1980; Kearney and Peebles 1973). Omitting saguaro, the relationship is stronger ($R_s = -.57$; $p < .00$). It is our opinion that the second calculation provides the more reliable test of the observed and expected rank order because our predictive model lacks a systematic method for controlling for the effects of differential preservation among taxa. Two decades ago Minnis (1981) pointed out that controlling for differential preservation is problematic and impedes any effort to compare among taxa. We feel that the plant tissues listed in Table 4.2 except saguaro are comparable because all of them preserve well in archaeological deposits.

APPLICATION OF THE MODEL TO THE ISSUE AT HAND

We assess the competing characterizations of Early Agricultural period land use by applying the diet breadth model, using osteofaunal and paleobotanical remains, to two research questions. One addresses the degree of similarity between osteofaunal and paleobotanical assemblages from Early Agricultural period, Early Ceramic period, and Hohokam period sites in southern Arizona. The other addresses the nature of changes that are apparent when the composition of the assemblages is considered in finer detail.

The first question addresses the contention that Early Agricultural period subsistence efforts did not differ greatly from the more recent subsistence efforts of the Hohokam. If that is correct, one would not expect statistically significant diachronic changes in diet breadth. Strong changes in diet breadth, on the other hand, indicate that subsistence practices were not static; instead, one or another resource became a more consistent target of subsistence efforts. The second question is an empirical one. If diet breadth did change, it should also be the case that the more-frequently used resources had the highest return rates with respect to some desired nutrient such as calories. There should be strong trends or other patterns that allow one to recognize the emergence of one or a few dominant resource use strategies. It should be possible to identify the emergence of a dominant subsistence strategy that replaces or substantially reduces the importance of other strategies.

These questions are addressed in two analyses. In the first, we show that diet breadths remained broad through the Early Agricultural period during the San Pedro (1200–800 BC), and Early (800 BC–400) and Late Cienega (400 BC–AD 150) phases. Diet breadth contracted sharply during the Early Ceramic period (AD 150–650), and continued to contract during the Hohokam Pioneer (AD 650–750), Colonial (AD 750–950) and Sedentary (AD 950–1150) periods.

CHANGES IN DIET BREADTH

Figure 4.4 illustrates the trend in the mean number of identified plant taxa among macro-

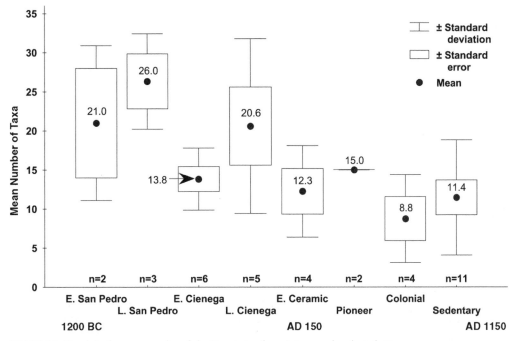

FIGURE 4.4. Trends in the mean number of plant taxa in southern Arizona archaeological sites.

botanical assemblages at phase or period-contemporaneous sites in southern Arizona. The occupations represented in Figure 4.4 span the interval from the San Pedro phase (1200–800 BC) of the Early Agricultural period (1700 BC–AD 150) through the Rincon phase (AD 950–1150). Assemblages from Early Agricultural period sites are consistently more diverse than the assemblages from later sites, with diet breadth declining by almost half from the San Pedro phase. The trend is statistically significant using Spearman's rank-order correlation when site age is compared against taxonomic diversity, with a moderate correlation ($R_s = -.44$; $p < .01$).

As Figure 4.5 illustrates, the average number of taxa in southern Arizona faunal assemblages also decreased through time, but it fluctuated to a greater degree than was observed in the macrobotanical assemblages. It is quite clear that Early Agricultural period assemblages were more diverse than Early Ceramic and Pioneer period assemblages. The *complete* trend, including Colonial and Sedentary period sites, is not very strong

or statistically significant ($R_s = -.26$; $p = .18$), owing to an increase in faunal diversity in the Colonial period. However, when Colonial and Sedentary period sites, essentially, sites more recent than AD 750, are excluded from the analysis, the downward trend is both strong ($R_s = -.51$) and statistically significant ($p < .03$). We attribute the increase in diet breadth that occurred in the Colonial and Sedentary periods to anthropogenically induced changes in the local landscape. These changes are discussed later.

PLANT RESOURCE GROUPS AND LAND USE STRATEGIES

Based on commonalities in their locations, seed sizes, and requisite harvesting and processing tool suites, we have defined eight groups of food plants that we call "resource groups." The evidentiary details that support the definition of these groups include a lengthy investigation of plant phenology and summaries of ethnographically or ethnohistorically documented uses (Diehl 2001), drawing upon a very broad range

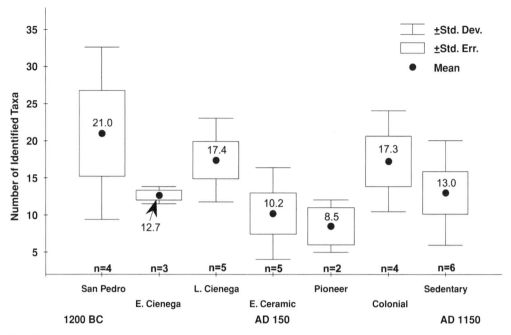

FIGURE 4.5. Trends in the mean number of animal taxa in southern Arizona archaeological sites.

of literature both anthropological (for example: Cane 1989; Moerman 1998; Simms 1987) and phenological (for example: Adams 1988; Kearney and Peebles 1973). The categories of plant resources include crops, high-density floodplain weeds, low-density floodplain weeds, desert tree legumes, cacti, non-floodplain wild grasses, local shrubs and distant resources.

CROPS

Crops are deliberately planted cultigens that have been anthropogenically transformed to have large fruit or seeds and that are highly—if not exclusively—dependent on humans for their successful propagation. In the Greater Southwest prior to the Early Ceramic period (AD 150) the only confirmed cultigen in macrobotanical specimens is maize; seed fragments identified as "cf. *Phaseolus* sp." were observed at Las Capas and Los Pozos, and other sites have intermittently produced squash or gourd seed fragments, and pollen that may represent cotton. From AD 150 through AD 1000, the list of confirmed domesticates expanded to include new varieties of maize (*Zea mays*), several vari-

eties of beans (*Phaseolus acutifolius, P. vulgaris* and *P. lunatus*), at least two varieties of squash (*Cucurbita pepo* and *C. moschata*), and cotton (*Gossypium* sp) (see Adams 1994; Ford 1981; Galinat 1988; Upham et al. 1987, 1988).

The tool inventories associated with crops include general purpose containers such as baskets and storage pots, and the mano and metate grinding tool kit. During mid-first millennium AD, the ground stone tool kit used by prehistoric southwesterners diverged from generalized seed processing tools into both general-purpose and crop-dedicated forms (Diehl 1996). The divergence roughly accords with the first uses in the Southwest of "flour corn" varieties of maize that offered greater yields per unit of planted land (Diehl 2005; Upham et al. 1988). Among manos used to grind maize, the need for increasing efficiency for processing ever greater quantities of maize continued to drive changes in maize tool technology (Diehl 1996; Lancaster 1984; Mauldin 1993).

Crops offered numerous advantages over many wild resources. They were uniquely controllable, and planting costs replaced search costs in the effort to obtain them. It is assumed that crops were locally grown, within a kilometer or two, and that transport costs were therefore negligible. Apart from cotton, harvesting costs were low. Little movement was required to completely harvest a patch and remove the large fruit and seeds from supporting tissues. Processing costs only included grinding, when practiced, and cooking. We have not attempted to account for planting costs. Indigenous Southwestern agricultural practices relied on the digging stick to break up soils around planted loci. Initial land clearing efforts may have required only modest work if burning was used to clear vegetation. The effort expended to clear vegetation and construct irrigation canals could have been amortized over several years of use. We suspect that the planting costs, where irrigation ditches were not used, were minimal.

HIGH-DENSITY FLOODPLAIN WEEDS

High-density floodplain weeds are wild, nondomesticated plants that thrive in fallow fields, on the margins of active agricultural fields, and in floodplains. Their locations are predictable, although there is a small search cost associated with their use, and they provide much lower yields per hectare than domesticated plants. Harvesting costs for these plants are higher than for domesticated plants, entailing more activity to strip or beat seed heads into containers, possibly with attendant losses to scattering. Subsequent processing steps include parching to remove closely fitting glumes, bracts and capsules, and, in some cases, shelling, prior to subsequent grinding or cooking. Examples of this kind of plant include pigweed (*Amaranthus* sp.), goosefoot (*Chenopodium* sp.), tansey mustard (*Descurainia* sp.), and sacaton grass (*Sporobolus* sp.). The associated tool technology includes baskets for collection and storage, and parching or winnowing trays. Depending on the strategy, it is possible that chipped-stone tools were used in the collection process. Where grinding was desired, basin metates and small manos were also used.

LOW-DENSITY FLOODPLAIN WEEDS

Low-density floodplain weeds are wild, nondomesticated plants that thrive in fallow fields and on the margins of active agricultural floodplains, but in less pure stands than high density weeds. These include starchy seed types, such as purslane (*Portulaca* sp.), false purslane (*Trianthema* sp.), and intermittently occurring oddities such as the nightshade or ground cherry type seeds (*Solanum* sp. or *Physalis* sp. seed type). Owing to their more dispersed growth habits, these resources provide much lower yields per hectare than the high-density weeds because they have higher search and harvesting costs, and higher transport costs. The associated suite of tools was the same one used for the high-density weeds, so it is likely that the processing costs were similar to the costs associated with high-density weeds. The search and harvesting costs associated with the use of low-density weeds, however, were much greater than with the use of high-density weeds.

DESERT TREE LEGUMES

Desert tree legumes more or less equate with mesquite (*Prosopis* sp.) pods. The requisite technology included heavy stone pestles, and mortars either made of tree stumps or formed in bedrock outcrops. The processing effort was labor intensive and involved repeated episodes of pounding and winnowing in baskets. The desired product was a meal made from the sweet, starchy mesocarp (a layer of tissue enclosed by the pod that surrounds the hard seeds within the pods). It is generally assumed by Southwestern archaeologists that the seeds, which were protein rich but very hard, were discarded except under circumstances of extreme need; it was common practice among the Pima and Papago in southern Arizona to discard the seeds (Doelle 1976, 1978; Gasser 1982). As was the case with the floodplain weeds, mesquite was locally available on floodplains, alluvial fans, and low terraces on the margins of floodplains.

CACTI

Ethnographically documented uses of cacti, especially saguaro, include the harvesting of the fruit with poles, heat treating to singe off the glochids and spines, and subsequent processing in pots, ultimately fermented, or drying on screens (Crosswhite 1980). Saguaro seeds were often dried, parched, ground into a meal, and consumed with other food. The associated cactus fruit harvesting technology included baskets or vessels for gathering fruit, a fire or other heat source for singeing spines, tongs, sticks or poles for knocking down fruit, and on some occasions, knives for splitting the fruit prior to seed removal. When the goal of fruit harvesting was to produce a beverage, the fruit were added to water in a ceramic vessel and boiled down to a thick syrup (Crosswhite 1980). Otherwise, fruit could have been dried for storage and consumed later as either a stand alone food or as an additive in some other preparation. The fruit harvesting technology included task-specific items such as tongs and poles, and general-purpose tools such as baskets, vessels, parching and winnowing trays, grinding stones, and stone knives.

Cactus fruit taxa that are common in prehistoric assemblages in southern Arizona typically include saguaro (*Carnegiea gigantea*), and prickly pear (*Opuntia* spp.), and, much less frequently, pincushion (*Mammillaria* spp.), and barrel (*Ferocactus* spp.) cactus. Most of the cacti may be found concentrated on the rocky slopes of foothills surrounding river basins. Their use could not easily have been "embedded" in other resource use strategies (Binford 1980), since lower elevation bajadas are not the best sources of other kinds of resources such as wood or game; during the month of July, however, the energetic costs of unsuccessful long-distance hunting forays, if they were attempted, could have been partially offset by harvesting cactus fruit during the return trip.

NON-FLOODPLAIN WILD GRASSES

Non-floodplain wild grasses are low-density grasses that grow in locations away from floodplains. The most commonly occurring taxa include bentgrass/muhly (*Agrostis* sp./*Muhlenbergia* sp.) type, stinkgrass (*Eragrostis* sp.), panic grass (*Panicum* sp.), and bunchgrasses.

Their definitive characteristic is that they do not occur in dense or nearly homogeneous stands. Most of them are not confined to floodplains or their margins, but instead are dispersed throughout the Tucson Basin and the surrounding foothills and montane regions. Harvesting costs for grasses are generally quite high and provide low energy return rates (Cane 1989; Simms 1987). They could have been obtained and processed using the same suite of tools applied to high- and low-density floodplain weeds.

LOCAL SHRUBS

This is a catch-all category that includes woody plants, except the tree legumes, that produce seeds with an ethnographically documented use as food. The taxa that occurred most frequently in plant assemblages included chia (*Salvia* sp.), saltbush (*Atriplex* sp.), and creosote bush (*Larrea tridentata*). There is no obvious associated tool technology, although any use of the seeds would almost certainly have entailed parching, winnowing, and grinding. These taxa generally occur away from floodplains on river terraces and alluvial fans, where they often compete with mesquite. These may have been gathered as an embedded task during the acquisition of other resources, perhaps only when higher priority resources could not be located.

DISTANT RESOURCES

This is another catch-all category. It covers resources that were not generally available along the floodplains, alluvial fans, terraces, or foothills in the intermontane basins. These include grapes (*Vitis* cf. *arizonica*), walnuts (*Juglans nigra*), pinyon nuts (*Pinus edulis*), and juniper (*Juniperus* spp.) seeds. They are so infrequent in assemblages as to scarcely warrant inclusion, yet to not do so would run contrary to the goal of applying a diet breadth model in the first place. In order to fully evaluate models of resource selection, it is necessary to identify resources that may have been available but that were not routinely used.

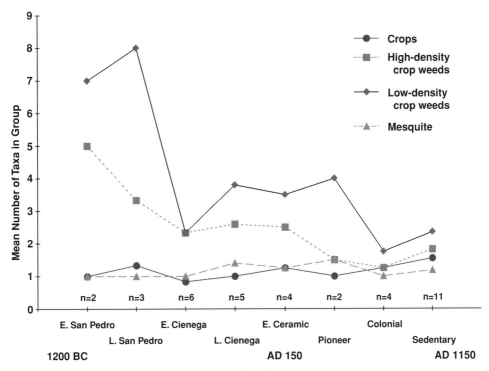

FIGURE 4.6. Trends in the mean number of plant taxa in four plant groups.

TRENDS AND DISCUSSION

Figure 4.6 and Figure 4.7 chart the diachronic trends of taxonomic diversity within plant groups. As Figure 4.6 shows, the taxonomic diversity of cultigens remained both static and low. The trend for cultigens is complicated, however, by the fact that for much of the covered interval, only three taxa were available—maize, beans, and squash. It should be noted that in reports where two kinds of a cultigen were reported, for example, the beans *Phaselous vulgaris* (common bean) and *Phaseolus acutifolius* (tepary bean), these were treated as two different taxa, as one would expect. Beans and squash preserve poorly because they do not produce a hard, inedible by-product that is routinely discarded as a consequence of use. Maize cupules (an anatomical part of the maize cob) are, in contrast, extremely durable and inedible. These qualities make maize more visible in the archaeological record than other cultigens. Returning to Figure 4.6, we see that diversity also changes little among desert legumes. More inter-

esting in Figure 4.6 is the decline in the taxonomic diversity of high- and low-density floodplain weeds. In Figure 4.7 we also observe declines in the diversity among the remaining four plant groups. Distant resources, which were never important, more or less vanished from plant assemblages after the Late Cienega phase. The diversity of wild grasses declined as well.

Although the details within the plant groups are not shown, the points of convergence are easily listed. Maize is the preeminent crop among other plants in that group. As time progressed, people focused increasingly on goosefoot, pigweed, and tansey mustard. The retention of high-density floodplain weeds apparently occurred at the expense of the low-density floodplain weeds and the wild grasses, since none of the latter two resource groups occur with high frequencies or ubiquities in macrobotanical assemblages. Among the cacti, the slight reduction in average diversity reflects the primary use of saguaro and prickly pear cactus fruit.

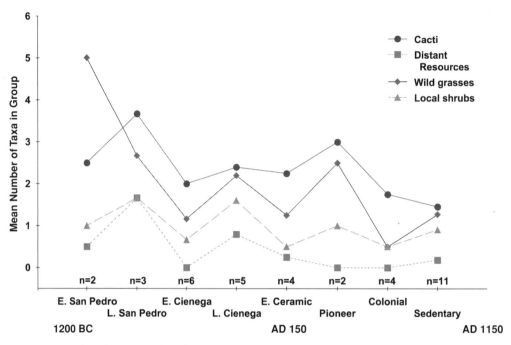

FIGURE 4.7. Trends in the mean number of plant taxa in four additional plant groups.

The preponderance of maize and high-density floodplain weeds, and the reduced dependency on grasses and low-density weeds in the Early Ceramic Period (AD 150–650) and Hohokam (AD 650–1150) assemblages suggests that floodplain land use intensified over time. Reduced cover and browse—habitats for certain wild animals—was probably one of the consequences of intensified floodplain land use. As is discussed below, inspection of the osteofaunal assemblages suggests that alterations in the floodplain habitat may have affected the distribution and availability of game animals in the vicinity of settlements.

FAUNAL RESOURCES AND LAND USE STRATEGIES

Comparisons of the animal use ratios from the different occupations also show some interesting temporal trends. The artiodactyl to lagomorph ratio and the large mammal to small mammal ratio both measure changes in the relative importance of large animals. The ratio of large to small mammals closely follows the cottontail-to-jackrabbit ratio. It declines through the Early Agricultural, Early Ceramic, and Hohokam Pioneer period, and increases during the Hohokam Sedentary and Classic periods in much the same way that the osteofaunal diversity increased. The decreases in the artiodactyl and large mammal ratios that occurred during the Early Ceramic period (Figure 4.8; Early and Late Cienega phases) co-occurred with the decrease in the cottontail-to-jackrabbit ratio. We suspect that the change was associated with intensified land-clearing on floodplains. Intensified human occupations near the floodplains would have caused reductions in local artiodactyl populations through the reduction of plants that were their primary food supply. Alternatively, the decline in lagomorph, large mammal, and artiodactyl ratios is a result of changes in human patch preferences. For this explanation to apply one would have to argue that hunting for jackrabbits, which were available in greater quantities away from floodplains and farther from villages, was preferred to hunting

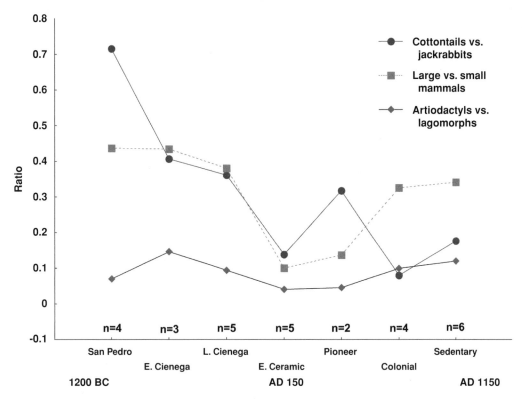

FIGURE 4.8. Trends in animal bone ratios in southern Arizona archaeological sites.

large animals, or cottontails, in floodplains and closer to villages. The energetic returns from such a strategy are inconsistent with the selective tendency towards optimization that we have already inferred. Jackrabbits, however, can be hunted more efficiently using communal tactics, thereby increasing their energetic returns.

Based on the changes illustrated in Figure 4.8, it is clear that the cottontail-to-jackrabbit ratio declined throughout the Early Agricultural period. The decline apparently continued through the Early Ceramic (AD 150–650), Colonial (AD 750–950) and Sedentary (AD 950–1150) periods. The temporary upturn in the cottontail-to-jackrabbit ratio during the Pioneer period (AD 650–750) provides a brief exception to the trend. The trend in the cottontail-to-jackrabbit ratio may reflect a decline in cottontail populations near sites. The decline may have resulted from agricultural land-clearing and the spread of settlements. Land and brush clearing for settlement space and agricul-

ture reduced the amount of low ground cover. Cottontails require well-distributed vegetation to hide from predators, while jackrabbits prefer a more open environment because they use speed and agility to evade predators (Bayham and Hatch 1985; Szuter and Bayham 1989). To the extent that declining cottontail populations are attributable to land clearing, the trend in the osteofaunal remains supports the conclusion that agriculture intensified throughout the period considered in this study.

Does the subsequent rebound in the large animal ratio during the Hohokam, Colonial, and Sedentary periods mean that floodplain use was less intense? We do not think so, because the ratio of cottontails to jackrabbits remained quite low during the Colonial period and increased only slightly during the Sedentary period, and the plant assemblages continued to show an almost exclusive dependence on floodplain resources. Instead, we suspect that the increased use of large animals in the Colonial and Sedentary periods indicates that Hohokam farmers engaged in more frequent and longer-distance hunting excursions (Speth and Scott 1989). Stated another way, we suspect that there was an increase in logistical mobility (Binford 1980; Kelly 1992) related to specialized foraging bouts. One object of these forays was to obtain protein to supplement a diet increasingly specialized on carbohydrates of lower nutrient quality. Beans provided an important protein contribution to the diet during the Hohokam periods, but it is unlikely that beans provided sufficient levels of all necessary proteins.

WHAT TRIGGERED THE INTENSIFICATION OF FLOODPLAIN FARMING AROUND AD 150?

The diet breadth model predicts that increased reliance on abundant high-return rate resources will cause the least productive ones to be excluded from the diet. The paleobotanical evidence, however, indicates that the introduction of a very-high-return resource, maize, did not cause diet breadths to contract significantly for at least 1350 years (1200 BC through AD 150).

Other material indicators that either suggest increased sedentism or increased dependence on maize are also absent from Early Agricultural period sites. Ground stone tool designs were not affected by the introduction of cultigens. The same tools that were available during the Archaic Period continued to be used without change until the middle of the first millennium AD. Only after roughly AD 550 were trough metates and specialized maize-grinding manos developed (Diehl 1996; Lancaster 1984; Mauldin 1993). The durability and form of house construction is a very regular cross-cultural indicator of the frequency of residential moves (Binford 1990; Diehl 1992; Whiting and Ayers 1968). Early Agricultural period structures were for the most part flimsy, small, and consistent with the kinds of structures that are generally built by people who change primary residences one or

more times each year (Diehl 1992; Gregory 2001; Gregory and Diehl 2002). The construction of disposable houses during the San Pedro and Cienega phases suggests that subsistence-settlement strategies were not revolutionized by the introduction of cultigens. It was not until the Early Ceramic period, starting around AD 150, that forager-farmers built more durable structures that made greater use of substantial posts and earth in their construction than Cienega phase structures. As Wills (1992) observed, the use of maize for at least a full millennium without significant morphological changes in maize kernel anatomy suggests that the selective changes often observed under intensive cultivation were delayed, arguing against intensive maize farming or primary reliance on maize. The situation did not change until the middle of the first millennium AD (Adams 1994; Upham et al. 1988). Studies of skeletal morphology of southern Arizona burials suggest that a "sedentary" existence did not come about until some time after the Early Agricultural period (Minturn et al. 1998). Rapid population growth, long-term site occupations, and true villages all remained absent throughout the Early Agricultural period (Gregory and Diehl 2002; Schurr and Gregory 2002).

It is obvious from the architectural, demographic, human osteological, macrobotanical, osteofaunal, and morphological (in maize) evidence that neither "sedentism" nor true "villages" came about as a consequence of the Early Agricultural period subsistence regime. Why not? Moreover, when diet breadth began to contract during the Early Ceramic period and, we infer, people began to rely more heavily on agriculture in lieu of wild resources, can we detect an event that initiated the change?

MAINTAINING DIVERSITY DURING THE SAN PEDRO AND CIENEGA PHASES (BC 1200–AD 150)

Why did use of cultigens have such a negligible immediate effect on food processing technologies or the organization of subsistence-settlement strategies? Moreover, why did diet breadth start to contract around AD 150, after a long period characterized by great breadth in a mixed economy of foraging and farming, and continue to contract thereafter? We suspect that wild foods were more prevalent in San Pedro and Cienega phase diets because maize cultivation made use of at least one highly risky technology: underground pit-storage. Studies of stored grain show that even when using modern high-technology storage devices, large quantities of the annual harvest are lost to predation and infestation (Bala 1997; Boxall and Calverly 1986, 20; Christensen and Meronuck 1986, 96), leading to losses of nutrient quality, increased sterility, and spontaneous low-oxygen combustion among stored grains (Bala 1997; Christensen and Meronuck 1986, 31–40; Nash 1985, 9, 230). Although prehistoric cultigens produced higher return rates at harvest time, in-ground spoilage in all varieties of stored wild and domesticated seeds may easily have exceeded 30% (Bar-Yosef and Meadow 1995). Moreover, Early Agricultural period farmers lived on the floodplain, and experienced intermittent overbank floods into residential and storage areas. These episodes, one hopes, occurred infrequently because they probably destroyed 100% of the remnant stored surplus from previous years. Even when stored foods were not rendered inedible or poisonous to humans, loss of seed viability may have promoted high variance in crop yields. Given the inadequacy of Early Agricultural period storage technology, maize cultivation was probably extremely risky, despite high average yields at harvest time in good years.

Early Agricultural period farmers attempted to mitigate the effects of in-storage yield loss in two ways. One very important approach was to continue to rely on a wide range of wild plants. In this way, early forager-farmers reserved as much as possible of their bulk stored grains for late winter and early spring fallow seasons, and for planting in subsequent years. They may also have retained access to wild taxa by establishing long-term social control of the best patches of wild foods through established land-use claims, as the Papago did with saguaro

camps (Crosswhite 1980, 20). By continuing to make extensive use of wild foods, early forager-farmers mitigated the high risk entailed in relying on stored cultigens. In any given year, the partial or even nearly complete failure of the agricultural system was offset by the continued use of extensive and intensive foraging for wild plants and animals.

The other risk mitigation strategy was to irrigate, a strategy that may have doubled the yields of maize (Mabry 2000). By maximizing production through irrigation, early farmers ensured that they would reap the greatest benefit from any seeds that germinated and matured to fruition. Although all seeds could not be expected to germinate, those that did managed to provide the maximum yield per plant.

WHAT HAPPENED AROUND AD 150?

Around AD 150, at the start of the Early Ceramic period, the introduction of ceramic storage jars changed the nature of subsistence by reducing in-storage grain losses. As a direct result of the improved storage properties of ceramics, the dependence on crops increased. This change occurred at the expense of wild plant and animal use, and diet breadth contracted in both the plant and osteofaunal assemblages.

Archaeological assemblages from the Early Ceramic period (AD 150–650) yield the first true high-quality ceramic containers. Based on the sizes and shapes of body sherds and rim sherds, and on the reconstruction of some vessels, seed jars (tecomates) were the dominant vessel form (roughly 85% of all rim sherds) during the Agua Caliente phase (AD 150–550; Heidke et al. 1998, 519; Heidke and Habicht-Mauche 1998) of the Early Ceramic period (AD 150–650). In contrast, Early Agricultural period vessels include only two seed jar rim sherds; almost half of the vessel forms from Early Agricultural period sites are small, non-utilitarian objects (Heidke et al. 1998, 503). The one reconstructed Agua Caliente phase (AD 150–550) jar from Santa Cruz Bend had a storage capacity of 27.5 liters or roughly five gallons (Heidke et al. 1998, 519). In comparison with

Early Agricultural period vessels it is unprecedented. No reconstructable Early Agricultural period vessels have been found, but ceramic experts think they were very small. According to Heidke et al. (1998; and Jim Heidke, personal communication 2002), the Early Agricultural period jars were comparable in size and shape to wild gourds—or softballs. The use of high-quality ceramic vessels protected grains from insect and animal predation, and provided better insulation from temperature and humidity changes, thereby reducing the prevalence of microbial infestation. In-storage yield losses were probably substantially reduced by the widespread use of the new vessel technology. Studies of modern grain storage systems consistently show that insulation of grain from temperature variation, moisture, and bacteria substantially reduces the loss of stored grain, helps maintain the nutrient quality of grain stored for food, and helps maintain the viability of grain stored for seed (Bala 1997; Boxall and Calverly 1986; Christensen and Meronuck 1986; Nash 1985).

As a result of the introduction of high-quality storage jars, the effective yields of agriculture increased, and risk (variance) and average loss in the amount of grain lost in storage decreased. Seeds stored for future planting remained viable for longer intervals, and when planted they grew to fruition in greater proportions than in prior centuries. Seeds stored for direct consumption retained their nutritive value longer, and fewer instances of spoilage were encountered. Crop cultivation became an increasingly productive subsistence strategy. At the same time, although the in-storage losses of wild plants were reduced by the new technology, the risk associated with the use of wild foods did not change much. They were not planted resources and were, therefore, still less predictable with respect to yield and the timing of their availability. The net energetic returns associated with the use of wild grains did not improve as dramatically as the returns from crops. We suggest that these changes were the source of the decline in diet breadth in both the plant

and osteofaunal assemblages documented in this paper.

CONCLUSION

Risk management may have been a primary concern to all prehistoric occupants of the Santa Cruz River floodplain, and our discussion necessarily simplifies a complex situation. Nevertheless, paleobotanical and osteofaunal assemblages accord remarkably well in showing that the nature of subsistence changed dramatically when high-quality storage jars were introduced. Early Agricultural period diets were relatively broad. During the Early Ceramic period, prehistoric groups shifted to a subsistence strategy that more heavily emphasized floodplain plant resources, both wild and domesticated. The consequent habitat modification that resulted from land clearing affected the local animal populations. During the Hohokam occupations after AD 550, plant diet breadths continued to narrow as crops became the primary source of calories. Long-distance hunting efforts increased after AD 750, during the Colonial and Sedentary periods. The increased use of nonlocal faunal resources may reflect an attempt to increase the levels of protein intake in an otherwise carbohydrate-rich diet.

The Early Agricultural period subsistence regime was a complicated one. In some ways it was more complex than subsequent Early Ceramic period and Hohokam subsistence regimes because Early Agricultural period forager-farmers used a greater variety of resources, and made greater use of wild resources than their descendants. The full range of behavioral implications for the wide range of resources pursued by Early Agricultural period forager-farmers is, however, not immediately obvious. Considering the flimsy nature of the architectural construction and the absence of any effects from the introduction of cultigens on food processing technologies, it is suggested that during the San Pedro and Cienega phases, a flexible subsistence and settlement strategy was used. This subsistence strategy may have encompassed considerable residential mobility, involving the seasonal abandonment of floodplain villages for other locations by most, if not all, members of the co-residential social group.

High residential mobility combined with extensive floodplain land use and irrigation systems is not a scenario that many scholars have considered. Certainly, highly mobile farmers have not been frequently documented among the myriad of ethnographic case studies of horticulturists (but see Graham 1994 for one example). Our research indicates, however, that Wills (1992) and Crown and Wills (1995) were near the mark when they suggested that cultigens were an important but not necessarily primary resource during the Early Agricultural period. Certainly Wills's concept of Early Agricultural subsistence is better supported in our data than claims that there were few if any substantive differences between Early Agricultural period land use strategies and subsequent Hohokam ones (for example, B. Huckell 1995).

A second problem with Early Agricultural period research lies in the absence of a good heuristic language for discussing the many ways that humans can incorporate both wild and domesticated plants into their land use strategies. Gregory and Diehl (2002) objected to the terms "agricultural dependence" and "sedentism" because both terms, and the simplistic use of attribute lists to invoke those terms, mask significant behavioral variation. As a result, there has been a tendency to write about the Southwestern Early Agricultural Period as the "transition to agriculture" and to describe post-transitional populations as "maize [or agriculture] dependent." Smith (2001a) has suggested a more descriptive approach, and his term "low-level food production" captures the sense of the subsistence economy that we envision for the Early Agricultural period in southern Arizona. Gregory (2002) suggested that the nature of residential occupations may be characterized by their place in the dimensions of settlement duration, continuity, and occupation intensity.

The Early Agricultural period is perhaps best characterized, then, by combining Smith's and Gregory's nomenclature. Sites were occupied briefly—no more than a year or two at a time. Sites were occupied discontinuously; the effort to harvest wild resources may have drawn most if not all occupants away from sites for protracted intervals. The term "residential mobility" was introduced by Binford (1980; see also Kelly 1992) to describe this kind of abandonment practice, and seasonal abandonments of Early Agricultural period villages were probably a normal event in the annual subsistence cycle. Sites were not intensely occupied. Indeed, despite their large size, most Early Agricultural sites were occupied by a few extended families at most (Gregory and Diehl 2002; Schurr and Gregory 2002).

The concept of a "transition" from foraging to farming or from hunting to farming implies that subsistence must be primarily and heavily organized around one food procurement strategy to the exclusion of others. The terms also imply that the incorporation of cultigens into the array of possible subsistence strategies was a transitive, unstable state between two more commonly documented stable states. Instead, our findings show that in the prehistoric Southwest the introduction of maize on or prior to 2000 BC[9] was obviously an important event since maize was rapidly incorporated into the general diet. The use of maize undoubtedly entailed shifts towards the use of floodplain resources at the expense of other resources. The development of irrigation canals followed quite quickly during the San Pedro phase (1200–800 BC).

The evidence points to an interval that lasted at least 1350 years, the San Pedro and Cienega phases, in which the use of maize resulted in no reductions in diet breadth, no effects on food processing technology, minimal reductions in residential mobility, no significant genetic changes in maize, and no apparent population increases. If one includes the preceding unnamed period from 1700 BC to 1200 BC in which maize was present, then the interval of "no impact" was 1850 years.[10] *That interval is longer than the entire subsequent human occupation of the Southwest.* It is likely that, in terms of residential mobility and stability of subsistence practices, the most viable long-term resource use strategy in the Southwest cannot be described using categories like "forager," "farmer," "sedentary," or "nomadic."

In light of our findings we suggest that archaeologists studying contexts in which maize or other cultigens were first introduced must face and address the possibility that the range of human behaviors involving early experiments with crops, or even with irrigation canals, may not be adequately represented by the innumerable nineteenth and twentieth century ethnographic case studies of people who used these technologies. To envision and describe the life ways of nascent farmer-foragers, we may have to entertain general behavioral ecology models that may have few, if any analogs among ethnographic case studies of small-scale farming. After all, such studies were based on observations of a world that is at least 3000 years removed from the contexts in which small-scale farming first occurred in the Southwest.

NOTES

1. The following sites provided macrobotanical and osteofaunal data: Las Capas (AA:12:111, San Pedro phase); Los Pozos (AZ AA:12:91, Late Cienega phase; Gregory, ed. 2001); Clearwater (BB:13:6, Early Cienega phase; Diehl, ed. 1996); Donaldson (EE:2:30, Late Cienega phase; B. Huckell 1995); Wetlands (AA:12:90, Early Cienega phase; Freeman, ed. 1997); Milagro (BB:10:46, Late San Pedro phase; B. Huckell et al. 1994); Lonetree (AA:12:120, Pioneer and Sedentary periods; Bernard-Shaw 1990); West Branch (AA:16:3, Pioneer period; Huntington 1986); Sunset Mesa (AA:12:10, Sedentary period, Ciolek-Torrello et al. 1999; Lindeman 2000); Los Morteros (AA:12:57, Sedentary period; Wallace 1995); Cerro Juanaquena (Early Cienega phase, Robert Hard, personal communication), Coffee Camp (AA:6:19, Early and Late Cienega phases, Halbirt and Henderson 1993); Redtail (AA:12:149, Pioneer and Colonial periods; Bernard-Shaw 1989); Square Hearth (AA:12:745, Early Ceramic, Sedentary and Colonial periods; Mabry, ed. 1998); Stone Pipe (BB:13:425, Early and Late Cienega phases and Early Ceramic period; Mabry, ed. 1998); Valencia Vieja (BB:13:15, Early Ceramic period, Wallace 2002), Santa Cruz Bend (AA:12:746, Early and Late Cienega phases; Mabry, ed. 1998), Valley Farms (AA:12:736, Late San Pedro phase; Well-

man 2000), Tanque Verde Wash (BB:13:68, Sedentary period; Elson 1986), and Valencia (BB:13:15, Sedentary period, Doelle 1985). Several unnamed sites from the Corona de Tucson Project were also included (B. Huckell et al. 1987). They were EE:1:152 (Sedentary period), EE:1:154 (Colonial period), EE:1:155 (Sedentary period), EE:1:157 (Sedentary period), EE:1:158 (Sedentary period), and AZ EE:1:160 (Sedentary period). Additional osteofaunal data from El Arbolito (EE:1:153, Early Ceramic period), the Dairy Site (AA:12:285, Pioneer period, Fish et al. 1992), Fastimes (AA:12:384, Colonial period, Czaplicki and Ravesloot 1988), Hodges (AA:12:18, Early Ceramic period, Swartz 1991), Houghton Road site (AZ BB:13:398, Early Ceramic period; Ciolek-Torrello 1998), Romero Ruin (Early Ceramic period, Swartz 1991), and Waterworld (AA:16:94, Colonial period, Czaplicki and Ravesloot 1989) were included.

2. *Zea mays*: Although maize is one of the best documented food plants in the world, the effort to estimate the return rates from prehistoric maize is complicated by many factors, most notably the lack of information about phenology and yields. The maize observed in Early Agricultural period deposits was probably poor stuff. It was a popcorn (Adams 1994), with small cobs. That the cobs were small is inferred from the tiny cupules and from the few intact cob segments from Las Capas and Los Pozos, none of which exceed 2 cm in length. Cross-sections of cob segments suggest that the maize grown at Las Capas may have been a string-cob variety with an average diameter (kernels excluded, cupules included) of 6 mm, and a rachis diameter that averaged 2.2 mm. It is unlikely that the typical specimen exceeded 10 cm in total length, but that estimate is generous, I suspect. Using regression equations for yield obtained by Doelle (1980) and Kirkby (1973), these cobs probably never yielded more than 300 kg/ha in irrigation settings; Kirkby's estimate for 1000 BC Oaxaca corn (300 kg/ha) should probably be viewed as the theoretical maximum yield from Early Agricultural period maize under favorable farming conditions. It is assumed that harvesting and transport costs were minimal (12 Cal/kg) owing to the close proximity of fields and the absence of any need to parch and winnow the grains. Doelle (1978) estimated that maize grinding burned 350 Cal/hr. Other experimental studies have established maize grinding rates. Wright (1993) achieved grinding rates of 624 to 864 grams/hour using manos and metates patterned after Pueblo I Anasazi sites.

For ease of calculation a grinding rate of .75 kg per hour is assumed to be the *maximum* rate at which Early Agricultural period farmagers could grind maize, since the basin type metates and manos that they used were general purpose grinding tools that were much less efficient than subsequent Southwestern manos and metates (see Diehl 1996). Maize provides 3600 Cal/kg (Ensminger et al. 1994). So the net energetic return rates are derived as follows: (3600 Cal/kg[gross] − 12 Cal/kg [harvest] − 466 Cal/kg [processing])*.75 kg/hr = 2341 Cal/hr. It should be noted, however, that since early maize was a popcorn, a less costly and perfectly viable strategy was to pop the dried corn and consume it directly or grind the popped kernels (which would have markedly reduced labor costs). So the theoretical maximum return rate for early maize is as great as the harvest rate less 12 Cal/kg. The one factor not calculated here is the energetic cost expended in field preparation and planting.

3. *Carnegiea gigantea:* Saguaro has two economically important edible yield components, seeds and fruit. Doelle (1980) observed mean saguaro cactus fruit harvest rates of 2.2 kg/hr (seeds and fruit pulp) in thirteen foraging bouts. Doelle derived saguaro cactus seed yields of .294 kg per kg of harvested fruit. Saguaro seeds provide about 5280 Cal/kg (Ross 1941, cited in Doelle 1980). The dehisced fruit of prickly pear, a good proxy for saguaro, provides about 1100 Cal/kg (Ensminger et al. 1994). A harvesting cost of 68 Cal/kg (Doelle 1976, 1978) and a 5 km transport cost of 32 Cal/kg (see Jones and Madsen 1989) are assumed for the combined fruit, for a 100 cal/kg harvesting and transport cost. If we assumed that cactus fruit was dehisced and dried for later consumption then the processing tax imposed on the fruit was nominal. This is not the way that saguaro fruit were handled by the Papago (Crosswhite 1980), but, lacking pots, Early Agricultural Period farmers probably did not have the option of producing reduced cactus syrup or fermented wine. So the return rate from cactus *fruit* is estimated as follows: (1100 Cal/kg*(1-.294)*2.2 kg/hr)-(100Cal/kg(1-.294)*2.2kg/h)r= 1708 Cal/hr-155cal/hr = 1553cal/hr. The return rate for cactus seeds, however, entailed the usual processing costs for drying, parching and grinding. For analogs about small seed grinding we must cast a broad net. Wright (1994) surveyed ethnographic studies of foragers living in semi-arid environments and noted seed grinding rates for grass seeds and grasses/sedges of 5 to 6 hr/kg using tools that are quite similar to those used by Early Agricultural period farmers. Cane (1989, 105) is the source for Wright's 5 hr/kg grinding rate, and Cane's western Australians ground their grass and sedge seeds after softening them in water. Canes rates for grinding goosefoot (5.3 hr/kg) were comparable. A small-seed grinding rate of .20 kg/hr is assumed. It is again assumed that grinding requires about 350 cal/hr as Doelle estimated for maize. The net energy return pre unit weight of saguaro *seed* is estimated as follows: ((5280 Cal/kg - (.294*100cal/Kg))-350cal/hr*(5 hr/kg)) = 5251 Cal/kg-1750 Cal/kg = 3501 Cal/kg. Multiply the net return per unit weight by the limiting factor imposed by the grinding rate (.2 kg/hr) and the net return rate is 700 cal/hr for seeds. Summing the returns from fruit and seeds we obtain a final energetic return rate of 2253 Cal/hr.

4. *Prosopis juliflora:* Experimental and ethnographic studies by Doelle (1980) indicate a reasonable mean harvest rate of 3.0 kg unprocessed pods per hour. Processing: pounding, winnowing and sifting, provides a fine meal, mesquite "flour," roughly equivalent to 30% by weight of the gross pre-processing pod weight. Processing transforms pods to meal at a rate of 2.4 kg pods/hour (Gasser 1982) which works out to .72 kg meal/hour. One kilo of mesquite meal provides 3470 Cal (Ensminger et al. 1994). So the gross energy production rate from mesquite is 2498 Cal/hour, without accounting for any of the energetic costs of harvesting or processing. Mesquite processing is labor intensive, and requires the use of a heavy mortar and pestle and winnowing trays. It is assumed that harvesting mesquite requires 150 Cal/hr (at 2.5 Cal/minute; from Doelle 1976:67). The energetic costs of pounding mesquite have not been estimated to my knowledge, but it is assumed that the effort is comparable to grinding corn (350 Cal/hr; from Doelle 1978). The net return rate for processed meal, then, is: 2498 Cal/hr [gross yield]- 150 Cal/hr [to harvest] - 350 Cal/hr [to process] = 1998 Cal/hr [net yield].

5. *Chenopodium* sp. Wild goosefoot seeds were observed in many of the samples. The sizes of the observed seeds were entirely within the range normally observed for wild taxa. It follows that yields from the seeds in the Las Capas samples were substantially lower than the yields from domesticated *Chenopodium quinoa*, which has been observed to yield 449 kg/ha in small-scale farms in Ecuador (MAG 1985 cited in Koziol 1993). Domesticated pigweed (*Amaranthus palmeri*) commonly returns 200–250 kg/ha using modern

farming methods (Williams and Brenner 1995, 155–156). Under non-cultivated circumstances it is expected that the best yield that one could expect from wild *Chenopodium* was 50 kg/ha it is assumed that similar optimum returns could be expected from wild pigweed. Examining Great Basin resources, Jones and Madsen (1989) estimated harvest rates for a number of small-seed taxa that were routinely used by Great Basin foragers. Harvest rates varied from .5 kg/hour (for bullrush) to .06 kg/hr (for pickleweed). Probably pigweed and goosefoot in southern Arizona compare well with the best Great Basin resources, however, and they may have been harvested at a rate of .70 kg/hr. Amaranth seeds contain 3500–3890 Cal/kg, and domesticated goosefoot (*C. quinoa*) about 3740 Cal/kg. I use 3740 Cal/kg as a reasonable estimate for "cheno-ams" (as they are often classified by paleoethnobotanists). Seed harvesting required stripping seed heads into a basket, or burning patches of seed-bearing plants and gathering the seeds. Assuming that the activity used about 60 Cal/hr, then 75 Cal were required to harvest one kilogram. The post harvest return per kilogram was 3665 Cal. Applying the processing rate of .2 kg/hr that was earlier assumed for saguaro seeds, and subtracting the 1750 Cal required to grind it, provides a net return of 1927 Cal/kg and a return rate of 383 Cal/hr.

6. *Descurainia* sp. Tansy mustard seeds are assumed to have relatively high harvesting costs since, by inspection, it grows nowhere in the Tucson Basin at densities that compare favorably with goosefoot or amaranth. It is assumed that tansy mustard was harvested at a rate of .20 kg/hr (better than grasses but worse than goosefoot or pigweed),

and yielded 3660 Cal/kg (FEIS 2004). The post harvest return rate was roughly 3585 Cal/kg. Subtracting the usual small-seed grinding cost (5 hours at 350 Cal/hr) leaves 1835 Cal/kg. Processed at a limiting rate of .2 kg/hr to grind gives a final return rate of 367 Cal/hr.

7. Grasses (Gramineae) have not been broken down into details of harvesting rates because there is virtually no basis for comparison among them. Dropseed (*Sporobolus* sp.) was the best among the Tucson Basin grasses in terms of patch density, but there are no quantifiable numbers for assessing harvesting rates or per-hectare yields. Jones and Madsen (1989) discussed grasses with harvesting rates in the vicinity of .13 kg/hr. If grasses yielded 3600 Cal/kg and the processing cost was 50 Cal/hour, then the post harvest return was about 3300 Cal/kg. Subtracting the processing cost (5 hours at 350 Cal/hr) leaves 1550 Cal/Kg and a net return rate of 310 Cal/hr.

8. The Spearman rank-order correlation coefficient ("rho") is a nonparametric test of the proportion of variability accounted for by the relationship between two ranked ordinal variables. It does not require normal distributions.

9. The Clearwater site (AZ BB:13:6) is an Early Agricultural period site also located in the floodplain of the Santa Cruz River in Tucson (Diehl 1996). Recently, maize (*Zea mays*) cupules recovered from a buried sand dune along an extinct channel of the river were identified by Diehl and verified by Karen Adams. The AMS date returned was 3410 +/−40 radiocarbon years (delta C13 = −10.4), yielding a calibrated age of BC 2140–1910 (Beta 160381).

5

A Formal Model for Predicting Agriculture among the Fremont

K. Renee Barlow

People living in the Fremont region (eastern Great Basin and northern Colorado Plateau) cultivated maize for more than 700 years, from AD 600 to 1300. In many respects, Fremont material culture is similar to other Southwestern archaeological traditions. However, the people who produced Fremont assemblages continued to rely on hunting and the collection of wild plants throughout the Formative period, with archaeological evidence supporting rather extreme interassemblage diversity in the importance of agricultural crops relative to local, indigenous food sources. In this chapter, the archaeological record of the Fremont is briefly reviewed, and a formal model is presented that predicts when foragers should have invested time in agricultural activities versus hunting or collecting wild foods. The model predicts that foragers will farm when the expected marginal energetic return for a particular farming activity (kcal/hr) is greater than the immediate return rate for foraging (kcal/hr), not as a function of potential or average harvest yields (kcal/ha) per se. The implications of this model for expecting spatial and temporal diversity in agricultural investments among Fremont foragers and farmers are discussed.

Found primarily in Utah north of the Colorado River, Fremont archaeological sites include pithouse villages and rancherías, adobe-walled granaries and pueblos, masonry structures, and distinctive regional styles of pottery, rock art, ground stone, and projectile points. Figure 5.1 shows the approximate locations of several dozen excavated sites which have played important roles in interpretations of Fremont lifeways. Most assemblages date to between AD 600 and 1400 (Aikens 1966; Jennings 1978; Madsen 1989; Marwitt 1986; Massimino and Metcalfe 1999; Talbot and Wilde 1989). The people who produced these assemblages cultivated maize and were contemporary with Basketmaker and Puebloan farming cultures in the Virgin, Kayenta, and Mesa Verde regions to the south, and hunter-gatherers in the Great Basin and on the Columbia Plateau.

Although synchronous with hundreds of Basketmaker agricultural hamlets and villages in neighboring Puebloan areas (e.g., Blackburn and Williamson 1997; Decker and Teizen 1989; Lipe 1993; Matson 1994; Matson and Chisolm

TABLE 5.1

TIME PERIOD	ARCHAEOLOGICAL ASSEMBLAGES IN THE FREMONT REGION
500 BC–AD 300 Late Archaic/ Transitional	Mainly Archaic camp assemblages, a handful with the addition of maize and arrow points. Also some open Archaic habitation sites with shallow pithouse or wickiup-like structures, but these are without maize.
AD 300–600 Hunting, Gathering and Maize Horticulture	Most sites are still Archaic camps, but maize is often present. Also several dozen habitation sites with Archaic points, Archaic ground stone, exterior hearths, bell-shaped storage pits, slab-lined cists, and/or shallow habitation structures. Sites with habitation structures often contain the remains of indigenous plant foods, typically are aceramic, and some yield maize.
AD 600–800 Expansion of Horticulture and Fremont Ceramic Technology	The earliest ceramics are securely dated to this period. Still some Archaic camp assemblages, but a shift from several dozen sites with maize and ceramics to the predominance and near ubiquity of maize and ceramics on sites around or shortly after AD 800. Pithouses are still fairly rare.
AD 800–1300 Diverse Fremont Agricultural/ Horticultural Economies	Hundreds of camps and habitations yield diagnostic Fremont ceramics, maize, ground stone and arrow points. Many habitation assemblages also include stone balls, ceramic figurines and pipes. Pithouse hamlets and villages are common, small pueblos are rare, wickiups are rare, and isolated granaries are found in high frequencies in some parts of the region. Regionally distinct styles of ceramics, rock art and projectile points develop.
AD 1300–1400 Late Fremont	Rapid decline in the frequency of assemblages with pottery, maize, and architecture.

1991), sites (500 BC to AD 300) in the Fremont region consist primarily of Late Archaic camps with the addition of maize and the bow and arrow in only a handful of assemblages. Table 5.1 outlines changes in assemblages during the agricultural transition in the Fremont region. Early sites with maize include Cowboy Cave (Figure 5.1), the Alvey site, Steinaker, the Elsinore burial, Clydes Cavern, and several sites in the Fremont River drainage (Geib 1993; Geib and Bungart 1989; Talbot and Richens 1996; Wilde et al. 1986; Wintch and Springer 2001; Winter and Wylie 1974). It appears that during this time some Archaic foragers in the Fremont region began incorporating maize horticulture into seasonal hunting and plant collection strategies.

Between AD 300 and 600, the archaeological record still consists mainly of Archaic camps, but with the addition of several dozen open, aceramic hunter-gatherer/horticultural habitation sites. These assemblages commonly include Archaic dart points, arrow points, Archaic ground stone, exterior hearths, bell-shaped storage pits, the remains of indigenous plant foods, and often maize. Some also contain shallow, dish-shaped habitation floors that may be the remains of wickiups or shallow pit structures (e.g., Geib 1993; Gruebel 1996; Schroedl 1992; Talbot and Wilde 1989; Tipps 1992). One

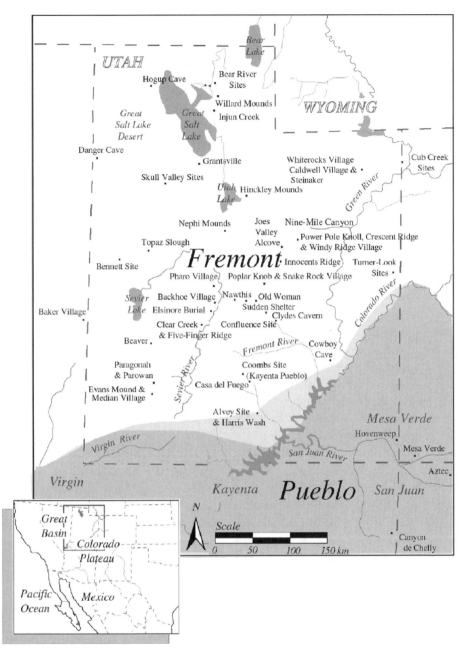

FIGURE 5.1. Map showing the approximate locations of important sites in the Fremont region (after Barlow 2002).

FIGURE 5.2. Fremont artifacts include (clockwise from upper left) an Ivie Creek black-on-white bowl from Pharo Village, a Sevier Gray incised grayware jar with applique from Nephi Mounds, a leather Fremont moccasin from Hogup Cave, two Parowan-type projectile points from Median Village, two clay figurines and three groundstone balls from the Old Woman Site, and Fremont dent maize hafted on a stick (center) from Harris Wash. (Artifacts courtesy of the Utah Museum of Natural History.)

such habitation in the Escalante area, Casa del Fuego, includes the remains of a shallow pithouse with more than fifteen burned structural beams, seventeen post-holes, two Elko points and one small indeterminate arrow point, but no interior hearth. The site dates to approximately AD 410–550, yet yielded no maize (Tipps 1992). An associated exterior surface, probably a processing and cooking area, included ash, burned rock, ground stone, and three possible hearths. In contrast, the Confluence site (approximately AD 220–650) yielded the remains of several shallow pithouses with interior hearths and eleven exterior features, including bell-shaped pits and an exterior hearth. Located in the San Rafael Swell area, this aceramic assemblage included beads, Elko points, ground stone, charred maize and maize pollen, pricklypear pollen, and charred *Chenopodium* seeds. Overall, assemblages from this period suggest that Archaic lifeways persisted throughout the region, but with maize horticulture playing an increasingly important role, perhaps in winter food storage, for some households or bands of foragers.

Between AD 600 and 800, the frequency of assemblages with both pottery and maize increased dramatically in the Fremont region. Assemblages from this time anticipate the diagnostic Fremont material culture traits that dominate the archaeological record from AD 800 to 1300. The overall character of the archaeological record suggests that during this period the economic importance of maize horticulture became more widespread, perhaps concomitant with the diffusion of ceramic technology.

Figure 5.2 illustrates some of the attributes of material culture which distinguish Fremont assemblages from contemporaneous archaeological traditions in the Southwest. Artifacts include a local variety of dent maize that often has twelve to fourteen rows and is commonly hafted on sticks (center); grayware ceramic jars which are sometimes decorated with appliqué or incising (upper right); grayware bowls (rarely slipped) with painted geometric designs (upper left); single rod and bundle basketry; regionally distinctive arrow points; leather moccasins (lower right); trough metates with a shelf and a second, smaller grinding depression; groundstone balls (lower left); broad-shouldered anthropomorphic figurines adorned with appliqué necklaces, hair knots, waistbands, shoulder decorations, and kilt-like accouterments (bottom center); and broad-shouldered anthropomorphic rock art figures with necklaces, horns or headdresses, earrings, and sometimes waistbands or other apparel.

Across the Fremont region, the overall configuration of sites is reminiscent of Basketmaker and Puebloan assemblages. At Caldwell Village in northeastern Utah (Figure 5.1), for example, Fremont remains include twenty-two pit structures, midden deposits, thousands of ceramic sherds, nine human burials (most interred in the floors of structures), several grayware jars, trough metates, manos, stone balls, bone awls, whistles, beads, and gaming pieces dating to about AD 1000 (Jennings 1978; Marwitt 1970, 1986). A few sherds of exotic, Puebloan pottery were also recovered. Just south of the Great Salt Lake, Fremont sites near the modern community of Grantsville, Utah yielded the remains of approximately 200 rectangular and circular pit structures clustered in small groups of about six to eight and scattered for several miles along two drainages (Steward 1933). Eight of these were excavated by Julian Steward during his brief tenure at the University of Utah (1930–33), resulting in the recovery of three human burials, a cache of maize, pieces of adobe, charred logs, an adobe-rimmed hearth, projectile points, basketry fragments, metates, manos, obsidian, a tubular pipe, grayware sherds that included fingernail-impressed and black-on-gray designs, a clay figurine, a stone bowl, and the remains of nine grayware jars in one structure and five black-on-gray bowls in another. About 135 km to the south, Pharo Village yielded the remains of three rectangular pit structures and eleven rectangular, coursed adobe surface rooms (Marwitt 1968). Charred beams (AD 1190 to 1260) and artifacts include thousands of ceramics, some with appliqué, incised, and black-on-gray geometric designs, a clay figurine, manos, metates, tubular pipes, stone balls, beads, bone awls, pendants, and dice. Twenty-four whole or nearly whole vessels include bowls (Figure 5.2, upper left) and wide-mouthed jars. Two human burials were found in midden deposits north of the occupation area.

In central Utah, the Old Woman site consisted of three large circular pithouses; a three-room, adobe surface structure; and rectangular, adobe-walled granaries (Taylor 1957). Artifacts include five clay, anthropomorphic figurines (Figure 5.2, bottom), two coiled baskets, several grayware jars and bowls, sherds with incised, black-on-gray and applique designs, worked sherd pendants and spindlewhorls, projectile points, scrapers, bifaces, bone awls and gaming pieces, ground stone manos, metates, balls (Figure 5.2, lower left), and several different types of exotic Puebloan pottery. In southwestern Utah, the site of Evans Mound consisted of the remains of dozens of pit structures, twenty-six of which were excavated by the University of Utah in the 1970s (Berry 1974; Dodd 1982). Other features included two multiple-room, rectangular, adobe granaries, five exterior living areas, and three human burials. Pithouses were circular to rectangular and represent multiple occupations (AD 1000 to 1200). Artifacts include basketry, six incised and corrugated grayware jars, three black-on-gray bowls, thousands of sherds, some decorated with incising, corrugation, fugitive red and black-on-gray designs, worked and drilled sherds, ceramic pipes, a figurine fragment, seventy-seven manos and metates, seven stone balls, projectile points, bifaces, scrapers, drills, bone awls, bone gaming pieces, a bone whistle, a quartz crystal, two shell ornaments, and exotic ceramics from neighboring Puebloan areas.

These five sites are not unique in size or richness of remains, but represent hundreds of larger, smaller, and similar sites throughout the Fremont region, a few dozen of which are shown in Figure 5.1. As a whole, they suggest broad similarities in technology, habitation types, and overall settlement pattern between the Fremont and the makers of Basketmaker and Puebloan assemblages. Talbot (2000; also see McDonald 1994; Upham 2000) has even argued that the people of the Fremont region maintained active trade networks with other Southwestern farmers, and that socioeconomic relationships with them increased after AD 900.

The subsistence practices of the Fremont also appear to fit within the parameters of other Southwestern groups. The classic cultigen suite of maize, beans, and squash, supplemented by lo-cal varieties of amaranth and chenopodium, are represented, and several sites have yielded evidence of irrigation facilities (e.g., Metcalfe and Larrabee 1985, Talbot and Richens 1996). Maize is nearly ubiquitous in Fremont assemblages, and the archaeological record indicates that it was an important dietary staple in some locations. The remains of a few individuals even have bone chemistry similar to Basketmaker and Pueblo burials from the four-corners region (Coltrain 1993; Coltrain and Leavitt 2002; Decker and Tieszen 1989; Matson and Chisolm 1991), suggesting that maize and other C4 plants (e.g., amaranth, saltbush, shadscale, and dropseed) were important components of prehistoric diets. They may have contributed up to 80% of the calories consumed if meat (e.g., bison, pronghorn antelope, bighorn sheep, mule deer, jackrabbit, cottontail) was not an important dietary element (0%), or up to about 60% of calories consumed if meat accounted for approximately 30–40% of the diet (cf. Decker and Tieszen 1989).

THE FREMONT PROBLEM

In spite of its similarities to other Southwestern agricultural complexes and consistent association with maize, however, hunting and gathering remains a persistent, defining element of Fremont lifeways (Aikens 1970; Madsen 1979, 1989; Madsen and Simms 1998; Simms 2000; Upham 1994). At the Evans site, for example, cultigens include maize and beans, and edible, indigenous plant remains include pickleweed, amaranth, sunflower, serviceberry, sagebrush, saltbush, brome grass, sedge, chenopodium, beeweed, cryptantha, Indian rice-grass, piñon pine, bulrush, globe mallow, juniper, dropseed, wildrye, and cattail pollen. Recovered faunal remains include mule deer, pronghorn antelope, mountain sheep, jackrabbit, cottontail, and prairie dog (Berry 1974; Dodd 1982). However, rather than a consistent diet or mobility strategy in any subregion or set of sites, diversity is a hallmark of the Fremont (e.g. Sharp 1989; Simms 1986). Occupants continued to rely on hunting and the

collection of wild plants throughout the Fremont period, with archaeological evidence supporting an unusual degree of variation between assemblages in the relative importance of agricultural crops (Barlow 1997, 2002; Madsen 1979; Madsen and Simms 1998; Simms 1986). Nearly all assemblages include maize and Fremont grayware, but the quantities of decorated wares, figurines, stone balls, moccasins, Utah-type metates, and other Fremont cultural markers vary greatly. Sites such as Baker Village, Pharo Village, and Caldwell Village have the attributes of sedentary or semi-sedentary agricultural villages, whereas sites in Topaz Slough, Fish Lake, Skull Valley, the Bear River marshes, Nine Mile Canyon, and the Fremont River drainage may represent enclaves of foraging/farming strategies that incorporated maize agriculture, ceramics, and other components of Fremont technology into lifeways with high residential mobility (Madsen and Simms 1998; Morss 1931; Simms 1986; Simms et al. 1997; Smith 1994; Spangler 2000).

Interassemblage diversity is so extreme that archaeologists have argued for decades about which sites should be included in the definition of Fremont, and which should be separated into different archaeological cultures or regional variants of the Fremont (for summaries, see Aikens 1966; Madsen 1979, 1989; Madsen and Simms 1998; Marwitt 1970). Clearly, maize farming in this region was not an "all or nothing" transition that was either entirely rejected or accepted as a way of life (cf. Upham 1994). Rather, maize agriculture appears to fit within a broad spectrum of foraging and farming strategies which include highly mobile hunter-gatherers at one end, semisedentary farmers on the other. Many Fremont households may have husbanded maize and used ceramic technology, but incorporated these technologies into mobile foraging and farming strategies. Topaz Slough, for example, located in the western desert of Utah (Figure 5.1), represents a Fremont assemblage associated primarily with hunting and gathering activities (Simms 1986; for a similar site near Fishlake see Janetski et al. 1999). Radiocarbon dated to approximately AD 1000–1100, excavated features include the remains of two small brush structures similar to those used by Historic period hunter-gatherers, and exterior concentrations of fire-cracked rock and ash. Artifacts include 403 Fremont ceramics, mostly grayware, six projectile points, lithic debitage, and ground stone. Possible food remains include one corncob fragment, numerous saltbush seeds, and the burned remains of jackrabbits, snakes, and a large unidentified mammal.

In Skull Valley, south of the Great Salt Lake, a series of six Fremont camps yielded concentrations of fire-cracked rock, the remains of a brush structure, and shallow pits filled with ash and charcoal. One of these sites was excavated in the 1990s (Smith 1994), and was radiocarbon dated to approximately AD 600–900. Artifacts include ground stone, lithics, and three Fremont grayware sherds. Food remains include a single corncob, several hundred chenopodium or amaranth seeds, saltbush, pepperweed, and *Sueda* seeds, and Phragmites pollen. In Nine Mile Canyon, a tributary of the Green River, several hundred sites (AD 650–1200) include a few clusters of one to five pithouses, and dozens of sites with masonry granaries and/or habitations situated high above the canyon floor (Spangler 1993, 2000; also see Gillin 1938; Gunnerson 1969; Morss 1931). The rock art along the canyon is spectacular, but middens are absent and artifacts are sparse at all sites. In sharp contrast with sites like Caldwell Village, Pharo Village and Evans Mound, ceramics are rare and consist mostly of nonlocal types, suggesting transient use of the canyon, perhaps seasonally while planting, harvesting, and storing crops (Spangler 2000).

In south central Utah, dozens of Fremont sites are located along the Fremont River and its tributaries. The Fremont culture was originally named for these sites, investigated by Noel Morss in the 1920s during the Claflin-Emerson Expedition for the Peabody Museum of Harvard (Morss 1931). With the exception of the nearby Coombs site, a large Kayenta pueblo, most assemblages suggest high mobility, with camps and facilities for collecting and storing wild foods and agricultural produce. Morss described small rock shelters with slab-lined storage cists, circular basalt boulder-lined habitation structures, and a small, freestanding adobe storage structure. Rock art and human burials were fairly common, and assemblages included projectile points, debitage, large quantities of faunal remains, moccasins, baskets, snares, tule mats, planting sticks, arrows, feathers, cordage, bone awls, mountain sheep horns, elk antlers, anthropomorphic figurines, manos, metates, a mortar, hides from bison, mountain sheep, elk and deer, cedar bark, salt, piñon nuts, maize cobs, kernels and husks, beans, and squash seeds and rinds. Fremont maize and ceramics were consistently found, but notably sparse in frequency. Morss concluded:

> This culture was characterized by cave sites with a slab cist architecture similar to that of the Basket-maker and Pueblo I periods; by a distinctive unpainted black or gray pottery; by the exclusive use of a unique type of moccasin; by a cult of unbaked clay figurines obviously related to, but more elaborate than Basket-maker III figurines; by abundant pictographs of distinctive types; and by a number of minor features which tended to identify it as a Southwestern culture (Morss 1931, iv)

Recent investigations in the Fremont drainage have similarly yielded the remains of numerous short-term camps and occupation features dating from 400 BC to AD 1200, including a small slab- and adobe-lined pit structure with beads, projectile points, lithics, ground stone, a figurine fragment, burned bone and maize; a basalt boulder-lined structure with interior hearths; an earth oven filled with charcoal, sand, and fire-cracked rock; ash and charcoal-filled stains and pit features; and numerous exterior hearths, some slab-lined and some with maize, (e.g., Barlow et al. 2002; Winch and Springer 2001).

FORAGING VS. FARMING: AN OPTIMIZATION MODEL

Much has been written about the potential effects of environment and climate on Fremont assemblages. Most arguments are based on implicit assumptions about the economics of farming versus foraging. Hypothesized increased summer rainfall is generally argued to have had a positive effect on maize yields, perhaps preceding geographical expansions of maize farmers and/or the spread of farming and sedentary adaptations (e.g., Berry 1974; Jennings 1978; Lindsay 1986). A popular alternative theory is that indigenous population increase warranted resource intensification, and farming, albeit less efficient than foraging, provided an overall increase in food (Hard 1986; Janetski 1997; Madsen 1982). Within the Fremont period, apparent interassemblage differences in the importance of maize agriculture are usually thought to be structured by opportunities to farm in situations amenable to higher crop yields versus less favored agricultural locations (Berry 1974; Jennings 1978; Lindsay 1986; Simms 1986). The sharp decrease in sites with Fremont material traits after AD 1300 is often argued to have been the result of sustained regional drought and cooling temperatures, although competition with migrating Numic foragers is sometimes nominated as a concurrent factor (e.g., Berry 1974; Coltrain and Leavitt 2002; Jennings 1978; Jennings and Norbeck 1955; Lindsay 1986; Simms 1986). While it is likely that each of these agents—proposed global or regional changes in climate, population increase, or movement of peoples—influenced the timing of expansions and contractions of agricultural economies on a regional scale, and perhaps strongly (e.g., Lindsay 1986); it is suggested here that these models are too general to elucidate the rich patterning that characterizes the archaeological record of the Fremont. Rather, foragers living in the area prehistorically likely responded to local foraging and farming environments on an annual basis. In particular, the abundance of high-ranked indigenous animal and plant foods and the effects of local soils, available groundwater, and expected precipitation and growing season temperatures on potential maize yields. That is, prehistoric foragers and farmers responded to the expected energetic return rates (kcal/hr) for

time spent in various foraging and farming *activities* at different times of the year in different locations. The aggregate of these decisions, made year after year for 700 years, resulted in the archaeological record. It is at this level that we must look to understand the mosaic of farming and foraging patterns that is Fremont.

To better understand the behavioral processes that contribute to variation in the economic importance of agriculture, a formal model is presented that predicts when a forager should increase or decrease investments in farming activities. Farming here is seen not as fundamentally different from foraging, but simply as the sum of a series of farming activities which may include: burning or clearing the land of brush, trees or other vegetation; cultivating the soil; making amendments to the soil such as adding composted vegetation; planting, building and maintaining irrigation facilities; weeding young plants; hilling around plants; watering by hand; guarding young plants and maturing crops from birds, rodents, deer, dogs, people, and other potential predators; harvesting agricultural produce; transporting, storing, and processing produce for consumption (Barlow 1997). Time spent farming is assumed to be analogous to time spent in activities such as traveling to wild food patches; hunting game animals; collecting wild plant foods; transporting them back to camp; and processing them for storage or consumption. Each activity, whether farming or foraging, is undertaken with the anticipation that a return in food energy will be realized.

An agricultural cycle is a period that includes the seasonal scheduling of all effort towards producing an agricultural crop, including investments in fields and agricultural facilities prior to the growing season, from the end of one harvest to the end of the next. In many regions this period corresponds roughly to an annual cycle or calendar year, but in others may be a period of only several months or seasons. The agricultural cycle concept is a common one in societies that rely heavily on agricultural crops, and it is used here to facilitate conceptual comparisons of seasonal farming efforts and seasonal foraging efforts. However, the "agricultural cycles" that we are familiar with are modeled here as the outcome, not the cause, of foraging and farming decisions.

Overall energetic return rates are assumed to be a function of energetic returns for both time spent foraging (F) and farming (H); foraging returns are a function of time spent in foraging activities (f), including harvesting, processing, and storing wild plant foods; and farming returns are a function of time spent in farming activities (h), including planting, harvesting, processing, and perhaps storing agricultural yields. The foragers' expected energetic return rate for time spent foraging and farming is

$$g(F, H) = \frac{F + H}{f + h}$$

where $F = g(f)$ and $H = g(h)$ and where F is the average gain for all time spent foraging during an agricultural cycle; H is the average harvest, or expected gain during an agricultural cycle for farming given a particular level of farming investment; f is the average cost or time spent foraging during the agricultural cycle, and the time required to process F; and h is the average cost or time spent farming to produce H during the agricultural cycle, and also the time required to harvest and process H.

Foragers are expected to spend the optimal time in foraging activities (f) and farming activities (h) to maximize the rate of gain for foraging and farming [$g (F, H)$] during the agricultural cycle. Implicit in this argument are the following assumptions and constraints:

· Time spent foraging and time spent farming are mutually exclusive, i. e., an hour spent foraging cannot also be spent farming,

· Time spent farming results in an anticipated increase in maize yields at harvest time,

· Time spent foraging and farming is costly, and individuals are expected to adopt foraging and farming strategies that maximize the rate of caloric gain for time spent in both during the agricultural cycle.

Implicit in these constraints, as in all optimal foraging models, is the assumption that individuals who employ efficient production strategies will leave more offspring or more successful offspring than less productive foragers, because they gain extra resources or extra time, or both, to invest in their family, offspring or mates (Barlow 1997, 2002; also see Kaplan and Hill 1992; Krebs and Kacelnik 1991; Simms 1987; Stephens and Krebs 1986; Winterhalder and Smith 1992).

The next equation, then, describes the circumstances when foragers would do better economically to invest the next increment of time farming (dh), rather than spending the next unit of time hunting or collecting wild foods which are immediately available (df). On the left side of the inequality, the overall return rate for foraging and farming includes variables to describe the rate of increase in harvest yields, (H' (h)), or the first derivative of H when the next small increment of time is spent farming (dh). On the right side, the overall return rate for foraging and farming includes variables to describe foraging return rates (F' (f)) when the next small increment of time is spent foraging (df). This inequality models the "decision" to spend the next unit of time in agricultural activities, and predicts when foragers should begin farming:

$$\frac{F + H + H'(h)dh}{f + h + dh} > \frac{F + H + F'(f)df}{f + h + df}$$

The forager is simply expected to farm when the average return rates for foraging and farming, plus the additional returns expected for spending the next unit of time farming, are greater than the average return rates for foraging and farming, plus the additional returns for spending the next unit of time foraging. The expected, average return rates for foraging(F/f) will vary with the types and abundance of local resources, and their spatial and temporal distribution. The average annual return rate for farming (H/h) will also vary with local conditions (e.g., Barlow 1997, 2002), likely structured by average temperatures during the growing season, length of the frost-free season, precipitation, soils, etc. Increases and decreases in time spent in these activities (h) will result in differing expected harvests and so, ultimately, will also influence overall returns for time spent foraging and farming ($g(F, H)$).

The average amount of time spent either foraging (f) or farming (h) may vary from zero hours to all time devoted to subsistence. However, to examine whether the *next* small unit of time should be spent farming (dh) or foraging (df) let us assume that this small increment of time represents an equal cost to the forager, regardless of whether it is spent farming or foraging: say one hour. For the purpose of this exercise, then, if $df = dh = 1$, Equation 2 quickly reduces to:

$$H'(h) > F'(f)$$

WHEN SHOULD FORAGERS FARM?

This solution indicates that *a forager should spend the next hour, or day, farming when the rate of calories gained from additional cultivation is greater than the immediate return rate for spending the next hour, or day, foraging* (compare Charnov 1976). Rather than the overall rate for farming versus the average return rate for foraging (e.g., Barlow 2002; Diehl 1997), the marginal return rate for farming activities relative to the immediate return rate for foraging should have the greatest influence on a forager's decisions to farm. That is, expected increases in future harvest yields with time spent farming today, versus present foraging opportunities regardless of farming investments already made in the current agricultural cycle (Barlow 1997).

Immediate foraging opportunities ($F'(f)$) will change seasonally during the agricultural cycle, and will vary from area to area even within regions defined by living or prehistoric cultures. Spring in one location may yield few foraging alternatives, but in another there may be numerous greens or hunting opportunities. Similarly, summertime may yield an abundance

of ripening fruit or seeds in one place while in another opportunities to collect wild plant foods may be comparably sparse. Ecological variation should also structure spatial and temporal differences in the marginal return rates ($H'(h)$) for investing the next hour in a particular farming activity. Some types of farming activities should intrinsically result in larger increases in harvest yields than others, but climate and environment will also influence the expected results of cultivation efforts. For example, early in the frost-free season, a forager spending eight, sixteen or twenty-four hours planting maize might consistently increase harvest yields from 0 to an expected ten bushels per acre. However, spending the same amount of time weeding the maize field later in the season may only increase expected yields from ten to twelve bushels per acre. Under these circumstances, a forager might usually plant maize, but whether she invests time weeding should be strongly influenced by foraging opportunities at "weeding time." Likewise, whereas the first eight or perhaps twenty-four hours of weeding in a field might yield an expected two bushels per acre increase, the fiftieth or one hundredth hour likely would not, as the expected gains associated with weeding probably diminish over time. Consequently, more variation is predicted in time spent weeding, both year to year and between households or communities, than in the amount of time spent planting crops.

Similarly, the marginal energetic returns for time spent just harvesting a field of ripe maize would be enormous, likely comparable to or higher than some of the highest ranked foraging opportunities in the Great Basin and Greater Southwest. In contrast, the expected increase in returns for time spent hoeing a field by hand for up to hundreds of hours—one, two or three times, as seen ethnographically in Latin America (Barlow 1997, 103)—would likely be much less and highly variable. In an arid desert environment, time spent watering may result in large increases in harvest yields relative to alternative foraging opportunities. However, in some montane settings, on floodplains, or in regions with tropical or monsoonal precipitation patterns, moisture may not be a constraining factor. In those locations, pre-planting field preparation activities like clearing land of vegetation, and perhaps weeding later during the summer, would likely result in larger increases in maize harvests. Again, whether the forager spends time in some subset of these activities, or chooses to forage, will depend on the expected marginal return rates for each.

Maize farming should be viewed not as a transition from "being" a forager to "being" a farmer, but as the outcome of a series of foraging decisions made at various points throughout the growing season. The aggregate of these decisions result in individuals, households or communities being classified as foragers or farmers, or something in between. Even if the appropriate time frame for optimization is an entire year, foragers and farmers should be flexible in the range and intensity of cultivation activities that they engage in, particularly in environments with spatial, seasonal, or annual variation in foraging opportunities and farming constraints. For this reason, a patterned mosaic of foraging and farming strategies is predicted among the Fremont (sensu Upham 1994). *Farming investments should only have intensified when higher-ranked foraging opportunities diminished, and Fremont farmers should have decreased farming efforts during the times and in the locations where higher-ranked foraging opportunities were abundant.*

IMPLICATIONS FOR FREMONT FARMERS AND FORAGERS

Differences in the agricultural strategies pursued during the Fremont period were likely structured by variation in both local foraging opportunities and the effects of local ecology on the marginal return rates for various types of cultivation activities, not average or expected maize harvests per se. Fremont farmers and foragers should have varied local farming strategies to maximize their energetic efficiency during all time allocated to subsistence. In regions where the expected return rates for foraging opportunities during the spring and summer were very similar to the expected marginal returns for various pre- and post-planting farming activities, such as soil preparation, weeding, and hand watering plants, the greatest variation in foraging/farming strategies is predicted. In contrast, greater investments in farming, and consequently less inter-site variation in Formative assemblage characteristics, are expected when the marginal yields for farming activities are uniformly greater than most foraging opportunities. However, at no time during the Formative period are farmers expected to have abandoned foraging in the sense that they ignored high-ranked fauna and plant foods simply because it was "time" to perform a particular type of cultivation activity. Rather, the amount of time invested in cultivation activities should have varied from place to place, being influenced by both seasonal foraging opportunities and differences in marginal farming returns. Even sedentary farmers should have often abandoned their agricultural fields during the growing season to pursue higher-ranked foraging opportunities.

In general, the energetic return rates for time spent in agricultural activities in the Fremont region were likely lower than those in most parts of Latin America today. Most of the region lies between 4000 and 6500 ft in elevation, and the length of the frost-free season varies locally from about 80 to 180 days (Lindsay 1986). Modern precipitation averages just under ten to approximately fifteen inches per year in most of the region, with more precipitation only at higher elevations (Oregon State University 2000). In addition, maize is a tropical grass and thrives on summer rainfall, but today the western and northern portions of the Fremont region receive mainly winter moisture (e.g., Lindsay 1986). It is sometimes argued that the Formative period was characterized by increased summer rainfall. Evidence cited includes increased quantities of maize, maize pollen, grasses, and grass pollens in archaeological sites, and increased dune building at a few

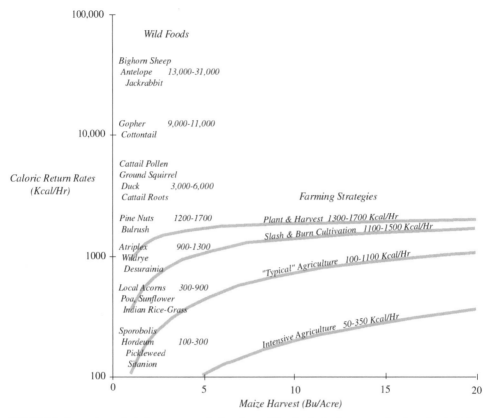

FIGURE 5.3. Comparison of caloric return rates for foraging and farming in the Fremont region from data in Barlow 1997; Barlow and Metcalfe 1996; Jones and Madsen 1991; Madsen et al. 1997; Simms 1987 (from Barlow 2002).

Great Basin locations (e.g. Coltrain and Leavitt 2002; Currey and James 1982; Lindsay 1986). Other sources of paleoenvironmental data, including packrat middens, pollen profiles, and deuterium variations, indicate a general increase in temperature in the Great Basin and Greater Southwest around 2000 years ago, with decreases in some populations of piñon pine, juniper, ponderosa pine, and Douglas fir (e.g., Betancourt 1990; Lindsay 1986; Long et al. 1990; Thompson 1990). However, it is not yet clear what effect this temperature change had on potential maize yields across the Archaic to Fremont transition. Fine-grained, tree ring, and reconstructed crop yield data from the southwest Colorado suggest that annual variation in rainfall was generally quite high during the For-

mative period from ~ AD 600 onward (Burns 1983; Van West 1994).

A number of previous studies have estimated average return rates (kcal/hr) associated with a variety of farming and foraging strategies in the Great Basin and Greater Southwest (e. g., Barlow 2002; Barlow and Metcalfe 1996; Diehl 1997; Jones and Madsen 1991; Madsen and Kirkman 1988; Madsen et. al. 1997; McCarthy 1993; Raven and Elston 1989; Simms 1987; for review see Zeanah and Simms 1999). Estimated rates of energetic gains associated with maize farming in the Fremont area range from 50 to 1700 kcal/hr (Barlow 2002). Figure 5.3 compares the expected return rates (kcal/hr) for four hypothetical farming strategies and common foraging opportunities in the Fremont region (from Barlow 2002).

Caloric return rates (kcal/hr) are plotted for wild foods along the y-axis, while caloric return rates for farming (kcal/hr) are plotted with gray curving lines relative to differences in expected maize harvests on the x-axis. Rather than ranking various farming activities relative to foraging opportunities, however, average farming return rates have been calculated based on reconstructed maize yields for farming in southwest Colorado from AD 650–1350 (data from Burns 1983; see discussion in Barlow 1997, 183–190), from field investment strategies observed among subsistence farmers in Mexico, Guatemala and Peru (Cancián 1965; Hastorf 1993; Stadelman 1940; Tax 1963), and from foraging cultivators in South Africa and southern Utah (Hitchcock and Ebert 1984; Kelly 1976).

Expected harvest yields vary from one to twenty bushels per acre, and predicted farming strategies include (1) a plant and harvest horticultural strategy in which foragers invest only fifty hours, or five to six person-days per acre, (2) slash and burn agriculture that includes 200 hours of labor, or about twenty person-days per acre, (3) "typical" subsistence agriculture investments of 400 hours per acre, and (4) an intensive maize agriculture strategy of 800 hours per acre, seen only in a few communities in Latin America (Barlow 2002). In general, caloric return rates for farming (kcal/hr) increase slightly with average maize harvests, but differences in time invested in fields have a much greater effect on overall success. Foragers would always do better economically to collect pine nuts and bulrush seeds, where available, than to spend additional time cultivating maize for decreasing marginal returns. However, when foraging returns are somewhat lower, in the neighborhood of about 300–900 kcal/hr, foragers would do better to spend time in cultivation than to leave fields to collect lower-ranked seed such as *Sporobolis*, *Hordeum*, pickleweed or *Sitanion*. These data suggest that increasing investments in farming in the Fremont region should coincide with decreases in foraging yields, not increased maize harvests per se.

On the other hand, even when expected maize harvests were comparably low, perhaps three to five bushels per acre, the predicted returns for just planting and harvesting maize was 1200 to 1700 kcal/hr. This places maize horticulture in the range of some of the highest-ranked plant foods associated with women's foraging strategies, in the Fremont region and elsewhere, but significantly lower than the expected returns for most hunting opportunities (Barlow 2002). Maize cultivation at low investment levels is predicted among prehistoric foragers given three conditions: (1) women were collecting similarly ranked plant foods, such as pine nuts and bulrush seeds, (2) growing season temperatures and moisture were sufficient to produce a maize crop of approximately three bushels per acre, and (3) seasonal land use patterns in which there was at least a moderate probability that the forager would be returning to the planting location at harvest time. Under this scenario, maize is expected to become a component of hunter-gatherer diets long before a material transition to farming would include the full suite of sedentary "Puebloan" characteristics and should have continued to be an element of foragers' diets in some locations even when full-time farming was not a tenable economic strategy.

This type of low-investment horticulture is not without precedent in the Southwest. Isabel Kelly (1976) reported a similar ethnographic case among the Southern Paiute foragers and cultivators. An informant of the San Juan Paiute of southeastern Utah and northeastern Arizona reported in the 1930s that his grandfather raised maize when he was a child, and that maize, pumpkins, beans, watermelon, cantaloupe, and sunflower were cultivated when he was an adult. His father:

> selected an open site (hence no need of clearing), near spring. Worked soil "with any kind of stick"; with his hands, dug ditch from spring in order to water plot. Planting not in rows. Apparently little cultivation; occasional weeding by hand. Planted in spring; thereafter left site to gather wild foods ripe in summer; returned to harvest agricultural products. (Kelly 1976, 192)

TABLE 5.2

	HIGH MARGINAL RETURN RATES FOR FARMING ACTIVITIES	LOW MARGINAL RETURN RATES FOR FARMING ACTIVITIES
High Return Rates for Foraging during the Growing Season	Narrow diet breadth, with only high-ranked wild plant foods and cultigens. High mobility, but variation in farming investment corresponds with annual variation in growing season temperatures, moisture, soils, other factors that strongly affect anticipated crop yields. Mostly "slash and burn" agriculture.	Narrow diet breadth with only high-ranked wild plant foods and cultigens. Mobility/land use patterns correspond to seasonally available high-ranked wild foods. Expect low investment agriculture, including "plant and harvest" strategies. Storage facilities near numerous wild-food collection areas.
Low Return Rates for Foraging during the Growing Season	Diets should include high- to moderate-ranked wild plant foods. Many low-ranked wild foods ignored during the growing season in favor of increased agricultural labor. Expect some "typical" field investment strategies and greater sedentism, with less variation in farming strategies overall. Storage facilities adjacent to habitations.	Broadest diets include high- to low-ranked plant foods, although maize was likely as important as many wild plant foods. Intensive field investments may occur, also expect long-distance travel to other resource patches. High residential mobility sometimes expected. Field investments should fluctuate with opportunities to collect wild foods.

Other wild foods that were collected and sometimes stored during the agricultural cycle included deer, antelope, mountain sheep, rabbits, rats, porcupine, wildcat, pine nuts, yucca fruit, mescal, cacti, wild onions, and various berries and small seeds, and the overall pattern of foraging included a number of seasonally occupied residences.

CONCLUSIONS

Throughout the Fremont region, and the Greater Southwest in general, spatial and temporal variation in the amount of time that foragers spent farming should correlate negatively with local foraging opportunities, but positively with the marginal returns for tilling, watering and weeding maize plants. Table 5.2 provides a simplified set of predictions for various environmental contingencies. In areas where high-ranked hunting and collecting opportunities were most abundant—with, for example, bighorn sheep, antelope, deer, ducks, pine nuts, bulrush seeds, and cattail pollen, berries, and root food—and where potential farming locations included well-watered alluvial sediments conducive to maize agriculture, variation in prehistoric investment in farming facilities (e.g., habitation, storage, and irrigation features) should be associated with annual differences in marginal farming returns relative to local foraging opportunities. In these locations farming efforts should not be intensive. Instead, slash and burn agricultural strategies, or field investments of about 150 to 200 hours per acre, are expected. Diets should be narrow in the sense that many lower-ranked plant foods that are locally available, and perhaps even abundant, (e.g., acorns, *Poa*, sunflower, Indian ricegrass, *Sporobolis*, *Hordeum*, pickleweed and *Sitanion*) should rarely be pursued over potential opportunities to farm. Even though archaeological assemblages may not suggest full-time, sedentary farming, these people would have greater overall caloric return rates, and better nutrition and health, than many other foraging/farming populations.

In contrast, the model predicts that most sedentary farmers in the Fremont region, or foragers with cultivation strategies that approach levels of field investment common among subsistence maize farmers in Latin America (i.e. about 400 hr/acre) were likely spending more time in farming and foraging activities that yielded increasingly lower marginal returns. Although there may have been a few locations in the Fremont region where farming resulted in consistent, plentiful maize production with comparably small amounts of effort, most areas likely required large investments to produce harvests comparable to those of subsistence farmers in Latin America. The least variation in farming investment between sites and temporal components in the Fremont region are expected where potential foraging returns were lowest but the marginal return rates for farming—or expected *increases* in harvests with field activities during the growing season—were moderate to high. Diet breadth might include many locally available, moderately ranked plant foods such as acorns, bluegrass, wild sunflower and Indian rice-grass, but farmers should pursue a wider range of farming activities before pursuing very low-ranked foraging opportunities such as pickleweed or squirrel-tail grass.

In areas where foraging returns during the growing season were high but expected increases in harvest yields with field activities were low, maize agriculture should have been incorporated into seasonal foraging strategies. Only low-investment farming efforts, perhaps "plant and harvest" or "slash and burn" strategies of less than 100 to about 200 hr/acre, are expected, and low-ranked wild plant foods

should rarely be pursued. Sedentary farming is not expected.

Perhaps somewhat counterintuitively, the most intensive farming investments are expected in areas with relatively low return rates for foraging and farming during the growing season, particularly if the expected marginal returns for increased field activities were low, but higher than the expected returns for foraging or moving to another field. However, increasingly lower-ranked foraging opportunities, including both a wider array of local plant foods and the use of high-ranked foraging patches further away from agricultural fields, should have become more attractive. Greater logistical organization is expected, with increasing specialization in site types and general use of space (sensu Binford 1980). Consequently, it is predicted that farming became a "way of life" not when farming was great, but when foraging alternatives were poor. Deteriorating environmental conditions should have led to increased farming investments, with the abandonment of more sedentary farming practices when higher-ranked wild foods or alternative economic opportunities were available. Diets should generally be very broad, including even very low-ranked wild foods, but significant year to year variation in field investments should correspond to fluctuating environmental conditions that affect both foraging opportunities and potential agricultural harvests.

Testing these expectations will require (1) collection of ethnographic and environmental data among modern maize farmers to estimate the energetic costs and gains associated with various farming activities—such as tilling, planting, weeding and watering, and harvesting maize fields—in various ecological settings, (2) environmental studies correlating these data with the environments surrounding archaeological sites in the Fremont region (sensu Van West 1994), and (3) fine-grained paleoenvironmental studies in the vicinity of Fremont sites that focus on late Holocene ecology to reconstruct prehistoric foraging opportunities (sensu Grayson and Cannon 1999), and (4) a re-examination of the archaeological data pertaining to Fremont diet and agricultural strategies.[1]

NOTE

1. This research was supported in part by a research fellowship from the Department of Anthropology, University of Utah, in 1994–5. An earlier version of the model was developed in my Ph.D. dissertation (Barlow 1997), and benefited greatly from discussions with Jack Broughton, Kristen Hawkes, Duncan Metcalfe, Alan Rogers, and Drew Ugan. I am also indebted to the Utah Museum of Natural History, especially Kathy Kankainen, Wendi King, and Duncan Metcalfe, for the beautiful photograph of Fremont artifacts in Figure 3, and to Jude Higgins for identifying typographic errors. I thank Joel Janetski, Doug Kennett, Duncan Metcalfe and Bruce Winterhalder for insightful comments on various drafts of the manuscript. Finally, I thank Paul Fife, professor of mathematics at the University of Utah, for comments and criticisms of the model and equations. All errors that remain are my own, and are probably the result of not following all of the excellent advice that I was given.

6

An Ecological Model for the Origins of Maize-Based Food Production on the Pacific Coast of Southern Mexico

Douglas J. Kennett, Barbara Voorhies, and Dean Martorana

Maize-based food production was well-established on the Pacific coast of southwestern Mexico by ~2600 B.P.[1], the beginning of the Late Formative Period. Biogeographical and genetic studies indicate that this cultigen was originally domesticated in Central Mexico by ~9200 B.P., and microbotanical studies suggest that it was widely dispersed to people living in several parts of Mexico and Central America by ~7500 B.P. People living in the Soconusco region during the Archaic Period (~7500–3500 B.P.) were foragers that may have supplemented their diets by cultivating morphologically wild plant species and some cultigens. Microbotanical studies suggest that people in this region added maize to their diets between 6000 and 5000 B.P., but a commitment to maize-based food production did not occur until 2400 years later (2600 B.P.). Based on the paleoecological record for the region and central place foraging theory, we develop a subsistence-settlement model for pre-village, Archaic Period, forager-horticulturalists and evaluate this model with the available archaeological evidence for this interval. We then use an adapted form of the Lotka-Volterra predator-prey model, cultivator-cultigen,

to explore the initial adoption of maize and the development of more intensive forms of maize-based food production in the area. Based on this analysis, we argue that the long-term delay between the introduction of maize and maize-based food production resulted from the relatively low energetic returns of early maize relative to other resources available in the region.

The emergence of food production is inarguably one of the most significant developments in the environmental history of our planet (Redman 1999; Roberts 1998; Dincauze 2000) and a fundamental turning point in human history (Childe 1951; Cohen 1977; Cowan and Watson 1992; Flannery 1973, 1986a; Gebauer and Price 1992a; Gremillion 1996a; Harris 1996b; Hayden 1990; Henry 1989; O'Brien and Wilson 1988; Price 2000a; Price and Gebauer 1995a; Rindos 1980, 1984; Smith 1998, 2001a; Watson 1989; 1995; Zeder 1995; Zohary and Hopf 2000). Originally characterized as a "revolution" (Childe 1951), and more recently as a transition (Price and Gebauer 1995b), true dependence on food production was often preceded by the low-level use of domesticated plants and animals by people who were essentially foragers (Smith 2001a). Mixed foraging and farming, still practiced today by the Mikea of Madagascar (Tucker, this volume), persisted for millennia in some regions, well after the domestication of key cultigens, and is considered to be a stable and highly successful subsistence strategy within certain ecological contexts. Nevertheless, the persistence of low-level food production often did give way, at different times, to the development of more intensive forms of agriculture involving terracing, irrigation (Doolittle 1990), and other more sophisticated agroecological techniques (e.g., raised fields; Fedick 1996). Once more intensive food production, with its associated surpluses, was established it fueled the development of socially stratified, politically centralized, and technologically innovative state-level societies (Diamond 1997; Nichols and Charlton 1997; Zeder 1991). It also underpins the exponential population growth, urbanization, and environmental destruction evident throughout the world today.

Intense human-plant interaction resulting in changes in the distribution and genetic make-up of plant populations influenced prehistoric foraging and horticultural strategies long before the emergence of intensive agriculture and the reliance upon a few key cultigens (Rindos 1984; Price and Gebauer 1995a; Piperno and Pearsall 1998; Watson 1995). However, the most successful cultigens were often domesticated in primary centers and dispersed into other regions where prehistoric foragers and horticulturalists were living (Diamond and Bellwood 2003; Hastorf 1999; Smith 1998; Wills 1995). It is important to understand how and why prehistoric foragers in various parts of the world incorporated key cultigens into their subsistence regimes (Winterhalder and Goland 1993, 1997), and how these shifts in subsistence altered prehistoric settlement strategies and land use.

In some cases, it is clear from the archaeological record that agriculturalists migrated into the territories of hunter-gatherers and ultimately replaced or subsumed them into their economies (Ammerman and Cavalli-Sforza 1984; Bogucki and Grygiel 1993; Cavalli-Sforza 1996; Diamond and Bellwood 2003). However, the transmission of domesticates through preexisting exchange networks also accounts for the rapid spread of domesticated plants and animals into many regions (Gregg 1988; Hastorf 1999, Piperno and Pearsall 1998). Recent studies suggest that the details of this transformation varied greatly throughout the world (Barton et al. 1999; Blumler 1996; Hart 1999; Price and Gebauer 1995a). The principles of Human Behavioral Ecology (HBE; Winterhalder and Smith 2000) predict that the adoption and use of domesticated plants and animals outside the parent region is contingent upon: (1) the availability and productivity of wild resources in the new area, (2) the fecundity and adaptability of the cultigen or domesticated animal species to the new area, and (3) population dependent and independent restrictions, e.g., territoriality, creating localized decreases in wild resources (resource depression; Barlow 2002; Broughton 1999; Cannon 2003).

Food production in Mesoamerica—principally the cultivation of maize, beans and squash—was relatively widespread by the Early Formative Period (~3500 B.P.; Flannery 1973) and by this time the peoples of Mexico and adjacent regions are generally classified by archaeologists as farmers (Flannery 1973; Smith 2001a). Subsistence strategies, however, were diverse and dependent upon differing ecological contexts; substantial reliance on food production occurred earlier in the highlands when compared to the coast, where people combined the cultivation of maize, beans, and/or squash with wild resources from wetland and littoral environments (e.g., fish, shellfish, etc.; Blake et al. 1992a; Clark and Blake 1994; Coe and Flannery 1967; Kennett et al. 2002). The most recent botanical and genetic studies suggest that maize, beans, and squash were domesticated in Central Mexico during

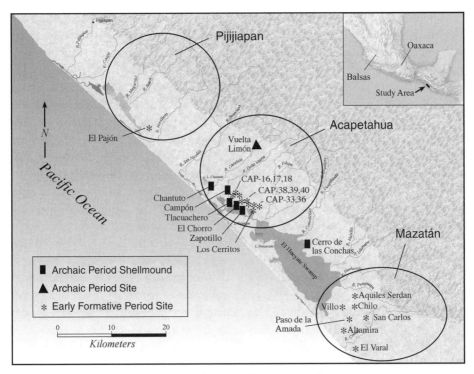

FIGURE 6.1. Study area showing the position of Archaic and Early Formative Period sites.

the Early Holocene (~10000–8000 cal. B.P., Matsuoka et al. 2002; Smith 1997b; Sonnante et al. 1994). Although these three cultigens were grown together after 3500 B.P., each appears to have its own domestication history that ultimately led to the symbiotic effects of growing these plants together in fields (Flannery 1973), a strategy that persists today throughout Mesoamerica. Reliance upon this triumvirate was preceded in many areas, e.g., Tehuacán Valley, Valley of Oaxaca, by a variety of mixed foraging and possibly horticultural strategies, and ultimately low-level food production–the supplementary use of maize, beans and/or squash occurring throughout much of the Early and Middle Holocene (Flannery 1986a; Smith 2001a). In some locations the low-level use of domesticated plants like squash persisted for at least 5500 years prior to a full commitment to food production (Smith 2001a).

In this chapter we analyze how people living in the Soconusco region of southwestern Mexico (Figure 6.1) responded to the arrival of one of these cultigens—maize. Biogeographical and genetic studies point to Central Mexico, the Balsas River region or Oaxacan Highlands, as the most likely area for early maize domestication (Figure 6.1 [inset], Benz 1994, 1999; Doebley 1990; Gonzalez 1994; Matsuoka et al. 2002; Wang et al. 1999). Macrobotanical evidence from dry caves in the mountains of Mexico indicate that domesticated maize had spread through this region by at least 6250 B.P. (Piperno and Flannery 2001); microbotanical studies of pollen and phytoliths from the tropical lowlands of Central Panama and Mexico suggest a far-reaching dispersal of maize as early as 7500 B.P. (Piperno and Pearsall 1998; Pope et al. 2001; Piperno 2001b). We do not assume that maize was the first cultigen to be used by the people of the Soconusco, but this plant is of particular interest because its use appears to have partially led to the transition to more intensive forms of food production and the emergence of cultural complexity during the Early and Middle Formative Periods (3500 to 2700 B.P.; Blake 1991; Blake and Clark 1999; Blake et al. 1995; Clark 1994; Clark and Blake 1994). Maize is also the most visible domesticate in both the micro- and macro–botanical record in Mesoamerica (Feddema 1993; Jones and Voorhies 2004; Kennett et al. 2002). Maize pollen and phytoliths dating to between 6000 and 5500 B.P. are evident in sediment cores from the Pacific coast of Guatemala, just south of the Soconusco (Neff et al. 2003). Maize phytoliths have also been recovered from Late Archaic Period archaeological deposits in the region dating to ~4600 B.P. (Jones and Voorhies 2004); and small maize cobs have been recovered from Early Formative Period contexts (~3500–3000 B.P.; Blake et al. 1992a; Feddema 1993). During the Late Archaic and Early Formative Periods, maize was used at a relatively low level and in combination with locally available wild resources, particularly from wetland and littoral environments. By the end of the Middle Formative Period (~2600 B.P.) agricultural communities dotted the coastal plain, and food producing economies emphasizing maize were well developed. However, wild foods continued to play an important role in some parts of the Soconusco throughout time (Blake et al. 1992a). The central question here is how a resource like early maize with poor energetic returns became a dominant feature of the subsistence economy in the region.

To model the transition to maize-based food production we first outline the paleoecology of the Soconusco with an emphasis on the biotic zones that parallel the coastline in bands. These biotic zones contained different resource types and densities offering a variety of opportunities for early foraging peoples. Based on these paleoecological data we develop a central place foraging model for pre-village (Archaic Period) forager/horticultural populations in the region and present the fragmentary archaeological evidence currently available. These data generally support the model, but continued testing will be needed for verification. We then turn to the development of maize-based food production in Mesoamerica, with special attention to the domestication of this plant and the morphological changes that it underwent during the Holocene; from a low productivity plant resembling teosinte, to the more productive forms of modern maize used in the region today. To simulate the dynamic responses of foragers in the Soconusco region to the appearance of maize of different types, we use an adapted form of the Lotka-Volterra predator prey model. Based on this model we predict the responses of foragers in the Soconusco to the introduction of maize at various times, and compare this to the available archaeological record for the Archaic and Formative Periods.

PALEOECOLOGY OF THE SOCONUSCO REGION

Maize was not domesticated in the Soconusco,[2] but introduced from elsewhere in central Mexico. Therefore, it is important to outline the social and ecological context into which this cultigen was introduced. Detailed environmental and paleoecological overviews for the region are available elsewhere (Clark 1994; Feddema 1993; Voorhies 1976, 2004), and in this section we summarize the pertinent paleoecological details with an emphasis on (1) the distribution and abundance of wild resources available to pre-village foragers/horticulturalists; (2) the early domesticates that may have been available; (3) environmental changes impacting the availability of these resources through the Holocene; and (4) the impact that human exploitation may have had on these resources through time.

The Soconusco is a tropical lowland region at ~15° N. latitude that stretches ~240 km along the Pacific coast from the Mexican-Guatemalan border to Pijijiapan, Mexico (Voorhies 1989a: Figure 6.1). This northwest-southeast trending coastal plain, which is flat and low-lying, is

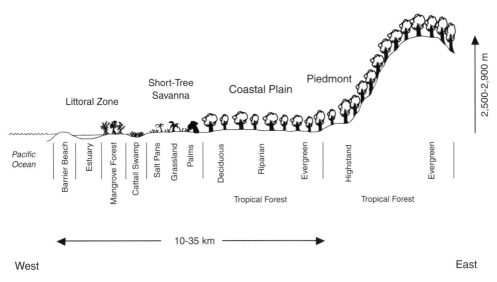

Sierra Madre Occidental

Piedmont

Short-Tree
Savanna

Coastal Plain

2,500–2,900 m

Littoral Zone

Pacific
Ocean | Barrier Beach | Estuary | Mangrove Forest | Cattail Swamp | Salt Pans | Grassland | Palms | Deciduous | Riparian | Evergreen | Highstand | Evergreen

Tropical Forest

Tropical Forest

10-35 km

West

East

FIGURE 6.2. Cross section of the Soconusco region showing geographical features and primary biotic zones.

flanked by the Pacific Ocean to the west and the Sierra Madre Occidental to the east (Figure 6.2). The width of the plain varies from 10 km near Pijijiapan to 35 km at the border between Mexico and Guatemala. The Sierra Madre rises 2500–2900 m along the eastern edge of the coastal plain, with the highest peak in the region reaching an elevation of 4110 m at the peak of the Tacaná volcano, straddling the Mexican-Guatemalan border. The rivers flowing out of the Sierra Madre form wetlands and lagoons along the seaward margin of the coastal plain; barrier beaches are well-developed along this stretch of coast, natural canals form a sheltered peri-coastal waterway along the entire seaward edge of the region. Archaeological sites, including ones dating from the Archaic to the end of the middle Formative Period (7500–2600 B.P.), are found on the inland side of the lagoon system and inland on the flat coastal plain (see Figure 6.1; Clark 1994; Kennett et al. 2002; Voorhies 1976, 2004; Voorhies et al. 2002).

Ambient air temperature in southwestern Mexico is relatively warm and stable through much of the year (Annual Mean: 26°C; Range: 20–36°C), but the region is influenced by highly seasonal tropical monsoonal rains (Annual mean: ~1500 mm; Vivó Escoto 1964). Rainfall is heaviest between April and October (~1200 mm, wet season) and much more limited between November and March (~200 mm; dry season). There is also a spatial gradient in the amount of rain that falls within the region; the highest precipitation falling in the mountains and the least falling near the coast. Rivers swell during the wet season transporting sediment out of the highlands onto the coastal plain, replenishing the rich alluvial soils that today support commercial agriculture of bananas and oil palms. Pericoastal environments are also flooded during wet season months, significantly reducing the amount of habitable dry land near the estuarine zone. Resource availability in the littoral zone peaks during the dry season (Kennett and Voorhies 1996). There may also be a general reduction in terrestrial biomass on the coastal plain during the dry season, particularly if arid conditions persist for extended periods. Stable carbon and oxygen isotopic analysis of mollusk shells from prehistoric sites in the region indicate that this tropical monsoonal rainfall regime persisted during the Archaic and Formative Periods (Kennett and Voorhies 1995, 1996; Kennett et al. 2002; Voorhies et al. 2002) and phytolith and pollen records show the stability of tropical forest growth with the exception of the large anthropogenic effects of burning and forest clearance recorded in these proxy records starting after 5000 B.P. (Jones and Voorhies 2004).

At the time of European contact (~AD 1520), the Soconusco was part of the Aztec Empire and, at the time, was well-known for its forest and agricultural products (Clark 1994; Gasco and Voorhies 1989, 75; Voorhies 1989a). Tribute items from this region paid annually to the Aztec Emperor included a diverse range of tropical bird skins, feathers, spotted animal pelts and cacao beans, by this time a highly prized domesticated tree crop traded widely in Mesoamerica (Gasco and Voorhies 1989).

Monsoonal rainfall patterns and differences in drainage in the region create several environmental zones that parallel the coast (see Figure 6.2). These environmental zones include, from the ocean to interior : (1) the littoral zone (including swampland); (2) tropical short-tree savanna, seasonally inundated and sometimes swampy; (3) forested coastal plain; and (4) piedmont forest. Each of these environmental zones contain several biotic communities (Clark 1994). The compressed nature of these environmental zones provided prehistoric people with a diverse range of economically valuable plants and animals within a relatively small foraging radius of 15–30 km depending upon settlement location within the region. However, the distances were great enough between these zones that prehistoric foragers and farmers had to decide where to establish settlements, determining which resources to exploit residentially and which to collect logistically[3] (see central place foraging below).

Resource-rich estuaries and wetlands formed along this section of coast with the sta-

bilization of sea-level between 9000 and 7000 B.P. (Fairbanks 1989; Kennett and Voorhies 1995, 1996). In this region the resources of the open ocean are difficult to access because of very heavy seas, consequently offering few subsistence opportunities for people with simple maritime technology (Clark 1994; Voorhies 1976). Large green sea turtles once laid their eggs on these beaches seasonally, with crabs and shellfish available on beach margins (Table 6.1; Coe and Flannery 1967; see Feddema 1993 for a comprehensive list of resources from different zones). Small animals occupied beach scrub fringing these long stretches of beach. Behind these barrier beaches, still-water aquatic habitats supported a wide range of marine and estuarine fish, mollusks, and crustacea, along with a variety of resident and migratory bird species (Voorhies 1976). It is also likely that shrimp were available during the dry season months in estuarine-lagoon systems open to the ocean (Clark 1994; Voorhies et al. 1991). A series of barrier beach ridges, visible in aerial photographs, show evidence for sequential progradation of the coastline after the stabilization of sea-level that included the infilling of estuarine lagoons. Lagoons are still present today in the Acapetahua portion of the coast (see Figure 6.1), and support several modern fishing and shrimp cooperatives. Large open lagoons also existed to the north (Pijijiapan) and south (Mazatán) of Acapetahua, but many have subsequently filled during the last 7000 years, creating salt pans, tropical savanna, and freshwater marsh systems (e.g., El Hueyate marsh; see Figure 6.1). The interior edge of these estuaries was bordered with a narrow, well-developed strip of mangrove forest and herbaceous swamps that today support a variety of edible plant and animal species. Most notable is the rich array of fauna and migratory waterfowl found in the El Hueyate swamp located toward the southern end of the study region (Alvarez del Toro 1985; Clark 1994).

A tropical short-tree savanna occurs immediately inland of the coastal wetlands. It consists of dispersed palm trees with an understory of

TABLE 6.1

Selection of Plants and Animals from Different Environmental Zones in the Soconusco

LATIN NAME	COMMON NAME	LZ	ST	CP	P	BIOTIC COMMUNITY
Agaronia testacea	mollusk	✓				beach
Anadara reinharti	clam	✓				beach
Chelonia mydas	green sea turtle	✓				beach
Coendou mexicanus	porcupine	✓				mangrove
Crocodylus astutus	river crocodile	✓				estuary/river
Ctenosaura similis	black iguana	✓				beach scrub
Dasypus novemcinctus	armadillo	✓				beach scrub
Goniopsis pulchra	small crab	✓				mangrove
Lutjanus colorado	red snapper	✓				estuary/river
Mycteria americana	stork	✓				estauary
Mytella falcata	mussel	✓				estuary
Ocybode occidentalis	beach crab	✓				beach
Ostrea columbiensis	oyster	✓				estuary
Polymesoda radiata	marsh clam	✓				estuary
Sesarma sulcatum	crab	✓				mangrove
Procyon lotor	raccoon	✓				mangrove
Sciades troschelii	marine catfish	✓				estuary/river
Strombus galeatus	snail	✓		✓	✓	beach
Tamandua tetradactyla	collared anteater	✓		✓	✓	mangrove
Peneus spp.	shrimp	✓				estuary
Centropomus sp.	snook	✓				estuary
Caiman crocodilus	cayman	✓				swamp
Cairina moschata	duck	✓				swamp
Cichlasoma timaculatum	bass	✓				swamp
Iguana iguana	water iguana	✓				swamp
Lepisosteus tropicus	gar	✓				swamp
Chrysemys scripta	black turtle	✓				swamp
Staurotypus salvinii	snapping turtle	✓				swamp
Acrocomia mexicana	coyol palm		✓			palm forest
Crescentia cujete	calabash		✓			palm forest
Quercus oleoides	oak		✓			palm forest
Sabal mexicana	fan palm		✓			palm forest
Scheelea liebmannii	corozo palm		✓			palm forest
Dasyprocta punctata	agouti		✓			grassland
Lepus flavigularis	hare		✓	✓		grassland
Nasua narica	coati		✓			grassland
Sylvilagus floridanus	cottontail		✓			grassland
Urocyon cinereoargenteus	grey fox		✓	✓	✓	grassland
Brosimum alicastrum	breadnut			✓	✓	tropical forest
Carica papaya	papaya			✓		tropical forest
Ficus glaucescens	black fig			✓	✓	tropical forest
Persea americana	avocado			✓	✓	tropical forest
Psidium guayaba	guava			✓	✓	tropical forest
Spondias mombin	hog plum			✓	✓	tropical forest
Persea americana	avocado			✓	✓	tropical forest

(continued)

TABLE 6.1 *(Continued)*

Selection of Plants and Animals from Different Environmental Zones in the Soconusco

LATIN NAME	COMMON NAME	LZ	ST	CP	P	BIOTIC COMMUNITY
Sterculia mexicana	chestnut			✓	✓	tropical forest
Theobroma cacao	cacao			✓	✓	tropical forest
Agriocharis ocellata	wild turkey			✓	✓	tropical forest
Alouatta villosa	howler monkey			✓	✓	tropical forest
Ateles geoffroyi	spider monkey			✓	✓	tropical forest
Coendou mexicanus	porcupine			✓	✓	tropical forest
Dasypus novemcintus	armadillo			✓	✓	tropical forest
Felis pardalis	ocelot			✓	✓	tropical forest
Felis yagouaroundi	jaguarundi			✓		tropical forest
Lutra annectens	river otter			✓	✓	tropical forest
Nasua narica	coati			✓	✓	tropical forest
Odocoileus virginianus	white-tail deer			✓	✓	tropical forest
Panthera onca	jaguar			✓	✓	tropical forest
Procyon lotor	raccoon			✓	✓	tropical forest
Tapirus bairdii	tapir			✓	✓	tropical forest
Tayassu tajacu	collared peccary			✓	✓	tropical forest
Ctenosaura pectinata	iguana			✓	✓	tropical forest
Quercus oleoides	oak				✓	tropical forest
Sylvilagus brasiliensis	forest rabbit				✓	tropical forest

Note: See Feddema 1993 for complete list. LZ = littoral zone; ST = short tree savanna; CP = coastal plain; P = piedmont.

grass and other herbaceous plants. This zone floods annually during the rainy season due in part to poorly draining soils. Parts of this zone positioned close to the brackish water estuary can be saline, and saltpans sometimes appear during the dry season. The soils in some other low lying sections of this zone are not salty and remain humid well into the dry season. The pith of *Palma real* is edible, as is the nut of the coyol palm (Clark 1994, 67), and it is likely that palms were an important dietary component for preagricultural populations in this region, as elsewhere in Central America (Hoopes 1995; Piperno and Pearsall 1998). As palm sap can be fermented this may have served as an alcoholic beverage prior to the production of maize beer (Blake et al. 1992a; Piperno, this volume). Medium and small sized game, including deer, peccary, armadillos, and tigrillos, are attracted seasonally to this zone (Clark 1994; Helbig 1964; Table 6.1), where important building ma-

terials are also found in abundance (e.g., palm thatch and wild bamboo; Clark 1994). Today the area is primarily used for grazing cattle (Clark 1994).

The coastal plain proper was once covered with a mix of tropical deciduous forest, riparian formations, and evergreen tropical forest (Clark 1994). A gradient of forest types, from evergreen forest near the mountains, to tropical deciduous forest closer to the coast, results from variations in rainfall and drainage on the coastal plain. Rivers and seasonal streams divide the coastal plain into a mosaic of riparian and forested habitats. This mosaic was home to at least 20 different mammal species, 126 bird species, 51 different reptile species, and 21 species of fish (see Clark 1994, 73 and Appendix 1). A selection of these is presented in Table 6.1. This list includes several species such as tapirs and peccaries that are no longer found in the region today (Voorhies 1976) due to their extirpation by humans. Many kinds of fruit-bearing trees also are available in this forested environment, including sapodilla, cacao, papaya, avocado, guanabana, and guayaba (Clark 1994). The best agricultural lands also occur within this well-drained zone, and horticulture, principally the exploitation and ultimate cultivation of root crops, likely started relatively early in this and other tropical forests (Piperno and Pearsall 1998). Forest clearance would have created small microhabitats in the forest, and paleoenvironmental records for the region suggest that burning and forest clearing started with the earliest visible occupation of the coast and intensified during the Formative Period (after 3500 B.P.) as maize-based food production became more established in the region (Jones and Voorhies 2004). Burning promotes the growth of herbaceous plants and tubers, so would have provided the needed space for fields, but this practice would also have reduced the habitat preferred by larger game animals such as deer and peccary. Today, large pastures are maintained over vast parts of this zone while extensive oil palm and banana plantations and cattle ranches cover much of the region.

The piedmont zone that borders the coastal plain is covered with lower montane rain forest due to higher annual rainfall (Miranda 1975). The rain forest has a high canopy (25–40 m) with dense undergrowth. Once the density of game animals was relatively high in this zone. It is likely that people living in communities on the coastal plain during the Archaic and Formative Periods hunted game in the piedmont region. The lower piedmont is particularly productive because it is well drained, receives plentiful rain, and has highly fertile soil (Table 6.1). Seasonal temperature variations are greater at higher elevations, reducing the growing season for maize, and either limiting the productivity of certain tropical lowland plant species or excluding them altogether (e.g., cacao; Clark 1994).

Determining the frequency and distribution of plant and animal species within each of these environmental zones during the Archaic and Formative Periods is difficult due to natural and substantial human-induced changes to the environment. The archaeological record for the region is fragmentary, leaving gaps in our current knowledge regarding environmental fluctuations during the Holocene. Radical changes in coastal habitats occurred until sea-level stabilized between 9000 and 7000 B.P. As sea-level stabilized after 7500 B.P., open and productive estuarine lagoons formed along the coast. Tropical deciduous and evergreen forests also covered the coastal plain by this time (Jones and Voorhies 2004). Marsh habitats were more restricted in the Early Holocene compared to today, but developed more fully during the Middle and Late Holocene as estuarine lagoons filled with sediment. The monsoonal rainfall regime was operating in this region by at least 7500 B.P. (Kennett and Voorhies 1995, 1996; Voorhies et al. 2002), but annual, decadal, centennial, and millennial climatic changes are evident in proxy climate records from elsewhere in Mexico and Central America (Voorhies and Metcalfe n.d.). Forest burning and clearing is also evident in pollen records for the region starting as early as 7000 and intensifying after 3500 B.P. Burning provided space for growing root crops, and possibly maize, but the destruction of forest habitat and hunting surely had decreased encounter rates with medium and small animals.

RETURN RATES FOR TROPICAL LOWLAND RESOURCES

The adoption of maize and the development of maize-based food production in the Soconusco region resulted from a series of individual decisions regarding diet choice made by people over several millennia. These choices were made in specific socioecological settings that resulted from changing environmental conditions, both natural and human induced, and fluctuating social landscapes impinging on the availability of resources, especially territoriality and increases in social complexity. Optimal foraging theory (OFT) predicts that foragers will economize with respect to dietary choice, selecting resources, or patches, that maximize the rate of energy gained per unit energy expended in locating, catching/ collecting, and processing prey. Dietary choice is therefore constrained by the availability of resources and social factors limiting access to them such as food taboos or territoriality. Given these environmental and social constraints, the most efficient food acquisition strategies available, it is argued, would be favored by natural selection because extra resources, or time saved, can be invested in additional offspring or provisioning existing offspring or mates. Nutrition and overall health have also been directly correlated with fertility and child mortality rates in different societies (Butz and Habicht 1976; Hill et al. 1987; Moseley and Chen 1984).

Ranking wild resources from highest to lowest returns helps determine the most likely dietary mix in a region and can be used to predict changes in diet breadth when ecological conditions change (e.g., depressed availability of higher ranked resources; Cannon 2003). Whether or not a new cultigen is incorporated into the dietary regime of a forager should be related to the availability of highly ranked wild resources and overall diet breadth (Winterhalder and Goland 1997). Ethnographic studies support the notion that caloric returns, rather than food preference, are robust predictors of diet choice (Hill et al. 1987; Winterhalder and Smith 2000). These studies also show that the size of a resource alone is not a good predictor of these dietary rankings, because resource value results from the caloric value of the resource minus the costs of acquisition and processing. Estimating return rates in prehistoric settings is challenging because each estimation depends upon encounter rates, procurement/processing techniques, and transportation costs, all of which are not directly knowable from the archaeological record. The costs and benefits of exploiting certain types of resources must be inferred from ethnographic studies within similar ecological contexts where this kind of economic data is collected and quantified, and/or from experimental studies that estimate resource return rates for labor investment in producing various technologies.

We examine two ethnographic studies from other tropical forest settings in the New World to garner the economic data needed to estimate return rates for different resources since firsthand observations of foraging practices in the Soconusco region are not available because traditional systems of agriculture and food extraction have given way to larger-scale ranching and cash-crop agriculture. One of these studies was conducted by James Nations and Robert Nigh (1980) among the Lacandon Maya, a small-scale farming/foraging population that re-colonized a portion of the southern Maya lowlands (Chiapas, Mexico) several centuries ago. Re-colonization of this region followed a long period of tropical forest regeneration that ensued with the collapse and abandonment of this area by the Classic Period Maya (AD 250–900; Webster 2002). We consider the foraging practices of these people to provide an apt analogy to the strategies practiced by early foraging and farming populations in the Soconusco region. Unfortunately, detailed information regarding the return rates of different plants and animals were not recorded in this study. To remedy this situation we turn to a second study conducted among Aché foragers who occupy a section of tropical forest in the Amazon and where a detailed study of return rates on a similar suite of resources has been conducted (Hill et al. 1987). We recognize that these data are not ideal, but we argue that they provide at least an approximation of dietary rankings in the forested coastal plain and piedmont zones within the Soconusco region. Ultimately, we are interested in comparing return rates of locally available wild resources with estimated rates of return for maize agriculture at various points in the past (see Tables 6.4 and 6.5 for estimated rates of return for maize-based food production).

The Lacandon Maya practice a diverse land-use system that capitalizes on different resource types from the primary and secondary forest and a variety of aquatic habitats; marshes, rivers, lakes, and streams (Nations and Nigh 1980, 8). At the heart of the Lacandon system is a form of slash-and-burn, or swidden, agriculture, where

TABLE 6.2
Selection of Plants and Animals Targeted by the Lacandon Maya of Chiapas, Mexico

SPECIES	COMMON NAME	USE
Crassidix mexicanum	grackle	meat
Cuniculus paca	paca	meat
Dasyprocta mexicana	agouti	meat
Dasypus novemcinctus	armadillo	meat
Didelphis azarae	oppossum	meat
Mazama americana	brocket deer	meat
Procyon lotor	racoon	meat
Sciurus aureogaster	red squirrel	meat
Sciurus deppei	forest squirrel	meat
Sylvilagus brasiliensis	rabbit	meat
Odocoileus virginianus	white-tailed deer	meat
Tayassu tajacu	collared peccary	meat
Annona scleroderma	wild annona	fruit
Brosium alicastrum	breadnut	fruit, seeds
Chamaedorea sp.	guatapil palm	heart, fruit, roofing
Diospyros digyna	zapote prieto	fruit
Ficus sp.	amate	edible bark; fiber
Inga spuria	chalahuite	fruit
Manilkara zapota	sapodilla	fruit
Pachira acuatica	water spote	fruit
Persea americana	wild avacado	fruit
Pachychilus indoirum	river snail	meat
Pomacea flagellata	apple snail	meat
Astyanax faciatus	sardine	meat
Ictiobus mevidionalis	pig fish	meat
Rhamadin guatemalensis	catfish	meat
Hyla baudini	tree frog	meat
Thynophrynis dorsalis	marsh frog	meat
Dermatemys mawi	river turtle	meat
Kinosternon sp.	small mud turtle	meat
Crocodylus acutus	yellow river crocodile	meat
Crocodylus moreletti	swamp crocodile	meat

Note: Data from Nations and Nigh 1980.

portions of the tropical forest are cleared and burned to grow maize and other domesticated plants (discussed below). Fields are used for several years, then abandoned to regenerate into forest. Areas of secondary forest growth, and presumably other naturally cleared areas, provide young shoots and saplings and attract a variety of game animals (Nations and Nigh 1980, 17; Table 6.2). Of these animals, white-tail (*Odocoileus virginianus*) and brocket (*Mazama americana*) deer are hunted most frequently. Because of this, their populations are monitored closely; there is some evidence to suggest that deer populations are managed to a certain degree. Although deer are the favored game in this area, a range of medium and small game animals, paca (*Cuniculus paca*) and collared peccary (*Tayassu tajacu*), are also targeted. These animals spend much of their lifecycle in primary forest habitats and aquatic-terrestrial ecotones;

TABLE 6.3

Return Rates for Selection of Animals Analogous to Those Present in the Soconusco Region during the Archaic Period

	SCIENTIFIC NAME	CAL/HR/PERSON
Brocket deer	*Mazama americana*	15,398
Biaju fruit	*Philodendron sellam (ripe)*	10,078
Coati	*Nasua nasua*	7,547
Virella fruit	*Campomanesia zanthocarpa*	6,417
Collared peccary	*Tajassu tajacu*	6,120
White-tipped peccary	*Tajassu pecari*	8,755[1]; 5,323
Paca	*Cuniculus paca*	4,705
Pretylla fruit	*Ficus sp.*	4,414
Brovilla fruit	*Casimiroa sinesis*	4,181
Kurilla fruit	*Rheedia brasilense*	3,245
Pychikytalla fruit	*Annoa sp.*	2,835
Membe fruit	*Philodendron sellam (unripe)*	2,708
9-banded Armadillo	*Dasypus novemcinctus*	13,782[2]; 2,662
Palm fiber and shoot	*Arecastrum romanzolfianum*	2,436
Palm fiber starch	*Arecastrum romanzolfianum*	3,219[3]; 2,246
Challa fruit	*Jacaratia sp.*	2,549
Boilla fruit	*Chrysophyllum gonocarpum*	2,884
Palm nut	*Acromia totai*	2,243
Large palm larva	*Calandra plamarum*	2,133
Roots	*Dioscorea hispida*	1,739
Palm growing shoot	*Arecastrum romanzolfianum*	2,356[4]; 1,584
Capuchin monkey	*Cebus apella*	1,370
Small palm larva	*Rhynophorus palmarum*	1,331
Bamboo larva	*Unknown*	936

Note: See Hill et al. 1987 for details. 1) First number does not include tracking time. 2) Second number includes optional processing time. 3) Men's return rate is listed first. 4) First number is for animals encountered in the forest and the second is for animals excavated from underground.

reductions in game animals associated with primary forest destruction are well documented in the Lacandon region. The forest also provides a range of edible fruit, bark, or in the case of several palms species, shoots and edible piths or hearts, and a range of reptiles, amphibians, fishes, and invertebrates (e.g., snails) are taken from rich freshwater habitats.

Similar to the Lacandon Maya, the Aché of Paraguay combine small-scale farming activities with hunted and gathered wild foods from the tropical forests of the Amazon (Table 6.3; Hill et al. 1987, 5). Although there are clear differences between the Amazon and the tropical forests of Mexico, a comparison of the resources used shows that many of the same mammal species

and a comparable range of fruit trees, palms, and other edible plants were targeted by both groups. Further examination of the return rates recorded in the Aché case indicate that larger animal species are among the highest-ranked resources, edging out many of the available plant species in the Amazon forest. Some animal species have return rates that fall below or within the range of most plants, most notably paca and monkey, owing to high pursuit and/or processing time (Hill et al. 1987). Fish, armadillos, rabbits, and grasshoppers, if effectively taken in large numbers, can have return rates that rival the largest and most naïve game animals (see Madsen and Schmitt 1998). Post-encounter processing costs can cause highly varied rates of return for the same resource (e.g., palms; Hill et al. 1987). We suspect that tubers were one component of the diet in the Soconusco region during the Archaic Period; however, as in other parts of the world (Flannery 1973), we have no direct archaeological evidence for this practice (see below). Modern-day foragers in tropical forests of the Philippines have return rates on wild tubers between 484 and 1739 cal/person/hour (Eder 1978). Piperno and Pearsall (1998) have pointed out that if the larger animal taxa were reduced in the tropical forest, wild and domesticated tubers were likely exploited along with other low-ranking plant species.

Return rates for tropical forest resources should be considered relative to those found in the littoral zone. Of these, the archaeological record suggests that fish and shellfish were the most important in the Soconusco region (Clark 1994; Kennett et al. 2002; Voorhies 1976; Wake et al. 2004).[4] The most abundant and concentrated shellfish species in the littoral zone are marsh clams (*Polymesoda radiata*). Several studies provide information regarding the return rates on the collection of somewhat comparable species of shellfish. Based on experimental work, Jones and Richman (1995) determined that mussel beds on the central coast of California produced about 500 cal/person/hour. In a classic ethnographic study of shellfishing among the Anbarra of Northern Australia in Arnhem Land, Meehan (1977, 524) determined that skilled women collecting clams (*Tapes hiantina*) had return rates in the range of 1000 cal/person/hour. More recently, Bird and Bliege Bird (2000) have quantified the relative return rates for different shellfish species from the reefs of the Meriam Islands of Australia (Torres Strait). In this study, the profitability for adults collecting shellfish varied greatly (300 to 6200 cal/person/hour), and was dependent upon the species targeted. Sunset clams (*Asaphis violascens*) are the most comparable to the species available in the brackish water lagoons of the Acapetahua Estuary and these provide return rates of approximately 400 cal/person/hour. Based on these data we suspect marsh clams

had return rates of between 500 and 1000 cal/person/hour.

Similar to shellfishing, return rates for fishing are dependent upon the overall productivity and character of the targeted fish species and the technology available at the time of capture or harvest. Many sophisticated fishing techniques and devices are known from ethnographic and ethnohistoric studies around the world (Aswani 1998; Lindström 1996; Winterhalder 1981b). Lindström (1996) has conducted a comprehensive study of return rates for fishing with ethnohistoric and experimental data from the Truckee River Basin on the western edge of the Great Basin (California/Nevada). Although these data were collected from a riverine context, it provides at least a proxy for fishing in the Soconusco littoral zone. Lindström calculated return rates for different types and sizes of fish using various fishing technologies. The key observation is that return rates for fish are highly variable and dependent upon the technology used, the season of capture, spawn or non-spawn, and the size of fish (200 to 40,000 cal/person/hour). The small size of some fish vertebrae found in Archaic Period shellmounds in the Soconusco suggest that nets were being used (Cooke et al. 2004). Based on comparable technology in Truckee River Basin, we estimate that fishing in the Soconusco wetlands would produce return rates in the 2000–5000 cal/person/hour range, somewhat comparable to small-sized game and a range of fruit bearing trees and palms. This estimate does not include the manufacture and maintenance of nets, fishing tackle, and boats, investments that would have reduced return rates significantly.

Once reasonable return rates are established for different food types, the economic rational of HBE and the diet-breadth model can be used to make several predictions about prehistoric foraging behavior that can be tested subsequently with archaeological data. The model predicts that as the abundance of higher-ranked prey species increases, the variety of resource types will decrease. Logically, the reverse also follows: if the abundance of high-ranked resources decreases, diet-breadth will increase. This means that potential prey types will enter a forager's diet based on the abundance of higher-ranked resources and not simply contingent upon immediate value. The availability of high-ranked resources is often population dependent. In other words, as the density of human foraging population increases, the availability of the highest-ranked prey species, such as deer populations, will usually decrease. Climate change may also decrease the availability of high-ranked prey as this clearly occurred at the end of the Pleistocene Epoch throughout much of the New and Old Worlds (Piperno and Pearsall 1998). In the Soconusco case, the archaeological record suggests that the highest-ranked species in the Holocene included medium and small sized game animals and fruit.

As a result of the spatial compression of biotic communities in the Soconusco region, people living on the coastal plain could exploit a variety of resource zones within a 15–30 km radius of their villages. Diet choice has ramifications for settlement location; foragers in this region decided where to establish base camps, which resources to exploit residentially, and which to exploit logistically. Where settlements were located was related to the natural differences in resource density and seasonal availability. The degree of mobility at any given time would also have been restricted by territoriality and subsistence practice, whether foraging or farming. Once foragers established encampments, additional constraints on resource acquisition were imposed by the transportation costs incurred from central place foraging. We now turn to central place foraging theory and our best estimates of Archaic Period subsistence and settlement prior to the development of more intensive maize-based food production during the Formative Period.

CENTRAL PLACE FORAGING IN THE SOCONUSCO

Central place foraging theory provides a point of departure for modeling pre-village, Archaic Period foraging strategies and the development of settled village life and food production in the Soconusco region. Based on the compressed nature of habitats along this stretch of coast, foragers could choose among a number of alternative locations. Important factors for selecting residential base locations in this region included the availability of drinking water, firewood, and well-drained land to establish a community. Based on these criteria, potential settlement locations were available on slightly higher locations along the inland periphery and islands of the littoral zone, seasonally within the short tree savanna, on the coastal plain, and in the piedmont zone. But not all these zones are equally attractive. Prior to the historical excavations of drainage canals, seasonal flooding in the short tree savanna would have periodically reduced the availability of suitable settlement locations, but old sandbars and small knolls would have provided dry, habitable locations throughout the year. Social factors, particularly territoriality, which would limit the location of settlements on the coastal plain, increased with population growth, environmental infilling, and controlled access to resource patches by certain individuals and groups in the region during the Formative Period (Blake and Clark 1999). The biotic communities, from the littoral zone to the piedmont, provided a diverse range of resources that had variable rates of return. Resource return rates also fluctuated seasonally. For example, in the littoral zone, shrimp and fish increased during the dry season compared with the wet season. Beyond base-level criteria for water, fuel, etc., central place foraging theory provides a set of principles for estimating the optimal settlement locations in the region. The model predicts that, all other variables being equal, foragers will select residential base locations that maximize net central place foraging returns given the pursuit, handling, and transport costs of different sets of resources in each biotic zone (Cannon 2003).

Based on central place foraging principles we would predict that, in the absence of restrictive territorial behavior of other groups and human induced resource depression, Archaic

Period residential bases would have been positioned on the coastal plain adjacent to rivers. Most of these inland locations did not flood on an annual basis and provided easy access to wood for fuel and building. They also were well-positioned for people to exploit a diverse range of animal and plant resources, including deer and valuable tree crops like avocados. Clearing patches in the forest through burning would have promoted the growth of some plant species (Piperno and Pearsall 1998) and possibly attracted deer to feed on new plant growth. Although seasonal fluctuations in forest resources would have been present, perhaps they were well-balanced on an overall annual basis. Over time, population-dependent increases in burning of tropical forest and more intensified hunting near the residential bases would have led to reduced populations of deer and peccary, the expansion of diet breadth, more distant logistical forays, and ultimately the relocation of residential bases. In this changing context, toward the end of the Archaic Period, the coastal littoral zone may have become a viable zone for residential bases.

The establishment of residential bases on the coastal plain during the Archaic did not preclude the use of resources from other, more distant, biotic communities through logistical foraging and/or sexual division of labor (Zeanah 2000, 2004). All resource zones in the Soconusco region would have been within a 15 km foraging radius of residential bases located in the middle of the coastal plain. Which resources were exploited depended upon people's overall dietary breadth at residential bases, along with the pursuit, handling, and transportation costs of more distant resources. These criteria place limitations on the types of resources pursued (Cannon 2003); how they are processed (Bird and Bliege Bird 1997); and the load size needed to make a trip pay off (Barlow et al. 1993). The maximum transport distance (MTD) is an index, developed by Jones and Madsen (1989) in the Great Basin, that takes these variables into consideration, MTD being the distance that a resource can be car-

ried before the calories in the load are exceeded by the costs of procuring and transporting it. Given load and volume limitations (~30 kg [or 64.3 liters], Jones and Madsen 1989; Zeanah 2000), the model predicts that people foraging at distant locations will limit themselves to resources of high net value.

Central place foraging theory also has direct implications for how resources are processed during logistical foraging expeditions. Large animal taxa will be butchered with greater attention to the best cuts of meat and, in some instances, weight restrictions will require that a portion of the edible meat be consumed at the kill site or left behind (Zeanah 2000). Drying meat, to reduce water weight, may also be practiced to maximize the net resource delivery rate to residential bases. Processing techniques like these should be reflected in the archaeological record. That is, skeletal elements associated with high utility body parts, e.g., femura and humeri, should be more frequently deposited at residential bases and low utility skeletal elements should occur at logistical foraging camps. Resources in the coastal littoral zone also would have been attractive to foragers living on the coastal plain. Many littoral resources can be collected en masse (e.g., mollusks, fish, shrimp) and processed to maximize net delivery rate to people living in the interior. If residential bases were positioned on the coastal plain, then these littoral resources were likely collected en masse and processed to maximize net delivery rate to residential bases: shrimp dried; fish gutted, beheaded, split and dried; and clams steamed open and the meat extracted and dried (Voorhies 2004; Voorhies et al. 1991).

Ethnographic studies in the Meriam Islands suggest that the degree of shellfish processing is contingent upon travel distance, processing costs, and the proportional value of the resource (Bird 1997; Bird and Bliege Bird 1997). The shell-to-meat ratio in most species of shellfish makes processing advantageous if transport distances are long, although there may be some advantages to keeping shellfish in their shell

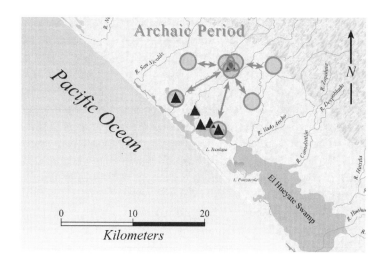

FIGURE 6.3. Central place foraging model for pre-village (Archaic Period) foragers in the Soconusco region (~7500–3,500 cal. yrs. B.P.).

(storage, etc., Kennett 1998). The archaeological implications of processing at special purpose locations in the littoral zone are that shrimp remains, even if preserved, would be rare, cranial elements of fish might be prevalent, and mollusk shells should be common. Shellfish could be collected throughout the year, but people would more frequently visit the littoral zone when shrimp and fish were more available during the dry season. Evidence for permanent occupation of these locations in houses, burials, diverse faunal and tool assemblages should be lacking.

Our Archaic Period central place foraging model for the Soconusco region is displayed in Figure 6.3. In this model, we predict that residential bases were positioned on the coastal plain near rivers. In this period, the forest was cleared from around these central places; wild plants were collected from various forested environments; deer, peccary, and small game were hunted in the vicinity of settlements; and people fished along river courses. Based on the low-level cultivation of some domesticated plants elsewhere in Mesoamerica we suspect that some cultigens were grown close to these settlements. Longer distance logistical trips to the piedmont zone and elsewhere on the coastal plain were employed to hunt larger game animals, and similar forays were used to collect resources in the littoral zone, perhaps more fre-

quently during the dry season months when resources were more abundant.

ARCHAIC PERIOD SUBSISTENCE AND SETTLEMENT DATA

Much of the Archaic Period archaeological record is deeply buried below alluvium and thus fragmentary (Michaels and Voorhies 1999; Voorhies 1996; Voorhies and Kennett 1995), but the data available generally support the central place foraging model proposed here. The archaeologically detectable Archaic Period occupation of the Soconusco coastal plain coincides with the stabilization of sea level between 9000 and 7000 B.P. (Fairbanks 1989). The best evidence for the presence of people during the Archaic Period comes from a series of six large shellmound sites positioned in a line along the coast (Clark 1994; Drucker 1948; Kennett and Voorhies 1996; Lorenzo 1955, Navarrete n.d.; Voorhies 1976, 2000b, 2004). Five of these sites are located in the Acapetahua Estuary, and the other site, Cerro de las Conchas, is situated near the inland margin of the El Hueyate swamp (see Figure 6.1). Shell deposits at Cerro de las Conchas date to between 7500 and 5500 B.P. and currently provide the earliest evidence for human occupation of the Pacific coast of tropical Mexico (Voorhies 2000a; Voorhies et al. 2002). The shellmounds in the Acapetahua Estuary

FIGURE 6.4. Photograph of a Late Archaic Period shellmound (El Chorro) in the littoral zone of the Acapetahua region.

date later, between 5500 and 3500 B.P., but are similar in character to Cerro de las Conchas. Although these shellmounds represent the earliest recognizable human occupation of the coast, earlier sites were probably covered by sediments deposited during the late Pleistocene/early Holocene marine transgression or subsequently by the actively prograding coastline (Voorhies and Kennett 1995). It is likely that small groups of people were living along the coast from the onset of the Holocene. This suspicion is based on clear evidence for human occupation of other parts of Middle America during the terminal Pleistocene and early Holocene (Cooke 1998; Cooke et al. 1996; Cooke and Ranere 1992; Brown 1980; Ranere and Cooke 1991; Piperno and Pearsall 1998; Zeitlan 1984; Zeitlin and Zeitlin 2000).

Work completed at the shellmounds along the Soconusco coast suggests that they were special purpose locations used for exploiting littoral resources, rather than permanently occupied settlements (Kennett and Voorhies 1996; Michaels and Voorhies 1999; Voorhies 1996, 2004; Voorhies et al. 1991). The shellmounds are impressive prehistoric features that form artificial islands within this wetland environment (Figure 6.4). They range in size from 0.20 to 1.17 hectares and are between 3 and 11 meters in

height (Voorhies 2004). Relative to other early sites in the region, they are highly visible in aerial photographs because they are periodically cleared and used in a variety of ways by people living in the littoral zone today. Excavations at these shellmounds indicate that they consist of densely packed layers of marsh clam shell (*Polymesoda radiata*) dating to the aceramic Archaic Period, with an overlying stratum of dark soil containing artifacts, principally ceramics, from later time periods. The Archaic Period deposits are distinctively bedded, with alternating burned and unburned layers of marsh clam shell, that we have interpreted as representing periodic use, rather than continual settlement (Kennett and Voorhies 1996; Michaels and Voorhies 1999; Voorhies 2004). This interpretation is also supported by the general absence of domestic features such as house floors and formal hearths,[5] a very low diversity of tools, faunal assemblages showing an intensive focus on shallow water lagoonal systems (fish, clams, and possibly shrimp; Kennett and Voorhies 1996; Michaels and Voorhies 1999; Voorhies et al. 1991; Voorhies 1996, 2004). Seasonality data indicate that early in the Middle Archaic Period littoral resources were procured throughout much of the year with an emphasis during the dry season months (Voorhies et al. 2002).

A sediment core placed in the wetlands adjacent to the Chantuto shellmound revealed that the mound extends well beyond its present base. Repeated excavations, and in one case coring, have failed to reach the bottom of any one of these massive accumulations of shell. Terminal dates for these shellmounds fall between 3500 and 3000 B.P. appearing to be coeval with a settlement shift to residential bases positioned just inland of the permanent wetlands, perhaps in the seasonally flooded zone.

Based on the seemingly logistical nature of these shellmounds, we have hypothesized that interior basecamps were positioned on the coastal plain, probably in forest clearings close to surface water and to wild and possibly domesticated food plants (Kennett and Voorhies 1996; Michaels and Voorhies 1999; Voorhies 1996, 2004), as predicted by our central place foraging model. Unfortunately rapid sedimentation rates on this flat coastal plain, associated with seasonal flooding, have obscured much of the record for early interior settlement in the region. A pedestrian survey of the region revealed few sites on the inner slope of the coastal plain that predated the Late Formative Period (Voorhies 1989b). In 1991, we surveyed rivers between Pijijiapan and Tapachula in order to discover deeply buried Archaic Period deposits (Voorhies and Kennett 1995). During this survey we discovered one aceramic cultural deposit buried between two and two and a half meters below the surface, but exposed in a natural river cut on the Cacaluta River. Subsequent excavations of this site (Vuelta Limón, see Figure 6.1) unearthed a variety of tools, including groundstone, hammerstones, flakes, and fire cracked rock, suggesting that it was a basecamp (Michaels and Voorhies 1999; Voorhies 1996, 2004). Unfortunately bone and charred seeds were not preserved in these alluvial deposits. However, the absence of ceramics and a single radiocarbon date place the site's terminal occupation at 3800 B.P., near the end of the Archaic Period. Vuelta Limón is located upstream from the Chantuto shellmound in the Acapetahua Estuary, which also dates to the end of the Late Archaic Period, and we suspect that foragers based at this interior location collected and processed shellfish at Chantuto for transport back to Vuelta Limón. Pollen and phytolith data from the site suggest that palms were in heavy use as building material, and possibly a food source, and that maize pollen was present at very low levels indicating the use of this cultigen by the terminal Archaic Period (see below; Jones and Voorhies 2004). Phytolith data from Vuelta Limón and Tlacuachero, a shellmound site positioned in the coastal littoral, both show evidence for forest disturbance during the Late Archaic Period (after 5000 B.P.).

Although the record is fragmentary, the available data suggest that pre-village foragers in the Soconusco established settlements in forest clearings on the coastal plain and foraged logistically in the littoral zone. It is also likely that these people foraged logistically in the piedmont zone for larger animal taxa, and at other locations on the coastal plain. The material record from the shellmounds strongly supports this hypothesis, as does the more limited evidence for stable interior settlement from Vuelta Limón. Intensive exploitation of highly localized marsh clams from the shallow lagoons in the estuary, combined with large-scale processing through cooking and drying, is also in line with the expectations of central place foraging theory: investment in processing was economically viable given the costs of transporting heavy shells back to interior settlements. Intensive exploitation of shellfish in this way also suggests that diet-breadth was relatively broad starting as early as 7500 B.P., as evidenced at Cerro de las Conchas. This suggests to us that populations of larger animal species were low on the coastal plain due either to predation pressure or because the environment would not support high populations. As a response, human dietary breadth was wide enough to include small marsh clams. The available data also suggest that these settlement and subsistence strategies were remarkably stable for thousands of years (7500 to 3500 B.P.). It was in the context of wide diet breadth and stable subsistence settlement strategies that maize was first introduced to and experimented with in the region. We now turn to the current state of knowledge regarding the domestication and dispersal of maize as a first step in modeling the incorporation of this culti-gen into the Soconusco dietary regime.

DOMESTICATION AND DISPERSAL OF MAIZE

Interest in the domestication of maize has a long, and somewhat controversial, history ex-tending back to the 1930s (Mangelsdorf and Reeves 1939), and a great deal of academic en-ergy has focused upon establishing the progen-itor of this important cultigen, argued either to be an extinct wild pod corn (Mangelsdorf 1974, 1986) or the wild grass teosinte (Beadle 1972, 1977, 1980; Galinat 1975, 1988, 1992, 1995). Several species of teosinte (*Zea* spp.) are native to tropical environments in southern Mexico and parts of Guatemala and Nicaragua (Iltis and Benz 2000; Sanchez-Velasquez et al. 2001), with some varieties adapted to semi-arid high-land environments above 1800 m (e.g., *Zea mays* subp. *mexicana*) and others distributed in wetter lowland tropical environments below 1800 m (e.g., *Zea mays* subsp. *parviglumis*). The most recent, and generally accepted, genetic work supports the hypothesis that maize was originally descended from teosinte and was do-mesticated at ~9200 years ago in southern Mexico; either in the Balsas River Valley (Doebley 1990), or in the highlands of Oaxaca (Matsuoka et al. 2002). These genetic studies suggest that *Zea mays* subsp. *parviglumis* (teosinte), found growing today on well-drained, karstic slopes in the Balsas River Valley (400–1800 m elevation), is the closest wild ancestor to all modern races of maize (Doebley 1990). However, genetic studies also indicate that, of the extant races of maize found today throughout the New World, the most primitive forms occur in the Oaxacan highlands (above 1800 m; Matsuoka et al. 2002). These data suggest that maize was do-mesticated outside the modern distributional range of the most likely progenitor species (Z.

mays subsp. *parviglumis*). Possible explanations for this perplexing pattern are that: (1) wild teosinte (subsp. *parviglumis)* was introduced from the Balsas valley to the highlands where it was subsequently domesticated (Matsuoka et al. 2002, 6084); (2) early Holocene environments favored *parviglumus* at higher elevations (Mat-suoka et al. 2002, 6084)[6] compared with its modern distribution; or (3) the present distribu-tion of extant landraces of maize do not reflect the ancient distribution, and maize was domes-ticated at low elevations in the Balsas River val-ley.

Although genetic studies suggest that maize was domesticated early in the Holocene, this has not been corroborated with botanical evi-dence from well-dated archaeological contexts (e.g., carbonized plant remains, pollen, or phy-toliths). Work currently underway in the Balsas River Valley is designed to locate early prehis-toric contexts that may contain well-preserved micro- or macro-botanical remains (Piperno, personal communication, 2004). The earliest available evidence for *Zea* comes from microb-otanical studies in central Panama and along the Gulf Coast of Mexico (Tabasco). *Zea* starch grains have been recovered from early grinding stones at Aguadulce Rockshelter in central Panama (slightly before 7000 B.P.; Piperno, this volume) and *Zea* phytolith assemblages of the same age have been recovered from prehis-toric sediments at Aguadulce and Cueva de los Ladrones, another rock-shelter site in central Panama (Piperno and Pearsall 1998; Piperno et al. 1985). *Zea* pollen grains dating to ~7100 B.P. were also recently recovered from archaeologi-cal contexts and wetland sediments in the tropi-cal lowlands of Tabasco (Gulf Coast of Mexico), coeval with the first evidence for forest clearing in the region (Pope et al. 2001). Several microb-otanical studies carried out in Northern Belize (Pohl et al. 1996), coastal Guatemala (Neff et al. 2003), coastal Chiapas (Jones and Voorhies 2004), and the Gulf Coast (Rust and Leyden 1994) indicate that maize was one of several cultigens consistently used in the lowland trop-ics, at least at low levels, by 5000 B.P. These data help substantiate the early occurrences of *Zea* in Panama and suggest a far-reaching dispersal of maize through the lowland tropics between 7500 and 7000 B.P.

The earliest evidence for *Zea* in the highlands of Mexico comes from fully domesticated maize cobs directly dated to 6250 B.P. at the site of Guilá Naquitz in the Valley of Oaxaca (Benz 2001; Piperno and Flannery 2001). These new dates are slightly earlier than the direct dates on maize cobs from San Marcos and Coxcatlán caves in the Tehuacán Valley (~5500 B.P.; Benz and Iltis 1990; Benz and Long 2000; Fritz 1994a; Long et al. 1989; Smith 1998), originally recovered by MacNeish and studied by Mangelsdorf in the 1950s and 1960s (Mangelsdorf et al. 1967). After decades of work in the highlands, and the clear identification of prehistoric deposits dating prior to 6250 B.P. (Flannery 1986a), micro- and macro-botanical evidence for either teosinte, or a primitive form of domesticated maize, is thus far absent (Piperno and Flannery 2001). Early dispersal of maize through the lowland tropics, and the late arrival of a fully domesticated species of maize in the highlands, supports the hypothesis that maize was domesticated at low elevations in the Balsas River Valley and dispersed widely through the lowland tropics prior to its use in the highlands of Mexico.

There are different varieties of domesticated maize, each with its own agroecological potential and environmental preferences: highlands vs. lowlands, frost resistance, pest resistance, etc. In fact, many landraces of maize are adapted to specific elevations and environments, and are distinct enough that some scholars have argued that maize was domesticated from several different ancestral stocks of teosinte (Galinat 1988). The early *Zea* phytoliths found at Aguadulce Rock shelter in Central Panama dating before 7000 B.P. are morphologically similar to those found in the glumes and rachis of Balsas River teosinte and primitive forms of domesticated maize (Reventador and Maiz Ancho; Piperno, this volume; Piperno and Pearsall 1998, 221). Phytoliths in later deposits at the same site are morphologically similar to modern varieties of maize. These data suggest that a primitive variety of domesticated maize was present in Panama just prior to 7000 B.P., well outside the natural range of its progenitor, *Zea mays* subsp. *parviglumus*. Maize macrofossils dating to this early time do not exist, but the primitive form of the phytoliths themselves suggest that this cultigen was morphologically similar to teosinte; with the possible absence of the distinctive cob and its kernels at least partially enclosed by a hard glume (Piperno and Pearsall 1998, 223). These traits made early *Zea* resistant to insect infestation and fungal diseases (Piperno, this volume), but would have contributed to higher post-harvesting processing costs.

The first *Zea* pollen grains (~7100 B.P.) found on the Tabasco coast are small, falling within the range recorded for wild teosinte (48 to 49.8μm; Pope et al. 2001). These data are consistent with the data from Central Panama for an early dispersal of a primitive form of maize through the lowland tropics. Shortly after 7000 B.P., phytolith and pollen assemblages from both Central Panama and Tabasco appear to be morphologically similar to modern maize. However, small *Zea* sp. pollen is relatively abundant at the sites studied in Tabasco until 4500 B.P., and indicates great variability in the morphology of this cultigen through this time (Pope et al. 2001). This suggests early dispersal and continued use at some locations of a primitive form of maize, with subsequent alterations possibly occurring outside of southern Mexico where it was originally domesticated.

Changes in maize did not stop after the clear development of morphologically modern maize, just as distinctive adjustments continue to be made to this plant today (Abbo and Rubin 2000; Martinez-Soriano and Keal-Klevezas 2000). The early maize cobs from Guilá Naquitz (~6250 B.P.) and the Tehuacán valley (5500 B.P.) are remarkably variable in character, but all had rigid rachis that required grain removal by humans if they were to be dispersed and propagated—a clear indication of domestication

(Benz 2001, 2104). Several morphological attributes in these early cobs are intermediate between teosinte and maize, and support the ancestral relationship between these two species (Benz 2001). The earliest maize cobs from Guilá Naquitz were small having fewer rows (two to four) of grain when compared to many modern maize varieties (Benz 2001). Some of the small maize cobs from the Tehuacán valley, thought to be early, have also now been shown to date later in time, but co-occur with cobs of varying sizes until about 4500 B.P. (Benz and Long 2000; Long et al. 1989). This is consistent with the pollen data from Tabasco indicating a mix of small teosinte, and large maize pollen grains starting as early as 7000 B.P., with the persistence of small *Zea* pollen until 4500 B.P. (Pope et al. 2001).

The Oaxacan and Tehuacán specimens suggest that human selection between 6250 and 4500 B.P. sought to maintain or increase the productivity of maize by promoting the naked-grained phenotype and increasing the number of grain-bearing spicklets (Benz 2001). However, the full-sized cobs that we associate with modern maize may not have developed until as late as 3000 B.P. (Benz and Long 2000), when there is clear botanical and stable carbon isotope evidence throughout much of Mesoamerica for more intensive forms of maize agriculture and larger cob sizes (Ambrose and Norr 1992; Benz and Long 2000; Blake et al. 1992a, 1992b; Clark 1994; Feddema 1993; Kirkby 1973; Sheets 2002; Smith 1997a). Evidence from several areas suggests that the varieties of maize available between 4000 and 3000 B.P., although fully domesticated, had relatively small cobs and were not as productive as many varieties of modern maize. A limited number of maize casts in clay from the site of Salinas La Blanca (Middle Formative; Cuadros Phase; ~3000 B.P.; Coe and Flannery 1967), located on the coast of Guatemala, suggest that maize cobs were slightly smaller than many modern varieties. Charred maize cupules and cob fragments (N = 2280) recovered from a series of Early Formative Period (3500 to 3000 B.P.) sites

in the Mazatán region of coastal Chiapas, Mexico have 12 row cobs, but are between 20–40% the size of modern maize in the region today (Blake et al. 1992a, 1992b; Feddema 1993).

Not all domesticated varieties of maize have the same agroecological potential, particularly in the lowland tropics, while the types of maize available in Mexico and Central America changed through time. Some of these varieties certainly would have had low return rates relative to other wild alternatives. For instance, one of the hypotheses regarding the late use of teosinte in the highlands, or of an early form of domesticated maize, is that *Setaria* (foxtail grass) cultivation was much more productive (Flannery 1973). This is supported by early evidence for *Setaria* seed exploitation and consumption from Early Holocene coprolite samples collected from dry caves in Tehuacán and Tamaulipas (Callen 1967a). The initial decision to invest time in maize cultivation in the Soconusco region was contingent upon the maize varieties introduced to the region at various times, with the productivity of these varieties correlated to the available alternatives. We now turn to the difficult task of modeling the relative productivity of maize-based food production through time in the Soconusco region.

RETURN RATES FOR MAIZE-BASED FOOD PRODUCTION IN THE SOCONUSCO

In order to compare the economics of foraging vs. farming in the Soconusco, we must estimate the net return rates of maize-based food production during the last 9200 years, the purported date for maize domestication in Central Mexico. Traditionally, farmers in this region annually grew two to three crops of maize, but today in some areas the development of large plantations on the coastal plain has pushed the milpas into more marginal areas of lower piedmont. Maize is grown less often in the lower coastal plain because much of this area has saline soils and/or is flooded during the rainy season (Clark 1994; McBryde 1947), and people living in this zone are also more likely to be engaged in other economic pursuits such as fishing or saltmaking. Corn and beans were grown together; the first crop planted in May at the beginning of the wet season and harvested in August at the end of the rainy season. The second crop was planted in September and harvested in December and a third crop was sometimes planted in January in humid soils halfway through the dry season then harvested in April (Clark 1994). This third crop was usually planted within old stream channels or on the lower coastal plain close to the water table. Harvested corn was stored in large ceramic vessels or in the rafters of houses (Clark 1994), providing the necessary seed-stock for subsequent crops and food for leaner times of the year. Crops grown on the lower coastal plain were at the greatest risk of failure because of unpredictable changes in rainfall resulting in dry conditions as well as the risk of crop destruction through flooding.

Detailed ethnographic data on the traditional agricultural economy in the Soconusco are not available, but other studies have focused on analogous situations in the lowland tropics of Mesoamerica. We rely upon two ethnographic studies conducted in the Maya lowlands that appear to us to provide the best baseline economic data for establishing estimated return rates for maize agriculture in the Soconusco, the Lacandon Maya of southern Mexico (previously discussed; Nations and Nigh 1980) and the Kekchi Maya that occupy a section of the tropical lowlands in Guatemala (Carter 1969). Both the Lacandon and Kekchi Maya are relatively recent immigrants into these forested habitats and therefore face similar opportunities and challenges to the pioneer populations living in the Soconusco during the Early and Middle Holocene.

We start with the Lacandon Maya of Chiapas, Mexico. These people practice a form of swidden or slash-and-burn agriculture that is widely used by small, relatively dispersed, populations in the lowland tropics of Mexico and Guatemala. In this agrarian system patches of primary and secondary forest are cut, dried, and burned to fertilize the soil and to make way for a suite of domesticated plant species, princi-

pally maize, but including many other plants as well (Nations and Nigh 1980). A range of criteria, including soil and vegetation types, are used to evaluate a potential field location, preferentially locating these fields in well-drained locations. Farmers generally cut primary or secondary forest during the dry months of January, February, and March burning this debris in a highly controlled fashion during the months of May or June. Maize is planted with a digging stick in May or June as the annual rains begin to fall, and a second planting is done 10–15 days later in areas where corn is not sprouting. These fields are planted and harvested for between two and five years and then left to regenerate into forest as other areas are cut and burned to create new fields. Cut fields take approximately 20 years to regenerate into primary forest, so at any given time the land surrounding a Lacandon settlement is a mosaic of primary forest, secondary forest at various stages of regeneration, and fields under cultivation. In the Lacandon case, plots cut from primary forest produce approximately 45 bushels of shelled corn per acre (2.8 metric tons per hectare; Nations and Nigh 1980, 11). This estimated yield is well within the range for other slash-and-burn farmers living in the lowland tropics of Mesoamerica (33 to 50 bu/acre, see Barlow 2002, 71; Stadelman 1940) and for traditional farmers in the Soconusco region (~44 bu/acre for first harvest; Clark 1994). Slightly smaller yields are reported for crops planted in fields cut from secondary forest and for the second crop when two are grown in the same field annually.

To our knowledge the most comprehensive study of labor requirements necessary for slash-and-burn agriculture in a lowland tropical setting were conducted by William Carter among the Kekchi Maya of Guatemala (Carter 1969). In this study, data was collected on the time allocated to a variety of agricultural tasks including: (1) selecting field locations, (2) cutting (slashing) low-story vegetation, (3) felling large trees, (4) creating fire breaks to control fires, (5) firing vegetation, (6) planting corn, (7) fencing sections of gardens to protect crops, (8) tending, watching

TABLE 6.4
Kekchi Maya Labor Costs for Maize-based Food Production

ACTIVITY	PRIMARY	LONG FALLOW	SHORT FALLOW
Site Selection	4	2	2
Slashing	24	40	30
Felling	107	0	0
Firebreaking	4	9	9
Firing	2	1	1
Planting Maize	16	16	16
Fencing	2	2	2
Watching	16	16	16
Weeding	1	20	38
Reeping	35	40	35
Granary Building	8	8	8
Carrying	37	46	37
Storing	19	20	19
Total	275	221	212
Return Rate	1801	1845	1854

Note: Labor costs (person hours per acre) are for maize fields cut into primary forest (8+ years growth), long fallow plots (4–7 years growth), and short fallow plots (1–3 years growth); data from Carter 1969. Final row is the calculated return rate for maize-based food production given yield estimates of 45 bushels of shelled corn per acre and the labor costs associated with the different types of fields (cal/person/hour; see text).

and weeding fields, (9) harvesting (reaping), (10) carrying the harvest to granaries, (11) building granaries, and (12) storing crops. These data are shown in Table 6.4 for fields cut into primary forest (8+ years growth), long fallow plots (4–7 years growth) and short fallow plots (1–3 years growth). These data reveal that the average labor input per acre of land cleared in primary forest is 275 person hours; for land cleared in long fallow plots is 221 person hours, and for land planted in short fallow plots of corn stalks and weeds is 212 person hours. In both the Lacandon and Kekchi Maya cases, there is a slight preference for clearing secondary growth simply because it takes less work to clear these fields. However, the benefits of planting in fields cut from primary forest are that these plots of land can produce slightly higher yields in the first year and weeding is less arduous when compared to low fallow plots. Table 6.4 shows clearly that the gains in labor cost made by not clearing primary forest are largely lost due to the rapid incursion of weeds into these secondary plots, together with the labor required to remove them.

Given the yield and labor investment data presented above we can now estimate the return rate for maize-based food production on the Soconusco coastal plain. This estimate only applies to farmers using relatively modern varieties of maize with high yields and therefore does not apply to populations living in this region prior to ~3000 years ago (see below for these estimates). We calculate the caloric return rates (cal/person/hour) following the procedure established by Barlow (2002). In this estimate, the return rate (cal/person/hour) for maize farming is equal to:

$$\frac{[x \text{ bu/acre}]\,[25.2 \text{ kg/bu}][3550 \text{ kcal/kg}]}{\Sigma y \text{ hr/acre} + [x \text{ bu/acre} *43.55 \text{ hr/bu}]}$$

Where x bu/acre is equal to the bushels of shelled, dried maize kernels harvested per acre;

TABLE 6.5

Estimated Return Rates for Maize-based Food Production in the Soconusco at Different Intervals during the Holocene

	BU/ACRE	HR/ACRE	PROCESSING (BU/HR)	RETURN RATE CAL/PERSON/HOUR
3000 BP-Present (modern-2 crop)	45.00	212	43.55	1854
4499–3001 BP (60% modern)	27.00	221	45.72	1600
7000–4,500 BP (40% modern)	18.00	275	47.90	1416
7100 BP	10.10	212	50.08	1259
9200 BP	2.43	100	52.26	958

25.2 kg/bu represents the average weight (kg) of shelled, dried maize kernels per bushel; 3550 kcal/kg equals the caloric value for maize; ∑y hr/acre equals the time in all field activities (clearing, planting, weeding, etc., see Table 6.4); 43.55 hr/bu, this equals the time needed to grain, pound, and grind one bushel of harvested, dried maize into meal using stone manos and metates (see Barlow 2002). Estimated return rates for growing maize in different field types, e.g., primary forest, etc., are presented in the final row of Table 6.4. These are based on yield estimates of 45 bushels of shelled corn per acre, which seems reasonable given the similarity between Lacandon maize yields and those recorded historically in the Soconusco region (Clark 1994). Post-harvest processing costs of shelling and grinding dried maize into meal are also accounted for in this estimate and represent between 45 and 90% of all time spent farming (Barlow 2002, 72). Based on this model, we estimate the return rates for maize-based food production in the last 3000 years to be between 1800 and 1860 cal/person/hour, a range dependent upon the type of field planted; whether in primary forest or long/short fallow plots.

Estimating maize productivity in the past is more difficult and must be inferred from harvesting experiments and macrobotanical remains (Flannery 1973, 1986a). Table 6.5 outlines our best estimates for maize productivity during the last 9200 years, since its initial domestication. Pollen and phytolith assemblages

from Tabasco and Central Panama (Piperno and Pearsall 1998; Pope et al. 2001), suggest that a primitive form of maize had dispersed out of Central Mexico sometime between 7500 to 7000 B.P. The early phytolith assemblages in central Panama, dating before 7000 B.P., are similar to those found in the glumes and rachis of teosinte and suggest that early maize had small, hard kernels, closer to the progenitor species than modern maize (Piperno and Pearsall 1998). Our calculations for the earliest collection and cultivation of *Zea* in Central Mexico (~9200 B.P.) is based on teosinte harvesting experiments conducted by Flannery and Ford in the 1970s (*Zea mays.* subsp. *mexicana*; Flannery 1973, 1986a). In these experiments teosinte produced approximately 2.43 bushels of seed per acre. We assume lower in-field labor costs compared with modern maize farmers because wild stands of teosinte were likely managed rather than planted and most of the initial labor costs were limited to time spent harvesting (~100 hrs). However, we have increased the estimate for post-harvest processing by 20% because kernels were harder and more difficult to process.[7] Therefore we suspect that the return rate for the earliest maize harvests in the central highlands of Mexico prior to the spread of this domesticate was approximately 960 cal/person/hour. This low estimate for early maize is not surprising given that return rates for most wild grasses fall below 1000 cal/person/hour (O'Connell and Hawkes 1981; Simms 1987).

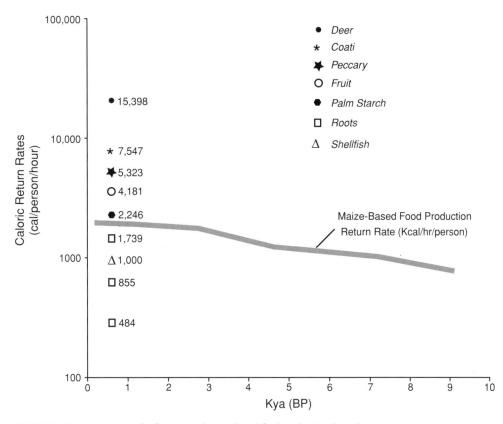

FIGURE 6.5. Energetic returns for foraging and maize-based food production through time.

We estimate the yield of the primitive maize that spread out of Central Mexico (ca. 7100 B.P.) to be comparable to teosinte from Flannery and Ford's highest yield plot located in an abandoned maize field (10.10 bu/acre). Assuming that maize was grown at a low level and that forests were already cleared near Archaic Period settlements we use a labor cost estimate of 212 hr/acre for this early maize, comparable to labor costs in fields where trees have been cleared (see Table 6.4). Field costs are increased after 7000 B.P. based on pollen and phytolith evidence from cores and archaeological sites in the Soconusco region suggesting intensified forest clearance (Jones and Voorhies 2004). Yield estimates after 7000 B.P. are calculated as a percentage of traditional maize productivity in the Soconusco and early macrobotanical evidence

for small, but increasing, cob sizes in Mesoamerica (Benz 2001; Benz and Long 2000; Blake et al. 1992a; Clark 1994; Feddema 1993; Long et al. 1989). Processing costs after 7000 B.P. are decreased incrementally until 3000 B.P. when morphologically modern varieties of maize are thought to be widely available in Mesoamerica.

Figure 6.5 shows the estimated changes in maize productivity through time relative to a selection of wild resources that were available in the region during the Archaic Period. Compared with other alternatives, maize, particularly early varieties of maize, was ranked relatively low, within the range of some small animals and most plant foods. Initially maize probably had lower return rates than locally available tubers and palms, but was higher in protein than these plant foods (Piperno and Pearsall 1998). A possible added benefit of early maize was also the high sugar content of its stalk and the potential of using this sugar juice for making beer (Smalley and Blake 2003). Therefore, it would appear that the initial incorporation of maize was a response to decreases in the availability of higher ranked prey items and increases in diet breadth or the benefits of this plant for brewing beer; or perhaps a combination of these two factors. The logistical exploitation of small, although highly localized, mollusks by 7500 B.P. is an indication that diet breadth had significantly expanded by this time and that populations of larger game animals had been reduced. The reduction of larger prey after 7000 B.P. was probably exacerbated by deforestation associated with developing agroeconomies. We now turn to an adapted form of the Lotka-Volterra predator-prey model to explore the variables involved in the incorporation and intensification of maize-based food production. We develop several variants of this model to explore the adoption and commitment to maize-based food production. These variants are then considered against the available data for the region.

A CULTIVATOR-CULTIGEN MODEL

An adapted form of the Lotka-Volterra predator-prey model is employed here to explore the interactive and symbiotic effects between human foragers and *Zea* in the Soconusco region. This model was originally designed to explore the synergistic population effects between predators and their prey. The basic assumption of the model is that predator population sizes are related to prey population sizes, and vice versa, and that a functional response occurs between the two—the rate of prey capture by a predator is a function of prey abundance (Gotelli 1998).

The Lotka-Volterra model is the simplest model of predator-prey interactions and was developed independently by Lotka and Volterra.[8] It has two variables, P and V, and several parameters: V is the density of prey, P is the density of predators, r is the intrinsic rate of prey population increase, δ is the capture efficiency coefficient, b

is the reproduction rate of predators per prey eaten, and m is the predator mortality rate. This mathematical model shows how predator populations keep populations of prey species in check. If the predator population is relatively low, the prey population will increase in size, and often results in population cycles that are stochastic in form.

In order to better match reality in terms of human/environmental interactions, we adapted the Lotka-Volterra model to the cultivator (human)-cultigen (maize) relationship that developed in the Soconusco region. Cultivator-cultigen interactions are unlike the relationship between predator and prey because plants, particularly potential cultigens, respond differently to human predation, intensified collection, and consumption. Cultivation and consumption can lead to selective increases in seed size, greater plant densities, and overall increases in cultigen productivity (e.g., Rindos 1984), rather than decreases in density or size. The cutting and burning of forest habitat and the creation of fields also increases the overall density and yield of cultigens due to economies of scale and sometimes creates a functional increase in cultivator population levels. This idea is supported by the close correlation between maize productivity and population densities in the Valley of Oaxaca, Mexico (Kirkby 1973). We argue that this model is appropriate for exploring the interactive processes at work in proto-agricultural biotic communities because net increases in cultigen acquisition, leading to more intensified food producing practices, are a function of changes in the rate of harvesting efficiency and cultigen density rather than intrinsic increases in cultivator population; although the context for adopting these cultigens in the first place may be related to population-dependent reductions in higher ranked prey. Further, the density and rate of cultigen harvest are also dependent on the food-quality being produced due to the demands of the cultivator.

We employ one variant of the Lotka-Volterra model known as the type III functional response. This model allows for changes in feeding be-

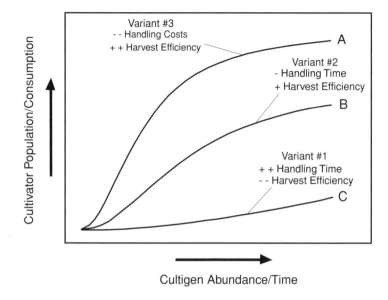

FIGURE 6.6. Graphical representation of three simulations (300 iterations each) of the Lotka-Volterra model with incremental changes in handling costs and harvest efficiency.

havior in response to resource density and availability. The functional response can occur when (1) cultivators switch to cultigens or other resources that become more common; (2) increases in harvest efficiency changes with the abundance of cultigens; and/or (3) costs of food production change, e.g., economies of scale. The quantitative expression of the type III functional response can be expressed (Gotelli 1998):

$$\frac{dN}{dt} = \frac{kV^2}{D^2 + V^2}$$

In this equation: dN/dt = feeding rate, t is the total amount of time a cultivator spends consuming a cultigen, or potential cultigen, and it includes search time plus time spent consuming a cultigen; k is equal to $1/h$, where h is the maximum return rate as influenced by the time necessary to harvest and consume a cultigen; V is equal to cultigen abundance or density; D is equal to $1/\delta h$ where δ represents the abundance of a cultigen given a certain feeding rate that is affected by harvest efficiency and the impact that a cultivator has on the per capita growth rate of the cultigen. As δ becomes larger, the per capita growth rate of the cultigen is depressed more significantly by the addition of a single cultivator.

To operationalize this ecological model we employed ECOSIM, a simulation package that combines object-oriented programming with a modern graphical interface.[9] Figure 6.6 shows the results of three simulations (300 iterations each) reflecting increases in cultivator consumption rates as a function of cultigen abundance. In these simulations, the feeding behavior of the cultivator is influenced by increases in harvest efficiency and diminishing handling time, the return rate. These variables functionally respond to changes in resource density and yield throughout the course of the simulation. Based on changes in harvest efficiency and handling time, we ran three different variants of the model for comparison against the archaeological record in the Soconusco region (following section). Each variant is shown in Figure 6.6. All three variants assume that harvest efficiency, measured as return rate, was high enough that maize was incorporated into the diet of foragers living in the region. This is related to the abundance of higher ranked prey and overall diet-breadth relative to the return rate for maize-based food production at that time, as discussed previously.

VARIANT #1 (40% OF MODERN MAIZE YIELD). Curve C (lowest) in Figure 6.6 assumes high handling costs (275 hr acre [within field] + 47.90 hr/bu [processing]) and low harvest efficiency (18 bu/acre; 1416 cal/person/hour) for maize-based food production. This isocline shows small increases in cultigen abundance through time and equally small increases in cultivator population levels and consumption rates. Initial use of maize may have occurred in forest clearings near settlements on the coastal plain with small increases related to the process of artificially changing early maize density and fecundity through burning and clearing forest habitat. The costs of food production entailed in clearing forests, preparing fields, and husbanding seedlings, along with the high costs of processing, limited rapid increases in cultivator population levels, and consumption rates. We would also expect this type of functional response during the early stages of plant domestication in Central Mexico, and with the initial dispersal of primitive maize before 7100 B.P., if return rates were high enough for maize to be targeted by foraging populations.

ARCHAEOLOGICAL TEST EXPECTATIONS FOR VARIANT #1. If this variant is correct we would expect early evidence, in the form of cobs or kernels, for the use of maize in midden deposits at residential bases on the Soconusco coastal plain. This cultigen would be one of several plant foods collected and consumed after this time and should be reflected in diverse macrobotanical and faunal assemblages of palms, tubers, maize, small and large animals, etc. Low-level use of this plant would be expected with small incremental increases in use though time, until other higher-ranked resources were depressed, or more productive varieties of maize became available. The best evidence for maize consumption should come from residential bases on the coastal plain. Small quantities of maize pollen and phytoliths should also be present in these archaeological deposits and in regional environmental records. Maize pollen may slowly increase through time along with indicators for burning (charcoal), forest clearance (decreases in tree pollen and phytoliths), and disturbance (increase in grass pollen and phytoliths). Stable carbon isotope data on human bones should indicate a slight increase in the consumption of C4 plants early on, with gradual increases evident through time.

VARIANT #2 (60% OF MODERN MAIZE YIELD). Curve B in Figure 6.6 assumes intermediate handling costs (221 hr/acre [within field] + 45.72 hr/bu [processing]) and intermediate harvest efficiency (27 bu/acre; 1600 cal/person/hour) for maize-based food production. Once maize was adopted, this isocline shows more rapid increases in cultivator population levels, and hence consumption rates, relative to increases in abundance through time. Similar to Variant #1, the initial use of maize likely occurred in forest clearings near settlements on the coastal plain, but the commitment to maize-based food production occurs more quickly. We would expect this type of functional response if a more productive variety of maize arrived into the region, via exchange, along with agroecological knowledge.

ARCHAEOLOGICAL TEST EXPECTATIONS FOR VARIANT #2. If this variant is correct, we would expect to find a small number of maize cobs and kernels of intermediate size in midden deposits at residential bases in the Soconusco. More rapid increases in the quantity and relative proportion of maize, compared with other plant foods, should be evident in the record. In other words, low-level use of maize would give way to more focused and specialized use through the interval. Similar to Variant #1, the best evidence for maize consumption should come from residential bases on the coastal plain. As maize-based food production became more viable, resources with smaller return rates, particularly resources with low rates of return that were collected logistically (e.g., mollusks), would be dropped from the diet. Compared with Variant #1, the expectation here is that maize pollen and phytoliths would increase more rapidly through time, along with indicators for a developing agroeconomy. Stable carbon isotope data should indicate a slight increase in the consumption of

C4 plants initially followed by clear evidence for C4 plant consumption soon after, rather than the more gradual changes expected in Variant #1.

VARIANT #3 (MODERN MAIZE). Curve A in Figure 6.6 assumes handling costs close to modern maize in the lowland tropics (212 hr/acre [within field] + 43.55 hr/bu [processing]) and the highest harvesting efficiency for maize-based food production (45 bu/acre; 1854 cal/person/hour). This isocline, and the behavior it reflects, would be expected if modern maize were introduced into a new region with an existing agroeconomy. It shows the most rapid increases in cultivator population levels, and hence consumption rates, relative to increases in cultigen abundance through time. The commitment to maize-based food production would be rapid and the build-up should be instantaneous in the archaeological record. High capture efficiency and minimal handling time in this case are attributable to the prolific nature of modern maize and an existing agricultural economy.

ARCHAEOLOGICAL TEST EXPECTATIONS FOR VARIANT #3. If this variant is correct, we would expect to see a relatively high proportion of large maize cobs and kernals entering the archaeological record. Rapid increases in the quantity and relative proportion of maize compared with other plant foods would be instantaneous archaeologically. Forest burning and clearing would be punctuated, rather than gradual. In other words, there should be no evidence for low-level use of maize, it would be used at a high-level from the beginning. The use of logistical foraging would be abandoned immediately as people invested heavily in forest clearance, field preparation, and other agroeconomic activities. Storage facilities would become prominent features immediately as subsistence pursuits became more specialized and diet-breadth is reduced. Large quantities of maize pollen and phytoliths should appear abruptly in archaeological deposits and in regional sediment cores. Stable carbon isotope data should indicate a sudden increase in the consumption of C4 plants followed by continued use at a high level.

ADOPTION OF MAIZE IN THE SOCONUSCO

The fragmentary paleobotanical and archaeological records from the Soconusco region currently support Variant #1 of the Lotka-Volterra cultivator-cultigen model, initial low-level use of maize followed by gradual increases in consumption rates through time that ultimately resulted in a reliance on maize-based food production. The earliest evidence for the use of maize in the vicinity of the Soconusco comes from the Pacific coast of Guatemala with maize pollen and phytoliths present in non-archaeological sediments dating to between 6000 and 5500 B.P., along with evidence for burning and forest clearance (Neff et al. 2003). Maize phytoliths were also recovered at Tlacuachero, a Late Archaic Period shellmound in the Acapetahua region (see Figure 6.1), dating to ~4600 B.P. (Jones and Voorhies 2004). The macrobotanical evidence for maize; of carbonized cobs, cupules, and kernels comes from Early Formative Period (3800–3000 B.P.) archaeological assemblages in the Mazatán region (Blake et al. 1992; Feddema 1993). Increases in burning and forest clearance, visible in sediment cores and archaeological sites, also appear to be relatively gradual with some punctuated burning events that could represent periods of more intensive farming, at least in certain locations (Jones and Voorhies 2004; Neff et al. 2003).

The appearance of maize at ~6000 B.P. did not have an immediate effect on Archaic Period subsistence and settlement practices of people living on the Pacific coast of southern Mexico. Evidence from the Middle Archaic Period site of Cerro de las Conchas (7500 to 5500 B.P.) suggests continued logistical exploitation of littoral resources. Although maize was clearly in the region, no evidence for maize cultivation was recovered from Cerro de las Conchas (Voorhies et al. 2002). This is true also of the early part of the record at Tlacuachero, a later shellmound in the Acapetahua region. At Tlacuachero changes in marsh clam harvesting strategies are evident in an oxygen isotope seasonality study (Kennett and Voorhies 1996). Prior to 5000 B.P. marsh clams were harvested at this location throughout the year with an emphasis during dry season months. A similar shellfish harvesting profile is also evident at Cerro de las Conchas (Voorhies et al. 2002). After 5000 B.P., however, marsh clams were more frequently harvested during wet season months. This culminated at ~4000 B.P. with harvesting solely during wet season months (Kennett and Voorhies 1996). The shift in seasonal harvesting patterns is coincident with the appearance of maize phytoliths at 5000 B.P. We interpret this change as reflecting the greater need during the wet season to obtain resources rich in protein from the littoral zone as a consequence of the seasonal difficulty in obtaining game animals and riverine fish from the coastal plain. Intensive harvesting of marsh clams, as evidenced by these massive shell-mounds, ended between 3500 and 3000 B.P.

Our model predicts that the best evidence for early maize cultivation will come from interior settlements on the coastal plain. As previously detailed, complex geomorphological processes have obscured and erased early archaeological sites and ancient land surfaces on the coastal plain. Much of what we know about Archaic Period subsistence and settlement comes from the highly visible shellmound sites along the coast, which we argue only represent part of the overall subsistence and settlement pattern in the region. Therefore, our interpretation of early maize cultivation remains tentative until interior settlements are located and tested. Vuelta Limón, a site on the inner coastal plain that we think was an Archaic Period basecamp, dates to the latest part of the Archaic Period (~3800 B.P.), although the length of its occupation is unknown. The presence of maize phytoliths across portions of the site suggest at least a low-level commitment to maize cultivation by this time.

In the Acapetahua region the earliest visible agricultural villages (Early Formative, 3500 to 2600 cal. yrs. B.P.) were positioned in a line

within or near the seasonally flooded wetlands on the inland side of the Acapetahua Estuary (Figure 6.7; also see Figure 6.1). A similar distribution of Early Formative sites is evident in the Pijijiapan area to the north, particularly the site complex of El Pajón (Paillés 1980), and in the Mazatán region to the south (Blake 1991; Blake et al. 1992a; J. E. Clark 1991, 1994; Lowe 1975), where Early Formative settlements are positioned near the El Hueyate marsh (Figure 6.1). Indeed, Early Formative Period sites are found in or near these distinctive wetland contexts along the coast of Guatemala (Arroyo 1994, 1995; Coe 1961; Coe and Flannery 1967; Estrada Belli 1998; Love 1989, 1993) and into northern El Salvador (Arroyo 1995). Excavations at Los Cerritos, an Early Formative Period site in the Acapetahua region (3400–3100 B.P.; see Figure 6.1 for location; Kennett et al. 2002), suggest a mixed foraging and food-producing economy. Shellfish continued to be collected, but not in such vast quantities as previously. Fish from estuarine habitats dominate the faunal assemblage, but many other reptiles and mammals also were targeted. Phytolith data suggest that maize was grown in the vicinity of the site and that squash (*Cucubitaceae*) and wild tubers (e.g., *Canna* sp.) also may have been cultivated. The strategic position of this settlement between the highly productive littoral zone and dry land suggests to us that the people living at this location were not fully committed to an agrarian lifestyle.

Excavations at several sites in the Mazatán region also suggest mixed foraging and food production during the Early Formative Period (3500 to 3000 B.P.; Blake et al. 1992a). These sites have diverse faunal assemblages that contain a wide range of wild animal species from wetland habitats that were in close proximity to these settlements. Of the seven wild and domesticated identified plants, maize, beans, and avocado were the most abundant (Feddema 1993). Maize was found at the sites of Aguiles Serdán, Chilo, Paso de la Amada, and San Carlos (Figure 6.1). Most of the remains were maize cupules and kernels, but some cob

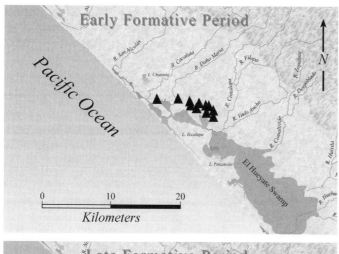

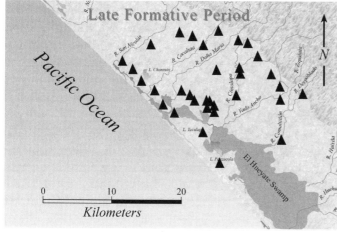

FIGURE 6.7. Early (~3500–2600 B.P.) and Late (~2600–1800 B.P.) Formative Period settlement distribution based on two regional surveys (Voorhies 1989b; Voorhies and Kennett 1995).

fragments were also identified. These data suggest that maize was small (20–40% modern) and that it was not yet a focal resource. Stable nitrogen and carbon isotopic analyses of Early Formative Period human skeletal remains support this hypothesis (Blake et al. 1992b).

A systematic pedestrian survey of the Acapetahua region suggests that settlements were evenly distributed across the landscape by the Late Formative Period (~2600 B.P.; Voorhies 1989b). This suggests to us that maize-based food production was well established in the region by that time. Excavations at the Late Formative Period site of Izapa substantiate this inference (Lowe 1982), as do excavations at La Blanca, a large political and economic center on the northern coast of Guatemala dating to this

period (Love 1993). Nitrogen and carbon isotope data suggest increases in maize dependence by this time (Blake et al. 1992b).

SUMMARY AND DISCUSSION

Visible evidence for maize cultivation appears in the Soconusco region and vicinity between 6000 and 5000 B.P. The first indication of the presence of this cultigen in the form of phytoliths and pollen comes from coastal plain sediments in Guatemala dating to between 6000 and 5500 B.P., and co-occurring with evidence for burning and forest disturbance (Neff et al. 2003). The availability of maize at this time did not stimulate an immediate transformation to maize-based food production, and we suspect that this cultigen was used at a low level in conjunction with a variety of wild and domesticated plants—perhaps similar to the low-level use of maize by the Mikea of Madagascar (Tucker, this volume).

In the Acapetahua region, evidence from Tlacuachero suggests that the appearance of maize phytoliths at ~5000 B.P. was coeval with the onset of gradual changes in the seasonal collection of littoral resources, particularly marsh clams (Kennett and Voorhies 1996). By 3500 B.P., marsh clams were effectively dropped from the diet, but fish, reptiles, and other littoral resources continued to be procured through the early Formative Period (3500 to 3000 B.P.). By then, the diet included some cultigens, including maize, beans, squash and avocadoes (Feddema 1993). In other words, mixed foraging and food production persisted through the early Formative Period.

Additional evidence for mixed foraging and food production through the Early Formative Period comes from an apparent shift in regional settlement during this time. Logistical use of littoral resources from interior base camps dating to the Archaic Period was replaced apparently by a shift to residential bases in intermediate locations between the coastal wetlands and the coastal plain. This settlement pattern is perplexing because the best agricultural lands are on the inner coastal plain, away from the littoral zone. One possible explanation for this pattern is that interior settlements are deeply buried under the alluvium and await future discovery. Another possibility is that population increases and persistent hunting on the coastal plain through the Archaic Period reduced the abundance of medium- and large-sized game animals. In this scenario, overall reductions in central place foraging returns stimulated the establishment of residential bases close to the littoral zone where fish, birds, and reptiles were abundant and their pursuit was more cost effective from settlements close to the wetlands because transportation costs were reduced.

The distribution of late Formative Period settlements (~2600 B.P.) over the entire width of the Soconusco coastal plain suggests that maize-based food production was well established by this time, if not earlier. Excavations of late Formative Period sites in the Mazatán region of Mexico and in the adjacent Guatemalan coast substantiate this inference. However, hunted and collected wild foods continued to be of great economic importance to people living in the region throughout prehistoric time (Blake et al. 1992a).

The early dispersal (7500 to 7000 B.P.) of maize through the lowland tropics, as seen in Tabasco, Mexico and Central Panama, is not visible in the known archaeological and palaeoenvironmental records from the Soconusco region. Absence of early maize may indicate that this cultigen did not pass through the Soconusco on its way to Central Panama. This seems to us unlikely given the similarity in lowland tropical habitat and the natural route of dispersal out of Central Mexico and down the Pacific coast. There are three other possible explanations for this pattern. The first, and least likely, is that the dates for early maize in central Panama are too early. The second is that maize was grown at such low levels in the Soconusco between 7500 and 6000 B.P. that it has thus far remained undetected in environmental records and archaeological sites, which are both seriously restricted. The third explanation, favored by us, is that return rates for maize cultivation were unfavorable at this early time, relative to the available alternatives in the Soconusco, and foragers chose not to cultivate it. This is most comparable to the situation in the Mexican highlands where it appears that the annual grass *Setaria*, which has higher return rates than teosinte, was preferred to early maize (Flannery 1973, 1986a).

Once maize entered the diets of foragers after 6000 B.P. it was used at low levels until the beginning of the late Formative Period (~2600 B.P.). Why such a delay? In the Soconusco, as elsewhere, there would have been several impediments to successful maize cultivation. As operationalized in the Lotka-Volterra cultivator-cultigen model (Variant #1), the investment of time and energy in planting, weeding, watering, and harvesting decreased the energy gained from this cultigen compared to other wild alternatives. This would include opportunity costs associated with cultivation, that is, the time invested in clearing forest and other tasks related to food production would have detracted from the time spent hunting deer, fishing, and collecting wild tubers. This, we argue, resulted in the slow growth of cultivator populations and associated slow growth in cultigen abundance. Technological limitations also may have contributed to this delay. Heavy dependence on dried seeds such as maize kernels and beans requires soaking and prolonged cooking. Seeds can easily be soaked in wooden bowls, gourds, or even leaf-lined pits, but protracted cooking requires direct heating that was not available until the development of ceramic technology. This may be one reason for the more rapid commitment to maize-based food production after the advent of ceramic technology in the Soconusco at ~3800 B.P. It is also possible that the net energy return from maize farming was heavily discounted (i.e., devalued, see Chapter 1, this volume), as it is among the Mikea of Madagascar (Tucker 2001, this volume), because of the delayed return to investment and the risks associated with crop failure.

CONCLUSION

Central place foraging theory predicts that foragers in the Soconusco region would have established residential bases in clearings on the forested coastal plain near rivers. The model also predicts that foragers would have hunted and collected the mix of wild animal and plant foods that maximized central place foraging returns within the vicinity of these settlements. This did not negate the use of longer distance logistical forays to hunt and collect resources in the piedmont and littoral zones, but these resources would have been hunted, collected, and processed in ways that maximized net delivery rates to centralized residential bases. The fragmentary archaeological data from the Soconusco support this model, with Vuelta Limón being a

centralized residential base, and the shellmounds representing specialized logistical foraging locations where littoral resources were collected and processed prior to transport back to residential bases elsewhere on the coastal plain. Predation pressure on the largest animal species, leading to resource depression at interior locations, would have increased diet breadth and promoted more frequent logistical forays. Persistent logistical use of littoral resources suggests that this strategy was stable for ~4000 years, between 7500 and 3500 B.P.

The microeconomic principles of the diet breadth model predict that maize would have entered the dietary regime of Soconusco foragers as higher ranked prey items were reduced and dietbreadth expanded to include lower-ranked plant foods such as maize. Gradual increases in the use of maize after 6000 B.P. are supported by the palaeoenvironmental and archaeological records currently available. These data fit the Lotka-Volterra cultivator-cultigen model (Variant #1) showing initial low-level use of maize followed by gradual increases in the commitment to maize-based food production. We argue that the delayed commitment to maize-based food production resulted from the initial response of foragers to a resource of low, but increasing, value. Due to the fragmentary nature of the palaeobotanical and archaeological records we stress that this model requires further testing. More systematic survey work is needed to locate Archaic and Early Formative period settlements deeply buried under alluvium on the coastal plain. Additional sediment cores also are needed in the Mazatán, Acapetahua, and Pijijiapan areas to define sub-regional differences in maize use in the Soconusco through time.

NOTES

1. Ages are expressed as calibrated calendar years before present (B.P.).

2. Soconusco is an adaptation of the Aztec name for this region.

3. Logistical foraging involves the strategic use of distant resources by people living at more centralized residential bases. People often travel

long distances, exploit and process a resource, and return to residential bases with the resource to provision their households.

4. Shrimp were probably an important resource, but are invisible in the archaeological record. Shrimp larvae enter the estuary, which serves as a nursery. During the dry season they grow appreciably and are easily captured with simple technology. These juvenile shrimp are an important aspect of the subsistence and cash economy in the region today.

5. Evidence for structures is present on one clay surface discovered at Tlacuachero, but this floor construction and the structures that were upon it, appear to be unique (Voorhies et al. 1991).

6. This is highly unlikely because drier conditions during the Late Pleistocene would have pushed Balsas teosinte downslope (Dolores Piperno, personal communication 2004).

7. However, it is possible that early maize was popped rather than ground or that the stalks and seeds were eaten green. This would have significantly reduced post-harvest processing costs.

8. Lotka-Voltera predator-prey model:

$$\begin{cases} \dfrac{dV}{dt} = rV - \alpha VP \\[2ex] \dfrac{dP}{dt} = bHp - mP \end{cases}$$

9. The program used is ECOSIM (Beta-Version), Empresarios Agrupados A. I. E. Mogallones, 3, 28015 Madrid, Spain.

7

The Origins of Plant Cultivation and Domestication in the Neotropics

A BEHAVIORAL ECOLOGICAL PERSPECTIVE

Dolores R. Piperno

During the past 20 years, evolutionary biologists have broadened the study of Darwinian processes by drawing on elements from the ecological and behavioral sciences, and asking questions relating to why as well as to how. As a result, flexible decision making by animals, local ecological circumstances, and rapid, phenotypic-level adjustments are viewed as fundamental to evolutionary change. The transition from foraging to farming is, at its heart, an evolutionary transformation, but to avoid a serious paradigm lag with modern biological principles and ensure that our theories can accommodate complex and learned human actions, archaeologists must incorporate these now-standard approaches to adaptive change in biology.

This paper uses behavioral ecology, specifically optimal foraging theory (OFT), to examine the origins of plant cultivation and domestication in the American tropics. It reviews the present empirical evidence for early food production in the Neotropical forest, and evaluates four main questions relating to the why and how of agricultural origins, as seen from the perspective of human be-

havioral ecology (HBE). Using two important genera of American plant domesticates, Cucurbita and Lagenaria, the paper also compares and contrasts the major tenets of HBE with those of other evolutionary programs in archaeology, such as co-evolution, and examines how well the assumptions and predictions of each approach are met by archaeological data.

Lastly, it is argued that HBE can be used to explore nomothetic explanations for food production origins because it, alone among the existing generalizing theories, can be applied across cultural and environmental boundaries.

Seasonal tropical forests, those that receive a prolonged period every year during which little to no rain falls, do not carry the distinction enjoyed by their rainforest relatives, despite the fact that they have been of far more use to humans for a longer period of time. It is in these forests that the highest biomass of comestible plants and animals and the most fertile soils for agriculture occur, and before they were cut for agriculture or converted into pasture, seasonally dry forests occupied large areas of the Central and South American landmasses (Figures 7.1a and b). Molecular biological and botanical studies of the modern flora tell us that many wild ancestors of crop plants are native to the seasonal tropical forest, where they can still be found in large stands reproducing successfully without a human hand (e.g., Doebley 1990; Olsen and Schaal 1999; Sanjur et al. 2002). Accumulating evidence from archaeology and paleoecology indicates that human manipulation of these plants gave rise to early, independent, and major systems of agriculture (Piperno and Pearsall 1998).

This paper examines the applicability of foraging theory to the question of the origins of food production in the American tropical forest[1]. I use foraging theory to identify important environmental and social variables that were acting on selection pressures and subsistence choices on the eve of the Neolithic and test predictions regarding dietary choice and breadth using archaeological data on early *Cucurbita* domestication. I ask four main questions, (1) why did plant food production start in tropical America and other nuclear cradles around the world, (2) why did it start when it did, (3) out of the many thousand species of plants that were available to prehistoric food producers, why were so few of them domesticated, and (4) should domestication itself be the focus of our studies, or are other socioecological processes antecedent to, and coincident with the transition from foraging to food production actually more significant? Lastly, I argue that foraging theory can be used to construct a nomothetic explanation for food production origins because it, alone among the existing generalizing theories (see Piperno and Pearsall 1998, 10–18), can be applied across cultural and environmental boundaries.

FORAGING THEORY, AFFLUENT FORAGERS, AND THEIR RELEVANCE TO FOOD PRODUCTION ORIGINS

I begin by questioning a major tenet of prehistoric economic reconstructions; that the transition from foraging to food production carried with it decreasing returns to labor. Although this negative relationship between work effort and agricultural production is now taken for granted in many discussions of agricultural origins (e.g., Hayden 1992; Hillman 2001; Norton 2000), there is little evidence to support it. The issue is important for a number of reasons. The notion that turning to cultivation was a last resort for foragers, initiated late in human evolution only when growing human populations had outstripped the food supply, largely derives from the perceived labor-intensiveness of plant cultivation. And if early farming was routinely more labor intensive than foraging, optimal foraging theory may not be well-suited to model the process. OFT is, after all, partially predicated on the assumption that subsistence strategies that substantially lower the efficiency of procuring food are not likely to be evolutionary success stories.

This assumption seems legitimate under many circumstances that involve small-scale social groups. In addition to the obvious subsistence benefits accrued from accumulating food expeditiously, efficient strategies may lead to increased fitness in other ways; for example, by decreasing exposure to environmental risks and liberating more time for other essential activities separate from the food quest such as child care and technological innovation (Kaplan and Hill 1992; Smith and Winterhalder 1992b). It seems reasonable to predict, therefore, that human foragers were not given to choosing and then perpetuating strategies that significantly lowered their foraging efficiency, or tolerating conditions that seriously eroded their resource return rates without adaptive innovations, unless they were constrained by social and political factors; e.g., significant social and economic commitments beyond the household such as superordinate political structures. Why, then, are early food producing strategies widely seen to have been considerably more labor intensive than foraging?

Perceptions of the relative laboriousness of foraging and food production have been colored, arguably more than any other factor, by the notion that the hunters and gatherers remaining

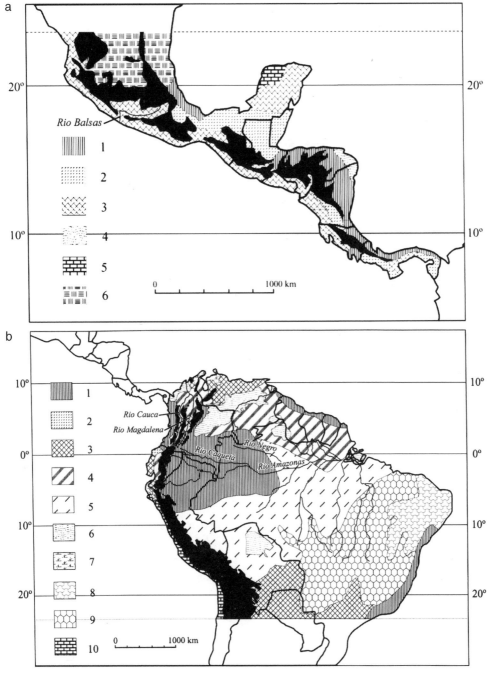

FIGURE 7.1. (a) The major types of forest and other vegetation types in the lowland American tropics of Middle and Central America. Areas in black indicate elevations above 1500 m above sea level 1. Tropical evergreen forest; 2. Tropical semi-evergreen forest: 3. Tropical deciduous forest; 4. Savanna; 5. Low scrub/grass/desert; 6. Mostly cactus scrub and desert; (b) The major types of forest and other vegetation types of South America; 1. Tropical evergreen forest (TEF); 2. Tropical semi-evergreen forest (TSEF); 3. Tropical deciduous forest (TDF); 4. Mixtures of TEF, TSEF and TDF. TSEF and TDF grow over substantial areas of the southern parts of the Guianas and south of the Orinoco river; 5. Mainly semi-evergreen forest and drier types of evergreen forest. Floristic variability can be high in this zone and includes fairly large patches of savanna and terrain with low trees; 6. Savanna; 7. Thorn scrub; 8. Caatinga; 9. Cerrado; 10. Desert (Piperno and Pearsall 1998, Figure 2.2).

on the planet when ethnography became a profession are affluent. That is to say, positive elements define relationships between human population numbers and available resources, overall abundance and quality of the food supply, and amount of daily leisure time. This view of foragers, which emerged from the Man the Hunter conference in 1966 (Lee and DeVore 1968) and was given a wider notoriety by Sahlins (1972), has come to dominate some contemporary interpretations of hunting and gathering, despite the fact that it has been challenged on the basis of a number of empirically-supported concerns (see Kaplan 2000 for an excellent review of the issue).

For example, the time allocation studies used to support assertions that foragers spend little time in the food quest are considered by several researchers to be unreliable because of the short duration of the studies used to estimate work effort, and an inattention to the negative effects of seasonal and longer-term fluctuations in the resource base (Bettinger 1991b, 48). Various investigators also note how modern foragers may suffer from chronic caloric (e.g., fat and carbohydrate) insufficiency, and that some societies rely to some degree—often seasonally—on agricultural produce, derived either from commercial sources or via exchanges with neighboring groups practicing agriculture (Kaplan 2000; Milton 1984). Moreover, with the application of optimal foraging models and a more thorough cost-benefit accounting of the activities that constitute subsistence work, e.g., the transportation and processing of food, it became clear that some foragers spend considerably more effort getting food from the wild to the edible state than was previously believed (Hawkes and O'Connell 1981; O'Connell and Hawkes 1981). Finally, an examination of the affluence issue using a combination of foraging theory and population ecology indicates that the under-utilization of resources and modest work effort occasionally characteristic of foragers is better explained by the fact that working longer hours and intensifying production might lead to overexploitation of wild resources than by an assumption

that foragers have "limited needs and wants" (Winterhalder 1993; Winterhalder et al. 1988).

Beginning in the 1980s, themes relating to hunter-gatherer affluence were carried into archaeological research. Human occupations in the Near East, North America, and Europe dating to the past 10,000 years and earlier characterized by fairly large, possibly permanent settlements with signs of technological and social sophistication, but lacking evidence for domesticated food products, were thought to represent a type of archaeological analog to affluent foragers, called "complex hunters and gatherers" (Price and Brown 1985). This view, that not all prehistoric foragers were ordained to a life in small and highly mobile groups of simple social structure, is well taken. Complexity is a loaded word, however, and a premise that significant population growth, resource intensification, and social inequality were within the reach of hunters and gatherers in virtually any ecological circumstance could lead to the same problems inherent with presupposing that most modern foragers live at culturally-determined levels of prosperity or deprivation. With the advent of better procedures for plant recovery and identification, some of the complex hunter-gatherers discussed in Price and Brown (1985) were shown to have possessed cultivated foodstuffs (e.g., Asch 1995; Crawford 1992). The possibility that other complex foragers, like the Late Epipaleolithic Natufian cultures of the southern Levant, were also food producers remains to be evaluated (Harris 1998), so that we are still not sure where and when in prehistory the term complex forager can be applied.

What is clear is that a considerable amount of social, technological, and economic *variability* probably existed among prehistoric hunters and gatherers (Kelly 1995). A major focus of our enquiries should be describing and explaining this variability using sensible theory and as much empirical evidence as we can bring to bear on the subject, with the ultimate objective being to elucidate under which socio-ecological circumstances foragers became food producers and under which circumstances they were less inclined to do so. Foraging theory is particularly well-suited to assuming a major role in this endeavor (Winterhalder and Kennett, this volume). In the tropical forest, as elsewhere, energetic efficiency is a major influence on foraging decisions. Energetic return rates, in fact, are the single best predictor of foraging patterns among modern tropical hunters-gatherers (e.g., Alvard 1993; Gragson 1993; Hames and Vickers 1982; Hill and Hawkes 1983; Hill et al. 1987). Energy production and efficiency can therefore be comfortably placed at the heart of a scrutiny of why foraging strategies change.

I rely in particular on the diet breadth model of optimal foraging (Hawkes and O'Connell 1992; Hill et al. 1987; Winterhalder 1981a) for a number of reasons[2]. After considerable scrutiny in biology it has been judged to be a "paragon of robustness" (Winterhalder 1986, 372), and it makes a number of valuable, and sometimes counterintuitive, predictions concerning food choice and subsistence change that are highly relevant to food production origins. First, resources will enter diets as a function not of their own abundance but of the abundance of higher ranked resources; those that yield a higher net acquisition rate, or NAR, of calories. Second, a decline in the abundance, called encounter rate, of higher ranked resources leads to the exploitation of lower ranked resources. Third, foragers will now choose a broader diet because it results in a higher return rate than could be achieved by investing ever greater search effort in locating increasingly rare items. As dietary breadth increases under these conditions, overall foraging efficiency decreases.

Using a combination of optimal foraging and population biology models (Winterhalder and Goland 1993), which can be powerful illuminators of resource selection and intensification and associated demographic trends, the following relationships between human population number and resource change can be predicted. If newly incorporated resources are dense, high-yielding, and resilient to human predation (high r), a reduction of search time can lead to smaller foraging radii, increases in residential

stability, greater investments in storage and food processing, and increases in human population number. If, however, newly incorporated resources are not dense and resilient, then longer and more mobile foraging might be required to maintain the same net caloric intake, and human population number could remain stable or even decrease (Winterhalder and Goland 1993).

Many of these expectations closely conform to hypothetical and archaeologically-documented processes linked to the emergence of food production, including the broad spectrum revolution (Flannery 1969; Hawkes and O'Connell 1992; Hayden 1992). As several behavioral ecologists concerned with human behavior have indicated (Hawkes et al. 1997; Kaplan and Hill 1992), the diet breadth model is particularly well suited for studying major directional changes in human subsistence over time because of its ability to make robust, qualitative predictions of prey choice and dietary diversity. Examining subsistence choices over long time periods with the diet breadth model thus does *not* require short-term or absolute precision in predicting which resources foragers will choose. A finding, in those rare cases where archaeological data are likely to be dependable enough to permit such a detailed reconstruction, that not all subsistence items in an archaeological set match the predictions of an optimal diet does not invalidate the use of the model to study important processual questions, such as human economic decisions, changes in dietary breadth through time, and their determinants. In the cases where paleoecological data are robust across the Pleistocene/Holocene boundary, they may serve as proxies for changing resource distribution and, hence, foraging costs in the absence of detailed archaeological records on subsistence.

THE RETURN TO LABOR
OF FORAGING AND FARMING
IN THE TROPICAL FOREST

If we agree that, all things being equal, energetic concerns were major constraints on foraging decisions, and that natural selection should have favored more efficient strategies at the expense of less efficient ones, we can look to experimental and other investigations of foraging and farming for what has become a significant corpus of data pertaining to the return rates or energetic profitabilities of various food resources in the tropical forest and other types of environments.[3] The return rates presented in Tables 7.1 and 7.2 include animals of various sizes and wild, above- and below-ground plant structures from a number of different types of ecosystems—savannas, deserts, tropical forests. The following generalizations about the return to labor from exploiting these resources can be made: (1) large and medium-sized animals typically give the highest rates of returns of calories of all resources considered; smaller animals often give lower return rates than do larger animal species, (2) primarily because of their high collecting and processing costs, plants are often less profitable than animals, and (3) tubers and fruits consistently give higher return rates than seeds, which often are the lowest-ranked in any regional and cross-regional set of resources.

The following comments and caveats are raised by these generalizations. First, high resource density can sometimes counteract the effect of resource size, and hence the employment of a mass collecting strategy with an appropriate technology may sometimes determine the return rate for a resource more so than its package size. A spectacular example is the very high return rate derived from mass collecting grasshoppers in the Great Basin (up to 33,000 kcal/hr) (Madsen and Schmitt 1998). However, where processing accounts for the majority of the overall handling in collection plus processing costs, as is to be expected with many plants, resource density usually will have far less effect on return rates. Second, larger animal body size may not always result in lower handling times and higher return rates for faunal resources. Killing larger and more ferocious animals after encountering them, for example, may have proved difficult for hunters using simple spear-wielding technologies, raising the costs of exploiting these animals.

Third, ecological factors may affect the return rates of the same class of resources. For example, monkeys, which account for a large portion of the animal biomass in tropical forest, have lower caloric return rates than do many smaller terrestrial animals and plants (Tables 7.1 and 7.2), in part because their arboreal habitat and agility necessitate a longer pursuit. Similarly, high spatial dispersion of tropical plants and extended collecting times required for them contribute to lower return rates for tropical forest roots and tubers than for underground plant organs of savannas and deserts, which are more densely distributed (Table 7.2). Fourth, where the landscape is heterogeneous, e.g., patchy, and a variety of closely ranked and low-cost resources exist in close proximity, a diet with some considerable variability may well exist despite the abundance of larger animals that would otherwise be expected to narrow the dietary range considerably (Simms 1987).

Fifth, some coastal resources, particularly sea mammals and even small fish captured en masse by nets, may have fairly high profitabilities (Perlman 1980; Rick et al. 2001; Yesner 1987). Because a number of environmental and cultural factors such as the class of resources exploited and availability of seaworthy boats cause substantial variability in coastal productivity, assessing the costs and benefits of maritime strategies is a more complex issue than deciphering terrestrial resource patterns (Perlman 1980; Yesner 1987). Estuaries may assume particular importance because they are rich in fish, shellfish, and other resources and permit simple, energetically efficient land-based strategies (Cooke and Ranere 1997), but productive estuaries require stable sea levels and warm surface waters. Available data suggest that riverine fish, which constitute essential resources for many tropical groups, are often more expensive to exploit than terrestrial game, and that, although the diversity of species is higher at tropical latitudes, many species are lower in fat and consequently in calories (Gragson 1993).

Overall, the evidence indicates that when compared with resources from other habitats,

TABLE 7.1
Caloric Returns from Hunting Large and Small Game and Other Animal Prey from Various Environments

ANIMAL	CAL/HOUR/PERSON	ENVIRONMENT
Buffalo	200,000	Coastal savannas of Australia[a]
Wallaby	50,000	
Mule deer and bighorn sheep	17,971–31,450	Great Basin desert[b]
Antelope	15,725–31,450	
Jackrabbit	13,475–15,400	
Cottontail Rabbit	8,983–9,800	
Ground squirrel	5,390–6,341	
13-lined ground squirrel	2,837–3,593	
Ducks	1,975–2,709	
Moose and caribou	11,950 (early spring)	North Ontario Boreal
	11,280 (fall); 6,050 (winter)	Forest[c]
	6,050 (winter)	
	5,920 (summer and fall)	
Muskrats	2,500 (spring trapping)	
	2,370 (fall hunting)	
	1,330 (fall hunting)	
	250 (spring trapping)	
Beaver trapping	1,640 (early winter)	
Hare snaring	1,900	
Waterfowl	1,980 (post-break-up)	
	1,190 (pre-freeze-up)	
Net fishing	9,680 (spring, net 3)	
	6,390 (fall, net 6)	
	5,320 (summer, net 5)	
	3,180 (spring, net 5)	
	2,260 (summer, net 4)	
Deer (brocket)	15,398	Tropical Forest, Paraguay[d]
9-banded armadillo	13,782, 2,662*	
White-lipped peccary	8,755, 5,323+	
Collared peccary	6,120	
Paca	4,705	
Large palm larva	2,133	
Small palm larva	1,331	
Capuchin monkey	1,370	
Dusky leaf monkey	1,620	Tropical Forest, Malaysia[e]
White handed gibbon	1,490	
Giant squirrels	1,060	
Macaques	480–780	
Squirrels	330–480	
Birds	230	
Shellfish, *Hippopus*	5,500	Reef flat, Torres Straits,
Shellfish, *Lambis*	2,500	Melanesia[f]
Shellfish, *Strombus*	1,200	
Shellfish, *Asaphis*	<500	
Shellfish, *Nerita*	<500	

Note: An asterisk (*) means the first number for animals encountered on the surface, the second number for animals dug up. A plus sign (+) means the first number includes time spent following tracks and the second number only includes after animal is heard or seen.
[a] Jones 1980; [b] Simms 1987; [c] Winterhalder 1981b; [d] Hill et al. 1987; [e] Kelly 1995; [f] Bird and Bliege-Bird 2000.

particularly faunal-rich savannas and open woodlands, the tropical forest is likely to reward foragers with low returns of calories (Tables 7.1 and 7.2). A variety of factors are responsible. The limited condition of light on the forest floor permits little in the way of herbaceous plant growth on which ground-dwelling animals can feed and, consequently, terrestrial herbivory is a minor way of life and game animals are few in number. Tropical forest animals available to human hunters are small, often arboreal, which, in addition to other negative factors relating to pursuit time, places a serious constraint on body size, and exist in low biomass. Except for white-lipped peccaries, which may travel in groups of more than 100 individuals, the animals tend to forage alone or in small family units, and to be shy. The brocket deer, which yields high benefit-to-cost ratios once encountered, and paca are also nocturnal.

Tropical forest plants are poor in calories, widely dispersed in space, and often contain high amounts of toxic chemicals and other defenses that make them expensive to process into food. Significantly, wild plants with large, underground storage organs (roots, rhizomes, tubers, and corms) that might serve as good energy sources grow at very low density in the mature forest (Hart and Hart 1986; Hladik and Dounias 1993). Recent surveys of wild yams (*Dioscorea* spp.) and other edible roots and tubers (e.g., Marantaceae) in mature, semi-evergreen forest on Barro Colorado Island, Panama, similarly indicate a low density of standing stems (<1 ha^{-1}) (D.R. Piperno, field notes). Once encountered and dug up, many of these are small. There are native, wild yam species with larger tubers, but they typically reside deep in the ground and are heavily defended by spines, chemicals, and/or abrasive calcium oxalate crystals (D. R. Piperno, field notes). Tubers, though exploited by Aché foragers of Paraguay, were sufficiently expensive as to exclude them from the ranking of the first 20 Aché resources, whose lowest return rate was 1331 kcal/hr (small palm larvae) (Hill et al. 1987). Root exploitation in tropical savannas of Venezuela and Colombia,

where plant density was higher than in forests, similarly yielded a return rate of less than 1200 kcal/hr, without the costs of processing considered (Hurtado and Hill 1987). Thus, data from the New World tropics are in accord with those from the Old World that wild roots and tubers are dispersed, occur in low densities, are expensive to process, and with their return rates likely to be low.

This evidence runs counter to the traditional notion that life in the tropical forest should have been easy for foragers because of high plant productivity and diversity associated with equatorial latitudes (Lee and DeVore 1968; Roosevelt 1989; but see Perlman 1980). When energetic considerations play major roles in food choices and human adaptations, a checklist of edible species available in any ecosystem becomes a poor predictor of food abundance and quality, and of the economic and demographic characteristics of the people occupying that habitat. I do not agree with researchers who have suggested that the tropical forest can provide a full-time living only for people with some access to a cultivated food supply (e.g., Bailey et al. 1989; Hart and Hart 1986). Rather, when interfluvial forests of higher soil fertility outside of the poorest examples from the Amazon Basin are considered,[4] sufficient terrestrial game probably exists to allow small groups of mobile foragers to satisfy many of their nutritional needs by focusing on meat and deriving supplemental inputs from plants and invertebrate food sources (Piperno and Pearsall 1998, 63–68). Examples exist of Neotropical foragers who today derive most of their calories from animal game, not plants (Hurtado and Hill 1987; Stearman 1991), and who appear to be meeting their subsistence requirements. This counterintuitive subsistence strategy at low latitudes may have been typical of some tropical forest foragers of the past. Expectations of affluence for foragers are not likely to be met, however, and most prehistoric foragers, like the few surviving today, probably existed at low population densities and were mobile, so as to maintain food intake

TABLE 7.2
Caloric Returns of Wild Fruits, Seeds and Underground Plant Organs

PLANT	TYPE	CAL/HR/PERSON	ENVIRONMENT
Gambel oak	Acorns	1,488	Great Basin[a]
Descurainia pinnata (Tansymustard)	seeds	1,307	
Lewisia rediviva (bitteroot)	roots	1,237	
Pinus monophylla (pinyon pine)	nuts	841–1,408	
Elymus Salinas	grass seeds	921–1,238	
Ten other grass species	seeds	138–702	
Typha latifolia	roots	128–267	
Calochortus nuttali (sego lily)	roots	207	Northern Rocky Mountains[b]
Lomatium hendersonii (biscuitroot)	roots	3,831	
Lomatium canbyi	roots	143	
Ipomoea costata	tubers	6,252, 1,769	Australian desert/scrub woodland[c]
Solanum centrale	fruits	5,984	
Two *Cyperus* sp.	roots	4,435*, 848	
Acacia coriacea	tree seeds (unripe)	4,333	
A. coriacea	tree seeds (ripe)	<676	
A. aneura	tree seeds	580	
A. cowleana	tree seeds	552	
Other *Acacias*	tree seeds	538	
Five grass species	seeds	261, 405, 668, 1,226	
Chenopodium sp.	seeds	652	
Four *Ipomoea* sp.	tubers	1,300, 1,701	Australian coast[d,e]
Dioscorea sp.	roots	2,000–2,500	Australian coast[e]
Ficus sp.	fruit	4,419	Paraguay Tropical Forest[f]
Casimiroa sp.	fruit	4,181	
Rheedia sp.	fruit	3,245	
Arecastrum sp.	trunk palm starch	2,246	
Acrocomia sp.	palm nut	2,243	
Dioscorea luzonensis	roots	484	Phillipine tropical forest[g]
Dioscorea hispida	roots	1,739	
Dioscorea sp.	roots	855	Malaysian tropical forest[h]
Three *Vigna* sp.	tubers	884, 1,967, 3,240	African savanna[i]

Note: Return rates in underline indicate processing not included. Italics indicate cooking not included. An asterisk denotes a higher value obtained from the river floodplain.
[a] Simms 1987; [b] Smith and Martin 2001; [c] O'Connell and Hawkes 1981; [d] Jones 1980; [e] Jones and Meehan 1989; [f] Hill et al. 1987; [g] Eder 1978; [h] Endicott and Bellwood 1991; [i] Vincent 1985.

on favorable terms (e.g., Charnov 1976; Hill et al. 1987; Stearman 1991).

In light of this, an essential question becomes, how did the return rate for foraging in the tropical forest compare with that for early food production? Return rates from various strategies in and of themselves mean little in this discussion because the decision taken by nascent farmers to cultivate some plants "has to be understood in terms of their previous decision-making pattern, the options open to them, and that new situation" (Flannery 1986b). If, as argued above, most human foragers and simple farmers under little demographic or social pressures would be little inclined to practice subsistence strategies that lower the rate of food accumulation, then the instances of early food production we can identify archaeologically—those that did not fail—should have been marginally profitable enough at the outset to sustain the habitual practice of this activity.

Table 7.3 provides examples of comparisons among overall energy returns from foraging and farming in the tropical forest[5]. For the Machiguenga, a southern Peruvian group of farmers who grow large amounts of manioc and maize, both the caloric and protein returns from horticulture substantially exceed those from hunting or gathering in the forest and fishing. Hames (1990) also states that Yanomamö horticulture is five or six times more efficient than hunting and adds that similar trends probably hold for many other Amazonian groups. It is also significant that mean foraging return rates for Aché and Cuiva were lower than returns from Machiguenga farming because these foragers have some of the highest rates of food accumulation reported for modern hunters and gatherers (Hill et al. 1987; Hurtado and Hill 1987). The Cuiva hunt and gather in tropical savannas.

A last bit of data from tropical America comes from Barlow's (2002) studies of maize farming under slash-and-burn techniques in five different areas of Mexico and Guatemala, where returns were between 1500 and 1800 kcal/hr. Not surprisingly, these values are less than those of the Machiguenga, whose plots

were heavily planted with starch-dense manioc. As with plant collecting, growing roots and tubers may provide higher profitabilities than cultivating seed plants. Data available for Near Eastern grasses indicate that return rates for wild wheat (1986 kcal/hr) and hand-tilled and harvested domesticated wheat (1815 kcal/hr) are very close (Simms and Russell 1997). There may have been little overall difference between the energetic efficiency of foraging and early farming in the Near East. Time-allocation studies elicit the same trends. Aché men, who, as just mentioned, achieve respectable return rates from hunting and gathering, spend 6.5 hr/day acquiring and processing food while foraging in the forest and only 3 hr/day when farming. Aché women spend 3.75 hr/day foraging and 2.7 hr/day farming (Hawkes et al. 1987). Hames's (1990) survey of time allocation among tropical foragers, simple horticulturists, and advanced horticulturists indicates little difference in labor time among the three, with simple horticulturists having somewhat more leisure time than the other two types of food accumulators. Although energetic return rates and other types of quantified information on the costs of simple farming systems in the tropical forest and elsewhere are limited, available data indicate that returns for tropical horticulture are likely to be greater, not less, than returns from hunting and gathering. There is no evidence indicating that early horticultural practices yielded significantly less to labor than had the last tropical forest foraging practiced on the eve of the Neolithic.

RESOURCE PROCUREMENT IN THE LATE PLEISTOCENE AND EARLY HOLOCENE NEOTROPICAL WORLD

If we view the transition from foraging to food production as a replacement of one set of alternative economic strategies by another, and if the return to labor played a significant role in the evolutionary selection of these different economic strategies, then how do we identify and

TABLE 7.3
Return Rates of Alternative Subsistence Strategies in the Neotropics

ACHÉ MEAN FORAGING RETURNS, PARAGUAY TROPICAL FOREST

	CAL/HOUR/PERSON
Men	1,253
Women	1,087

From Hill et al. 1987.

CUIVA MEAN FORAGING RETURNS. VENEZUELAN SAVANNAS

	CAL/HOUR/PERSON	REMARKS
Men	3,001	Mostly hunted game; handling time not included. Processing not included
Women	1,125	99% Roots

From Hurtado and Hill 1987.

MACHIGUENGA SLASH AND BURN AGRICULTURE: MANIOC AND MAIZE, PERUVIAN AMAZON

	CAL/HOUR/PERSON	PROTEIN CAPTURE (g/hr)
Machiguenga Gardens (Food Production)	3,842	45
Machiguenga Forest (Hunting and Gathering)	116	7.3
Machiguenga Fishing	214	38

All numbers from Keegan (1986); based on figures provided by Johnson and Behrens 1982, and Johnson 1983.

SLASH AND BURN AGRICULTURE: MAIZE, LOWLAND TROPICAL MEXICO AND GUATEMALA

CAL/HOUR/PERSON

1,400–1,800

From Barlow (2002).

study the conditions that changed the return rates of wild resources such that the cultivation of some of them became more advantageous than full-time foraging? Changes in return rates of a sufficient magnitude likely to elicit new adaptations can be associated with major, natural changes to the environment, as oscillating climate and vegetation bring changes in resource density and distribution and necessitate a series of new options for humans with regard to the availability, exploitation, and procurement of plants and animals. They can also be a product of human population growth that results in the depletion of various animal and plant prey that may reduce their encounter rate and lead to the incorporation of lower ranked resources (Stiner et al. 1999; Winterhalder and Goland 1993). These kinds of changes are sometimes visible archaeologically by size diminution through time of harvested species (e.g., Stiner et al. 1999). Technological innovations may also affect resource return rates by changing the collecting and processing or handling time for resources (Hawkes et al. 1997).

In looking for conditions that transformed plant and animal communities and foraging return rates in tropical America before the initiation of food production, climatic and vegetational perturbations associated with the close of the Pleistocene are an obvious place to start. Human population densities on this recently-colonized landscape were very low between ca. 14,000 and 10,000–8000 B.P. (Cooke 1998; Dillehay et al. 1992; Ranere and Cooke 2003), making human demographic pressure on resources an improbable factor in economic change. Moreover, shifts in subsistence strategies are more likely to have been particularly conspicuous during and after periods of pronounced environmental change, a scenario that archaeological records spanning the Pleistocene/Holocene transition in the Near East, tropical America, and New Guinea seem to support (Haberle 2002; Hillman 2001; Lentfer 2002; Piperno and Pearsall 1998). And where paleoecological data are robust across the Pleistocene/Holocene boundary, they can serve as proxy indicators for changing resource distribution and foraging costs independent of, and as is often useful, in place of detailed archaeological records on subsistence.

Theories that closely associate climate change with agricultural origins have frequently met with negative reactions from anthropologists for varying reasons. Climate change is often cast into the set of single-factor or prime mover types of explanations, which are seen to be overly simplistic, or simply irrelevant, because they are not culturally motivated and do not provide realistic appraisals of possible cultural responses other than food production (e.g.,

Wagner 1977). In a seminal paper on the origins of agriculture, David Harris (1977, 183) offered these lucid points:

> The fundamental objection to explanations that regard climate change as a primary stress factor is that they fail to demonstrate precisely how a secular change in climate affects hunter-gatherer subsistence patterns. They rest on the assumption that climatic change induces adjustments in the distribution and density of the plant and animal communities on which forager populations depend, but they usually fail to specify the nature of those adjustments with sufficient precision that a hypothesis may be tested against empirical evidence. They also suffer from the inadequacy and ambiguity of the evidence itself, as uncertainties surrounding the interpretation of the Near Eastern palynological record clearly demonstrate.

Using foraging theory to examine the domestication process disassociates climate from the status of a prime mover exerting a unidirectional influence on cultural decisions, setting climate more appropriately within the domain of environmental variability, from whose derivative sets of alternative resources efficient-minded foragers make informed decisions about the food chase. It is these changing human actions, of course, that drive evolutionary and cultural change (Winterhalder and Kennett, this volume). And the often inadequate and ambiguous paleoecological records on the Pleistocene to Holocene transition that Harris rightly complained about have given way to reconstructions of Late Quaternary environments that are increasingly impressive in their detail and chronological control, including in the lowland Neotropical forest.

The conventional wisdom that the lowland tropical forest was immune to the climatic changes that impacted higher latitudes during the last ice age has been overturned by a substantial body of evidence indicating that the tropical biome was subject to dramatic Quaternary environmental oscillations. During the final 10,000 years of the last glacial cycle (between ca. 20,000 B.P. and 10,000 B.P.), the period of most intense interest to us because it accommodates virtually all accepted chronologies for human colonization of the Americas (Dillehay 1997; Dillehay et al. 1992; Meltzer et al. 1994), the Neotropical world was a considerably cooler and drier place than it is today (for a detailed summary of the evidence, see Piperno and Pearsall 1998, 90–100). Temperatures were at least 6°C lower and precipitation was reduced in the order of about 30 to 50%. Glacial-age atmospheres also contained much less CO_2 (about 180 ppm) than they would during the early Holocene (about 280 ppm).

These conditions resulted, depending on the area and elevation considered, in the following: (1) replacement of much of the seasonal tropical forest by types of open vegetation similar to today's thorn woodlands, thorn scrublands, and savannas, (2) partial replacement and reduction of lowland evergreen rain forest by arboreal elements now primarily confined to drier types of forest, and (3) an 800 to 1200 downward slope movement of some forest elements generally confined today to cool and high mountainous areas above 1500 m. Figures 7.1a and 7.1b present the modern, potential vegetation for the lowland Neotropics. Figures 7.2a and 7.2b show the vegetational patterns reconstructed for the tropical lowlands between ca. 22,000 and 10,500 B.P., based primarily on paleovegetational data derived from lake and swamp sediment cores.

Much light has been shed in recent years on why tropical environmental conditions during an ice age were so profoundly different from modern conditions. Formerly thought to be incompatible physical forces of the Pleistocene climate, cooling and drying are now understood to be ice age co-actors. For example, significantly cooler sea surfaces documented at low latitudes contributed considerably less moisture to the air through evaporation, thereby reducing atmospheric water vapor content and precipitation over tropical land surfaces (Webb et al. 1997). The net effects of the peculiar combination of low temperature, precipitation, and atmospheric CO_2 on Pleistocene tropical plant communities are under considerable discussion. Questions under evaluation include whether low CO_2 or in-

creased aridity caused the widespread expansion of open, savanna-like types of vegetation with many C4 plants at the expense of C3-dominated forests (Cowling and Sykes 1999; Huang et al. 2001). New empirical studies of lakes from Mexico and Guatemala show that vegetational shifts from C3-dominated forests to C4-dominated grasslands in the tropics were unlikely without significant reductions in precipitation (Huang et al. 2001). Moreover, low CO_2 concentrations acting independently of climatic influences probably cannot account for the fact that many lakes from Guatemala to southern Brazil were substantially lower or completely dry during the Late Pleistocene (Piperno and Pearsall 1998, 96–97). The tropical ice age climate appears to have been both substantially drier and cooler.

What are the implications of these reconstructions of late Pleistocene and early Holocene environmental conditions for late-glacial and early post-glacial human exploitation of the tropical flora and fauna? It can be predicted that the most significant vegetational and faunal shifts, and potentially the greatest changes in foraging return rates between ca. 12,000 B.P. and 9000 B.P., took place in areas now marked by strong seasonality of rainfall, where the modern, potential vegetation is tropical deciduous forest and drier types of semi-evergreen tropical forest (modern annual precipitation from ca. 1200 to 2500 mm) (Figures 7.1a and b). These areas include much of the Pacific watershed of Central America, large parts of northern South America (including the Orinoco drainage in Venezuela and the northeastern fringe of Amazonia comprising the southern Guianas and northeastern Brazil), the southern and southwestern stretches of the Amazon Basin, and parts of Bolivia. Here, savanna/thorny scrub vegetational communities were prevalent during the Late Pleistocene. They undoubtedly were homes to many of the more than 30 genera of now-extinct, large- and medium-sized grazers and browsers like mastodont-like gomphotheres (*Cuvieronius* and *Haplomastodon*), mammoths (*Mammuthus*), glyptodonts (Glyptodontidae), giant ground sloths (*Eremotheirum*, *Megatherium*, and Mylodontidae),

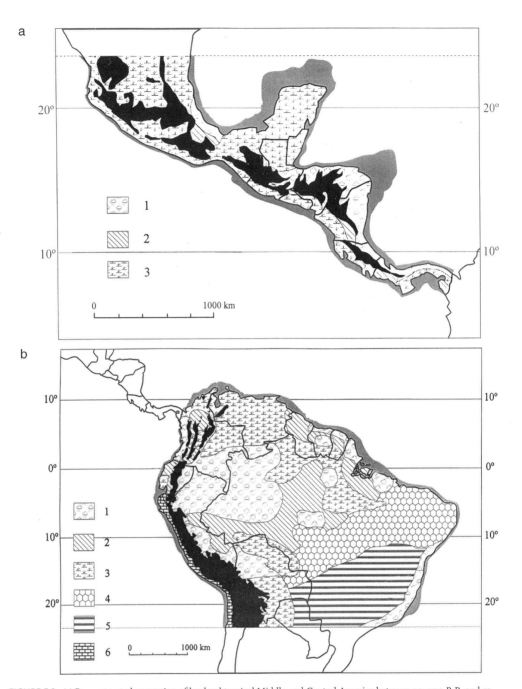

FIGURE 7.2. (a) Reconstructed vegetation of lowland tropical Middle and Central America between 20,000 B.P. and ca. 10,500 B.P. (b) Reconstructed vegetation of lowland tropical South America between 20,000 B.P. and ca. 10,500 B.P. Areas in black indicate elevations above 1500 m above sea level. Gray represents Pleistocene shoreline. Explanation: 1. Largely un-broken moist forest, often with a mixture of presently high-elevation and lowland forest elements. In some areas, montane forest elements (e.g., *Podocarpus, Quercus, Alnus, Ilex*) are conspicuous. Annual precipitation is lower than today, but sufficient precipitation exists to support a forest; 2. Forest containing drier elements than characteristic today. High-elevation forest elements occur, especially in moister areas of the zone. Areas near the 2000 mm precipitation isohyet and areas with sandy soils may contain savanna woodland. The vegetation may be patchy; 3. Mostly undifferentiated thorn woodland, low scrub, and wooded savanna vegetation. Some regions (e.g., Guatemala) have temperate elements (e.g., *Juniperus*). Areas receiving greater than 2000 mm of rainfall today may still support a drier forest, as in 2. River- and stream-side locations support a forest; 4. Quite possibly, a drier vegetation formation than 5 (below), with fewer trees and more open-land taxa. Paleoecological data are lacking for the zone; 5. Fairly open and humid forest containing many presently high-elevation taxa (e.g., *Ilex, Podocarpus, Rapanea, Symplocus*) combined with elements of the modern semi-evergreen forest and cerrado. Precipitation is lower than today but northward shifts in the southern polar fronts and other factors ameliorate precipitation reduction. The modern, seasonal forest/cerrado vegetational formations of the region are not present until about 10,000 B.P.; 6. Desert/cactus scrub (modified from Piperno and Pearsall 1998, Figure 2.4).

giant capybaras (*Neochoerus*), flat-headed peccaries (*Platygonus*), and horses (*Equus* [*Amerhippus*]). The Joboid and fluted Clovis and fishtail projectile points made by pre-Clovis and Clovis human populations, respectively, in Central and South America between ca. 13,000 B.P. and 10,000 B.P. were designed to spear and kill such animals (Dillehay et al. 1992; Ranere and Cooke 2003), and hunting in drier and more open areas during the late Pleistocene was probably a highly profitable pursuit.

In addition to a high animal biomass, the savanna/thorny scrub, late-glacial floristic communities probably contained dense associations of dry-land cacti and legumes (e.g., *Opuntia*, *Prosopis*, *Agave*), which offered an appreciable high-quality and low-cost, edible biomass, with little cost of processing. These plants can still be found in number today along the dry, Pacific littoral of Central America and similar areas of lowland South America, their interglacial "refugia" to which they retreated at the close of the Pleistocene. They were probably exploited by human populations in the lowlands, as they were at higher elevations in Mesoamerica (Flannery 1986a, b).

We should not lose sight of the fact that in some regions, such as the Pacific watershed of Central America, the late-glacial environment was probably a patchy and heterogeneous one in which different mixes of high-profitability animal and plant resources could have easily been exploited together (see Piperno and Jones 2003). Edge habitats, where early successional forest growth met the open terrain and where an abundance of browse was available for game to feed on, were more extensive on the late Pleistocene landscape. In such circumstances, where a variety of closely ranked and low-cost resources were available, use of optimal foraging models do not predict that the largest animals would be exploited to the exclusion of medium-sized and some smaller game and plants, or that short-term dietary variability would not occur (Simms 1987).

With regard to glacial and post-glacial subsistence strategies, fluctuations in atmospheric concentrations of CO_2 may also have been very important because CO_2 significantly influences the rate of photosynthesis and plant productivity (Cowling and Sykes 1999; Zhao and Piperno 2000). CO_2 concentrations were 33% lower than pre-industrial values (PIV) until ca. 12,500 B.P., when they were still 25% lower than the PIV, not rising close to PIV values until about 9000 B.P. (Barnola et al. 1987). It is well understood that C3 plant water-use efficiency and biomass are significantly reduced under lower CO_2 levels such as those that characterized the Pleistocene. C4 plants (many grasses, excluding rice, bamboos and the Poaceae of higher tropical elevations and latitudes) and CAM plant taxa (all the cacti), which photosynthesize carbon more efficiently, are relatively more competitive and better adapted to atmospheres deficient in carbon dioxide (Cowley and Sykes 1999). The great majority of crop plant wild progenitors—all roots and tubers, pulses, tree crops, non/grass herbaceous seed plants, and also wheat, barley, rye, and rice—are C3 species. These plants probably became relatively more profitable to exploit as the Holocene conditions were established. Sage (1995), in fact, proposes the interesting idea that low CO_2 levels would have substantially inhibited the development of effective cultivation systems during the Pleistocene.

A considerable amount of paleoecological data from the tropical lowlands indicates that ice age conditions generally persisted until between ca. 11,000 and 10,500 B.P., when the climate rapidly turned warmer and wetter, and elements of seasonal tropical forest moved from their glacial locations and began to replace most of the savanna/thorny scrub floristic associations. Some of these trees must have been harbored in better-watered areas along streams and river courses within easy pollen dispersal range of sites because they enter pollen and phytolith records soon after the major climatic snap marking the end of the Pleistocene; climatic and vegetational reversals to glacial-like conditions resulting from the Younger Dryas can't be detected in most lowland tropical records. By about 10,000 to 9000 B.P., depending on the region, paleoecological records indicate that where a Pleistocene landscape had supported savanna-like vegetation, species-rich, seasonal tropical forests now flourished (Compare Figures 7.1a and b and 7.2a and b). As high-ranking resources diminished in density and became more dispersed, the cost of searching for them increased, foraging efficiency declined, and a broader set of lower profitability plant and animal resources were incorporated into diets.

In contrast to the situation just described, paleoecological data show that where the modern potential vegetation is tropical, evergreen forest or moister types of semi-evergreen forest (e.g., modern annual precipitation between 2500 mm and 4000 mm) largely persisted during the Pleistocene (Figures 7.2 a and b). There was likely always a big block of forest in the northern, western, and perhaps central reaches of the Amazon Basin, for example, where even a 50% reduction in precipitation would have brought enough moisture for forest growth. The Caribbean watershed of Central America from Panama to Guatemala, where forests are mainly ever-wet, represents another large, contiguous area that probably remained under forest cover throughout glacial cycles. In such areas, it can be predicted that foraging return rates following the end of the Pleistocene saw comparatively little change between 11,000 and 10,000 years ago. Far fewer game animals were lost to extinctions, and one type of forest was replaced by another, with little consequence for the abundance, distribution, and potential profitability of resources useful to humans.

In summary, the single most important factor driving subsistence changes after the close of the Pleistocene probably was the dramatic decline in foraging return rates associated with the demise of glacial-period resources and expansion of forests into regions where open land vegetation had prevailed during glacial times. The removal of many mega- and large- to medium-sized fauna from a resource set

and the need to practice foraging full-time in a tropical forest would immediately force subsistence options in the direction of lower ranked resources, and substantially broaden the diet breadth. Following the diet breadth model, people would have started to cultivate some plants as soon as the net return from subsistence strategies involving plant propagation exceeded those resulting from full-time foraging (Kaplan and Hill 1992). Using paleoecological data to predict the threshold at which this might occur, the time period between ca. 10,000 and 9000 B.P. is likely to be highly significant. This is when the closure of the landscape by advancing forest occurred and foraging return rates were declining significantly. It would not have taken long before economic strategies that incorporated the cultivation of plants were more profitable than full-time foraging. If true, then food production origins in the lowland Neotropics should be sought during the early Holocene in the seasonal tropical forest.

JOINING THE MODEL AND THE EMPIRICAL EVIDENCE ON AGRICULTURAL TRANSITIONS

The archaeological and paleoecological evidence attesting to an early development of foraging and food production in the lowland Neotropics, the plants involved that can be identified using presently available techniques, and other aspects germane to the process relating to settlement, technological, and land use strategies are presented in detail elsewhere (Piperno 1998; Piperno in press; Piperno and Pearsall 1998; Piperno et al. 2000a, b; Pope et al. 2001). Figures 7.3 and 7.4 provide a summary of the relevant developments arranged in parallel with a calibrated and uncalibrated carbon 14 chronology, and a map showing the location of the sites. The evidence is currently strongest in a region from lower Central America to northwestern South America comprising Panama, Ecuador, and Colombia. Here, combined microbotanical studies; pollen, phytoliths, and starch grains, indicate that human manipulation of Neotropical plant species—including maize (*Zea mays*), squashes and gourds (*Cucurbita moschata, C. ecuadorensis*), arrowroot (*Maranta arundinacea*), manioc (*Manihot esculenta*), lerén (*Calathea allouia*), and yams (*Dioscorea* spp.)—leading to their domestication took place in the early Holocene (10,000–7000 B.P.). Tree crops (e.g., palms and avocado [*Persea americana*]), which provided essential dietary fats and cooking oils as well as important ingredients for making *chichas* (fermented beverages), were probably involved in these horticultural systems. We cannot, however, say at this time which early archaeological remains of tree fruits, often abundantly represented in early sites, are from wild and which are from cultivated plants.

Paleoecological data provide correlative lines of evidence and indicate that beginning at 7000 to 5000 B.P., depending on the region, crops were grown in the context of an agroecology created by slash-and-burn techniques of field preparation. Hence, earlier systems of food production seem to have been simple and inexpensive kinds of horticulture practiced largely in house gardens and other near-residential locations, which did not involve significant field preparation and the progressive removal of primary forest trees over large areas, and thus did not leave such kinds of signatures on paleoecological profiles. Some paleoecological records (e.g., from Panama and Brazil) attest to considerable forest burning and the creation of smaller-scale forest openings between ca. 11,000 and 7000 B.P.[6]

Archaeological foot surveys and excavations in Panama, Ecuador, Colombia, and northern Peru show that between 10,000 and 5000 B.P. settlements were generally small, often covering less than one hectare, and located beside lakes, secondary watercourses, and seasonal streams, whose bits of alluvium could have been used for planting. Settlement organization appears to have been something like the modern, tropical hamlet and hamlet clusters in which no

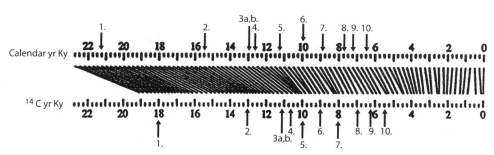

1. LGM (Last Glacial Maximum)
2. Monte Verde occupied
3a. Clovis entry into tropical America
3b. Specialized coastal exploitation at Quebrada Jaguay and Quebrada Tacahuay, southern Peru
4. End of the Pleistocene
5. Forest reclaims the lowland tropical landscape upon early Holocene warming and precipitation increase
6. First evidence for plant cultivation and domestication; *Cucurbita* at Vegas, Ecuador and Guilá Naquitz Cave, Mexico
7. Introduction of *Cucurbita* at Peña Roja, Colombian Amazon
8. Introduction of maize and manioc into Central Pacific Panama; slash-and-burn agriculture starts there
9. Maize pollen at San Andrés, Caribbean Coast of Mexico
10. Earliest maize cobs at Guilá Naquitz Cave; Formative Period (arrowroot, cotton, productive maize) begins at Real Alto, Ecuador.

FIGURE 7.3. Calendar year and associated carbon 14-year chronology for some major developments in Central American and South American prehistory related to the initial peopling of the continents, resource use, and early plant cultivation and domestication. The combined carbon 14 and calibrated year age scale (X 1000) is reprinted from Figure 1 of Bartlein et al. 1995 with kind permission from Elsevier.

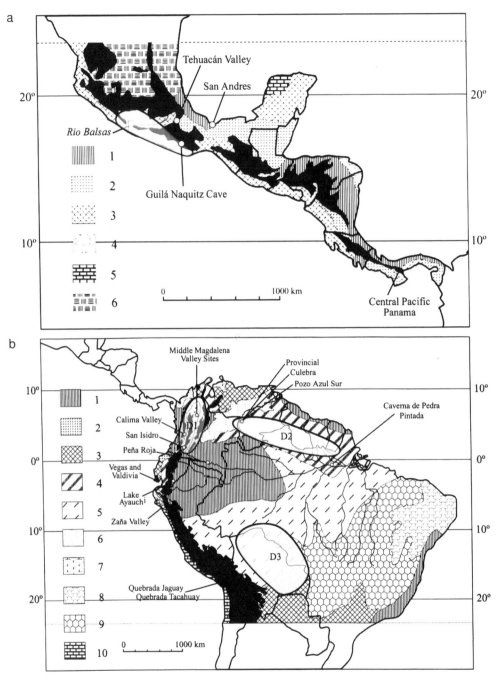

FIGURE 7.4. Sites in the lowland Neotropics occupied and/or containing evidence for plant cultivation and domestication between ca. 11,000 and 5000 carbon 14 yr. B.P. Ovals represent likely domestication areas for various, important lowland crop plants as follows: Mexico: maize (*Zea mays*) and squash (*Cucurbita argyrosperma*); also possibly jícama (*Pachyrhizus erosus*). South America; D1 : sweet potato (*Ipomoea batatas*), squash (*Cucurbita moschata*), arrowroot (*Maranta arundinacea*), achira (*Canna edulis*—lower, mid-elevational in origin); also possibly sieva beans (*Phaseolus lunatus*), yautia or cocoyam (*Xanthosoma saggitifolium*), and lerén (*Calathea allouia*); D2: yam (*Dioscorea trifida*); also possibly yautia (*Xanthosoma saggitifolium*), lerén (*Calathea allouia*), and chile peppers (*Capsicum baccatum*); D3: manioc or yuca (*Manihot esculenta*), peanut (*Arachis hypogaea*), chile pepper (*Capsicum baccatum*), and possibly squashes (*Cucurbita moschata* and/or *C. maxima*) and jack bean (*Canavalia plagiosperma*). Notes: People in the American tropics appear to have been engaging in early plant cultivating and domesticatory relationships with plants over wide geographic areas. Likely areas of origin for other lowland, pre-Columbian cultivars include the wet forests of the northwestern Amazon Basin (*Bactris gasipaes* [the peach palm] and possibly *Sicana odorifera* [cassabanana]), southwest Ecuador, where another species of *Cucurbita*, *C. ecuadorensis*, was semi-domesticated during the early Holocene. southwest Ecuador/northern Peru (*G. barbadense* cotton), and the Yucatan Peninsula (*G. hirsutum* cotton) (modified from Piperno and Pearsall 1998, Figures 3.18, 3.19, 4.5, and 4.8).

more than one to a few nuclear families share a residential community, and the nuclear family is the main unit of production and consumption. Sedentary village communities did not begin to widely emerge in the tropical forest until the fourth millennium B.P.

Although findings of similar antiquity involving different plant species will probably be discovered in other regions, the oldest evidence for plant cultivation and domestication in tropical America, as in highland Mexico (Smith 1997b), involves *Cucurbita* spp. (squashes and gourds). In modern squashes and gourds, phytolith size bears a close relationship to fruit and seed size, and, as is the case with seeds, there are no phytoliths from wild *Cucurbita* as large as those that occur in domesticated plants (Piperno et al. 2000b; Piperno and Stothert 2003). Phytoliths recovered from deposits dating to the terminal Pleistocene period (10,800 to 10,000 B.P.) in two preceramic sites in southwest Ecuador belonging to the Las Vegas culture are indicative of wild *Cucurbita* exploitation. Large *Cucurbita* phytoliths of a size indicating they were from domesticated varieties and that they probably resulted from a local domestication of the only species of *Cucurbita* native to the region, *Cucurbita ecuadorensis,* occur in deposits from the same two sites dating to between about 10,000 and 7000 B.P. (Piperno et al. 2000b; Piperno and Stothert 2003). Direct AMS dating of carbon trapped inside these phytoliths confirmed that domestication occurred between 10,100 and 9300 B.P. (Piperno and Stothert 2003). Other subsistence remains from the deep and dense Las Vegas preceramic middens, e.g., a wide variety of mollusks, including mangrove species, 25 categories of marine fish, crab, rabbit, deer, squirrel, opossum, and rodents, locate this early horticultural horizon firmly within a broad-spectrum subsistence strategy involving an intensive exploitation of coastal resources, including estuaries, that emerged at ca. 10,000 B.P.

Other evidence for an early Holocene development of horticulture in northern South America includes stone implements that ap-

pear to be hoes, some of which are beautifully polished. These occur at sites in the Middle and Upper Cauca Valley, Colombia (Calima Valley and San Isidro on Figure 7.4b), and are well-dated to between 9000 and 7300 B.P. (Gnecco and Salgado López 1989; Herrera et al. 1992). These tools, together with studies of the Calima sites' soils, strongly suggest that plant cultivation was being practiced, although we cannot yet specify which species were being manipulated. *C. moschata* squash, root crops such as arrowroot, sweet potato, lerén, and tree fruits like the avocado would be among the prime candidates. Phytolith evidence from Peña Roja, located in wet, evergreen forest of the Colombian Amazon, indicates that lerén and a domesticated species of *Cucurbita* arrived by ca. 8000 B.P. Maize and manioc starch grains retrieved from the surfaces of grinding stones from the Aguadulce Rock Shelter, Panama, well-dated to ca. 7000 to 6000 B.P., indicate even earlier cultivation and domestication in their respective birthplaces, southwest Mexico (Doebley 1990) and South America (Olsen and Schaal 1999).

Recently reported analyses from molecular biology and archaeobotany shed new insights on the question of maize domestication and spread. The rachids, cupules, and seed bracts from teosinte (wild maize) and maize contain phytoliths that can be distinguished from one another because the production and morphology of these phytoliths is largely controlled by an important genetic locus called *teosinte glume architecture 1 (tga1)* (Dorweiler and Doebley 1997). Thus, phytolith analysis may yield information on phenotypic changes that occurred during the transformation of teosinte to maize. At the Aguadulce Rock Shelter, Panama, where, as noted above, maize starch grains occurred on early grinding stones, phytolith assemblages identical to those found in the glumes and rachids of teosinte were isolated from sediment strata dating to shortly before 7000 B.P. (Piperno and Pearsall 1998, 221–224; Piperno et al. 2000b). Because the phytoliths are unique to *Zea* and teosinte is not native to Panama, the phytoliths probably originated from a primitive race of maize whose glumes and cupules were more silicified, and thus better defended from insects and fungal diseases. Stratigraphically above this zone and throughout the remainder of the sequence, cob phytoliths are modern in morphology, suggesting a change in glume hardness or size that made kernels easier to process after ca. 7000 B.P. in Panama.

These and other microfossil data from south of Mexico accord well with a recent study that estimates a ca. 9000 cal yr. B.P. date for maize domestication on the basis of a molecular clock (Matsuoka et al. 2002). Interestingly, these molecular data also suggest that the oldest surviving maize is from highland Mexico, despite the fact that maize's wild ancestor is naturally distributed today at lower elevations in the Balsas River Valley. The new molecular work raises the possibility that maize's origins may not be uncovered in warm and relatively wet zones of Mexico, as archaeologists, inferring from previously reported molecular data, have supposed (e.g., Piperno and Pearsall 1998; Smith 1998, 155). Early archaeological sequences from the highlands, however, show no evidence for an exploitation of teosinte prior to the appearance of an already completely domesticated maize, as would be expected if maize was of highland derivation (Piperno 2001b; Piperno and Flannery 2001). This issue will not be resolved until archaeological data from the Balsas River Valley and other lower-lying regions of southern Mexico become available. The oldest surviving maize varieties may inadequately reflect prehistoric lowland maize diversity.

Although empirical data for plant and animal consumption during the late Pleistocene and early Holocene periods are admittedly slender, the following trends in subsistence, settlement, and technology merit discussion. The end stages of the Pleistocene and beginning of the Holocene, by which time the last of the faunal extinctions occurred and forests were advancing rapidly on the landscape, are marked by what appears to have been a technological and economic transition to a broader diet with increased emphasis on lower ranked plant and other foods of lower trophic levels. These include a variety of tropical forest tubers, roots, seeds, and coastal resources. This finding conforms to the predicted cultural response to decreasing foraging return rates under optimal foraging strategies.

Unfluted and fluted projectile points and their associated tool kit complexes (heavy end scrapers, perforators, and burins) used to hunt and process now-extinct mammals disappear from most archaeological complexes by ca. 10,000 B.P. (Cooke 1998; Ranere and Cooke 2003), whereas several different types of plant grinding technologies, such as edge ground cobbles, boulder milling stone bases and small, flat milling stones, and the aforementioned hoes first occur in sites from Colombia, Ecuador, and Panama between about 10,000 and 8000 B.P. (Stothert 1985; Ranere 1992). Such kinds of plant-specialty implements are absent in earlier occupations from these and other regions of the Neotropics, indicating that plant exploitation was a less important or less systematic activity during the late and terminal Pleistocene periods, and also that the types of plants exploited for the most part did not require intensive processing as do seeds, roots, and nuts. Direct evidence from starch grains and phytoliths residue analysis of the grinding stones from Panama and Colombia demonstrates that they were used to process roots, tubers, and seeds from a variety of tropical forest plants (Piperno in press; Piperno and Pearsall 1998; Piperno et al. 2000a).

The termination of the Pleistocene also yields the first demonstrable evidence for committed and specialized exploitations of marine fauna. The early Holocene Vegas occupations of southwest Ecuador have already been discussed. In southern Peru, where little land was submerged by rising sea level, people using nets from ca. 11,000 B.P. to 10,500 B.P. at Quebrada Jaguay and Quebrada Tacahuay focused on capturing selected species of mollusks, small, calorie-rich fish, and sea birds (Keefer et al. 1998; Sandweiss et al. 1998). Important questions include whether such kinds of maritime adaptations were taking place at other coastal localities where the oceans perhaps were not as productive, and if they occurred even earlier.

In summary, available evidence indicates that when the Pleistocene ended, people turned their attention to the plants and animals of the seasonal tropical forest and other resources occupying lower trophic levels and increased the breadth of their diets. Paleoecological reconstructions combined with the corpus of data on the return to labor of exploiting modern resources, indicate that the tropical forest plants and animals that expanded onto the landscape after ca. 10,500 B.P. were far more expensive to capture and convert into food than those that were available or more abundant before the ice age ended. Thus, early dietary broadening and associated technological changes probably were effected under conditions of decreasing foraging return rates brought on by the decline of higher ranked animals and plants.

The social units responsible for the earliest foraging and farming in tropical America appear to have been small, egalitarian, and organized at the level of the household. Thus, they do not meet the requirements of social models for agricultural origins, which have status-conscious big men fostering or coercing the accumulation of agricultural surpluses and labor-intensive foods in order to enhance the power of individuals or groups (Hayden 1995a). These social phenomena occur long after the beginnings of food production, when sedentary village life became established. The relevance of social factors to economic transitions is more realistically sought in these later time periods. Large surpluses fueled by agricultural economies containing a few highly productive crops would have captured the attention of accumulating individuals who recognized the exploitative value of manipulating people who produced such surfeits.

Although optimal foraging theory appears to provide a cogent exposition for the transition from foraging to food production, later features of agricultural intensification, which are outside the purview of this paper, are not easily explained by simple models from evolutionary ecology. Social factors mentioned above and others, e.g. population pressure arising from the success of small-scale food production and competition over good agricultural lands, no doubt were influential in fueling the development of agricultural economies. Nonetheless, because the environment can be defined broadly to include "anything external to an organism that impinges upon its probability of survival and reproduction" (Winterhalder and Smith 1992, 8), behavioral ecological studies using multiple goals and measures may be well suited to examining social relationships and competition under food-producing modes of production, together with their roles in the emergence of social stratification.

Finally, if one considers the collective molecular, botanical, archaeological, and paleoecological evidence, there is substantial support for the idea that seasonally dry tropical forest gave rise to many crop plant species and/or supported early horticultural systems that incorporated crops domesticated elsewhere on the seasonally dry landscape (Figures 7.4a and b). Some of these regions include: (1) the Balsas River Valley, southwestern Mexico, the putative cradle of maize and possibly *Cucurbita argyrosperma* (the cushaw and silver-seeded squashes), (2) the Cauca and Magdalena Valleys of Colombia, probable homes to several important crops, including sweet potato, lerén, arrowroot, and *Cucurbita moschata*, the single most important species of squash utilized by indigenous inhabitants of the lowland Neotropics, (3) southwestern Ecuador, where a native species of *Cucurbita*, *C. ecuadorensis*, was probably semi-domesticated during the early Holocene, (4) southwestern Brazil/eastern Bolivia, the probable birthplace of manioc, peanuts, and other crops, (5) an area comprising southern Venezuela/southern Guianas/northeastern Brazil, where root crops, including the American yam, *Dioscorea trifida*, likely were domesticated, and (6) central Pacific Panama, where squash (*C. moschata*), maize, manioc, arrowroot (*Maranta arundinacea*), and possibly yams (*D. trifida*) arrived from their domestication locales in Mexico and South America between ca. 8000 and 6000 B.P.

In contrast, regions supporting ever-wet forests today, where forests persisted during the Pleistocene, were responsible for the development of relatively few important starch- and protein-rich crops.

IF PLANT FOOD PRODUCTION WAS A MORE EFFICIENT AND EVOLUTIONARY SUCCESSFUL STRATEGY OF FOOD PROCUREMENT THAN FORAGING, WHY DID IT TAKE SO LONG TO DEVELOP?

Students of agricultural origins who are skeptical of theories that incorporate climate change as an influential element in the process have justifiably asked the following question: if the environmental oscillations associated with the end stages of the Pleistocene were influential in the global transitions from foraging to food production, why didn't the six to seven major glacial to interglacial passages that occurred previously during the past two million years, and that probably caused similar ecological cascades, lead to these transitions sooner (e.g., Hayden 1992)? A single, overriding, and quite possibly crucial difference between the termination of the last major glacial period and those six to seven terminations and interglacials that preceded it may have been the presence of anatomically and cognitively modern people, who by 14,000 B.P. had occupied every major continent on the globe, including both hemispheres of the Americas (Dillehay 1997).

Archaeologists, paleoanthropologists, and now molecular biologists are less willing to accept the proposition that the behavior of hunters and gatherers prior to the emergence of anatomically modern humans about 100,000 years ago was qualitatively the same as that of people practicing foraging on the eve of agriculture (e.g., Enard et al. 2002; Foley 1987; Klein 1999, 2001; Kuhn and Stiner 2001; Mellers 1996; Niewoehner 2001). In comparing the archaeological records of middle Pleistocene or middle Stone Age occupations, equivalent to Mousterian and dating from ca. 250 ky ago to as late as ca. 30,000 B.P. in southern Europe, with those

of the Later Stone Age or Upper Paleolithic (between ca. 50,000 and 12,000 B.P.), marked differences in settlement strategies, diets, technology, and, arguably, social interactions and networks, become apparent (for recent reviews see Klein 2001 and Kuhn and Stiner 2001).

The possible implications of these differences are important. Economically rational behavioral responses to resource fluctuations of a kind associated with the end-Pleistocene environmental changes, or responses that became necessary because human population growth resulted in the over-exploitation of resources (Stiner et al. 1999) required the ability to efficiently capture what were often higher-cost, smaller game, plants, and shellfish, and faster, more elusive birds and lagomorphs, and convert them into digestible foodstuffs. This, in turn, necessitated significant alterations to hunting gear; implements related to plant gathering, processing, and preparation; and the social relations of production. Evidence for these innovations is absent until after the origination and spread of anatomically modern humans 100 ky ago, and many of them do not appear or become common until the Upper Paleolithic (ca. 35,000 B.P.) and later (e.g., Klein 1999; Kuhn and Stiner 2001). A late (ca. 100 ky ago) acquisition of language suggested by a recent molecular analysis (Enard et al. 2002) obviously would have been crucial in this regard.

Between 130 and 110 ky ago, Mousterian/ middle Stone Age societies in the Near East, Europe, and southern Africa passed through a strong glacial termination and interglacial period climatically similar to the last such transition (Muhs et al. 2001). Their tool kits and diets, however, bear no resemblance to those of hunters and gatherers who navigated the latter stages of the Pleistocene and the onset of the Present Interglacial in ways that permitted specialized exploitation of coastal resources, efficient capture of small and elusive game, and intensive harvesting and processing of plant foods. The fact that Mousterian populations didn't collect slow-moving, easy-to-harvest prey like tortoises and shellfish sufficiently intensively to cause their over-exploitation, but that Upper Paleolithic populations did (Stiner et al. 1999), probably also speaks to differences in the cognitive and behavioral capabilities of Middle Paleolithic and Upper Paleolithic societies that resulted in less effective food procurement strategies during earlier periods. Arguably, the most parsimonious explanation for the chronology of the origins of food production is that a behavioral capacity for the types of resource exploitation and management practiced by modern foragers and farmers evolved with our own species, *Homo sapiens*, no earlier than about 100 my ago, and perhaps as late as 50 my ago (Klein 2001). Thus, the convergence of the cultural, ecological, and evolutionary factors necessary for the emergence of agriculture probably did not occur until the end of the Pleistocene.

Richerson et al. (2001) argued recently that extreme climate variability during the final 60,000 years of the Pleistocene had as much to do with the timing of agricultural origins as did the end-Pleistocene environmental changes. Their position is that strong, millennial and shorter-term oscillations in climate before 12,000 B.P., which are well documented from Greenland ice core isotopic analysis, made the development of reliable agricultural systems impossible. I am skeptical about this theory for a number of reasons. There is considerable evidence that during those rapid climate shifts between ca. 70,000 and 15,000 B.P., atmospheric CO_2 concentrations, temperatures, and in some regions, precipitation, were always considerably lower than during the Holocene (Barnola et al. 1987; Jouzel 1999). Hence, potential food resources were probably not altered in ways such as occurred at the end of the Pleistocene, when shifts in selective pressures and the development of alternative economic strategies that included plant cultivation resulted.

The few pollen records dating to between ca. 70,000 and 15,000 years ago with millennial- and shorter-term levels of precision provide empirical evidence that vegetational re-assortments and structural transformations to the biota like those associated with the latest foraging and earliest food production did not occur sooner (e.g., Behling et al. 2000; Roucoux et al. 2001). In northeastern Brazil between 40,000 and 15,000 B.P., for example, warmer and ". . . wetter periods were apparently too short for an expansion of humid flood plain or mountain forests" (Behling et al. 2000, 991), the present interglacial vegetation.

WHY WERE SO FEW PLANT SPECIES DOMESTICATED?

A noteworthy attribute of agricultural origins all over the world is that, out of the thousands of plant species that were available to early farmers, just a small percentage of them were domesticated. For example, it is estimated that only 30 of the approximately 7500 species of the world's grasses became subjects of human production strategies (Harlan 1999), including just two genera of native American grasses, *Setaria* and *Zea*, and only *Zea* was demonstrably domesticated. Although we have little control on early root and tuber exploitation, it would appear that a single species of the large genus *Manihot* with more than 100 species well-distributed in Mexico and South America was domesticated, a single time, in the Brazilian Amazon (Olsen and Schaal 1999). Many species of the yam-producing genus *Dioscorea* grow in the Americas, yet only one native to northeastern South America, *D. trifida*, was clearly ennobled and disseminated to other regions of the Neotropics. What factors gave rise to these patterns?

Oft-discussed reasons why certain plants and not others become foci of human exploitation and production include life history habits (annual vs. perennial), nutritional value and palatability, shelf life, and genetic variability and amenability to artificial selection in planting beds. All these factors may have important effects on the domestication process, but exactly how is often unclear, and more than a few exceptions to the rules occur. For example, the wild ancestors of many crop plants possess highly fibrous, bitter and/or toxic fruits, seeds, and roots, and a hard and rigid fruitcase completely envelops wild maize kernels.

These plants could not have been particularly easy to process and turn into food.

Behavioral ecology has the potential to elucidate this issue. There is little understanding of the proximate mechanisms; that is, the cognitive and other processes directly underlying human and other animals' decisions about food procurement (Krebs and Davies 1997). It is likely, however, that in human beings "rules of thumb" guides exert strong influences on resource choice (Winterhalder 2001). These rules originate in natural and cultural selection on foraging rules, or from experience gained from following adult mentors during childhood (Winterhalder 2001). One such rule of thumb may have concerned the often positive relationship between resource size and profitability.

For example, annual plants, besides yielding quick and more reliable returns to human labor from year to year, often produce much heavier and larger seeds and underground plant organs than do perennials. Exploitation and domestication in the Cucurbitaceae, a large family where only nine of approximately 350 available American species, six of them in the genus *Cucurbita*, were brought under human control, seem to be closely correlated with fruit and seed size. Wild *Cucurbita* fruits and seeds are considerably more stout than many other members of its family. The Cucurbitaceae genera *Sicana*, *Sechium*, and *Cyclanthera* also gave rise to domesticated species in the Neotropics, and few to no other annual cucurbits have fruits the size of the wild progenitors (T.C. Andres, pers. comm. 2003). Preliminary studies are showing that Balsas teosinte grains—even after removal from their fruit-cases—are larger than many other wild, Neotropical grass grains, including its close relative *Tripsacum* (Piperno, laboratory notes).

Old World trends in domestication appear to be similar. Wild einkorn is robust and large-seeded, and not surprisingly, return rates of exploiting large stands of this grass (2300–2744 cal/person/hr), and probably large-sized wild emmer and barley as well, are considerably higher than those of exploiting many other species of smaller-grained wild grasses (Table 7.2) (Russell

1988). Wheat, barley, pearl millet (*Pennisetum*), and sorghum (*Sorghum bicolor*) cultivated under traditional methods also yielded higher rates of return than did the aforementioned wild grasses (Russell 1988).

Cost-benefit factors other than those related to size probably mattered, too. For example, grains that for other reasons were more easily threshed, winnowed, and prepared into food than others were likely early foci of attention. More such cost/benefit and size data are required on wild progenitors of crop plants and numerous other exploited and unexploited wild species, but it seems that simple size, and its cost/benefit consequences, can explain why some of the plants that were taken under cultivation and domesticated were so chosen for early farming strategies. Prehistoric foragers/early farmers were unlikely to have given serious attention to plants that did not show potential of yielding a better profitability than the available wild or cultivated alternatives in the flora. It is also possible that some individual species with promise as potential cultivars were neglected because of the high productivity of their post-glacial terrestrial and marine ecosystems, e.g., in the arid highland valleys of Mexico and on the coast of Peru, which may have favored the persistence of foraging in those regions longer than in others after the Pleistocene ended (see Piperno and Pearsall 1998, 233–235).

A predicted result of such kinds of fitness-enhancing, rules of thumb, and similar sculptors of cultural plant exploitation would be that long periods of experimentation with a fairly large and diverse set of species, especially those with similar life history and nutritional qualities, would not occur before the establishment of productive farming systems. Such a scenario runs *contra* to co-evolutionary models of agricultural origins, which imply that protracted mutualisms between people and plants involving an unconsciously-motivated dispersal and increase of density of useful plants, largely resulting from human habitat interference around sites, preceded plant use intensification and cultivation (Rindos 1984). When such kinds of mutualisms began is not specified, nor considered important. Moreover, a high diversity of dietary species is expected for a long period of time before the emergence of agricultural economies under co-evolutionary scenarios, mostly because humans would not be deliberately choosing specific taxa for manipulation and production. The paucity of plant remains from archaeological sites dated to the late through terminal Pleistocene and early Holocene periods has made these issues difficult to evaluate. With regard, however, to an early exploitation of the Cucurbitaceae in the Americas, four cases exist, including two new examples from the lowland tropics, that shed some light on the problem.

The fruit rinds of virtually all genera in the Cucurbitaceae produce phytoliths recognizable in archaeological sediment samples (Piperno 1998; Piperno et al. 2000b). These highly durable mineralized structures provide a useful way to follow early exploitation in this important group in the tropical forest, where seeds and fruits are rarely preserved. At two Las Vegas preceramic sites in southwest Ecuador, where cultural deposits date to between ca. 10,800 and 7000 B.P. and sediments are phytolith-rich, the only cucurbit phytoliths derive from *Cucurbita* and *Lagenaria*. The latter is a gourd of African origin that was probably dispersed from the Old World to the New by ocean currents, and then utilized and widely disseminated by humans at an early time in the Americas. As discussed above, a significant increase in the size of *Cucurbita* phytoliths at Vegas between ca. 10,000 and 7000 B.P. indicates domestication during the early Holocene.

In Panama, rock shelters with phytolith-rich cultural deposits spanning the ca. 10,700 to 3000 B.P. period similarly demonstrate the exploitation of just *Cucurbita* and *Lagenaria*. The *Cucurbita* seems to have arrived as a domesticated plant by ca. 8000 B.P., and was probably the species *C. moschata* moving out of northern South America (Piperno et al. 2000b, unpublished data; Sanjur et al. 2002). Interestingly, a wild gourd, *C. sororia*, is apparently native to Panama, where it still can be found growing in

the vicinity of the sites. No evidence of its utilization by pre-Columbian people can be detected in the archaeobotanical records, however. Many other genera and species of cucurbits grow in these regions of Ecuador and Panama today, and would have been available when the sites were occupied. Moreover, systematic human disturbance of the Panamanian tropical forest through firing and small-scale forest clearing is ancient, dating to terminal Pleistocene times (Piperno and Pearsall 1998), and though many species of cucurbits would have responded to such activity by invading disturbed areas near habitations, there is no evidence from the archaeobotanical records that people ever utilized these plants.

A highly selective exploitation of the Cucurbitaceae is also evident in highland Mexico. Just three genera of cucurbits, *Cucurbita*, *Lagenaria*, and *Apodanthera* are represented in the well-preserved macro-fossil records from the Tehuacán (Cutler and Whitaker 1967) and Oaxaca Valley (Guilá Naquitz Cave) (Whitaker and Cutler 1986). Guilá Naquitz yielded the earliest evidence for domesticated *Cucurbita* (*C. pepo*) in Mesoamerica, dated to 9000 B.P. (Smith 1997b). Wild-type *Cucurbita* fruits and rinds were found in earlier deposits. Remains of *Apodanthera*, a wild melon whose seeds are eaten by indigenous people today, were scarce; the Tehuacán investigators raised the possibility they were modern intrusives. Local ecological conditions may have contributed to cucurbit representation at Guilá Naquitz (Whitaker and Cutler 1986), but such factors less convincingly explain the selection of utilized cucurbits at Tehuacán because other genera and species of the Cucurbitaceae were probably common in the barrancas near the sites. It is also noteworthy how the Tehuacán and Oaxaca inhabitants appear to have been drawing most of their plant calories and protein from a relatively small set of wild species available to them (Smith 1967, 1986), perhaps illustrating how food procurement efficiency shaped their overall subsistence strategies.

The number of sites for which information is available remains limited, but if this pattern persists it would indicate that early human experimentation with a substantial number of species in the Cucurbitaceae was not a typical strategy for those societies who developed or adopted the earliest domesticated squashes and gourds. Experimentation need not have been a necessary part of formulating a diet, and long, mutualistic associations between foragers and the plants they subsequently brought under cultivation and domesticated may not have been commonplace because energetic efficiency was a primary determinant of foraging decisions. Following simple optimal foraging strategies, and sometimes led by rules of thumb guides (bigger is often better), Pleistocene foragers arguably preferred resources providing higher return rates than the alternatives, some of which would nonetheless come to dominate some post-glacial ecosystems and diets in the interglacial world. Early Holocene foragers probably focused from the first on the most profitable wild species in this set, from which they created the earliest crop plants.

SHOULD WE BE SEEKING THE ORIGINS OF PLANT DOMESTICATION OR THE ORIGINS OF PLANT CULTIVATION? BEHAVIORAL INFLUENCES ON THE EVOLUTION OF DOMESTICATION

The commonplace focus on domestication as the preeminent event in people/plant relationships during the past 12,000 years is understandable, since domesticated plants provide higher yields, and economies based on them can easily spread—with or without people—and replace non-food-producing economies. This focus, however, makes some investigators uncomfortable, particularly those who work in the tropics. In the root- and tree-dominated crop plant systems of lower latitudes, plants often cannot be tidily placed into wild, cultivated, and domesticated categories. Rather, there are many intermediate stages between the manipulation of plants in their wild states and their movement to prepared plots (Balée and Gély 1989; Harlan 1992a; Harris 1989). Furthermore, prehistoric

horticultural practices in the tropics, like many still existing today, may have involved almost as many morphologically "wild" as "domesticated" plants, even after a protracted period of time, and it is unlikely that all early cultivated plants acquired characteristics associated with a domesticated status, either in part or in full (Harlan 1992a; Harris 1989).

These concerns dovetail with the growing realization among prehistorians working at higher latitudes that the appearance of recognizably domesticated plants may have been preceded by a protracted period of systematic cultivation of morphologically wild forms, called pre-domestication cultivation or non-domestication cultivation (Asch 1995; Hillman and Davies 1992; Kislev 1997). Cultivating a plant does not inexorably lead to the appearance of domesticated traits, and when the domestication process occurs, both biological—coming from the plant's genomic or life history traits—and behavioral—coming from the people who are cultivating the plant—influences are often involved. Hillman and Davies (1992) have shown very well how it takes the right combination of harvesting and sowing strategies to convert wild wheat and barley into domesticated strains, even though only a few, seemingly malleable genetic loci control the relevant phenotypic features in these plants. If, for example, early cultivated cereals were harvested by the most common, and least effort, method of gathering grasses employed by recent foragers who heavily rely on grass seeds—beating grain heads into baskets—rare, tougher-rachised phenotypes would not have been advantaged, and domestication as such would have been stymied (Hillman and Davies 1992). It is only when people who, for whatever reasons, made the decision to harvest grains with sickles or by uprooting whole plants that the path to domestication proceeded.

As one of the world's leading experts on the genetics of maize describes, the creation of maize from its wild ancestor teosinte, *Zea mays* subsp. *parviglumis*, similarly may not have been a straightforward event, resulting as it did from: "a series of improbable mutations . . . the conversion of teosinte into maize is so improbable that it is difficult to imagine that it happened several times" (Doebley 1990, 16, 24). At least five different regions of the teosinte genome had to be changed under cultivation before the plant acquired the architecture, soft and reduced glumes, and cob that turned it into maize. It seems possible that at some point during the process humans began to consciously choose some of the harvesting, or sowing, or storage strategies they knew were more likely to result in the increase of plants possessing desirable, domesticated traits.

The possibility of an early horizon of pre- or non-domestication cultivation is currently receiving more attention in the Old World than in the New (but see Asch 1995 and Bray 2000), but some good candidates for non-domestication cultivation have already been described from highland Mesoamerica. Seeds of *Setaria* spp. (foxtail millet) were present in high quantity in human feces from the Tehuacán Valley by ca. 7400 B.P., and at the Ocampo Caves, Tamaulipas, Mexico by ca. 5400 B.P. (Callen 1967a, b). This is before maize can be demonstrated by present evidence in either region, potentially making *Setaria* the earliest cereal of the Mexican highlands. At Ocampo, the species was identified as *Setaria geniculata*, a perennial grass, and an increase in grain size over an approximately 1500-year-long period attesting to a degree of artificial selection was noted. Many of the *Setaria* grains seem to have been no larger than those typical of wild plants, however. At Guilá Naquitz Cave, high quantities of a type of morphologically wild runner bean (*Phaseolus* spp.) suggested to the excavator that between ca. 10,600 and 8500 B.P., people may have been artificially increasing their density by cultivating them (Flannery 1986a, b). If true, the runner beans would be the New World's first cultivated legume. In these cases, therefore, domestication was not a rapid process and plant cultivation did not inevitably lead to phenotypic changes.

Plant domestication is perhaps best thought of as a form of speciation in the way that some biologists conceptualize speciation, as a relatively rare event brought about by sets of different processes sometimes involving both genetic and ecologically-driven behavioral attributes, that may or may not require long temporal periods. What may *not* have been so rare in agricultural evolution, and were probably more commonplace occurrences during end-Pleistocene and post-glacial times than we thought, were non-domestication cultivation and protracted instances of pre-domestication cultivation. One might argue, in fact, that the crucial shift was when people turned to the practices of preparing plots specified for the propagation of plants, and repeatedly sowed and harvested in such plots, whether or not these practices led to phenotypically-altered plants recognizable as domesticates.

Such practices required, or perhaps forced, changes in mobility, division of labor, stone tool technology, food storage strategies, and settlement and social attributes from those characteristic of foragers to those more typical of full-time farmers. Unlike the practices of protecting, tending, and casually replacing wild species in their natural settings, this behavioral adaptation was disposed to inducing the development of superior, domesticated species, e. g., with non-shattering rachises, large and naked grains, edible fruit flesh, and large and non-poisonous roots, and the establishment and spread of food-producing economies. When this economic strategy emerged is an easier question to answer at present than where and how many times it arose. The evidence is clear on this point—as early as during the final stages of the Pleistocene, but not earlier than that, when anatomically and apparently cognitively modern people faced for the first time the profound ecological perturbations that accompanied the close of a major glacial cycle.

Perhaps some day, with more perfect archaeological records, we will be able to discern in how many regions of the world foragers intensified their use of post-glacial resources in ways that resulted in the systematic propagation of certain plant species, and then we can speak with more confidence to the issues of how and how often food production independently emerged.

Until that time, we should be cautious about assuming (e.g., Rowley-Conwy 2001) that only rarely did hunters and gatherers become food producers in prehistory.

BEHAVIORAL ECOLOGY AS A GENERAL MODEL FOR THE ORIGINS OF PLANT FOOD PRODUCTION

As students of human behavior, we want to understand why and how such a crucial development as agriculture arose. Those of us who are inclined to think in ecological and evolutionary terms and look for parsimony will pursue universal explanations. This is not to say that we have little interest in how the origins of food production subsequently led to local economic and social developments in various regions around the world, only that our immediate focus is on the origins, not the subsequent local developments. Regardless of our theoretical proclivities, we must incorporate intentionality into our models because conscious human decision-making must have driven important aspects of the process (Watson 1995). Changes that were brought to time spent in foraging, search area size, scheduling of resource acquisition, and settlement mobility (Flannery 1986a), as well as the particular species that occupied the first root and seed beds, are a few examples. Moreover, the decision to cultivate plants was surely not hidden in the sub-conscious of any beginning farmer, but was underlain by a set of well-conceived and thought out expectations, which sometimes were met and sometimes not. I suspect that nascent farmers were confident that by growing some of the plant species they had been harvesting in the wild, they could increase their yield of food per unit area of land exploited, decrease their search area for resources, and not work harder than they had been previously. Regardless of whether this is true or not, nothing in my reading of the behavioral ecological literature indicates to me that short-term intentionality should be denied as a source of the cultural traits and variability on which natural or cultural selection act.

The search for general patterns underlain by universally applicable processes is a fundamental pursuit of science. It leads to "testable truths," unlike explanations usually advanced in the humanities that result in "persuasive truths" (Ridley 2001), for which I prefer the less gentle term persuasive speculation. As most of us know first hand, it is easy to persuasively speculate, and harder to formulate theories, explicitly lay out their assumptions, and recover empirical data that judge how reliable they are so that we can alter them if need be. Until not very long ago, we were handcuffed to persuasive speculations by methodological limitations on the recovery of dietary and paleoenvironmental data, but we increasingly have at our disposal the right types and combinations of archaeobotanical and other techniques to gather knowledge so that it can be distilled into testable truths.

As a first stride when contemplating a nomothetic explanation, if it can be shown that anything went during the early development of food production—that is, if its initial stages proceeded at widely different times along many disparate pathways in its cradles of origin—then a search for generalizing processes should cease. The near-synchroneity of food production origins in at least seven widely dispersed and ecologically disparate regions of the world, however, should be our first signal that a single, underlying process may have been at work everywhere. That these synchronous origins occurred when or shortly after the world's fauna and flora were experiencing profound, climatically-driven shifts should then lead us to consider universal theories grounded in ecology and evolution.

In considering the transition to food production as an evolutionary process whose workings were put in motion at the end of the ice age, but whose outcome varied from region to region depending on local socioecological circumstances, foraging theory satisfies, perhaps uniquely, the requirements of a general model. When, on the present evidence, the systematic cultivation of plant foods did not follow upon the end-Pleistocene ecological perturbations, human responses nonetheless triggered considerable dietary broadening with shifts to r-selected plant and animal dietary items, reductions in mobility, and technological innovations, all of which were uniquely characteristic of end- and post-glacial times. These transformations are the expected answers to resource change and instability when food procurement strategies largely conform to the logic of foraging theory, and they are documented in virtually every region of the world where a good archaeological record exists (e.g., Cowan and Watson 1992; Flannery 1969; Price 2000a; Price and Gebauer 1995a; Rick and Erlandson 2000). That they also are necessary prerequisites to practicing food production as we understand it, whether as a pristine or secondary development, further underscores my point.

Other explanations for the "broad spectrum revolution," such as population pressure (Cohen 1977) and risk reduction (Flannery 1986b), or as a response to the new availability of resources in the post-Pleistocene world (McCorriston and Hole 1991) do not apply as equally well in different regions of the globe, which saw substantial variability in all of these conditions, as does foraging theory. The fact that many plants apparently cannot provide the energetic return rates needed to favor the selection of food-producing strategies in their local ecological spheres helps to elucidate the question of why broad-spectrum economies did not become food-producing economies everywhere upon the termination of the Pleistocene. Foraging theory allows that subsistence decisions are reversible, so one might guess that in the cases where cultivating plants was attempted but was not profitable enough, nascent farmers returned to full-time foraging. These cases, though interesting, will not easily be documented archaeologically.

It was sometimes the case, as in Europe (Price 2000a), that decisions taken by indigenous foraging societies about how to exploit the post-glacial biota pre-adapted them, in ways both ecological and social, to the incorporation of exogenous, domesticated plants and animals. That the gene pools of some modern Europeans have primarily Upper Paleolithic and not Neolithic roots (Gibbons 2000) probably has much to do with the fact that the post-Pleistocene occupants of Europe responded to the end of the Pleistocene with economically rational subsistence strategies.

In conclusion, behavioral ecology is a powerful model for studying the transition from foraging to food production because it offers testable hypotheses supported by existing data for the following fundamental questions: (1) why human societies initiated plant cultivation; because its incorporation into subsistence economies resulted in a more energetically-efficient strategy than full-time hunting and gathering; (2) when they initiated it; it became a better strategy when ice age terrestrial and coastal resources were replaced by those of the present interglacial period; (3) which plants they chose for their early gardens and fields; cultural search images and resource choice may have been fundamentally shaped by rules of thumb guides as to which resources are most profitable, themselves shaped by Darwinian selection; and (4) how they practiced early farming; in the tropics, small-scale planting in plots near residences provided profitable alternatives to full-time foraging in the post-glacial forest. In the Neotropics, foraging theory can also explain why many important crop plants were domesticated in the seasonal, not in the ever-wet lowland forest. It was in the seasonally dry forest that the most dramatic shifts in the distribution and abundance of resources and decline of foraging efficiency occurred, and here also existed plants that provided the return rates necessary for the emergence of food-producing strategies.

This is not to say that behavioral ecology will provide all the answers to the questions we ask. But we can best understand which pathways toward food production may have been motivated more by social and other imperatives outside the spheres of ecology and evolution when we have tested the assumptions of foraging theory and identified which of them are supported or violated.

NOTES

1. The following working definitions are used throughout to maintain clarity as to what kinds of food production systems are under discussion. Cultivation and farming refer to the preparation of plots specified for plant propagation and repeated planting and harvesting in such plots. A cultivated plant or cultivar refers to those that are planted and harvested, regardless of their domesticated status. Horticulture and agriculture denote, respectively, small-scale plantings (e.g., house gardens), which typically contain a range of dietary, medicinal, and utilitarian species, and large-scale—in the tropics usually swidden or slash-and-burn—field systems, in which domesticated plants are common and often dominate as staple crops. Domesticated species are those that have been genetically altered from the wild form through human artificial selection and normally are dependent on human actions for reproduction. Food production is used to envelope all types of plot preparation and planting behavior including cultivation, horticulture, and agriculture.

2. Because I am exploring the applicability of optimal foraging theory, I largely leave aside the issues of risk reduction and resource security. There is substantial evidence that in simple groups of tropical foragers and horticulturists, food sharing in the form of extensive household exchange is the most important tactic used to counter risk (e.g., Hames 1990; Hill et al. 1987). Furthermore, risk-generated responses that alter the diet breadth at the expense of energetic efficiency are predicted to occur only when the expected food intake is much higher or lower than the minimum needed to prevent a shortfall (Winterhalder 1986, 1990). These conditions probably did not characterize tropical America on the eve of food production; people were neither awash in food surpluses nor experiencing severe short-falls. For these reasons, it is likely that risk-sensitive behaviors assumed more prominent roles in structuring human economic decisions in the tropical forest after the development of agricultural systems and village life.

3. Despite the fact that major constraints on human settlement and population number in tropical forests have often been linked to protein (game) abundance, a considerable amount of evidence indicates that obtaining calories may pose more serious problems for some foragers. Milton (1984), for example, showed that fisher-farmers in Amazonia existed at much higher population densities than neighboring hunter-gatherers primarily because they had an ample supply of carbohydrates even though they experienced seasonal shortages of protein. The hunter-gatherers were limited mainly by severe seasonal and annual shortages of carbohydrates from wild resources. A similar situation is documented in the rain forest of Zaire, where Mbuti pygmies, although having ample meat resources year-round, experience severe seasonal shortages of starch-dense foods from wild plants (Hart and Hart 1986).

4. The Amazon region offers what are among the poorest and the richest environments for human exploitation in the world. The best habitats, the floodplains (*varzea*) of the middle and lower stretches of the river, account for only about two percent of the land area of the Basin, are rich in wild protein and carbohydrates, and would have given early societies little incentive to cultivate plants. The poorest environments, the upland forests, have poor soils and low useable plant and animal biomass, and were probably too harsh to support a transition from foraging to farming. These factors may account for the extra-Amazonian or Amazon-periphery origins of most important Neotropical crop plants (see Figure 7.4).

5. I recognize that comparisons of modern tropical foraging and farming are drawn from instances of evolved horticultural traditions, and from ecosystems that have been altered from those first encountered by prehistoric foragers. These concerns are balanced by the facts that estimates for foraging efficiency are not derived from obviously degraded environments (e.g., the Aché and Machiguenga live in species-rich tropical forest where game animals are still common), and that modern slash-and-burn planting systems are considerably more labor intensive than the simple door-yard, garden horticulture envisaged for the earliest tropical farming, which did not require extensive land preparation. The modern analogs, while not perfect, are acceptable for framing the argument.

6. All carbon 14 dates in the manuscript are uncalibrated. For information on calibrated years for all dates, see Figure 7.3.

8

Costly Signaling, the Sexual Division of Labor, and Animal Domestication in the Andean Highlands

Mark Aldenderfer

Relatively little is known of the emergence of animal husbandry in the Andean highlands. In this chapter, I explore the use of diet breadth models, costly signaling theory, and other models derived from human behavioral ecology to examine how animal husbandry appeared around 4400 years ago in the Rio Asana valley of far southern Peru. It is generally accepted that animal husbandry was adopted in the region as a risk amelioration strategy. However, since animal herds need time to grow before they can be harvested, this seems unlikely. Instead, a model that examines differences in men's and women's provisioning strategies within a costly signaling framework shows how animal husbandry could have been adopted not to buffer risk, but instead to augment and extend men's status competition as long as women were able to feed their families. The model helps to explain changes in women's labor allocation, status, and roles across the transition from a forging to a herding subsistence strategy.

Although our understanding of the empirical outlines of the process of plant domestication in the Andean highlands has improved substantially over the past 30 years, it remains the case that models of the domestication process for the region are few. Most research conducted on the topic has been focused upon the identification of potential cultigens and their domestication status, dating their contexts accurately, and identifying general patterns in the distribution of wild, cultivated or domesticated species across the highlands as well as into other adjacent ecological zones (Castro and Tarrago 1992; J. Hawkes 1989, 1990; Pearsall 1992, 1995). Compared to the rest of the world, however, scholars of South America have yet to develop a robust corpus of models for the domestication process.

There is good and bad in this. The bad is that it is difficult to compare in a systematic way domestication trajectories in South America, such as they are known, with other, better-studied areas of the world. The good, however, is that because relatively few models have been created, the best practices of modeling from other historical contexts can be borrowed and employed in the region. One of the more compelling sources of these models is human behavioral ecology (HBE).

My goal in this paper is to outline how models derived from HBE, specifically costly signaling theory, can provide useful insights into how plants and animals were domesticated in the Andean highlands. For this paper, I define the highlands as that set of lifezones that are found within an elevation range between 3000–4800 m above sea level, and although they are characterized by considerable local variability due to the structure of high mountain and high plateau environments (Aldenderfer 1998, 2–4), at a more general level they include the high valley systems of the arid western flanks of the Andes, wet and dry puna (or altiplano), and the *suni*, which is the puna environment found in the Lake Titicaca basin (Aldenderfer 1989, 120–126). This elevation range is consistent with the "Andean high elevation agricultural complex," defined by Pearsall (1992, 196), which includes cultigens such as the potato (*Solanum tuberosum*; and other Solanaceae), oca (*Oxalis tuberosa*), ullucu (*Ullucus tuberosum*), maca (*Lepidium meyenii*), quinoa (*Chenopodium quinoa*), canihua (*Chenopodium pallidicaule*), and mashua (*Tropaeolum tuberosum*). All but mashua and maca became important subsistence staples for the pre-conquest peoples of this region.

I am specifically concerned with the development of agro-pastoral economies in the Andes between 4600 and 4400 B.P.[1], and how these might have emerged from a foraging adaptation (Aldenderfer 2002). The Andes have much more in common with the Near East and Africa than with the rest of the Americas in this case, for it is the only New World locus of animal domestication of significant economic importance. Both the llama (*Lama glama*), used primarily as a cargo animal but also for meat, and the alpaca (*Lama pacos*), used primarily as a source of high quality wool, were domesticated from indigenous camelid species (the guanaco, *Lama guanicoe*, and vicuña, *Vicugna vicugna*, respectively). Further, current models of the domestication process in the Andes assert that animals were domesticated before (Hesse 1982a,

b; Wheeler 1995) or simultaneously with plants (Kuznar 1993; Pearsall 1989). These models have much in common with those proposed by Marshall and Hildebrand (2002) for Africa, where they show that while cattle may have been herded as early as 9000 B.P., plant domesticates did not appear until 4000 B.P., and that by Russell (1988), who has made a similar argument for the temporal priority of animal domestication in both North Africa and the Near East.

Those models giving temporal priority to animal domestication over plant cultivation are based upon the assertion that animal herding would have been a more reliable subsistence strategy in patchy, unpredictable environments than any strategy reliant primarily upon plant procurement. In Marshall and Hildebrand's model, foraging peoples focused upon hunting would have turned to the herding of animals so as to avoid or buffer risk, while in Russell's, hunters would have turned to herding as the return rates from hunting were diminished by population growth. In the Andes, Hesse (1982a, b) has made an argument for the origins of camelid herding in the hyperarid environs of northern Chile around 4000 B.P., with plant domesticates appearing in the diet at least 2000 years later. His reasoning is similar to that found in the Old World examples: in risky, patchy environments, animal herding buffered risk better than did any strategy based upon plants. In contrast, Pearsall (1989) and Kuznar (1993) have created models of a mutualistic, or co-evolutionary, process that highlights the simultaneous domestication of chenopods and the husbandry of camelids. Here, once low-ranked plants are added to the diet they increased in abundance in animal pens, corrals, and middens associated with habitations.

While each of these models is plausible as an explanation of the origins of herding from a foraging lifeway, none is entirely satisfactory. Russell, for example, calculates an optimal diet that includes secondary products, such as milk, and then compares this diet to various agricultural yields. As Alvard and Kuznar (2001, 306) note, while secondary products such as blood and milk may have reduced the opportunity costs of animals such that it was more profitable to herd, rather than hunt, them, it is unlikely that these products were the initial stimulus for herding. As for herding animals to buffer risk, Alvard and Kuznar (2001) have shown that while in the long run animals, especially small-bodied herbivores, may become a reliable and consistent resource, when compared to plants, it is hard to see how foragers could turn to herding rapidly to buffer short term risks since herding necessarily creates a significantly delayed return on initial investment. In such instances, foragers may well have had to continue reliance upon a mixed economy until herd sizes grew to a size sufficient to simultaneously serve the subsistence needs of the herders, while providing a sufficiently large herd size for reproduction to occur. The co-evolutionary models of Pearsall and Kuznar offer one way in which potential herders could create sufficiently large herds while buffering long-delayed returns on investment.

But a more difficult problem that none of these models can overcome is the lack of consideration of process. The transition to a herding lifeway is only partially about calculating an optimal diet in a particular setting, because any explanation of the process must also account for probable changes in social relationships and the allocation of labor as well. An *in situ* transformation of subsistence economy from a foraging to a herding lifeway would have necessarily involved significant changes in rights of access to land, the disposition of pastoral products, the division of labor, and measures of prestige and status (Ingold 1976; Paine 1971; Smith 1990; Aldenderfer 2002, 390–91). Herders tend to define ownership of land within kin groups, and deny others access to it. Rights of access to pastoral products lies within the domestic sphere, and are not generally shared beyond the household. A sexual division of labor is common in pastoral societies, but the role of women's labor in these societies stands in sharp contrast to that of women in foraging societies. Whereas in most foraging societies women are usually the

most important provisioners of their families, in pastoral societies, their direct contribution to the diet is far smaller. Further, women have limited rights of disposition of the products of pastoral production, which instead tends to be controlled by men. While women's labor is important to societal reproduction, women in herding societies have lower status than women in foraging groups. Finally, men get status and prestige by having large herds and by being able to provide kinsmen, especially sons, with animals to start their own herds. In contrast, men in foraging societies tend to obtain status through successful hunting and the consequent sharing of meat beyond the domestic unit.

What is needed, then, are models capable of defining an optimal diet and that can simultaneously capture the changes in labor, status, and the decision making process of agents engaged in a transition from a foraging lifeway to one based upon herding. To that end, I blend two approaches frequently employed in human behavioral ecology: diet breadth models and costly signaling theory as a means by which to explore this transition. I will use the diet breadth model to examine men's and women's contributions to diet during this transition, and then turn to costly signaling theory to explain how men may have turned to herding rather than hunting within a carefully defined environmental and social context.

I will explore the utility of this blended approach through a case study of the transition from hunting and gathering to herding at Asana, which is located in the high sierra-puna rim environment of the western flanks of the south-central Andes (Aldenderfer 1998; Figure 8.1). At Asana, the transition from a hunting and gathering lifeway to one dominated by herding seems quite abrupt as measured in archaeological time. The final cultural level of the Qhuna phase (foragers) at Asana is dated to 4580 B.P., whereas the first level of the following Awati phase (herders) dates to 4340 B.P. The dates overlap at two standard deviations, and are thus statistically indistinguishable. Putting this aside for the sake of discussion, the transition could have taken as few as

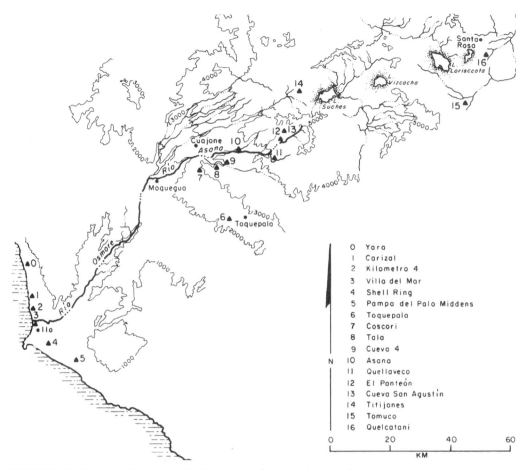

FIGURE 8.1. The Río Asana drainage showing the locations of major Archaic period sites.

0   Yoro
1   Carizal
2   Kilometro 4
3   Villa del Mar
4   Shell Ring
5   Pampa del Palo Middens
6   Toquepala
7   Coscori
8   Tala
9   Cueva 4
10 Asana
11 Quellaveco
12 El Panteón
13 Cueva San Agustín
14 Titijones
15 Tomuco
16 Quelcatani

KM

20 years and as many as 500. Importantly, there is no stratigraphic discontinuity between the two levels; no discernable sterile layer separates them, and neither layer is very thick. However, the archaeological record clearly indicates that a fundamental change in lifeway took place in a relatively short time at Asana.

DIET BREADTH MODELS

Diet breadth models are some of the simplest, yet most powerful, models used in optimal foraging theory. The fundamental premise of the model is concerned with predicting whether a forager will or will not take a resource upon encounter. Resource acquisition is divided into two parts: the costs of searching for the resource, and the costs associated with processing it once

captured or selected. Resources are ranked by their post-encounter return rates, which are simply the measure of energy return (as measured by some currency) after search and processing costs have been considered (Kelly 1995, 78). The decision to take a resource upon encounter thus depends on the quality of the resource, its density (which affects search costs), and its processing costs (which affects return rates). The key assumption of the model is that the forager is attempting to maximize energy returns. As Kelly (1995, 86–87) notes, the model makes a number of important observations about the composition of human diets: resource abundance alone cannot be used to predict the presence of a resource in a diet, as search costs for high-return-rate resources decrease, diets will expand regardless of the abundance of a low-ranked resource, and if a higher-ranked resource becomes available, lower-ranked resources will be dropped from the diet no matter what their abundance. Variants of the model have been applied with considerable success to ethnographic (Hawkes, et al. 1982; Hill and Kaplan 1992; Winterhalder and Smith 2000) and archeological contexts (Simms 1987; Broughton 1997; Madsen and Schmitt 1998; Stiner and Munro 2002).

COSTLY SIGNALING THEORY

Costly signaling theory is based upon the premise "that expensive behavioral or morphological signals are designed to convey honest information benefiting both signalers and the recipients of these signals." (Smith and Bliege Bird 2000, 246). In effect, it is all about how honest communication is delivered and received. Signals delivered must convey accurate and reliable information about some important underlying quality of the signaler, such as overall health status, resource control, competitiveness, cleverness, or ability. To be effective, the generation of signals must impose a cost on the signaler that is directly linked to the quality being advertised. The requirement that the signal be costly is important, because it reduces the frequency of bluffing or false signals. By imposing a steep cost on the signaler, it ensures that the recipients of the signal are convinced that the signaler indeed has the qualities advertised. The payoff to the signaler

> comes from being chosen as a mate or ally or deferred to as a dominant in mating, cooperative, or competitive contexts, respectively. The payoff to the signal recipient comes from the usefulness of the information inferred from the signal: he or she should be able to evaluate the signaler's qualities as competitor, mate, or ally by attending to the signal rather than through more costly means of assessing the signaler's abilities, qualities, or motivations. (Smith and Bliege Bird 2000, 246)

As applied to humans, costly signaling theory has been used to explain so-called "wasteful" behaviors, such expensive public displays and ceremonies, and importantly, sub-optimal subsistence decisions. Sosis (2000) shows that from an optimality perspective, Ifaluk men should seldom engage in torch fishing, which is physically strenuous and characterized by very low return rates. They should instead adopt other strategies. Sosis argues that torch fishing is an honest signal that advertises a man's strong work ethic, because it is observable (it takes place at night and the audience, particularly women who have few other ways of obtaining reliable information about men's work, can easily track the activities), costly (it takes a great deal of energy to hunt in this fashion), reliable (it is directly tied to provisioning and resource consumption), and is beneficial (men will presumably be selected as a potential mate or ally, and women will have better information for choosing their mates).

Among men's activities in foraging societies, hunting has been identified by many ethnographers as a prime venue for display and signaling, particularly in the pursuit of large game (Hawkes and Bliege Bird 2002). Although women are known to hunt small game and rodents, cross-culturally, men spend most of their effort pursuing large-bodied animals. Moreover, in most foraging societies, meat is considered a collective good, and is widely shared beyond the hunter's immediate household. As Hawkes and Bliege Bird (2002, 59) show, traditional explanations of this activity pattern—that hunting is the most efficient energy or protein extraction strategy and that women do not contribute substantial amounts of animal protein to the diet—are invalid in some empirical settings, and it has been observed that men often hunt large-bodied game when other prey types and choices offer superior return rates.

Hunting is now widely viewed through the lens of costly signaling theory as a kind of competitive display, wherein men signal through their efforts and successes that they are indeed worthy mates, reliable allies, and potential leaders. Although men may simultaneously provision their families, they may also use meat as an honest signal within a framework of status competition. Shared meat is not necessarily a nutritional benefit that will be returned to the hunter in some scheme of balanced reciprocity but is instead a demonstration of skill and prowess that will be repaid in other currencies (Wiessner 2002). Viewed in this manner, the hunting and sharing of large-bodied game can be an honest signal in that it is observable (game is widely distributed, and all present directly see and benefit from that distribution), costly (in that men may have to work longer hours or pursue prey species distant from the residential base; see Hill and Hawkes 1983), reliable (meat is obviously tied to provisioning), and finally, beneficial (there are direct nutritional benefits to the consumption of meat, and the provider gets immediate attention from the process; they may also enjoy long-term benefits). In short, while hunting may provide nutritional benefits, it can also enhance one's competitive advantage vis-à-vis others while simultaneously providing benefits to others.

I will use costly signaling theory in this paper to explore how hunters may have made a decision to husband and conserve prey not on the basis of conservation being a more efficient subsistence strategy, but one that took a familiar activity—hunting—and transformed the status benefits derived from it through competitive display into another arena of resource procurement—herding.

THE ECOLOGICAL SETTING OF ASANA

Asana is found on the north bank of the Río Asana, one of the major tributary streams of the Río Osmore (or Moquegua; Figure 8.1). This perennial stream courses through two major environmental zones: the sierra and puna rim. The sierra can be divided into two zones, the lower high sierra (2500–3400 m) and the upper high sierra (3400–3800 m). Significantly, Asana is found at the ecotone between these two zones. The lower high sierra is drier, and consequently, is characterized by lower primary productivity when compared to the upper high sierra. Eleva-

tions above 3800 m are described as puna rim, which consists of a series of plant communities found in an elevational range from 3800–4800 m and which are interdigitated in the narrow valleys and gorges of the headwaters of the major streams and their tributary *quebradas* along the western cordillera of the Andes. Unlike the puna, which is characterized by broad, open plains dotted with springs and cut with numerous streams, the puna rim is constrained by steep slopes, and consequently, plant communities found within it are smaller and more tightly packed.

PLANT RESOURCES FOR HUMANS AND ANIMALS

In the Río Asana drainage, the lower high sierra (2500–3400 m) is dominated by four plant communities. Aside from the small streamside community that contains small evergreen shrubs and widely scattered *molle* trees (*Schinus molle*), the other three communities are dominated by *Franseria meyeniana* (Figure 8.2), a perennial shrub, and include a number of other grasses and herbs, the most important being *Chenopodium petiolare*, a close relative of the domesticated Andean grain quinoa (*Chenopodium quinoa*). These communities differ primarily in plant density, and therefore, productivity. Kuznar (1993, Table 8.1) has estimated that one of these communities (*Franseria meyeniana* dry aspect) has high densities of *Chenopodium petiolare*, making it very productive. However, plant densities in each of these communities are highly dependent upon rainfall. Therefore, provided that seasonal rains were sufficient, this represents a productive zone of use during and immediately after the rainy season.

The upper high sierra (3400–3800 m) has the most complex ecology in the region, but two plant communities—*Fabiana weberbauerill*, regular and dry aspect, and *Balbisia-Verbena-Diplostephium*—comprise about 42% of its area. Both are good sources of high quality forage for animals, but of all the upper high sierra communities, only *Balbisia* has significant densities of *Chenopodium petiolare* (ca. 17 kg seeds/ha). Two different communities—tola *Cherodesma*

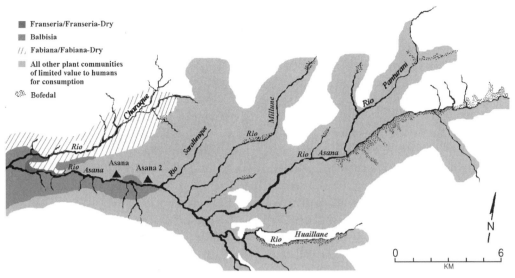

FIGURE 8.2. Location of high-quality plant patches in the Río Asana valley.

and tola pampa—are important from 3600 to 3800 m. The former is rather sparse, but since it is barren, annual grasses and herbs grow thickly and rapidly given sufficient rain, and often attract animals to them. Tola pampa is dominated by bunch grasses and tola (*Parastrephia lepidophyllum*). This community has a high productivity, but because its dominant plant is not preferred forage for any species, it has little resource potential for humans. Another important community is the tolar, which is dominated by tola and bunch grasses, most commonly *Stipa ichu*. While extensive (35% of upper high sierra land), and characterized by high productivity, the palatability of its major species for the indigenous animals is low.

Another important community is that based upon the queñua (*Polylepis besseri*), the only major tree species found in the high sierra. This community comes in two variants—an open forest that is found on hill slopes ranging in elevation from 3800–4000 m, and a closed forest found along the stream course. Together, these account for ca. four percent of the total area of the high sierra. These communities are the natural habitat of the taruca (*Hippocamelus antisensis*), but they can also be used by the guanaco. Finally,

very small bofedales (*Distichia moor*), are found scattered throughout the high sierra. Although small in area, they are the preferred forage of the vicuña (*Vicugna vicugna;* see discussion below).

The vegetation of the puna rim is less varied than that of the high sierra. Two landforms predominate: dry lands (pampa) and wet lands (bofedal) (see Figure 8.2). The dry lands are dominated by bunch grasses (i.e. *Calamagrostis amonea, C. brevifolia, Stipa ichu, S. brachyphylla*) and composite shrubs (*Parastrephia lepidophylum, P. lucida, Baccharis macrophylla, Chersodoma iodopappa*). Wet lands are dominated by mats of *Distichia muscoides* (*t'iña*) and *Oxychloe andinum* (*khuli*). Upon this mat grows a number of grasses including *Calamagrostis crysantha* and *C. rigescens*. Bofedales are important sources of forage for herbivores in the puna rim.

The puna rim is dominated by two plant communities: pampa (35%) and puna desert (37%). The pampa is similar to the high sierra pampa although it contains less palatable bunch grasses. The puna desert is typical of the dry puna of southern Peru, Bolivia, and northern Chile, and it is a barren and unproductive region avoided by the Aymara pastoralists of the region. Although puna bofedales comprise only

2.5% of puna lands, they are the most critical resource for puna rim pastoralists and for the vicuña. These are highly productive wetlands, and vicuña cannot thrive without them.

MAJOR ANIMAL SPECIES:
GUANACO, TARUCA, VICUÑA

Three large herbivores are found in the Rio Asana valley: guanaco (*Lama guanicoe*), taruca (*Hippocamelus antisensis*), and vicuña (*Vicugna vicugna*). Each species is characterized by territorial family groups and bands or troops of males living between them. Of the South American camelids, the guanaco has by far the greatest behavioral flexibility in terms of range, diet, and social behavior (Franklin 1982). They have an elevational range from sea level to approximately 4200 m, and depending upon resource availability and abundance, are either migratory on a seasonal basis, or fully territorial. How far they migrate, however, is not clear, although Franklin (1982, 481) notes that they may move up and down within valley systems, or laterally between river valleys. Unfortunately, there are no studies available that have identified migratory ranges nor the severity of the conditions required for migration. Guanaco can both graze and browse, and this is the basis of their flexibility. They are known to eat grasses, forbs, and shrubs, are able to digest forage more effectively than most domesticated animals, including the domesticated camelids, and can inhabit extremely arid environments (Franklin 1982, 482).

Guanacos typically have a number of social groups, the two most important being the family group, which includes a single adult male, females, and their offspring younger than 15 months, and the male group (Franklin 1982, 482). When possible, the male of the family group defends a feeding territory year-round, although females without young may leave the group during the austral summer. Franklin (1975, 168) notes that guanaco in the high sierra of the Peruvian Andes maintain family territories. Guanaco family territories in Tierra del Fuego averaged 29.5 ha, varying with forage quality (Franklin 1982, 482), and average densi-

ties of guanaco ranged between 1 guanaco/8 ha to 1/19.2 ha (Franklin 1975, 194–195). Male groups consist of immature individuals living well away from the family groups, and while they apparently have no defended territory, they can generally be found in a single area or zone. Solo, non-territorial males circulate around and between these different groups. Franklin (1975, 195–96) reports that of the 326 guanacos observed at Guanacón of the central Peruvian Andes, 74% were in family groups while 23% were in either male troops or were solitary animals.

Group size and density are highly variable, and family groups are regulated more by the fluidity of social structure and the aggressiveness of the territorial male. As Franklin (1982, 483) notes, while group territory size declines with higher densities of preferred forage, mean group size apparently is not directly predictable from forage quantity alone. Kuznar (1990, 126) suggests that the maintenance of family territories tends to keep average group size significantly below carrying capacity predicted by forage density.

Unlike the guanaco, the vicuña are strictly grazers, and their preferred forage is the vegetation that is typically found at puna rim and puna bofedales. Moreover, as Franklin (1982, 477) notes, the animal is an obligate drinker, meaning that the animal must drink water once or twice a day during the dry season (see also Vilá and Roig 1992). Because of these limits, the vicuña has relatively little behavioral flexibility, and is found at elevation ranges from 4200 to 4800 m. Because of their diet, then, they are essentially tied to bofedales large enough to maintain group size, although they are able to eat bunch grasses when necessary.

According to Franklin (1982, 477), "vicuña social organization is based upon a year-round system of resource defense polygyny with permanent feeding and sleeping territories." Like the guanaco, the vicuña have two basic social groups: family groups and male groups. Permanent family groups consist of a single male and associated females and their offspring. These groups occupy the best areas of pasture within the bofedales. Average family group compositions have been reported as 1 male, 4.4 females, 1.84 young at Huaylarco (Koford 1957, 164), and 1 male, 3.2 females, and 1.9 yearlings at Pampas Galeras (Franklin 1982, 478). The territory sizes of vicuña family groups average between 12.8 and 20 ha (Franklin 1982, 479; Koford 1957, 170). Data from Parque Lauca, Chile, suggests that 1.01 to 2.67 ha bofedal lands can support a single adult vicuña (CONAF 1983, 23–28). Group size remains constant year-round, and changes only when juvenile males are expelled from the group or a new female is acquired by the dominant male. These groups are essentially sedentary since their feeding and sleeping territories are generally close.

Two other family groups have also been defined: the marginal territory group and the mobile family group (Franklin 1982, 479). Both of these groups are slightly smaller than the permanent group since they occupy less productive territories. Because of this, they are obligated to move more frequently for forage and water. Consequently, these groups are slightly less predictable in terms of their location than are permanent family groups. Male groups are composed of non-territorial males, with group size ranging from two to over 100 animals (Franklin 1982, 479). These animals live in poorer habitat types, and move long distances between feeding areas to avoid conflict with territorial males. Male groups, then, have the greatest mobility and range when compared to all other social groups, and further, have the greatest variability in group size. Of all of the social groups of vicuña, then, the male group, while the largest, is the most unpredictable in location. Unlike the guanaco, territory size, group composition, and population density for the three family groups of the vicuña are highly correlated with forage density, and according to Franklin (1982, 480), this is apparently due to the territorial male's ability to defend and maintain the boundaries of the territory. This means that these groups are very predictable in terms of size, composition, and location. Koford (1957), in his study of the vicuña population of

Huaylarco, notes that of the 200 vicuña that made up the local population, 125 were in family bands (62.5%), with the remainder (75; 37.5%) in male troops.

As a cryptic species, taruca prefer highly dissected environments generally near forested habitats such as groves of queñua (*Polylepis* spp.). While these trees have been observed growing at elevations up to 4600 m, they are generally confined to elevations below 4200 m, and in that range they form thickets of varying size and density. The diet of the taruca is poorly understood, but apparently they avoid larger bunch grasses and prefer to eat smaller plants close to the ground surface (Kuznar 1990, 135; Roe and Rees 1976, 725), although reports from Chile and Argentina indicate that their diet is relatively broad, and includes both graze and browse (CONAF 1983, 9; Mengoni 1986, 68).

Taruca are territorial and inhabit home ranges that vary between 0.25 to 2.0 km^2, and are found in three types of groups: mixed male/female groups and their offspring, with an average size of 9.5 individuals; a male group ranging in size from a single animal to five animals, with an average of 1.8 animals/group; and finally, a female group with an average size of 4.2 animals/group. In regional population composition, each group contributes 53%, 22%, and 25%, respectively, to the total. Densities of taruca vary considerably, ranging from a low of 0.3 km^2 at Pampas Galeras, 1.2 km^2 at La Raya, and between 0.7 and 0.95 km^2 in the Río Asana drainage of the western flanks of the Andes (Kuznar 1990, 136).

PLANT AND ANIMAL PRODUCTIVITY IN THE RIO ASANA VALLEY

Chenopods have been studied in the Andes for decades (Mujica 1994), but surprisingly little attention has been paid to their wild ancestors. Kuznar (1990, 1993) reports his botanical research in the Rio Asana valley along the western flanks of the Andes, and has described in detail a series of experiments designed to evaluate the natural productivity of wild chenopods and the

TABLE 8.1
Chenopodium Productivity and Distribution in the Río Asana Valley

COMMUNITY	PLANTS/HA	TOTAL AREA OF COMMUNITY	MEAN AND RANGE OF PRODUCTIVITY
Franseria[a]	70,000	707 ha	70 kg/ha; 55–94 kg/ha
Balbisia[a]	1,667	404 ha	17 kg/ha; 13–22 kg/ha
Corral communities[b]	—	0.92 ha	4921 kg/ha
Mean and range of total productivity, *Franseria* community			49,400 kg; 38,885–67,165 kg
Mean and range of total productivity, Balbesia community			8,160 kg; 6,240–10,560 kg
Total productivity corral patches[b]			467 kg

[a] Data from Aldenderfer (1998, Table 2.6).
[b] Data from Kuznar (1993); plant counts and mean values not available.

time required to process them. Two different forms of chenopods grow naturally in the Río Asana valley: *Chenopodium petiolare* (quinuay) and an unidentified species locally named quinua *chibo*, or goat quinoa (Kuznar 1993, 259–60). Chenopods grow rapidly during the rainy season (December–April), and persist on the stalk for months longer until they are eaten or their stalks break due to progressive desiccation. Modern goat pastoralists cultivate small patches of quinuay on the middens near their residential structures (Kuznar 1990). Although these chenopods are found scattered throughout the valley in small, discontinuous patches distributed in part by a mutualistic relationship with goats, they are primarily concentrated in two plant communities in the high sierra: the *Franseria meyeniana*, a dry community of the lower high sierra, and the *Balbisia* community of the upper high sierra. Kuznar (1993, Table 8.1) has estimated that these communities have natural stands of chenopods totaling 70,000 and 1600 plants/ha, respectively. He has further calculated that individual plants of either species produce from 0.79 g to 1.39 g of seeds per plant, averaging 1.0 g/plant, thus resulting

in 70 kg/ha and 1.6 kg/ha in the respective plant communities. As a comparison, estimates of the productivity of domesticated *Chenopodium* using traditional agricultural practice (not using fertilizer) in Peru and Ecuador range between 400–800 kg/ha. (Hernández and León 1994). Unfortunately, we do not have good estimates of individual patch sizes of chenopods in the Asana valley, but given the high density of plants in the *Franseria* community, I will assume that patches are smaller than 1 ha in size. Table 8.1 presents basic data on the total wild chenopod productivity of the patches in the Rio Asana valley.

Another factor that may have served to increase the amount of chenopods in the valley is the above-mentioned mutualism between goats and these species. Kuznar (1993) has noted that chenopod densities are extremely high in and around the corrals of modern goat pastoralists in the Río Asana valley. Not only do goats transport seeds in their coats, they also defecate large numbers of these seeds in their corrals since chenopods are preferred forage for these animals. This process produces very high densities: at 15 pastoral camps in the valley totaling 952 m[2], the total seed production in this aggregated area is 467 kg (Table 8.1). Koford (1957, 160) and Franklin (1975) have both observed similar vegetation growth, but of different species, in natural dung piles for both vicuña and guanaco. While the number of such mutualistically-generated patches would depend on the number of territories, and would probably be individually smaller and of lower density than the modern patches, these patches would nevertheless have the advantage of being predictable in their location given the territorial habits of these species.

The density and size of any animal population is dependent upon the natural productivity of their habitat and the behavioral ecology of the animals that inhabit it in terms of dietary preferences and territorial maintenance. Although the quantity of resources places an absolute limit on the population density of any species, this measure may not be the best for wild animals because other concerns, such as territoriality, mating patterns, and other dietary considerations also influence the distribution of wild animals on the landscape. Each of the wild herbivores considered in this study—guanaco, taruca, and vicuña—have a social structure based on family groups that defend territories. For instance, based on calculations of stocking rates (an estimate of the number of hectares of land one animal needs for foraging, expressed as the number of hectares per animal per year), 0.28 ha bofedal/vicuña could support an average family band of six to seven individuals, thus requiring a territory of only 1.5 to 1.75 ha, far less than 10% of territory sizes actually observed. This is reflected in Franklin's (1982, 480) statement that "Although habitat resources probably dictate group size within the feeding territories, they to not regulate it; the territorial male does." Therefore, considerations beyond the gross amount of forage influence the size of vicuña territories. Clearly, then, while the puna rim could in theory support large numbers of vicuña, it cannot do so due to their behavior. Also, since they are obligate drinkers, they are tethered to water. Therefore, in estimating the economic potential of the puna

rim, the productive potentials of the abundant dry lands can be ignored since the only limiting resource is the bofedal.

Yet another consideration is niche selection. The vicuña specialize on bofedal lands, and have developed a highly efficient dentition that allows them to more quickly and rapidly eat the plants that grow in this community. Thus while the taruca and guanaco find these plants palatable, they cannot compete with the vicuña for this preferred forage effectively. Further, their preferred habitat lies within the *queñual* forest, which provides them with cover and shelter. These two factors, then, essentially eliminate the taruca from consideration as a species of major importance on the puna rim. A similar case can be made for the guanaco, although in this instance, the criterion for niche selection appears to be the altitudinal range of the animal, since it is generally found at elevations below 4200 m, suggesting that it was rarely, if ever, found in the puna rim.

Therefore, given these constraints on habitat and niche use in these animals, the following figures are realistic estimates of wild animal abundance in Andean environments: one guanaco/8–20 ha of high sierra land, one vicuña/2 ha bofedal or one vicuña/6.5 for 10 ha bofedal and environs, and 1 taruca/30 for 100 ha of upper high sierra land and *queñual*. Using estimates of high sierra and puna area based on the community vegetation surveys completed by Kuznar, it is possible to compute total numbers of animals present in each environmental zone (Table 8.2). The puna bofedal has higher per hectare animal productivity than any habitat in the high sierra, and further, given the behavioral characteristics of the vicuña, their presence in and around the bofedal resource patch is very predictable. In contrast, although both the guanaco and taruca are territorial animals, their overall numbers are relatively low per hectare of animal productivity. Consequently, their territories and home ranges would necessarily be larger than those of the vicuña, and therefore, their spatial predictability would be lower as well.

TABLE 8.2
Estimated Animal Productivity, Río Asana Valley

ENVIRONMENTAL ZONES	TOTAL AREA
Lower high sierra	2,125 ha
Upper high sierra	1,800 ha
Puna rim queñual	1,007 ha
Puna rim bofedal	400–600 ha
Total number of animals present	
Lower high sierra	0.05–0.13 animal/ha
Guanaco[a]	106–266
Modal territories[b]	13–33
Upper high sierra	0.06–0.16 animals/ha
Guanaco[c]	140–350
Modal territories[b]	17–43
Taruca[d]	28–93
Modal territories[e]	6–19
Puna rim	0.5–0.65/animal/ha
Vicuna[f]	200–390
Modal Territories[g]	21–41

[a] Estimate based upon one animal to 8–20 ha of high sierra land.
[b] Estimate based on average family size of six, with ca. 74% of population in family group.
[c] Estimate based upon one animal to 8–20 ha of high sierra land and puna rim queñual.
[d] Estimate based upon one animal to 30–100 ha of high sierra land and puna rim queñual.
[e] Estimate based upon average family size of five, with 100% in some social group.
[f] Estimate based upon one animal to two ha bofedal or 6.5 animals to 10 ha bofedal lands and environs.
[g] Estimate based upon average family size of six, with 62.5% of population living in family group.

Since the guanaco is extinct in the Río Asana valley and the taruca pushed into marginal habitats by overhunting and competition with domesticated herd animals, it is not possible to observe their territories in the field. However, it is possible to estimate their general sizes and locations based on the known behavioral ecology of these animals. In narrow valleys such as those typical of the western flanks of the Andes, sedentary guanaco family groups have territories linearly distributed along the valleys (Franklin 1982). Animals use the flanks of the slopes for sleeping areas and food, and move to the valley bottoms for both forage and water. Territories tend to be adjacent along the length of the valley, and are tightly packed. Vicuña have a similar territorial organization, although they are focused upon bofedales. At night, the animals move into the slopes surrounding the bofedal or water source. Before sunrise, the animals begin to move toward the bofedal, grazing as they do so. They begin to return to the slopes in the early afternoon. All of this activity takes place within their territories (Vilá and Roig 1992, 294; Franklin 1982). Like the guanaco, their territories are packed linearly within valleys. Taruca have similar territorial characteristics. They tend to remain hidden in the *queñual* during the day, and forage within it at night.

The concept of territory is useful, because it can be used as a proxy measure of a resource patch. That is, since each of these species is highly territorial, the location of the territory is predictable, although the exact location of the animals within it may not be known with certainty. Given their habits, it is virtually certain that the animals will be somewhere within that territory. We can use this to determine the number of modal territories within each of the environmental zones. A modal territory is simply the

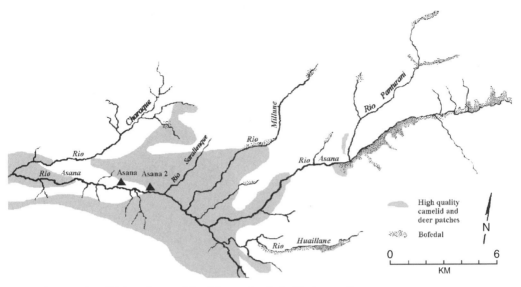

FIGURE 8.3. Location of high-quality camelid and deer patches in the Río Asana valley.

area required by an average family group for each of the species. To calculate the number of modal territories, one must know the proportion of animals in the entire population that reside within family groups as well as the average family group size. Using estimates of 74% of guanaco, 62.5% of vicuña, and 100% of taruca living in family groups, and average family sizes of six, six, and five animals, respectively, it is possible to estimate the proportion of the population living in family groups and thus the number of modal territories within each environmental zone (Table 8.2).

While it is important not to reify these numbers, they do provide some interesting comparisons. If we assume each modal territory to be a patch, it is clear that the environmental zone with the most patches, on average and in average years, is the upper high sierra, followed by the puna rim and the lower high sierra. That the puna rim has fewer patches makes sense since the bofedal is able to support larger numbers of animals. Likewise, the lower high sierra has few patches simply because the plant communities are the least productive in the entire valley system. The larger number of patches in the upper high sierra is obviously deter-

mined by the presence of two non-competing species—guanaco and taruca—inhabiting the same zone.

PATCH LOCATIONS AND TRAVEL TIMES

For the most part, high quality plant and animal patches in the Río Asana valley are discontinuous except in the immediate vicinity of Asana, where there is some overlap (Figures 8.2 and 8.3). Plant patches tend to be located downstream from Asana, whereas animal patches lie upstream.

However when viewed from a travel time perspective, the majority of all high quality resource patches are found within a eight-hour round-trip travel time from Asana (Figure 8.4; Table 8.3). Only the vicuña patches in the puna rim, and chenopod and guanaco patches in the extreme lower high sierra are found at round-trip travel distances greater than eight hours. Even with loads typical of foraging or hunting peoples, most of the high quality resource patches in the Rio Asana valley are located within what is generally considered to be the daily foraging radius commonly observed within a residential context (Bettinger et al. 1997, 897).

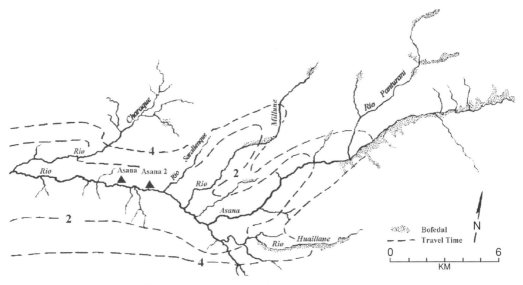

FIGURE 8.4. Travel times in the Río Asana valley. Contours are isochrons in two-hour increments.

THE ARCHAEOLOGY OF ASANA

Asana, located in the upper Río Moquegua valley of far southern Peru is found at an elevation of 3430 m. The site was occupied over an 8000-year span, and for most of this time, it served as a short-term residential base for mobile foragers who hunted taruca and camelids and who gathered wild plants, mostly chenopods (Aldenderfer 1998). Mobility was characterized by intra-and inter-valley movement, and except for a very short period from ca. 9800–9500 B.P., where foragers moved from coast to highlands, patterns of land use were focused upon an elevational continuum from 3000–4800 m, signaling the advent of permanent high elevation land use in the south-central Andes.

However, the start of the Qhuna phase (4600 B.P.) marks a significant change in settlement and subsistence patterns. Instead of making a number of limited residential moves throughout the year, the foragers living at Asana appear to have been relatively sedentary. Residential architecture at the site increases in both size and internal complexity, and refuse disposal patterns signal long-term habitation. Residential structures average 9 m²

of covered floor space, suggesting the presence of larger extended families when compared to earlier periods. Each occupational level of this phase has at least five large residential structures present, and it is likely that more were present. Although habitation was permanent, no storage facilities were found associated with the residential structures. Activities performed at Asana are consistent with residential use, and reflect the full range of domestic processing and maintenance tasks, such as a minor amount of hide preparation and gear manufacture and repair. The residential structures were grouped around a single public structure that was used as a dance floor, public space, or near the end of the occupation, as a probable focus of intensive, restricted worship.

Settlement patterns and the kinds of lithic materials used to fashion chipped stone tools show that subsistence practice was constrained within an elevational continuum from 3000–4000 m. All lithic raw materials found at the site come from high sierra sources, and only two rock shelters in the valley—Cueva 4 located downstream from Asana at ca. 3400 m, and Quellaveco, found

TABLE 8.3
Round-trip Travel Times to High Quality Resource Patches in the Río Asana Valley from Asana

SPECIES/LOCATION	MINIMUM TRAVEL TIME[a]	MAXIMUM TRAVEL TIME[a]	TOTAL AREA[b]	PROPORTION OF HIGH QUALITY PATCHES WITHIN EIGHT-HOUR ROUND TRIP[c]
Guanaco, lower high sierra	3 (3.75)	10 (12.5)	2,125 ha	90%
Guanaco, upper high sierra	0.5 (0.63)	4 (5)	1,800 ha	100%
taruca	1.0 (1.25)	6 (7.5)	1,007 ha	100%
vicuña	6 (7.5)	12 (15)	500 ha	20%
chenopods all communities	0.5 (0.63)	10 (12.5)	1,187 ha	90%

Note: Travel time does not include search or processing time.

[a] In hours, unburdened travel (see Aldenderfer 1998, 10–15 for an explanation of the computation of travel times; for burdened travel (load estimated at 15 kg), multiply travel time by 1.25 (figure in parentheses).
[b] Compiled from Aldenderfer (1998, 41–45).
[c] Eight-hour round trip is based upon one-way (return to Asana) burdened travel time.

upstream at an elevation of 3800 m—show signs of Qhuna phase occupation. Activity performance within the shelters was limited to lithic reduction, retooling, and possible gear maintenance. No ground stone tools were found in them. Since both shelters have very limited viewsheds and a narrow range of activities performed, it is likely they served as the temporary camps of foragers moving up and down the valley, and not as hunting blinds or field camps. A number of open-air lithic scatters with Qhuna phase materials are found upstream from Asana as well, and these fall in an elevational range of 3600–3800 m. None of these contained ground stone, and again, activity performance was limited to retooling and lithic reduction.

Subsistence was based primarily upon hunting taruca and camelids and intensive exploitation of a local form of *Chenopodium*. Unfortunately, preservation of paleoethnobotanic materials at the site was extremely poor, and consequently, quantitative estimates of plant use cannot be made. However, every residential structure had at least one large *batan* (metate) embedded in its floor, and there was significant investment in the shaping of smaller hand stones used for seed grinding. Although seed processing, indicated by the presence of small hand stones and batanes, occurred in earlier phases, the intensity of seed processing in Qhuna times is far greater than any of these. There is no evidence of animal pens or corrals, and the faunal assemblage reflects the local consumption of animals with little exchange with adjacent groups. The faunal assemblages of the phase show that whole animals were returned to the site with minimal field processing. This is based on the observation that head, phalanges, and metapodials are all present in expected frequencies. For the first time, small mammal and rodent bones are found at sites of the Qhuna phase, suggesting that compared with previous occupations of the site, diet breadth had increased. Because the faunal assemblage is highly fragmented, most likely to produce bone juice or grease, it is not possible to quantify the proportions of taruca versus camelids taken. Indeed, the Qhuna phase faunal assemblages are the most highly fragmented, again suggesting the intensive use of much of hunted animals for consumption.

At the start of the Awati phase (4400 B.P.), settlement in the valley was markedly different and was anchored by two residential bases—Asana and El Panteon—found some 17 km apart in distinct ecological zones. El Panteon is found immediately adjacent to a large bofedal which maintains high quality pasturage year-round. Only a single residential structure is found in each of the Awati occupational levels at Asana, and the average covered floor area of the structure is only 4.2 m². The single residential structure at El Panteon dating to this phase is similar in size and shape, but was not fully excavated. This structure could not have been used by a large co-residential group, and most probably reflects the presence of a single family. Both sites are dominated by a small animal corral defined by the presence of dung-derived soils and bounded by small postmolds. Activity performance at both sites is characterized by small tool maintenance, retooling, and gear repair. Small ground stone tools are present, but in very limited numbers, and no large batanes are present, a striking change from the previous phase.

Settlement patterns and the kinds of lithic materials used to fashion chipped stone tools show that subsistence practice ranged across an elevational continuum from 3000–4800 m, much greater in scope than that of the Qhuna phase. Although the majority of the lithic materials used by Awati phase peoples comes from the high sierra, significant proportions of materials are now found from the puna rim (the area surrounding El Panteon), and the more distant high puna. Aside from a small rockshelter near El Panteon (Cueva San Agustin), none of the other rockshelters in the Río Asana valley showed signs of Awati phase use. Further, none of the small open-air sites found between 3600–3800 m had Awati phase points found within them. Instead, Awati projectile points are found as stray finds up and down the valley and in some of the smaller quebradas that flow into the Río Asana. This pattern of dispersal was probably generated by loss during hunting, and does not indicate a pattern of field camp or logistical site utilization.

Although the presence of small grinding stones indicates that seed processing was still practiced, it is clear that the intensity of seed use is far lower than in the Qhuna phase. The faunal assemblage is dominated by camelid remains, but taruca are very rare, and small mammals and rodents drop out of the assemblage. Packet data show that whole animals were consumed on site, but in stark contrast to the Qhuna phase assemblages, the faunal assemblages from both sites are dominated by low-utility parts, primarily heads, phalanges, and metapodials. High-utility parts, such as ribs and femora, are conspicuous by their absence. Those faunal elements present are highly fragmented, reflecting a continued practice of bone juice and grease production.

Kuznar (1990) has argued that based on the presence of yearling animals at Asana, the site was occupied during the dry season (austral winter), and that El Panteon was occupied in the wet season, or austral summer. This pattern of land use is consistent with what is known of modern goat pastoralists in the valley today. However, since the number of yearling faunal elements is very small and non-diagnostic as to species, this argument is not well-grounded. No matter what the season of occupation, however, it is clear that the Awati phase marks the transition from a foraging to a herding lifeway in the Río Asana valley.

In summary, a number of dramatic changes took place in the Río Asana valley from 4600–4400 B.P. A near-sedentary lifeway based on intensive plant utilization and hunting developed in the valley and supported a modest population for at least a time. This was replaced rapidly by a herding lifeway that appears to have supported a much smaller population. The impressive public architecture of the Qhuna phase disappeared and was not replaced, further implying dramatic changes in other social domains, including those articulated with labor, status, and societal reproduction.

Viewed from a diet perspective, plants (the chenopods) fell in rank, and small mammals and rodents dropped out of the diet altogether. Again, while quantitative estimates of the proportion of hunted faunas in the Awati phase diet cannot be made with any certainty, the taruca disappeared from the diet as well. Whatever caloric returns these resources offered were apparently replaced by herded animals. Whatever the cause of this transition, there is no evidence for rapid or dramatic climate change. In fact, this part of the late Holocene is, if anything a period of climatic amelioration, with increasing rainfall characteristic of high elevation environments across the south-central Andes (Baker et al. 2001). And while a replacement argument for the appearance of herding at Asana is plausible, there remains the difficult problem of identifying the source location of the replacement population (Aldenderfer 2002). The transition to herding, then, in the Río Asana valley seems driven not by external factors but instead choices made by agents within their local ecological and social setting.

WOMEN'S WORK, MEN'S WORK, AND RETURN RATES IN THE QHUNA PHASE

Both the archaeology and spatial positioning of Asana suggests that the foragers who occupied the site during the Qhuna phase obtained most, if not all, of their resources during daily foraging trips within a residential context. No field or logistical camps associated with plant processing are known to have existed in the valley during this phase, while at Asana, plant processing was intensive. The faunal assemblages show that whole animals were being returned to the site with minimal field processing, judging from the high frequencies of low-utility head, phalange, and metapodial parts present. And the only field camps known from Qhuna phase are located upstream from Asana, along the terraces of the river below the queñual forest, the prime habitat of the taruca, and within an average 2.5 hour round-trip travel time (Aldenderfer 1998, 47). Simple observation suggests that Asana as a residential site was located in an "optimal" place in the landscape.

This begs the question, however, of just how resources were procured by the site's inhabitants and how labor was allocated to that end. To gauge the "optimality" of Asana's placement, we must now turn to a consideration of women's and men's labor and the return rates for that labor. Evaluating return rates can provide us with useful information about how labor roles may have been transformed as herding became the basis of subsistence, and further, whether these transformed labor roles could have permitted societal reproduction during that transition. Also, through the analysis of the division of labor and return rates, we can examine the argument that herding was adopted as a risk buffering response to environmental uncertainty and variability.

The question of the rigidity of the sexual division of labor has become a major research topic in the study of foraging peoples over the past two decades. Once viewed as a cross-cultural universal in which males and females cooperated to provision themselves and their children, as viewed from the perspective of human behavioral ecology it is now widely recognized that males and females have different subsistence strategies that may or may not converge (Bliege Bird 1999; K. Hawkes 1996; K. Hawkes and Bliege Bird 2002). Women's reproductive fitness benefits from parental investment, and therefore, they tend to adopt provisioning strategies that have return rates sufficient to feed themselves and their children on a consistent basis. Such strategies benefit from the tendency for related women to forage and share cooperatively. In contrast, males may benefit more from provisioning strategies that increase the number of mating opportunities obtained through widespread sharing of meat. As discussed above, men may hunt large game despite low return rates in hopes of obtaining meat so as to "show off" and thus prove

TABLE 8.4
Return Rates for Strict Division of Labor Subsistence Strategy

	NUMBER OF HUNTERS OR COLLECTORS			RETURN RATES
Men's foraging returns	1	2	3	
Guanaco	17,448	8,724	5,816	17,448
Taruca	8,738	4,369	2,912	8,378
Women's foraging returns				
Chenopods, 6 hour collection	5,328	10,853	15,984	894
Chenopods, 8 hour collection	6,926	13,853	20,778	894

Notes: All hunting and collecting conducted within the foraging radius; travel time to patch not included. Return rates are based on total kcal/hr of meat and fat of single adult animals; see Aldenderfer (1998: Table 9.5). Return rate for vicuña is 7,490 kcal/hr. For chenopods, estimates are based on experimental data reported by Aldenderfer (1998: Table 9.3).

themselves to be a reliable potential ally and to obtain social attention (K. Hawkes 1990, 1991). Alternatively, males hunt to provide collective goods to non-kin so as to compete for status, "and, ultimately, for the material and fitness-enhancing correlates of status, such as mates, food, or territory." (Smith and Bliege Bird 2000, 259; Wiessner 2002). Regardless of which explanation proves valid in any empirical setting, it is clear that women's and men's foraging goals should be considered separately in any analysis of the optimal diet.

Although a number of potential foraging strategies can be postulated for the foragers of Qhuna phase Asana, I will examine two: (1) women as the exclusive collectors of chenopods, and men as the exclusive hunters of taruca and camelids, and (2) a strategy of cooperative hunting taruca and camelids by both men and women supplemented by chenopod collection by women. These two strategies provide the clearest alternatives for labor allocation and the calculation of resource rankings. Vicuña are not considered in either model because Qhuna phase foragers did not have access to vicuña patches. To calculate foraging efficiency, I use Winterhalder et al's (1988, 325) equations under equilibrium conditions (also see Zeanah 2004, 9). The results of these calculations for each of these strategies is presented in Tables 8.4 and 8.5.

As expected, the foraging efficiency of the guanaco and taruca are far higher than that of the chenopods, which suggests that men's hunting is capable of providing sufficient calories for provisioning small families. However, just how hunting is accomplished matters considerably. The optimal return is for a single hunter to kill one prey animal within the foraging radius. Obviously, as the number of hunters increases, the payoff diminishes proportionately as long as only one animal is taken. If we assume a family size of five, and with each member requiring 2500 kcal/day, a total of 12,500 kcal is required to provision it. Viewed from this perspective, men should only hunt guanaco if provisioning is the goal of their subsistence efforts, and they should always hunt alone. Further, this calculation does not take into account the probability of failure, which to some extent would be only moderate since the guanaco is a territorial animal and the location of the family group's territory is fairly predictable.

Taruca hunting has a lower foraging efficiency and return rate. Despite the territorial behavior of this species, it is cryptic, meaning that hunting taruca would involve higher search costs once arriving at a patch. Modern inhabitants of the Río Asana valley claim to use dogs to hunt taruca today; the dogs are trained to chase the animal and to bring it down, and it is killed by people following the chase (Kuznar

TABLE 8.5

Return Rates for Collective Hunting Subsistence Strategy

SPECIES	TOTAL KG AND KCAL/FAMILY GROUP	RETURN RATE PER NUMBER OF PARTICIPANTS[a]		
		6	8	10
Guanaco	460/300,880[b]	50,146	37,610	30,088
Taruca	188/128,966[c]	10,747	8,060	6,448
Vicuña	220/179,760[d]	29,960	22,470	17,976

[a] Based on two hours of pursuit time per participant.
[b] Estimates based on family group including one adult male (110 kg), three adult females (80 kg each), and two juveniles (55 kg each; Aldenderfer 1998, Table 9.6).
[c] Estimates based on family group including one adult male (52 kg), two adult females (42 kg each), and two juveniles (26 kg each; Aldenderfer 1998, Table 9.6).
[d] Estimates based on family group size including one adult male (50 kg), three adult females (40 kg each), and two juveniles (25 kg each).

1990, 135–136). Another effective strategy that could be used to hunt these animals would take advantage of two of their behavioral characteristics: their territoriality and their tendency to descend to the river bottoms to escape pursuit. If a group of hunters could get above their territories, they could essentially "beat" the animals down slope where they could be taken by hunters awaiting them there. A material correlate of this strategy may be the Qhuna phase open-air sites, which lie just below the queñual slopes. However, this hunting strategy has the added cost of increasing the number of hunters, thus diminishing the return rate unless more than one animal is taken.

Although the foraging efficiency of the chenopods is quite low, the return rates per gatherer per collecting day within the foraging radius are relatively high, and since they are additive—more gatherers are capable of obtaining more of the resource until the patch is exhausted or within-patch search time increases significantly—it is clear that two gatherers are capable of provisioning a family of five, including a slight surplus, from within the typical foraging radius if they spend 10 hours/day directed at gathering pursuits. This is somewhat longer than many known ethnographic foragers living in similar arid environments, and it suggests that children may well have been

drawn into the subsistence quest if family size was small. However, the evidence from Qhuna phase Asana suggests that families were likely larger than five individuals. Even if they had as many as eight members, however, three chenopod collectors could still provision the entire group over the course of an eight-hour collecting day. These calculations also show, however, that a subsistence strategy based upon intensive chenopod collection may well have been risky in the face of drought, because any shortfall of precipitation would have reduced the number of plants, especially in the lower high sierra, and would have forced gatherers to spend longer days collecting either by increasing search and processing time within patches or travel time to more distant patches beyond the foraging radius.

Since Qhuna phase Asana was a sedentary occupation, could chenopods have supported its population year-round? As Table 8.1 shows, there are approximately 1000 ha of high quality chenopod patches in the Rio Asana valley within the eight-hour foraging radius. Assuming each hectare produces an average of 70 kg/ha, these patches could support just over 250 people/year assuming 2500 kcal/person/day. Although we do not have a firm estimate of population size at Asana for each occupational level of the site, the number of domestic structures present and

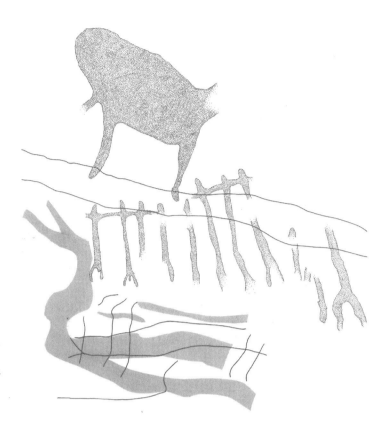

FIGURE 8.5. Representation of collective hunt strategy. Note the line-up of anthropomorphs. From Cueva Cimmarona, a small rock-shelter near the Río Asana drainage.

their sizes suggest that the total population may have been 50–60 individuals.

At first glance, the collective hunting strategy appears to be highly efficient (Table 8.5). Custred (1979) and Rick (1980, 328–29), among others, have argued that the most efficient hunting technique for the vicuña family group is a collective, surround technique in which animals are driven into cul-de-sacs or are prevented from moving with a human blockade. This technique is used today by Andean herders who surround vicuñas to shear their wool. A group of 20–30 people surround the family group or male troop, and gradually push the animals into a tight knot. Individual animals are sheared, then released. Hunters could just as easily surround a family group and kill all of its members. This strategy is illustrated in the rock art of the Andean highlands (Figure 8.5), and could have been extended to both the guanaco and the taruca. With six participants hunting guanaco, it has the highest re-

turn rate of all of the procurement strategies, and even with ten participants, it has a return rate greater than three collectors of chenopods working six hours. The taruca collective hunting strategy is less efficient than the guanaco strategy, primarily because of the smaller body size of the prey within the family group, and has return rates comparable to two chenopod collectors working a six-hour day.

However, there are two problematic features of the collective hunting strategy, one short-term and the other long-term. The short-term problem is getting enough people to encircle the family group effectively. Six individuals appears to be the absolute minimum, and clearly, larger numbers of people are preferable. The number of participating individuals in ethnohistorically recorded surrounds ranged into the many hundreds; these were sponsored by leaders of complex societies, however, and are not comparable to those likely to have been done by early

Andean hunters. It is obvious that as the numbers of participants increased, the return rate would diminish proportionately.

The long-term problem is concerned with the issue of resource conservation and hunting strategies. Consensus is beginning to emerge that foraging peoples reliant upon hunting do not conserve game, and tend to take numbers of prey in excess of the maximum sustainable yield in many instances (Alvard and Kuznar 2001). The reasons for this are multiple, and indeed, foraging theory predicts that hunters will tend to maximize short-term returns at the expense of long-term consequences, and that hunters take prey as predicted by typical diet breadth or central place models regardless of the "prey species' vulnerability, reproductive value, or state of local depletion." (Alvard and Kuznar 2001). If this had been the case, it would have been relatively easy for hunters to quickly decimate local populations of camelids and taruca, which were never present in very large numbers (see Table 8.2).

Whether this occurred in the Río Asana valley is unknown. Based on excavation data from the Junín puna, Rick (1980; Rick and Moore 2001) has made a strong case that Andean hunters were resource stewards. He argued that hunters, no matter what strategy they employed, could have easily identified male animals in camelid family groups due to their tendency to move forward toward predators as the other members of the family group retreated. I have argued that conservation may have occurred in the Río Asana valley of the western flanks of the Andes (Aldenderfer 1998, 285–87), but have re-evaluated this position in a more recent publication, and have shown that a "cultural logic" of short-term benefits chosen over long-term considerations may in fact be a better explanation of Andean hunting strategies (Aldenderfer 2002, 405). Indeed, as I shall discuss below, the use of this hunting strategy may have been a contributing factor to the ultimate herding, rather than hunting, of the guanaco.

Likewise, it is difficult to estimate the labor trade-offs chenopod collectors may have made to participate in these hunts. Should they have been successful, they would have obviated the need for daily collecting trips to provision families. However, this has to be balanced against the probability that the return (the amount of meat) for any individual in that collective labor investment would have been shared across a much larger number of people unlike the returns from chenopod collection, which would have been shared only within the family. This would have certainly reduced the payoff substantially, and as a consequence, women may have resisted participation in these hunts if probabilities of failure and a potentially large pool of participants was deemed to be too large.

In summary, an optimal diet for Qhuna phase foragers was based upon women's collecting of chenopods and men's hunting of guanaco within the foraging radius. Taruca hunting was lower ranked and would have been a secondary hunting pursuit for men. The faunal evidence from the site supports this inference: NISP counts of taruca make up far less than one percent of the total assemblage (Aldenderfer 1998, 231). Collective hunting strategies may have been employed as well, but women may have resisted participation in them because payoffs for their labor may not have sufficiently provisioned their families (children). Although chenopod collection could have supported the entire Qhuna phase population at Asana, any substantial lack of rainfall or change in its periodicity could have led to short-term provisioning crises. Given the relatively low return rates for the chenopods, it would have been difficult to store large enough quantities to alleviate such crises unless larger numbers of collectors (i.e. men) were employed to that end. Indeed, the lack of obvious storage facilities at Asana suggests that this strategy was not employed unless it was needed.

THE TRANSITION TO HERDING IN THE AWATI PHASE

Given this baseline, we can now explore how herding may have been adopted in the Río Asana valley during the Awati phase. Alvard and Kuznar (2001) have proposed an interesting and useful model for the transition from hunting to herding from an HBE perspective. They view animal herding as a kind of prey conservation, in which long-term benefits of herding outweigh the short-term benefits of taking encountered prey immediately. They argue that there are certain necessary, but not sufficient, conditions that create a context within which this transition occurs: competition for hunted resources becomes intense due to local population growth within a residentially sedentary context, the consequent formation of defendable territories, and the perception among hunters that hunted prey are valued, but *private*, goods. Finally, a key assumption is that the benefits of husbanding depend on the value of animal resources to individual fitness (Alvard and Kuznar 2001, 301). Here, men's fitness may be enhanced either by provisioning for themselves and close kin, or by engaging in behaviors that may increase the number and quality of their mating opportunities.

The key to understanding how this transition occurs within this context is that long-term discounted, deferred returns (i.e. those obtained from conserving) must be higher than the short-term returns from hunting. To explore this, they use the concept of the maximum sustainable yield (MSY), which is the rate at which a prey species can be taken without causing a decline in population size and thus yield. The MSY is based upon the reproductive rate of the species and the total number of animals that can be sustained within a given ecological context (as measured by the carrying capacity). The scenario painted by Alvard and Kuznar is that as return rates from hunting begin to drop, due to competition in the face of resource depression, individuals decide to conserve the resource or hunt it. Ultimately, the outcome of this decision is based upon the resource's value and its discount rate. The discount rate is defined as "the economic measure of the rate at which current income is valued over future income" (Alvard and Kuznar 2001,

297). In other words, the discount rate measures the time depth people take into account when deciding the costs and benefits of any future subsistence-related decision. The higher the discount rate, the more likely it is that hunters will favor short-term thinking (i.e. take the prey on encounter) rather than conserving the prey for future use. As Alvard and Kuznar (2001, 299) show, for any MSY strategy to be selected, "...the reproductive rate of the resource population must be greater than the discount rate—the rate of return from the best current alternative investment." Smaller-bodied prey have faster intrinsic rates of growth than do larger ones. Thus herders beginning with two goats, which have a maximum intrinsic growth rate of 0.7, can achieve a herd size of 100 animals in 24 years. In contrast, large-bodied animals, such as cattle, with maximum intrinsic growth rates of 0.25, would take 72 years to achieve a herd size of 100 animals. Not surprisingly, the return rate for the goat population, as measured in kcal/year, rises at a substantially faster exponential growth rate than does that for cattle or other large-bodied species (Alvard and Kuznar 2001, 301).

Herding smaller bodied animals appears to make good economic sense, but hunters still have to decide between immediate or delayed returns (see Woodburn 1982). What, therefore, is the appropriate value of the discount rate? The discount rate is what leads a hunter to decide to consume immediately or conserve prey for future use. Also, given that herd growth is a process and not an event, what kinds of changes in labor deployment and resource procurement are required by both males and females to achieve their often divergent fitness goals?

Alvard and Kuznar (2001, 303–04) established their discount rate based on research by Rogers (1994), who posited that from the perspective of natural selection, the discount rate depends upon the rate of population growth, the average relatedness between the individuals and their offspring, and the length of the generation. Using a generational length of 30 years, and assuming an average coefficient of relatedness of 0.5 between parent and offspring, Rogers shows that the discount rate is 2.4%, which corresponds to conditions of zero or very flat population growth. Alvard (1998) has argued on the basis of modern ethnographic data on foraging peoples that in prehistoric times, although long-term population growth rates may have hovered around zero, there were periods of time at which growth rates varied between zero and five percent. Using these figures, they show that the prey body size at which hunting and herding provide the same return is approximately 40 kg. Only when discount rates are low will animals with body sizes larger than 40 kg be herded since the opportunity costs of hunting them would be too high.

How do these predictions correspond to the transition to herding in the Await phase in the Río Asana valley? Qhuna phase settlement patterns suggest that at least one of the conditions of the Alvard and Kuznar model—residential sedentism within a territorial context—is satisfied. Whether Asana was experiencing significant population growth—one of their other conditions—is more equivocal. There is no question that population of Asana during the Qhuna phase was substantially greater than that of the preceding Pisi Mara phase, but it is far from clear that population grew in the Qhuna phase. The total number of residential structures in each excavated level is the same, although the largest domestic structures are found in the final occupational levels of the site. Given that the population was tethered to the high sierra, while population growth rates may not have been high, it is reasonable to postulate that over time, competition between hunters for prey may have increased, especially if collective hunting strategies were occasionally employed. This would have had the effect, if practiced frequently, of exceeding the MSY of guanaco populations in the valley over time. Finally, while we cannot know if the guanaco became an economically defendable private good, it would have been labor intensive to defend these territories from others. In summary,

most of the conditions of the Alvard and Kuznar model are tentatively satisfied based on the available data from the Qhuna phase at Asana.

Although the conditions of the model are satisfied, its predictions are not. Recall that adult guanacos have an average weight of 110 kg, while adult taruca average 52 kg. Given this model, it is the taruca that should have been herded rather than the guanaco, which we know in the Río Asana was the species herded. What explains this discrepancy between the archaeological record and model predictions?

In the case of the taruca, all of its behavioral characteristics mitigate against successful herding. They are territorial, but large amounts of time and labor are required to hunt them. They are difficult to locate because they tend to remain hidden and solitary during the day. It is likely that the increased labor costs associated with managing them, such as employing larger numbers of people to mind and direct them, would have significantly reduced the return rates of such a strategy. From a woman's labor perspective, the time spent herding taruca would not have contributed sufficiently to provision her children and close kin. In fact, as I have shown above, taruca are conspicuous by their absence in Awati phase faunal assemblages, suggesting that despite their continued presence in the valley, their value had declined considerably.

Alvard and Kuznar (2001, 306) offer a number of explanations for how larger-bodied animals may have eventually been herded. As I noted above, if the discount rate is low, larger-bodied animals may be herded. One way for this to occur is for population growth rates to decline substantially or to crash. When viewed across the phase boundaries, population numbers in the valley decrease dramatically. Asana in the Qhuna phase had up to 50 inhabitants, while in the Awati phase, it had no more than a single family that apparently moved between two residential locations. It seems plausible that the observed population decline into the Awati phase may have contributed to the decision to herd. However, given the substantial settlement reorganization that took place in the valley, a decline in the discount rate seems to offer only a partial, and incomplete, solution to this question.

A simpler answer to this question is that the guanaco was the only prey species in the high sierra that *could* be successfully husbanded. Although none of the wild South American camelids are particularly easy to tame (Moore 1989, 91–96), the known behavioral flexibility of guanaco social groups suggests that it is more easily tamed and managed into different social formations. Clearly, the return rates from hunting, either through overexploitation of the resource or a change in the discount rate following a significant population decline, made returns from husbanding feasible.

Can costly signaling theory provide further insights into how these decisions were made in the past? Recall that costly signaling theory asserts that while hunting often provided nutritional benefits to hunters and their kin, as well as non-kin through sharing, it is also a form of competitive display, wherein hunters work longer hours or pursue non-optimal prey to achieve non-nutritional benefits from other members of the social group. These may include enhanced mating opportunities, improved possibilities of alliance formation and coalition building, and more consideration from others. These benefits can obviously enhance men's fitness. Hunting, therefore, provides a means by which status can be improved. I argue here that a decision to husband animals may be seen from a costly signaling perspective as an alternative means by which a man can signal his positive qualities to potential mates and allies. We know that in established herding societies, the primary measure of men's status is the size of his herd, with larger herds denoting high status. Formerly hunted animals (collective goods) become private, a necessary condition for prey conservation to occur (Alvard and Kuznar 2001). Under these conditions, hunters may chose to conserve and defer benefits for future consumption, rather than to consume the resource

immediately. In effect, this kind of decision lowers the discount rate. That is, emerging prey conservator-herders (our former hunters) now accept high opportunity costs to forgo taking prey immediately. Of course, this decision is contingent upon others seeing this as an honest signal of ability, foresight, and capacity. This perception would be intensified as herd sizes grew larger over time. Prey conservators who lacked the skill to tame animals, adequately protect their herds, or obtain sufficient pasturage for steady herd growth would fall in status rankings.

This scenario is consistent with a number of predictions derived from costly signaling theory. Since herds are quite visible, in that they are corralled and penned in public view, they offer an honest, observable signal of quality. The signal is costly since the former hunter has chosen to accept higher opportunity costs of not taking the prey immediately, and by investing labor to protect and augment the resource over a long time frame. It is reliable as well since the conserved prey can be translated easily into other resources that provide direct fitness benefits to the herder and his family, and finally, it is beneficial for both the signaler (his degree of quality is obvious), and for the observer, since the signal is unambiguous. Note that this is also consistent with the observation that it is not the meat per se that is important as the signal, but what the meat actually means as it reflects on the skill of the hunter. In effect, from this perspective, our emerging prey conservator-herder can have his cake and eat it too—he gets status through herd display, but yet is not under a burdensome obligation to share the profits from his hard work. Remember, what the signal recipient gets from this is an honest, direct measure of the man's underlying fitness-related qualities. Unlike in most foraging societies, meat is not widely shared beyond the household in pastoral societies, although this tendency may be modified by bond of sibling cooperation and marriage. Thus when animals are slaughtered, their meat is consumed within the family or a far more limited social circle than is

TABLE 8.6
Comparison of Return Rates for Natural and Corral Patches of Chenopods

	NUMBER OF COLLECTORS			RETURN RATES
Women's foraging returns	1	2	3	
Natural chenopods, 6 hour collection	5,412	10,824	16,236	902
Corral chenopods, 6 hour collection	10,188	20,376	30,564	1,698

Notes: Estimates of kcal/hr for natural patches based on experimental data reported by Aldenderfer (1998: Table 9.3); for corral patches, see Kuznar (1993). All collection performed within the foraging radius.

common in foraging societies. Limited sharing is consistent with the new measure of status—larger herd sizes. Gifts of animals occur in most pastoral societies, but consistent with the predictions of evolutionary theory, it is practiced within families when gifts are given to sons and daughters upon marriage so that they may start their own herds (Flannery et al. 1989).

How does women's work fit into this scenario? Is the decision to forgo short-term consumption one that is sustainable, and if so, what kinds of labor deployment are necessary for societal reproduction to continue? Since men are choosing to trade high opportunity costs for status competition, the returns once obtained by their hunting must be made up for by other subsistence choices. Also, new costs associated with herd management and care must also be assumed by the co-residential group. How can this new cost be managed?

This problem is now compounded by a change in settlement. Awati phase peoples had two residential bases, one in the upper high sierra at Asana, and the other on the puna rim at El Panteon. While 90% of the high quality chenopod patches can be found within the foraging radius of Asana (see Table 8.3), none of these are found within the foraging radius of El Panteon. If we assume that the entire co-residential group made the move between these sites, this means that women were not near the resource patches they used in Qhuna phase times to provision their families for a significant part of

the year. If we assume that these incipient herders spent 182 days at each residential base, two chenopod collectors, given the smaller family size in Awati times, could not have provisioned a family of five for that period during an eight-hour collecting day within the foraging radius, and could barely have covered resource needs collecting over a ten-hour day (Table 8.4). Since they are right at the edge of being unable to collect enough to satisfy daily provisioning requirements, they cannot also provide returns sufficient for storage for the remainder of the year. Clearly, it would have been advantageous for women to stay as long as possible at Asana in order to satisfy their provisioning goals. Were there other options available?

Recall the mutualism models of Kuznar (1993) and Pearsall (1989), who argue that dense patches of chenopods would have been created next to residential sites in and around animal corrals as herding became more important. As I have shown above, the density of these stands can be quite high. Using Kuznar's (1993) figures, the productivity per hectare of these stands of chenopods created in corral contexts 4670 kg/ha, is almost 70 times greater than the productivity of natural stands! However, each individual patch in Kuznar's sample is quite small (average patch size at corrals is 63 m^2), and they are widely dispersed across the valley. However, increased density of these plants does improve their harvesting efficiency by reducing search (or travel) time between plants in a patch. Kuznar (1993, 262) estimates that by reducing the walking time between plants, it is possible to collect 511 g/hour, effectively doubling return rates (see Table 8.6). Assuming that these corral patches are harvested by two collectors over a six-hour collecting day, these small patches could have provided an additional 75 days of provisioning for a family of five. One obvious problem with this scenario is that these patches do not become established until the herds of husbanded animals are established, and at least in the short run, then, this resource, while growing through time, would not have provided sufficient returns for significantly more daily provisioning.

These data suggest then, that instead of moving the entire co-residential group back and forth between these two residential bases on a seasonal basis, women would remain at Asana for much of the year, while men took their growing herds to the puna rim during the dry season, where bofedales would provide permanent pastures. This would allow women to continue to provision their families more effectively by remaining near the high sierra chenopod patches, and it would provide the herded animals with new pastures. This type of residential pattern is common in the Andes today. For instance, in the community of Chichillape of southern Peru, men and boys take animals into higher elevations during the wet season, where pasturage and forage are abundant following the rains, and construct simple structures known in Aymara as *anaqa* (Palacios Rios 1977, 159). Women and older family members remain at the lower elevation residential site. The animals remain at higher elevation until the forage there is exhausted. The season of the residential move at Asana during the Awati phase would have been different, however. Men and women would have lived at the site during the wet season, when chenopods became abundant, and the men would have moved the herds to the puna rim during the dry season to graze on the permanently available bofedal vegetation.

Changes in settlement also provides males with the opportunity to hunt the vicuña, which resides in small, predictable patch locations in the puna rim. As can be seen Tables 8.4 and 8.5, once vicuña can be taken from within the foraging radius, as is possible at El Panteon, they increase their rankings and make them worthwhile to hunt. This is especially true for the collective hunt strategy as long as sufficient labor could be mobilized. As Alvard and Kuznar (2001, 306) note, hunting remains common in many pastoral societies, and would have been especially important as a provisioning tactic during a prolonged transitional period between hunting and herding, as would have been the case in the Andes given the relatively slow maximum rate of increase of the camelids. Under this scenario, women may have moved to El Panteon at some point in the dry season to provide labor for herd management as men moved off to hunt vicuña or to assist in collective hunts. They thus became more dependant upon men's hunting as a provisioning strategy, and in so doing, may well have begun the process of diminishing their status and their rights of control over the distribution of resource production. In effect, men's labor and status as achieved through the costly signaling of growing a herd becomes more critical for societal reproduction than it had been in Qhuna times.

How might chenopod domestication fit into this scenario? Kuznar's (1993) experiments with wild chenopods in the Río Asana valley have shown that unlike the domesticated plant quinoa, which usually has a single, thick stalk that contains the bulk of the seeds, the wild chenopod quinuay is a much smaller plant that has a large number (5 to 25) of short stalks, each of which contains seeds. These stalks grow radially from the plant, and tend to bend to the ground. To harvest the plant, it is necessary to either bend low or actually sit on the ground to pull the seeds from each stalk, or cut the stems below the seed bundle, and then remove the seeds. Tschopik (1948, 501) reports that Aymara in the modern era pull the plants from the ground and beat them on threshing grounds, or in some instance, break the heads of the plants off. In each case, however, the labor is tedious and difficult, and as I have shown, return rates are very low given the search and handling time required. The only way in which return rates could have been improved substantially would have been for the intentional modification of the plants to increase the numbers of seeds per plants, and to reduce the number of stalks that needed to be stripped and processed. Women collecting chenopods in corral patches probably began experimenting with these plants, and through their manipulations, may well have set the plants on a course toward domestication as Rindos (1984) and others have argued. This process of manipulation would have been relatively easy in corral patches because the plants are more closely packed. These observations suggest that the mutualism models offered by Kuznar and Pearsall are plausible under these conditions in Andean settings.

CONCLUSIONS

The combined use of costly signaling theory and simple diet breadth models, when considered in detail with the sexual division of labor and the recognition that men and women may have different provisioning strategies, provides further insight into the *process* of how herding became established in at least one region of the Andes. Since women and men may have distinct provisioning strategies, it becomes important to examine their foraging strategies separately, and to determine just what each strategy could have contributed to the diet. In the case of Qhuna phase Asana, women could have provisioned their families through chenopod (and probably other plants as well) collecting, and the archaeological record from the site supports an inference that their labor was intensive and critical for social reproduction. Men in the Qhuna phase first hunted guanaco, then taruca, and again, data recovered from the site demonstrate convincingly that hunting strategies were consistent with general model predictions. How much this hunting contributed to the diet is not known.

The transition to herding in the Awati phase was examined using Kuznar and Alvard's (2001) model of animal husbandry or herding as prey conservation. Potential herders must decide when it is more profitable to forgo taking prey on encounter and to defer these immediate benefits in anticipation of obtaining larger ones in the future. This decision is based is on the return rate for immediate resource consumption compared to future returns if conserved, which is mediated by the discount rate. Since most hunting peoples have very high discount rates (always take prey on encounter if it is in the optimal diet), what circumstances would lead to the decline of discount rate? Costly signaling theory provides insight into how the discount rate might have been lowered. If men's hunting is in great part not about provisioning per se, but about status competition, men may well spend more time and effort doing it than return rates from it would support. As prey became more scarce, and competition for hunters increased, prey may have become a private, or at least contested, good, and under those circumstances, hunters may have decided to protect the resource and defer consumption *as long as* they could continue to derive competitive status advantages by so doing, thus lowering the discount rate. However, this process would have required the re-allocation of labor to maintain societal reproduction during the period of the transition (which would have been protracted) and in the case of the Río Asana valley, it meant changes in settlement patterns. Women would have become more dependent upon the returns from hunting and herding, as it became more difficult to provision their families from their own collecting efforts, and this in turn may have led to the diminishment of their status, which is commonly observed in pastoral societies.

Although I have shown this model to be plausible and the predictions generated from it consistent with data recovered from excavations at sites in the valley, it is far from being demonstrated. However, I also believe that it presents a compelling alternative to models of the domestication process in the Andes which assert that herding was a response to environmental risk. If anything, the model developed in this chapter shows that herding, at least in the short run, was highly risky and that some men capitalized on this risk to their own reproductive benefit. Further, it could only have been successful if women's labor was re-allocated.

Testing this or any other model derived from HBE sources is fraught with significant problems and obstacles. As Zeanah (2004, 28) notes, archaeologists have yet to develop a set of reliable middle-range propositions and tools that can be used consistently to examine the archaeological record from the perspective of HBE models. Although the basic requirements for the successful testing of an HBE model are those we would wish to have in any archaeological setting, HBE models demand high-quality environmental reconstructions, fine-grained settlement pattern data, and sufficient excavation at key sites in the settlement system so as to reconstruct activity performance and diet within a seasonal framework. And it should be obvious that while HBE models have general applicability, they can only be tested locally. That is, models must be tuned to specific paleoenvironmental and cultural historical settings and should not be extended unnecessarily. Taken together, these data can then be directed at two complementary reconstructions: alternative provisioning possibilities based upon gender and settlement patterns consistent with those provisioning strategies.

The necessity of these requirements figures prominently in the debate between William Hildebrandt and Kelly McGuire versus Jack Broughton and Fred Bayham about changes in hunting practices during the Middle Archaic period in California (Hildebrandt and McGuire 2002; Broughton and Bayham 2003; Hildebrandt and McGuire 2003). Hildebrandt and McGuire have proposed that an observed shift in hunting strategies during the Middle Archaic toward the taking of artiodactyls is inconsistent with the predictions of optimal foraging theory, and that the faunal data from these sites are better explained by a costly signaling model, which

they label in their paper the "showing off" hypothesis. Broughton and Bayham counter that the most parsimonious explanation for this shift is that males turn to hunting large-bodied game such as the artiodactyls because ameliorating climatic conditions at the start of the late Holocene have substantially increased their numbers. Further, they assert that this is consistent with the predictions of optimal foraging theory, and that appeal to costly signaling models here is unnecessary. In his discussion of the debate, Zeanah (2004, 27–28) notes that while his own analysis of changing foraging patterns in the Carson Desert of western Nevada during the late Holocene bolsters the argument made by Hildebrandt and McGuire, he also asserts that their model is not directly testable because, among other things, it has a wide geographic scope and limited settlement pattern and paleoenvironmental data. In effect, the model, while plausible, is not "local enough" since alternative provisioning strategies within a well-defined settlement system cannot be evaluated, and given this situation, plausible reconstructions of men's and women's contribution to the diet and how these may have changed cannot be developed.

Zeanah's model is a good example of how to build a testable HBE model, and one that is applicable to this discussion. For his Carson Desert setting, Zeanah has copious and high-quality paleoenvironmental reconstructions that allow him to recreate plant and animal communities at different times in the past. Further, through ethnography and ethnohistory, he is able to create species lists of both major and minor resources critical to the indigenous peoples of the region. Combined with data on plant and animal productivity and experimental data on harvesting efficiency, these sources of information create the basis for the reconstruction of alternative provisioning strategies by gender on a seasonal basis. Although Zeanah reconstructs these strategies as averages (that is, without considering interannual or seasonal variability), a dynamic model could represent variability effectively. Alternatively, as I have argued elsewhere (Aldenderfer 1998, 278–79), while average values for return rates may not capture decision making with precision, they do provide insight into human decision making at a heuristic level, and deviations from this modal state on modeling outcomes can be evaluated and estimated.

Zeanah then integrates these alternative provisioning strategies with fine-grained settlement pattern data from the region, and develops a model of central place foraging based upon them. He shows that in the period before AD 1250, it is probable that women's foraging decisions drove the establishment of central places. They were located near high-quality plant patches that varied on a seasonal basis. In contrast, men's activities were focused on the logistical hunting of large-bodied game from these central places.

Viewed from this perspective, the limitations of the model I have presented are obvious. While we have excellent data on site distributions and activity performance in the time periods most critical to the transition to herding from hunting, and therefore, can construct plausible models of settlement patterns, our data on the productivity and distribution of plant species important to the diet and high-quality paleoenvironmental reconstruction of the transitional period are poor, thus making it difficult to create truly robust estimates of provisioning strategies of men and women. However, the trend of the model is clear: even using a single major plant species—the chenopods—women would have been able to provision their families without a significant contribution from men's hunting returns. Comparisons with ethnography bolster this contention; San and Hadza women often capture small mammals during the foraging trips, thus adding protein to the diet. Women in the Asana valley could have done so as well, and the faunal data do show presence of small numbers of rodent and small mammal species. Within the contexts of these limitations, I argue that the model I have presented is plausible, but hardly tested in the classic sense of the term.

At least two other guanaco domestication trajectories could be explored through this model. In Chile at the extreme northern limits of the Atacama desert in the Puripica river drainage, Nuñez (1981) and Santoro and Nuñez (1987) report on a series of sites that appear to reflect a trajectory toward sedentarization from 4800–4000 B.P. within a context of possible animal and plant domestication. Hesse (1982a, b) notes that the faunal remains, most probably guanaco from Puripica 1, one of the key sites in the region, reflect incipient herding and animal management. The role of plants, however, is limited, although grinding stones are said to be present in the assemblage. Hesse (1982a) argues that given the extremely fragile environment of the region, an optimal strategy would have been to focus hunting strategies on the most predictable resource in the drainage, the camelids. Plants would have been of secondary importance given their low abundance and low predictability. If anything, chenopod densities in the arid Atacama would have been significantly lower than those in the Río Asana drainage throughout this period. Hesse further argues that herd management would have been an important risk-buffering strategy, and management would have led rapidly to their domestication by ca. 4000 B.P. The second is from northwestern Argentina, where Olivera and Elkin (1994) argue that guanacos may well have been domesticated by 4000 B.P. Unfortunately, both regions have limited paleoenvironmental reconstructions and therefore, plausible reconstructions of alternative provisioning strategies will be extremely difficult to develop.

No matter what the empirical setting, however, it is apparent that models derived from the full spectrum of human behavioral ecology have a prominent role to play as we begin to improve our understanding of the process of plant and animal domestication in the Andean highlands.[2]

NOTES

1. Dates are expressed as uncalibrated calendar years before present (B.P.).

2. Acknowledgments. This material is based upon work supported by the National Science Foundation under Grant No. BNS 8822261, an award from the H. John Heinz III Charitable Trust, four awards from Northwestern University, and a Regents Junior Faculty Fellowship from the University of California. This paper has been informed by many discussions with Nathan Craig, who helped me think through the many implications of costly signaling theory. I also wish to thank Douglas Kennett and Bruce Winterhalder for working with me so patiently as this paper evolved through a series of incarnations. They have been excellent editors and advisors. All errors of interpretation are mine alone.

9

Human Behavioral Ecology, Domestic Animals, and Land Use during the Transition to Agriculture in Valencia, Eastern Spain

Sarah B. McClure, Michael A. Jochim, and C. Michael Barton

Most applications of Human Behavioral Ecology (HBE) to questions of agricultural origins have focused on plant domestication in archaeological contexts in the New World, where domestic animals were generally less important in early agricultural societies. In contrast, domestic animals play an important part in subsistence strategies and land use in Old World early agricultural societies. In this chapter, we examine the role of domestic animals in changes of land use during the transition to, and consolidation of, food producing economies in Valencia, Spain. Using the behavioral ecological model of ideal free distribution as a heuristic concept, we show the tight linkage between agricultural subsistence strategies, herd management, and long-term dynamics of human land use. Two broadly different herd management strategies were stable for long periods of time and the shift from one to the other was tightly linked with socioecological changes during the Neolithic.

In recent years, ecological approaches to the origin of and transition to agriculture have been popular, especially in research conducted out-side of Europe (e.g., Cowan and Watson 1992; Harris and Hillman 1989; Price and Gebauer 1995a; Smith 2002). These include studies founded in Human Behavioral Ecology (HBE), focusing on co-evolutionary processes, risk minimization strategies, resource selection, or a combination of these as explanatory or exploratory models for understanding the adoption of domesticates into prehistoric subsistence practices (e.g., Barlow 2002; Blumler et al. 1991; Gremillion 1996a; Hawkes and O'Connell 1992; Layton et al. 1991; Piperno and Pearsall 1998; Rindos 1980, 1984; Winterhalder 1993; Winterhalder and Goland 1997).

Risk minimization is often called upon to explain the move from foraging to farming-based subsistence economies (see Winterhalder and Goland 1997; Redding 1981). In these models, domesticates, usually plants, are regarded as risk minimizers; initially adopted to diversify the existing resource base. Through co-evolutionary processes (Rindos 1980, 1984) or simple intensification, the efficiency of the resource as a food source rises. In this view, domesticates gradually became the dominant subsistence resources, and risk minimization strategies shifted to a focus on diversification through use of fall-back wild resources, plot dispersal, and perhaps other mechanisms (e.g., Blumler 1996; O'Shea 1989; Winterhalder 1990; Winterhalder and Goland 1993, 1997). These approaches have been effective in a variety of archaeological contexts, primarily when dealing with the origins of plant domestication and the gradual shift towards widespread food production. These studies are based on the concepts of foraging theory, in that they share the assumption that individuals will adjust their behavior to maximize the payoff or minimize the risks of various foraging and farming activities. For example, Gremillion (1996a) used diet breadth and opportunity cost models from optimal foraging theory to identify when an introduced crop would be adopted by agriculturalists. She argued that the adoption of a new resource is possible in times of abundance as well as in scarcity, but with different goals: efficiency maximization in the former, and risk minimization in the latter. Using the models as a heuristic device, she then examines the introduction of the peach into the subsistence regime in the southeastern U. S. and the regional differences in the intensity of maize agriculture. Especially for those with relatively low energetic contributions she concluded that the adoption of new crops can result from decisions to minimize subsistence risk (Gremillion 1996a, 199).

Applications of foraging theory to agricultural contexts with domestic animals are rare, and tend to focus on the initial stages of animal domestication (e.g., Redding 1981; Alvard and Kuznar 2001). Although foraging theory has been widely applied to hunting activities archaeologically and in the ethnographic present (see Winterhalder and Smith 2000), it seems ill-suited to the analysis of domestic animals, which appear to provide a stable, readily available source of meat without the costs of pursuit time and transportation associated with hunting wild animals (see Barlow 2002; Cannon 2003; Grayson and Cannon 1999). An exception is the ethnographic research by Mace (1990, 1993a, 1993b), who has developed a model for explaining investment in herds and agriculture among agropastoralist societies in Sub-Saharan Africa. The dynamic optimality modeling she employs investigates the adaptiveness of pastoralist subsistence strategies for long-term household survival (Mace 1993a) and transitions between cultivation and pastoralism, based on the assumption that farming and herding households adopt strategies that maximize their chances of remaining viable over a generation or longer (Mace 1993b). The modeling suggests that household wealth plays an important role in the subsistence decisions made—whether in the context of a shift to more agriculture or in management strategy of animals—and is a key factor in determining the optimal strategy of a household. In other words, there is no single optimal strategy for farming or pastoralism, or the combination thereof. Mace's research shows that an optimality-based model is effective for understanding the interplay between domesticated plants and animals in subsistence decisions, although the implications of this for archaeologists are limited by the extent to which we can generate the necessary data for evaluating the model from Neolithic contexts.

Foraging theory in general provides a multitude of approaches, some of which may be more useful than others for understanding the transition to agriculture and addressing contexts that include domestic animals. In this chapter we employ the ideal free distribution model, from behavioral ecology (Fretwell and Lucas 1970), to explore the dynamic relationship between domestic resource management and land use, and focus on the cultural and economic developments in Valencia, eastern Spain, during the Neolithic. In the following, we briefly outline the cultural developments of the Neolithic in Valencia and describe the diachronic nature of agricultural production in the region. Secondly, we describe the ideal free distribution model. We then discuss the relationship between domestic animal management and land use in Neolithic Valencia.

Finally, we suggest a model of Neolithic land use and how the ideal free distribution model may be a useful heuristic device for understanding the changes in the subsistence-settlement patterns that occurred in this region.

THE BEGINNINGS OF AGRICULTURE IN EASTERN SPAIN

In Europe, the origin of food production is usually explained by the introduction of farming techniques to a region via colonization by farmers or through indigenous adoption of farming practices, and subsequent processes of dispersion such as acculturation and/or migration (Bernabeu et al. 1993; Bernabeu et al. 2001; Price 2000b). The archaeological record in different parts of Europe suggests that this transition was highly varied. Agriculture became established quickly and apparently exclusively in some regions, whereas others show long-term survival of distinct foraging and farming populations in close proximity, with varying degrees of interaction (e.g., Barnett 1995, 2000; Binder 2000; Bogucki 2000; Clark 1990; Dennell 1985; Halstead 1996; Jochim 2000; Keeley 1996; Price 1996, 2000b; Thomas 1996; Tringham 2000; Whittle 1996; Zilhao 1993; Zvelebil 1986a, 1996; Zvelebil and Lillie 2000). For example, in central Europe the transition to agriculture is marked by the rapid appearance of agriculturalists known as the Linearbandkeramik (LBK) culture group. The archaeological record for LBK is dramatically different than for the late Mesolithic hunter-gatherer groups in Germany. Late Mesolithic sites were generally ephemeral and contain the remains of collected wild foods. Contemporary LBK sites were larger and contain uniform house structures that suggest a high degree of residential stability. The settlements were strategically placed on productive loess soils and contain the charred remains of cultigens, domesticated animal bones, ceramics, and polished stone axes that were likely used to clear fields (Jochim 2000). This situation has long been considered a good example of agricultural migration and displacement of indigenous hunter-gatherers. Current research also suggests that dispersion of domesticates, farming techniques, and knowledge into non-farming areas and their adoption by local foragers may have played an important role in the transition to agriculture (Jochim 2000). A similar but prolonged transition from foraging to farming is evident in southern Scandinavia, where indigenous hunter-gatherers traded with nearby farmers for nearly a millennium, then made a rapid shift to an agricultural lifeway (Price 2000c; Price and Gebauer 1995a).

In eastern Spain (Figure 9.1), archaeological evidence indicates that the first domesticated plants (einkorn wheat, *Triticum monococcum*; barley, *Hordeum vulgare*; and legumes such as Haba beans, *Vicia faba*; lentils, *Lens culinaris*; and peas, *Pisum sativum*) and animals (sheep, *Ovis aries*; goat, *Capra hircus*; cow, *Bos taurus*; and pig, *Sus domesticus*) were introduced into the region by 5600 BC (Bernabeu et al. 1993; Bernabeu et al. 2001; Martí and Juan-Cabanilles 1997). The remains of these domesticated animals and plants are often found together with Cardial pottery, a distinctive type decorated with impressions of the Cardium shell. Cardial ceramics are considered to be part of the Impressed Ceramic Complex, the first pottery assemblages to be found widely distributed throughout the western Mediterranean (Bernabeu 1995; Martí 1998). The domesticated plants and animals are generally considered to be of Near Eastern origin (Hopf 1991; Nguyen and Bunch 1980), despite potential wild progenitors of pigs and cattle in the area (see Rowley-Conwy 1995).

In the western Mediterranean, researchers generally interpret Cardial assemblages in one of two ways; either as (1) a colonization of farmers or (2) an indigenous adoption of domesticated animals and plants by foragers in the region (e.g., Barnett 1995, 2000; Bernabeu et al. 1993; Bernabeu et al. 2001; Bernabeu 1996; Donahue 1992; Martí and Juan-Cabanilles 1987; Martí 1998; Zilhao 1993, 1998, 2000). Few data are currently available to address this question on a large scale. However, several studies focused on the Neolithic occupation of Portugal, Spain, and southern France

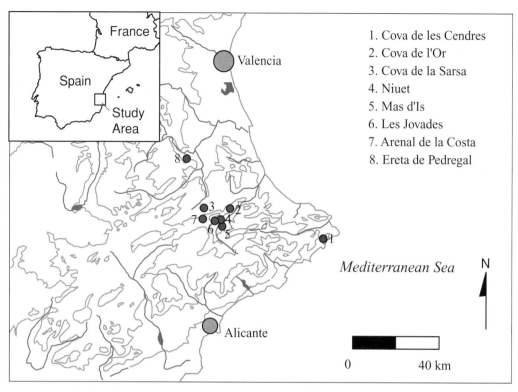

FIGURE 9.1. Archaeological sites in Valencia mentioned in text.

(Arnaud 1982; Barnett 1995, 2000; Barton et al. 1999; Barton et al. 2004; Bernabeu 1995, 1996; Binder 2000; Zilhao 1993, 1998, 2000), suggest that the introduction of agricultural practices to the Iberian Peninsula may have resulted from a combination of colonization and adoption by local hunter-gatherers (see Bernabeu 1996; Price 2000b, 2000c; Zilhao 2000).

The chronology of the Valencian Neolithic is reconstructed largely from archaeological sequences from two cave sites: Cova de l'Or and Cova de les Cendres (Martí and Juan-Cabanilles 1987, 1997; Martí 1998) (Figure 9.1), and primarily based on changes in pottery styles rather than the documentation of changing economic activities (Bernabeu 1989). The Neolithic is divided into two phases (Table 9.1), with subdivisions based on decorative shifts in ceramics (Bernabeu 1995). Neolithic I (5600–4500 BC) is defined by the predominance of decorated ceramics, primarily impressed and incised wares, including Cardial Ware, which appears

in assemblages to varying degrees. Cardial impressed ceramics persist after 3800 BC in some parts of Valencia, but drop out of many assemblages across the Iberian Peninsula (Bernabeu 1989, 1995, 1996; Martí and Juan-Cabanilles 1997). Highly decorated wares decline during the subsequent Neolithic II (4500–2400 BC) phase in favor of undecorated ceramics. The final Neolithic II or Chalcolithic (HTC) (2400–1800 BC) is defined by the presence of "Bell Beaker" vessels, a characteristic form of pottery that marks the transition from the Neolithic to the Bronze Age in the region (Bernabeu 1995; Bernabeu and Pascual 1998).

In stark contrast to the early farming communities of the eastern Mediterranean (e.g., Nea Nikomedea in Greece or sites throughout the Levant; Bar-Yosef and Belfer-Cohen 1992; Byrd 1992; Whittle 1996), evidence in the Valencia Province for aggregated settlement is not strong until the Neolithic II, several millennia after the introduction of domesticates and agricultural

TABLE 9.1

Chronology of the Neolithic in Valencia, Spain

TIME PERIOD	DATES	CERAMIC CHARACTERISTIC
Neolithic I (NI)	5600–4500 BC	predominance of decorated ware, including Cardial
Neolithic II (NII)	4500–2400 BC	decline in decorated ware
Chalcolithic (HCT)	2400–1800 BC	Bell Beaker vessels

techniques to the region (Barton et al. 1999, 2002; Martí 1998; Martí and Juan-Cabanilles 1987, 1997; Whittle 1996). The settlement pattern appears to shift from dispersed, relatively ephemeral settlements in the Neolithic I to aggregated villages, such as Niuet and Arenal de la Costa (see Figure 9.1), later in the Neolithic II phase. These villages are characterized by labor investment in built facilities and internal organization: ditches, storage areas, and wattle and daub constructed houses, and they are located in similar ecological settings in larger valley bottoms and in upland valleys (Bernabeu 1993, 1995; Bernabeu et al. 1994; Pascual 1989). Although relatively little is known about early Neolithic open-air sites, current research by Bernabeu et al. (2002, 2003), Barton et al. (2004), and others (e.g. Bosch et al. 2002) suggest that some degree of settlement aggregation may begin during the Neolithic I in some areas.

Settlement aggregation has been interpreted as a shift from agriculturalists to "campesinos," connoting an intensification of agricultural subsistence practices and corresponding changes in social organization and cultural behavior (Martí and Juan-Cabanilles 1987; Martí 1998), including the emergence of social stratification and intensified exchange relationships with more distant groups, such as in Andalucia in southern Spain, several hundred kilometers away. As Barnett (2000) has recently suggested, the Neolithic in the western Mediterranean presents an interpretive challenge as it represents the rapid and early appearance, but slow assimilation of production-based economies among

emergent agricultural societies (see also Zvelebil 1986b). In other words, agriculture was the focus of subsistence activities well before characteristic features of agricultural societies, such as aggregated villages, are identifiable archaeologically. In Valencia, the available record suggests that domestic plants and animals were in use for over a millennium before aggregated farming villages became widely established in the region. Taking up this challenge, we suggest that the nature of domestic animal and plant management in the particular ecological landscape of Valencia affords insights into these developments. We now summarize what is known about early agricultural strategies in Valencia and then evaluate these data within the framework of the ideal free distribution model.

THE NATURE OF EARLY AGRICULTURE IN VALENCIA

The reconstruction of early agricultural activity in any region is never an easy task. In Valencia, as is the case across most of the western Mediterranean, excavated Neolithic I data come almost exclusively from cave and rock shelter deposits. The only exception is ongoing research at the early Neolithic open-air site of Mas d'Is that so far has produced small floral and faunal samples that are still under study (Bernabeu 2001, personal communication). On the other hand, most Neolithic II subsistence data derive from open-air sites, with little from caves and rock shelters, making comparisons between time periods difficult. Results of archaeological

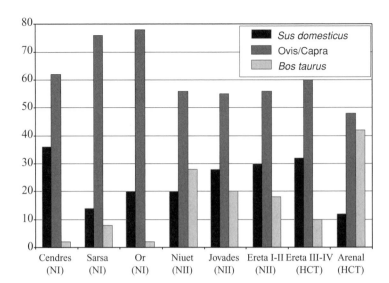

FIGURE 9.2. Relative percentage of identified domestic faunal remains from seven sites in Valencia. Parentheses indicate chronological placement of site (after Bernabeu 1995; Bernabeu and Pascual 1998; Pérez 1999).

surveys in the region suggest that Neolithic I settlement was located on the valley floor (Barton et al. 1999; Bernabeu et al. 1999), surrounded by fertile soils and close to water sources. In the Neolithic II, villages are found in similar locations to Neolithic I sites, but others are positioned in more marginal areas, such as along valley margins and in higher elevation valleys. In all cases, however, Neolithic II villages are close to water sources, often located at the convergence of streams and rivers. Neolithic II settlements are more readily identified on the surface than Neolithic I sites because of their greater density of archaeological material.

Despite the lack of quantitative data from Neolithic faunal and floral assemblages, some patterns of domesticated plant and animal use are evident more generally in the archaeological record. Domestic legumes, wheat, and barley were grown from Neolithic I onwards (Badal et al. 1991), and it appears that additional cultigens were not added to this suite of cultivated plants later in the Neolithic (Bernabeu 1995). Wheat and barley are regularly found mixed together at Neolithic I sites in Valencia, a common pattern throughout the western Mediterranean during the early Neolithic. This has been interpreted as evidence for intercropping of these two species (i.e. cultivation within

the same plot; Bernabeu 1995; Bernabeu and Pascual 1998). However, in the Neolithic II, individual cultigens are found spatially segregated within archaeological deposits, with 95% of carbonized seeds encountered in an archaeological context, e.g. storage pit, from a single species, suggesting that the cultivation strategies were more focused. Alternatively, this pattern may be the result of differences in storage and consumption patterns between the Neolithic I and II.

Faunal assemblages at Neolithic sites indicate that goats, sheep, cattle, and pigs were the primary domesticated animals tended in the region (Figure 9.2). In addition to these domesticated animals, a variety of wild taxa, such as deer (*Cervus elaphus*) and rabbits (*Oryctolagus cuniculus*) continued to be taken (Bernabeu 1995; Pérez 1999). Sheep and goats (ovicaprids) are numerically the most economically important domestic animal in all Neolithic sites studied, particularly during Neolithic I when the bones of these animals dominate faunal assemblages. The dietary importance of pigs and cattle appears to change more dramatically within the suite of domestic animals over the course of the Neolithic (Bernabeu 1995; Pérez 1999). Figure 9.2 shows the relative percentage of identified domestic faunal remains from seven sites in eastern Spain. During the Neolithic I, 62–78% of the domestic animal assemblages consist of sheep and goats. Pigs are the second largest proportion of domestic animals, ranging from 14–36% of the assemblages. In contrast, only very few cows are documented (2–8%). In the Neolithic II sites of Niuet, Les Jovades and Ereta de Pedregal (Phase I–II), sheep and goats continue to dominate assemblages (~55%), and pigs remain in the 20–30% range. Notably, these sites show a significant increase in cow bone in comparison to the Neolithic I assemblages. During the Neolithic II, 20–30% of the domestic fauna found at archaeological sites are cattle bones. Generally, the relative importance of pigs is greater than cattle in all of the sites published, but cattle surpass pigs in some Chalcolithic (Copper Age) assemblages such as Arenal de la Costa (see Figure 9.1 for location).

A possible exception to this pattern is found at the Neolithic I open-air site at Mas d'Is, where two of the three bones found at the site were cattle bones (Bernabeu 2002, personal communication). In comparison, the faunal analysis at the open-air Neolithic I lake settlement of La Draga in Catalunya revealed almost 30% cattle bones with 25% pig and 30% sheep and goats of the total number of identifiable bone recovered (Bosch et al; 2002, Figure 115). However, the analysis of minimum number of individuals evidences that only 10.9% of the identified animals at La Draga are cattle, 12.3% pig, and 46.7% sheep and goats (Bosch et al. 2002, Figure 116), mirroring Neolithic I domestic animal assemblages elsewhere (see Pérez 1999). The predominance of cattle bone at Mas d'Is, as well as the higher number of identified cattle bones at La Draga, may well be due to taphonomic differences in survival rates of animal bones among species.

Diachronic changes are also found in herd composition and kill patterns of several species (see Bernabeu 1995). In the Neolithic II, more animals, especially cattle, sheep, and goats, reached adulthood than in the Neolithic I, suggesting a shift from a primary use as a meat

source to additional uses of secondary products such as milk, labor, and wool. This change in animal management has been noted throughout the Iberian Peninsula (Pérez 1999). Recently, Pérez (1999) summarized faunal data from several sites across the Iberian Peninsula and identified changes in herd management during the Neolithic II. Overall, cattle remains rise relative to other domestic taxa in the Neolithic II with a concurrent decline in ovicaprid bones. Pig bones generally remain constant through time. The dietary importance of wild animals, such as deer, wild boar, and rabbit, remained relatively constant throughout the Neolithic, but varied between sites (Pérez 1999). Charcoal studies of Niuet and Les Jovades (Badal 1993, 1994) show that in the second half of the Neolithic II, forested areas were limited to higher elevations. This is also evidenced by the low percentages of wild forest animals such as deer in archaeological assemblages at Niuet and Les Jovades (Pérez 1999, 97).

FARMING STRATEGIES IN THE VALENCIAN NEOLITHIC

The data from Neolithic sites in Valencia suggest two distinct forms of agriculture. The Neolithic I was a hoe-based farming strategy with relatively high yields that was conducted in well-watered regions and on the most fertile soils (Bernabeu 1995). By exploiting fertile land immediately around a settlement, it is thought to broadly resemble the traditional Mediterranean *el huerto* system of garden-plot cultivation. In this system, fields are located close to habitation sites and cultivation is more or less continuous, often without fallow or only short fallow periods. Rotation of cereals and legumes is frequent; other kinds of treatment such as manuring are possibly used. This planting strategy was complemented by ovicaprine husbandry, managed primarily for meat production and pastured in close proximity to habitation sites and agricultural fields. However, high productivity patches may have been limited and were dependant on the available soils and water. Therefore they may not have been amenable to significant intensification

(Bernabeu 1995). Areas may have been too small to support large aggregations, or may have been too quickly depleted for long-term occupation by larger groups. In general, however, this kind of locally focused, concentrated land use typified early Neolithic agropastoral systems elsewhere in the Mediterranean (Hill 2000; Rollefson and Kohler-Rollefson 1992).

During the Neolithic II a new farming strategy emerged. Much more extensive areas of less fertile upland soils were cleared and planted, facilitated by the possible introduc- tion of the oxen-pulled plow. This is more sim- ilar to the traditional Mediterranean farming system known as *secano*, or dry land farming (Bernabeu 1995), in which larger plots are ro- tated between winter and spring cereals, lying fallow over a longer three-year rotation. Due to the geographically extensive nature of this sys- tem, the distance between the villages and plots were larger (Bernabeu 1995). With more area in cultivation, herds had to be grazed in fallow fields or at greater distances from settlements. Herd management also shifted to a more diver- sified focus that emphasized secondary prod- ucts, such as milk products, wool, and labor, in addition to meat.

IDEAL FREE DISTRIBUTION

The ideal free distribution (Fretwell and Lucas 1970) is widely used in non-human population ecology, making it one among a small set of fundamental behavioral ecology models (Suther- land 1996). It seeks to represent habitat selec- tion choices of individuals based on the evolu- tionary framework that individuals will maximize fitness. Originally employed in stud- ies on bird populations (Fretwell and Lucas 1970), the ideal free distribution model has since been applied to a variety of animal species. Anthropological applications include the spatial pattern of salmon fishing boats off the coast of Canada (Abrahams and Healey 1990) and sperm whalers off the Galapagos Islands and in the north Pacific in the nineteenth century (Whitehead and Hope 1991).

With its focus on habitat selection, the model of ideal free distribution can be used to explore how individuals use and distribute themselves across a landscape under a variety of social and environmental conditions. A habitat is defined as the area where a species is able to colonize and live (Fretwell and Lucas 1970, 18). A landscape may be divided into different habi- tats, potentially of different sizes. Habitat selec- tion is based on the suitability of the habitat, and both population-density dependent and in- dependent factors may play a role in a habitat's suitability. The distribution of individuals among habitats is therefore determined by the relative suitability of available habitats (Fretwell and Lu- cas 1970, 19). This point ties in with Brown's (1969) concept of the buffer effect: at low popu- lation densities, individuals tend to live predomi- nantly in the better habitats. At higher popula- tion densities, a larger fraction will be found in poorer habitats (see also Sutherland 1996, 7). A habitat's *basic suitability* is defined when popu- lation density is close to zero. This is the first step in ordering habitats, and, by definition, no two habitats have equal basic suitabilities (Fretwell and Lucas 1970, 21).

The ideal free distribution (IFD) makes sev- eral assumptions. First, all individuals have the information to select and the ability to set- tle in the most suitable habitat available. There are no barriers, social or otherwise, that would prohibit this behavior. This optimization as- sumption is the "ideal" in the IFD. Second, all individuals are free to shift their habitat selec- tion in response to local population density. As a result of this adjustment, all individuals within a local population will come to have identical expected success rates: there is equal access to resources within the habitat. This as- sumption provides the "free" in ideal free dis- tribution. The model assumes that individuals are able to enter any habitat on an equal basis with existing residents. Furthermore, all indi- viduals are alike in their needs and therefore in their assessment of habitats.

It is key to the model that habitat suitability will change as a result of the density of individuals

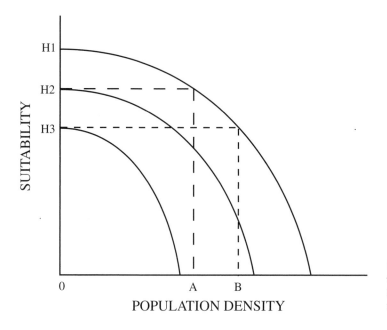

FIGURE 9.3. Ideal free distribution model (after Fretwell and Lucas 1970, 24; Sutherland 1996, 5).

exploiting it. The value of a habitat may decline because of *interference* or *depletion*. Interference results in the short-term decline of intake rate that decreases a habitat's suitability due to the presence of others (Sutherland 1996, 7). Examples of interference include increases in fighting and stealing, and under these conditions resources are simply less accessible. Depletion, on the other hand, works in the long term and is defined by the actual removal or reduction of resources caused by immediate consumption or degradation of the environment through time.

Figure 9.3 graphically shows the expectations of the ideal free distribution model (after Fretwell and Lucas 1970, 24). In this figure, habitat 1 (H1) has a higher suitability than habitat 2 (H2), with basic suitability defined at zero population density. However, with increase in population, the suitability of the habitat declines. When density reaches point A, the suitability of H1 is equal to H2 with zero density. With increased population, individuals will now settle in both H1 and H2. This pattern continues with habitat 3 (H3). When population density reaches point B, suitability is equal between H1, H2 and H3. With an increase in population,

individuals will now settle in H1, H2, or H3. The general process is the following: if individuals are making the best habitat choice available to them, then they will distribute themselves first in the best resource location, and when the suitability there has dropped to the suitability level of the next-ranked habitat, they will move so that their relative densities equalize the marginal suitabilities of the two habitats. This distribution is an equilibrium because no individual can gain by moving. As populations continue to increase, densities within each habitat will rise, and more habitats will be occupied.

ALLEE'S PRINCIPLE

Another type of change in suitability is found in Allee's principle. This states that habitat suitability measured by the survival and reproductive rates of individuals residing there may initially rise with increasing population size, up to some maximum (Allee et al. 1949). Only when population size increases beyond this threshold do survival and reproduction begin to decrease (Figure 9.4). In effect, at low densities there are increasing returns to scale. Among agricultural communities, an example of this might be

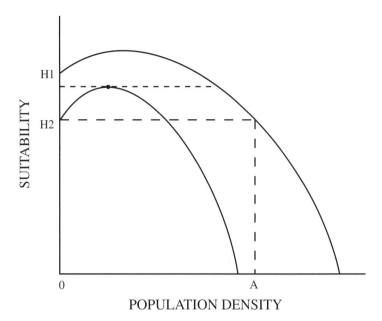

FIGURE 9.4. Allee's principle (after Fretwell and Lucas 1970, 25; Sutherland 1996, 11).

investment in irrigation systems or field terraces. The terracing of hillsides requires a great amount of labor input, and a minimum number of individuals to tend the structures; the potential returns of farming are greatly increased by enlarging the area available for farming.

Figure 9.4 shows two habitats that respond to population density and exploitation in a manner consistent with Allee's principle (after Sutherland 1996, 11; Fretwell and Lucas 1970, 25). In this situation, individuals will settle in habitat 1 (H1) and enjoy an increase in suitability of their habitat until they reach a population density threshold. This increase in suitability may also be termed "secondary suitability." Further increases in population density will decrease the secondary suitability of H1 until population density A, when the suitability in H1 equals the suitability at zero density in H2. With a further increase in population size, individuals will now settle in H2 and H1. However, in accordance with Allee's principle, the suitability of H2 increases with a growing population, while the suitability of H1 is decreasing. Secondary suitability is higher in H2 than at H1 at this point, making it advantageous for individuals to move from H1 to H2. With the assump-

tions of the ideal free distribution, individuals will continue to move into H2 until the suitability in H2 reaches its threshold. At that point, individuals will fill both habitats so that the marginal suitability of the two is equal (see above). The model predicts that due to these changes in suitability, even a very small change in population density may result in a very large change in distribution (Fretwell and Lucas 1970).

As shown above, land use patterns in Valencia change from Neolithic I to Neolithic II. The ideal free distribution model provides a theoretically grounded framework for understanding the settlement shift visible in the Neolithic. It identifies a set of factors and processes that may be influencing habitat selection and population distribution, and makes predictions about how these should change with changes in population density, habitat suitability, and related factors. Habitats will be settled in order of their basic suitability, and will be occupied in densities that equalize their marginal suitabilities. Livestock management involves use of the landscape to ensure that domestic animals are an economically viable resource. This spatial component of animal management is an important factor in estimating a habitat's suitability. Neolithic domestic animals of eastern Spain provide different meat yields, have differing potentials to provide secondary products, and their lifespans and survival needs may be more or less suited to subsistence practices more generally implemented by farmers. Similarly, animal management strategies—and their attendant costs—also vary according to taxa and according to the uses to which animals are put. The management strategies employed for domestic animals affects the suitability of a habitat. Below, we examine the potential returns and costs of Neolithic animal husbandry in eastern Spain. Subsequently we examine the spatial components of animal management and their implications for habitat choices in light of the IFD.

MANAGING DOMESTIC ANIMALS IN SPAIN

The diachronic patterns evident in faunal assemblages suggest changes in animal management during the course of the Neolithic, with pigs and cattle becoming a greater percentage of domestic animal assemblages in the Neolithic II. We summarize the temporal and spatial implications associated with the documented shifts in domestic animal assemblages at Neolithic sites, and we look at some of the behavioral characteristics of each of the domestic animal species found in Neolithic Spain to gauge the spatial and temporal needs that farmers had to reconcile to make animal management worthwhile.

CATTLE

Prior to their extinction in the seventeenth century, aurochs (*Bos primigenius*), ancestors of domestic cattle (*Bos taurus*) were found extensively across Europe, including Spain. Prehistorically and historically, wild cattle are most commonly associated with wooded landscapes. Since cattle lack upper incisors, they primarily rely on plants that are easily torn, such as grasses, leaves, and the branch tips of woody plants.

The domestic cattle found in Neolithic contexts are thought to have been introduced from the eastern Mediterranean (Bernabeu 1995; Martí

1998; Pérez 2002) and not domesticated locally despite the presence of wild cattle in the region prior to the Neolithic. Cattle are present in low frequency in Valencian Neolithic I, but their importance increases notably during the Neolithic II. Furthermore, kill patterns document a change in herd management in the Neolithic II, when more animals reached adulthood, marking a shift from use primarily as a meat source to milk production and labor (Bernabeu 1995; Pérez 1999). The latter is clearly supported by bone pathologies on the articulations of extremities found only in Neolithic II assemblages that seem to indicate use as draught animals for plows and/or carts (Pérez 1999).

Modern cattle do not have a specific breeding season, and calving can occur at any time (Gregg 1988, 103). Farmers can control the breeding season by restricting a bull's access to heifers, providing farmers the opportunity to dictate when calves and associated lactation take place. To achieve this end, a farmer must spatially separate the bulls and heifers to create a breeding season. This means a greater investment in pens to keep the animals separate.

Cattle provide farmers with a wide array of products, such as meat, milk, blood, leather, bone, and labor. Gregg (1988) has tabulated the amount of meat and milk production a herd of cattle would provide, as well as its required grazing area. Our estimates are taken from Gregg (1988) and based on modern, unimproved cattle (Dyson-Hudson and Dyson-Hudson 1970) and estimates of Neolithic cattle sizes. On average, a single mature cow can provide 1.78 liters of milk surplus daily and a meat offtake of ca. 225 kg, while requiring an average of 1.5 ha (3.7 acres) of pasture (Bakels 1982) or 1 ha (2.47 acres) of forested land per month for grazing (Bogucki 1982) (Table 9.2). Steers or castrated bulls are difficult to identify archaeologically (Grigson 1982), but they provide a range of advantages to farmers. Castration speeds weight gain in cattle and makes the animal easier to handle. An older steer, also called an ox, provides the strongest and most reliable source of labor.

SHEEP AND GOATS

Although mountain goats (*Capra pyrenaica*) were present in Valencia during the early Neolithic, domestic goats (*Capra hircus*) were introduced to the region from the Near East (Nguyen and Bunch 1980; Pérez 2002) and not domesticated locally. Domestic sheep and goats (ovicaprids) combined dominate all of the Neolithic I and II faunal assemblages in the Province of Valencia, comprising 48–78% of domestic animal assemblages (Figure 9.2), and show an increase in the ratio of sheep to goats through time (Bernabeu 1995; Bernabeu and Pascual 1998; Pérez 1999).

After bearing young (one to two per year), sheep lactate for an average of 135 days, whereas goats lactate for 210 days. Redding (1981) estimates that the daily average surplus of milk from sheep is 0.33 l and goats is 0.38 l. The meat offtake is approximately 50% of the live weight, resulting in ca. 12 kg for adult females and 5 kg for lambs and kids (see Gregg 1988) (Table 9.2).

Changes in slaughter patterns of both sheep and goats suggest a corresponding change in herd use between the Neolithic I and II. In the Neolithic I site of Cova de l'Or (ca. 5500–4900 BC) the vast majority of ovicaprids killed were under three years of age (Bernabeu 1995). This pattern is found at other Neolithic I cave sites throughout the Mediterranean, and contrasts with Neolithic II villages, where the majority of animals were harvested after reaching adulthood (Bernabeu 1995). As with cattle, this pattern suggests the increased use of milk products and wool in addition to meat.

PIGS

Wild boar (*Sus scrofa*), the ancestor of the domestic pig (*Sus domesticus*), is found throughout the European continent and remains a popular game animal in Valencia. It is very difficult to separate the two species in archaeological assemblages, which has led some researchers to argue for an indigenous domestication or very late introduction of domestic pigs in parts of the western Mediterranean (e.g. Rowley-Conwy 1995). However, the introduction of pigs to Mediterranean islands as part of an initial agricultural package is well documented (Pérez 2002), and substantiates the possibility that pigs were introduced in other parts of the western Mediterranean as well. It is generally assumed that domestic pigs were introduced to Valencia along with the suite of domestic animals; the separation of wild from domestic animals in archaeological sites is based on osteological metric analyses. Throughout the Valencian Neolithic, pigs comprise the next largest percentage of domestic faunal remains at archaeological sites after combined ovicaprids, although cattle come to nearly equal pig remains in some Neolithic II contexts (Bernabeu 1995).

Meat production is the primary advantage of pig farming. Pigs are the most prolific breeders (up to 15 piglets a year) of all domesticates in the western Mediterranean. Pigs mature rapidly, can live up to 20 years, and provide the highest caloric meat yield of any of the available domesticates. Preferring nuts and fruits, pigs are omnivorous, and can convert refuse and spoilage into a nutrient-rich food source. Prehistoric pigs were much smaller than modern pigs, and their meat offtake per adult animal is estimated at ca. 15–25 kg (Glass 1991; Gregg 1988; Jacomet and Schibler 1985; Müller 1985) (Table 9.2). However, keeping pigs has its challenges. As Zeder (1996, 1998) points out, pigs have higher water requirements, a lower heat tolerance, and cannot convert cellulose-rich grasses into proteins. In arid environments they are usually kept close to home with access to shade and wallow (Zeder 1998). Pigs congregate in smaller groups where they follow a dominant individual, often an older sow. This tracking behavior is easily transferred to a human swine herder (Zeder 1996). Unlike other domesticates being discussed here, pigs are not easily moved over great distances. It is likely that during the Neolithic, movement was limited to short seasonal trips between river bottoms and oak forested hillsides (Zeder 1996).

THE ROLE OF SECONDARY PRODUCTS

To what extent were milk, wool, and labor important products of early domesticates? Did they

TABLE 9.2

Domestic Animal Products, Area Requirements, and Birthing Rates

TAXON	MEAT OFFTAKE (kg)	MILK OFFTAKE PER DAY (LITERS)	MILK ENERGETIC RATE (kcal/kg) (RUSSELL 1988; REDDING 1981)	REQUIRED GRAZING AREA PER ANIMAL PER MONTH (ha)	NUMBER OF LACTATION DAYS	AVERAGE NUMBER OF YOUNG PER YEAR	MORTALITY RATE (%)	INTRINSIC RATE OF INCREASE (RUSSELL 1988)	FINITE RATE OF INCREASE (RUSSELL 1988)
Cow (*Bos taurus*)	225	1.78	839	1–1.5	200	1	20	0.033	1.034
Sheep (*Ovis aries*)	12–20	0.33	1096	0.1–0.15	135	1	32	0.061	1.063
Goat (*Capra hircus*)	12–20	0.38	668	0.1–0.15	210	2	42	0.109	1.115
Pig (*Sus domesticus*)	15–25	0	0	n/a	0	5–6	n/a	n/a	n/a

Note: Unless otherwise noted, data from Bogucki (1982) as summarized in Gregg (1988). Values for pig (*Sus domesticus*) are estimates for smaller, prehistoric pigs as opposed to modern breeds (Bogucki 1982).

influence decisions to domesticate or adopt certain species, and if so, how? Sherratt (1981) systematically called into question the use of secondary products in early Neolithic times. His study compiles the evidence for the use of the plow and cart, and the production of milk and wool in the Old World, with emphasis placed on the Near East and Europe, and concludes that secondary products only came into use several millennia after the spread of agriculture, well into the Valencian Neolithic II. Pictorial documentation from archaic Sumerian Uruk in southern Mesopotamia and pictograms on Akkadian period cylinder-seals from Mesopotamia and Assyria show that the plow and cart were in use by the third millennium BC. Archaeological evidence in central Europe dating to the third millennium BC and later, in the form of grave goods, ceramic vessel design, and rock art, show cattle yoked to carts or plows. Sherratt suggests that milking and wool manufacture were a late development in animal domestication. Early domesticates were not genetically modified enough to provide good and stable sources of milk and wool. Wooly sheep are a late phenomenon, appearing after several millennia of human selection. As for milk, Sherratt points to lactose intolerance among humans and low yields among animals as the main deterrents of early production practices. He argues that high milk and wool production emerged through time by active human selection of animal populations. A decrease in lactose intolerance and concurrent manufacture of milk products, in turn, is the result of millennia of human-animal interrelationships.

Many of his arguments have been questioned by archaeologists working in Europe (e.g. Gregg 1988; Rowly-Conwy 1995). Historic documents exist only from the third millennium BC onwards, serving *terminus antes quem*, rather than for dating of the use of secondary products. Furthermore, there is disagreement over the influence of lactose intolerance on the desirability of milk products. Fermentation of milk lowers the lactose content of cheese, yogurt, and similar products (McCraken 1971; Sherratt 1981). Even now there are high levels of lactose intolerance,

yet modern populations continue to consume fermented milk products. Sherratt himself argues for milk product consumption after the third millennium BC. Despite presumed evolutionary changes in cattle during the Neolithic (Sherratt 1981, 276), it still remains unclear why milk manufacture could only have taken place after several millennia of agriculture.

In addition to meat, cattle may provide milk and labor. The identification of milk production in archaeological contexts is difficult, and is mostly based on herd composition through the identification of kill patterns. The use of cattle (especially steers or oxen) for labor can be deduced from kill patterns as well as bone pathologies caused by physical stress. Sheep and goats also may be kept for milk and wool. Wool production is very difficult to identify directly archaeologically, and is usually indicated by textile production artifacts, such as spindle whorls or loom weights. Finally, while pigs provide a very stable and secure source of meat, they do not offer any other services or products other than refuse management.

Table 9.3 shows a ranking of domestic animals found in the Valencian Neolithic. In terms of caloric returns from meat alone, cattle rank the highest, followed by pigs then ovicaprids. The ranking changes when secondary products are added to the mix of energy return potential. When ranked by milk yield, cattle again rank highest, followed by goats and sheep. However, when ranked by the energetic rate of milk (kcal/kg), sheep rank highest, followed by cow and goat. In terms of reproductive capacity, pigs rank the highest of all of the domestic animals available. The finite rate of increase (Table 9.2; Russell 1988) shows the average rate at which a herd might grow. These data are not available for pigs, but differences in rate of increase are visible among goats (the highest), sheep, and cattle. The risk of herd loss was likely another element playing into agropastoralists' decisions at the time. Species react differently to climatic fluctuations, and management strategies may be influenced by pastoralists' desire to maximize herd stability (Mace and Houston 1989; Mace

TABLE 9.3
Domestic Animals in Descending Rank Order According to Different Characteristics

ARCHAEOLOGICAL RECORD	MEAT OFFTAKE	MILK YIELD	ENERGETIC RATE OF MILK	LABOR	REPRODUCTIVE CAPACITY
sheep and goat	cow	cow	sheep	cow	pig
pig	pig	goat	cow	pig, sheep and goat	goat
cow	sheep and goat	sheep	goat		sheep cow

Note: Compiled from Gregg 1988; Glass 1991; Redding 1981; Russell 1988.

1990, 1993a, 1993b; Redding 1981, 1982). The relative importance of domestic animals based solely on meat offtake is very different than if milk and reproductive capacity are considered.

ANIMAL MANAGEMENT COSTS

Managing domestic animals must take into account total extraction costs as well as returns. Time and labor for butchery and meat preparation should be generally equivalent to the extraction costs incurred for wild animals. However, herd management and its attendant costs can vary between domestic taxa, including the extraction and processing of some secondary products—especially milk, wool, and animal labor. In terms of management strategies, the domestic animals of Neolithic Valencia have different life histories and behavior, which, to a large extent, define a set of temporal and spatial needs that must be maintained and organized by a farmer.

Although pigs are comfortable foraging in woodland areas, they are difficult to supervise in such terrain, entailing search costs if humans are to harvest their meat. Domestic pigs are generally kept close to houses for use in refuse management, and, due to their need for shade and wallow, pigs often require a human-made shelter. Furthermore, pigs are not very mobile and require at least a part of the household to remain in proximity to the habitation.

Sheep and goats are much more mobile than pigs, and can be taken to a wide range of areas for long or short stays. However, these an-imals consume relatively large amounts of cellulose-rich plant materials (one hectare grazing area can supply 150 kg cattle vs. 133 kg sheep or goat meat offtake; Gregg 1988) and must be brought into fresh pasture regularly. Due to their agility, goats can reach leaves of trees and shrubs inaccessible to sheep, which allows them to forage more diverse resources. On the other hand, sheep move and feed in fairly tight groups and can graze in open vegetation more efficiently than goats (Halstead 1981, 324; Williamson and Payne 1965, 284–5). Sheep to goat ratios therefore inform us not only of the herd management goal (herd stability or protein maximization, see Redding 1981, 1982), but also of a farmer's spatial organization.

In a meat production strategy, herds of sheep and goats are kept small and many young animals are slaughtered at an early age. Only a few animals are allowed to mature to adulthood, providing greater meat packages and ensuring the reproductive survival of the herd. In a milk producing strategy, more lactating females are kept and herds are generally larger. Kill patterns show a preference for adult animals. Bucks and rams are lone animals, so in both strategies a spatial segregation between them and the does/ewes and young is expected. This separation can occur with relatively little investment by the farmer. However, the animals must be kept out of fields. Depending on the size of the herd, this may mean tethering the animals individually, or constructing a corral.

Alternatively, people may erect fences around their fields to keep out all free-ranging herbivores (wild or domestic). In either case, some sort of supervision while grazing near fields is necessary, and these options are potentially visible archaeologically.

Of all the domestic animals available in the Valencian Neolithic, cattle have the highest time and space requirements. As stated earlier, calving can occur at any time of the season, so if a farmer wants to control herd size and calving season, bulls and heifers must be kept apart from one another. Although they need less fodder per unit of body weight than sheep and goats (Clutton-Brock and Harvey 1978; Halstead 1981), cattle require large amounts of grazing area and/or leafy fodder. Also, they cannot thrive in as diverse a range of vegetation communities as can ovicaprids.

In a meat management strategy, cattle herds are small and consist of a bull and several heifers, with calves slaughtered at a higher rate. In a milk production strategy, more heifers must be kept to produce sufficient milk, increasing the grazing area needed. If oxen are kept for labor, these too need space for grazing away from plots, although the grazing area may be supplemented by bringing fodder to the animals. All of this requires an infrastructure and labor investment much greater than for the other animals.

Management costs seem notably lower for ovicaprids than for other Neolithic domestic animals in Mediterranean environments. They can be supported on small patches of landscape and on more diverse forage than cattle. Their smaller size and more regular breeding schedule also make them more manageable. While cattle better survive the cool humid climates and dense forests of northern and central Europe, they lose this advantage in the mesic and seasonally arid Mediterranean. Ovicaprids are not as prolific as pigs, but they require fewer built and maintained facilities and can thrive in a wider variety of habitats. Although ovicaprids do not consume refuse like pigs do, neither do they potentially compete with humans for food as do the omnivorous pigs.

We hypothesize that these overall lower management costs gave ovicaprids a net higher return across the Mediterranean in the early phases of the Neolithic, in spite of lower package size than cattle and lower reproduction rate than pigs. The potential for milk and wool secondary products helped maintain this high ranking in the Mediterranean over time. In the Neolithic II of Valencia, however, socioeconomic changes in the form of population aggregation and associated shifts in settlement in conjunction with different agricultural practices increased the net return rate of both cattle and pigs relative to ovicaprids. In a positive feedback relationship, these latter domestic taxa also helped to make these changes possible. Below, we discuss how the ideal free distribution concept provides a heuristic structure to address the interrelationships between cultivation, animal management, and long-term dynamics of human land use in the Neolithic of the western Mediterranean using this consideration of the relative costs and benefits of each of the domesticated resources (see Table 9.3).

DOMESTIC ANIMALS, LAND USE AND IDEAL FREE DISTRIBUTION DURING THE VALENCIAN NEOLITHIC: A MODEL OF CHANGE

As described above, the Neolithic I agricultural strategy may be characterized as a dispersed settlement focusing on the most productive landscape patches for hoe-agriculture, complemented by relatively small numbers of domestic animals. Of the domestic species available, sheep and goats were favored because of their low management costs. Neolithic I farmers utilized few high-ranking patches per household in an intensive fashion, farming a patch until fertility declined making it more productive to shift to another equally high-ranking patch. In terms of the ideal free distribution, we see these patches as being part of one habitat (Figure 9.5, H1). We have argued that domestic animals were kept for meat production. Sheep and goats

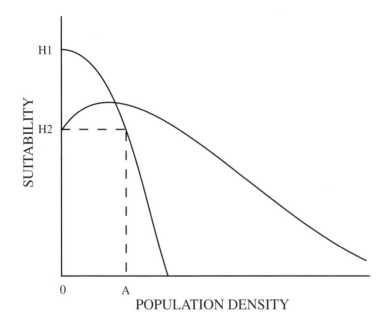

FIGURE 9.5. Adapted ideal free distribution and Allee's principle models for the Neolithic in Valencia, Spain. Habitat 1 (H1) represents settlement during Neolithic I, habitat 2 (H2) represents the Neolithic II settlement pattern.

complimented the plant management strategy by allowing humans to harvest resources in patches that would rank low for hoe-agriculture, such as abandoned fields and upland areas beyond the easily cultivated valley bottoms. In this context, sheep and goats would have been more favorable than higher-ranking cattle and pigs by minimizing the area needed for pasture and fodder. Sheep and goats also are easily moved from one area to another. Farmers could thus convert inedible vegetation into meat and access wild resources not available in the valley bottoms by letting their livestock graze in these upland areas.

However, this strategy had some long-term and unforeseeable consequences. Sheep grazing closely crop ground foliage, preventing the regeneration of seedlings, while goats preferentially browse leaves and twigs, especially new foliage, preventing seed generation. By farming more productive alluvial soils in the valley bottoms and then shifting these fields to intensive pasture for sheep and goat, where the latter are particularly efficient foragers, farmers would have put the lands at a higher risk of major erosion during the winter rainy season when vegetation cover is at a

minimum. Deforestation and increased sediment transport is evidenced by palaeobotanical and palynological data by the end of the Neolithic I (e.g., Badal 1990; Badal et al. 1994; Bernabeu and Badal 1990; Dupré 1988; Fumanal 1986; Fumanal and Dupré 1986). Changes in human population density would further have complicated this situation. Figure 9.5 shows the decline in the suitability of H1 with increased population density. Over time, high-ranking patches for hoe agriculture became scarcer, while sheep and goat grazing degraded areas farther afield. In essence, this farming strategy was likely an unintentional, expansive process with irreversible ecological consequences that resulted in the decline of suitability for this habitat. Notably, this was not simply a population-dependent decline in suitability, as indicated for classic ideal free distribution modeling described above, but a reduction of basic suitability that permanently lowered the ability of this habitat to support agropastoralists independent of subsequent shifts in population density.

The long-term response to the growing shortage of patches suitable for the Neolithic I agricultural pattern was to begin exploiting another habitat (Figure 9.5, H2) for agriculture during the Neolithic II. This was accompanied by more extensive clearance of woodland and use of ox-drawn plows. In some respects, this also represents a different socioecological niche. At some point in the late Neolithic I, the suitability of the originally unoccupied valley margins (H2) began to match that of the heavily exploited and depleted riverine floodplains (H1). Due to the permanent drop in the suitability curve for H1 habitats favored by Neolithic I agropastoralists, the new H2 habitats occupied by Neolithic II populations—and their new socioecological niche—remained favored over alternative habitats even with subsequent density-related declines in suitability. The Allee effect (Figure 9.5) for H2 is based on the necessary investments made in agricultural architecture, such as terracing. As is often the case in a shift to another habitat, occupation of this habitat entailed greater labor input per return with more extensive land-use, now a tactic comparable in returns to the best yields available in the more localized but depleted bottom lands. Numerous large storage pits at Les Jovades testify to sustaining a sizable sedentary population (Bernabeu 1993, 1995; Bernabeu and Pascual 1998; Pascual 1989). Archaeological evidence from a number of cave sites shows a shift in use of caves as corrals for sheep and goats during the Neolithic II (Badal 1999). The labor investment in constructing corrals suggests that larger herds of livestock were kept in the cave for longer periods of time. Farmers were thus using areas farther from villages for prolonged periods. These corrals would house ovicaprids while farmers could hunt and gather in upland areas.

This shift also had other, associated repercussions to human subsistence practices. These changes conform to predictions of other behavioral ecology models, especially the diet breadth model of optimal foraging theory. In Neolithic I contexts, the success of el huerto agropastoralism made a few domesticates a high ranking set of resources—i.e., a high caloric return for labor invested in cultivation and processing—with a corresponding reduction in diet breadth over

prior Mesolithic foragers. The subsequent decline in the productivity and availability of el huerto habitats of highest suitability (H1) may have meant a corresponding change in the use of domesticates as labor investment costs increased relative to caloric return with the shift to extensive Neolithic II agropastoralism.

The diet breadth model predicts that people will diversify their diet in response to the loss of high-ranking resources. In fact, some evidence suggests that one of the behavioral responses of farmers to these challenges during the Neolithic II may have been a notable increase in the use of wild plants and animals while tending domestic animals away from villages (Martí and Juan-Cabanilles 1987, 119–124). This is a counterintuitive pattern for an expanding agricultural economy, but in line with predictions of foraging theory. As the overall return of the subsistence system declined, resources formerly neglected because of low value relative to pursuit and handling costs should now become attractive. A more geographical consideration may also be important here: relocation to valley margins may have put people into closer proximity to species newly attractive to collectors.

Consistent with the Allee effect, we propose that the suitability of this new habitat for farming activity (Figure 9.5, H2) began to rise thanks to labor investment, improved technology, and changes in domestic animal management. Domestic animal management shifted from a focus on meat production to meat and milk production strategies, with a greater use of cattle and pigs. In conjunction, a more fundamental reorganization of scheduling and labor may have accompanied the economic changes. With a greater number of animals per settlement or household than in the Neolithic I, different members of a family (e.g., the young or old) may have been charged with activities such as feeding and milking, while others may have invested more time and labor into the construction of corrals and pens. Scheduling of activities would have been dictated in part by the animals' needs and in part by the demands of more extensive plant agriculture.

Mace (1993a, b) and Mace and Houston (1989) offer additional explanations for this kind of shift in strategies related to long-term viability of households. Reasons for such a shift could include changes in risk management strategies based on household wealth and a greater investment in farming as the subsistence focus. For instance, Mace and Houston (1989) demonstrate that in their study area in sub-Saharan Africa the optimal ratio of camels to goats for long-term household viability depends on total household wealth. The probability of a household remaining viable is dependent on the number and type of stock held. Their model predicts the herd species composition that a household should keep to maximize its long-term viability and shows how this is influenced by changes in household wealth (Mace and Houston 1989, 187–188). Goat herds grow at faster rates than camel herds, but they are more liable to heavy losses in droughts. In addition, camels have higher food yields (1:8 ratio) and can be traded for a greater amount of other food sources than goats (Mace and Houston 1989, 189–191). Based on these parameters, the optimal species mixtures vary depending on general household wealth. Poorer households should not invest in camels until total livestock wealth is well above the minimum wealth at which a household could theoretically exchange goats for a camel (Mace and Houston 1989, 192). After this point, the majority of the household's wealth should be invested in camels. In times of household wealth decline, camels can then be exchanged for goats, with investment in camels again only when the herd size has increased. Mace and Houston's (1989) study is particularly interesting in light of herd management changes during the Neolithic in Valencia. The increase in high yield, but higher risk cattle relative to sheep and goats in the Neolithic II may be an indication of greater household wealth than in the Neolithic I. A complementary idea focuses on the role of farming relative to domestic animal management (Mace 1993a, b). Shifts in farming practices in the Neolithic II, such as use of the plough, may have increased agricultural yields

and provided the basis for increased household wealth, allowing the animal management strategy to shift towards high yield, high risk cattle. If Neolithic II households were indeed wealthier than in the Neolithic I, new light would be shed on other socioeconomic changes documented during the Neolithic II, such as the emergence of social hierarchies and the development of long-distance exchange. At present archaeological data are lacking to test this hypothesis, but it remains an intriguing idea.

Furthermore, during the Neolithic II, land-use broadened to include upland areas with marginal soils in plant agriculture as well as grazing areas for animals in an extensive manner. This strategy is analogous to a shift to central place foraging (e.g., Barlow 2002; Cannon 2003; Grayson and Cannon 1999). People appear to have aggregated in locales best able to exploit remnant valley bottoms, extensive upland fields, and a new environmental mosaic, created largely by human activity, for a differently balanced suite of domestic animals (Figure 9.6). The IFD model also shows that changes in population density, although a factor in settlement shifts, did not have to be large in order to produce a great shift in land use. A marginal increase in population density in the Neolithic I habitat (valley floors) may have prompted initial settlement of valley margins, where a growing population began using the oxen-drawn plough and may have constructed terraces, enhancing the secondary suitability of the habitat. This process would appear as a qualitative shift and may have rapidly drawn population and settlement away from the riverine margins.

CONCLUSIONS

In this chapter we have attempted to illustrate how ideas from behavioral ecology, specifically the ideal free distribution, can be used heuristically to address fundamental issues in the transition to agriculture in eastern Spain. The Neolithic in Valencia is characterized by the quick and early emergence of production-based economies in the Neolithic I (by 5600 BC) and

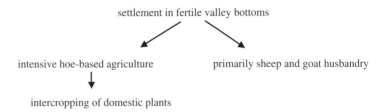

NEOLITHIC I

settlement in fertile valley bottoms

intensive hoe-based agriculture   primarily sheep and goat husbandry

intercropping of domestic plants

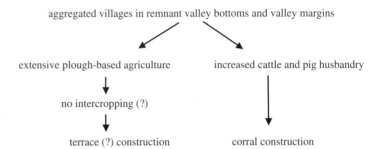

NEOLITHIC II

aggregated villages in remnant valley bottoms and valley margins

extensive plough-based agriculture   increased cattle and pig husbandry

no intercropping (?)

terrace (?) construction   corral construction

FIGURE 9.6. Idealized Neolithic subsistence systems in Valencia, Spain.

the slow development of aggregated village communities and associated shifts in habitat in the Neolithic II. By looking to habitat selection models, behavioral ecology has given us a theoretically grounded framework to analyze changes in settlement and subsistence practices as phenomena that are inextricably linked. Our study has shown that when the valley floors used intensively by Neolithic I farmers declined in suitability, they were faced with the challenge that their farming strategy, which was stable for more than a millennium, was no longer viable. In response, people in the Neolithic II shifted to a second habitat, valley margins, that increased in its secondary suitability through the adoption of a new technology, the plough, and possible investment in agricultural architecture. Farmers changed their habitats, intensified their domestic resources in innovative ways by shifting domestic animal management strategies, and expanded their use of the landscape. Changes of household wealth during the Neolithic II may help explain the shifts in animal management strategies, but this remains to be tested. Despite the stability of Neolithic I farming strategies, it is this Neolithic II pattern that remained a stable strategy for many millennia afterwards with irreversible ecological consequences, including the creation of much of the modern Mediterranean landscape. Behavioral ecology has given us a set of tools to examine a fundamental shift in human prehistory from a different perspective, and provided new questions to be examined with the archaeological record.

10

Breaking the Rain Barrier and the Tropical Spread of Near Eastern Agriculture into Southern Arabia

Joy McCorriston

Farming came late to Arabia, about 5000 years ago, long after the beginnings of agriculture in the Levant 10,000 years ago. The adoption of domesticates in Arabia occurred piecemeal as Arabian foragers and herders adopted specific animal and crop components over a period perhaps as long as four millennia, beginning well after a Levantine agro-husbandry package was in place. Despite the relative proximity to and contacts with domestication "centers" in Africa and South Asia, non-Levantine domesticates, except African cattle, were unavailable to Arabian foragers in early prehistory. Levantine crop domesticates faced a rainfall barrier across most of Arabia with high heat and summer precipitation, making herd animals the most likely domesticates to spread. With the middle Holocene recession of the Southwest Asian monsoon, peoples facing aridity also experimented with water management technologies, an essential pre-requisite for the adoption of Southwest Asian cereals and legumes. Climate change provided an important catalyst for adopting crop domesticates after cultivation began in areas where cattle herds anchored pastoralists to diminishing water sources.

Greeks and Romans called southern Arabia "Arabia Felix" for its plant life and great wealth in plant products, yet Yemen's prehistoric peoples adopted food production late and incrementally between the middle sixth and third millennium BC. Why did foraging persist through the first half of the Holocene in a land that, thereafter, gave rise to great civilizations built upon agricultural surpluses and a far-flung trade in spices, incense, and plant balms? Were early South Arabians simply unaware of plant domesticates from adjacent regions, or did the continued pursuit of wild resources outweigh the benefits of food production? The juxtaposition of southern Arabia to the Levant, East Africa, and South Asia suggests that foragers could have selected domesticates from distinct packages of plants and animals originating in these three independent centers of domestication (e.g., Garrard 1999; Harlan 1992b, 67–68; Meadow 1996). Yet paleoecological analysis in southern Arabia indicates that there were almost no opportunities to grow crops without irrigation, leaving domesticated animals as the most highly valued and probable first domesticated resource. The initial adoption of domesticated animals allowed a growing population of foragers to continue foraging in a mixed foraging-pastoral economy that was stable and viable for a long time rather than switch to food-production-based economies.

The question of how and when farming and husbandry entered southern Arabia has wider implications for the development and spread of early agricultural systems from primary domestication centers. Egypt, Europe, South Asia, and Central Asia all offer archaeological cases of a spread of domesticates and agricultural techniques from the Levant (e.g., Wetterstrom 1993; Halstead 1996; Price et al. 1995; Dennell 1992; Meadow 1996; Harris et al. 1993; Harris and Gosden 1996; Diamond and Bellwood 2003). In many cases, the Levantine domesticates spread together as an agro-husbandry package that included sheep, goats, cattle, pig, cereals, pulses, and a sedentary lifestyle. Yet southern Arabia's incorporation into the expanding periphery of farming systems was likely different, for current evidence suggests that southern Arabian foragers acquired just a few of the domesticates from each of the three source regions and recombined these domesticates in a staggered and innovative process. For nearly 4000 years from the middle sixth to the early third millennium BC, South Arabia's population, like many other societies worldwide, continued a predominantly foraging lifestyle akin to low-level food production (Smith 2001a). Low-level food production may take many forms, but its salient characteristics are the cultivation of wild or domesticated plants and the herding of animals often as minor components of long-term and stable economies.

Several factors explain the Arabian transition to agriculture, in which only a few domesticates were incorporated into foraging systems at different times and in different cultural contexts (Cleuziou and Tosi 1997). One important aspect is the availability (or lack thereof) of domesticates through contacts with domestication centers outside Arabia. Changes

in foraging strategies brought about by Arabian environmental change in the middle Holocene also played an important role. Regional climate records indicate that summer rainfall was reduced across the peninsula during much of the middle Holocene. Local environmental effects of this climate change varied dramatically, offering new opportunities and constraints to foragers living along the coast, in the highlands, and in the inland deserts. Highland foragers and later forager-pastoralists are of particular interest, for influences from eastern, western, and northern domestication centers intersect in the southern and western Arabian highlands.

By the end of the moist early Holocene, 4500 BC[1], these highlanders had established permanent dwellings (Fedele 1988, 34; Kallweit 1997, 8; McCorriston et al. 2003, 76–77). Highlanders had acquired domesticated cattle (likely African) in the early Holocene (Fedele 1990, 38), and coastal foragers had acquired caprines and cattle (Uerpmann and Uerpmann 2000, 48–49; Cattani and Bökönyi 2002, 46). Nevertheless, it was the middle Holocene (fourth millennium BC) invention of technology suitable for irrigation that allowed South Arabians to adopt Levantine domesticated winter crops such as wheat and barley. No one knows exactly what people sought to achieve with these earliest water management strategies. Were these strategies for cultivating wild plants to eat or to enhance browse for cattle livestock or wild game? Or were foragers trying to control increasingly unpredictable and violent floods in terrain they were loath to abandon during flooding? Whatever the motivating factors, water management was the technological context that later (third millennium BC) fostered cereal-based food production in Arabia.

Optimization models from human behavioral ecology (HBE) predict that new domesticates will be adopted as existing high-ranked resources became sufficiently rare or unpredictable (Gremillion 1996a, 199). Microeconomic theory also predicts that hunters will adopt animal husbandry under conditions of increased prey scarcity (with increased prey value), recognized ownership of prey (or territory), and greater returns from deferring use of food (Alvard and Kuznar 2001, 297). In the southern Arabian case, the adoption of food production was staggered across a lengthy time frame with the adoption of cattle, caprines (both middle sixth millennium BC), and cereals (late fourth millennium BC) into different cultural contexts and changing environmental circumstances. Archaeological data still lack the resolution that would allow accurate assessment of the significance of domesticates like cattle in the early Holocene. But HBE models and changing environments suggest that their significance grew through time so that people eventually adopted cultivation strategies (like irrigation) to ensure continuous access to cattle and the wetlands upon which they depended.

THE ARCHAEOLOGY OF THE ADOPTION OF DOMESTICATES IN SOUTHERN ARABIA

A recent pan-Arabian review by Cleuziou and Tosi (1997, 124–127) details the evidence for foragers' use of domesticated animals from the middle sixth millennium BC and documents an intensified pattern of exchange between foraging groups in Arabia and outsiders. Data across the Arabian peninsula remain scant, and vast areas lack even basic archaeological study, so in many areas the arguments about which crops and animals were first adopted remain somewhat conjectural. Widely scattered archaeological evidence points to highland foragers incorporating domesticated cattle into an economy that retained a significant emphasis on hunting wild animals, such as gazelle and wild asses (Cleuziou and Tosi 1997, 124; Fedele 1990, 38; see also Cattani and Bökönyi 2002). Fishing and mollusk collection remained important to the herders who first adopted domesticated sheep and goats along the eastern Arabian coasts (Uerpmann and Uerpmann 2000, 49; Cleuziou and Tosi 1997, 124). Even as foraging, herding, and fishing continued to provide the mainstay of coastal Arabian

subsistence, contact with Mesopotamians, who had introduced caprines and could have offered cereals, persisted (Oates et al. 1977, 232; Roaf and Galbraith 1994, 778; McClure and al-Shaikh 1993, 113–118; Méry and Schneider 1996, 81; Uerpmann and Uerpmann 1996, 131–136). Nearly four thousand years after the first evidence for animal husbandry, geomorphological and archaeobotanical evidence of the third millennium BC shows the adoption of cereal-based food production in the highlands (Ekstrom and Edens 2003, 28) and oasis margins of the interior desert in southern and eastern Arabia (Cleuziou and Costantini 1982, 1181–1182; Costantini 1990a, 190–200). In southwest Arabia, laminations from annual flooding of fields under cultivation began accumulating in the irrigated wadis of the desert fringe by 3000 BC (Brunner 1997, 196; Brunner and Haefner 1986, 82; Francaviglia 2000, 646).

From the earliest documented southern and eastern Arabian Holocene sites, archaeology indicates that foragers experienced both direct and indirect contact with peoples in distant domestication centers. The evidence includes lithic technology (Inizan 1988, 39; Cleuziou and Tosi 1997, 124; Charpentier 1996, 5), raw materials such as obsidian (Inizan 2000, 12), bitumen (Lawler 2002, 1791), and ceramics (Oates et al. 1977, 232; Roaf and Galbraith 1994, 778; McClure and al-Shaikh 1993, 113–118, Uerpmann and Uerpmann 1996, 131–136). By the time oasis farming began around 3000 BC, economically specialized activities along Arabia's eastern coastlines indicate exchange within the far-flung Bronze Age "World System" (Charpentier 2001, 43 1994; Edens 1999a, 83–84, 1994, 214–217), and these contacts continued between Arabia's inland settlements and food-producing peoples elsewhere (e.g., Weisgerber 1987, 269–270; David 1996, 31–34; Blackman et al. 1989, 74; Cleuziou 1992, 95–97; Cleuziou and Tosi 1994, 756–757; Blackman and Méry 1999, 24; Méry and Schneider 1996, 81–93; Lombard 1981; Moorey and Roger 1974, 55–59; Cleuziou and Vogt 1985, 257–258; Mackay 1943, 199–200, Plate LXXIX; Weeks 1999, 59–61; Ratnagar 2001, 118; Tosi 2001,

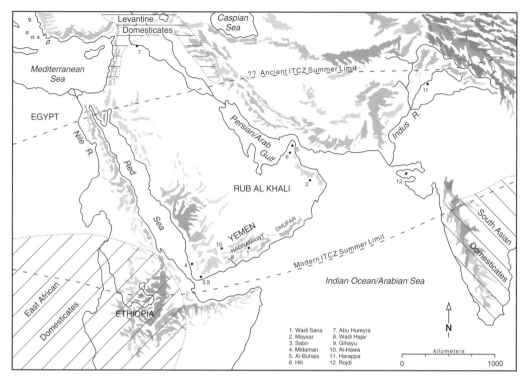

FIGURE 10.1. Map of the Indian Ocean/Arabian Sea with three domestication centers. The indicated former summer limit of the Inter-Tropical Convergence Zone (ITCZ) is a speculation based on paleoenvironmental and archaeological evidence from southern Mesopotamia, the Arabian Peninsula, Rajasthan, and the African Sahara.

145–148; Newton and Zarins 2000, 171). Contact with Mesopotamia, the Indus civilization, and East Africa offered ample opportunities for the introduction of domesticated plants and animals and knowledge of food production as it became available in these regions.

Southern Arabia, a region that includes Dhufar, Mahra, and Hadramawt, offers the ideal setting to examine the origins of food production in Arabia (Figure 10.1). Three crucial factors converge: these are geographic position, climate history, and tight integration of archaeological and paleoenvironmental records. Southern Arabia lies at the crossroads of ancient exchange networks that connected people living in three independent centers of domestication-the Levant, East Africa, and South Asia-and therefore South Arabian foragers likely had access to domesticates adapted to different environmental and cultural settings. From the Levantine (Eastern Mediterranean) region came winter crops such as wheat and barley, while potential African

domesticates included summer millets and sorghum. South Asia (Indian sub-continent) provided indigenous summer crops, including small summer millets, gram (summer pulses), and sesame. All three regions also offered different domesticated animals, including Levantine goats, Levantine cattle and African cattle (Bradley and Loftus 2000, 249; Hanotte et al. 2002, 338). A new archaeological sequence from the Southern Arabian highlands (McCorriston et al. 2003) provides a localized, landscape history of the development of low-level food production and a new testing ground for HBE predictions of resource availability, use, and optimization in Arabian foraging strategies.

THE RASA[2] PROJECT: WADI SANA ARCHAEOLOGICAL-PALEOECOLOGICAL SEQUENCE

In highland Wadi Sana, one of the major drainages of southern Yemen's southern plateau, new archaeological data, summarized and updated here (McCorriston et al. 2003, 69–83), suggest adoption first of cattle, then irrigation, and finally caprine herding. Cattle herding probably began in the mid-late sixth millennium BC. By the fifth millennium BC, people had developed landscape management practices such as burning to enhance wild resources; by the fourth millennium BC they used stone and earthen dams for water management.

Hunter-forager peoples occupied the southern highlands from the early Holocene climatic optimum in the seventh millennium BC, and their hearths and living surfaces—littered with retooling and fashioning debris for projectile points—can be traced on aggraded silt terraces in front of rock shelters. From the beginning of the fifth millennium BC, mobile peoples established campsites on the alluvium of middle Wadi Sana. RASA fieldwork has yielded new sequences of closely integrated archaeological horizons and paleoecological data in natural sediment beds (McCorrriston et al. 2003; McCorriston and Oches 2001; McCorriston 2000). Paleoenvironmental proxies include sedimentary sequences up to 8 m thick, magnetic and pedological properties of wadi fill deposits, and a vegetation record from dated hyrax middens (McCorriston et al. 2003, 67). Charcoal recovered from hearths preserved in the alluvium suggests a xeric parkland vegetation of medium-sized trees, most of which can still be found infrequently today. A series of weak paleosols attests to stable land surfaces that could support comparatively lush vegetation in an area today devoid of most plant life (<1% cover) and most precipitation. People possibly managed this ancient vegetation through burning, for the sediment record contains extensive burnt surfaces, contiguous with hearths. As with comparable evidence from highland northern Yemen, paleosols also contain charcoal flecks that may stem from deliberate woodland clearance (cf., Wilkinson 1997, 844, 859). If deliberate, these fires were probably set to enhance tender plant growth for browse. Domesticated cattle probably appeared by 5000 BC.

From intensive archaeological investigation of middle Wadi Sana (McCorriston et al. 2005), the most significant evidence of human aggregation appears with the construction of ritual structures from the middle-late fifth millennium BC (cf., McCorriston et al. 2003, 83). These are widely scattered (20–200 m apart) on or within the surfaces of wadi fill and on adjacent bedrock and gravel terraces, suggesting that their builders were among the last to experience a fairly moist alluvial landscape before widespread erosion set in. Excavations indicate that these 2–5 m diameter structures, built of massive upright slabs, had a life-cycle, were occupied at least for cooking, and were probably deliberately filled with stone, perhaps from their upper walls, at the end of their internal use. This cycle could take about five generations (100–200 years). They could have been houses, but they are widely scattered and fairly isolated one from another. Once filled, they may have served as markers or ritual platforms and be associated with an intense ritual focus on cattle, possibly domesticates. As the most substantial evidence for human communities in middle Wadi Sana, these appear about 1000 years before evidence for water management and prior to middle Holocene aridification.

Whether or not people deliberately set periodic fires, they did initiate management of seasonal runoff into the wadi at the end of the early-middle Holocene moist phase. Ancient check dams lie buried in silt and gravel deposits and sometimes extend for tens of meters across an eroding surface. Several water management structures can be dated to the fourth millennium BC, a period during which Wadi Sana experienced drying conditions. Sediment studies indicate the termination of sedimentation in the middle Wadi Sana by the end of the fourth millennium BC and a shift to predominant down-cutting. Check dams buried in sediments therefore most likely pre-date the most severe environmental changes associated with changing hydrology (McCorriston and Oches 2001, 675; McCorriston et al. 2003, 77–79), but were probably constructed as overall rainfall began to decline and perhaps concentrate into a shorter season. While it remains to be fully established that changing precipitation caused the hydrologic change, the timing coincides with the pan-regional monsoon weakening and the southward shift of the Inter-Tropical Convergence Zone (ITCZ) (Overpeck et al. 1996).

Water management may have continued in Wadi Sana as rainfall patterns shifted, but archaeological traces in the form of check dams are much more difficult to date (they probably continue to be built) after the end of the fourth millennium. Most cultivators probably shifted to permanent water sources at the springs of Ghayl bin Yumain, at the southern source of Wadi Sana. Hunters or herders may have camped with goats in several shallow caves. There are a few prominent Iron Age (fifth to first century BC) fortresses along Wadi Sana's narrowest passes, and these may have been linked to limited agricultural activities near the springs. But most evidence for human occupation and land management disappears after the fourth millennium BC. There are traces of occupation in rock shelters, including simple grafitti perhaps by caravaneers and rock drawings by itinerants. As in other regions of Arabia, a variety of monuments and cairns in distinctive styles mark both funerary and territorial activities of mobile people (Cleuziou and Tosi 1997, 127–128; Braemer et al. 2001, 29–42) whose use of Wadi Sana's resources probably differed substantially from their cattle-herding predecessors. If sedentary occupation had occurred, even under more arid circumstances and therefore in a different preservation environment, archaeologists would still detect occupational remains. For example, house sites are evident and dated to the middle second millennium BC in nearby Wadi Idim, where an active spring was a critical resource (McCorriston 2000, 139–143).

Wadi Sana's paleoenvironmental records correspond to a regional middle Holocene pattern. A peninsula-wide recession of the southwest Asian (summer) monsoon (Burns et al., 1998, 501; Kutzbach 1981, 61; Kutzbach et al. 1996, 624; Prell and Kutzbach 1987, 8413–14; McClure

1976, 755–756, 1984; Roberts and Wright 1993, 207–209, 218; Prell and Van Campo 1986, 526–527; Van Campo et al. 1982, 59; Fontugne and Duplessy 1986, 81, 85; Whitney et al. 1963, 33) brought important localized changes in rainfall, vegetation, ground and surface water distributions and intensity, and the distributions of wild game that depended on them. As rainfall dwindled (probably with greater concentration of available rainfall in increasingly restricted seasonal bursts) groundwater recharging was affected (Burns et al. 1998, 500), with an important and deleterious effect on springs and seeps at the interface of porous and hard rock layers. Today one can easily see the tufa from former spring deposits and the organic beds of dried marshes distributed along the margins of now-arid wadis. Not all such deposits date to the early Holocene, but some do (McCorriston et al. 2003, 65). Seasonal flooding must also have diminished, placing stress on important fruit-bearing trees like 'ilb (*Zizyphus spina-christi* L.) and restricting the range of cattle to the few permanent water sources that remained. Possibly cattle herders restricted their mobility to these permanent water sources for the benefit of their cattle. Under these circumstances, they probably needed to add lower-ranked resources such as small-seeded grasses, forbs, and reed or rush tubers, cultivated with the check dams they constructed by the fourth millennium BC (McCorriston and Oches 2001, 675; see also Wilkinson 1999, 186).

MIDDLE HOLOCENE ENVIRONMENTAL CHANGES ACROSS SOUTHERN ARABIA

New archaeological and paleoecological evidence is also emerging elsewhere in the western Arabian highlands (e.g., Wilkinson 1999; Garcia and Rachad 1997; Edens 1999b; Edens et al. 2000) and interior deserts (e.g., Inizan et al. 1997; Braemer et al. 2001, 42; Zarins 2001, 34–54; de Maigret 1996), and this new evidence suggests regionally specific Arabian culture histories and environmental sequences. Central Arabia's early Holocene lakes dried up by the fifth millennium BC (McClure 1976, 755–756, 1984), ending a phase of woody cover and surface water in the Ramlat as Sabatayn of central Yemen (Inizan et al. 1997). Throughout the early Holocene, drainage from southern and southwestern Arabia's mountains formed a single fluviatile system draining through Wadi Hadramawt-Masila to the Indian Ocean and readily linking foraging peoples along its tributaries (Cleuziou et al. 1992, 6–8). In the highlands of northern Yemen, this early-middle Holocene period saw greater precipitation and less evapo-transpiration than the present day, resulting in higher lake levels and cooler conditions, with swampy, foggy basins and wooded slopes (Wilkinson 1997, 852). Geologists have now dated extensive paleosols formed under more humid conditions by stable vegetative cover where soil formation is now outstripped by erosion. Such paleosols ceased forming during the fifth to third millennium BC (Fedele 1990, 33; Brinkman 1996a, 202–205; Marcolongo and Palmieri 1990, 139; Wilkinson 1999, 190). Major hydraulic changes in the Dhamar plateau of northern Yemen date to the middle fourth millennium (Wilkinson 1999, 189–190), echoing the changes apparent in the fluvial system of Wadi Sana. Growth rates and isotopic composition of cave speleothems[3] from northern Oman and Dhufar indicate that during the early-middle Holocene, strengthened monsoon circulation resulted in higher rainfall and lowered surface-water evaporation. Speleothem growth slowed during the fifth millennium BC—another indication of more arid conditions across the Arabian Peninsula (Burns et al. 1998, 500). An apparent time lag in the effects of diminished precipitation from Central Arabia's deserts to the southern and western highlands may be real or may reflect differential preservation of paleorecords: for example, paleolacustrine deposits may have lost upper (latest) layers to post-lacustrine deflation.

HBE, ARABIAN FORAGING PATTERNS, AND RESPONSES TO ENVIRONMENTAL CHANGE

What would have been the effects of aridification on Arabian cattle-herding plant foragers in the middle Holocene? Wadi Sana offers some of the earliest Arabian evidence for cultivation, and by the late fourth millennium, terraces and Levantine crops were present in the Dhamar region of Northern Yemen (Ekstrom and Edens 2003, 28; Wilkinson 1997, 844; Wilkinson 1999, 185), coinciding with the period of monsoon recession. The circumstances of long-term foraging in southern Arabia suggest that changes in *constraints* (or "auxiliary conditions and parameter values," Winterhalder and Kennett, this volume) on prey choice were balanced and partly offset by the selective and staggered introductions—first of domesticated animals and intensified plant cultivation strategies, followed by the adoption of domesticated plants.

The widest and most successful applications of HBE in archaeology historically have invoked diet breadth (= resource selection/prey choice) models to predict and explain archaeological data (e.g., Winterhalder and Goland 1997, 128). Such models require identification of three key components—constraints, currency, and choices—for archaeological application (Kaplan and Hill 1992, 176–177; Winterhalder and Smith 2000, 54). *Constraints* refers to the options available and includes the range of available prey and environmental conditions that sustain and limit prey and prey density. *Currency* may refer to energy, nutrients, or in human cases, social value gained and expended in food procurement. None of these model components can be directly measured in the archaeological record, but their relationships in the model cue archaeologists to suspect changes in one component when others change (Winterhalder 2002a, 206–208). During 3000 years of what Smith (2001a) has called "low-level food production," the value of newly introduced domesticated resources was first to redress and maintain the currency of wild Arabian resources rather than to provide immediate food alternatives to them.

For example, under the circumstances of low-level food production, in which "not all roads lead to agriculture" (Smith 2001a, 24), foragers may employ intensification strategies to enhance access to valued resources (prized wild game), whether by increasing the resource abundance or lowering its variability through greater energy inputs. Use of domesticated lactating female goats to extend the range of hunters would allow them to encounter game at (brackish) water sources not otherwise habitable for humans (Cleuziou and Tosi 1997, 126; Lancaster and Lancaster 1999, 112; cf., Close and Wendorf 1992, 68). The earliest Arabian evidence for what can unequivocally be termed pastoralism (at Jebel al-Buhais in eastern Arabia, Uerpmann and Uerpmann 2000) coincides with the onset of arid conditions of the middle-late Holocene, which imposed changing constraints on foraging by widening the distances between remaining potable water sources. The evidence from earlier sites and from other contexts (like Wadi Sana) suggests that domesticated cattle and caprines had been introduced without becoming immediately the mainstay of pastoral economies (e.g., Cattani and Bökönyi 2002, 44–51; Garcia and Rachad 1997; Fedele 1990, 38). The introduction first of cattle, then later caprines, supports the energetic expectations of Russell (1988, 159) that pastoral strategies should evolve in the absence of agriculture (in marginal dry-farming lands) and that cattle, the larger animal, offers better opportunities for delayed returns (Alvard and Kuznar 2001).

Scenarios for the introduction of domesticated animals, which are not further explored here, do not explain the long-delayed introduction of crop agriculture, for much of Arabia's highlands had overall sufficient moisture for farming in the early Holocene. To explain the introduction of crops, one must first consider Arabia's basic foraging patterns, sustained, apparently, within the long-term context of low-level food production and pastoralism before the impacts of aridification.

FORAGING PATTERNS

Probably three early Holocene foraging adaptations existed, each corresponding to a different ecological zone and including (1) the coastal plain, (2) the desert interior, and (3) the southern Arabian highlands. While some of the same resources were available in all three zones and prehistoric exchange systems and mobility operated among them, there were nevertheless significant differences. Environmental reconstructions of these zones and resources may be largely inferred from modern resource distributions and paleoclimate models. Reconstructions of human behavioral adaptations in southern Arabia rely on analogy with the foraging preferences of peoples in comparable environments elsewhere in Arabia and beyond. What follows is a highly provisional model of forager response to paleoclimate change in southern Arabia.

COASTAL PLAIN FORAGING

Much of the southern Arabian early Holocene coastline lies below sea-level (stabilization at 7000 years ago). Subsequent uplifting on the Red Sea side of the Arabian peninsula and along the Arabian Gulf has countered the effect of subsequent (middle Holocene) sea level transgression, so that at a coarse scale, coastlines have remained more or less stable since the middle Holocene (Sheppard et al. 1992, 22–31). Many of the most ancient forager camp sites in this zone surely lie submerged along the coastal shelf of the modern Arabian Sea (Indian Ocean), which would have extended the coastal plain by several kilometers in flat areas. A wider coastal plain would have provided greater estuarine resources with brackish swamps of mangrove (*Avicennia marina*) and extensive lagoons, as has been found in northern Oman (Charpentier et al. 2000).

Coastal foragers would be restricted to sources of fresh water, which constrains the size of populations, their distribution, and their mobility (Cartwright 1998, 100). Along the South Arabian coast today, surface sources of fresh water are relatively scarce, but fresh water lies sometimes only a few meters below the surface. Shallow wells are easy to dig through the sand dunes and loose sediments filling dry pre-Quaternary river beds. Such wells can water animals and limited plantings alike, but wells are highly localized. The only "river" in all of Arabia is the spring-fed stream in Wadi Hajar. Springs occur where uplifted and rifted formations expose a juncture between porous and harder rock at locations along the coastal escarpment.

The Arabian Sea provides special resources for coastal dwellers. In the winter, sea turtles nest along the beaches and can be easily caught and their eggs retrieved. Mollusks abound in different environments—*Terebralia palustris* living year-round in the slow-moving water of mangrove stands; limpets and gastropods (especially top, turban, and cone shells) accessible on rocks and in rocky pools during calmer winter months; bivalves like clams, oysters, and mussels in the sand and mud and attached to rocks, mangrove roots, and driftwood; spindle (conch-like) shells, cowries, lobsters, octopi, oysters, and clams where winter divers could reach them. In-shore reef-fishing with spears and nets would yield grouper, snapper, wrasse, grunt, bream, mullet, herring, and sardines, while pelagic fishing with trolling hooks would be the strategy for taking dolphinfish, tuna, and kingfish, again in winter months. Upwelling during the summer monsoon generated fantastically rich nutrients for sea-life (Sheppard et al. 1992, 44–51), but also brought temperature inversions and coastal storms that severely limited human access to fishing and rough-water mollusk-collecting.

Shorebirds and their eggs, the latter available in the spring months, offer another valuable resource to coastal foragers. Ground-nesting terns and tropical birds occupy coastal cliffs; grebes, pelicans, spoonbills, and flamingoes can inhabit mangrove swamps, lagoons, and mudflats. Migrants abound in the winter months. Although greater early Holocene summer precipitation would enhance vegetation and groundwater, in the early Holocene the coastal plains still experienced drier winter months than summer, as they do today. Plants tend to fruit at the end of summer rains, providing foragers only with vegetative parts high in cellulose during other parts of the year. Plants with edible tubers, corms, bulbs, and rhizomes are few in the Arabian flora.

Foragers could access rich shellfish, fish, and fowl during winter months, but would have faced a highly seasonal environment with high summer temperatures, stormy seas, and summer plant growth limited to vegetative mass. These factors, although mitigated in the early Holocene by higher summer moisture than today, nevertheless discourage year-round collection. The coastal environment offered both high seasonal variation and high predictability of resources, many of which could be anticipated at fixed nesting grounds, beds, reefs, mangrove swamps, or springs. Under these circumstances, foragers tended to practice low residential mobility with tethering to water sources during the winter months when diverse aquatic resources were abundant and accessible. One may speculate that summer monsoon restrictions on some aquatic resources would encourage greater use of others (e.g., mollusks and crabs from mangrove swamps), perhaps encouraging storage of fish and shellfish products (El Mahi 2000, 101–104). Alternately, foragers could increase residential mobility during summer in response to seasonally abundant surface water and reduced fishing opportunities (Kelly 1995, 125–128). This presupposes that foragers could and did remain on the coast year-round, a conjecture as yet lacking archaeological evidence to support it (Cartwright 1998, 102; Charpentier et al. 2000, 82).

Archaeological evidence for forager economies along the southern Arabian coast is scarce. A recently excavated early Holocene shell midden at Gihayu west of Aden suggests that coastal fishermen camped repeatedly (but not necessarily year-round) on one stable location situated between lagoon and coast. The net weights, knives, scrapers, and a variety of hammerstones and tools on pebbles are "typical of fishermen and mollusk gatherers' settlements" (Amirkhanov et al. 2001, 9). Mortars and grinding stones also occurred and may have been used in the preparation of plant foods, perhaps the tubers of rushes (*Typha* sp.) and seeds of salt bush (*Suaeda fruticosa*) and other plants in the Chenopodiaceae. Mollusk shells dominate the archaeofauna, with bivalves typical of stony sea bottom or rocky shore environments. Other prey included fish, mammals, and turtles.

Although diverse archaeological surveys have recovered stone tools typical of early Holocene foragers elsewhere along the coast, the socioeconomic patterns practiced by their makers remain poorly understood. From the Red Sea coast, shell midden sites indicate heavy reliance on mollusks and crabs from mangrove swamps and, perhaps to a lesser extent, hunted game (wild asses) and eggs (ostrich shell). (Domesticated cattle may also have been present (Tosi 1986, 406–408; Cattani and Bökönyi 2002)). Certainly the best-known sequence of Arabian coastal adaptation comes from northern Oman on the Arabian Gulf where middle Holocene foragers employed nets and carved fish hooks to exploit marine resources while accumulating shell deposits from coastal habitats and bone from terrestrial hunting (Charpentier 2001, 34; Charpentier et al. 2000, 75–82). Although settlement patterns have yet to be fully defined, seasonal mobility seems likely. Foragers transported flint from highland sources three kilometers away (Charpentier 2001, 41), and sites lack the dense deposits of mangrove-specific species one would expect if these swamps provided year-round settlement opportunities. There may have been a zonal seasonal transhumance to inland mountains practiced by coastal foragers: this pattern probably occurred among the earliest pastoralists and continues in Dhufar among cattle and goat herders today (Uerpmann et al. 2000, 232; El Mahi 2001, 134–138).

DESERT INTERIOR FORAGING

Today the Arabian desert is hyperarid (<50 mm rainfall per year) with few wells and widely spaced oases around the vast Empty Quarter, or Rub al Khali (See Figure 10.1). This is the environment most dramatically affected by middle Holocene monsoon recession: in the early Holocene, vast permanent lakes filled the basins of a sub-desert open parkland where acacias, bunchgrasses, resin trees (especially myrrh), and thorny scrub grew along seasonal stream beds and fringed the reedy lake margins (Lézine et al. 1998).

Desert foragers were restricted to sources of fresh water, available on a permanent, perennial basis in shallow lakes, which were widely dispersed across the Empty Quarter. These lakes attracted large game—wild cattle, wild asses, ibex, gazelle, possibly wild camels, and ostriches—and undoubtedly served as winter refuges for migratory birds. Like the African Saharan lakes of the early Holocene (Harlan 1992b, 60), those in Arabia probably had annually variable and retreating margins that sprouted a rich bed of annual seed-bearing grasses (e.g., *Panicum*, *Pennisetum* sp.), and forbs (e.g., *Cassia* spp. *Indigofera* spp., *Crotalaria* spp., *Tephrosia* spp., *Rumex* spp.) at the onset of the dry season. At the dry season's end, foragers could gather small tubers (*Cyperus* spp., *Typha* sp.) or the seeds of bitter melon (*Cucumis colocynthus*). These resources, along with acacia pods and other edible tree fruits (e.g., *Zizyphus spina-christi*), would likely have been seasonally available (especially at the beginning of the dry season) in drainages throughout what today is a hyperarid desert. Game birds such as grouse, partridge, francolin, and chukkar, and various small mammals (e.g., hares, foxes, gerbils) and reptiles were encountered year-round, but may have been most highly valued during summer months when larger game could range more widely and thereby have been less easy to acquire. Eggs—ostriches' and game birds' in particular—would have provided a welcome resource at the end of winter and beginning of summer when migrant birds moved north. Swarms of desert locusts offered an intermittent bounty in the years in which they proliferated.

During the wetter summer months, when lake-margins flooded, pools appeared in various locations throughout the savanna. These pools would have seasonally reduced the distances between water sources and may have fostered wider, more even distribution of large game, especially herbivores. Hunters who placed high priority on such prey would opt for greater logistical mobility to encounter them in the dry season, while residential mobility might be expected to increase during the wet season (Kelly 1995, 126).

The best archaeological evidence of early-middle Holocene lake margin adaptation comes from the Ramlat as-Sabat'ayn lake of al Hawa, which filled for at least 500 years (probably longer) in the seventh to sixth millennium BC. Archaeologists have recovered the surface remains of hearths associated with animal bones, ostrich eggshell, and neolithic-type stone tools used as arrow tips, other projectile tips for hunting, scrapers, knives and grinding implements such as mortars, bowls, and grinding stones (Inizan et al. 1997, 141–143). It remains difficult to reconstruct forager socioeconomic patterns, but there is no evidence of permanent settlement. Campsites (mostly surface scatters) suggest high residential mobility by small foraging bands, who left few remains. Some foragers either ranged for, or most likely traded widely, sea shell and mother-of-pearl decorations and highland obsidian (of African origin) (Inizan et al. 1997, 143; Inizan 2000, 12). Ostrich eggs, widely prized as water (or honey?) containers, may have been one of several desert resources exchanged for obsidian and shell; the locus of such exchanges, if they took place, was almost certainly the intervening highland regions between coast and desert.

SOUTHERN ARABIAN HIGHLAND FORAGING

Southern Arabia's highland zone stretches for several hundred kilometers inland between the narrow coastal plain and the vast Empty Quarter of the interior (see Figure 10.1). Annual rainfall in the South Arabian highlands may have been as high as 350 mm per annum prior to the middle Holocene retreat of the summer monsoon, and would easily have supported gallery forests along seasonally-charged streambeds and open parkland on sediments accumulating in pre-Quaternary drainage channels. There appears to have been a major geomorphological shift in the middle Holocene that resulted in downcutting through early Holocene sediments: one result of this shift is a change in preservation environments and poorer archaeological records (i.e., deflated sites) of later Holocene inhabitants (McCorriston et al. 2003, 64–67). Notwithstanding this preservation bias, there appear to have been more early Holocene inhabitants, supported by foraging in a substantially richer and more predictable highland environment (McCorriston et al. 2005). The highlands comprise several distinct zones, including a moist and much-faulted coastal escarpment with short, narrow drainages infrequently charged with water; the high plateau with broad drainage basins; and inland-draining wadis with short slopes and easy passage between plateau and bottomlands serving as natural passage from highlands to Arabia's interior.

Highland foragers could depend on perennial spring waters seeping laterally from the interface between porous and hard rock layers along the cliffs of the wadis. Furthermore, there was surface water available in seasonal summer creeks and floods and extensive ponding in the wadi bottoms and upland hollows that would have lasted at least until the spring. Increased early Holocene moisture fostered much more plant growth than found today and supported an abundance of wild game. In addition to the gazelles, ibex, baboons, hyena, and leopards that one can still see today, wild cattle and giant buffalo were also present in the gallery forests of the wadi bottoms. Grasses, shrubs, and trees provided extensive cover for game birds and small mammals, and migrant birds would have spent the winter at springs and reed-fringed ponds.

Plant biomass was higher in the southern Arabian highlands than coastal or desert regions. Edible plant foods included the pods of acacia, drupe of *Zizyphus*, cattails and tubers of reeds, nutgrass tubers, and the seeds of a range of small-seeded forbs and grasses akin to those available in the interior. With a higher density and diversity of flowering trees, honeybee nests and their sweet combs were likely available and may have played a role in forager resource choice and exchange systems.

At highland archaeological sites, stone tools include projectile tips suitable for spear or javelin hunting of large and medium mammals, as well as arrow points, scrapers, cutting and boring tools, and ground stone mortars suitable for pounding seeds, dried fruits, and fruit pods. Rock art from western Arabia suggests that cattle and giant bovids were prized prey (Garcia et al. 1991) before their incorporation as domesticates into long-term herding-plant-foraging strategies. Year-round water is necessary to support cattle, and foragers could have expected to encounter them in the wadi bottoms, where standing water pooled perhaps for most of the dry season after summer rains. While rainfall, secondary plant productivity (flowering and fruiting), honey production, migratory fowl, and mammal calving followed a sharply seasonal pattern, there was nevertheless an overall higher productivity than the Arabian interior, suggesting that highlands could support greater population densities.

Some of the earliest evidence for sedentism in Arabia comes from highland sites in the form of house sites (e.g., Fedele 1988, 34; Zarins 2001, 36–45; McCorriston et al. 2003, 76–77). These pre-date most evidence for middle Holocene precipitation decline, and therefore sedentism may be best understood as the outgrowth of successful early Holocene foraging strategies and opportunities rather than as a response to climate change. That so little is known of Arabia's early and middle Holocene highland foragers represents a vital gap in our archaeological knowledge within the region. If highlanders indeed were the most dense and sedentary of Arabia's foraging populations, then they are also the people most likely to have practiced resource management strategies and technologies important in the adoption of plant domesticates and agriculture. Elsewhere, a packing/sedentism model has been widely associated with conversion from (forager-based) low-level food production to food production economies (e.g., Flannery, 1969; Harris 1998; Bar-Yosef and Belfer Cohen 1992; Close and Wendorf 1992; Hassan 1984; Haaland 1995). The packing/sedentism model

developed with the assumptions that fertility shifts and population growth directly impact resource tenure and mobility (Rosenberg 1990, 1998). In highland southern Arabia, pastoral-cultivators burning off vegetation and later building check dams managed packed territories and resources that ultimately proved insufficient for cattle and their keepers as the monsoon rains diminished. They turned to caprine pastoralism and to farming.

THE UNAVAILABILITY OF AFRICAN AND SOUTH ASIAN CROPS

African and South Asian crops, best suited to the summer rainfall that fell in Arabia during the early Holocene, were domesticated late and thus not available to travel between Africa and Arabia or South Asia and Arabia in the early-middle Holocene. Contact between Eastern Africa and Yemen dates to at least the sixth millennium BC (Inizan 2000, 12). But many domesticates like sorghum (*Sorghum bicolor*), millets (*Eleusine coracana, Pennisetum glaucum, P. typhoides*), and teff (*Eragrostis tef*) (de Wet 1977) evolved much later in time, up to the first millennium BC (Rowley-Conwy et al. 1999, 58; Haaland 1995, 168–171; Wigboldus 1996, 79–80) and after long cultivation (Wasylikowa and Dahlberg 1999, 24; Wasylikowa et al. 1997, 935–940; Stemler 1990, 96; Haaland 1995, 159–164, 168–171). The earliest dates on pearl millet (*Pennisetum glaucum*) from the south-western Sahara and from sub-Saharan West Africa suggest cultivation began around the middle second millennium BC (van der Veen 1999, 5; Amblard 1996, 423, 425; D'Andrea et al. 2001, 345–346). Other crops such as Ethiopia's indigenous teff (*Eragrostis tef*), finger millet (*Eleusine coracana*), noog (*Guizotia abyssinica*), ensete (*Ensete ventricosum*), coffee (*Coffea arabica*) and qat (*Catha edulis*) remain poorly documented in the archaeological record with no conclusive evidence for early-middle Holocene use. In several cases, the earliest dated African crops have appeared outside Africa: African finger millet from (South Asian) Harappa and Rojdi dates to the mid third millennium BC (Weber 1998, 270–271; cf., Fuller 2002, 277–281), and African teff appears as ceramic impressions from first century BC Yemen (Soderstrom 1969, 401). Sorghum remains problematic and much contested, with the earliest dates on ceramic impressions from Yemen and Oman (Cleuziou and Tosi 1997, 128; Costantini 1990a, 192–193; Cleuziou and Costantini 1982, 1181–82; cf., Willcox 1994, 462) and on plant remains from South Asia (Fuller and Madella 2002, 334–335). African crops, along with cotton (*Gossypium herbaceum*) (Betts et al. 1994, 497) and non-humped cattle (*Bos taurus*) (Grigson 1996, 64; Close and Wendorf 1992, 67–68), emerged piecemeal from very diverse sub-Saharan environments and cultural practices.

Indian archaeobotany and archaeozoology enjoy a comparatively long history, with reasonable certainty about the dates and South Asian context for the introduction of Levantine domesticates, such as goats, wheat, and barley (Costantini 1984; Meadow 1996, 393–395). The (less documented) development of indigenous South Asian domesticates such as native South Asian millets (including *Setaria verticillata, Pannicum sumatrense, Paspalum scrobiculatum, Echinochloa colona*) (Kajale 1991, 164–165; Weber 1998, 267–268; Fuller and Madella 2002, 334–336; Fuller 2002, 293), and gram pulses (*Vigna* spp., *Cajanus cajan, Macrotyloma uniflorum*) occurred in the fourth millennium BC (Fuller 2002, 292–5). Zebu or humpback cattle (*Bos indicus*), domesticated in India (Meadow 1987, 898–899, 1984, 329; Matthews 2002, 440–1), appear to have been an early export across the Indian Ocean (Grigson 1996, 64; Hanotte et al. 2002, 337). Sesame (*Sesamum indicum*) was available from middle-late third millennium in South Asia (Fuller 2002, 294–295; Nayar and Mehra 1970, 28–29; Bedegian 2004; cf., Potts 1997, 67–68).

In sum, Levantine plant and animal domesticates, along with African cattle, were the earliest available to southern Arabian foragers. Archaeologists more or less agree that indisputable evidence for domesticated plants and animals appears widely during the Pre-Pottery Neolithic B during the ninth to eighth millennium BC (Garrard 1999, 82; Table 10.1). Researchers find marked differences in the plant and animal domesticates used at different sites. (e.g., Willcox 1996, 150–151; van Zeist 1988, 58–59; Rosenberg and Redding 1998; Horowitz with Lernau 2003). Not until the Middle Pre-Pottery Neolithic B did a common package of fully domesticated plant and animal resources—sheep (*Ovis*) and goats (*Capra*), wheat (*Triticum monococcum, T. dicoccum*), barley (*Hordeum sativum*), lentils (*Lens culinaris*), peas (*Pisum sativum*), flax (*Linum usitatissimum*), and finally cattle (*Bos taurus*) and pig (*Sus scrofa*)—emerge as agriculture across the broad culture area of the Fertile Crescent (Hole 1984, 99; Garrard 1999, 76–78). Thus one may assume that Arabian foragers had access to Levantine farming no earlier than around the mid eighth millennium BC.[4] Thereafter, summer rainfall posed a significant impediment to the transfer of cereals southwards.

LEVANTINE CROPS AND THE TROPICAL RAIN BARRIER

Highland aridification and especially the invention of water management technologies in the fourth millennium BC broke the tropical rain barrier that constrained the southward transfer of Levantine domesticated crops. Summer rainfall (carried by monsoon winds during the more northward extent of the ITCZ or Inter-Tropical Convergence Zone) fell across southern Mesopotamia (Sirocko et al 1993), Arabia (Blanchet et al. 1997, 191, 194; Sanlaville 1992, 8–14), southern Sahara (Panchur and Hoezlmann 1991; Haynes 2001, 121, 138), India (Deotare and Kajale 1996, 25; Wasson et al. 1984, 386), and possibly even the extreme southern tip of Jordan (Frumkin et al. 1991, 199; Henry et al. 2003, 21–22) during the early Holocene. Such rainfall would extend the natural range of tropical crops sown in summer and harvested in autumn-winter, such as sorghum, millets, sesame, and summer pulses (gram). Certainly the moisture balance in many highland regions would

TABLE 10.1

Domesticates and Dates from the Levant, East Africa, and South Asian Sub-continent

DATE (CALIBRATED)	LEVANT	SOUTH ASIA	AFRICA	ARABIA
post 1000 AD			(in Ethiopia) wheat, barley, pulses	
300–1000 AD				
300 BC–300 AD			**sorghum**	
1000–300 BC				dum palm, dom fruit, tef
2000–1000 BC			**pearl millet**	
3000–2000 BC	**safflower, tree fruits**	sesame, sorghum, finger millet, foxtail millet		camels, ? sorghum, flax, complex irrigation
4000–3000 BC	**olive**	?cotton, gram, native millets	?cotton	wheat, barley, pulses ? broomcorn millet
5000–4000 BC			(in Egypt) wheat, barley, pulses, flax, caprines	**check dams & terraces**
6000–5000 BC	grape	wheat, barley, goats, zebu		cattle, caprines, dates
7000–6000 BC			**African cattle**	
8000–7000 BC	**Levantine cattle, pigs**			
9000–8000 BC	**wheat, barley, pulses, flax, caprines**			
10000–9000 BC	**rye**			

Note: Boldface indicates an indigenous plant or animal thought to be domesticated in the region listed. All references are cited in text.

have permitted cultivation of such crops assisted by early water management technologies. The paleorecords, particularly records from cave speleothems and paleolacustrine pollen, indicate that winter precipitation in Arabia was negligible throughout the early Holocene. Late Pleistocene-early Holocene winds across Arabia's central and northern deserts came predominantly from the southwest and west (Whitney et al. 1963, 35; El-Moslimany 1983, 142). While the strength of winter storm tracks was stronger and did decline in the middle Holocene, southern Arabian winter rainfall had never been sufficient to support a Mediterranean or continental vegetation adapted to winter precipitation. Widespread aridification therefore meant diminished *summer* moisture for semiarid tropical plant communities.

A net decrease in precipitation would have had multiple and varying local effects, among them increased surface runoff and down-cutting as vegetative cover diminished and soils were exposed to greater erosion risks from seasonal flood waters. Springs dwindled and died as waters that once seeped along the juncture of hard limestone and porous overlying shales failed to emerge along the vertical faces of deeply incised wadis and faulted blocks. Marshy backwaters and seasonally recharged pools disappeared. Like the Central Arabian lakes, these early Holocene water sources were visited by herder-foragers, who faced greater distances between dwindling perennial water sources. People faced with these changing conditions could adopt one of several strategies, such as decreasing territorial ranges, so as to remain close to predictable water resources, or adopting new resources and schedules that allowed them to maintain, increase, or alter their ranges to collect food. These choices certainly varied with geographic and cultural variables across the middle Holocene Arabian landscape, and while there is no room to explore all possible regional differences here, several points common to all Arabian contexts deserve discussion.

First of all, lack of Arabian winter rainfall necessarily imposed constraints on adopting and growing Levantine domesticated plants, the earliest crops known to have been available to Arabian herder-foragers. Mediterranean wheats, barley, legumes, and flax all grow with 300–600 mm of winter (November-March) rainfall and rely on a long day length through spring-summer to flower and bear seeds. Today's wild cereal relatives (wild barley, wild oats, wild emmer, wild einkorn, wild rye) primarily show differences in tolerance to drought (Blumler 2002, 103–104), with varying vernalization requirements for highland and lowland strains of the same species (Blumler, personal communication). This implies that high heat and summer aridity in Mediterranean climates (rather than winter climate variables) place the greatest regional constraints on cereal crops (Blumler 2002, 103). High summer temperatures and humidity (i.e., Arabian) outside the Mediterranean zone would similarly constrain cereals sown to germinate under summer rainfall. One may also assume that ancient wheats adapted to

Mediterranean conditions needed spring and summer daylight hours of Mediterranean latitude to initiate flowering that yields grain. If foragers moved wheats and other Mediterranean-adapted cereals into the tropics with summer rainfall, they would have to plant early enough in summer for long daylight hours to trigger flowering. But high summer temperatures and moisture limit this option to cool highland regions in the tropics (Figure 10.2).

From the northward spread of cereals into Europe and Eurasia, one may recognize the selection for growth habits of early domesticates that ensured crop survival in continental winters. Agriculture in continental climates relies on strongly vernalized cereals—these are varieties and introductions of new genes that allowed cereals a winter vegetative stage (vernalization) after autumn sowing in continental climates (summer and winter rainfall). Spelt and bread wheat (*Triticum spelta, T. aestivum*) likely acquired this character from a wild steppe grass (*T. tauchii*) (Tsunewaki 1968, 77), allowing wheats and similarly genetically selected cereals to spread northwards across the Alps and central Asian steppe in the fifth to fourth millennia BC. Wheats and other higher latitude crops need cool temperatures for germination, also limiting their growth in the hot tropics (Evans 1993, 135–136; c.f., Blumler 2002, 102, 104). Across Arabia, this effectively restricts agriculture to autumn planting and winter growth, except perhaps for the southwestern highlands.

Autumn-sown domesticated wheats and other crops eventually spread southward. Winter cereals and legumes first appear in Egypt's Nile Valley and the Nile-fed Fayyum basin around 5000 BC (Wetterstrom 1993, 201), and there is no doubt that autumn Nile flooding provided all the necessary moisture for their winter-spring growth in early Egyptian agriculture (Butzer 1976, 48–50; Hassan 1984, 60–62). Likewise, the sixth millennium BC introduction of winter cereals to South Asia relied on winter precipitation in Pakistan's Kachi Plain (Costantini 1984). By the middle Holocene (sixth millennium BC), the Upper Indus floodplain gradually turned to destabilization

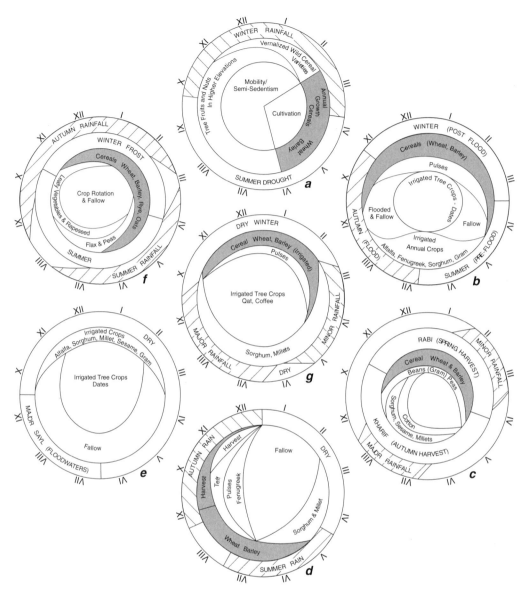

FIGURE 10.2 A-G. Seasonal growth cycles of cereal crops in a) epi-Paleolithic-Neolithic Levant, b) Egypt (adapted from Has-san 1984, 61; Butzer 1976, 49) c) Baluchistan, d) Ethiopia (adapted from D'Andrea et al. 1999, 108–109), e) recent pre-industrial Yemen (Tihama lowlands), f) temperate Europe , g) recent pre-industrial Yemen (northern highlands). In each diagram, concentric bands indicate season of crop production, but band width and shading is unrelated to crop importance. Center text indicates activities that occur year-round and/or inter-annually. Shaded Levantine cereals show the importance of vernalized crops for transfer to Europe and the tropics. A diagram of the wild resources preferred by non-agricultural foragers in the Levant (a) has been included to show the spring growth of non-vernalized varieties.

with reduced soil formation and channel migration. This phase was followed by the resumption of weakened soil development and establishment of fourth to third millennium Harappan sites (Schuldenrein et al. 2004, 793). Under these more stable conditions, farmers could better predict floods to use simple "sailabi" (innundation) techniques (Meadow 1996, 395–396; Fuller and Madella 2002, 348–350) to produce winter cereals, the original staple crops of Harappan farming (Weber 1998, 270–271; Costantini 1990b). Levantine crops eventually became established in East Africa's and Yemen's cooler highlands where they now flourish under a summer rainfall regime in high elevations that offset the climate coincidence of high temperatures and high humidity. No definitive evidence suggests Near Eastern crop introductions to Ethiopia any earlier than the first millennium BC (D'Andrea et al. 1999, 105–107; Brandt 1984, 176–184), possibly via Yemen's southwest highlands.

Without water management and conservation techniques to support growth of Levantine domesticates adapted to Mediterranean rainfall and photoperiod, plants dependent on winter rainfall for spring growth could not spread into most of Arabia as (summer) rainfed crops. Summer rainfall provided virtually all moisture, as can be deduced from paleovegetation. In Wadi Sana there are scant data on which types of plants constituted the expanded cover over early Holocene paleosols, but the few ancient wood charcoal fragments identified thus far are from trees adapted to monsoon precipitation (McCorriston et al. 2003, 75). Paleobotanical evidence pointing to plant ecology elsewhere in the Arabian peninsula is also sparse, but palynological records suggest early Holocene summer rainfall in the southern interior (Inizan et al. 1997, 146; Whitney et al. 1963, 34) and the Gulf (El-Moslimany 1983, 142–144), as does the isotopic composition of perennial grasses that once stabilized dunes (Whitney et al. 1963, 27). Moisture was also greater in the southwest highlands. Research there has yielded soil profiles containing pollen and phytoliths suggestive of grassy savanah interspersed with scrub and occasional woodland thickets and pocketed by marshy stands around lakes on the (now dry) valley floors (Wilkinson 1997, 852).

Most Arabian foragers would therefore have to depend on summer rainfall for plant cultivation and would find African and South Asian crops more appropriate. In a comparable African example, Jack Harlan has highlighted the importance of decrue cultivation techniques—in which summer-ripening millets and other annuals might be harvested in the enhanced moisture margins of lakes that expanded during spring and summer rainfall—at the margins of early Holocene Saharan paleolakes (Harlan 1992b, 60).

The decrue technique could also have been an option for foragers camped at the margins of Arabia's paleolakes, where equipment such as grinding stones and mortars may reflect a focus on seed and tuber harvests comparable to Saharan early Holocene foraging (Barakat and Fahmy 1999, 44). But any early foraging groups that encountered Levantine crop domesticates could only use them if able to water crops with irrigation from perennial flow or by soaking soils with heavy annual floodwaters sufficient to water a crop throughout the winter or spring growth season, as occurred in the Egyptian Nile basin (Hassan 1984, 61–62). This technology existed by the third millennium BC in major South Arabian drainages (Francaviglia 2000, 646; Brunner and Haefner 1986, 82; Brunner 1997, 196; Coque-Delhuille and Gentille 1998, 89), but its use in the fifth millennium remains a matter of conjecture. In the few highland instances such as Wadi Sana, catchment areas for the earliest water management structures are very limited. With the present data archaeologists can only speculate about cultivation practices, but we can be certain that water management technology must have been a necessary precursor to adopting domesticated crops.

What then, were cattle-pastoralist foragers cultivating in Wadi Sana between 5000 and 3000 BC? The terrain adjacent to their checkdams was marshy and annually inundated at least through the summer months. The dams may have served to retain water in post-flooding fields or ponds that provided moisture throughout the winter. Such moisture could have watered cattle, and it could have offered a decrue context for sowing and harvesting the small seeds of native grasses and forbs. Arabia was not without cultivable plant resources of her own. Recent discoveries of late sixth to early fifth millennium BC carbonized date stones from Dalma Island in the Arabian Gulf show that the date fruit served as an edible, perhaps even cultivated, resource (Beech and Shepherd 2001, 87). Bronze-age date stones and wild *Zizyphus* pits (from dom, a native tree) were recovered from Ra's al Jinz (Oman) (Costantini and Audisio 2000, 145). Domesticated date trees are irrigated and tended near perennial water

TABLE 10.2

Archaeological Phases of the Holocene in Wadi Sana, Hadramawt, Southern Arabia

DATE (CALIBRATED)	PHASE	DESCRIPTION	SITES
300 BC–present	V	Nomadic pastoralists in modern environmental conditions	trilith cairns
1200–300 BC	IV	Iron Age caravans and fortresses in modern environmental conditions	Old South Arabic grafitti, Qalat Hubshiya
3000–1200 BC	III b	Hyper-arid conditions, some cairns probably associated with tribal territories of pastoralists	numerous undated cairns, Shi'b Munayder houses near springs
4000–3000 BC	III a	Monuments and ephemeral traces left by mobile foragers and herders in an arid middle-late Holocene environment	Wadi Shumlya Gravel Bar flint workshop, Wadi Sana Rockshelters
4500–4000 BC	II	Pithouses and checkdams built as early-middle Holocene aridification began	Wadi Shumlya Gravel Bar, 2000-009-1, Wadi Sana pit house 2000-037-3
6500–4500 BC	I	Rock shelter and open encampments during the early Holocene climatic optimum.	Wadi Shumlya hearths and burnt surfaces, Khuzmum Rock shelters

sources throughout Arabia today, and date palms flourished where sophisticated spate irrigation provided additional runoff (Hehmeyer 1989, 38–40; Levkovskaya and Filatenko 1992, 247, 251). In considering potential cultivation uses of fifth to fourth millennium BC highland check dams in South Arabia, the importance of enhancing moisture for edible tree cultivars—date palm, dom fruit (*Zizyphus spina-christi*), *Acacia gerrardii*, *Balanites aegyptiaca*, *Zizyphus leucodermis*, *Z. mauritiana*, *Allophylus rubifolius*, and *Monotheca buxifolia* as well as indigenous wild grasses such as *Panicum turgidum* and *Pennisetum divisum*, deserves further exploration (Ghazanfar 1994; El-Moslimany 1983, 174). Once an indigenous context for cultivation was established, Levantine crops could be adopted.

MIDDLE HOLOCENE CLIMATE CHANGES AND THE ADOPTION OF CAPRINES AND CEREALS

If most Levantine plant domesticates could not move south before the invention of irrigation systems delivering adequate winter-spring season moisture, aridity-tolerant Levantine domesticates—especially goats and sheep—could. Archaeological evidence points to their sixth to fifth millennium BC introduction along the Arabian Gulf coast (Uerpman et al. 2000, 231–232), and their adoption by mobile groups throughout the arid Arabian interior in the fourth millennium BC (Cleuziou and Tosi 1997, 127), possibly as desalinization systems that allowed herder-foragers to maintain or expand their territorial ranges in a landscape of increasingly brackish water sources. A recent synthesis of the data for sixth millennium BC occupation of eastern Jordan's arid steppe suggests that foragers there had taken up caprine herding as an additional component of pre-existing hunting-cultivating-collecting strategies (Martin 1999, 100). Such people thrived independent of sedentary villagers in Mediterranean regions to the west, suggesting a model for similar groups throughout arid Arabia. While summer rainfall regimes might impose limits on the southward spread of cereals, caprine and cattle herding could have passed early into Arabian forager economies and developed, at least among some groups, as low-level food production.

Aridification had predictable effects: one must suppose that the middle Holocene monsoon recession dramatically changed the constraints on pastoralist-forager groups across Arabia. As interior early Holocene lakes dried up, their surface areas affected by annual flooding would shrink, providing ever-diminishing land (lake perimeters) for decrue cultivation of wild annuals and pressing desert foragers into alternative strategies (like their Saharan counterparts; Hassan 2000, 18–20). Arabian archaeology has not yet produced the data to model prehistoric population dynamics on a regional or peninsular scale, but regionally-focused research (e.g., Braemer et al. 2001, 43; Uerpmann et al. 2000; Breton 2000, 49; McCorriston et al. 2005) can offer guesses about population sizes and pressures. These were surely related to increasingly territorial practices such as the middle Holocene settlement of oases and the construction of highly visible cairn burials and later, charnel houses for communal burials (Cleuziou 1997, 407–409). Highland pastoralist-cultivators had experimented already with water management in the form of checkdams and terraces, and these technologies could be modified either to enlarge catchments or extend a water application period as rainfall became increasingly sparse. Adoption of domesticated Levantine cereals as existing high-ranked resources became sufficiently rare or unpredictable could only occur in the context of these established technologies in the Southern Arabian highlands.

CONCLUSIONS

South Arabian archaeological research still struggles to document when and how the adoption of domesticated plants and animals into indigenous foraging systems occurred. The archaeological record has not yet indicated the plants cultivated by pre-farming pastoralists in Arabia, nor are there sufficient cases to examine fully the timing and contexts of cattle domestication. Increasingly arid middle Holocene conditions might have encouraged reliance on indigenous Arabian resources such as camels and dates, whose domestication histories remain a fascinating puzzle for future research (Beech and Shepherd 2001, 87), but whose genetic ancestors and prehistoric manipulation may lie in Arabia. What is clear is that the adoption of domesticates in Arabia and in larger context, across the Near East (to include Egypt, Arabia, and Anatolia), took a long time and occurred piecemeal, even though a Levantine agro-husbandry package was in place by the middle Pre-Pottery Neolithic B (eighth millennium BC). Interpretations have been influenced by the European record showing that the Levantine agro-husbandry package moved with farmers to (Mediterranean) Greece, but the spread of Levantine crops and animals elsewhere followed different trajectories (such as the transfer of selected domesticates to low-level food producers), influenced in part by environmental constraints and climate changes.

Non-Levantine domesticates were not available for Arabian foragers in early prehistory. Therefore, in the face of a rainfall barrier, pastoralism was most likely to spread. The adoption of cattle, possibly from Africa, prior to the adoption of Levantine caprines in the Southern Arabian highlands meets the basic predictions of HBE (Alvard and Kuznar 2001; Russell 1988, 140–143). Cattle offer better opportunities for delayed returns and in marginal dry lands meet the energetic expectations that pastoral economies should develop in the absence of agriculture. However, it should be noted that moisture availability restricted the option of cattle pastoralism to regions of sufficient perennial water availability. The Wadi Sana record strongly suggests that water management and plant cultivation began in the context of cattle pastoralism in territories around water sources.

Adjustments in water management probably led to new irrigation techniques that did, much later, permit cultivators to adopt Levantine domesticates. Middle Holocene environmental changes, including reduced rainfall and its local effects, provided an important catalyst for adopting crop domesticates as local plant resources dwindled and plant cultivators restricted their mobility. Barley and wheat were staple crops in middle third millennium BC settlements (Costantini 1990a, 190–200; Cleuziou and Costantini 1982) and clearly remained important in the sophisticated irrigation economies of later Arabian states and their peripheries (Hehmeyer 1989, 41). In southern Arabia, it was the development of landscape management areas where people already practiced cattle pastoralism that ultimately allowed Levantine winter cereals to move south, breaking the tropical rain barrier.

NOTES

1. Throughout this paper I have used calendar dates BC to provide a coherent, single temporal framework for the non-specialist. Arabian prehistory is conventionally described by uncalibrated radiocarbon dates (B.P.) prior to the third millennium BC, which has historical dates, stylistic parallels and material imports, and easily resolved calibration issues. I have converted uncalibrated prehistoric radiocarbon dates, sometimes with awkward citation of only a millennium or two in which fall multiple possible intercepts of the calibration curve.

2. RASA stands for "Roots of Agriculture in Southern Arabia" and is a multinational interdisciplinary collaboration among American, Yemeni and other scholars in archaeology and paleoecology.

3. These are precipitates from cave waters dripping through carbonate rocks.

4. For a review of archaeological finds of crops and domesticated animals in Arabia and controversies surrounding sorghum, the reader should consult Cleuziou and Tosi (1997), de Moulins et al. (2003) and Edens (forthcoming). For long-term manipulation of tree crops—date and 'ilb—consult Beech and Shepherd (2001), Cleuziou and Costantini (1982, 1181), and Hehmeyer (1989, 38–41).

11

The Emergence of Agriculture in New Guinea

A MODEL OF CONTINUITY FROM PRE-EXISTING FORAGING PRACTICES

Tim Denham and Huw Barton

In this paper, foraging theory is used to explore how agriculture arose from pre-existing subsistence practices in the Highlands of New Guinea. In the first half of this paper several key lines of evidence for prehistoric subsistence practices from the early to mid Holocene are reviewed. These reviews provide a foundation for differentiating agriculture from other subsistence practices in the region. In the second half of the paper, several themes from foraging theory are adopted to show behavioural continuity in the emergence of agriculture from pre-existing foraging strategies in the Highlands of New Guinea.

We propose that hunter-gatherers were able to subsist permanently in the rain forests of Highland New Guinea, and that agriculture emerged gradually and not as a revolution, from pre-existing subsistence practices. Hunter-gatherers during the terminal Pleistocene and early Holocene in Highland New

Guinea employed two strategies to increase the productivity and reliability of key foraging patches. Firstly, there is palaeoecological evidence for considerable environmental manipulation through the clearance and burning of vegetation. Secondly, archaeological evidence indicates the movement of plant and animal species by people during the terminal Pleistocene and early Holocene in the Melanesian region. In this paper, the focus is on plant exploitation as early agricultural practices focused on plants, not animals. Through increasing environmental manipulation and a greater reliance on perennial starch sources such as taro (*Colocasia esculenta*) and bananas (*Musa* spp.), hunter-gatherers were able to subsist permanently in tropical rain forests in the interior of New Guinea. These foraging strategies were based on "vegecultural" practices of plant propagation. We argue agriculture arose from these pre-existing foraging strategies through gradual, and possibly largely inadvertent changes in the intensification of plant use and the level of residential mobility. The changes in land use documented at Kuk Swamp, the main wetland archaeological site in Highland New Guinea, were not isolated local events or a point of origin from which agricultural practices spread. They were an agricultural expression of a more widespread process of human-plant interaction and environmental modification in the Highlands of New Guinea.

The remainder of the introduction raises questions concerning concepts of agriculture, the timing and nature of its emergence in the Highlands of New Guinea and the value of foraging theory for understanding agricultural origins. In the second section of this paper, several environmental and prehistoric contexts are reviewed to orient the reader to key lines of evidence and argument relevant to an investigation of prehistoric plant exploitation in this region. In the third section, an interpretation of the emergence of agriculture from pre-existing strategies of plant exploitation in Highland New Guinea is proposed that uses several themes from foraging theory.

A WORKING DEFINITION OF AGRICULTURE

The terminology used to define "agriculture" is confusing and many conceptual schemas attempt to account for the diverse ways in which people obtain their subsistence (Harris 1996a). In this paper, agriculture is defined as the deliberate movement, planting and cultivation of plants within cleared plots, with associated transformations including plant morphogenesis (due to selective pressure) and to people's engagement with their environment (due to cumulative landscape modifications) and with each other (due to changing sociocultural practices) (after Harris 1996a; Hather 1996; Ingold 1996; Spriggs 1996; Yen 1989). Agriculture is a historically contingent, ecological, and social practice for which there is no single diagnostic marker.

On the one hand, morphogenetic changes to plants need not mark domestication or be coincident with agriculture as such transformations reflect selective pressures that are initiated by a range of intentional and unintentional practices (after Hather 1996; Jones et al. 1996). The rates of morphogenetic change for different species, varieties of the same species, and plant parts furthermore are highly variable (Jones and Colledge 2001), as are the persistence of these traits once selective pressures are relaxed (Dumont and Vernier 2000). In addition, many plants are transplanted today into gardens from wild forms in the Highlands of New Guinea with little genetic transformation of the species (after Powell 1970a; Yen 1985). The absence of morphogenetic transformations in cultivated food plants in the tropics consequently is not definitive evidence for or against the presence of agriculture.

On the other hand, the independent emergence of agriculture need not yield dramatic and unilinear demographic growth, environmental degradation, sociopolitical hierarchies, or a package of associated cultural traits (Thomas 1999, 7–33), although it is often associated with some of these elements. In New Guinea, agriculture may have led to gradual population growth, environmental degradation, and the spatial expansion of some language groups over thousands of years (after Pawley 1998, 684). These processes were however gradual, spatially and temporally variable, and did not result in stratified societies.

AGRICULTURE IN NEW GUINEA: DIFFUSION OR INDIGENOUS INNOVATION?

There are two main schools of thought regarding the origins and transformation of agriculture in New Guinea. Traditional orthodoxy views agriculture as having diffused from a center of domestication or hearth in Southeast Asia (e.g., Sauer 1952, 24; Vavilov 1992, 127, 430). According to this view, domesticated plants and animals and agricultural technology diffused to

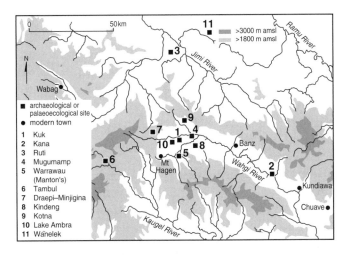

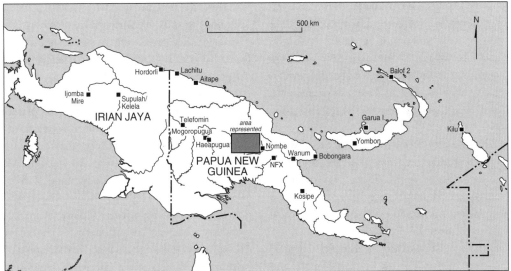

FIGURE 11.1. Map of New Guinea showing sites referred to in the text with inset of Upper and Middle Wahgi Valley. Papua New Guinea is the country that includes the eastern half of the island of New Guinea and surrounding islands, with the Indonesian province of Irian Jaya or West Papua occupying the western half. The island of New Guinea, sometimes referred to as mainland New Guinea, has a mountainous interior referred to as the Highlands and which usually denotes land above 1200 m above mean sea level (AMSL).

New Guinea from Southeast Asia with Austronesian expansion, which is marked by the Lapita cultural complex in Island Melanesia that dates to approximately 3300–3100 Cal B.P., or slightly earlier (Jones and Spriggs 2002). On linguistic, as well as archaeological, grounds Austronesian influence on New Guinea did not occur for another 1000 years (Spriggs 1995), which accords with the near-absence of Lapita pottery from the mainland, excepting the Aitape sherds (Figure 11.1; see Terrell and Welsch

1997). Earlier contact between Austronesians and mainland New Guinea may have occurred through West Papua, although there is currently a lack of evidence. It seems implausible that there was no contact and, hence, transmission of domesticated plants and agricultural techniques between New Guinea and Austronesian colonists of the Bismarck Archipelago.

Opposed to this perspective are claims for much earlier and independent agricultural origins by c. 10,200 Cal B.P. on New Guinea, which accompanied climatic amelioration after the end of the last glacial maximum (LGM), i.e., post 21,400 Cal B.P. (18,000 B.P.; see Golson 1977a, 1991a; Golson and Hughes 1980, Yen 1991). Golson and Yen proposed that agriculture developed in the lowlands with the upward movement of crops and practitioners accompanying the altitudinal expansion of mixed forests into the Highlands, i.e., land above 1200 m elevation (Golson 1991b, 82; Yen 1991). According to this view, many plants used by early agriculturalists were considered to have originated in the lowlands, such as bananas (*Musa* spp.) and taro (*Colocasia esculenta*). The wild types of these plants were not available in montane environments, with present-day altitudinal tolerances being a product of agronomic selection, e.g., *Colocasia* taro (Yen 1995, 835). However, the original altitudinal range and distribution of some wild types, such as *Colocasia esculenta* var. *aquitilis*, are poorly known (Matthews 1991, 1995).

Haberle proposed a similar model in which the mid-altitude inter-montane valleys, and not the lowlands, were the locus of agricultural emergence (Haberle 1993, 299–306, 1998, 4–5). He cited Bourke's (n.d.) information on altitudinal tolerances to suggest that a range of agricultural staples were present in the inter-montane valleys during the late Pleistocene. Climatic variability at the beginning of the Holocene led to the emergence of more intensive cultivation techniques. New plant management practices arose from pre-existing plant procurement and production strategies in order to maintain subsistence levels when confronted with significant environmental change.

The claims for indigenous and independent agriculture are based on multiple lines of archaeological, geomorphological and palaeoecological evidence (Golson 1977a, 1991a; Golson and Hughes 1980). These ideas, however, have not received universal acceptance due to the lack of published evidence, the near-absence of archaeobotanical material in key archaeological sites, and the uncertain function of archaeological remains (Bayliss-Smith 1996, 508–9;

Smith 1998, 142–3; Spriggs 1996, 528–9). For example, it is unclear whether some features represent agricultural practices, other subsistence activities, or natural processes (e.g., Denham 2004).

THE APPLICATION OF FORAGING THEORY TO HIGHLAND SUBSISTENCE

The aim of this paper is to use elements of foraging theory to develop a model to show how intensive forms of environmental and plant manipulation, culminating in agriculture, developed from pre-existing foraging practices in the interior of New Guinea. In formulating an indigenous model of agricultural origins, any clear evidence pre-dating Austronesian arrival by c. 3500 Cal B.P., at the earliest, is significant. Although Austronesian diffusion into Melanesia undoubtedly transformed pre-existing subsistence strategies, the introduction of plants, technologies and practices, and resultant transformations are poorly defined for mainland New Guinea.

Previous attempts to understand subsistence practices in Highland New Guinea from the late Pleistocene to early Holocene are unpersuasive because they do not fully characterize hunter-gatherer subsistence and occupation within rain forests of the interior (e.g., Groube 1989; Golson 1991b; Harris 1995). These positions do not show how significant changes in environmental manipulation, resource availability, an increasing reliance on starch staples, and changing diet breadth facilitated the development of more intensive agricultural practices from pre-existing foraging strategies. In this paper, foraging theory is used to characterize subsistence in the late Pleistocene and to show how agriculture developed from pre-existing foraging practices in the early Holocene.

Research attempting to elicit the foraging behaviours of a wide variety of animal species has shown that there are general behavioral patterns influencing the actions of individuals and that these behaviors are not species specific (e.g., Krebs and Davies 1997; Stephens and

Krebs 1986). These studies were applied to modern hunter-gatherers with similar success in determining the rules that generally influence the foraging choices made by humans (e.g., Hawkes et al. 1982, 1991; Heffley 1981; O'Connell and Hawkes 1981; Smith 1981; Winterhalder 1977, 1981a).

Hunter-gatherers are faced with a range of foraging opportunities and constraints in their use of landscapes. People cannot always be in the same place as resources, and ideal food items may not always be available in a given locale. There are also physical limitations to what the human body can tolerate in terms of digestive capability and energy expenditure. Resource acquisition is a trade-off between the amount of energy available to a forager and the amount of energy that must be expended in its search, pursuit, or capture. A negative energy balance is obviously an unsustainable strategy, and maintaining a positive energy balance may be confounded by issues of food dispersal and abundance, processing costs such as toxin removal, and inter- and intra-group competition for the same resources.

Several theories allow us to make predictions about how foragers may have used a given set of ecological resources. These include rate maximizing theories of diet breadth (MacArthur and Pianka 1966), patch choice (Winterhalder 1981b), foraging time, i.e., marginal value theorem (Charnov 1976; MacArthur and Pianka 1966), and choice of prey relative to travel time, i.e., central place foraging (Orians and Pearson 1979). An underlying assumption common to all these theories is that long-term survival is related to the efficient use of energy in the pursuit of food.

We are unable to discuss prehistoric diet in Highland New Guinea in any detail, largely due to limited archaeobotanical information on the range of food resources exploited in the past. We can, however, use foraging models to infer the likely range of strategies employed by hunter-gatherers in general terms without knowing precisely what was eaten and how it was captured or collected. Using foraging theory we can model innovative scenarios for foraging strategies that have no modern analogs in the Papua New Guinea Highlands.

We propose that hunter-gatherers were able to subsist permanently within the rain forests of Highland New Guinea by maintaining small foraging groups and high residential mobility. We also suggest that these groups were not passive users of their environment but actively manipulated successional stages of plant growth through burning. This behavior encouraged the growth of high-ranked plant resources such as starchy tubers, and increased the spatial predictability of game animals. A wide range of energy-rich starchy plants in the tropics readily reproduces through vegetative rather than sexual reproduction. These plants can establish themselves from root, tuber, and stem fragments, a factor that was possibly fundamental to the emergence of early horticultural systems in the Highlands. Human preference for these plants and subsequent movement of plant parts such as stored tubers into new campsites, cleared areas, and recently burned areas, would have increased the relative abundance of these resources and raised the productivity of frequently used foraging "patches" over time.

The archaeological and palaeoecological evidence from the highlands supports such a hypothesis with unequivocal evidence of landscape clearance associated with occupation in the Pleistocene. We cannot prove that humans were moving plants into the Highlands during the late Pleistocene phases of occupation, but the available archaeological evidence suggests that translocation of plants and animals was a strategy used by some hunter-gatherer groups at this time and was certainly occurring in the early Holocene. The evolutionary "pay-off" to groups exploiting such a strategy, even at low intensity in an otherwise resource depauperate environment, would have been high.

ENVIRONMENTAL AND PREHISTORIC CONTEXTS

Several general and specific contexts require consideration in order to understand how agriculture may have arisen independently in the Highlands of New Guinea. General contexts include geography and climate, and proxy signatures of agriculture from the archaeological record. Specific contexts include the archaeobotanical evidence for the presence and use of specific plants, palaeoecological evidence of landscape transformations associated with prehistoric practices, and archaeological remains of these practices at wetland sites in the Highlands. These specific contexts currently provide the key lines of evidence for interpreting how modes of plant exploitation changed through time.

ENVIRONMENTAL SETTING

Several large inter-montane valleys run along the Highland spine of New Guinea. The valley floors lie between 1200 and 1900 m above mean sea level and have low gradient rivers with adjacent wetlands. These wetlands filled through organic and subsequent inorganic sedimentation during the late Pleistocene and Holocene. The interfluves consist of mountain ranges rising several hundred meters above valley floors with considerably higher peaks, e.g., Mount Hagen at 3700 m.

The wetland archaeological sites currently of most significance for determining the origins of agriculture in New Guinea are situated in the Upper Wahgi Valley. The upper reaches of this valley are wide and mantled in debris flow (lahar) deposits from an eruption of Mount Hagen at least 200,000 years ago, with overlying and aggrading wetland deposits up to several miles wide (after Hughes et al. 1991, 229–30). The three Upper Wahgi Valley sites (Kuk, Mugumamp, and Warrawau) are of most significance and are situated in wetland margin locations between 1560 and 1590 m altitude. These wetland margins are transitional environments subject to seasonal, interannual, decadal, and millennial variations in hydrology, soil formation and ecology.

The Upper Wahgi Valley has a lower montane humid climate with an average annual temperature of 19°C and annual rainfall of c. 2700 mm (Hughes et al. 1991, 229). Climates are relatively aseasonal and dominated by local orographic effects rather than regional weather patterns, with little resultant variability in mean monthly rainfall, humidity, and temperature (Powell et al. 1975, 2). Estimates of tree-line altitude suggest glacial retreat commenced at 18,000 Cal B.P. (Haberle et al. 2001), with accelerated climatic amelioration from 14,000 Cal B.P. prior to stabilization at approximately 10,000 Cal B.P. (Brookfield 1989; Haberle 1998, 4). Late Pleistocene fluctuations in climate, recorded in the northern hemisphere and proposed as a trigger for agriculture, e.g., Younger Dryas (Hillman 1996), are not clearly identifiable in environmental records for the southern hemisphere (Chappell 2001). Slightly warmer, wetter, and more stable climates existed during a hypsithermal between 10,000–6800 Cal B.P. in the Highlands (Brookfield 1989), with El Niño Southern Oscillation (ENSO) events and climatic conditions similar to the present commencing from 5700–4500 Cal B.P. (Haberle 1998, 5).

SETTLEMENT AND MATERIAL CULTURE

The earliest settlement on mainland New Guinea dates to at least 40,000 years ago at Bobongara on the Huon Peninsula (Groube et al. 1986), with slightly younger but comparable dates from Lachitu on the north coast (Gorecki 1993) and for island Melanesia (Pavlides and Gosden 1994). Initial colonization of New Guinea may have occurred much earlier because the island formed a contiguous landmass with Australia during much of the Pleistocene, where the earliest dates suggest initial colonisation between 60,000 and 50,000 years ago (Roberts et al. 1994). Excavations at Kosipe (White et al. 1970) and Nombe (Mountain 1991) suggest human presence in the mountainous interior of New Guinea by at least 30,500 Cal B.P.

Subsistence practices in the Highlands are not well defined for the Pleistocene and parts of the Holocene. Most interpretations consider that the Highlands were used on a seasonal, temporary basis during the Pleistocene for the procurement of energy-rich kernels of *Pandanus* spp.

(Bulmer 1977, 69; Golson 1991b, 86–8; Hope and Golson 1995, 823; White et al. 1970, 168–9). The collection of *Pandanus* nuts was accompanied by hunting, as evidenced from faunal collections from caves and rock shelters (Mountain 1991). Few proxy signatures of a transition to agriculture are present in the lithic, faunal, or macrobotanical assemblages recovered from cave and rock-shelter excavations (after Bulmer 1966; Christensen 1975; Mountain 1991; White 1972). Potentially the most significant proxy signatures, which are briefly discussed here, are a change in stone tool technology and two late Pleistocene habitations.

First, stone tools dating from the early Holocene in the Highlands are predominantly represented by informal flaked stone technologies with the addition of ground axe/adzes at or before 6800–5700 Cal B.P. (Christensen 1975, 33). Although the introduction of hafted edge-ground tools would have facilitated forest clearance, this technological shift is not well dated and need not be coincident with the beginning of agriculture. Groube (1989) has proposed that people altered their rain forest environment using waisted blades, dating to at least 40,000 years on the Huon Peninsula (Groube et al. 1986). These blades were used from first colonization for "judicious trimming, canopy-thinning, and ring-barking, and perhaps, with the aid of fire, some minor felling" (Groube 1989, 299). These tools were used to disturb the forest canopy, thereby promoting the growth of favored species, and to aid the harvesting of those species, e.g., extracting the starch-rich pith of sago (*Metroxylon sagu*) and cycads (*Cycas* spp.; Groube 1989, 293).

Second, two open sites of late Pleistocene antiquity are noteworthy as potential evidence for sedentism: NFX in the Eastern Highlands (21,400 Cal B.P., Watson and Cole 1977) and Wañelek in Madang Province (17,900 Cal B.P.; Bulmer 1977, 1991). Both open sites are presented as evidence of late Pleistocene habitation in the Highlands, although their significance is qualified by difficulties of interpreting the structural remains at NFX (Golson 1991b, 86)

and limited publication of features at Wañelek (cf. Bulmer 1973). The poorly-defined buildings indicate periods of reduced residential mobility. Irrespective of these methodological problems, these structures need not be significant in terms of agriculture because they could have been used seasonally or occasionally for hunting and the procurement of periodically fruiting plants (i.e., *Pandanus* species).

In sum, the prehistory of the interior of New Guinea provides only a limited image of forager subsistence and mobility. By contrast, in Island Melanesia a new picture of rain forest use and hunter-gatherer mobility is emerging. From the interior rain forests of New Britain, excavations at Yombon, 35 km from the coast, have recovered a number of retouched chert tools from layers dating to around 40,000 Cal B.P. and 16,800 Cal B.P. (Pavlides and Gosden 1994). Highly mobile groups manufactured the tools on-site from a local, currently buried, chert source and the artifacts represent the strategic use of inland rain forest resources. On Garua Island off New Britain, excavations and survey have recovered a complex prehistory of landscape use throughout the Holocene (Torrence et al. 2000). From at least 10,000 years ago hunter-gatherers were highly mobile and produced hafted multipurpose obsidian tools that were continuously maintained as groups ranged over relatively large areas (Kealhofer et al. 1999). Over time expedient forms of tool use became more frequent, and there is evidence of raw material stockpiling and lowered residential mobility. Plant residues on stone tools indicate that site function changed over time from single purpose activities to multiple tasks (Fullagar 1992). These temporal trends are argued to reflect a gradual transition from low intensity land management from at least the beginning of the Holocene, to more intensive forms of plant cultivation by the mid-to-late Holocene (Torrence et al. 2000).

ARCHAEOBOTANICAL EVIDENCE OF PLANT USE

Ethnobotanical and ethnographic studies of subsistence practices in the interior of New

TABLE 11.1

Contemporary Altitudinal Tolerances for Some Plants Potentially Present in Inter-montane
Valleys of Highland New Guinea during the Late Pleistocene

SCIENTIFIC NAME	COMMON NAME	USUAL ALTITUDES (m AMSL)	EXTREME ALTITUDES (m AMSL)
Starch Sources			
Colocasia esculenta	taro	0–2400	0–2740
Dioscorea alata	greater yam	0–1900	0–2100
Dioscorea bulbifera	potato yam	0–1800	0–1920
Dioscorea nummularia	nummularia yam	0–1850	0–1950
Musa spp.	Fe'i banana	0–1900	0–2060
	diploid banana	0–1880	0–2030
	triploid banana	0–2290	0–2580
Pueraria lobata	pueraria	0–2300	0–2740
Saccharum officinarum	sugarcane	0–2550	0–2730
Setaria palmifolia	highland pitpit	0–2700	0–2720
Zingiberaceae	ginger	0–1900	0–2200
Vegetables			
Abelmoschus manihot	Aibika	0–1850	0–2110
Commelina diffusa	wandering jew	0–?	0–2390
Oenanthe javanica	Oenanthe	1100–?	0–3400
Rungia klossii	Rungia	1000–2700	0–2720
Solanum spp.	nightshade	0–2700	0–2740
Fruit and Nut Species			
Castanopsis acuminatissima	Castanopsis	650–2350	570–2440
Pandanus brosimos	(wild) karuka	2400–3100	1800–3300
Pandanus julianettii	karuka	1800–2550	1450–2730
Rubus moluccanus	red raspberry	0–2150	0–2250
Rubus rosifolius	red raspberry	950–2800	700–2900

Note: based on Haberle 1993, 299–306; Mike Bourke n.d. and pers. comm. 2002; Jack Golson pers. comm. 2002. Inter-montane valleys are defined as above 1200 m. The occurrence of plants is estimated based on a maximum depression of 600–780 m for the lower montane boundary (Hope and Tulip 1994 in Hope and Golson 1995, 820).

Guinea provide invaluable information on the range of utilized plants (e.g., Powell and Harrison 1982; Powell et al. 1975) and animals (e.g., Majnep and Bulmer 1990). The current evidence suggests that people utilizing the interior of New Guinea, and particularly the Highlands, were oriented more towards plants than fauna for their subsistence since initial settlement (e.g., Groube 1989; White 1996). Archaeobotanical evidence and phylogenetic investiga-tions suggest a broad range of plants were present or used starting in the late Pleistocene and continuing into the Holocene. These plants include fruit and nut bearing trees, the main starchy staples of Pacific agriculture, and a range of other vegetables (Table 11.1).

ARBORICULTURE

Arboriculture in the tropics is generally represented by the well-preserved tough endocarps or husks of nuts (Christensen 1975; Yen 1996, 1998), although the presence of other edible species can also be inferred from pollen, seed, and wood assemblages (e.g., *Castanopsis* spp., *Ficus* spp.; Powell 1970b). Several archaeobotanical collections document early and middle Holocene use of a wide range of fruit and nut bearing trees in Lowland Melanesia (Gorecki 1992; Hayes 1992; Swadling et al. 1991) and Highland New Guinea (Donoghue 1988). Based on archaeobotanical collections in the lowlands, Yen has proposed that canarium almonds (*Canarium* spp.) were indigenous to New Guinea (1990, 262) and subject to selection, inter-island transportation, and domestication, particularly *C. indicum*, from the early Holocene (Yen 1996, 41).

Haberle (1995) proposed a similar long-term trajectory for the selection and domestication of *Pandanus brosimos* (wild form) to *Pandanus julianettii* (domesticated form) from the late Pleistocene in the Highlands. Palaeoecological and archaeological evidence for human disturbance and settlement, respectively, within the interior rain forests of New Guinea indicated over 20,000 years of activity prior to the earliest putative evidence of horticulture (1995, 207–8). *Panadanus brosimos* would have provided a reliable food source in the Highlands during the last glacial cycle and was subject to selective pressures resulting from sustained exploitation (Haberle 1995, 208). Over time, domesticated varieties of *Pandanus brosimos* developed (i.e., *P. julianettii*), which were subsequently transplanted below 2400 m in the Holocene, the usual lower altitudinal limit of the wild form.

The nuts of *Canarium* spp. and *Pandanus* spp. are highly nutritious, high in fat (66–69 g/ 100 g), protein (12–14 g/100 g) and calories (Powell 1976, 117). The kernel of *Canarium* spp. yields approximately 2500 KJ per 100 g of nut flesh (Coronel 1992, 105). The seasonality of fruit production varies considerably in response to climatic stimuli across the Highlands and yields fluctuate considerably from year to year

(Bourke 1996). The husbanding of wild plants, however, requires no more than clearing away competitive growth to open up the canopy and encourage fruit production (Groube 1989, 299).

STARCHY STAPLES

The starchy components of plants, among the most highly ranked in terms of diet breadth, are rarely preserved as tissues unless they were carbonized prehistorically (e.g. Hather 1992; Hather and Kirch 1991). Recent research aimed at recovering preserved starch granules from the surface of stone and shell tools (Barton and White 1993; Fullagar 1992, 1993; Loy et al. 1992) and soils from archaeological contexts (Barton et al. 1998; Therin et al. 1999) is beginning to shed light on the use of palms, rhizomes, and tubers by Pleistocene tropical foragers in Melanesia.

Recent archaeobotanical studies in lowland Melanesia have identified the residues of several Pacific staples on stone tools. Staples include taro (*Colocasia esculenta* and *Alocasia macrorrhiza*) dating to c. 32,500 Cal B.P. at Buka in the Solomons (Loy et al. 1992). At Balof 2 in the Bismarck Archipelago, *Alocasia* sp. and *Cyrtosperma* sp. dating from c. 16,800 Cal B.P. and yam (*Dioscorea* sp.) dating from 12,300 Cal B.P. have been reported (Barton and White 1993). Starch staples have recently been documented from prehistoric contexts at Kuk in Highland New Guinea. Discoveries include starch grains of *Colocasia* taro on artifacts and *Musa* banana phytoliths (including *Eumusa* morphotypes) in sediments from 10,000-year-old contexts, and the presence of probable ginger (Zingiberaceae) or possible palm phytoliths on tools from 7000–6400 Cal B.P. (Fullagar et al. 2002; Lentfer 2002).

The antiquity of these staples in Melanesia challenges previous portrayals that they were Southeast Asian domesticates introduced by Austronesians. Pre-Austronesian subsistence in Melanesia, including the Highland interior of New Guinea, was not devoid of perennial, high-caloric sources of food (pace Golson 1991b; Hope and Golson 1995, 827). The presence and deliberate human use of these major starch staples of Pacific agriculture in Melanesia prior to Austronesian contact opens up new interpretative possibilities for the development of subsistence practices in the region.

OTHER VEGETABLES

People in the Highlands use hundreds of other plants for food, construction, medicines, and ritual purposes (Powell 1976; Powell et al. 1975). Archaeobotanical assemblages of seeds and wood from late Pleistocene and early Holocene contexts at several wetland sites in the Highlands, including Kuk, contain numerous edible species (Powell 1970b, 1982a; Powell et al. 1975). Several present-day food plants occur in prehistoric contexts at Kuk including: *Cerastium* sp., *Coleus* sp., *Oenanthe javanica*, *Commelina* sp., and *Solanum nigrum* (all mainly from at least 6500 Cal B.P. onwards); *Rubus rosifolius* is present throughout the sequence; and *Rubus moluccanus* only occurs in Pleistocene sediments. Although most species are undiagnostic because today they occur in numerous habitats, they indicate the range of species available for human use in the past (Powell 1982b, 32).

Direct evidence of cultivated plants is relatively rare in Highland archaeological contexts, the exceptions being gourd (*Lagenaria siceraria* or *Benincasa hispida*) from a middle Holocene context at Warrawau (Golson 2002) and a macrobotanical sample of sugarcane (*Saccharum officinarum*) from a putatively middle Holocene context at Yuku (Bulmer 1975, 31). The age and identifications of both finds are, however, uncertain (Golson 2002; Daniels and Daniels 1993, 6; respectively). Saccharum sugarcane was formerly grown in monocultural plots in parts of the Highlands and was a major food source in the past (Daniels and Daniels 1993, 2–4).

*ARCHAEOBOTANICAL VISIBILITY
OF PLANT DOMESTICATION*

At present, it is not possible to determine if these archaeobotanical finds are domesticated or wild varieties. Little research has tracked the morphogenetic impacts of human selection on nut, pollen, seed, starch grain, and phytolith morphologies for prehistoric or contemporary populations of Pacific food plants (exceptions being Donoghue 1988; Haberle 1995; Yen 1996). These studies lack the resolution and sample sizes of Southwest Asian (Hillman 1996) and neotropical domesticates (Piperno and Pearsall 1998). Without such studies, the phylogenetic relationships between wild and domesticated varieties and species cannot be matched to plant macro or microfossils. However, several cultivated plants in contemporary New Guinea horticulture have reproductive mechanisms suggestive of anthropogenic selection (e.g. the development of parthenocarpy in *Musa* bananas and the loss of flowering in the greater yam, *Dioscorea alata*). These characteristics may well represent human transformations of pre-existing wild forms to develop a more productive variety or species.

Lebot (1999) has reviewed the biomolecular signatures for most of the major Pacific staples including *Colocasia* taro, *Musa* bananas, the greater yam (*Dioscorea alata*), giant taro (*Alocasia macrorrhiza*), breadfruit (*Artocarpus altilis*), and *Saccharum* sugarcanes. Based on a range of genetic research, Lebot concluded that these plants were domesticated in Melanesia and that "New Guinea and some parts of Melanesia have been important centers of diversity for species that also exist in Asia" (Lebot 1999, 626). His conclusion accords with some previous hypotheses, e.g., the domestication of a wild variety of taro (*Colocasia esculenta* var. *aquatilis*) in the Melanesian region (Matthews 1991, 1995), and undermines traditional interpretations that domesticated plants in New Guinea diffused with Austronesian dispersal. Although biomolecular techniques enable some determination of genetic variability, domesticated varieties, and the locus of domestication, they require chronological calibration using contemporary samples and archaeobotanical finds, which are currently sparse.

If the archaeobotanical finds are taken in conjunction with the biomolecular data, the two lines of evidence are mutually supporting. The former show the presence and use of a several major staples in Melanesia prior to any known contact with Southeast Asia. The effects of anthropogenic selection on these plants in Melanesia during the late Pleistocene and early Holocene are suggested by their modern-day reproductive strategies and biomolecular composition.

REVISED SCENARIO

An important component of the argument about forager occupation of primary tropical rain forest relates to potential return rates from collected resources. Previous arguments about availability of carbohydrates within the rain forest focused on the availability of fruits and *Dioscorea* yams (e.g. Bailey et al. 1989; Bailey and Headland 1991; Headland 1987). Although some yams are thought to be indigenous to New Guinea (Powell 1976) and grow at Kuk (see Table 11.1), their geographic origins are uncertain. Other starchy resources were certainly available to Pleistocene hunter-gatherers within the New Guinea rain forest including: the rhizomes of Araceae and Zingiberaceae; the starchy interior of several species of palm (e.g. *Metroxylon* sago); the fruit and pseudo-corm of *Musa* bananas; and *Pandanus* nuts. Unlike the yam family, members of the Araceae and Zingiberaceae (both potentially present at Kuk) are shade-tolerant species adapted to living in the low light conditions of primary rain forest. While there is as yet no available data regarding the density and distribution of these plants in these environments, they are known to be a common component of herbaceous vegetation throughout Melanesia (Richards 1996, 122).

Phytogeographic and phylogenetic studies are corroborated by recent archaeobotanical, palynological and residue analyses. In particular, the presence and use of so many major caloric sources alter possible scenarios of pre-Austronesian subsistence in New Guinea. The archaeobotanical evidence supports the possibility of broad-spectrum plant use in Melanesia

starting in the late Pleistocene. The earliest direct evidence of plant use in the Highlands of New Guinea comes from the early Holocene, i.e., *Colocasia* taro residues at Kuk. Rather than being a non-center or secondary center for introduced Austronesian domesticates, an emerging picture suggests the Melanesian region is a primary center of crop domestication and dispersal. Many of the major staples of Pacific agriculture were present as wild forms in New Guinea and domesticated there, with new varieties of the same species being introduced by Austronesians from areas of domestication and/or use in Southeast Asia and Indo-Malaysia. These findings have major implications for considerations of hunter-gatherer subsistence ecology and the independent origins of agriculture in the Highlands of New Guinea.

HUNTER-GATHERER SUBSISTENCE AND ENVIRONMENTAL MANIPULATION

In terms of vegetation response to climate change, from the Last Glacial Maximum (LGM) to around 13,000 Cal B.P., many mid-altitude valley floors were blanketed with *Nothofagus* beech-dominated forests. Golson proposed that these beech forests were monostands, with few utilizable species other than *Pandanus* spp. being present (Golson 1991b). His interpretation accords with the ecology of *Nothofagus*-dominated forests in contemporary high altitude areas of Papua New Guinea (Read et al. 1990) and West Papua (Hope 1976, 124–5). At the beginning of the Holocene, the floors of the major inter-montane valleys between elevations of 1200 and 1960 m "were invaded by lower altitude taxa, leading to a complex mixed forest" (Hope 1996, 178). Pollen diagrams document an increased presence of *Castanopsis, Lithocarpus, Podocarpus,* and other mixed forest species. The demise of beech stands in the mid-altitudes was accompanied by an increased "floristic and structural complexity" (Hope et al. 1988, 603). Golson identified a broad spectrum of floral resources potentially utilized in the mixed forests including: vegetables, (e.g., *Rungia klossii* and *Oenanthe javanica*); the major staples consisting of *Musa* bananas, *Saccharum* sugarcane, *Colocasia* taro and "yam-like tubers, apparently of the genus *Dioscorea*" (Golson 1991b, 87); nut and fruit-bearing trees (especially *Castanopsis-Lithocarpus* spp., *Elaeocarpus* spp. and *Ficus* spp.); vines with fruits; and fungi (after Golson 1991b; Hope and Golson 1995).

According to these interpretations, the rain forests of lower montane New Guinea were utilizable only on a seasonal basis during the Pleistocene. With a change in forest composition, there was greater potential for occupation based on a range of resources starting in the early Holocene. In contrast, Haberle (1993, 299–306; 1998, 4–5) proposes that a much broader range of plants was present throughout the late Pleistocene and was sufficient for subsistence. In terms of arguments regarding the occupation of tropical rain forest by hunter-gatherers (e.g. Bailey and Headland 1991; Bailey et al. 1989; Headland 1987; Kuchikura 1993; Sillitoe 2002), a major factor not sufficiently considered in previous debates is the ability of humans to deliberately and inadvertently manipulate their environment. We propose that burning and plant translocation were two strategies employed to increase resource availability within patches of montane rain forest in the late Pleistocene.

ANTHROPOGENIC DISTURBANCE OF THE RAIN FOREST

The extent and changing severity of anthropogenic disturbance signalled in pollen diagrams can be used as a surrogate measure of the scale and intensity of human subsistence practices on the environment (Haberle 1994, 2003; Piperno and Pearsall 1998, 167–320). The impacts of low-intensity uses, such as the collection of *Pandanus* kernels, may be minimal, whereas forest clearances to prepare patches and promote plant diversity require greater intervention and are more likely to be archaeologically visible. The sensitivity of the environment to anthropogenic impacts also requires consideration as it varies in response largely to climatic factors.

The earliest anthropogenic disturbances of Highland vegetation date to almost 40,000 Cal B.P. at Haeapugua (Haberle 1998), Kosipe (Hope 1982), and Supulah in the Baliem Valley (Haberle et al. 1991; Hope 1998). These burning events may represent crop-procurement practices intended to enhance the productivity of favored plants, such as *Pandanus* spp. (Hope and Golson 1995, 822–3). In the late Pleistocene and early Holocene, more intensive clearances occurred in large inter-montane valleys between 1400 and 1650 m elevation (Table 11.2; see Figure 11.1). Charcoal values indicate increased burning in the region as a whole from 20,200–14,100 Cal B.P., with local variability between 14,100–10,200 Cal B.P. (Haberle et al. 2001, 264). Burning and clearance were not synchronous or cumulative. For example, elevated charcoal and disturbance taxa frequencies at Lake Haeapugua from 26,000–11,400 Cal B.P. were followed by invasion of swamp forest (Haberle 1993, 214–5, 1998, 11) and two early episodes of prolonged clearance followed by forest recovery occurred at Telefomin (Hope 1983). In contrast, the record for Kelela Swamp in the Baliem Valley shows cumulative disturbance from before c. 7800 Cal B.P. to the present (Haberle et al. 1991).

Two unpublished pollen diagrams from Kuk record anthropogenic burning and disturbance of the forest from c. 19,000 and c. 17,000 Cal B.P., although there were no concomitant increases in forest taxa (Powell 1984). Haberle has more recently completed a third unpublished pollen diagram for the early to middle Holocene and from associated archaeological contexts at Kuk (Haberle 2002). From c. 10,000 Cal B.P., there is the creation and maintenance of a mosaic of vegetation communities including primary forest, secondary forest, swamp forest, and open grassland. A coincident peak in charcoal particle frequencies suggests fire was the cause of vegetation change. The record of vegetation clearance accords with previous interpretations of human-induced erosion rates from c. 10,000 Cal B.P. within the Kuk catchment (Golson and Hughes 1980, 296–8; Hughes

TABLE 11.2
Selection of Late Pleistocene to Early Holocene Clearances in New Guinea

SITE	LOCATION	ALTITUDE (m AMSL)	INITIATION (CAL B.P.)	REFERENCE(S)
Mid-altitude, inter-montane sites				
Kelela Swamp	Baliem Valley	1420	pre–7,800	Haberle et al. 1991
Telefomin	Ifitaman Valley	1500	21,400–18,500 13,500–9,100	Hope 1983
Kuk Swamp	Wahgi Valley	1560	pre–10,200	Powell 1984 Haberle 2002
Lake Haeapugua	Tari Basin	1650	17,400–14,100	Haberle 1998
High and low altitude sites				
Lake Wanum	Markham Valley	35	9,500	Garrett-Jones 1979
Lake Hordorli	Cyclops Mountains	780	13,000	Hope and Tulip 1994
Laravita Tarn	Mount Edward Albert	3780	14,100	Hope and Peterson 1976
Ijomba Mire	Discovery Valley	3720	c. 13,000	Hope 1996

Note: See Figure 11.1.

et al. 1991). These changes are not climatic as they occur during a period of relatively stable, warmer and wetter conditions (Haberle et al. 2001). By c. 6500 Cal B.P., the Kuk diagram shows a highly altered rain forest environment. The Kuk vicinity is an open environment dominated by grassland, with forest at a distance from the wetland.

Anthropogenic degradation of primary forest pre-dating 6100–5700 Cal B.P. also occurred at Lake Ambra and Draepi-Minjigina in the Upper Wahgi valley. These two sites record changes from undisturbed primary forest in the late Pleistocene and disturbed environments with higher percentages of woody non-forest species by the mid Holocene (Powell 1970b, 1982a, 218). The intervening period is missing from the chronologies at both sites. Another pollen spectra at Warrawau depicted secondary forest from the beginning of the diagram at c. 5700 Cal B.P. (Powell 1970b, 155–9; Powell et al. 1975, 43–4, 46–8). Secondary forest was represented by light-demanding species including *Trema* sp., *Acalypha* sp., *Macaranga* sp. and *Dodonaea* sp. These Wahgi Valley sites record a

further decline in forest cover up to 4500 Cal B.P. with concomitant rises in grass frequencies (Powell 1982a, 218).

Beyond the Wahgi Valley, "[b]y 4500 Cal B.P. considerable areas of forest had been cleared throughout the [H]ighlands" (Powell 1982a, 224). A minor recovery of the forests occurred in the Wahgi Valley after 4500 Cal B.P. (Powell 1982a, 218), although it was not dramatic and the following 1800–2400 year period represents stabilization of a disturbed environment. Across the Highlands, however, the record is variable during the Holocene with some sites recording forest clearance, regeneration, or relatively pristine forest. For example, Nurenk Swamp at 1950 m elevation shows no signs of clearance until 300 years ago (Hope et al. 1988, 614).

Despite much variability, several general trends are visible in the palaeoecology of the Highlands. As climates ameliorated after the LGM, people occupied the large inter-montane valleys more frequently, for longer periods, and depended more heavily on an expanding resource base (Golson 1991b, 89). The Highland

TABLE 11.3
Archaeological Phases at Kuk Swamp, Wahgi Valley

PHASE	DESCRIPTION	AGE (CAL B.P.)
1	Amorphous palaeosurface	10,220–9910
2	Mounded palaeosurface	6950–6440
3	Rectilinear field systems (early sub-phase)	4350–3980
	Rectilinear/dendritic field systems (late sub-phase)	pre-3260–2800
4	Rectilinear field systems	1940–1100
5	Rectilinear field systems	420–260
6	Rectilinear field systems	260–100

Note: Phase 1, 2, and 3 dates are based on recent research (Denham 2003a). Phase 4, 5, and 6 dates follow Golson 1982.

clearances are among the earliest anthropogenic clearance of vegetation anywhere in the world (Flenley 1979, 122). Forest clearance within the inter-montane valleys of New Guinea was not synchronous, cumulative, or ubiquitous during the late Pleistocene and early Holocene. By the middle Holocene, anthropogenic disturbance of the rain forests was more widespread and more severe, with some areas degraded to grassland.

PLANT TRANSLOCATION

There is evidence for the deliberate translocation of plants and animals within Melanesia during the Pleistocene and Holocene. Based on archaeobotanical collections in the lowlands, Yen proposed that *Canarium* spp. were indigenous to New Guinea (1990, 262) and subject to selection, inter-island transportation and domestication during the late Pleistocene (Yen 1996, 41). There is also considerable evidence for the Pleistocene translocation of marsupials from mainland New Guinea to the Bismarck Archipelago and Timor (Spriggs 1997, 53–5; White 2004). These translocations show the deliberate, intentional movement of species in order to diversify food sources on neighboring islands.

There is no direct evidence of plant transloca-tion in the Highlands of New Guinea during the Pleistocene, but it is indicated in the early Holocene by the *Colocasia* taro at Kuk (associated with Phase 1, 10,220–9910 Cal B.P., see below;

Fullagar et al. 2002). Taro is a lowland crop whose modern altitudinal range is a product of anthro-pogenic selection for cultivation (after Yen 1995, 835). Taro would not be expected to be present above 1500 m elevation approximately 10,000 years ago unless people had brought the plant into the Highlands. The context of the *Colocasia* residues, being present on a used edge of a stone tool in an anthropogenic plot within a cleared and managed valley ecosystem, are suggestive of de-liberate movement and planting.

ORIGINS OF AGRICULTURE AND WETLAND ARCHAEOLOGY

Multi-disciplinary investigations directed by Jack Golson were undertaken in the 1970s and 1980s at Kuk Swamp (referred to as "Kuk"), Wahgi Valley, Western Highlands Province, Papua New Guinea. Six prehistoric phases of wetland management for agriculture dating from 10,000 to 100 Cal B.P. were subsequently identified (Table 11.3; Golson 1977a). Kuk is the type-site for wetland archaeological investiga-tions in the Highlands, and is cross-correlated with finds from other sites.

The more recent phases of drainage (Phases 4, 5, and 6) are rectilinear in form, are unques-tionably associated with agriculture, and are not considered further in this paper. The earlier three phases (Phases 1, 2, and 3) are more amorphous and are not directly analogous to contemporary

TABLE 11. 4

Cross-correlation of Kuk Phases to Other Wetland Archaeological Sites in the Interior

SITE NAME	ALTITUDE (m AMSL)	PHASES	PRINCIPAL PUBLICATIONS
Tambul	2170	3	Golson 1997
Minjigina	1890	4	Lampert 1970; Powell 1970b
Mogoropugua	1890	5–6	Golson 1982
Haeapugua	1650	3–6	Ballard 1995
Kindeng	1600	n/a	Jack Golson, pers comm 2001
Warrawau (Manton's)	1590	2–3, 5	Golson et al. 1967; Lampert 1967
Kotna	1580	5	Jack Golson, pers comm 2002
Kuk	1560	1–6	Golson 1977a; Golson and Hughes 1980
Mugumamp	1560	2, 5–6	Harris and Hughes 1978
Kana	1480	2?–5	Muke and Mandui 2003
Ruti	480	2?	Gillieson et al. 1985

Note: See Figure 1. The identifications of Phase 2 at Mugumamp and Warrawau post-date Kuk and at Kana and Ruti are provisional (Denham in press a).

horticultural practices. These three phases predate the known Austronesian influence on mainland New Guinea, although later Phase 3 ditch networks are contemporary to the Lapita cultural complex in Island Melanesia. The transition from Phase 2 to Phase 3 marks the emergence of rectilinear ditch networks. The early three phases, and particularly Phases 1 and 2 at Kuk, have partially-grounded claims for the early, pre-Austronesian, and independent origins of agriculture in New Guinea (Bellwood 1996, 484–7; Golson 1991a; Haberle 1993, 299–306; Yen 1990, 261–4).

Golson and colleagues have long asserted the artificial and agricultural character of the archaeological remains associated with the early three phases: "[they] represent mixed gardening [agriculture] with the intercropping of different plant species and allowance for their varying soil and moisture requirements" (Golson 1990, 145). Others are unconvinced by the early evidence for agriculture (Spriggs 1997, 62). New excavations at Kuk and a review of the site archive from previous excavations have yielded revised interpretations of the archaeological significance of Phases 1, 2, and 3 (Denham 2003a).

PHASE 1

Archaeological evidence of Phase 1 is unique to Kuk and formed the basis of claims for early and independent agricultural origins in the Highlands of New Guinea (Bayliss-Smith 1996, 508–9; Golson 1977a, 1991a; Golson and Hughes 1980). These interpretations were made with "somewhat less confidence" than those for Phases 2 to 6 (Golson 2000, 232). Phase 1 at Kuk was interpreted to consist of an artificial palaeochannel and associated palaeosurface with cut, anthropogenic features (Golson 1977a, 613–5, 1991a; Golson and Hughes 1980).

Renewed investigation of Phase 1 at Kuk casts doubt on previous interpretations (Denham 2004). Multiple lines of evidence previously proposed to indicate the artificial construction of the palaeochannel were reviewed and shown to be indeterminate in terms of origin. Cross-sectional and planform morphologies of the paleochannel are potentially consistent with natural drainage. The previously proposed traverse through a low hillock is not determinate because it occurs in compactional alluvial stratigraphy and along a pre-existing paleochannel cut.

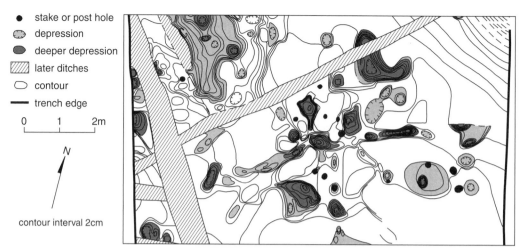

stake or post hole
depression
deeper depression
later ditches
contour
trench edge

0   1   2m

N

contour interval 2cm

FIGURE 11.2. Plan of Phase 1 palaeosurface at Kuk with shading to enhance topographic features.

Although there are no strong grounds to infer the anthropogenesis of the paleochannel, the interpretation of the paleosurface remains largely unaltered. The paleosurface comprises irregularly distributed and disorganized features (Golson 1977a, 613, 1991a, 485; Golson and Hughes 1980, 298–9). Although some paleosurface features represent natural drainage, others are clearly anthropogenic including stake and post holes, pits, and complexes of inter-cut features (Figure 11.2). The presence of a few artifacts, starch residues of *Colocasia* taro on stone tools (Fullagar et al. 2002) and phytoliths of *Musa* bananas (Lentfer 2002; Wilson 1985) confirms earlier interpretations of experimental cultivation of indigenous plants (after Golson 1991a, 484–5; Yen 1990, 262–3). Palynological and geomorphological records of forest clearance and erosion on adjacent slopes indicate the use of the wetland margin was part of a wider land-use strategy potentially analogous to shifting cultivation.

PHASE 2

Three sites in the Wahgi Valley are reported to represent unequivocal evidence of middle Holocene agriculture (see Table 11.4; see Figure 11.1): Kuk (Golson 1977a, 615–8), Warrawau (Golson 1982, 121) and Mugumamp (Harris and Hughes 1978). These sites were interpreted

to consist of large artificial watercourses associated with anthropogenic paleosurfaces. Similarly aged, more equivocal evidence of former agricultural activities was documented at Kana near Minj (Muke and Mandui 2003) and the Ruti Flats (Gillieson et al. 1985).

A recent review of the evidence at these latter two sites questions previous interpretations of age and agricultural origins, respectively (Denham 2003b). In contrast to previous depictions, the artificial construction of the paleochannels or ditch at Kuk, Warrawau, and Mugumamp is uncertain, and the inferred associations with paleosurfaces at each site are not well demonstrated (Denham 2003b). The paleosurfaces at the three sites are similar and for the Kuk site were characterised as (Figure 11.3):

> . . . a web of short channels, so disposed as to define roughly circular clay islands of about one metre diameter. . . . The intersections of these channels form small basins, whose bases are not only slightly lower than those at the central point of the [runnels] that connect them but also than the base level of the channels in the system that directly articulate with the major [paleochannels] (Golson 1977a, 616).

The paleosurfaces enabled the retention of water during periods of low runoff and the

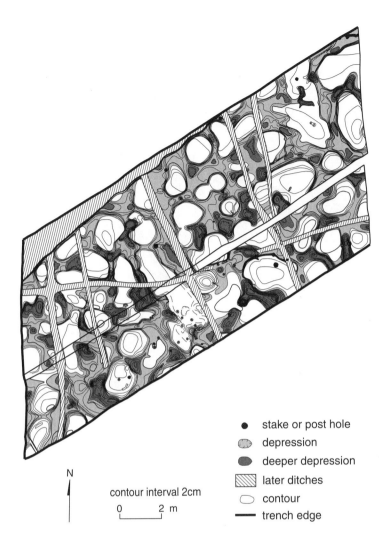

● stake or post hole

🌑 depression

🌑 deeper depression

▨ later ditches

◯ contour

▬ trench edge

N

contour interval 2cm

0   2 m

FIGURE 11.3. Plan of Phase 2 palaeosurface at Kuk with shading to enhance mounds and intervening drainage features.

drainage of water through the system during high runoff (Golson 1977a, 616). A less integrated paleosurface type was present at Kuk and consisted of more dispersed features that lacked an overall pattern (Golson 1977a, 616–7).

The anthropogenesis of paleosurfaces is demonstrated by regular feature types, associations of stake and post holes with the edges of deeper depressions, and artifacts, charcoal, and manuports in feature fills. Both paleosurface types at Kuk represent cultivation (Golson 1977a, 617). The integrated paleosurface represents small-scale micro-topographical manipulation of the wetland through the construction of mounds to enable the multi-cropping of plants with different edaphic requirements.

Water-tolerant plants, such as *Colocasia* taro, were planted along the edges and in the bases of shallower features, and water-intolerant plants, such as *Saccharum* sugarcanes, *Musa* bananas, and mixed vegetables were planted on the raised mounds (Golson 1977a, 616, 1981, 57–8; Powell et al. 1975, 42). Archeobotanical remains from feature fills, associated contexts and stone tool residues provide corroboratory evidence for the use of these plants at this time (after Fullagar et al. 2002; Haberle 2002; Lentfer 2002; Powell 1982b; Wilson 1985).

PHASE 3

Phase 3 drainage networks at Kuk are distinctive from earlier forms. The drainage networks

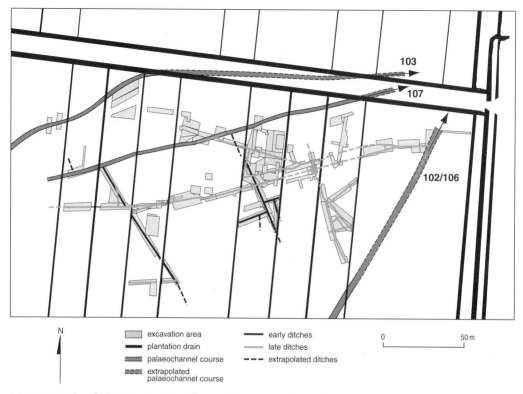

N

▨ excavation area	━━ early ditches
▬ plantation drain	━━ late ditches
▬ palaeochannel course	--- extrapolated ditches
▰▰▰ extrapolated palaeochannel course	

103
107
102/106

0   50 m

FIGURE 11.4. Plan of selected early and late Phase 3 drainage networks at Kuk.

are comprised of ditches that articulate with each other and major palaeochannels. The ditch networks were characterised as "a regular grid of drainage lines" (Powell et al. 1975, 42) and "open dendritic" (Golson 1977b, 49), but were not described in detail. Only a few associated "field" features were recorded (Golson 1981, 58; 1977a, 620).

Phase 3 ditches and ditch networks group into three sub-phases based largely on stratigraphic and tephrochronological correlations (Denham in press a; Figure 11.4): three early rectilinear ditch complexes predate 4350–3980 Cal B.P.; mid-late unarticulated ditches and poorly dated ditch pairs; and two late ditch complexes with dendritic, rectilinear and triangular components, pre-date 3260–2800. Cal B.P.

The initiation of ditch digging was an indigenous innovation within the Highlands that reflects an increasing reliance on relatively productive wetlands within a grassland landscape. Contemporary ditched drainage exists at several other wetlands in the interior of New Guinea (see Table 11.4).

A wooden spade dating to 4570–4150 Cal B.P. (ANU 2282; .985% at two sigma) at Tambul (2170 m) is broadly contemporaneous to early Phase 3. The Tambul finds represent an altitudinal expansion of agricultural activities into a marginal environment for many of the known cultivars (Bayliss-Smith 1985; Golson 1997, 145–6). The Tambul evidence complements Walker and Flenley's record of anthropogenic disturbance at c. 5100–3200 Cal B.P. (inferred ages) at Sirunki (2500 m) in Enga Province (1979, 339–40).

Several sites provide contemporary evidence to late Phase 3 including Warrawau and Kana in the Wahgi Valley and Haeapugua in the Tari Basin. The dates for ditches, crop remains, and implements at these sites are highly synchronous and combine to give an estimate of 2750–2150 Cal B.P. (Denham in press a). These sites represent a spatial expansion of agricultural activities through the Wahgi Valley, into the Tari Basin and, perhaps, into other inter-montane valleys.

CULTIVATION OF WETLAND MARGINS

The archeological evidence from Kuk and other sites represents human use of wetland margins from the beginning of the Holocene. The extent of human alteration is less dramatic than previously proposed for Phases 1 and 2 given the lack of evidence for the artificial construction of paleochannels. The Phase 1 and 2 paleosurfaces are suggestive of human alteration of the wetland margin for the cultivation of plants. This interpretation is consistent with microtopography, feature types, associated artifacts, charcoal, and archeobotanical remains of crop plants. Essentially the Phase 1 and 2 evidence corresponds to features within cultivated plots, whereas the Phase 3 ditch networks represent field systems.

FORAGING IN TROPICAL RAIN FORESTS: UNDERSTANDING SUBSISTENCE BEHAVIOR IN THE HIGHLANDS

How can these prehistoric lines of evidence be used to understand prehistoric subsistence behavior in the Highlands? While edible plant resources were generally poor in quality and probably widely dispersed in climax rain forest (Bailey et al. 1989), the Bailey and Headland (1991) hypothesis that the interior tropical rain forests away from the coasts represented a barrier or "green desert" to early modern human foragers is overstated. Recent papers critiquing the idea of hunter-gatherer subsistence within interior tropical rain forest continue to rely upon ethnographic analogy and data collected from groups that are now largely sedentary (e.g. Kuchikura 1993; Sillitoe 2002).

A review of hunting and gathering return-rates from Highland New Guinea presents, at first glance, good evidence in support of the "green desert" hypothesis for the Wola of the Southern Highlands (Sillitoe 2002). Vegetation across the valley is thick (mostly *Nothofagus* spp.),

with more settled areas supporting secondary woodland and cane grassland (Sillitoe 2002, 47). The Wola primarily support themselves through swidden horticulture and pig herding (Sillitoe 2002, 47). Sillitoe claims that during hunting and gathering, the Wola expend four times more energy than they gain (Sillitoe 2002, 46). Obviously such return rates would mean the rapid extinction of any group dependent upon this strategy. Sillitoe (2002, 56) also claims that two groups, the Siane and Maring have similar negative energetic returns from foraging alone. Other New Guinea groups, for which data is available, do not fare so badly and several, including the Etolo (Dwyer 1983, 1985) and Wopkaimin (Hyndman 1979), return positive energy gains from foraging (Sillitoe 2002, 58). Groups from the riverine lowlands, the Gadio Enga, Gidra, and Kubo, fare the best with a high protein and energetic intake from hunting and gathering activities (Sillitoe 2002, 59).

Sillitoe (2002, 69) suggests that human occupation of the Highlands was not sustainable without some form of horticulture or proto-horticulture. While people were probably using various practices to manage resource distributions within the rain forest, Sillitoe has left one important variable out of his equation: mobility. The Wola, like other New Guinea groups occupying the Highlands are sedentary farmers who live in permanent base camps. The typical foraging range of the Wola is between 2 and 3 kilometers and rarely more than 4 kilometers—well within a day's foraging radius from the settlement. What Sillitoe's data does support is the contention that New Guinea rain forest could not have supported large hunter-gatherer populations practicing low residential mobility. Due to the nature of resource distribution and density in the rain forest, a foraging group will rapidly exhaust even the most productive patches.

In order to understand prehistoric occupation of the Highlands, alternative scenarios of landscape occupation need to be developed that are not so reliant on specific and possibly inappropriate ethnographic analogies. Foraging theory is of great potential given that it enables human behavior to be modelled in very general terms. Several elements of foraging theory enable its general principles to be applied to concrete prehistoric contexts including: resource availability within the landscape, nutritional sources and diet breadth, and mobility. These elements can be reviewed in terms of the prehistory of Highland New Guinea, and the Upper Wahgi Valley in particular, to develop a framework for understanding hunter-gatherer subsistence and the origins of agriculture.

RESOURCE AVAILABILITY

Pre-existing models of hunter-gatherer subsistence and agricultural origins overlook three important contributors to resource availability in tropical rain forests in the Highlands. These are gap dynamics, the importance of ecotones, and anthropogenic manipulation of the environment.

GAP DYNAMICS AND RESOURCE OPPORTUNITIES

Climax rain forest is not homogeneous, but in a constant state of growth, breakdown, and regeneration. Processes of regeneration are spatially and temporally discontinuous and produce patchworks or mosaics of gaps, building phases, and stands of mature forest (Richards 1996, 51). Gaps are quickly colonized by herbs, climbers, and secondary growth species, thereby increasing the diversity of potential resources within the rain forest. Patches of secondary or disturbed habitat within the rain forest occur in predictable and unpredictable spatial locations. Gaps in the primary rain forest created by tree-throw, wind damage, landslides, or lightning strikes occur at irregular intervals and are largely at random, whereas ecotones and edge habitats are more predictable in location, being associated with riparian corridors, swamps, and particular vegetation communities (see below).

Gap size influences species composition. Small gaps favor shade-tolerant species, whereas light-tolerant plants prosper in larger gaps (Richards 1996, 215). Species diversity within gaps will rise initially and then gradually decrease as secondary forest becomes established.

Over time, the distribution of resources and relative productivity of patches changes in response to gap dynamics within the forest. Many wild plants such as tubers, palms, and fruit trees will benefit from an open or otherwise disturbed forest canopy (Groube 1989, 299; Piperno and Pearsall 1998, 75). Within the semi-evergreen forest on Barro Colorado Island in Panama, Piperno observed (Piperno and Pearsall 1998, 75) that even relatively casual human disturbance, such as the creation of trails, could lead to increased densities of favorable plant species. However, Piperno and Pearsall (1998, 75) caution that the significance of "natural gaps" is often overstated, with most being too small to induce changes in vegetation that would attract human foragers.

The spatial distribution of higher yielding "patches," coupled with the relatively poor distribution of edible forest resources in mature stands, may have strongly influenced forager behavior and residential mobility. In the same way that foragers must weigh up the choices about what to forage, they must also determine where best to expend their foraging efforts within the landscape. In an environment that is otherwise depauperate of edible resources, rich foraging patches, such as a stand of sago or area of disturbed forest, may represent return rates many times above the average of undisturbed primary rain forest. Such patches will become attractive targets for foragers and are likely to have strongly influenced the movement of foraging groups. Once within a foraging "patch," foragers are then faced with a second problem, when should they leave? Marginal Value Theorem (Charnov 1976) suggests that foragers will do best in terms of energy gain if they abandon the patch at the point that returns fall to that of surrounding or nearby patches. If the travel time between patches is also high, then foragers may only exploit the highest-ranked resources before moving on (Orians and Pearson 1979), thereby maintaining a high level of residential moves and a narrow diet breadth.

In the *Nothofagus*-dominated Pleistocene forests of Highland New Guinea, the limited gap dynamics within monostands was considered to contribute to low resource availability (after Golson 1991b). However, pollen diagrams suggest the floor of the Wahgi Valley had a mixed as opposed to homogeneous forest composition during the late Pleistocene. Resource availability at least on the valley floor and basal slopes was greater than previously characterized by Golson (after Haberle 1993, 299–306). Many useful and edible plants were present within the Wahgi Valley throughout the late Pleistocene, with their local availability dependent upon the magnitude and frequency of gap dynamics. Larger gaps in the rain forest, those likely to last for decades (Richards 1996, 53), were probably "mapped" and repeatedly targeted by foraging groups.

Small foraging groups at low density in this environment may have exercised high residential mobility in order to increase their chances of encountering useful resources in a relatively depauperate, unpredictable environment (after Piperno and Pearsall 1998, 61). The low density of plants and game also encouraged camp movement as edible resources within walking distance were rapidly depleted around the perimeter of settlements (see above). Although hunter-gatherer mobility was probably high for the earliest foraging groups occupying the interior forests of New Guinea, the level and intensity of residential mobility may have initially increased as humans began to modify their environment, thereby increasing patch numbers and relative levels of productivity. Only as the relative productivity of "patches" falls would foragers spend more time in each patch and broaden their diet breadth in order to recover sufficient food after a long journey. Consequently, early patterns of landscape use within the Highlands of New Guinea during the Pleistocene, or perhaps any tropical forest, may have no modern analogs.

FOREST-WETLAND ECOTONE:
A FOCUS OF ACTIVITY

Against this backdrop of high residential mobility in the rain forest, ecotones within the inter-montane valleys, e.g., wetlands and riparian corridors, were spatially restricted but productive locations that became foci of more continuous activity (cf. Kelly 1995, 121). A significant ecotone for food production within the Upper Wahgi Valley and other inter-montane valleys was the forest-wetland margin. As stated previously, the wetland margin was not stationary but fluctuated. The inherent instability and fluctuations of the wetland margins resulted in constant disturbance, maintained succession at an intermediate stage, and increased the diversity of species with greater productive potential for humans. Additionally, a unique range of water-tolerant species was present and available for exploitation, e.g., *Colocasia* taro. The wetlands were favored locations for extended occupation and targeted as rich foraging patches during logistical forays and residential moves. In addition to resource gathering, these ecotones became areas of experimentation for the cultivation of indigenous plants (after Golson 1977a, 614; 1991a, 484–5; Yen 1990, 262–3). The disturbance and manipulation of the environment on the wetland margin were similar to the activities occurring in the mixed forests on adjacent slopes, although they were probably initiated to encourage a different suite of plants.

The features associated with Phase 1 (c. 10,200 Cal B.P.) paleosurface at Kuk were attempts to manipulate the wetland margin to enhance productivity. The pits, runnels, and stake and post holes may represent "patch" features associated with digging, planting, and staking of plants. Geomorphology and paleoecology suggest similar practices were ongoing on adjacent valley slopes. By Phase 2 (6950–6440 Cal B.P.) the extent of wetland manipulation had changed, with semi-regular mounds being built to enable the cultivation of water-intolerant plants with water-tolerant plants on mound edges and within the intervening runnels and pits. Given the extent of anthropogenic modification, these plots were certainly planted. By early Phase 3 (4350–3980 Cal B.P.), ditch networks drained and demarcated cultivated, multi-cropped plots.

Based on the hypothesis developed here, people deliberately mimicked patches, ecotones, and plant distributions through clearance and burning, probably from initial settlement (after Groube 1989), and the deliberate movement of plants capable of asexual reproduction since the late Pleistocene. "Patches" of secondary forest, edge and disturbed environments, including the wetland margins, were crucial to the late Pleistocene human occupation of the Highlands. Modern humans were almost certainly aware of the importance of gap, edge, and secondary forest habitats and ecotones, and the variation in resources with altitude. Many of the important carbohydrate-rich plant foods that humans required existed within forest patches at different altitudes, for example, *Pandanus* nuts (mid-high), *Musa* bananas (low-mid), *Metroxylon* sago (low), and within wetland environments, e.g., *Colocasia* taro (low-mid).

Powell (1982b) has noted that many of the indigenous cultivated plants in the Highlands of New Guinea are not diagnostic markers of agriculture because most are also found in disturbed, edge and wetland habitats. Most cultivated plants were adapted to secondary and transitional habitats, such as the gaps and wetland margins exploited in the Upper Wahgi Valley. Through burning people were able to expand the total area of secondary forest and control the temporal phases of plant succession on dryland slopes and along the wetland margin. Contrary to previous interpretations, the earliest clearances in the Highlands encouraged the growth of a whole range of different species in different habitats, and not only *Pandanus* spp. People utilized a wide range of patches in different habitats and altitudes in order to access the broadest range of possible resources. For example, resources with altitudinal habitat ranges between elevations of 500 and 3700 m were accessible within a few days walk from Kuk.

At present, it is unknown whether many crop plants dispersed to the Highlands as wild or domesticated forms, and, if the former, whether people were directly responsible. It is uncertain, if people were responsible for dispersal, whether such dispersals were the product of deliberate or inadvertent activity. Wild yams (*Dioscorea* spp.) and *Colocasia* taro are present in the Upper Wahgi Valley (Powell et al. 1975, 21, 24–5). These species are not as productive as cultivated species or varieties and are rarely used today for food.

Based on documented translocations in Island Melanesia during the Pleistocene and the Highlands in the early Holocene, anthropogenic plant movement and replanting via asexual methods of propagation probably occurred in the Highlands during the Pleistocene. For species with tubers and rhizomes, this practice was relatively straightforward and possibly unintentional as well as deliberate. Many tubers can be stored for extended periods and were potentially transported as a food source. New growth is possible from either discarded tops or bases of the tuber in some species (Dounais 1996, 629; Wilson et al. 1998). Unwittingly, highly mobile foragers moving frequently from one rapidly depleted patch to another could have rapidly spread a wide range of plants throughout their foraging range as they carried, partially ate, and discarded unwanted but reproductively active plant portions (cf. Hather 1996). Plants discarded in areas of disturbed secondary forest, perhaps already cleared by burning, would be more likely to survive into new adult plants, adding to the diversity and density of preferred foraging patches.

Once in the Highlands, people exerted selective pressure on plants and began to deliberately replant them between patches. People may have known about the asexual reproduction of yams, aroids (taros), and some trees from roots, rhizomes, and suckers (Hather 1996). The intention was probably to move favored species and varieties between plots, but the net long-term effect was to move plants between regions. Over time, such a strategy would have increased patch productivity and reliability of return rates, but encouraged a greater reliance on fewer species and reduced diet breadth.

PRELIMINARY RETURN RATES AND RESOURCE RANKING

Little data is available to determine handling costs of many important food resources in New Guinea and the tropics generally. Table 11.5 has been compiled from several sources with differences in the methods of time and energy calculation. In several cases the data were not suitable for the required energy calculations and they are listed for comparative purposes only. These figures should be viewed as preliminary and coarse estimates.

Although energy intensive in its preparation, *Metroxylon* sago has the potential to provide an enormous energy return (Ulijaszek and Paraituk 1993). The figures provided for this lowland plant here are generated by sedentary horticulturalists, do not factor in any travel times to the resource "patch," and hence, probably over-estimate return rates for prehistoric foragers. Sago, as it is prepared today also requires that the palm be felled, split, and the interior pith chopped out and sieved, to produce the pure starch flour. While the technology required is not complex, the advent of hafted tools would have greatly increased return rates.

In terms of food resources in the Highlands, *Pandanus* nuts provide high return rates, although Sillitoe (2002, 61) notes that cultivated rather than wild varieties were collected in his study. Whether this factor would significantly affect the outcome of returns if only wild plants were used is uncertain, but cultivated varieties presumably provide higher returns than wild precursors or other species. The potential return rates vary but are generally quite high, which supports previous interpretations of *Pandanus* spp. nut collection as the basis for temporary, pre-agricultural subsistence in the interior of New Guinea (Bulmer 1977; Golson 1991b; Groube 1989; White et al. 1970). The returns of wild and feral yams overlap with that of *Pandanus* nuts, and wild yams may be consumed throughout the year and are not subject to wide seasonal fluctuations. Among the Semaq Beri of the Malay Peninsular observed by Kuchikura, variation in the intensity of yam gathering primarily depended upon the availability of ported stores of rice and flour (Kuchikura 1993, 89). As stores diminished the search for yams increased. Some species such as *Dioscorea pentaphylla* were often the targets of long treks and the tubers of *Dioscorea alata* were taken whenever encountered, regardless of food supplies at the time. Tubers of *D. alata* may weigh up to 60 kg though weights of between 5 to 10 kg are more common (Burkill 1935, 815).

There are no calculated figures available to make estimations of the return-rates of *Musa* spp. and aroid rhizomes of *Colocasia esculenta*, *Alocasia* spp., and *Cyrtosperma merkusii*. Almost all aroids contain bitter tasting oxalic acid and calcium oxalate crystals or raphides (Brown 2000, 276), which require some processing to remove and make the plant palatable. Preparation of bitter tasting yams and aroids is very similar and achieved through soaking, washing, or cooking. The extent to which different preparations of these starchy rhizomes would lower their returns within a foraging context is not known. If so, aroids would not be far behind many species of yam in terms of energy returns and may fare better in some cases as they prefer the moist, sheltered environments (Brown 2000, 43) that are characteristic of primary rain forest and may have been more widely and densely distributed than yams.

DIET BREADTH: AN INCREASING RELIANCE ON STARCH STAPLES

The point at which inadvertent activity became deliberate action is probably not visible in the Highland archaeological record. Sources of aroid and *Musa* starch were high-ranked resources because they enabled a high caloric return with little seasonal, annual or inter-annual variability in availability. Although other potential high caloric/nutrient sources existed, such as *Castanopsis* nuts and *Pandanus* kernels, the relatively high collecting and processing costs

TABLE 11.5

Preliminary Estimates of Energy Yields, Return Rates, and Resource Ranking for Some New Guinea Food Plants

PLANT NAME	PART EATEN	AREA	ENERGY kJ/100 g	RETURN-RATES cal/hr/person	RANK	SOURCE
Agaricus sp.	Fungi	Widespread?	97	18	5	Sillitoe (2002)
Amaranthus spp.	Leaves, young plant	Widespread, highlands	25–210			Powell (1976)
Colocasia esculenta	Tuber, leaves	Widespread	475			Powell (1976)
Colocasia esculenta	Leaves, petiole	Widespread	80–240			Powell (1976)
Cyrtosperma chamissonis	Rhizome	Jimi, New Britain	550			Powell (1976)
Canarium spp.	Nut	Lowlands	2700			Coronel (1992)
Dioscorea alata	Tuber	Widespread		598	3	Kuchikura (1993)
Dioscorea hispida	Tuber, leaves	New Britain		855–3770	3	Endicott and Bellwood (1991), Kuchikura (1993)
Dioscorea pentaphylla	Tuber	Widespread		1070	3	Kuchikura (1993)
Dioscorea spp.	Tuber	Widespread	676 (2)	1299	3	Kuchikura (1993)
Hibiscus manihot	Leaves, shoot	Widespread	130–197			Powell (1976)
Musa spp.	Fruit	Widespread	540			Powell (1976)
Oenanthe javanica	Leaves	Highlands	118	10	6	Sillitoe (2002)
Metroxylon sagu	Pith (sago)	Lowlands	1520	6979	1	Ulijaszek and Paraituk (1993)
Pandanus spp.	Nut	Widespread, highlands	2800	616–1468	2	Sillitoe (2002)
Saccharum officinarum	Cane sugar	Widespread	243			Powell (1976)
Alsophila spp.	Fern fronds	Widepread	180	134	4	Sillitoe (2002)

Note: Resource ranking based on ratio of energy produced to energy expenditure. In Sillitoe (2002), energy return rates calculated from figures provide foraging trip times and energy returns in weight and kJ; energy expenditure calculated at 780 kJ/hour per person, a figure that estimates slow walking over level terrain. In Kuchikura (1993), figures based on return rates calculated in kg/hour and where c. 1.52 kg of tuber yields an average of 1300 Cal food energy. The effort required to detoxify tubers of D. hispida are factored into the return rates in this table. On average 1 kg of D. hispida tubers required 11.4 minutes of work to remove toxins; in Ulijaszek and Paraituk (1993), data from original calculation in MJ.

and seasonality of these arboreal resources resulted in a lower overall ranking. Although these lower-ranked arboreal resources were still widely used, other starch sources became the focus of subsistence activities.

Some starch plants important to prehistoric inhabitants of New Guinea are now regarded as minor contributors to diet, e.g., some Araceae—except *Colocasia* taro—and *Zingiber* gingers, and do not feature prominently in current agricultural systems. As foraging theory clearly demonstrates, the presence and absence of food items in a diet is a function of their energetic ranking based on caloric or nutritional content and handling/processing times relative to alternatives, and not on relative abundance in the environment. Many species of importance to pre-agricultural communities, such as seeds in the Australian desert, were dropped from the diet as higher-ranking alternatives became available, such as processed flour (O'Connell and Hawkes 1984).

In Highland New Guinea, the plant resources that ultimately formed the corpus of "cultivated" varieties were high-ranked resources (e.g., Kuchikura 1993; O'Connell and Hawkes 1984). Resource availability increased due to higher densities of patches in different secondary growth stages and of starch resources within patches through inadvertent and deliberate planting. An important implication is that relatively sophisticated strategies of plant management by highly mobile hunter-gatherers, including burning and the translocation of plants and animals, emerged in the tropics. For much of prehistory, people did not invest heavily in cultivated plots within a limited geographical area, rather the spatial and relative aseasonal ubiquity of resources and their ease of exploitation facilitated high mobility, as seen among sago exploiters in the lowlands of New Guinea today (Roscoe 2002).

A MOBILITY AND STARCH-BASED UNDERSTANDING OF HUNTER-GATHERER SUBSISTENCE AND AGRICULTURAL EMERGENCE

The emergence of seed-based agriculture in seasonal climates required a very different set of initial conditions and hypotheses to developments in tropical rain forests (e.g. Barlow 2002). Seed-based agriculture utilizes lower-ranked resources, provides lower return rates, and requires greater investments of time in terms of cultivation, processing, and storage. These requirements limit mobility, encourage sedentism, and foster the development of attendant social structures to organize production and distribution. Given the limited contribution of seeds to New Guinean diet, the emergence of agriculture in New Guinea may have followed a different trajectory from cereal-based agriculture in Southwest Asia and Mesoamerica.

The archaeological expression of the tropical systems of cultivation would not be expected to resemble those of seed-based agricultural systems (after Harris 1996b; Piperno and Pearsall 1998). Most food crops in Highland New Guinea require minimal processing and are not stored for any appreciable time prior to consumption. Indeed, the return rates for most major starch sources in New Guinea are high, even when accompanied by intensive processing, e.g., *Metroxylon* sago (Roscoe 2002). The ubiquity, both spatially and temporally, of resources and their ease of exploitation may account for the limited development of social hierarchies among contemporary agricultural populations in New Guinea, with only weak political leadership being manifest in the persuasive guile of the big man.

A general model of broad-spectrum foraging behavior in the Highlands emerges for the Late Pleistocene that includes the deliberate creation of patches and the associated movement and planting of starch staples by foragers. The initial phases of hunter-gatherer occupation favored high residential mobility to access widely dispersed resources, such as *Pandanus* spp. Low intensity vegetation clearance through burning signified attempts to manipulate resource availability in patches and was potentially associated with the deliberate translocation of plants, as documented for Island Melanesia. These processes may have initially increased residential mobility. After 20,000 Cal B.P., the scale of anthropogenic impacts on the landscape intensified, although this may represent continuity of practices in an environment more vulnerable to disturbance. During the Pleistocene, wetlands served as foci of activity given their transitional environments and diversity of resources compared to adjacent slopes. The intensified disturbance of forests on the slopes and floors of the inter-montane valleys from the early Holocene, and the greater reliance on cleared patches, translocated plants, and decreased mobility are not explainable solely in terms of broad-spectrum foraging.

Within an increasingly domesticated landscape in the Upper Wahgi Valley during the late Pleistocene (after Yen 1989), more intensive, swidden-like practices may have originated from pre-existing mobile, forager practices. An increased reliance on productive starch resources and decreasing diet breadth in the late Pleistocene was expressed spatially by more restricted use of plots located within and potentially between different valley systems by the early Holocene. These plots, probably scattered to maximize resource availability in different environmental zones and different altitudes, were sufficient to guarantee subsistence.

At first, we suspect these plots were widely scattered. For instance, groups within the Upper Wahgi Valley used upland forests, valley slopes, and wetland margins, as well as low altitude resources. For inhabitants of Kuk, a whole range of fruit and nut bearing taxa not present at higher altitude, and potentially including *Metroxylon* sago, were present in the Lower Jimi Valley approximately 50 km away (Gillieson et al. 1985). Organized expeditions to the Lower and Middle Jimi Valley by groups in the Upper Wahgi Valley occurred historically to gather bush resources, to hunt game, and to obtain salt, stone axes, and other exchange valuables (Hughes 1977).

Through time, we argue that various factors constricted group mobility including an increased reliance on particular sources of starch, increased inter-group conflict with or without increasing populations, or the prevalence of malaria at lower altitudes. With limited mobility,

groups became increasingly reliant on intensively managed or maintained patches within a more restricted geographical area. A form of swidden cultivation emerged with plots dispersed within a relatively stable territory, potentially within one valley, to maximize access to available resources on slopes and wetland margins.

Phase 1 at Kuk may be evidence of an early form of plant management by highly mobile communities and not necessarily by sedentary groups. These archaeological remains represent a "patch" on the wetland margin used for cultivating specific plants, such as the wet cultivation of *Colocasia* taro. This patch was probably integrated into a spatially extensive scatter of patches that promoted *Pandanus julianettii* and *Pandanus antaresensis* at higher altitudes; *Musa* bananas, *Colocasia* taro, and minor yams (*Dioscorea* spp.) on adjacent valley slopes; and, a whole host of lowland fruit, nut, and starch bearing trees at lower altitudes.

Lower levels of residential mobility in New Guinea may only have occurred much later as the environment became increasingly degraded, and more intensive modes of subsistence were adopted. By approximately 6800 Cal B.P., the Kuk vicinity had degraded to grassland, with similar anthropogenic transformations being documented elsewhere in the Upper Wahgi Valley. The difficulties encountered in cultivating grasslands promoted the altitudinal expansion of cultivation to higher valley slopes (see Christensen 1975) and an increased reliance on wetland margins. More intensive forms of cultivation, such as mounding (Phase 2) and ditching (Phase 3 onwards), were responses on the wetland margin to an increasing reliance on a smaller resource base within grasslands. The increased labor investment in the construction and maintenance of mounds and ditches would have severely limited group mobility.

Throughout each period the emphasis was on developing patches, through burning and planting, that maximized resource availability in different environments. Initially, highly mobile hunter-gatherer groups undertook broad-spectrum foraging. Decreasing mobility through time corresponded to an increasing reliance on starch sources, a decreasing diet breadth and an increasing reliance on more spatially restricted and fixed distributions of patches within rain forests. Group mobility and access to geographically dispersed resources were further limited by increasing populations and other social pressures within an increasingly degraded environment. Subsistence behavior through time can be characterized as gradually changing through time. However, the outcomes in forms of subsistence practice were diverse and included hunting and gathering, swidden horticulture, and intensive wetland agriculture.

VEGECULTURE, BEHAVIOR AND AGRICULTURAL ORIGINS

A key feature of the subsistence model presented here is the biology of plant staples that are or were cultivars in recent agricultural systems. Many cultivated staples, particularly the yams, taros, bananas, and some nut trees can be asexually reproduced. In the case of the yams, new plants may be propagated in another location simply by replanting the crown or distal end of the tuber. Araceae and Zingiberaceae can also be propagated clonally via rhizomes and tubers or by planting above-ground tissue containing dormant sympodial buds (Hather 1996). Propagation of *Metroxylon* sago, *Musa* banana and some species of nut trees (e.g. *Pandanus* spp.) is also possible via asexual methods by planting suckers (Schuiling and Jong 1996; Stone 1992; Valmayor and Wagih 1996).

Though asexual propagation does not allow for genetic variation in new plants, changes to the physical environment can cause favorable and lasting changes to clonal phenotypes (Abraham 1997, 275; Chikwendu and Okezie 1989, 354–5; Dumont and Vernier 2000, 141). For example, experimental programs significantly altered the physical form of wild yam tubers within a score of years without any sexual re-

production in the plants. Changes in growth environment including exposure to sunshine, tending and weeding, and tillage and mound heaping were deduced to be major factors inducing favorable changes in tuber morphology (Chikwendu and Okezie 1989). These controlled variables could be mimicked by the simple strategies of vegetation clearance to promote secondary forest regrowth and clearance around individual plants to reduce competitive growth.

The particular biology of plants capable of clonal reproduction and the incredible fecundity of the tropics enabled the evolution of plant management systems in which "domestication" need not be seen as fundamental to the emergence of agriculture. In fact, as Hather (1996, 548) has pointed out, domestication—defined as a genetic change—may occur at any point along a plant management continuum as long as the plant continues to be under selective pressure. For tropical plant management systems, domestication may be incidental and not a key variable of the process.

Human foragers were aware of the growth habits and life histories of many key economic plant species since the late Pleistocene. Prehistoric foragers encouraged their growth through forest clearance (cf. Groube 1989; Bayliss-Smith 1996) and manipulated their distribution and density through the physical movement of plants or plant parts. Within this strategy of plant management, the inter-montane swamps, such as those occurring at Kuk, attracted a higher rate of visitation and perhaps a higher intensity of foraging than other patches of secondary forest. Whether by accident or intent, such locations gradually became populated with increasing numbers of starchy staples suitable for transport and vegetative reproduction from unspecialized portions of the plant. In this way, and due to the greater fertility of soils as much as by visitation, managed stands of starchy staples were potentially present at Kuk for thousands of years. We argue that the earliest agricultural evidence for human activity at Kuk (Phases 1 and 2) reflects the archaeological visibility of ongoing plant management practices, rather than the sudden emergence or a "revolution" in plant manipulation.

CONCLUSION

The origins of tropical agriculture have been previously portrayed as arising from a continuum of people-plant interactions (see Hather 1996; Harris 1989). In this paper, a model of Pleistocene foraging in the Highlands of New Guinea has been developed using several key concepts from foraging theory. These concepts include diet breadth and the Marginal Value Theorem. We applied these concepts to Highland's prehistory in order to show how: highly mobile foragers could have permanently subsisted in the rain forests of the interior of New Guinea, and agricultural practices represent continuity from preexisting foraging behavior.

Foragers employed two strategies, patch creation and plant translocation, to increase resource availability and permanently subsist in the interior rain forests. Following Groube (1989), we argue that these strategies were practiced from initial colonization of the island and that Pleistocene subsistence in tropical rain forests was predicated on anthropogenic transformation of the environment. Through time, the archeological and paleoecological visibility of subsistence practices increased. As people became increasingly reliant on starchy plants and lived within an increasingly degraded landscape, patch use became more intensive and spatially restricted and was accompanied by reduced mobility. The archeological remains of these subsistence practices are visible as Phases 1, 2, and 3 at Kuk.

The model proposed here requires further interrogation through new investigations of past and present subsistence practices in the Highlands of New Guinea. The archeobotanical, archeological, geomorphological, and paleoecological records for the Highlands are complementary but incomplete. A comprehensive register of the plants formerly grown and used requires compilation, although this lacuna is being addressed through the application of microfossil techniques, i.e., phytolith and starch grain analyses. Similarly, more information is needed on the distribution, nutritional value, and varieties of wild types of starch sources in the Highlands. Current information on these sources is anecdotal, with the majority of energetic information being obtained for the growing, harvesting, processing, and consumption of contemporary cultivars. Without new research, our understanding of prehistoric subsistence in the Highland interior of New Guinea will remain largely hypothetical.[1]

NOTE

1. This paper was written in 2002 and 2003. Tim Denham thanks Professor Jack Golson for permission to access and use materials in the Kuk site archive pertaining to investigations in the 1970s and 1980s. He is grateful to Dr. Simon Haberle, Dr. Carol Lentfer, and Dr. Richard Fullagar for permission to cite unpublished information arising from renewed investigations at Kuk in 1998 and 1999 and to Dr. Mike Bourke for permission to cite unpublished work on the altitudinal tolerances of crop plants in the Highlands. Hugh Barton thanks the AHRC (APN 10872) who finded his research and the writing of this paper. Both authors thank Graeme Barker, Robin Torrence, J. Peter White, and the volume editors for their comments on earlier drafts of this paper.

12

The Ideal Free Distribution, Food Production, and the Colonization of Oceania

Douglas Kennett, Atholl Anderson, and Bruce Winterhalder

Islands in Oceania were some of the last habitable land masses on earth to be colonized by humans. Current archaeological evidence suggests that these islands were colonized episodically rather than continuously, and that bursts of migration were followed by longer periods of sedentism and population growth. The decision to colonize isolated, unoccupied islands and archipelagos was complex and dependent on a variety of social, technological and environmental variables. In this chapter we develop an integrative, multivariate approach to island colonization in Oceania based on a model from behavioral ecology known as the Ideal Free Distribution. This ecological model provides a framework that considers the dynamic character of island suitability along with density-dependent and density-independent variables influencing migratory behavior. Unique among existing models, it can account for the episodic nature of certain aspects of the colonization process. Within this context we critically evaluate the role of foraging, low-level food production, and ultimately intensive food production, as important contextual variables that influenced decisions to disperse. We argue that intensive food production was one variable that contributed to decreasing suitability of island

habitats, stimulating dispersal, and ultimately migrations to more distant islands in Oceania.

The processes involved in the development of food production worldwide during the last 10,000 years were complex and spatially variable. At a minimum, they involved some combination of the following set of factors: (1) the expansion of diet-breadth during the late Pleistocene and early Holocene, leading to the development of co-evolutionary relationships between humans and potential domesticates (Richards et al. 2001; Rindos 1984; Stiner et al. 1999, 2000; Winterhalder and Goland 1997); (2) intensified exploitation of wild plants and animals by some prehistoric foragers (Henry 1989); (3) translocation of wild plants and animals by foraging groups and the management or cultivation of these wild species in some instances (Piperno and Pearsall 1998); (4) the initial domestication of plants and animals in several independent centers (Cowan and Watson 1992; Price and Gebauer 1995a; Smith 1998); (5) the adoption of these plants and animals by foragers living in adjacent regions, often in different habitats; (6) subsequent experimentation

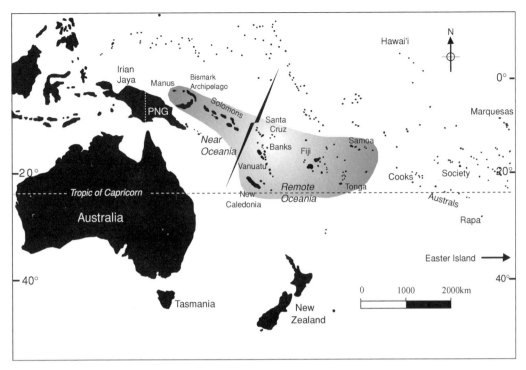

FIGURE 12.1. Map of Oceania showing the relevant islands and archipelagos.

leading to a reliance on food production or the stability of mixed subsistence strategies (low-level food production; Smith 2001a; Tucker, this volume); (7) continued transmission of new and improved domesticates through exchange networks (Hastorf 1999), and (8) the ultimate emergence of more intensive food production in certain locations (Smith 1998). Some of the consequences of food production included localized population growth, the spread of domesticated plants and animals along with agrarian knowledge and technology through exchange networks, the actual migration of food producers into regions occupied by foraging populations (Cavalli-Sforza 1996; Diamond and Bellwood 2003), and a general increase in human impacts on natural ecosystems (Bellwood 2001; Diamond and Bellwood 2003; Redman 1999). The demographic expansion of farming populations is linked to significant cultural, linguistic, and biological changes (Bellwood 2001). It has also been argued that the emergence of food production fostered the expansion of anatomically modern humans into previously unoccupied territory, most notably the colonization of ever smaller and more remote islands in the Pacific, Mediterranean, and Caribbean (Diamond and Bellwood 2003; Keegan and Diamond 1987; Kirch 2000; Kirch and Green 2001; Patton 1996; but see Anderson 2003a).

In this chapter we explore the dispersal of people into Oceania and the role that food production may have played in this complex social and ecological process. In particular, we are interested in the migration of people onto islands in Near and Remote Oceania (Figure 12.1).[1] Near Oceania consists of several large islands in the Bismarck Archipelago, positioned 100–200 km to the northwest coast of New Guinea, and the Solomon Islands, a series of smaller islands that stretch to the southeast. Prior to sea-level rise during the late Pleistocene and early Holocene, the Solomons formed a single larger island known as Greater Bougainville. Vanuatu and New Caledonia form the western boundary of Remote Oceania, which also includes 38 major archipelagos of 344 colonized islands in West and East Polynesia (Kirch 1984). West Polynesia encompasses the larger, aggregated archipelagos of Tonga and Samoa, plus some smaller archipelagos. In its early prehistory, Fiji is also regarded as West Polynesian. Except for New Zealand, islands in East Polynesia tend to be smaller and more dispersed.

All of the islands in Near Oceania lie within the tropics, but several islands in Remote Oceania are subtropical or are positioned farther to the south, and have temperate climates; for instance New Zealand lies between 35 to 45° south. Little seasonality in rainfall or temperature occurs close to the equator, but cooler temperatures and distinctive wet and dry seasons become more common to the south (Spriggs 1997; Anderson 2001a). The initial colonization of Remote Oceania involved a sixfold increase in minimum voyaging distances over those attained in Near Oceania (200 km) and distances of up to 3700 km were crossed to reach New Zealand and Hawaii.

The study of island colonization has a long history with a large body of literature developed during the last 30 years (Fitzpatrick 2004; Keegan and Diamond 1987). Much of this research was stimulated by MacArthur and Wilson's 1967 book entitled *The Theory of Island Biogeography*, and by the recognition that islands provide a well-bounded context for studying cultural evolutionary processes. In the late 1980s, Keegan and Diamond (1987) synthesized the literature on island colonization in various parts of the world and concluded that biogeographical principles, particularly their physical and geometrical properties, provided a useful framework for understanding the colonization process. They argued that climatic, geological, and oceanographic differences among islands shaped their terrestrial and marine productivity and influenced the ability of humans to colonize them. Superimposed on these ecological qualities are geometric properties influencing the likelihood that seafaring migrants will reach particular islands—factors like position, size, and the distance between pairs along likely routes of colonization. In this view, the likelihood that an island will be colonized decreases with distance, as does the possibility of follow-up assistance once an island is occupied. However, colonization of distant islands may be promoted by configurational effects. For instance, archipelagos consisting of larger aggregations of islands potentially provide greater resource diversity for colonists compared with individual islands. Island size also influences the probability of successful colonization because larger islands offer a greater quantity and diversity of habitats and resources.

Although physical and geometric properties are important for understanding island colonization, purely biogeographical models have shortcomings. Based on the geometry of position, distance, and size, they highlight the probabilistic elements of "blindly" reaching a particular island and surviving there. They do not help to analyze the reasons for initiating migration, nor the intentional or unintentional consequences of settlement for an island's resource potential, and thus for the long-term persistence of settlement. Although likely to be important, such factors are extraneous to biogeographic models.

In Oceania, explanations for island colonization can be grouped into push or pull models. Most push models invoke demographic pressure as the primary causal force initiating dispersal (Clark and Terrell 1978; Anderson 1996). It has been argued that population levels on islands generally increase with agricultural intensification, and eventually the population exceeds carrying capacity, stimulating segments of the population to move to adjacent islands. Pull models often propose a rapid dispersal of people through Oceanic island chains, as opportunistic foragers skim off the highest-quality resources (Clark and Terrell 1978; Anderson 1996; Davidson and Leach 2001) and quickly move on to the next propitious location. Although an improvement, the combination of biogeographic patterning and push-pull variables

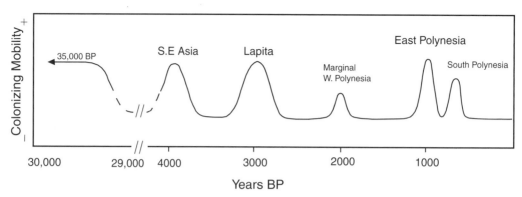

FIGURE 12.2. Colonization mobility in Oceania during the last 35,000 years (see Anderson 2001a).

does not capture the episodic nature of migratory behavior evident amongst humans and other animals (Diamond 1977), and evident in the archaeological data from Oceania (Anderson 2001b; Figure 12.2). Island colonization in Oceania also appears to be a dual phase process. Each episode seems to have a sedentary phase, perhaps representing a period of population growth, and a phase of high mobility and rapid dispersal. The speed of colonization during these unstable episodes does not suggest incremental demographic pressure, but is more reminiscent of rapid dispersal, triggered by opportunistic foraging behavior. It appears that a variety of contextual variables are at work; colonization of Oceania cannot be explained by invoking single variables.

In this chapter we develop an integrative, multivariate model for the colonization of Oceania within the behavioral ecology framework of the ideal free distribution (Abrahams and Healey 1990; Fretwell and Lucas 1970; Sutherland 1996). This set of ideas provides a simple framework that considers the dynamic character of habitat suitability along with density-dependent and density-independent variables that might influence dispersion and habitat selection by colonists in Oceania. In particular, we examine how food production might have influenced decisions to disperse and colonize remote islands. We argue that low-level food production (Smith 2001a), and later intensive food production, contributed to more rapid decreases in habitat suitability through degradation, but also

increased the overall carrying capacity of many remote island habitats. This particular point is set within a more general argument: low level and ultimately more intensive food production was one of several variables including population growth, dynamic impacts of exploitation on fragile island environments, technological development, and the inherent ecological suitability of various island groups in Oceania. The ability of human behavioral ecology (HBE) to integrate multiple contextual variables with an emphasis on behavioral responses to changing ecological conditions make it an ideal framework to explore the causes and consequences of human dispersal onto remote islands in Oceania.

IDEAL FREE DISTRIBUTION AND HUMAN MIGRATIONS

Two consequences of food production were localized population increase and the dispersion of agricultural populations into areas occupied by hunter-gatherers or regions not previously populated (Bellwood 2001; Diamond and Bellwood 2003). The migration of animals or people into new habitats often entails a series of complex behavioral responses to changing social and environmental conditions. Both density-dependent and density-independent influences may stimulate migration. Ultimately, an individual's or group's decision to migrate depends on the cost and likely success of relocating, and on the overall size, quality, and productivity of a homeland region relative to alternatives elsewhere. The overall productivity and suitability of a region can change for a variety of environmental and social reasons. Short- and long-term climatic changes may alter the distribution and availability of subsistence resources, as will changing subsistence practices and technology such as foraging or food production, fluctuations in the density of the human occupants, habitat degradation due to unsustainable exploitation, and changes in social cohesion or conflicts. Dense populations often deplete resources rapidly, but low density use can affect the availability and distribution of other plant and animal species on which a population depends (Sutherland 1996). Resource exploitation also can entail mutualistic and beneficial relationships between humans, animals, and plants, for instance by enhancing the suitability and resource richness of an environment (Rindos 1984).

Another consequence of larger populations is competition that lowers the overall suitability of a resource patch or habitat. Conspecifics deplete shared resources; interference can result from fighting, stealing, or control of resources or patches by individuals (Sutherland 1996). Territorial or despotic behavior by individuals or groups may also affect the suitability of a region and can stimulate the movement of people into adjacent, less desirable areas. Warfare and despotic behavior would be expected in regions that were environmentally or socially circumscribed (Carneiro 1970, 1978, 1988). In this context, the largest populations would aggregate in the most productive locations. Population increases, from endogenous growth or in-migration, and community fission would result in the infilling of more marginal zones. In some instances this would result in environmental "packing" and decreases in habitat suitability (Binford 1968, 1983). In addition, the territories of some groups may extend well beyond their immediate needs, thus forcing disenfranchised individuals to colonize more marginal habitats. Contests for smaller, more circumscribed sections of arable land would predictably become more frequent within this context. Warfare and

other forms of despotic behavior (e.g., cannibalism; Kantner 1999) also create social instability and may stimulate the dispersal of people well below the actual carrying capacity of a habitat (Kennett and Kennett 2000). The net result of these despotic behaviors is reduced habitat suitability leading to more rapid emigration.

THE IDEAL FREE DISTRIBUTION (IFD)

The IFD model provides an explanatory framework for predicting when individuals will disperse or migrate to a new habitat based on density-dependent changes in the suitability of the habitats available to them. Habitats are ranked by their quality, as assessed by the fitness of the initial occupant. Typically, fitness-related measures such as production of young or rate of food intake are used to measure quality or suitability (see Winterhalder and Kennett, Chapter 1, this volume; Figure 12.3). Quality is density dependent and declining with increasing population density due to competition. Competitors may use up resources directly, for instance by occupying living sites or by consuming and depleting food resources, or they may indirectly make resources harder to find or capture; for instance, by stimulating their dispersal or elevated wariness; or render them less desirable by contaminating or fighting over them. The former is known as depletion competition, the latter as interference competition. Sutherland (1996, 9) gives this example: "drinking a pub dry would be depletion whilst a crowd around the bar hindering access would be interference." In the case of the subsistence transition from foraging to food production, depletion would include density-dependent decreases in game animals; interference would encompass increases in erosion and the depletion of soil nutrients associated with more intensive land use.

For IFD purposes, a habitat is defined partly by scale—it is larger than the multiple patches that would be encountered in a single foraging trip and equal to or smaller than the whole range available to a group—and partly by economic characteristics—it is a relatively homogeneous zone of production with respect to the resources

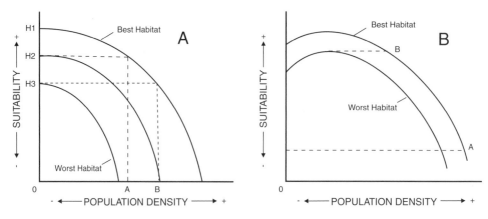

FIGURE 12.3. A) Ideal free distribution (after Fretwell and Lucas 1970, 24; Sutherland 1996, 5); B) Allee's principle (after Fretwell and Lucas 1970, 25; Sutherland 1996, 11).

available and a characteristic method of extracting them. Key to this definition: we expect each habitat to be characterized by a unique curve representing its suitability, as a function of increasing population density and exploitation. For instance, habitats in Oceania would include inland (initially forested), riverine, and coast (e.g. rocky shoreline, beach and reef). This definition recognizes that we may wish to analyze population distribution over contemporaneous, but spatially separate habitats. Or, the IFD can also be used to compare temporal shifts among the habitats that emerge on the same landscape if, for instance, climate change significantly alters its resource characteristics or a technological innovation provides a new means of exploiting the resources found there. The former would allow for the analysis of how a population distributes itself over a set of extant habitats; the latter would analyze choice with respect to "movement" to changing environmental or technological possibilities. Combinations are possible, and settlement of Oceania probably entailed both possibilities. In our very general IFD application we model two habitats defined by environment; small versus large islands, and two defined by shifting between modes of resource extraction; foraging versus food production (see below).

We assume that individuals will elect to reside in the *ideal* or best habitat available to them,

and that they are *free* or unrestricted in their movement to effect that choice. They are competitors of equal ability and access to resources. Under these conditions, habitat distribution will work out in the following manner. Colonizing individuals will locate first in the best habitat available. With increasing density due to immigration or to *in situ* growth suitability there drops. When it is diminished to the quality level of the second ranked habitat, further population growth stimulates immigration and populations will become apportioned between them. Because each individual is ready to relocate if another habitat offers an edge in suitability, the population distribution will equalize marginal qualities across all occupied habitats. This is an equilibrium distribution, a consequence of the marginal equalization of habitat suitability. At the IFD no individual has an incentive to relocate.

The IFD makes two general predictions: (1) the extant population distribution over available habitats will reflect an equilibrium that equalizes their marginal suitabilities; and, (2) the chronological sequence of habitat occupation and use; changing densities in a particular habitat; changes in the variety of habitats occupied will follow the pattern predicted by a particular form of the IFD curves (see Sutherland 1996, 1–14). In each case, empirical tests of quantitative predictions provide stronger results than qualitative assessments. Our application focuses mainly on a corollary of (2): continuous change in overall population size will result, by IFD predictions, in a process of habitat settlement and migration with important *discontinuous* properties. In particular, migration from larger islands should be more episodic than from smaller, and migration from agricultural populations more discontinuous than from foraging populations. Our evidence is meager and mainly qualitative, but the effort is interesting because no other model of comparable generality makes predictions consistent with the episodic character of human occupation of Pacific islands.

THE DESPOTIC VARIANT

The ideal despotic distribution (IDD) is a variant of the IFD highlighting differential access to resources. If interference arises among competitors of unequal abilities, or if by establishing territories, initial or superior competitors can protect themselves from density dependent habitat deterioration by successfully defending better resource opportunities, then the inferior competitors and those without territories are pushed to poorer habitats. Compared to the IFD, a despotic distribution will equilibrate with disproportionate numbers or densities in the lower-ranked habitats. This makes intuitive sense: by garnering disproportionate resources in the best habitats, the better competitors push their inferiors into habitats of lesser suitability. Because of this, the use of lower-ranked resource patches has been documented as a buffering strategy among a variety of bird species (Brown 1969; Meire and Kuyken 1984; Moser 1988). In fact, in empirical studies the ideal free distribution sometimes serves as a null hypothesis to measure the effects of interference competition and unequal resource access (Sutherland 1996).

THE ALLEE EFFECT VARIANT

There also may be density-dependent effects within habitats that make their suitability *increase* over some range of increasing population density. At very low population densities the overall survival rate may be low because of the difficulties associated with finding mates or problems with inbreeding depression (Allee et al. 1949; Sutherland 1996). Increasing density improves the suitability of the habitat for subsequent arrivals. Likewise, the subsistence system may be affected by positive economies of scale, where scale is determined by density. A growing population might increase the density of desirable resources by more completely maintaining forest cover in early stages of succession. It might facilitate technological improvements, from seed distribution to irrigation. The suitability of marginal areas might be improved once colonized, as forests were cleared and fields were prepared through plowing and terracing. Greater density may also offer protection from intruders or enemies.

Figure 12.3b shows the distributional consequences of the Allee effect. As before, initial settlement populates the highest ranked habitat, A. Whether from *in situ* growth or external immigration, increasing density eventually spills over into habitat B. However, because the suitability of habitat B *increases* with each addition, it draws population from habitat A, reducing density there. If the apex of the suitability/density curve for habitat B is higher than that for habitat A, and B is sufficiently spacious, the Allee effect conceivably will empty habitat A for a period, as individuals seeking a more salubrious habitat quickly migrate to this new and improving zone. Habitat B would show a rapid increase in population; the decline in habitat A could be quite dramatic. With an Allee effect, individuals might abandon areas that previously provided adequate payoffs, a pattern consistent with settlement unconformities evident in several parts of the world as agricultural populations replaced or subsumed hunter-gatherer populations (Bellwood 2001; Renfrew and Boyle 2000).

Whatever form it takes, the IFD shows how an incremental quantitative change in one variable such as population density or habitat suitability may lead to qualitative changes in another; the range of habitats occupied; their relative settlement densities. Moving from the IFD to the IDD and Allee variants portends qualitative changes of increasing magnitude. As with most HBE models, there are few limits on what kinds of variables one might accommodate in the IFD and its variants. For instance, climate change might shift the relative suitability (vertical position, thus relative ranking) of the curves. Habitats or subsistence practices highly susceptible to density dependent degradation will have steep downward slopes; those which generally are not so sensitive to population density will have more shallow slopes. Economies of scale in subsistence practice may cause the slope of the curve to be positive over certain ranges of density. The consequences of territoriality, social inequality, and economic exploitation for dispersion and habitat use can be represented in despotic versions of the model. Manipulation of these and other elements can be used to generate hypotheses about population distribution and migration based on a wide range of potentially causal conditions.

The IFD model does not explicitly include the cost of relocation, assuming that this is negligible when compared to the benefits of optimizing long-term habitat choice. This simplification is expedient for analytical purposes, but it may seem an especially unrealistic assumption in the case of initial spread over broad expanses of the Pacific. The issue here, however, is relative rather than absolute costs of relocation which can be thought to constitute a continuum broadly divisible in two. First, most of the islands in Remote Oceania, like those in Near Oceania, lie at distances which could be covered in a week or less of sailing, and it can also be argued (Anderson 2003b) that predictability of finding new islands was quite high within the main island band of the tropical south Pacific. Given the same sailing technology and a choice of favorable sailing conditions, the relative cost of relocation was small. Second however, there were some passages that were unusually long within the main band of Remote Oceanic islands, as between Vanuatu and Fiji,

or Samoa and the Cook Islands, and in addition there were several very long passages to the marginal islands of Hawaii, Easter, and New Zealand. Clearly the costs of relocation in these cases, especially to the margins, must have been higher than was common within the main island band. How much higher depends in part on what view is adopted of maritime technology. If Polynesian vessels and navigation were of a high order of capability (Finney 1979; Irwin 1992; Lewis 1994), then relocation costs to the margins must have been substantially lower than if the technology was relatively undeveloped (Anderson 2000a). On the other hand, the issue is also a perceptual one. Groups considering relocation in circumstances where the preferred choice was to sail off into the unknown had no way of estimating the relative cost of reaching a new island, and it is possible that, within the initial period of dispersal, the perceived relocation cost flattened to virtual invariance everywhere beyond the islands of an already-settled archipelago. Of course, when voyaging occurred after the period of initial dispersal, by which time some sense of Oceanic geography may have developed, then relocation costs could more reliably be factored into choices. An additional issue is the degree to which relocation might have generally coincided, or was not prompted by, periods of wind reversal on a millennial scale; in which case a high frequency of downwind sailing would also have reduced the relative costs of relocation (Anderson, n.d.b). These considerations are, as yet, inadequately researched, but relative insignificance of relocation costs can be assumed in the interim for the sake of exposition here.

As will become evident in the following sections, the islands of Oceania were colonized over a long period of time by people using a wide range of subsistence practices, from foraging to intensive food production. The size and productivity of these islands also varies greatly, from the large, more tightly clustered islands of Near Oceania to the smaller, more dispersed islands of Remote Oceania. As a starting point for

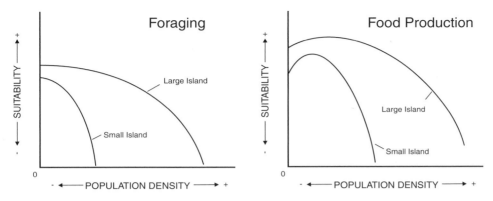

FIGURE 12.4. Hypothetical IFD models for mobile foraging and food production on small and large islands.

generating predictions, we distinguish between IFD curves for foragers and food producers, and those for large and small islands (Figure 12.4). The hunter-gatherer curves are negatively sloped reflecting population-dependent impacts on habitat productivity. On small islands they decline steeply and approach the x-axis at fairly low population sizes; on large islands they decline more gradually and approach the x-axis at significantly larger population sizes. By contrast, the food-producer curves evidence an Allee effect due to economy of scale and peak, before declining. On small islands the peak is fairly narrow and the plunge to the x-axis occurs at low population size; on large islands the peak is high and broad and the approach to the x-axis at quite large population sizes. Consistent with the observation that the earliest forms of food production were probably less efficient than foraging, at its best, we have ranked the initial suitability of food-production "habitats" below those for foraging in the same environment whether large or small island. We do not depict despotic behavior leading to resource defense, but it would put pressure on weaker competitors to emigrate by promoting more rapid plunges towards the x-axis, thus stimulating rapid dispersal.

The proposed set of IFD models allows us to more precisely predict episodes of colonization as a function of population density and mode of production. Specifically, hunter-gatherers are more likely to be mobile, and the pace of colonization likely to be more regular and more dependent upon island size. Food producers are likely to be less mobile, and the pace of colonization more episodic. This is because the Allee effect creates a period of "stickiness" to a new settlement, in which things are actually improving with increases in population size, negating any tendency for significant emigration in a new round of colonization for some time period. That delay will be longer the larger the island. Regardless of island size and mode of production, one of the most robust predictions of this model is that if habitats vary in terms of average rewards, then migratory behavior is expected to be episodic rather than continuous. Because this appears to be the pattern of migration in Oceania, a pattern not easily accommodated in alternative explanations, we believe the IFD may have explanatory merit. Our argument requires that we turn to Oceania, first to the specifics of island colonization and second to temporal changes in subsistence practices.

COLONIZATION OF OCEANIA

Archaeological evidence shows that the first pulse of colonization into Oceania was initiated during the Pleistocene Epoch between 35,000 and 29,000 years ago (see Figure 12.2).[2] These early colonists likely departed from the northeastern coast of New Guinea to occupy New Britain and New Ireland, the largest islands in the Bismarck Archipelago (Allen et al. 1988; Allen et al. 1989). Adjacent islands exhibiting evidence for Pleistocene age settlement include Buka, on the northern end of the Solomon Island chain, and Manus, positioned 200 km northeast of New Ireland (Fredrickson et al. 1993; Wickler and Spriggs 1988). During much of the Pleistocene, sea level was substantially lower than today and New Guinea was connected to Australia forming a super-continent known as Sahul. Anatomically modern humans colonized this landmass from Southeast Asia by at least 40,000 years ago (Allen 1994; Allen and Holdaway 1995) and perhaps as early as 55,000 B.P. (Roberts et al. 1994; Thorne et al. 1999). The crossing from Southeast Asia (also a landmass less insular and more extended by lowered sea levels, known as Sunda) to Sahul suggests that people had some rudimentary seafaring technology at this early time (Anderson 2000a; Clark 1991; Erlandson 2001).

Colonization of the Bismarck archipelago and adjacent islands by hunter-gatherers depended on the appropriate maritime technologies and knowledge (Irwin 1992). Given the close geographic proximity of these islands to New Guinea, however, relatively simple boats, even bamboo rafts, some of which occur naturally after floods, could have been used (Anderson 2000a). It is very unlikely that sails were employed as Horridge (1987) has proposed, because sailing technology worldwide has a mid-Holocene origin, including in China, one of the more likely sources of Pacific technology (McGrail 2003). The accessibility and suitability of some islands was also enhanced by lower sea-level stands in the Pleistocene. Between 35,000 and 29,000 years ago sea level was 40 and 70 m below current levels (Thorne and Raymond 1989). New Britain, New Ireland, and Manus were larger, but the water gaps between New Guinea and the Bismarcks were essentially the same. New Britain is visible across the 90 km gap separating it from New Guinea and there is two way intervisibility (<100 km) between all of the islands in the Bismarck archipelago except for Manus. This island is ~230 km from New Ireland and required a blind crossing of 60–90 km (Spriggs 1997). However, it is unclear how early in the Pleistocene Manus was colonized due to the absence of datable material at the base of Pamwak, the only Pleistocene-age site known on the island (Frederiksen et al. 1993). The island of Buka, in the Solomon archipelago to the south, was also colonized early (29,000 B.P.; Wickler and Spriggs 1988) and required a partially blind crossing of 175 km from New Ireland. At this time, Buka was the northern extent of a single island known as "Greater Bougainville" that extended southeast through the modern day Solomon Island chain. There is currently no evidence for colonization of Vanuatu or New Caledonia, or other more remote archipelagos, until after 3300 B.P. (Anderson et al. 2001a).

The next significant episode of island colonization in Oceania appears to be associated with the expansion of agricultural populations south from Taiwan through the islands of Southeast Asia between 5000 and 4000 years ago. This spread of people is inferred from the widespread distribution of archaeological assemblages containing Asian domesticates—the ubiquitous rice, pigs, and dog; red-slipped or paddle impressed pottery; ground stone adzes; distinctive shell and bone ornaments; and barkcloth beaters (Bellwood 1975, 1978, 1985, 1996, 2001). Biological and linguistic data suggest that the changes evident archaeologically were related to an expansion of Austronesian-speaking people that ultimately replaced or swamped the existing hunter-gatherer populations on each island (Diamond and Bellwood 2003). The appearance of ceramics in archaeological assemblages in the Bismarcks at 3300 years ago has also been interpreted as an extension of this expansion (Bellwood 1978; Shutler and Marck 1975; Spriggs 1990)—an intrusion into island Melanesia of new people with different subsistence regimes, settlement practices, and sociopolitical organization, known as the Lapita cultural complex in Melanesia and Polynesia. However, other scholars interpret the appearance of Lapita as the product of *in situ* developments within Island Melanesia (Allen and White 1989; Gosden 1992; Gosden and Specht 1991; Terrell 1989; White et al. 1988; see below).

Lapita-age settlements of 3300 to 2300 B.P. are identified by the presence of dentate-stamped or incised pottery (Anderson et al. 2001a; Kirch 1997). A recent inventory of archaeological deposits containing dentate-stamped pottery includes approximately 184 locations extending 4500 km from the Bismarck Archipelago, southeast to Fiji, Tonga, Samoa, and Wallis in the South Pacific (Anderson et al. 2001a; see Figure 12.1). The appearance of Lapita pottery east of the Solomon Islands represents the earliest known colonization of Remote Oceania (Kirch and Hunt 1988). Sites throughout the Lapita range are most commonly found in coastal contexts with overall densities on larger islands being lower than smaller islands (Anderson 2001a). If the frequency of Lapita sites is standardized using land area by island size, the number of Lapita sites in Near Oceania (1.74 per 1000 km^2) is virtually identical to Remote Oceania (1.69 per 1000 km^2), but within Remote Oceania the overall density of sites increases from west to east (1.24 per 1000 km^2 in Vanuatu/New Caledonia to 2.45 per 1000 km^2 in Fiji and West Polynesia; Anderson 2001a).

Although there are similar densities of Lapita sites in Near and Remote Oceania, the chronological range of these sites throughout the region is quite different. Recent dates from the Bismarck Archipelago suggest the appearance of Lapita pottery at around 3300 B.P. with the cessation of production occurring as late as 2000 B.P. (Anderson 2001a; Green and Anson 2000; Specht and Gosden 1997; Torrence and Stevenson 2000). Dates range between 3100 and 2600 in the Reef/Santa Cruz Archipelago; 3000 to 2700 B.P. for Vanuatu (Bedford et al. 1998; Spriggs 1997); 3000 to 2700 for New Caledonia (Sand 1997, 1999; 2000); 2900 to 2600 B.P. for Fiji (Anderson and Clark 1999); and 2850 to 2650 B.P. for West Polynesia (Tonga, Samoa and Wallis). These data suggest a 200–400 year lag between the initial settlement of Near Oceania and the first dispersal of people into portions of Remote Oceania. It also appears that colonization accelerated from west to east and that the persistence of the Lapita cultural complex was more fleeting in Remote Oceania (Anderson 2001a). When the overall number of sites is considered in Near and Remote Oceania, settlements were established much more rapidly in Remote Oceania (22–27 per century) when compared to Near Oceania (6–10 sites per century) (see Anderson 2001a and Anderson et al. 2001a).[3]

Recent archaeological studies suggest a long pause of perhaps 1500 years between the expansion of Lapita peoples into West Polynesia and the colonization of more remote islands and archipelagos in East Polynesia (Anderson 2002; Anderson and Sinoto 2002). New work in the Society Islands suggests colonization no earlier than 1000 B.P. (Anderson et al. 1999) and the current data from the Marquesas indicate early settlement dating to around 900 B.P. (Rolett and Conte 1995; Rolett 1998). On the remote fringes of East Polynesia, Easter Island was likely colonized by 1000 B.P. (Steadman et al. 1994), Hawaii at about the same time (Athens et al. 1999), and New Zealand (Anderson 1991, Higham et al. 1999) along with several other south Polynesian islands (Anderson and White 2001; Anderson and O'Regan 2000; Johnson 1995) by 800 B.P. We currently are reevaluating the early settlement history of Rapa in the Austral Islands, but it is likely that this remote island was settled no earlier than 800 B.P. (Kennett et al. 2003; Walczak 2001). Colonization of East Polynesia also includes the 25 "mystery islands" (e.g., Christmas, Norfolk, and Pitcairn Islands), colonized after 1000 B.P., then abandoned before European contact (Anderson 2001b, Anderson et al. 2002; Bellwood 1978). Thus, the data indicate that the colonization of East Polynesia was late and, despite vast geographic expanse, relatively rapid.

These new settlement data do not support the traditional view that eastward voyaging and colonization were relatively continuous once they were initiated by Lapita peoples (Kirch 1997, 2000; Irwin 1992). The idea that colonization was continuous has been supported by decreases in indigenous tree pollen and increases in charcoal sediments in a paleoenvironmental sequence collected from Mangaia in the Cook Islands interpreted as anthropogenic forest clearance starting as early as 2500 B.P. (Kirch 1996, 1997, 2000). Similar types of sequences have been used to argue for early settlement on Easter Island (1500 to 1200 B.P.; Flenley 1996; Parkes 1997; Parkes and Flenley 1990) and New Zealand (2000 to 1500 B.P.; Sutton 1987). However, recent studies in New Zealand suggest that ancient soil carbons are often washed into lake sediments and return anomalously old radiocarbon dates (McGlone and Wilmshurst 1999). Therefore, the lake core chronologies from Mangaia and elsewhere are suspect and should be carefully reevaluated. Furthermore, there is often a dichotomy between lake core data suggesting anthropogenic landscape modification and the earliest tangible archaeological evidence for colonization. For instance, Kirch (1996) excavated seven rock shelter sites on Mangaia and has a well-established chronology (40 radiocarbon dates) for human activities on the island starting at approximately 1000 B.P. Interestingly, the earliest levels of the Tangatatau Rock shelter site (~1000 B.P.) contained the bones of several extinct landbirds and these species do not appear in more recent strata at this or other sites on the island, suggesting the prehistoric extirpation of these species (Steadman and Kirch 1990). The presence and rapid extirpation of large landbirds (~200–300 years after colonization; see below) is consistent with other early settlement sites in East Polynesia (Anderson 2002). Based on these data we would argue that the deposits at Tangatatau Rock shelter represent some of the earliest settlement on Mangaia. Again, this is consistent with new evidence from elsewhere in East Polynesia (e.g., Anderson and Sinoto 2002) and our central thesis that colonization of the Pacific was episodic. We now turn to a more detailed analysis of subsistence strategies and the emergence of food production in Oceania.

SUBSISTENCE CHANGE AND THE ORIGINS OF FOOD PRODUCTION

The first people to colonize Near Oceania between 35,000 and 29,000 years ago were probably relatively mobile hunter-gatherers whose subsistence strategies were structured by the availability and distribution of wild foods. Terrestrial fauna were restricted to a narrow range of edible species that included lizards, snakes, rats, bats, and birds (Spriggs 1997), but coastal habitats like reefs and lagoons offered a rich array of marine foods (Flannery 1995). The tropical forests covering these islands provided little in the way of edible plant foods, but disturbed patches along rivers and coastlines, particularly wetlands, would have afforded staples familiar to early colonists (taro-*Colocasia esculata*; and sago palm, *Metroxylon*) (Spriggs 1997; Yen 1985, 1995). Forest disturbance and habitat manipulation during early settlement would have promoted the growth of these wild plants (Groube 1989; Yen 1995).

Evidence for settlement in Near Oceania prior to 20,000 years ago is relatively scarce. Only four sites can clearly be assigned to this early period (Spriggs 1997). Three of these sites are pericoastal rock shelters or caves that contain stratigraphic evidence for sporadic use during this early period (Allen 1991; Gosden and Robertson 1991). Simple flaked stone tool assemblages at these sites also suggest high mobility. Marine shells and fishbone are the most common constituents in these deposits. At the sites of Buang Meraback and Matenkupkum (New Ireland), the large size of shells suggests that the early inhabitants of this cave were foraging in relatively pristine shell beds (Spriggs 1997). The fishbone found in the lowest levels of Matenkupkum is also some of the earliest evidence for marine fishing in the world (~35,000 B.P.; Allen 1993). Useware and starch grains on stone tools from Kilu Cave on Buka Island (Solomons) suggest that maritime foraging was coupled with plant exploitation, including the use of *Colocasia* taro, a plant that later became an important agricultural staple in Melanesia and Polynesia (Loy et al. 1992). The importance of plants to these early colonists is also suggested by the open air site of Yambon, positioned in the forested interior of New Britain (Pavlides 1993; Pavlides and Gosden 1994).

Changes in settlement and subsistence in Near Oceania after 20,000 years ago are signaled by a break in the occupation of pericoastal rock-shelters. The caves and rock-shelters used after 20,000 B.P. are positioned 3–5 km from the coast at a slightly higher elevation (Spriggs 1997). Marine resource exploitation continued, but changes in shellfish assemblages are evident, particularly between sites occupied during the late Pleistocene and early Holocene. Some of these changes are easily attributed to habitat changes coincident with sea level rise or the formation of coastal estuaries associated with the stabilization of sea level between 8000 and 6000 B.P. (Spriggs 1997). Other changes in marine shell assemblages are attributed to intensified human exploitation strategies, their impact on intertidal resources, and subsequent adjustments of foraging strategies. For instance, when the Holocene (10,000 to 2000 BP) assemblages at Matenkupkum (New Ireland) are compared to the pre-20,000 deposits, a much wider range of small and large species are evident and the quantities of the largest species are significantly reduced (Gosden and Robertson 1991). A similar pattern is evident at Buang Merabak where an increased variety of smaller shell taxa are evident after 10,800 BP (Balean 1989; cited in Spriggs 1997). These patterns are consistent with heavy exploitation and depletion of high ranking resources and the consequent expansion of diet breadth, also documented by Anderson (1981, 1983) in New Zealand, Broughton in late prehistoric Northern California (Broughton 1999), Janetski in the Great Basin (Janetski 1997), and others (Butler 2000; Nagaoka 2001, 2002).

The fishbone collected from late Pleistocene and early Holocene deposits suggests contin-

ued exploitation of near-shore reef habitats but there is little evidence for intensified fishing after 10,000 B.P. A small number of shark teeth found in Holocene deposits (8400 B.P.) at the Balof 2 rock shelter in New Ireland provide weak evidence for fishing beyond the reef (White et al. 1991). There is substantial evidence for deliberate movement of wild animals from New Guinea to the Bismarcks and Solomon Islands during the late Pleistocene, followed by more intensive hunting of these animals during the terminal Pleistocene and early Holocene (Gosden 1995; Flannery and White 1991). Evidence from several rock shelter sites indicate the late Pleistocene introduction of a possum species (*Phalanger orientalis*) to New Ireland from New Guinea (Flannery 1995). A different possum species (*Spilocuscus kramer*) was introduced to the more remote island of Manus (Bismarck Archipelago) and evidence for the introduction of the bandicoot (*Echymipera kalubu*) and a small wallaby (*Thylogale browni*) comes from caves in New Ireland (Flannery 1995). In addition, a rat species native to New Guinea (*Rattus praeto*) has been discovered in 13,000-year-old deposits at the site of Panakiwuk, New Ireland (Flannery 1995). What appears to be the deliberate translocation of animal species to Near Oceania suggests that people may have been compensating for population density-dependent resource depletion with the introduction of new species (Anderson 2001a).

A similar pattern is evident in the floral records from early sites in Near Oceania. The presence of native almond seeds (*Canarium indicum*) in late Pleistocene and early Holocene sites in Near Oceania indicate the transplantation of this species from New Guinea where it is naturally widespread (Yen 1990), although whether by people or the flying fox, remains uncertain (Anderson n.d.a). Seeds in terminal Pleistocene (13,000 to 10,000 B.P.) deposits at Pamwak (New Ireland) and Kilu (Solomons) might suggest early arboriculture, in essence the deliberate planting, tending, and harvesting of trees (Spriggs 1997). Evidence for short-term forest clearance during the Early Holocene is visible in pollen records from New Ireland (Allen et al. 1989). *Colocasia* taro residues are evident on tools from late Pleistocene and early Holocene deposits and yam (*Dioscorea*) residues are present on two tools from the Holocene levels at Balof 2 (New Ireland; Barton and White 1993). This indicates continued low-level use of starchy plants from the Pleistocene into the Holocene.

There is also some evidence in Island Melanesia for the intensification of subsistence strategies during the Holocene. Pollen and charcoal evidence from several locations indicate short-term local clearance of forest and continuous, low-level burning in some areas. Shell and bone accumulations increased during the Holocene at the sites of Pamwak on Manus and formal artifact types, including shell and edge-ground stone axes, become more common (Spriggs 1997). A similar pattern is evident at the sites of Matenbek (New Ireland) where larger amounts of imported obsidian are symptomatic of intensified trade (Gosden 1995). Heightened exploitation of possum is also evident at several locations during the Holocene possibly providing the foundation for more stable, sedentary settlement at some inland locations (Marshall and Allen 1991; White et al. 1991). Several cave sites were also abandoned between 6000 and 5000 B.P. perhaps signaling reduced mobility and the consolidation of populations on the landscape. Wood structures found in the waterlogged deposits at the Apalo site (Arawe Islands) suggest a settlement stability at some locations between 4250 and 4050 B.P. (Gosden and Web 1994). These deposits also contained a large variety and quantity of seeds from trees (*Canarium*, coconuts, and others; Hayes 1992, cited in Spriggs 1997). Whether that suggests only an accumulation of shoreline flotsam in the waterlogged site (Matthews and Gosden 1997), systematic collection of naturally grown resources, or more formal arboriculture still remains uncertain. The predominant subsistence-settlement pattern evident in the records from across Near Oceania from 20,000 to 3300 B.P. is that of a mobile hunter-forager

strategy with some degree of localized intensification and sedentarization during the Holocene (Spriggs 1997).

By contrast, substantial changes in settlement and subsistence are evident in Island Melanesia after 3300 B.P. (Kirch 1997; Summerhayes 2000a). Pottery, including dentate stamped Lapita forms, appears in the record for the first time (Kirch 1997, 2000; Spriggs 1997; Summerhayes 2000a). New settlements were established on small, offshore islands and stilt houses were sometimes constructed over coastal lagoons. These communities were commonly larger than previously occupied residential bases (Anderson 2001a). Accelerated erosion evident in the geomorphological records surrounding these settlements is consistent with intensified gardening activities on adjacent hillslopes. The first undisputed appearance of domesticated animal bone of pig, chicken, and dog also occurs in these deposits (Spriggs 1997). The changes evident in the archaeological record are interpreted by some as a culmination of intensified subsistence practices in Island Melanesia during the Holocene (Allen and White 1989; Gosden 1992; Gosden and Specht 1991; Terrell 1989; White et al. 1988). Others (Green 1991; Kirch 1997, 2000; Spriggs 1997) hypothesize that these changes represent an influx of people and culture from island Southeast Asia, broadly linked with the Austronesian expansion out of China (Bellwood 2001, Diamond and Bellwood 2003). This hypothesis is supported by a variety of archaeological, linguistic, and genetic evidence (Bellwood 2001; Kirch 1997; Spriggs 1997); however it is likely that cultural developments during this time were complex involving intrusion, accommodation, integration, and innovation (Green 1991).

Spriggs (1997; Jones and Spriggs 2002) has described the early Lapita populations in Near Oceania as "full blown" agriculturalists, but the importance of food production is debatable based on the available data—particularly during the early stages of this cultural period. Lapita age sites (3300 to 2200 B.P.) in Near Oceania are commonly positioned on the coast near lagoons or close to natural openings in island-fringing reefs. Shells and fish bones preserved in these sites suggest the exploitation of fish and shellfish from a variety of marine habitats: coastal lagoons, reefs, and open ocean. Artifact assemblages contain fishhooks, lures, and netweights, the technology of relatively sophisticated fishing practices (Summerhayes 2000a). Food production is inferred from geomorphological studies showing increased erosion rates near Lapita age settlements (Spriggs 1997), presumably associated with deforestation and field preparation for taro and yams in hillside gardens, but such data are difficult to interpret because forest clearance can occur in the absence of food production (e.g., clearing for settlement; Anderson 1995, 2000b). Beyond these data, building a case for intensive food production is difficult due to preservation problems in tropical environments. Waterlogged sites in Island Melanesia—Mussau and Arawes Islands (Kirch 1989; Gosden 1992)—provide some evidence for the utilization of nuts, and possibly of arboriculture based on the presence of *Canarium* and coconuts, but evidence for taro, yams, breadfruit, and bananas are absent. Forest clearance and a form of "swidden" horticulture may be indicated by increased charcoal concentrations in sediment cores after 3000 B.P. Changes in pollen assemblages also indicate a decline in tree taxa and the Lapita adze kit may have been used to ring trees and clear forest. Pig, chicken, and dog bones are all found in Lapita faunal assemblages, but all domestic animal bone occurs in much lower proportions relative to undomesticated species—particularly fish. For instance, at the waterlogged site of Talepakemalai eighteen pig bones were identified in a vertebrate assemblage consisting of 14,148 bones (Kirch 1997).

Several scholars have argued that the colonization of more remote archipelagoes in the Pacific—Vanuatu, New Caledonia, Fiji, Tonga, and Samoa—was significantly dependent on agriculture (Kirch and Green 2001; Spriggs 1997). Indeed, evidence for rapid colonization of more remote islands between 3200 and 2700 B.P. is used as one line of evidence supporting the hypothesis that Lapita peoples had a well-developed food production economy (Spriggs 1997). It is true that terrestrial resources on islands east and south of the main Solomons are depauperate compared with the islands of Melanesia that were colonized during the Pleistocene. Indigenous land mammals are absent except for several species of bat. Large flightless birds were common on many of these more remote islands, but the overall diversity of avifauna was reduced. Plant diversity is also restricted in remote Oceania, and wild taro (*Colocasia* or *Cyrtosperma*), yams (*Dioscorea*), and bananas are absent (Green 1991; Spriggs 1997; van Balgooy 1971). With respect to Vanuatu, Spriggs (1997, 41) argued that, in the absence of domesticated plants and animals, human settlement may have been impossible, from which it was inferred that "transported landscapes" composed of taro, bananas, native almonds, breadfruit, pigs, chickens, and dogs carried in the canoes of early colonists were vital and allowed them to replicate their homeland economies (Kirch 1997).

The importance of food production to these early colonizing populations in Remote Oceania is largely hypothetical and not securely demonstrated (Anderson 2000b; n.d.a; Anderson and Clark 1999, Burley et al. 2001; Clark and Anderson 2001). Lapita settlements in Remote Oceania are generally positioned on old beach surfaces close to fringing reefs and lagoonal environments that provided a wide range of marine resources and clearly supplied the bulk of the diet (Kirch 1988; Burley 1998; Galipaud 1996). The size of these communities in Remote Oceania generally is smaller than equivalent sites in Near Oceania and settlement mobility appears to have been relatively high (Anderson 2001a; Clark 1999; Bedford et al. 1998, 1999). Similarly to Lapita assemblages in Near Oceania, marine vertebrates and invertebrates are common. Diverse kinds of fishing tackle, such as fishhooks and lures, point to the importance of maritime subsistence activities (Kirch 1997). Early Lapita deposits also contain terrestrial birds and reptiles that rapidly went extinct (Anderson 2002). Early colonists in Vanuatu focused on harvesting naturally occurring foods that resulted in localized resource depletion and frequent site relocation (Bedford et al. 1998). In New Caledonia, the early animals targeted and extirpated included a large megapode (*Sylviornus neocaledoniae*), a crocodile (*Mekosuchus inexpectus*), and a horned tortoise (*Meiolania* sp.) (Balouet and Olsen 1989; Balouet 1987; Sand 1996a, 1997). Similar faunal extinctions are evident in Fiji where there was another giant megapode (*Megavitiornis altirostris*) and another genus and species of mekosuchid crocodile (*Volia athollandersoni*; Anderson et al., 2001b, Molnar et al. 2002, Worthy 2000; Worthy et al. 1999). Likewise in Tonga, there were large, now extinct, iguanids (Pregill and Dye 1989; Steadman 1993). Animal extinctions were a product of direct hunting and habitat destruction, but all of the known species seem to have gone extinct before there could have been any serious competition with introduced domestic and non-domesticated (e.g., rats) animals.

Only chicken bone appears in reasonably early Lapita contexts in Remote Oceania, and even there it might not have arrived with the first settlers (Steadman et al. 2002). Carbonized plant remains are rare in Remote Oceanic deposits, and no cultigens are known from early Lapita contexts. The presence of garden snails (*Lamellaxis gracilis*) could provide early evidence for food production because it is a species that was probably translocated to Remote Oceania with taro planting stocks and associated soils (Kirch 1997). However, there is no evidence to show how early that might have occurred in the Lapita era. In addition, recently acquired and more firmly dated pollen and charcoal records from islands in Remote Oceania also suggest that food production played only a minor, if any, role initially (Anderson 2002). These newer records are starting to show a lag of up to 500 years between the appearance of burning and forest clearing activities for cultivation and the accelerated deforestation indicative of more intensive food production. In New Caledonia, where early Lapita sites date to between 3000 and 2900 B.P. (Sand

1997), charcoal levels in sedimentary cores increased after about 3000 B.P. and the diversity of tree pollen was reduced. However, large-scale deforestation is not evident in these records until 2500 B.P. (Stevenson 1999; Stevenson and Dodson 1995). A similar pattern is evident at several locations within the Fijian archipelago, sometimes coincident with evidence for increasing erosion (Anderson 2002).

Therefore, the case for early Lapita food production rests solely upon linguistic reconstruction (Kirch and Green 2001). Linguists have traced the root of modern Polynesian languages back to a proto-Oceanic language. Proto-Oceanic words for many of the domesticated plants, including taro, yam, banana, and breadfruit, and for aspects of the swidden agricultural system both suggest that food production has a long history in Oceania (Kirch 1997). These linguistic data, although intriguing, do not carry sufficient chronological precision, however, to validate the idea that early Lapita colonists practiced food production and carried domesticated plants and animals during the first push into Remote Oceania. Evidence for the movement of obsidian, adzes, and sometimes pottery (Burley and Dickinson 2001; Green and Kirch 1997; Weisler and Kirch 1996; Weisler and Woodhead 1995) over vast areas during the Lapita Period shows that the full suite of Oceanic domesticates could have become established in Remote Oceania through continued contact with populations in Island Melanesia following the initial colonization of more remote islands.

The importance of food production for early Lapita colonists is far from resolved and further field study will be required to test several alternative propositions. We offer the following testable hypotheses in lieu of a solid statement regarding the importance of food production to early Lapita populations. To start, due to the vagaries of the archaeological record we cannot completely rule out the hypothesis that early Lapita populations transported domesticated plants and animals to more remote islands in Oceania as a package. This remains an alternative hypothesis, although we find no compelling archaeological, linquistic, or biological evidence in its support at this time. Alternatively, we present two additional hypotheses. The first, favored by Anderson (n.d.a), is that the earliest Lapita colonists were effectively foragers who skimmed the highest ranked marine and terrestrial resources as they dispersed through Vanuatu, New Caledonia, Fiji, and into Western Polynesia (Anderson, n.d.a). The implication of this hypothesis is that early Lapita colonization outran the movement of most food production into Remote Oceania and that domesticates, other than the chicken, were introduced into the Lapita economy during the continuing migration process, probably in a piecemeal fashion, rather than as a package (Anderson n.d.a). The second hypothesis, favored by Kennett, is that the early Lapita economy combined a low-level food production package, as defined by Smith (2001a), of select domesticates: chicken and possibly taro, maritime foraging for shellfish and fish, and the exploitation of the most easily obtainable terrestrial foods (*Canarium* nuts, large birds, eggs, etc.). This mixed production strategy may have been similar to the low-level food production practiced by the Mikea of western Madagascar (Tucker 2001, this volume). In both propositions, foraging for wild foods was the most important strategy initially, but food production increased in importance as people impacted the availability of wild resources, and the abundance of easy prey diminished on each island.

Current archaeological data suggest a pause in colonization activities once Lapita settlements were established in the Fijian, Tongan, and Samoan archipelagos. After this time (~3000 B.P.), settlement pattern data for these island groups suggest: (1) increased number of settlements in coastal locations and other previously unoccupied islands within each archipelago; (2) reductions in settlement mobility (Clark 1999); (3) the expansion of populations into the interiors of larger islands (Clark 1999; Hunt 1987; Sand 1996b); and, (4) intensified agricultural practices, inferred from inland expansion and the development of terracing and irrigation systems. On Vanuatu, the presence of Malakulan

pottery across the landscape suggests the expansion of people into interior locations as late as 1000 years ago. Rapid increases in charcoal frequencies also occur in a core from the Rewa delta on the southeast coast of Viti Levu, Fiji, by about 2300 B.P. (Anderson 2002). This is consistent with the post Lapita phase record from Fiji indicating a depletion of easily gathered natural foods and an increased reliance on agriculture between 2300 and 1900 B.P. (Clark 1999). Inland areas started to be colonized late in the Lapita period, when settlements covered the landscape by 1000 B.P. Group conflict over territory is indicated by the establishment of fortified villages on the landscape by 1200 B.P. (Field 2004). In New Caledonia, intensified agricultural strategies are inferred from new sediment core data suggesting deforestation after about 2500 B.P. (Stevenson 1999; Stevenson and Dodson 1995), and population expansion into interior areas at 2000 B.P. that culminated around 1000 B.P. (Sand 1996b; Galipaud 1996). The first fortifications on the Loyalty Islands at 1800 B.P. are attributed to infilling of the landscape and territoriality (Sand 1996b). This context is more consistent with the despotic variant of IFD and would have stimulated emigration more rapidly.

The evidence for rapid colonization of East Polynesia (~1000 B.P.), if correct, suggests that migrations were initiated from West Polynesia in the context of: (1) increasing population density, (2) decreases in habitat suitability caused by erosion and soil degradation after an initial increase in habitat suitability for agriculture due to forest clearance and terracing; and (3) heightened interference due to territoriality and warfare. Once colonized, subsistence and settlement strategies varied between islands in East Polynesia, but early colonists generally combined the hunting of ecologically naïve flightless birds, large reptiles, and other easy prey, with maritime foraging/fishing and low-level food production. The dominant faunal constituents in early East Polynesian assemblages are near shore reef fish (e.g., 90.4% of assemblage at Tangatatau Rock shelter on Mangaia;

Steadman and Kirch 1990). However, these early faunal assemblages also contain the bones of flightless birds, which were often extirpated within the first few hundred years of occupation of each island. The rapid extinction of twelve species of Moas in New Zealand is well-known (Anderson 1989) though it was probably not as rapid as proposed by Holdaway and Jacomb (2000; see Anderson 2000c). A wide range of other animals was also extirpated (40 species of birds, 1 bat, 3–5 frogs; Anderson 1997, 2002; Worthy 1997) there and elsewhere in the archipelagos of East Polynesia. Heavy intertidal predation pressure, indicated by decreasing shell size through time, is also evident in shellfish assemblages from several islands (Steadman and Kirch 1990). This ubiquitous East Polynesian pattern is evidence for early and rapid extinction, extirpation, or reduction in the largest, or most accessible, animals on each island (Anderson 1981, 1984, 1988; Kirch 1996; Steadman 1989; Steadman and Kirch 1990; Steadman et al. 1994; Weisler 1995).

Intensive agricultural strategies were well developed in West Polynesia prior to the colonization of East Polynesia. The available records indicate that early colonists carried economically valuable plants and animals into East Polynesia. For instance, the early cultural strata at Tangatatau Rock shelter (~1000 B.P.) contain a rich carbonized plant record that includes taro (*Colocasis esculenta*), other root crops (*Cyrtosperma chamissonis*), banana (*Musa*), breadfruit (*Artocarpus altilis*), Tahitian chestnut (*Inocarpus fagiferus*), sugarcane (*Saccharum officinarum*), ti (*Cordyline terminalis*), and the sweet potato (*Ipomoea batatas*) (Hather and Kirch 1991; Kirch et al. 1995; Kirch 1996). Chickens (*Gallus gallus*), pigs (*Sus scrofa*), and dogs (*Canine*) are also evident in East Polynesian records relatively early (Steadman and Kirch 1990). However, an immediate commitment to intensive food production is not evident in the available records. Turning back to the Tangatatau Rock shelter example, the earliest levels contain large concentrations of native land birds and very few domesticated animal bones (chickens or pigs), but the latter increase through time as the frequency of native landbird species decreases (Steadman and Kirch 1990). The 25 mystery islands of East Polynesia appear to have been abandoned after the collapse of indigenous fauna and before agricultural intensification (Anderson 2001b, Anderson et al. 2002). In several of these instances it appears that only one or two domesticated plants or animals were successfully transported or propagated on these islands.

Some temperate islands, particularly the South Island of New Zealand, were also outside the range of successful cultivation of tropical cultigens. However, on islands that lacked such environmental limitations, or were not abandoned, intensified agricultural strategies appear to develop much more rapidly (~100–200 years) when compared to West Polynesia (~500–1000 years) (Anderson 2002). This parallels evidence for increases in sociopolitical complexity, territoriality, and warfare (Kirch 2000). Evidence for anthropogenic environmental changes of deforestation and erosion appear earlier and were more rapid in East Polynesia (Anderson 2002). This was related, in part, to the small size of these islands, but was also linked to the more developed nature of food production at this late date.

SUMMARY AND DISCUSSION

Hundreds of islands were colonized in Oceania after 35,000 years ago, and each island provided a new set of opportunities and constraints to potential colonists. Basic foraging models (Winterhalder 2001) predict that considerable temporal and spatial variability in colonizing behavior would have existed. Beyond the occupational histories of individual islands, there does appear to be temporal and spatial structure in the process of colonization. Current archaeological data strongly suggest that the migration of people to smaller, more remote islands and archipelagos was episodic and not continuous. Bursts of colonization activity were followed by longer periods of local population growth, environmental infilling, and intensification of subsistence strategies. Smaller, more remote islands with decreasing resource potential were colonized after periodic delays.

The largest landmasses (New Britain, New Ireland, and Greater Bougainville) in Near Oceania were first colonized by hunter-gatherers between 35,000 and 29,000 B.P. Archaeological evidence for this early time is limited, but suggests that foragers complimented the use of protein-rich intertidal resources with wild plant foods from wetland habitats. This included the exploitation of *Colocasia* taro, a plant species that later became an important Oceanic domesticate (Yen 1995). The periodic use of caves and rock shelters suggests that populations were highly mobile using the landscape extensively. After initial colonization the record suggests a long period of stasis with some evidence for small-scale increases in population after 20,000 years ago and again during the Holocene (~10,000–3500 B.P.; Spriggs 1997). This period saw the infilling of different environmental zones on larger islands and the colonization of smaller adjacent islands in the Bismarck Archipelago and Solomon Islands (e.g., Manus; Spriggs 1997). As populations increased, habitat suitability would have decreased due to resource depletion or interference, stimulating intensification or migration.

The presence of non-native species of trees and animals (e.g., chestnut and marsupial possum) in late Pleistocene deposits in Near Oceania (~13,000 years ago) suggests that people were actively manipulating the landscape and possibly compensating for exploitation-induced depression in the availability of naturally occurring foods (Anderson 2001b). Intensified subsistence strategies are evident at interior locations where possum were aggressively targeted (Marshall and Allen 1991; White et al. 1991), in Holocene shellfish assemblages suggesting increases in diet breadth, and perhaps in the development of arboriculture by about 4000 B.P. Population increases and the intensification of subsistence strategies occurred in the context of global sea level rise after 18,000 B.P. that reduced the size of islands in the Bismarks and inundated portions of Greater Bougainville to form the modern-day distribution of islands in the Solomons (Fairbanks 1989; Thiel 1987). Coastal wetlands would have become increasingly productive with the stabilization of sea level after 7000 years ago and may have contributed to intensified use of maritime resources after this time.

Despite several decades of work in Remote Oceania, there is no evidence for occupation east of the Solomon Islands prior to 3300 B.P. (Anderson et al. 2001a). The ideal free distribution model predicts that these more remote islands would have been colonized only when average subsistence returns there were equal to those in the Bismarck Archipelago or the Solomon Islands. Delayed colonization of these remote islands (~30,000 years) suggests that (1) population in the Bismarcks and Solomon Islands were not experiencing sharp decreases in habitat suitability, but perhaps the opposite, an Allee effect; (2) initial suitability of these remote islands was low; or (3) the dispersal of populations to these islands was restricted because of environmental, technological, or social barriers (e.g., territoriality). A combination of these factors likely contributed to delayed colonization of more remote islands in the Pacific.

Other factors may have impeded colonization as well. Clark and Kelly (1993) have argued that endemic malaria, common in the region today, caused high infant mortality and kept early populations in Near Oceania relatively low. It is also probable that resource availability in New Caledonia and Vanuatu, as well as other remote islands, was comparatively low due to their limited terrestrial plant and animal diversity (Anderson 2001a; Spriggs 1997). In addition, these islands are all south of the equator and are subject to greater seasonal differences in temperature and rainfall (Spriggs 1997). In the absence of agriculture and storage, seasonal resource shortfalls—likely to have been more pronounced during Pleistocene glacial conditions—would have constrained the viability of colonization. Current data suggest that these islands were unoccupied until the late Holocene so impediments due to resistance of earlier settlers were certainly not a problem, but environmental and technological barriers may have inhibited colonization. For example, the water gaps between islands were greater (over 300 km) and may have required more specialized maritime technology.

The appearance of Lapita settlements in the Bismarck Archipelago was a major threshold in Oceanic prehistory that represents either an outgrowth of indigenous developments (Allen and White 1989; Gosden 1992), an intrusion of Austronesian peoples from Southeast Asia (Bellwood 2001; Spriggs 1997), or a combination of the two (Green 1991). Lapita settlements were strategically positioned near or over, by means of stilthouses, coastal lagoons that were often on small islets adjacent to larger islands occupied by indigenous, non-Lapita, hunter-horticulturalists. The placement of settlements on smaller islands suggests that other island habitats were full or that Lapita peoples selected locations to avoid hostilities or endemic malaria that likely plagued indigenous communities in Near Oceania at the time (Clark and Kelly 1993). The frequency and size of Lapita settlements suggest that populations increased more rapidly relative to contemporaneous hunter-horticultural communities on adjacent islands. The economic engine for increased population growth probably consisted of intensive maritime foraging coupled with low-level food production that intensified through the interval. It is also possible that rapid population increase was partially related to reduced susceptibility of Austronesian populations to endemic malaria (Kelly 1999). Regardless, population increase in Lapita communities ultimately outpaced indigenous populations which were swamped or replaced.

Lapita migrants in Near Oceania entered landscapes that were depleted of larger game animals and other easy prey (Allen 1996). The productivity of intertidal resources like shellfish was also reduced, at least in some areas, because of sustained exploitation for thousands of years (Spriggs 1997). Lapita faunal assemblages indicate a clear maritime focus and improvements in seafaring with fishing technologies available

as early as 3300 B.P. Reductions in habitat suitability due to resource depression and interference were probably exacerbated by interference from hostile indigenous populations. It was in this context that, following a lag of several hundred years, voyaging and colonization activities increased and the more remote parts of Oceania—New Caledonia, Vanuatu, Fiji, Tonga and Samoa—were colonized between 3000 and 2800 B.P. (Anderson 2001a).

As the vigor of eastward colonization began to wane 2700 years ago, and Lapita pottery started dropping out of the archaeological record, there is increased evidence for reduced settlement mobility and intensified food production in Fiji, New Caledonia, Tonga, and Samoa (Clark 1999; Sand 1996b). Intensive food production in Remote Oceania is signaled by large-scale forest clearance, intensive erosion, and the movement of soils from hillsides to valley bottoms (Anderson 2002). This culminated in the settlement of interior locations and the terracing of hillsides to contain erosion and maximize the amount of cultivated land. Territoriality and social circumscription are suggested by the appearance of fortified settlements in lowland and upland settings (e.g., Best 1993; Field 2004), contributing to decreases in habitat suitability that would have promoted emigration. The emergence of more intensive strategies varies between islands, but they were well established throughout West Polynesia by 1000 years ago. Several forms of intensive food production were evident by this time, including terracing, pond-field cultivation of taro, and irrigation agricultural systems (Clark 1999).

If our current estimates for the colonization of East Polynesia are correct, then the population increases, environmental infilling, and agricultural intensification evident in West Polynesia occurred during a pause in eastward colonization activity that lasted for more than 1500 years (Anderson 2002). Many of the islands in East Polynesia were colonized rapidly after 1000 years ago and New Zealand was colonized as late as 800 B.P. Except for New Zealand, all of the islands in East Polynesia are relatively small and are not complex ecologically. The biological diversity on these islands is low, the productivity of marine habitats declines from west to east, and seasonal variations in temperature and rainfall become accentuated particularly on subtropical islands. Rapid extinctions of the largest landbirds and reptiles, evident archaeologically (Anderson 1989; Steadman and Kirch 1990), reduced the biological diversity of these islands further still.

Human ability to discover and colonize islands was dependent on factors of access, such as island size and remoteness, prevailing climatic and environmental conditions in relation to maritime activities, and the availability of seafaring technology and knowledge (Anderson 2000a; Erlandson 2001; Irwin 1992; Spriggs 1997). However, the data from Oceania are generally consistent with the predictions of the IFD model: the long interval between the initial colonization of Near Oceania (35,000 B.P.) and Remote Oceania (3300 B.P.) consistent with the IFD curve for foragers living on large islands; the more rapid succession of colonization episodes in Remote Oceania after the establishment of Lapita populations in West Polynesia more consistent with IFD curves for food producers on small islands. The 200–400 year pause in colonizing vigor after the first arrival of Lapita people in Near Oceania and the 1500 year pause in West Polynesia prior to the colonization of East Polynesia, if upheld archaeologically, is also consistent with the infilling of populations and the intensification of subsistence strategies in Near Oceania and West Polynesia respectively.

Thus, there appears to be a close match between the scale of this HBE model and the available archaeological data (c.f. Smith, this volume). IFD predictions are ones of central tendency, the probabilistic equilibrium result of a large number of individual decisions made over a time interval that allows for several rounds of adjustment in habitat choice. Likewise, the overall history of colonization in Oceania, as recorded in the archaeological record, smoothes highly localized decisions over sufficiently long periods of time and enough repetitions of migration events that patterning becomes visible at a scale concomitant to that of the model.

Nevertheless, the episodic nature of colonization now evident in the archaeological record could be the result of other historical processes. For instance, colonization episodes could have been triggered by periodic advances in seafaring technology, both of boats and navigational and other sailing skills (Anderson 2000a). Direct archaeological evidence for boats is uncommon and makes this hypothesis difficult to test. The neotraditional assumption is that celestial navigation techniques were well developed and that large double-hulled canoes existed prior to the colonization of Remote Oceania (Irwin 1992). Yet, the late Holocene appearance of Lapita assemblages coincides with a sixfold increase in voyaging range into the prevailing wind and likely signals the first arrival of the sail and possibly the outrigger (Anderson, 2000a, 2001c, n.d.a). Linguistic data, furthermore, suggest that the large double-hulled canoes were a relatively late development, certainly after the colonization of Fiji and West Polynesia (Blust 1997; Anderson n.d.a). The colonization of extremely remote islands in East Polynesia was probably contingent on the development of the double-hulled canoe (Anderson 2000a, 2001c). Developments in maritime technology, therefore, were one important component in the episodic nature of colonization, particularly for the discovery and assessment of remote islands. Given the probable nature of early sailing technology, particularly the likely absence of an upwind capacity (Anderson 2000a, 2001c), the larger numbers of voyages may have occurred during periods of wind reversal related to millennial scale changes in climatic and associated oceanographic conditions (Anderson n.d.b). Long-term climatic change may turn out to be another key element in explaining the episodic nature of the colonization of Oceanic islands.

An important assumption of the IFD model employed here is that the costs of relocating were small enough to be ignored. Setting sail across the Pacific without prior knowledge of habitable islands would have been risky and potentially costly, but it might not have been perceived in that light. In any event, we have assumed, for the sake of simplicity, that the locations of surrounding, uninhabited islands were known to emigrants, their position and relevant agro-ecological features having been scouted prior to colonization. To this extent, the decision to disperse would have been an informed one, and of relatively low risk and cost in transportation when considered relative to the lifetime scale of its consequences. In some cases this assumption may be unrealistic because of the distances traveled to Fiji, Easter Island, and Hawaii and the ability of early island explorers to return to their home islands given prevailing winds and limitations imposed by maritime technologies (Anderson 2003b, n.d.a).

Given these limitations we suspect that the colonization of islands involved a dispersal phase and a migratory phase (Anderson, n.d.a), the former being the outward, one-way initial occupation of islands, the latter a two-way process involving the movement of people back and forth between island groups along with food and goods. Dispersal would have been an exploratory phase when the resource potential of islands was assessed given available subsistence practices and technologies. This phase would have been riskier, and therefore more costly, than the migratory phase when more information was available regarding target islands. Therefore, we envision the colonization of islands as a process rather than an event. Regardless, population-dependent decreases in island suitability would likely stimulate dispersal and migration in much the same way, but the costs of dispersal would have been considerably higher relative to the follow-up migration process and would have contributed to the long pauses between colonizing episodes.

The distinction between dispersal and migration phases is important when considering the role that food production played in the initial colonization of Remote Oceania by Lapita peoples. We have proposed alternative hypotheses in response to the traditional assumption that food production was one of the primary contextual changes that stimulated the colonization of Remote Oceania (Kirch 2000; Spriggs 1997), a hypothesis that is currently not well supported by the available archaeological data. One proposition is that early Lapita peoples were mainly foragers who skimmed the highest-ranked resources from pristine island environments in Remote Oceania. The second proposition is that these people combined low-level food production of taro and chicken with foraging for wild food, both terrestrial and marine. Regardless, it is clear that food production was not essential for the initial dispersal of people into Remote Oceania in a strict economic sense. The known early Lapita assemblages in Near and Remote Oceania are dominated by marine resources and contain few, if any, domesticates. If early Lapita people were foragers (Hypothesis #1) then the decision to disperse was not stimulated by the perceived advantages of food production on smaller, more remote islands that would not have sustained foraging economies, increased productivity, and decreased subsistence risk. This would suggest that early Lapita peoples sailed away from low-level food production and that they only brought in domesticated plants and animals as the suitability of island habitats in Remote Oceania decreased with faunal collapse, one form of resource depression.

Alternatively, the combination of low-level food production and intensive maritime foraging in Near Oceania may have contributed to decreases in island habitat suitability during the 200–400 year period that separates the first appearance of Lapita peoples and their dispersal into Remote Oceania, in combination with long-term decreases in habitat suitability associated with a sustained, long-term occupation by hunter-gatherers. This mixed subsistence strategy would also have changed the perception of the overall resource potential of smaller, more remote islands while decreasing subsistence risk. Therefore, domesticates may have played a significant role in the decision to disperse even if the role of food production was minor initially, due to the local availability of wild resources. In the absence of competing populations, the earliest settlement on these islands would be expected in optimal locations for collecting marine and terrestrial resources and low-level food production. Less optimal locations in the interior are expected to develop later. Deforestation, sediment loading in valley bottoms, and terracing could have created an Allee effect where larger populations were possibly supported prior to environmental degradation. More despotic/territorial behavior would be expected with habitat infilling as would the intensification of agricultural strategies. Both would have contributed to more rapid emigration. Evaluation of this hypothesis is dependent upon larger-scale excavations in Early Lapita sites in Near and Remote Oceania coupled with new technology for detecting domesticated plants in environments unfavorable for the preservation of organic material, such as starch grain and phytolith analysis.

Food production appears to have been well developed before the colonization of East Polynesia and certainly contributed to relatively rapid decreases in habitat suitability that played an important role in the decision to emigrate. The availability of domesticated plants and animals to augment the depauperate environments of remote islands probably influenced the decision to emigrate. However, in a similar fashion to the Lapita colonization of West Polynesia, the initial generations of colonists were subsidized by naïve and easily captured game. Successful and persistent settlement of these ecologically impoverished islands was often dependent upon a rapid increase in agricultural production. Pollen and charcoal records from different islands indicate that extensive forest clearing and burning started within a century of colonization (Anderson 2002). Intensive agricultural production involving terracing, irrigation, and pond-field cultivation developed rapidly suggesting that domesticated plants and animals, along with extensive agrarian knowledge, were carried by early colonists. Direct archaeological evidence

for this is also available (Kirch 1996). The most productive island habitats were selected, and early colonists combined the hunting of ecologically naïve landbirds and reptiles with continued maritime foraging and agriculture. The rapid extinction of larger fauna caused by overexploitation was compensated by increased food production, which intensified in parallel with increased population density. In some cases, faunal collapse on islands with little agricultural potential resulted in abandonment (e.g., Pitcairn, Norfolk and 23 others; Anderson 2001b). On other islands rapid extinction resulted in agricultural intensification, rapid population growth, the formation of large villages, territoriality, and more centralized political systems founded upon hereditary leadership (Kirch 2000).

CONCLUSION

The proposed Ideal Free Distribution model provides a framework that considers the dynamic character of island habitat suitability along with density-dependent and density-independent variables influencing migratory behavior. The archaeological data from Near Oceania is consistent with the IFD curves for hunter-gathers living on large islands. Evidence for the more rapid colonization of Remote Oceania is consistent with IFD curves for food producers living on small islands. The model also accounts for the episodic nature of island colonization. The initial generations of colonists in Near and Remote Oceania were subsidized by relatively dense and easily captured populations of naïve game. This phase lasted several generations, the bounty and persistence of this windfall a function of island size. Declines in wild resources appear to have been offset by intensified foraging and the translocation of wild animals (Near Oceania) or efforts to replace these resources with expanding food production (Remote Oceania). In Remote Oceania the transition from dependence on an ephemeral local bounty of foraged resources to a stable and fairly productive regime of cultivation was the point of greatest risk for successful colonization, while it is clear from the abandonment of several islands after faunal collapse that it was not always successful (Anderson 2003b). The population that made it through this period of vulnerability, then experienced an Allee effect of increasing economies of scale in food production. Local habitat suitability grew as an effective system of agro-ecological production was developed. This phase was one in which population was locally tethered; it lasted for a relatively long interval before overpopulation, circumscription, and possibly environmental degradation began to reduce suitability, leading to a new round of emigration if suitable, uninhabited islands were available. The length of each phase in this cycle was a function of island size, which would mean that, once a colonization episode was initiated, small islands in East Polynesia would have been colonized rapidly and relatively continuously. The rapid development of social stratification in East Polynesia after colonization also accelerated the tendency for emigration.

Our formulation of this model is based on fundamental HBE principles, the IFD model in particular, and our interpretations of the available archaeological data in Oceania. The model predicts that colonization of Oceania would have been episodic and not continuous. New radiocarbon chronologies throughout Oceania should continue to confirm the episodic nature of colonization starting 35,000 years ago. The model also predicts that a relationship exists between population density and habitat suitability. Therefore, substantial population growth and reductions in habitat suitability should be clearly evident in the palaeoenvironmental and archaeological records in source archipelagos prior to the next episode of emigration. More rapid reductions in habitat suitability are expected with intensified food production strategies in that emigration would be expected prior to large-scale agricultural intensification. The most intensive food-producing strategies such as pondfields or terracing should be evident on

islands in East Polynesia late in prehistory when options for emigration were limited. We argue that this scenario is plausible, and testable. However, we note that others might be devised within the framework of the IFD, perhaps giving greater attention to social stratification and resource inequalities, and thus to a despotic variant of the IFD.

Our use of the IFD model also is qualitative and general, as is our assessment of its fit to the available archaeological data. A more robust application would develop out of independent quantitative information on available habitats, including measurement of their ranking (quality) and the response of their suitability to increasing human populations. The latter requires careful determination of the shape of the suitability/density curve. The information on migration and settlement required to test this model would include the sequence and timing of intra-island settlement of habitats, and inter-island migration, both relative to the population history and its density in particular locales. It also would require observations on the socioeconomic conditions pertinent to "free" or "despotic" regimes of resource competition. It is encouraging that this type of data is archaeologically accessible, and will eventually become available in sufficient detail to evaluate the explanatory potential of the IFD in this setting in a more quantitatively rigorous fashion.

NOTES

1. The islands of Micronesia are not considered in this paper, but the ideas explored here could easily be extended to that vast region.

2. All Pleistocene and early Holocene dates are reported in radiocarbon years before present and dates in the late Holocene are calibrated years before present.

3. This pattern could also be caused by differences in the amount of archaeological fieldwork completed in each region, but sustained work in both Near and Remote Oceania for the last 40 years would suggest that this is not the case.

13

Human Behavioral Ecology and the Transition to Food Production

Bruce D. Smith

HUMAN BEHAVIORAL ecology and foraging theory offer frameworks for considering and characterizing variation and change in human subsistence patterns, both across a range of environmental gradients and through time (Winterhalder and Smith 2000). Given that the initial domestication of plants and animals and the subsequent development and spread of agricultural economies and landscapes constitutes one of the earth's most significant environmental transformations, it is not surprising that there has been interest in exploring the utility of these theories and models for opening up new approaches and gaining a better perspective on this major transition in human history. This chapter offers a brief overview of some of the central questions and challenges involved in efforts to employ foraging theory and related behavioral ecology models to better understand domestication and agricultural origins.

SCALES OF ANALYSIS AND DATA RESOLUTION REQUIREMENTS

Perhaps the most obvious aspect of foraging theory and other behavioral ecology models that sets ory and other behavioral ecology models that sets

them apart from the wide range of alternative approaches to understanding change and transition in the archaeological record is their apparent small scale, "fine resolution" context of application, at the individual or small group level, rather than in terms of larger and longer-term societal level adaptive responses to "external pressures." In their concise and straightforward characterization of optimal foraging theory, for example, Winterhalder and Goland (1997) contrast the diet breadth model with other proposed approaches to explaining domestication and agricultural origins in terms of scale and specificity. They describe most previous explanations as involving "extensive" variables such as population growth, climate change, and technological innovation, which are generalized and normative, and which operate on the system level: "extensive variables are those measures that summarize population wide, interspecific (community level) or long-term (multi-generational) aspects of things biological" (Winterhalder and Goland 1997, 126).

In contrast, Winterhalder and Goland argue that optimal foraging theory derives considerable theoretical strength from the much smaller or "local" temporal, spatial, and ecosystem scale on which it is applied. Diet breadth modeling, for example, like foraging approaches in general, involves "intensive variables . . . those that characterize the behavior of an individual at a particular place and time. They refer to the situated properties of the organisms making up ecological sets; they potentially are subject to the direct action of selection" (1997, 126). Identifying the intensive variables of foraging models as being subject to the direct action of selection also suggests that within the framework of foraging theory the choice or selection of plant and animal resources at the local level, i.e. individuals, is potentially open to being predicted on the basis of higher level selection theories and assumptions. This question of the nature and strength of a predictive link between general evolutionary principles of selection and individual diet choice decisions will be considered later in this chapter, within a broader discussion of the necessary care and procedures which should be exercised in any efforts to predict archaeologically situated local events on the basis of general theoretical models or overarching frameworks of expectation. Setting this discussion aside for the moment, the small scale of application of foraging theory warrants closer consideration, both in terms of the importance of clarifying the range of scales within which foraging theory can be employed, and the potential constraints and limitations of archaeological data.

Archaeological research is carried out on a range of different social, spatial, and temporal scales of consideration; e.g. individual, family or household, settlement or community, polity, and various higher level sub-regional and regional geographical and cultural contexts, depending upon both the kinds of questions being addressed, and the quality and relative level of resolution of available relevant archaeological information. Within this broad range of different potential scales of archaeological analysis, which are open for consideration and which are the most appropriate to select when attempting to apply foraging theory to questions of diet choice and subsistence change? Winterhalder and Goland (1997) (see above) indicate that for-

aging theory applies at the scale of individual decisions at a particular time and place, and that this fine-resolution level of analysis carries with it considerable theoretical strength. A number of scholars, however, have cautioned that while foraging models are scaled to address individual decisions, archaeological deposits in contrast represent the accumulated and intermingled traces of many such resource selection events (Grayson and Delpech 1998; Gremillion 2002, 144). An important and as yet unresolved issue, then, is whether the "intensive" variables required to test foraging theory and behavioral ecology models in general can be observed and accurately measured in the archaeological record. Can sequences of temporally discrete individual decisions regarding resource selection be identified in the occupational episodes of ancient settlements? And if such individual resource selection decisions can't be recognized, to what extent can the "intensive variable" small-scale focus of foraging theory and behavioral ecology reasonably be expanded in terms of the necessity of considering larger pooled and therefore "normative" sets comprised of numerous resource selection decisions, before the ascribed "theoretical strength" of foraging theory is diluted? As Gremillion notes: "A model's performance may be difficult to assess because it exceeds the degree of resolution offered by the data" (Gremillion 2002, 144).

It is interesting in this regard, however, that in a number of the studies of present-day human societies which are frequently cited as providing supporting evidence for broad applicability of foraging theory, such as those of the Aché (Hawkes et al. 1982; Hill 1988; Hill et al. 1987), diet choice data is aggregated from the activities of all Aché foragers, and would appear to be representative of normative societal scale behavior sets, rather than reflecting individual diet choice decisions. Bamforth (2002, 439) indicates that such data aggregation practices are not unusual in optimization studies. If foraging theorists are comfortable using aggregated data sets in diet selection studies of present-day human societies, can archaeologists reasonably employ foraging theory at scales of analysis up to and including the community and polity level and perhaps beyond? At what point will cumulative aggregation of individual diet choice decisions and an expanding scale of analysis result in variables losing their "intensive" identity and theoretical strength and becoming normative and "extensive"?

Another important aspect of foraging theory is that it emphasizes the contextual consideration of diet-choice decisions, focusing on individual actions in particular cultural and environmental settings. This contextual approach is clearly compatible with archaeological efforts to consider settlement-scale subsistence analyses within a larger research framework of environmental and societal reconstruction. Like foraging theorists, archaeologists have long recognized the value of considering changes in human societies and economies as involving associated shifts in a range of relevant environmental and cultural variables over time.

When considered in a larger geographical context, the individual through polity scale, local setting context of foraging theory, along with Winterhalder and Goland's (1997) associated critique of more generalized and universally applicable explanatory models of domestication and agricultural origin, also gains a level of support from the growing recognition that like politics, domestication and agricultural origins are always local. More than a half-dozen independent centers of domestication have now been identified worldwide (Diamond 2002; Smith 1998), with human societies in each bringing different plant and animal species under domestication in different sequences at different times. In addition to these "primary" centers, other areas of the world also experienced their own distinctive developmental transitions as domesticates of various kinds, and in various combinations, were introduced into extant regional hunting and gathering economies. While a range of generic "extensive" variables have been proposed as playing prerequisite or causal roles in domestication and agricultural origins in a number of different world regions

(e.g. Richerson et al. 2001), each of these areas is also deserving of a closer-fit, more situated, and local scale analysis. Such analyses should incorporate a detailed understanding of the attributes of the indigenous species targeted for domestication as well as the larger set of plants and animals included in a society's subsistence economy and the broader biotic communities of the areas they occupied.

Along with being tightly focused contextually, foraging theory and behavioral ecological models are also targeted at short time frames, compared to models which look at change occurring over longer "multi-generational" periods of time. Foraging theory targets immediacy—the intra-generational "behavior of an individual at a particular place and time" (Winterhalder and Goland 1997, 126):

> The real stuff of evolutionary profundity lies in the local factors of an organism's experience: the constraints it faces, its actions and the consequences of those actions. Immediate details have the greatest causal efficacy in the evolutionary explanation of adaptive design.

Once again, the small-scale or short-term focus inherent in foraging theory and behavioral ecology approaches finds some level of support in the growing appreciation for the long and drawn-out nature of the distinctive developmental transitions from hunting and gathering through low-level food production to agriculture that unfolded in quite different ways in different areas of the world (Smith 2001a). Not only does each world region represent a unique developmental puzzle, requiring a good understanding of the particular local components of ecosystems and human subsistence systems, but each regional developmental sequence is also best viewed as actually being comprised of a linked linear set of discrete evolutionary steps or organizational changes: not as a single transformational episode but rather as a sequential set of linked puzzles. Each of these temporally discrete puzzles warrants attention and analysis in and of itself. Foraging theory would certainly provide a fine-grain temporal resolution appropriate for separate, stand-alone consideration of each of the many developmental shifts up through time that mark the long and complex transition from hunting and gathering to full agriculture. However one chooses to break down these long developmental processes for closer analysis, what is clear is that the spatial and temporal context of change, and the basic nature of each of the sequential episodes of transition in any given region, can be quite diverse.

Take, for example, the pre-Columbian developmental history of eastern North America. The Eastern United States provides one of the best documented records of the independent domestication of indigenous species and the subsequent, long delayed, emergence of agricultural economies. Early European accounts of the sixteenth and seventeenth centuries described various forms of maize-beans-squash agricultural economies as prevailing across much of the East, from New England to northern Florida. This widespread reliance on a generally similar agricultural economy at European contact, however, was not the result of a rapid and broad scale transition between two steady states—hunting and gathering and agriculture—that took place over some brief period in the past. The developmental history of the transition to food production in eastern North America in fact is a much more complex, interesting, and regionally variable story (Fritz 1990; Green 1994; Gremillion 1997a; Hart 1999; Smith 2002; Woods 1992). The crop trinity of squash, maize, and beans only coalesced in the East about three centuries prior to European contact, with the very late arrival of the common bean in the region (Hart and Scarry 1999). Maize arrived in the eastern United States by about 100 BC, more than a millennium earlier than beans, but apparently did not become a significant dietary component until after AD 900. Changing stable carbon isotope values and an increased archaeological visibility around AD 1000 marks its initial emergence as a central crop plant. Squash (*Cucurbita pepo*), the third crop plant in the trinity, in turn, was a local creation, domesticated from a wild eastern North American

Cucurbita gourd by about 3000 BC, long before the arrival of maize. Morphological changes in seed size and seed coat thickness in three other eastern plant species (marshelder, *Iva annua*; sunflower, *Helianthus annuus*; chenopod, *Chenopodium berlandieri*) indicate that they too were being deliberately planted by human societies (ergo domesticated) across an interior mid-latitudes area encompassing parts of present day Illinois, Ohio, Kentucky, Tennessee, Missouri, and Arkansas, as early as 2500 to 1500 BC.

Archaeological evidence for these earliest domesticates is still quite limited, however, and the exact timing and sequence of their domestication is still not yet clear. At the present time their domestication appears to have been an additive sequence of temporally and spatially distinct undertakings that extended over a period of perhaps 1500 years. Squash was the first species domesticated in the East, by about 3000 BC, followed by sunflower 750 years later at 2250 BC, marshelder after another 250 years, and finally, by 1500 BC, chenopod. All four of these local domesticates have relatively low archaeological visibility until about 200 BC—a century perhaps prior to the arrival of maize in the region, when they exhibit a clear if regionally diverse increase in representation in human settlements across the middle latitudes (Smith 2002).

When considered together in this manner, all of these temporally discrete episodes of change in eastern North America clearly represent a rich abundance of opportunities to independently employ foraging theory to address and better understand the separate individual evolutionary steps that occurred as human groups of the region followed various lengthy transitional trajectories from hunting and gathering to the maize-beans-squash agricultural economies described by Europeans in the sixteenth and seventeenth centuries (see, for example, Gremillion 1996a, 1997a, 1998, 2002). The separate domestication of squash, marshelder, sunflower, and chenopod between 3000 and 1500 BC, for example, would each seem to qualify for separate foraging theory consideration, as would their increase in dietary importance by 200 BC, the introduction of maize at 100 BC, its subsequent rise to a pan-regional scale central economic role around AD 900–1000, and the late arrival in the East of Mexican crop plants through the Southwest, including the common bean (*Phaseolus vulgaris*) and hubbard squash (*Cucurbita argyrosperma*) (Fritz 1994b). Additional independent opportunities for the application of foraging theory are represented by the diffusion of both indigenous and introduced domesticates into new areas of the East up out of river valleys into tributary stream settings, as well as by consideration of the selection, status, and role of plants such as little barley (*Hordeum pusillum*), erect knotweed (*Polygonum erectum*), and maygrass (*Phalaris caroliniana*), which while not yet documented as morphological domesticates may well have been managed and had similar dietary importance as the four identified indigenous domesticates. Foraging theory might also provide a new comparative perspective for considering what local factors influence why various indigenous domesticates play roles of differing importance in different areas of the East, and why farming economies centered on maize developed several centuries later in some parts of the lower Mississippi Valley than in other areas of the East (Fritz and Kidder 1993).

Eastern North America is not unique in providing a long-temporal sequence of linked but distinct developmental dietary shifts to which foraging theory might be applied. In Mexico, for example, almost 4000 years elapsed between the domestication of the region's first major crop plant—squash (*C. Pepo* ssp. *pepo*) at 8000 BC and the subsequent appearance of the second—the transformation of the wild grass teosinte into the crop plant maize by about 4300 BC (Smith 2001a). Certainly the initial domestication of these two major crops, separated by 4000 years of time, must have occurred in different environmental, subsistence, diet breadth, and cultural contexts, and provide the opportunity for separate independent foraging

theory consideration (see, for example, Flannery 1986b; Reynolds 1986).

The Near East, of all of the world's independent centers of domestication, offers the greatest number and variety of distinct species-level opportunities to apply foraging theory in order to gain a better understanding of the process of domestication and the development of food production economies. Barley, rye, emmer and einkorn wheat, lentils, goat, sheep, cattle, and pig were all domesticated in different parts of the Fertile Crescent at different times, and each represents a distinct stand-alone opportunity for foraging theory analysis and well-situated consideration of the changing value and utilization of a rich variety of food energy sources. As is the case in eastern North America and Mexico, along with other world areas, the Fertile Crescent and neighboring regions also provide ample opportunities for the application of foraging theory analysis to the subsequent diffusion and differential selective adoption of domesticates in a wide range of environmental and cultural landscapes, resulting in the development of regionally distinct crop and livestock complexes and agricultural economies (see McCorriston, this volume).

If the archaeological record is capable of providing the data resolution required, these approaches would appear to hold the promise of having broad world-wide applicability in providing new ways of approaching and better understanding each of the distinct sequential small-scale contexts of change in resource utilization and subsistence strategies, which when taken together over time, combine to trace the slow and regionally quite variable development of food production economies. However, as is the case with any proposed approach to understanding complex past trajectories of human cultural evolution, foraging theory also faces a range of potential pitfalls, including those having to do with placing too much faith in the value of general principles and universal laws in predicting and explaining patterns of past human behavior.

EPISTEMOLOGY

Anyone exposed to the extended epistemological discussions that took place among archaeologists and philosophers of science in the 1970s, can appreciate the importance of understanding the underlying epistemological foundation of human behavioral ecology and foraging theory and how these approaches can and cannot be applied in archaeological contexts. The danger would lie in mistakenly assuming that foraging theory and behavioral ecology take any sort of strongly deductive or covering law explanatory form. The potential for mistaking human behavioral ecology as essentially positivist and deductive in logical structure is partially due to the occasional (mis)use by foraging theorists of terms such as "covering arguments," "hypothetico-deductive," "deductive," and "deduce," which in formal logical contexts clearly indicate covering-law forms of inference; e.g. "HBE is an anomaly within sociocultural anthropology due to its hypothetico-deductive research strategy (Winterhalder and Smith 2000, 52; Optimal foraging theory can be classed with "analyses that begin with selection and that attempt to deduce its consequences for behavior in specified environmental circumstances" (Winterhalder and Goland 1997, 125).[1]

The possibility that foraging theory might be considered as qualifying for general covering law status, however, is not immediately evident, given that foraging models are "internalist" in that the causal focus is on humans making individual decisions: foraging theory is scaled at the level of individual or small-group intra-generational decision making regarding changes in resource selection. In addition, the particular details of resource access, the situational specifics that provide the proximate context for such decisions, are recognized as central to understanding and explaining the choices that are made. Within this internalist, small-scale, intragenerational context of decision making, shaped and structured by the particular immediate composition of available resources, however, individual human choice mistakenly might be assumed to be dictated by overarching rules—as being derived from higher level biological principles of selection. In terms of the logical structure of foraging theory, then, particular individual events or decisions regarding resource selection might be "explained" in that they logically follow—can be deduced—from a general law-like or universal principle that universally holds. The temptation would be to believe that predictive power and covering law explanatory strength could be derived from such overarching general laws of selection. It would then be these general or covering law principles which would determine the specific decisions that would be made, once the proximate variables regarding the availability and costs of available resources were factored in.

Something "loosely akin" (Salmon 1967, 18) to this general hypothetico-deductive method of inference provides the essential epistemological core for much of the research carried out in the sciences. There is no question that within the realms of physics, chemistry, biochemistry, etc., faith in, and employment of, overarching principles of varying reach are justified. But is such an epistemology appropriate for consideration of more complex biological and cultural behavior sets? Are there general laws or principles from which human decisions in any particular situation can be derived or predicted? By the mid-1970s archaeologists and philosophers of science had agreed that covering law models and hypothetico-deductive methods of confirmation were not appropriate for archaeological inference (Salmon 1975, 1976; W. Salmon 1967, 1973; Smith 1977, 1978; Wylie 1992).

Importantly, Winterhalder (2002a) clearly defines both the logical structure of foraging theory and the constraints inherent in archaeological inference in his discussion of a four-fold (Cells A-D) division of models according to their appropriateness of application in different scientific disciplines, based on the quality and quantity of data available (y-axis) and the degree of understanding in conceptual or theoretical terms (x-axis) that exists in different subject areas. Cells B and C, which contain many of the different kinds of models that can be employed in studies of human behavior or the historical and evolutionary sciences, differ from each other in significant respects. Cells B and C in Winterhalder's presentation are both constrained by limited data. Conceptual or theoretical understanding, however, is greater in Cell C than in Cell B, resulting in distinct differences between the two cells in terms of how models can be used, and how inference is constrained and structured. While certainly loosely drawn, this basic distinction between Cell B and Cell C—Cell C having a higher level of theoretical understanding—would seem to roughly correlate well with how confidently particular events can be predicted, derived, or deduced from overarching general principles; i.e. in Cell C they can, in Cell B they can't.

In concurrence with the consensus conclusion reached by interested philosophers of science, logisticians, and archaeologists a generation ago, Winterhalder places evolutionary archaeology squarely in Cell B, where it is appropriately paired with arguments by analogy ("analogic"—Winterhalder 2002a, 206) as the correct method of inference, and well outside the reach of Cell C deductive covering-law models. This does not mean that human behavioral ecology and foraging theory, even if they were proposed as qualifying for Cell C covering law hypothetico-deductive status, could not be employed in archaeological analysis and interpretation, only that they should be characterized and used under the same logical constraints as other Cell B models and explanatory frameworks.

The most obvious B Cell constraint or limitation to be imposed on foraging theory would of course be to sever any perceived explanatory or deductive, predictive link between an overarching principle of selection and the specific subsistence choice faced within a particular context of resource availability. Foraging theory, like other theoretical approaches and perspectives, are a rich source of situation-specific hypotheses regarding resource selection. Once formulated, however, such individual, situated hypotheses would derive no strength, no power, no advantage over other alternative hypotheses, from the

foraging theory from which they were generated. The only appropriate measure of the relative worth of alternative competing hypotheses, including those based on foraging theory, is how well they account for and are supported by currently available archaeological information, and the value and depth of plausibility considerations. Their status is achieved, not ascribed (Wylie 1992).

Winterhalder (2002a) also provides a description of the general "exploratory" and "evaluative" role of models in Cell B subject matter areas, and in so doing provides clear guidelines and reasonable expectations regarding the appropriate application of foraging theory to transformational questions documented in the archaeological record, including the process of domestication and agricultural emergence:

> With limited data and understanding (Cell B), models necessarily are speculative and provisional. The main activity is their evaluation. Here models help to define and isolate problems. They facilitate preliminary analyses. Evolutionary Archaeology and some life history and behavioral ecology models sit here. As theoretical understanding increases Cell C models can be used in an interpretive or inferential fashion. (Winterhalder 2002a, 208).

> The evaluative [Cell B] mode is focused on testing the model against observations. Evaluative statements commonly take the form: *If the assumptions of the model accurately reflect the referent situation, then* we expect the following observations. Here [Cell B] models provide provisional hypotheses and the analytical work lies in testing those hypotheses . . . The model is made subordinate to the empirical evidence (Winterhalder 2002a, 209). [bracket text added]

The phrase—"the model is made subordinate to the empirical evidence"—reiterates the key point that in Cell B subject matter situations (which encompasses evolutionary archaeology and domestication), any hypotheses regarding resource choice which are generated from foraging theory expectations and principles carry no predictive or explanatory weight with them. Whatever value they may have relative to other alternative hypotheses can only be measured in how well they account for the available relevant data. As Winterhalder points out (2002a), the seductive danger for anyone working in Evaluative Cell B situations with models characterized as also having Interpretive C Cell capacities is deluding oneself into the false belief that in fact one is working in Cell C Interpretive mode, where covering laws hold and specific hypotheses derive predictive weight and explanatory power from their mother ship covering laws:

> An analyst willing to pursue evaluation is seldom so disinterested as to eschew completely extrapolating to interpretive uses . . . as a consequence it can be difficult to discern the relative balance of evaluation and interpretation in a particular application. Judgements are further complicated if authors are not explicit. It is tempting for the advocates of a model to slip unintentionally from evaluative to interpretive modes with few discernable signals that they have done so. (Winterhalder 2002a, 209).

Winterhalder goes on to describe the evaluative mode as grading into the Cell C interpretive mode, and indicates that it is possible to offer "a *plausible* covering argument that the model applies to a situation" (2002a, 209), and this argument of plausibility "rather than by direct test" enables one to explain and interpret observations, and to further extend or generalize from them (Winterhalder 2002a, 209):

> [Cell C] statements take the form: because of its theoretical generality for social foragers, the producer-scrounger game likely characterized hominid hunter-gatherers, with the consequences x, y, and z for subsistence and social behavior. Interpretive use implies a model that is only weakly validated in either the theoretical or the empirical sense in that situation [Bracket text added.]

How does one decide if a model has a high enough plausibility rating to qualify for Cell C interpretive mode applications? Winterhalder (2002a, 209) suggests that "willingness to engage in the interpretive use of a model depends on" three criteria:

a. general confidence that the model captures the relationship it claims to represent; that is on prior testing in related contexts;

b. on the covering argument for suitability in this context;

c. on inability to make a more direct evaluative use of the model in this context [e.g. in the historical sciences such as archaeology] (Winterhalder 2002a, 209).

Given the use of modifiers such as *"plausible covering arguments"* and *" its theoretical generality . . . likely characterized"* (italics added), Winterhalder clearly is not suggesting these three criteria provide a justification on logical grounds for the elevation of any theory or model to "covering law" or "hypothetico-deductive" status, where a previously demonstrated universal application of the overarching principle substitutes for, and reduces the value of, any actual empirical evidence or testing.

Interestingly, the three criteria listed above closely conform to what takes place during *plausibility consideration* of hypotheses—an initial step in various supplemented hypothetico-deductive methods of inductive confirmation which are generally considered appropriate for archaeological inference (Salmon 1976; W. Salmon 1967, 1973; Smith 1977, 1978). When considered within the context of such methods of inductive confirmation, the logical outlines and limitations for useful application of foraging theory in archaeology can be outlined:

1. Covering Law and Hypothetico-deductive frameworks of inference are not appropriate for foraging theory, which can only reasonably be employed within an inductive format of confirmation;

2. Foraging theory potentially can be a rich and valuable source of situated small-scale hypotheses regarding domestication and other resource-selection decisions along the food production developmental trajectory;

3. Specific hypotheses generated on the basis of foraging theory principles or expectations

derive no predictive power or explanatory status from their source;

4. Once formulated, hypotheses are subjected to plausibility considerations—their prior probability is taken into account as an initial screening of their plausibility: "such plausibility considerations are logically separate from and prior to the actual testing of a hypothesis" (Smith 1977, 605). A number of authors have addressed the need for explicit and careful *attribute class* and *reference class* selection during plausibility consideration (Ascher 1961; Salmon 1967, 90–91; Salmon 1975, 461; Smith 1977);

5. Plausibility considerations in archaeological reasoning invariably take the form of argument by analogy, which calls for an explicit and detailed determination of the prior probability of all alternative proposed hypotheses on the basis of seven non-quantitative criteria (see Copi 1972, 358–362; Salmon 1975; Smith 1977):

   1. The number of situations shown to share the attributes in question.

   2. The dissimilarity of the situations shown to share the attributes. This is what M. Salmon is referring to when she discusses employing ethnographic cases from dissimilar subgroups of the reference class (1975, 461).

   3. The number of shared attributes.

   4. The number of inferred attributes.

   5. The significance of the shared attributes.

   6. The specificity of inferred attributes . . . .

   7. The number of points of difference between situations.

   (Smith 1977, 608)

The prior probability rating of a foraging theory generated hypothesis would thus be considered within the framework of argument by analogy and would involve explicit

presentation and assessment of well documented particular past situations of a similar kind (see Winterhalder's criteria 1 and 2 above) where empirical evidence supported the hypothesis;

6. Plausibility consideration in archaeological reasoning is followed by the formulation of a set of alternative hypotheses of non-negligible prior probability (multiple working hypotheses; Chamberlain 1965), each having a set of observational predictions. Hypotheses generated from foraging theory should not, then, be viewed in isolation, as the only potential solutions under consideration.

7. The relative strength of alternative competing hypotheses would then be established through empirical testing. This would involve developing sets of test implications or observational predictions for each, along with bridging arguments and, when needed, auxiliary hypotheses. Determining which hypothesis is best supported by the available archaeological evidence would then be based on the significance, number, and variety of observational predictions shown to be empirically true and false.

When considered within this larger context of the general consensus logical structure of archaeological inference, the central epistemological challenge facing foraging theory comes into clear focus. Given the inherent complexity and limited strength of archaeological arguments, researchers interested in employing foraging theory, as Winterhalder (2002a) points out, will constantly be confronted by the seductive lure of simply accepting, a priori, the universal applicability of foraging theory principles, rules, theorems, etc., and applying them in an interpretive, explanatory mode in specific transition to food production case study situations in lieu of any requirement for empirical data-based testing and confirmation. This dilemma facing foraging theory applications in terms of universal applicability versus a reliance on empirical testing and confirmation is well illustrated in the ongoing discussions regarding the economic role of acorns during the Natufian lead-up to initial plant domestication in the Near East (Barlow and Heck 2002). Based on the general expectations of foraging theory, acorns should have been a significant component in Natufian diets, given their energetic benefits and costs. But representation of acorns in Natufian archaeobotanical assemblages falls far short of foraging theory predictions. On one side, scholars adhering to a perspective of strict empirical observation might argue that given their relative absence in the archaeological record, acorns played at most a minor role in Natufian economies. Scholars strongly convinced of the predictive power of foraging theory could argue that the general model is more likely to reflect past reality than what is present in the archaeological record, and that acorns must therefore have been an important food source, irrespective of archaeological evidence to the contrary. The important contribution that foraging theory can make in such situations, and its appropriate epistemological application, is to show that theory and available data are at odds, while opening potentially rewarding new avenues of inquiry leading to a better understanding of the procurement, processing, and dietary significance of acorns in Natufian economies and possible reasons for their absence either from Natufian settlements or from Natufian diets.

THEORY

At least four aspects of foraging theory appear to open up interesting avenues of discussion regarding its application in archaeology and to questions of domestication and the transition to food production and agricultural economies. In terms of logical form, all four of these areas of discussion have to do with whether specific hypotheses generated from foraging theory will have non-negligible prior probability. That is, are the foraging theory reference classes composed of case study examples of previous empirically confirmed successful application of foraging theory sufficiently similar to qualify as being

appropriate and relevant to the diet choice decisions under consideration (see the seven criteria for establishing prior probability, listed above, as well as Winterhalder's criteria 1 and 2)?

The first of these questions regarding prior probability measures for foraging theory relates to the strength of the claim that foraging optimization and efficiency of caloric intake provides an acceptable correlate or proxy variable for reproductive fitness, success in contributing to the gene pool of the next generation, which in turn is a central mechanism in modern evolutionary theory. Is optimization in diet choice closely correlated to, and as strongly selected for, as reproductive fitness? Bamforth (2002) provides a lengthy critique of this central tenet of foraging theory, arguing that there is little if any support for the existence of a correlation between optimizing foraging behavior and reproductive fitness, even in those case study situations most often cited as providing justification for considering foraging theory as strongly linked to a central mechanism of natural selection:

> The link in the Aché data between foraging and reproductive success violates the assumption that explicitly underlies general optimization thought in anthropology, that is, that natural selection should prefer foragers who optimize, with optimization generally conceived as maximizing the efficiency of resource acquisition. . . . Reproductively successful hunters among the Aché do not appear to optimize. (Bamforth 2002, 439)

The ongoing debate regarding the fitness proxy status of foraging optimization is relevant to the current discussion in that it underscores the necessity of compiling appropriate reference classes in order to ascertain the prior probability of foraging-theory-derived hypotheses. Optimization behavior in subsistence related activities cannot be automatically assumed to confer selective advantage to individuals. As a result, if a hypothesis involving optimization behavior is to be considered as having non-negligible prior probability, it will not be because of the strength of the link between optimization behavior and natural selection, but rather will be based on the quality, quantity, and diversity of previously documented empirical case studies included in reference classes and subclasses.

A second prior probability question has to do with how to go about establishing appropriate reference classes for considering foraging-theory-derived hypotheses regarding the initial domestication of plants and animals. Foraging theory analysis of human societies began with the expansion of biological models and approaches beyond non-human application and into the realm of consideration of hunter-gatherer economies and decision making. An important assumption for this expansion of consideration would appear to be that human hunter-gatherers still operate largely as components under the constraints of ecological systems. They are subject to the same set of rules and selective pressures as other species components of biotic communities. But domestication of plants and animal, and the long sequence of diet choice decisions leading to food production and agriculture marks the escape of human populations from these "natural" rules. Humans along with their domesticates come under an entirely new set of selective pressures than those which hold sway over hunter-gatherers. Rather than just being another component within ecosystems, humans become the driving force in reshaping ecosystems and creating entirely new landscapes. Given that the transition to food production marks a major transformation in human history and a dramatic shift in the role of humans in controlling and shaping their environments, it would seem appropriate to establish separate reference classes involving animal studies, human hunter-gatherer studies, and those involving low-level food production societies. Comparison of these different reference classes in terms of the strength of empirical evidence of the role of optimization in subsistence activities could then provide a good way of assessing the prior probability of foraging-theory-derived hypotheses. Strong empirical support for foraging theory expectations across all reference classes would substantially strengthen the prior probability of a foraging theory hypothesis.

In contrast, if foraging theory expectations were documented in non-human and human hunter-gatherer reference classes, but not in low-level food production societies, prior probability could be seriously questioned. Related to this requirement for establishing clearly defined reference classes for consideration of hypotheses derived from foraging theory is the more basic question of actually identifying and documenting in a systematic way all of the empirical case studies of whatever kind that can be included in the various reference classes to be employed. Application of foraging theory to archaeological settings worldwide will, of necessity, involve assembling various reference classes according to a number of different environmental and cultural criteria (Smith 1977, 1978).

A third avenue of discussion regarding the applicability of foraging theory to contexts of domestication and the transition to food production involves the central explanatory role assigned to the concept of "initial contact" as employed in foraging theory. Winterhalder and Goland (1997) argue that the critical first step leading to domestication occurs when resource selection decisions "bring foragers into contact with potential domesticates" (p. 123). Initial contact is critical, then, and foraging models allow analysis of "the processes that brought human beings into regular contact with species that through coevolution became domesticates" (p. 128). In advance of this initial contact, the "transitional domesticate (TD) species in question . . . has a pursuit and handling efficiency that is somewhat too low to make it an element in the optimal diet" (p. 132). When the value of some higher-ranking resources slips, however, for any variety of reasons, then . . ." resource TD enters the diet and becomes subject to coevolutionary pressures such as described by Rindos (1984)" (p. 132). The explanatory focus, then, appears to be shifted away from domestication itself, to gaining a better understanding of the precursor resource selection decisions which "bring foragers into contact with potential domesticates" (PDs) and how these newly encountered PDs or TDs "enter the optimal diet, initiating the process of domestication under coevolutionary pressures" (Winterhalder and Goland 1997, 147).

There are several related difficulties in theory that cluster around this shift in explanatory focus away from the process of domestication itself to the earlier precursor "first" or "regular" contact with potential domesticates as they are first added to the diet. These difficulties call into question the existence of any causal link, other than that of distant prerequisite, between when and under what circumstances a potential human food source is initially added to the diet, and its subsequent transformation into a domesticate. Many of the plant and animal species brought under domestication in different world regions at different times by different human societies, for example, were significant wild food sources for a thousand years or more before they were domesticated. Given the substantial temporal separation between the "first contact" with, and subsequent domestication of, so many target species by human groups, it is hard to assign any explanatory value regarding domestication to a better understanding of decision making associated with initial dietary appearance. Any causal link between a species being initially selected as a food source and then subsequently transformed into a domesticate is further cast into doubt by the very high percentage of plants and animals that were economically important over long time spans and yet were never domesticated. Thus any modeling or analysis of resource selection and the initial entry of a food source into the diet of a human society would not seem likely to contribute to any better understanding of subsequent contexts of domestication.

A fourth theoretical issue, which again relates to the question of the need to establish non-negligible prior probability, and to the relevancy and appropriateness of reference classes, has to do with several of the encounter-contingent features or characteristics specific to the diet breadth or resource selection model, suggesting that, as a number of researchers have noted (e.g. Gremillion 2002), it is not well suited for application to many situations involving human foragers. Under the diet breadth model all decisions

regarding resource utilization are encounter-contingent and situated in the moment, without any premeditation, planning, or prior resource-specific objectives in mind. Each individual forager, whether human or non-human, moves through a landscape of resource opportunities according to a simple set of strict behavioral parameters: advancing at a measured rate of about two to three paces (5–10 meters) per minute, scanning across a 35-meter-wide targeting zone, and searching for all resources simultaneously: "upon encounter with a potential dietary item he or she must make a contingent assessment: pursue the present resource or continue searching in hopes of locating a more attractive one to pursue" (Winterhalder and Goland 1997, 128–129). Obviously, the standard diet breadth model is not the most appropriate of the various alternative foraging theory approaches available for modeling foraging and resource management behavior patterns of relatively sedentary human societies that are transitioning to food production economies in landscapes where many of their food resources, including potential or transitional domesticates, are patchy in distribution, seasonally available, well mapped, periodically monitored, and managed to varying degrees.

METHOD

Efforts to apply foraging theory to any of the long sequence of questions having to do with domestication and the transition to food production and agriculture in different regions of the world will face a set of related methodological challenges, all having to do with the degree of accuracy and level of confidence with which the energy cost and benefit values of individual resources can be quantified. Generating the numbers necessary for foraging theory analysis in an archaeological context of domestication is no easy task. Minimally it would require accurate *quantification* of both modern reference class and archaeologically recovered data of the following kinds: (1) size and density or abundance estimates for different food resource species in the past environment, including potential domesticates; (2) the human energy investment costs in acquisition and processing these resources; and (3) information from the archaeological record regarding the energy both obtained from targeted resources and expended by human consumers during a series of intra-generational time spans that bracketed the transition of interest, based on comparable, high resolution, representative, and short time frame data sets.

The first two categories of energy value estimates—resource abundance and acquisition costs—are arrived at through argument by analogy. In the case of environmental reconstruction and species density estimates, modern biological census data is sought for environmental settings similar to that which existed in the ancient study area. A range of complications often arise in projecting such modern biotic community data onto ancient landscapes. There are invariably reference class difficulties in accurately matching past landscapes with modern analogs, particularly when past study area catchment zones encompass a range of habitat types; e.g. main channel, backswamps, oxbow lakes, natural levees, uplands, tributary streams, etc. Population density values for various resource species are often of necessity drawn from a variety of different modern studies. In addition, past and present density values for a range of species can vary dramatically through multi-year cycles. Intervening changes in the species composition of biotic communities, particularly loss of predators and the introduction of invasive exotics, can also easily complicate attempts to accurately impose modern biomass estimates on past landscapes. While it is certainly possible to roughly estimate, in terms of range values, the abundance of different food resource components of ancient biotic communities, it will often be questionable whether such density value projections can meet the required confidence standard of quantifiable accuracy necessary for acceptable foraging theory analysis. It is important to keep in mind in this regard that numerical biomass density estimates presented for a species or resource component of any ancient ecosystem will reflect a series of imbedded assumptions

and modern analog data selections which can vary dramatically in source and quality.

Turning to another column of figures in foraging theory analyses of archaeological situations, estimates or projections of acquisition and handling/processing costs associated with past human utilization of various resources are even more difficult to establish with any reasonable degree of accuracy. Resource yield and acquisition costs obviously will have varied dramatically in many past environments during different seasons of the year, and human groups, using available technology, can be expected to have tailored their annual cycle to take full advantage of various seasonal "sale" opportunities, when resources predictably occur in localized, high density, low cost situations, such as the easy harvesting of fish trapped in the shallow shrinking backswamp pools of late spring in eastern North American River Valleys. The challenge comes in trying to gain a detailed enough understanding of the sophisticated and nuanced seasonal patterns of resource utilization employed by past human societies so that the full range of acquisition and handling costs can be specified with the degree of accuracy required for successful foraging theory analysis. In some areas, such as the Great Basin of the western United States, ethnographic descriptions of available technology, subsistence strategies, and seasonal patterns of resource utilization are quite detailed, providing a relatively good reference class for argument by analogy projections of general estimate resource acquisition costs for past human societies of the region. In many other regions of the world, however, ethnographic reference class information is either completely lacking or poorly documented, making resource cost estimation much more problematic. Given that the acquisition cost for a resource can vary dramatically depending upon season of the year; age, sex, and experience level of the human pursuer; and the nature of the available acquisition technology, it is important to not invariably rely upon a single standard cost estimate for a resource, irrespective of the particular situated context of individual resource selection events.

Another quite interesting and difficult to quantify variable involving resource yield and acquisition cost estimates that should be considered in any lead-up to domestication and transition to food production situations is the manner and the extent to which human resource management and intervention in the life cycle of targeted PDs and TDs may have substantially changed both energy input and output values. Many past landscapes were substantially modified by humans interested in improving the reliability and expected yield of resources. These management strategies (Harris 1996a) would have comprised difficult to recognize and quantify "indirect" labor and energy investments in resources, and would have resulted in increases in potential energy yield and foraging theory resource rank. Such management investment in targeted PDs and TDs represents a significant underconsidered complication and challenge for foraging analyses of the transition to food production in prehistory.

A final methodological complication for foraging theory applications involves the difficulties inherent in quantifying with the necessary degree of accuracy the dietary contribution of the full range of a past human society's plant and animal food sources, based on their representation in archaeobiological assemblages. While the analysis of plant and animal remains from archaeological contexts can provide a wealth of information regarding the relative dietary contribution of different plants and animals, when appropriately considered, there are a range of potential problems inherent in efforts at detailed full assemblage quantification and analysis. Perhaps the most obvious difficulty would come in even the most straightforward attempt to combine plant and animal assemblages into a single integrated rank order list of food resources based on their numerical value caloric contribution to the society being studied. Such simple merging of plant and animal assemblages in an effort to accurately quantify their importance in the diet of past societies has so far proven extremely difficult if not impossible, due to the absence of any good shared analytic standard of reference between plant and animal remains.

DISCUSSION

Human behavioral ecology and foraging theory hold considerable potential for providing new perspectives and opening new approaches on plant and animal domestication and the transition to food production worldwide. Their successful application in illuminating these complex developmental transitions, however, will be shaped, constrained, and focused by the array of epistemological, theoretical, and methodological issues, some of which are briefly considered above. Rather than constituting an argument in opposition to the use of foraging theory in studying the transition to food production, the various questions raised here are meant to provide general parameters or guidelines regarding how foraging theory can best be employed in studying these evolutionary processes. Limitations in archaeological data sets and the structure of archaeological inference impose clear constraints on the use of foraging theory and other behavioral ecology models. While human behavioral ecology and foraging theory can provide a wealth of new perspectives, approaches, questions, and hypotheses regarding domestication and the transition to food production, they should not be considered as imparting any explanatory authority or interpretive strength to these predictions or proposed explanations. The interpretive value of hypotheses generated from foraging theory can only be determined through empirical testing, assessment of prior probability, and consideration of observational predictions, relative to alternative competing hypotheses. At the same time, recognition of the limited availability and restricted relevance of many of the potential reference classes, as well as the difficulties inherent in accurately quantifying past resource abundance, acquisition cost, and human utilization values, renders problematic any attempts to fully and confidently employ behavioral ecology and foraging theory analysis in an explanatory, evaluative mode in archaeological situations.

These limitations, however, do not constrain the very valuable role that foraging theory can play in opening up new avenues of inquiry regarding the emergence of food production economies—as an inspiration and source for the creation of novel and provocative perspectives and hypotheses, and raising previously un-recognized questions and interpretive possibilities (Gremillion 1998, 149; 2002).

NOTE

1. Keep in mind that by definition, a deductive type of argument—in which a consequence is *deduced*—is one in which the conclusion *must* logically follow from the premises (Salmon 1963, 14; Salmon 1976, 377; Smith 1977, 78).

14

Agriculture, Archaeology, and Human Behavioral Ecology

Robert L. Bettinger

THIS VOLUME MARKS a turning point in the development of human behavioral ecology (HBE), whose past efforts have spoken to a research agenda largely crafted in the biological sciences by individuals interested in non-human species. The thrust of most HBE contributions has been to show that humans play by the same rules as other species, or at least to illuminate certain aspects of human behavior with reference to the behavior of other species. As a consequence, the HBE research agenda has historically targeted behaviors that theorists working with non-human species think are important (e.g., foraging behavior, habitat choice, etc.; Pyke, et al. 1977; Schoener 1971; Stephens and Kreb 1986). These behaviors are not necessarily spectacular, nor do they capture the imagination of the public, but they are important notwithstanding because theory implies they should be strongly determined by evolutionary processes whose basic principles are relatively well understood and give rise to robust and plausible models against which these behaviors can be compared (Kuhn 1962, 25). These behaviors are important because of their connection to theory.

The importance that anthropologists assign to agriculture, by contrast, does not hinge only—or even mainly—on its connection with theory. Theory and models are important in anthropology, but much of anthropology is not theory-driven. Anthropology has always had to confront an historical record that is dotted with important human achievements, and anthropologists have always been more or less aware that one of their jobs is to make sense of history in relation to these landmarks—certainly this is what the public expects them to do. Ideas vary about which landmarks are important, but the origin of agriculture certainly ranks near the top, along with things like the inventions of fire, language, stone tools, writing, and, less certainly, state-level societies. Anthropology is required to deal with developments like the origin of agriculture because their historical importance is self-evident. They are important *whether or not there are theories to explain them.* An issue to consider, then, in thinking about the connection between the theories of behavioral ecology and the origin of agriculture, is that the match might not be particularly revealing, the theories of behavioral ecology having been designed with other things in mind. The task of matching the two is made considerably more difficult by the special importance that anthropology attaches to landmarks like the origin of agriculture.

It is not a coincidence that these landmarks distinguish humans from other species; that is their point. In the minds of many anthropologists, they make humans a special case, and thus help distinguish anthropology as a separate discipline. The issue here is not whether humans are animals, subject to the basic theories of biology. Every anthropologist with an ounce of gumption accepts the biological basis of human life. The biology that makes humans like other animals, however, provides no special place for anthropology. The part left over— the "non-biological" component—provides that place. For many anthropologists, the size of this "non-biological" component, assuming it could be measured, does not matter. For them, anthropology and biology are separate because they address phenomena that are qualitatively, not quantitatively, different. Their claim is more than that the human case is "unique." The furry egg-laying platypus is unique, as indeed are all species, by definition, but only in the mundane, quantitative sense; this is nowhere seen to warrant a wholly separate discipline of "platypusology." For these individuals, the warrant for anthropology is that landmark achievements like agriculture are special enough to put humans in one category and all other living things in another.

In a way, then, exploring the connection between behavioral ecology and the origin of agriculture is really asking whether agriculture is a landmark human achievement, or whether, as with tool-using, its presence merely reaffirms the basic connection between humans and the rest of the biological world (cf. Rindos 1984). This is certainly what has made so problematic the early Holocene irrigation systems of New Guinea discussed by Denham and Barton in this volume (see also Golson 1977a). Antiquity itself is not the issue; Near Eastern agriculture is as old or older. The problem is that Near

Eastern agriculture laid the way for civilization and the state, and irrigation in New Guinea didn't—it wasn't a landmark in the same high-profile manner. Plainly, if this instance of irrigation was agriculture then agriculture per se was not a landmark. This might seem a small prejudice, easily overcome by trained anthropologists, but it is not. Specialists interested in aboriginal agriculture and its origins, for example, have long been aware that some Great Basin groups, e.g., in Owens Valley, diverted water to increase root and seed production (Steward 1930); very few of them know—or even care— that many more Great Basin groups diverted water to drive rodents from their burrows (Steward 1941). The behaviors are materially the same, but the connection with agriculture, and the connection of agriculture to higher levels of human achievement (e.g., state-level societies), makes crop watering important and rodent drowning not.

This is the kind of issue that makes the application of human behavioral ecology to the origin of agriculture so challenging. It is as much a matter of deciding whether there are connections as it is a matter of detailing those connections. These complexities are fully revealed in the remarkable range of ideas and hypotheses displayed in the contributions to this volume. One is particularly struck by the sophistication demonstrated in presenting data and theory, matching one to the other, and deciding what to do when one says the other is wrong. In biology, where experiments are possible, the best investigators are those clever enough to manipulate experimental conditions to produce a desired match between theory and data. Every archaeological excavation is in some sense an experiment, but archaeological data cannot be pushed around like lab rats. The archaeological record is what it is; at some level it speaks for itself—whether or not it matches theory. Unfortunately, this has not always prevented theoretical zealots from forcing their data into imagined matches with theory.

Critics of HBE have hinted that its proponents are prone to such imagination. Indeed,

Bamforth (2002) suggests an analogy between archaeological applications of HBE and the fanciful uses of general systems theory that were momentarily popular in archaeology in the 1960s and 1970s. I am an admirer of Bamforth and his work, but here he is wide of the mark. Let's be very sure about one point anyway: HBE theory and general systems theory are classes apart. The problem with general systems theory had nothing to do with how it was applied by archaeologists; the problem was the theory itself, a few good ideas but mostly smoke and parlor tricks (Salmon 1978, 177–178). Relative to that, the theory that underwrites HBE is a paragon of clarity, parsimony, and logic. Take foraging theory. It is grounded in neo-economic constructs and relationships with ancestries that go back to Adam Smith (1776) and Carl Menger (1951), and on principles that guide the business practices of countless commercial operations, from corner grocery stores to multi-million-dollar destination casinos. It is possible to question the relevance of foraging theory to a particular archaeological problem. Given the maturity of the theory and concepts in economics, biology, and anthropology, it is seldom possible to question that the models do what they say they do, or to suggest that their meaning is unclear. Systems theory was attractive because it was ambiguous; foraging theory is attractive because it is not. In the final analysis, this seems to be the real fear of critics: that the power of the theory that informs HBE increases the archaeological temptation to stretch the data to fit expectations—to see things that are not there.

There is nothing sinister in the HBE view of foraging, however. It arises from the more general belief that behavior is shaped by evolutionary processes. Foraging is thought to be particularly revealing because, among all the things that humans do, food-getting seems like the sort of thing that ought to be especially subject to selective forces that would reward rational action. Bamforth (2002, 438) doubts that archaeologists can actually test this proposition, however, because the relationship between foraging and fitness is indirect. In his view, since optimal foraging does not guarantee fitness, observing that foraging is optimal in a specific case says nothing about evolutionary processes acting on the connection between foraging and fitness; he converts a possibility, fitness may not be involved, into a negative absolute, no connection can be shown. Yet what matters here is not individual cases, but the larger body of evidence that emerges as when we test the implications of the foraging-fitness hypothesis against the archaeological record. If it repeatedly turns out to be wrong—if foraging behavior routinely is opaque to prediction on the fitness premise—then we'd obviously have to find some other way to explain foraging. But Bamforth seems to be saying something else, that even if foraging repeatedly turns out to be economically rational, the connection between it and fitness will remain problematic—presumably because rational foraging could be the result of something else. This reminds me of a fundamentalist minister who believed the world had been created in seven days, and knowing that I didn't, suggested that God had created things like fossils with the "appearance of age" as a test of faith—to sort out believers and non-believers. Perhaps this is what Bamforth has in mind—the gods have made humans merely to appear to be economically rational—just to mess with our heads.

Bamforth, however, may only be saying that the HBE view of foraging is simple common sense (Bamforth 2002, 438–439)—no different than that of, say, economists, who likewise assume that humans behave as though they were economically rational. "There is a close parallel between the development of theories in economics and population biology," as MacArthur and Pianka (1966, 603) observe. The difference lies in what rationality is thought to index. For the economist, rationality indexes utility in the abstract; economists do not stipulate the nature of utility from theory; they infer this empirically by observing "revealed" preferences. In HBE, by contrast, utility is specified with reference to evolutionary theory that gives priority to currencies closely related to fitness, food being one of these, prestige being another. If you told an economist to measure utility in calories and to see the world in terms of resource populations rather than markets, that economist would solve the diet breadth problem no differently than a human behavioral ecologist, but no economist would argue that utility ought to be measured that way. More fundamentally, economists are not at all concerned with why humans are economically rational, only with the implications that follow from that assumption. Rational behavior, of course, produces economic success, but economic success has no meaning except with reference to the standards of economic rationality; this is the crux of the formalist-substantivist debate in economic anthropology, in which the formalists took the economist's point of view (Dalton 1971, 6–7; Davis 1973, 1–29). For the economist it matters little why humans are economically rational—work of the gods, perhaps. HBE, by contrast, situates rationality in a larger theoretical context through a most plausible insight: economy in foraging contributes to fitness by making people or their babies healthier, by freeing up time to do other things to the same effect, or by reducing exposure to hazards.[1]

Among the contributors to this volume, Smith seems the most troubled by the archaeological use of HBE, particularly the possibility that foraging theory might not be the best tool for documenting and explaining the transition from foraging to farming. His concerns seem to center on two related issues. One has to do with the emphasis on individuals in foraging theory (methodological individualism; Bettinger 1991b, 152–153), the other with the overall quality of the archaeological record and our ability to test HBE models effectively.

INDIVIDUALS AND GROUPS

Optimal foraging theory (OFT) centers on the behavior of individuals under conditions given at a specific place and time. The archaeological record, on the other hand, commingles the behavior of many individuals over varying, but often long, periods of time. The scalar mismatch between the model predictions and data is obvious; whether it makes any difference is not. Smith (this volume) follows Thomas (1986) in thinking that it does. Whether commingling *per se* is a problem is a purely empirical question, depending on the amount of variation between individuals and conditions through time and across space. If all individuals were exactly the same and conditions never changed, commingling obviously would not matter. Neither would it matter much if individuals and conditions varied in a relatively stable way around some mean. It *might* matter, if conditions and individuals varied in a way that would make the mean a misleading measure of actual behavior— for example, if variation were distinctly bimodal: e.g., hunters clearly dividing into two groups, good and bad; or—more problematic and a major issue within HBE—male and female. It is clearly possible for individuals to vary by eyesight, strength, agility, and tools at hand in ways that would cause them to rank resources or adjust diet breadth differently, just as it is possible for technological or environmental change to reshuffle ranking and breadth over extended periods of time. It remains true, however, that unless one can specify how the many faceless individuals in the archaeological record differed, or how technology or climate changed over time, there are few ways of knowing whether any damage is done by ignoring these things. Do we know that prehistoric foragers must have differed in ability? Yes. Do we know that environmental conditions often varied over short intervals, even seasonally, in the past? Yes. Everyone who does archaeology knows these things, and that is not the question. The real question is, "Do we know enough about either to warrant rejecting the diet breadth model because it ignores them?" Generally not, but when we do, it often makes more sense to modify the model than to discard it—by dividing the record into periods in a way that controls for differences in climate and technology, for instance. In short, it is one thing to assert that people and circumstances differed in ways that affected decision making, and quite another to assert *a priori* that these differences led to decisions consistently at odds with, for instance, the diet breadth model. I am quite happy to grant that individual variation might lead to behavior that cannot be characterized by a mean; I am not prepared to grant that a case against the archaeological use of OFT is made merely by raising the possibility. In the absence of such evidence, or a theoretical reason for supposing otherwise, archaeological OFT makes a reasonable assumption: that the decisions made by many individuals over extended periods of time can be captured with reference to an average. Archaeologists do this all the time. I generalize in an analogous way, for example, when I employ projectile points as time-markers, as though they were all temporally equivalent, or as indicators of site function, as though they were all used in exactly the same way, propositions I know strictly to be untrue.[2]

CONTEXT OF RATIONAL ACTION

A more plausible objection to applying foraging theory to the commingled assemblages of archaeology has to do with the context of rational action. The diet breadth model, the foraging theory most commonly employed by archaeologists, is about the behavior of individuals in relation to the natural environment, yet for human foragers the social environment may well be more important. They live in groups of differing size and change their behavior accordingly. How much this matters depends on the nature of the social group, the interactions between its individuals, and the divergence in their interests. If foraging remains an individual affair, as frequently it does, the effect will be mainly one of competition: larger groups may decrease resource abundance enough to reward individuals who expand diet breadth. Here groups change the behavior of individuals, but not the context of that behavior.

In short, the presence of groups per se does not make diet breadth problematic. Indeed, pursuing the effect that groups have on individual subsistence behavior has long been an important area of HBE research (e.g. Bettinger and Baumhoff 1982. E.A. Smith 1985). Of direct relevance here, Winterhalder and Goland (1993) (see also Layton, et al. 1991) have argued from foraging theory that this group effect is critical to understanding the origins of agriculture; the Ideal Free Distribution model employed in several contributions to this volume deals with this as well. They suggest that population growth that depressed the abundance of high-ranked resources causing diet breadth to expand is likely connected with the initial use of many, generally low-ranked, plants that were eventually domesticated, setting the stage for agriculture (Flannery 1973). Smith (this volume) argues this is a classic case where HBE purports to answer a question that it actually begs. He allows that potential domesticates might have entered the diet with population growth but questions, on grounds of a temporal disconnect, whether that has much to do with the origin of agriculture. He points out that many domesticates entered human diets in wild form thousands of years before they were either intensively exploited or domesticated. Smith has a point here. Both population growth and the rational decision making that underwrites the diet breadth model should produce relatively rapid change, which does not seem to describe the prolonged interval of incidental, low-level food production that often precedes agricultural intensification. It is conceivable, however, that low-level food production is drawn out by the stable limit cycles (Belovsky 1988; Winterhalder, et al. 1988) that keep human and resource populations in constant motion as a consequence of their mutual interaction; human populations rise until resources become scarce, then fall as a result, allowing resources to rebound, in response to which populations then rise, and so on. In one plausible scenario, low-level food production appears when diet breadth expands during that part of the cycle in which human populations are large and resources scarce, and disappears with contracting diet breadth during the ensuing part of the cycle in which human populations are small and resources abundant, going full-round every century or so (Belovsky 1988, 351; Flannery 1973; Winterhalder and Goland 1993). Such intermittent, low-intensity selection on cultivars might well explain why full-blown agriculture took so long to develop.

Despite the anomalous time lag, the connection that Winterhalder and Goland (1997) make between the initial use and eventual domestication of important crops is surely cogent, but perhaps more akin to the stochastic connection between smoking and lung cancer. Smoking one cigarette will (probably) not produce cancer—even a lifetime usually does not; but surely the longer one smokes, the greater the chance. Fortunately, the tobacco company subterfuge that no precise connection between smoking and lung cancer has ever been shown, that most lifetime smokers never develop cancer, and so on, has been unsuccessful. The public is not misled: they know that smoking causes lung cancer. It seems similarly pointless to deny that there is a connection between the conditions that promote the use of potential domesticates and their eventual domestication. Foraging theory provides an elegant account of some of those conditions.

FORAGING THEORY AND COOPERATION

Granting all the above, applying foraging theory to archaeological assemblages is made much more complicated from a theoretical standpoint if those assemblages represent situations where individuals may benefit through cooperation by pooling costs and splitting profits (Winterhalder 1986). Cooperation is common among foragers, but awkward in the premise of self-interest on which OFT and HBE theory more generally rests. Economic self-interest only permits cooperation that produces, for individuals, greater benefits with less risk than doing something else—not cooperating. Cooperating, however, seldom nets as much as "cheating,"—contributing less than a full share of the costs while insisting on a full share of the benefits (Bettinger 1991b). Then, the temptation to cheat, and the fear that

others will cheat enough to reduce the split, may prevent cooperation altogether. This "prisoner's dilemma" is the crux of the tragedy of the commons (Hardin 1968), where cooperation in resource conservation is prevented because individuals find it too tempting to let others conserve while they continue to harvest. Self-interested individuals should only "cooperate" when their payoff is so large that losses to cheating do not matter. The payoffs of hunter-gatherer cooperation, however, likely fall short of that, especially in large-scale efforts (e.g., Waterman and Kroeber 1938), suggesting it is motivated by something other than economic self-interest (Boyd and Richerson 1988), which might lead to behaviors, hence archaeological assemblages potentially at odds with the predictions of foraging theory.

FORAGING THAT IS NOT FOOD GETTING

In the broader logic of HBE, of course, foraging is not an end but merely a means of increasing "fitness." Perhaps, then, cooperation in foraging is not about getting food but getting something else that adds to fitness. HBE itself provides one such possibility in the "costly signaling" hypothesis (Bliege Bird et al. 2001; Smith and Bliege Bird 2000), developed to account for the "show off" behavior commonly observed in foragers, as among the Aché for example (Hawkes 1991), where some hunters go to great lengths to contribute more than their fair share to the common pot. In the costly signaling hypothesis their subsistence effort is really a means of acquiring mating opportunities and allies; fitness is increased by economically suboptimal decisions promoted by a shift in the reference of decision making from subsistence to mating and partnerships. The implications for agriculture are obvious here. If foraging is not about food-getting, perhaps agriculture is not about producing food. Perhaps it is the costly signaling of aggrandizers interested in acquiring power, as Brian Hayden thinks (Hayden 1995a, b). If so, the costly signaling hypothesis suggests that early agricultural aggrandizers would likely cultivate species that (1) were highly desired, (2) were difficult to produce, and (3) came in packages large enough to be widely distributed. The hypothesis further implies—and this is quite important when thinking about the hypothesis in relation to the origin of agriculture—that too many costly signalers is not a viable solution—the behavior cannot be universal (Gintis, et al. 2001).

Even if somewhat affected by showing off, early agriculture would likely not be all that spectacular, and might well approximate the low-level food production envisioned by Smith (2001a)—at least if the Aché are any indication. For in the final analysis, Aché foraging is mainly about filling empty stomachs, which is why, despite the occasional show off, Aché foraging behavior as a whole maximizes rates of return in accordance with diet breadth (Hawkes, et al. 1982)—and would generate archaeological assemblages accordingly. By like reasoning, the settings of early agricultural experiments undoubtedly provided some margin for show-off aggrandizing but surely not enough to dominate subsistence behavior overall. In this case, while Piperno (Chapter 7) rightly questions Hayden's explanation of agriculture because it implies levels of status differentiation that are simply lacking at this time, the costly signaling variant, which implies such behavior in more limited scope (Gintis, et al. 2001, 104, 112, 116), remains a possibility. Perhaps showoff behavior can be more surely linked to the spread of agriculture as a coherent system than to its origin, as Piperno implies. Coltrain and Stafford (1999), for example, furnish evidence that consumption of corn was connected to status among the Fremont, suggesting that corn there might have been spread by those aspiring to control others, as Hayden thinks, or trying simply to acquire mates, as with costly signaling; the hypotheses closely overlap here.

TRUE COOPERATION

True forager cooperation, where cheating can but routinely does not occur, poses the greatest problem to the application of foraging theory to commingled archaeological assemblages. Foraging theory normally assumes that individuals engage in behaviors that are purely self-interested and that maximize their own foraging returns, hence utility. True cooperation requires individuals to accept less than that on the assumption that others will do the same, which requires an upward shift in the level of accounting, from the individual to the group. Individuals still make decisions, but their choices are now weighed in terms of the collective, or group, benefit. Where this is true, group selection is most likely responsible. Group selection, of course, is problematic in neo-Darwinian theory because it requires special conditions, thus more assumptions, than individual self-interest. It generally acts much more slowly and weakly than individual level selection (Soltis et al. 1995). That notwithstanding, group selection predicts resource rankings that are essentially identical to those of a standard diet breadth model (Schoener 1971). This is because in both cases the benefit of foraging that entails joint effort, e.g., game drives, is measured as a rate, by summing all costs and benefits as though they were equally split among the participating individuals, whether or not they are actually distributed that way.

The connection with agriculture is less obvious here, yet quite fundamental. As Bowles and Choi (n.d.) argue, investment in agriculture—and short of that, adaptive intensification of almost any kind—requires proprietary use of land and resources supported by some form of true cooperation. For example, I have argued along these same lines that hunter-gatherers are likely to intensify subsistence patterns only where group selection, or something like it, has evolved proprietary use rights that permit individuals who invest extra procurement effort, e.g., in acquiring resources for storage, to reap all or most of its benefits (Bettinger 2001, 172–181). This logic applies equally to agriculture. Territoriality and storage are only two of the many behavioral incentives that were likely necessary to promote agricultural experimentation and intensification. Neither is likely to evolve in any intensive form where individuals act in purely self-interested ways. No family is strong enough to defend its fields or stores of food in settings where everyone is motivated wholly by self-interest. The Mikea discussed by Tucker (Chapter 2) are a case in point. No Mikea family can afford to intensify agricultural production so long as Mikea cattle owners feel free to look the other way while their herds fatten on the crops of their farming neighbors. In the absence of a group ethic supporting proprietary use rights, there is only tolerated theft, a grudging transfer of resources that erodes the motivation to intensify or experiment.

THE ARCHAEOLOGICAL RECORD

Setting all the theoretical objections aside, it is quite reasonable to ask, as Smith does, whether archaeological remains can be quantified with sufficient precision to demonstrate that patterns are more consistent with foraging theory than some alternative. It is equally reasonable to ask, as he also does, whether enough can be known about prehistoric environments to generate the rankings and estimates of abundance needed to model diet breadth. I share Smith's concerns about the quality of the archaeological record, but if excavated faunal and floral assemblages will not sustain inferences as to the relative importance of various foods, more than foraging theory is at risk; a substantial fraction of any archaeological interpretation rests on knowing these things. Fortunately, we do not need to establish consumption in accordance with the diet breadth model at every site, any more than I need to be able to radiocarbon date every Rose Spring projectile point I find. Indeed, taken alone, individual assemblages, even sizeable ones, may not be especially revealing of economic decision making. Many assemblages, including small ones, in combination often speak more clearly to these patterns. These, in combination with knowledge of fundamental ecological relationships, can provide the information

needed to construct and test plausible models of diet breadth. Waguespack and Surovell (2003), for example, employ the relationship between body size and density in mammals (smaller body = higher density) to estimate the frequency with which different prey would have been available to Clovis hunters, and compare this to the observed frequency of those prey in Clovis faunal assemblages. Because large prey are more commonly represented in these assemblages than they should be, Waguespack and Surovell conclude Clovis foraging was highly selective, implying relatively narrow diet breadth and relatively abundant resources. This body size to density relationship is sufficiently robust to serve as a general source of OFT prediction. It predicts almost perfectly, for instance, the relative frequency of Aché kills, suggesting that the Aché take these species upon encounter as would be predicted by the diet breadth model, when diet breadth is quite broad (Figure 14.1).

Smith's real message seems to be one of caution: HBE has substantial promise but theories can be deceptive and archaeologists, like all scholars, can be prone to foolishness. To keep us from mischief, he advocates rigid adherence to protocol of scientific methodology that involves, among other things, comparing the performance of HBE with equally plausible theoretical alternatives. The problem here, and with the idea of multiple working hypotheses in general, is that when it comes to foraging behavior it is hard to know what the alternatives are or should look like. Indeed, that is precisely the problem. I am drawn to foraging theory because it generates hypotheses with clear implications for the archaeological record. I would very much like to explore ways of thinking about prehistoric human behavior in other than strictly economic and evolutionary ways, perhaps with reference to the deep-lying mental structures that interest Levi-Strauss (1964), who talks of decision making weighed in terms of "good thinking" rather than "good eating." But "good thinking" does not lead me to predictions about the archaeological record in the same way that

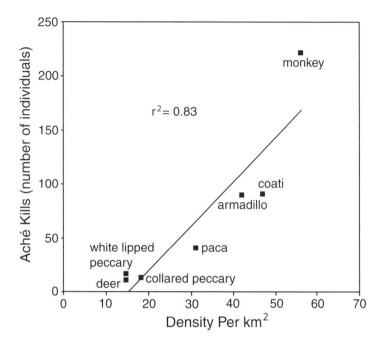

FIGURE 14.1. Density of mammals taken by Aché hunters predicts the frequency with which they are taken. Density estimated from body size (cf. Waguespack and Surovell 2003) using average body size (Hawkes et al. 1982: Table 1). Number of individuals taken is as given by Hawkes et al. (1982: Table 1).

"good eating" does, when I construe that with reference to foraging theory. Evolutionary psychology offers some possibilities in this regard but not with the precision of OFT. My more fundamental problem with the method of multiple working hypotheses is its suggestion that I should spend time developing plausible alternatives. In my view the responsibility for that falls squarely on those who doubt the hypothesis I'm working on; it keeps me busy enough as it is. The alternatives in which I am mainly interested are the null hypothesis and the "middle range" behaviors acting on the patterns on which my attention is mainly centered, for instance butchering and density-mediated destruction affecting the composition of faunal assemblages. These provide complication enough to justify my choice of HBE theory as the simplest, most parsimonious account of human behavior.

RETHINKING FORAGING MODELS

The simplicity of HBE theory is obviously an advantage but is also a weakness, because so much weight is placed on so few variables. The diet breadth model, for example, rests on the ratio of just two variables, time and energy. The choice of variables is obviously critical, but time and energy are pretty good. Energy certainly measures subsistence utility in a more general way than, say, protein or vitamin C; and time is so fundamental a cost that it scarcely needs defending. The problem is mainly in application. The model tells us how to weigh choices only in a general way (energy relative to time), for instance, and it does not tell us how the choices themselves should be defined. In theory, choices that produce the same rate of return should be equally attractive. In the real world, however, an activity that takes ten minutes and produces ten calories may not be equivalent to another that takes 100,000 minutes and produces 100,000 calories, the commitments of time being so different. Similarly, an activity that takes ten minutes and produces zero calories half the time and twenty calories the rest of the time is not really equivalent to another that takes ten minutes and produces ten calories every single time, the latter being so much more reliable. In this volume, the papers by Barlow and Tucker speak to these issues.

Barlow argues that to understand the transition to food production requires rethinking how subsistence choices are defined. The diet breadth model assumes that preferences for different choices are absolute. Individual prey types or foraging options, e.g., fishing or trapping, are either always avoided or always exploited. It follows that if agriculture is treated as simply another foraging option, the transition from foraging to farming can only be wholesale and abrupt; commitment to agriculture cannot be partial. Barlow argues that this is an artifact of the way this choice is defined, which artificially telescopes the whole of agriculture into a single activity, with a single energy-time ratio. At very coarse time-scales this does no great harm. As temporal resolution increases, however, it increasingly fails to predict what is seen in the many cases where agricultural beginnings display a long, low-level phase of food production. In light of this, Barlow argues it is more instructive to think about marginal rates of return in terms of short-term commitments, and of agriculture as comprising several separate short-term activities that correspond to individual phases of the agricultural cycle. Rather than committing to the agricultural cycle wholesale, individuals constantly weigh the costs and benefits of its individual components—planting, weeding, tending, harvesting, etc.—against those provided by foraging opportunities available at the same time. Planting is clearly critical to the others, but planting does not require weeding, or even harvesting. Sometimes people plant, weed, tend, and harvest; sometimes they just plant and harvest, and sometimes they don't plant at all. By this view, food production may enter the economy more gradually and not irreversibly, the emphasis shifting along with conditions that variously favor foraging or farming. Many have observed that things like prey abundance may—and often do—shift seasonally, requiring that diet breadth be calculated separately for each distinctive situation. Barlow extends that logic by showing how the importance of short-term decision making increases when a sequential array of agricultural behaviors are added to an existing array of foraging choices.

Tucker essentially comes to the same conclusion but in a different way. As does Barlow, he argues for the importance of short-term decision making: individuals constantly weighing alternative courses of action in keeping with changing circumstances. But where Barlow sees payoffs weighed in the usual way (energy divided by time), Tucker sees payoffs that incorporate time preference, i.e., aversion to postponed rewards. Payoffs are time-discounted; devalued according to the time they take to be realized, constantly changing with time and periodic alterations in discount rates. The time preference reflected in discount rates is partly a matter of risk. Long-term activities such as agriculture are inherently riskier than short-term activities because there is more time for things to go wrong (for an in-depth discussion of risk see Winterhalder, et al. 1999). Discount rates, however, also reflect opportunity costs. The discount rate for any single activity rises and falls directly with the perceived utility of its alternatives. Among the Mikea, the shifting utility of short-term foraging alternatively encourages and discourages long-term agricultural investment, preventing agricultural intensification. When food stockpiles are large, the Mikea choose to plant and tend corn rather than forage, because large stockpiles diminish the perceived utility of foraging for relatively small immediate returns, reducing the agricultural discount rate enough to make the perceived utility of a large future corn harvest more attractive than foraging. But as stockpiles diminish, the need to feed hungry mouths increases the perceived utility of foraging, and with it the agricultural discount rate, until the perceived utility of foraging for a relatively low immediate return exceeds the perceived utility of tending corn for a much greater, but postponed, return. Thus a vicious cycle: Mikea abandon their fields to weeds, thieves, and marauding cattle, insuring too little will be harvested and set aside to keep the family in the field tending their crop next year. If, as Tucker argues, farming returns are much better than foraging returns, Mikea could become successful farmers if only they would

TABLE 14.1
Effect of Discounting on Diet Breadth

	COATI	PACA
net kg	2.3	4.9
kcals	4436	9506
handling time (hr)	0.64	1.37
kcals/handling time	6964	6964
resource rank	1 (tie)	1 (tie)
kcals discounted by handling time @ 0.30	3724	6744
discounted kcals/handling time	5847	4941
resource rank	1	2

Note: Without discounting, coati and paca are equal in rank. If the discount rate is greater than zero (0) coati outranks paca. The discount rate is set arbitrarily here at 0.30 and time at 1.0, kcals being discounted according to the formula $kcals/(1+td)$, where t = time and d = discount rate.

adjust their discount rates. On that view, agriculture might be just a matter of attitude adjustment—"good thinking," as Levi-Strauss would have it. Alternatively, Mikea discount rates may be realistic—perhaps agricultural losses to climate cannot be avoided or losses to theft and cattle adequately remedied without fear of reprisal, even when fields are closely watched. If so, "good thinking" will run afoul of bad outcomes.

In any event, Tucker and Barlow see partial commitment to agriculture, whether among the Fremont or Mikea, as a response to long-term uncertainty that promotes short-term tactics. Barlow builds this into her models mechanically, by limiting choices to behavioral alternatives that are all short-term. The discounting approach saves that step because the linkage between uncertainty and short-term tactics is already captured in the discount rate, which measures uncertainty, and as it rises, increasingly favors short-term tactics with immediate rewards, i.e., as opposed to delayed returns (Woodburn 1980). The effect is illustrated in Table 14.1, which shows the energetic returns and handling times for two important Aché prey, coati and paca (Hawkes, et al. 1982). These animals return exactly the same amount of energy per unit of handling time but differ in size;

the larger paca requires more than twice the handling time of the coati. In the diet breadth model, the two are equal in rank, i.e., both are taken or both are ignored. However, if their returns are discounted by handling time at the same rate, the smaller coati, which requires less time, will outrank the larger paca, which requires more handling time, because discounting favors short-term tactics over long-term ones, as Barlow intuits.

It seems unlikely that short-term discount rate fluctuations of the kind described by Tucker alone are enough to explain why prehistoric foragers began to experiment with long-term tactics such as food production. It seems most likely that short-term variation will trigger innovative long-term tactics only when a more fundamental shift in time preference has already pushed subsistence behavior generally in a direction that favors long term tactics. The balance between population and resources is probably critical here, because time preference is sensitive to the overall abundance of resources, here energy. To see why this so, note first that foraging is not an end in itself but a means of enhancing fitness, which can be also achieved by non-foraging activities: seeking mates and allies, protecting mates and offspring, monitoring resources and potential allies. In this broader view, foraging and non-foraging activities compete for time and energy. This can lead to allocations of time and energy that are suboptimal with respect to foraging yet that enhance overall fitness. Costly signaling, for example, is wasteful only if it is viewed as foraging. In the larger picture, losses in the foraging part of the equation are offset by fitness gains in the non-foraging part. In actuality, the time and energy that costly signalers "waste" in foraging is not really being spent on foraging at all, on subsistence-getting; rather, time and energy are being *subtracted* from foraging and spent more profitably on non-foraging fitness. Resource (energy) abundance enters this picture on the assumption, following Winterhalder (1983, 75), that the marginal contributions of time and energy to non-foraging fitness are functions of their relative abundance. This means that when energy is relatively abundant, an additional increment of time will increase non-foraging fitness more than the additional increment of energy that could be obtained by investing the same amount of time in foraging. Because of this, and because foraging and non-foraging activities compete for time, *as energy becomes more abundant, less time will be spent on foraging and more time will be spent on the other things that enhance fitness* (Winterhalder 1983, 81). This model is sensitive to changes in resource abundance in a way that the diet breadth family of models is not. Most notably, it predicts that where resources are abundant, foragers will not maximize their energetic intake in accord with the standard models of OFT but will instead increasingly minimize the time spent foraging, spending the balance on non-foraging activities; they will tend to be *time-minimizers*. Conversely, as resources become scarce, foragers will tend to maximize foraging time and become *energy-maximizers* (Winterhalder 1983, 81; the same conclusion is derived less formally in Bettinger 1999b, 2001). Contrast this with the standard diet breadth model, where the relative value of time and energy never change, and time-minimizers are indistinguishable from energy-maximizers: optimal solutions minimize time and maximize energy at the same time.

In theory, the energy abundance that favors time-minimizing should lead to a diet breadth that is quite narrow—restricted to species with very high return rates (Winterhalder 1983). With human foragers, these rates will matter less than the absolute investment in time required by different resources, because the abundance that promotes time-minimizing generally occurs where population densities are quite low, favoring high residential mobility that enhances foraging and non-foraging fitness at once, e.g., by locating mates, opportunities for trade, superior foraging opportunities, and monitoring regional resources. Large package resources generally produce the highest rates of return, but they can also require commensurately large blocks of time that impede mobility. For this reason, when resource abundance favors time-minimizing, human foragers will find it most practical to achieve this using time preference as a simple rule of thumb, discounting resource return rates according to the amount of time involved.

Since time preference dictates subsistence choices at odds with those of standard diet breadth, energy will not be maximized per unit of time. In the paca-coati case in Table 14.1, for example, to maximize energy per unit of time—minimize time per unit of energy—requires that paca and coati be treated identically, both taken, both ignored. Time preference, however, dictates that the two be treated differently, coati ranking ahead of paca, because the former requires less handling time. Given the right conditions, this permits taking the coati while ignoring the paca, which will not maximize the rate at which energy is acquired. In this model, then, time-discounting squanders energy to save time, which makes sense when resources are so abundant and reliable that time can be more profitably spent enhancing fitness in other ways.

The model makes it possible to think about major trajectories of hunter-gatherer adaptive behavior—and about the place of food production within these trajectories—in a way that the diet breadth family of models precludes simply because they do not accommodate changes in the importance of time relative to energy. In broad stroke, when population densities are very low in relation to available resources, so that energy requirements are readily satisfied, hunter-gatherer strategies will be time-minimizing, not energy maximizing, and thus defy the predictions of the diet breadth model. By like reasoning, strategies will also defy those of the patch choice model (MacArthur and Pianka 1966). Behavior will be time-limited; foraging will be highly opportunistic, taking advantage of circumstances that favor relatively high returns in the short-term, often favoring smaller resource packages and short-term settlements overall.

As population increases relative to resources favoring energy maximizing, time preference will diminish. Resource rankings will gradually be reshuffled in accordance with standard diet breadth and subsequently vary in the way it predicts. In practical terms, energy will be maximized in relation to space by supporting more people per unit of space rather than in relation to time, as formerly with time preference. This is intuitively logical: competition in the form of other foraging groups decreases the opportunity costs of foraging and increasingly rewards hunter-gatherers who make do where they are, with what they can get, squeezing more and more energy from less and less space.

Because time preference leads to suboptimal return rates, the potential for population growth increases as time preference diminishes and return rates are optimized. Since population growth itself diminishes resource abundance in a way that favors energy maximizing and reduced time preference, the trend will be self-reinforcing—growth decreases time preference generating more energy per unit of space, which may generate further growth, further decreasing time preference, and so on. Where large population densities lead to scarce resources that favor energy-maximizing, there is no time preference, at least none related to energy abundance. Population density and realized return rates will no

longer vary directly but inversely: each subsequent increment of population growth will reduce return rates. Population may still continue to grow despite declining rates of return, because, as Winterhalder and Goland (1993) have so elegantly shown, population density ultimately does not hinge so much on rates of return in energy per unit of time as on resource reproductive capacities of energy per unit of space per unit of time. As argued above, population growth under these conditions can only be the result of strategies that maximize energy in relation to space rather than in relation to time. Continuing increases will hinge on the presence of resources with high reproductive rates, seed plants, for example.

This brings us finally back to Barlow and Tucker, both of whom depict situations where short-term tactics imply time preference that works against agricultural intensification. What is difficult to explain in either case is why, given this time preference, any effort at all is invested in agricultural production. Tucker lays this to seasonal differences in food on hand that affect short-term risk. When larders are full, short-term risks are minimal, so the discount rate falls enough to make farming attractive (a similar argument is advanced by Flannery 1986b). The key, then, would seem to be accumulation and its short-term effect on discount rates. Accumulation will be limited among time-minimizers, whose time preference promotes short-term tactics, hence limited returns. As foraging becomes more energy-maximizing, however, time preference may decrease enough so that resource accumulation may temporarily depress discount rates enough to encourage experiments with food production. Once started, the cycle is self-reinforcing only to an extent scaled by the amount of accumulation, which determines the length of its effect. Small accumulations sustain equally small investments in agriculture, as among the Mikea (and, evidently, the Fremont). By this view, those who have argued that experiments with agriculture begin when food is scarce (e.g. Cohen 1977), and those who have argued that it begins when food is abundant (e.g. Sauer 1952), are both right. Food must be scarce because time preference (hence resource abundance) needs to be low enough to be temporarily affected by resource accumulation. At the same time, food must be abundant because limited commitment to agriculture implies that time preference is still high enough to preclude full-time investment in long-term tactics. Obviously, neither the Mikea nor the Fremont would so easily give up on food production were not foraging so attractive. There is nothing in the discount rate-accumulation relationship that would seem to promote continued intensification because the effect of accumulation is self-limiting, again, as among the Mikea. Indeed, it seems quite possible that adding a little farming to an existing foraging repertoire might decrease uncertainty and increase overall quality of life in a way that would stabilize time preference and discourage further intensification. At the same time, anything that acted independently to increase levels of accumulation would promote greater investment in agriculture.

MODELS THAT INCLUDE SPACE

Archaeologists are particularly well positioned to observe the consequences of evolutionary processes as they unfold through time. The bulk of HBE, however, is not about change over time but about patterns and relationships at particular points in time, many of which play out across space in a way that is also archaeologically observable. Chapters in this volume deal with two such models: central place foraging theory (CPF) and ideal free distribution (IFD).

Central place foraging (Chapters 3 [Gremillion], 6 [Kennett et al.]) differs from the standard diet breadth model by requiring that foraging begin and end at a central place, adding to-and-from travel time to the overall cost of foraging. Insofar as human foraging is concerned, the usual insight is that when load size is fixed, say by the volume of carrying baskets, travel time may overshadow in-patch return rates

in a way that favors high-quality, low-return resources (many kcals per liter, few kcals per hour) over low quality, high-return resources (few kcals per liter, many kcals per hour). Thus, when there is no travel time, a 200 kcal load that requires one hour of foraging will be preferred to 300 kcal load that requires two hours of foraging (200 kcal/hr > 150 kcal/hr); however, with two hours of travel time the reverse will be true (200 kcal/3 hrs = 66.67 kcals/hr < 300 kcals/4 hrs = 75 kcals/hr). The implications of CPF for early agriculture and its intensification have to do with this size effect in reverse: travel time that makes low-return resources near at hand more attractive than high-return resources at a distance.

Gremillion's CPF model, for example, uses knowledge of central places and return rates in suboptimal as well as optimal settings to assess these effects on early low-level food producing in the eastern United States. Experimental data suggest that in this setting cultivated sumpweed (*Iva annua*) would have produced much higher returns than cultivated chenopods (*Chenopodium belandieri*) for gardeners residing in the best agricultural settings, located on the floodplains. However, travel time would have diminished these differences for gardeners who maintained their central places on adjacent hillsides, perhaps in response to competition, presenting a combination of many different local and distant foraging and farming opportunities that would be viable. At distances greater than 15 km, floodplain cultivation of any kind would have been unattractive relative to hillside cultivation, where experimental data suggest the two crops would have been about equally productive. Here, increasing travel time and the corresponding intensification of local production seem to explain an archaeologically observed pattern of mixed crop farming where simple return rates in the best agricultural settings might lead one to predict a more specialized pattern.

CPF can also be used to make inferences regarding agricultural intensification. Resources collected logistically should be especially sensitive to this, for instance. Those at the lower end of the spectrum may be dropped as agricultural production intensifies, as perhaps happened with coastal shellfish harvesting as part of the Archaic to Formative transition in Chiapas, discussed by Kennett et al. in this volume.

In Gremillion's CPF model, cultivators choose between alternative subsistence-settlement options on the basis of return rates without affecting those return rates. The Ideal Free Distribution (IFD) model (papers by McClure, Jochim, and Barton [Chapter 9] and Kennett, Anderson, and Winterhalder [Chapter 12]) (see also Belovsky 1988, 354; Fretwell and Lucas 1970) in contrast, assumes that such choices directly affect return rates and that population shuffles around in response. Among hunter-gatherers, return rates typically decrease as the number of consumers increases. Pressure on highly productive patches may quickly exhaust their potential, depressing return rates to the point that patches that were initially poorer become equally attractive, drawing some population there. With cultivation, on the other hand, return rates may actually increase at first, as settlements initially reach the size necessary to permit effective trade, the pooling of agricultural labor, etc., and as agricultural infrastructure such as forest clearing, terracing, etc, improves. This may actually draw inhabitants from settings that had been more attractive before this trade and cooperation emerged locally. At some point, however, additional arrivals merely add farming pressure, adversely affecting plot size, plot quality, fallowing intervals, and return rates. If return rates drop so far that other settings become more attractive, there will be out-migration. The important point here is that if foraging or farming populations are free to move in response to changing circumstances, regional return rates will tend to be in equilibrium, i.e., the same in all settings. That is, as return rates drop in one setting, population will move to those settings where they remain high. Immigrants depress return rates in their new setting, which now has more people, but out-migration increases them in their old setting, which now has fewer people. This continues until return rates are essentially the same every-

where. This is a simple but exceedingly important insight for archaeologists.

For one thing, it suggests that marginal settings, the ones we often overlook, can be particularly revealing of quality of life on a regional level, their use signaling that return rates overall have finally dropped in line with what little these depauperate environments can provide. The colonization of small islands in the Pacific, discussed by Kennett, Anderson, and Winterhalder [Chapter 12], provides one such example. In this sense, marginal settings provide a particularly clear test of theories about such things as intensification, sedentism, and agriculture, which are alternately attributed to resource abundance or scarcity. The cold, dry, resource-poor alpine tundra above 10,000 feet in the White Mountains east of Owens Valley, California, furnishes an example (Bettinger 1991a). A dramatic increase in alpine land use there at AD 600 coincides with subsistence intensification and the appearance of year-round villages on the much richer valley floor below, suggesting that all these changes occurred during a period when overall quality of life, as measured by regional return rates, was declining.

More generally, the logic that stands behind the IFD model—that rational decision making and population movement will adjust local return rates until they are in regional equilibrium—allows for reasonable inferences about the return rates of behaviors that have not yet been, and may never be, well documented archaeologically. This is simply because the logic of IFD allows one to extrapolate return rates from well-controlled settings to poorly controlled settings so long as the two are in IFD equilibrium. It is quite conceivable, thus, that in systems where both were present, settlements for foraging may speak more clearly to the productivity of low-level agriculture than can be inferred directly from the agricultural settlements themselves.

LOW-LEVEL FOOD PRODUCTION

The contributors to this volume seem broadly in agreement that the origin and early spread of agriculture is gradual and drawn out over time, in keeping with the trajectory of low-level food production outlined by Smith (2001a). The key archaeological evidence here is the gap between the time at which domesticates first appear in archaeological assemblages and the time at which they first come to dominate subsistence and settlement. The gaps are substantial: 4000 years in the eastern US, 5500 years in Mesoamerica, 3000 years in the Near East, and 1350 years in the southwestern US (Diehl and Waters, Chapter 5). Smith (2001a) does not purport to explain this phenomenon—he merely observes that it is inconsistent with the traditional notion of agriculture as a revolution and with classification schemes built around it. Contributors to this volume offer some specific explanations. McClure, Jochim, and Barton [Chapter 9], for example, argue that in prehistoric Spain, soil deterioration in the few places most favorable to agriculture forced settlement to shift gradually over time to places that demanded more intensive agricultural effort. In this case, agriculture intensifies slowly and gradually because it was in response to soil deterioration, the pace of which was slow and gradual. Diehl and Waters [Chapter 5], on the other hand, suggest that in the American Southwest the gap is due to technological barriers—that the effective use of corn required sophisticated ceramics that reduced storage risk, which were not perfected until relatively late in time. Things like soil deterioration and technological barriers were undoubtedly locally important in slowing the low-level transition, but the pattern is so general and widespread it seems more reasonable to regard them as symptoms of stability (rather than causes of it) in situations where change is generally unrewarding, as Kennett et al. [Chapter 6] suggest for maize agriculture in coastal Chiapas. If the rewards of reliable corn storage are too low, even relatively cheap innovations in ceramic technology may not produce a net benefit. If this is generally true, change will only occur because it cannot be avoided, as with soil deterioration.

This temporal lag between initial use of domesticates and commitment to agriculture is

intriguing from a theoretical standpoint simply because it is so long in relation to the evolutionary forces that are commonly believed to explain agricultural origins. Selection, population growth, and rational decision-making are so powerful they should have produced the observed change much more quickly. The prolonged low-level use of domesticated plants and animals suggests these forces must have been negligibly small or continually reversing, as with the stable limit cycles mentioned much earlier. Suppose, for instance, that corn growing rises to prominence because corn growers have a higher rate of survival than foragers or because corn growers end up with more food, which causes foragers to shift to corn growing. Under either scenario, if it takes 5500 years for corn growers to increase from 1% of the population to 50%, as in Mesoamerica, the advantages of corn growing would have to be so small (about 2.1%) that it would take 1000 years for corn growers to increase from 1% to just 2.3% of the population, and 2000 years for them to increase to 5.1% of the population.[3] Traits that remain so rare for so long are highly subject to elimination by population drift and drift-like effects in cultural transmission.

On the other hand, the lag time that characterizes the transition from foraging to farming is in keeping with group selection, which is relatively slow acting because it requires the social dissolution, i.e., cultural extinction, of whole groups rather than change in individual behavior which is comparatively rapid (Soltis et al. 1995). The group selection version of Mesoamerican example above, for instance, would give the advantage of corn growing to groups, not individuals, implying a cultural extinction rate of about 2.1% per generation for foraging groups, which seems reasonable. The behavior under group selection during the low-level transition would not be cultivation itself, but the host behaviors that encourage cultivation. Among these, storage is particularly important since, as we have seen in relation to the Mikea, anything that promotes accumulation will also promote investment in long-term strategies, including food production. The incentive of individual families or households to invest time and effort accumulating and storing food, however, varies directly with their autonomy in determining its consumption. In this sense, storage is inherently a social problem—a prisoner's dilemma where cooperation amounts to keeping your hands out of your neighbor's storeroom, a rule that encourages storage. Where stored food is a public good, where neighbors are constantly dipping into each others' storerooms, investment in storing will look much like Aché hunting, only a handful will invest really intensive effort—and will always expect something valuable that others have to give up in return. For storage to become general and self-reinforcing requires a change in the rules, a group consensus matched by group behavior to the effect that stored resources are off-limits to general claims. Individuals can seldom accomplish this (witness the penalties for hoarding in groups that share), but groups can do it. It is quite thinkable that such rules might evolve and be maintained locally in small groups by conformist and related forms of transmission, and that as a consequence such groups would fare better than groups lacking them, along the lines discussed by Soltis, Boyd, and Richerson (1995). The rate at which this occurs will determine the rate of transition to the group selected behavior. Soltis, Boyd, and Richerson (1995) suggest such group-level transitions require on the order of 1000 years or more, roughly the magnitude that characterizes low-level food production. What makes the group selection explanation particularly attractive entirely apart from timing, is the behaviors themselves—things like territoriality, land ownership, privatization, and storage. At root, all of them require that individuals voluntarily limit the expression of their individual self-interest.

As others have, Smith (2001a) has struggled to understand just where hunting and gathering leave off and agriculture begins, and, deciding this is pointless, simply identifies a "middleground" that includes many groups (Diegueno, Owens Valley Paiute, Northwest Coast) that are certainly hunter-gatherers—they differ in no major way from their neighbors except for the few activities that cause them to be put in this middle ground. Owens Valley Paiute moved easily by marriage into places where irrigation was impossible, just as their neighbors, who did not irrigate, experienced little trouble marrying into Owens Valley and participating in its irrigation projects (Steward 1970). What united the Owens Valley Paiute with their non-irrigating neighbors was the principle that harvested food was private food. What separated the Owens Valley Paiute from their non-irrigating neighbors was private ownership of land, yet the Owens Paiute shared this behavior with groups throughout California—groups not in Smith's middle ground—whose resource rich locations: acorn groves, fishing rocks, and seed patches were invariably privately held. Rather than put the Diegueno and Owens Valley Paiute in the middle ground and leave the rest of California out, it seems more reasonable to include them all and regard this middle ground as centering on the evolution of group selected behaviors that promoted subsistence intensification in general, which led to proto-agricultural practices in a handful of places.

ARCHAEOLOGY OR HUMAN BEHAVIORAL ECOLOGY

As noted at the outset, many fear that applying HBE theory to landmark human developments like the origin of agriculture (1) forces unseemly matches between data and theory, (2) strips away many things that make humans human, and (3) makes human behavior secondary in importance to Darwinian evolutionary theory. The papers in this volume prove the first fear groundless. They display substantial theoretical expertise, but the bulk of the discussion is about the archaeological data. No one is overtly trying to manipulate the data to produce a match with theory. The problem is more one of trying to see how a bewildering array of important archaeological facts—radiocarbon dates, plant remains, and faunal assemblages—are to be read in light of theory, i.e., how to think about the archaeological record in evolutionary terms.

As to the second fear, whether humans remain distinctively human in the presence of HBE theory remains an empirical question—indeed, it is a major topic of HBE research. However, if a large part of human behavior is the product of group selection, as I happen to believe, then human behavior will be distinctive in all the ways that anthropologists have always believed and at the same time subject to neo-Darwinian processes, of which group selection is merely a special expression. It is significant here that the warrant for group selection does not come from the mainstream of HBE but from a rather separate brand of work know as dual inheritance (or culture transmission; Boyd and Richerson 1985; for archaeological applications see Bettinger and Eerkens 1999; Shennan 2002), which concerns itself with the modes of cultural inheritance, i.e., how behaviorally relevant information is acquired and transmitted, and how this moves in relation to genes. A very large part of the human behavioral repertoire and its archaeological expression is substantially the product of imitation, instruction, and other forms of cultural transmission. The key insight of culture transmission theory is that to the extent these modes of transmission do not parallel, i.e., are asymmetric, to genetic transmission, human behavior will differ from what would be expected from the genetic model that underpins much of HBE. Culture transmission theory makes group selection much less problematic than it is in HBE (e.g., McElreath et al. 2003).

The chief drawback of transmission theory is that, to date, its predictions have been less specific than those of HBE, and thus harder to test. It is easy to see why this is so. HBE produces clear predictions about behavior because the context, especially technology and environment, are taken as givens. This or that group forages optimally given its environment and the tools at its disposal. Observing such behavior, and departures from it, is critical, of course, but a comprehensive approach to human foraging should also include a processual account of how the technology and the skills involved in its use were acquired in the first place. This is the problem Julian Steward (1938) confronted when developing his model of cultural ecology. His solution was to argue that many behaviors—especially subsistence and social behaviors—were the result of two *independent* forces, technology and environment. Environment dictated what was available; technology dictated what could be obtained from it. For Steward, humans did not adapt to a natural environment but rather a cultural environment, the "effective environment," determined by what could be obtained using available technology. Only by making technology at least partly independent of environment was Steward able to avoid the pitfall of environmental determinism, which makes technology and everything else wholly a function of environment. For Steward, technology was a function of culture and culture history. Culture transmission theory seeks a formal framework for understanding this aspect of the adaptive equation. Culture transmission and HBE are entirely compatible and there is much to be gained by joining the two to tackle difficult and important problems such as the origin of agriculture. Laland and Brown (2002) provide a useful summary of the different points of view and insights about the potential for building bridges between them.

Some of the connections are obvious. As noted more than once above, HBE recognizes that there are many paths to fitness that compete for time and energy—foraging, alliance-building, mate seeking, etc. Nearly all of these opportunities are pursued by means of behaviors that are culturally acquired and transmitted. On that view, cultural transmission is just another fitness-enhancing behavior that competes for time and energy. Henrich (2004), for instance, has noted that the effectiveness of cultural transmission is highly dependent on access to potential social models; complex behaviors require larger model pools than simpler ones. Complex foraging technology may save time or increase returns, but only if enough time and energy has been invested in maintaining communication with a model pool of requisite size.

A good deal of hunter-gatherer mobility is probably related to this requirement, especially where population densities are low. It is reasonable to think that the technologies and behaviors required to take full advantage of agriculture, e.g., ceramics for effective storage, likewise required large model pools. This may in part explain the long low-level transition to full-time agriculture, since, if population densities were initially low, the mobility needed to maintain contact within a large enough model pool would have worked against any form of agricultural intensification that tethered groups to fixed places. Clearly, then, there is much to be gained by incorporating dual inheritance theory into the larger HBE agenda and adding that dimension of culture to the investigation of important questions like the origins of agriculture.

Finally, as to whether HBE makes humans subservient to Darwinian evolutionary theory, it is not the archaeological proponents, but rather the archaeological critics, of HBE who seem to put theory ahead of the archaeological record. Bamforth (2002, 441) asks whether the application of foraging theory to archaeological problems has, "illuminated the operation of Darwinian processes in any substantial way"—as though illuminating Darwinian theory were what really mattered. Thomas (1986) makes the same point, invoking this quote from Gould (1980): "We take the evolutionary concepts formulated for us by students of modern populations and we try to show that ancient ones lived by the same rules. But where does this lead beyond exemplification based on imperfect data" (Gould 1980, 98). Whether archaeology has illuminated evolutionary theory is arguable. I think it has, but for me that has never been the point. I got into archaeology because I was interested in the past. I employ theoretical models to gain insights about it, adapting them to the problem at hand. Since I'm interested in prehistory, I think it quite reasonable to want to know, for example, whether Clovis

hunters were large game specialists or generalized hunter-gatherers—not because I'm interested in evolutionary theory, but because I'm interested in Clovis hunters. The models of HBE—diet breadth in particular—are there to provide helpful insights. If my work and that of others contributes something to evolutionary theory along the way, so much the better; but that is not my agenda. I am an archaeologist interested in prehistory. Darwinian theory is a means to that end, not an end in itself. It is quite evident that the contributors to this volume share that view.

NOTES

1. It is often incorrectly assumed that the foraging-fitness connection is more plausible if food is scarce than if it is abundant. This seems reasonable but is not. From a Darwinian standpoint, if food is really abundant, population will simply grow until it is not, and the problem will reappear. More fundamentally, where food is abundant, foraging may still determine fitness. Even if fitness comes from other things, it will still make sense to forage optimally, and thus free up time that can be used to obtain those things. This is dealt with in several sections below.

2. Quibblers will note that projectile point types are taken to represent a span of, rather than a point in, time, but the span itself is pure artifice. No one thinks every Rose Spring point was in use from the beginning to the end of that span—they represent many individual time points, some of which are more "representative" of the span (those in its middle) than others (those at either end).

3. This was computed using a variation of the equation provided by Soltis, Boyd, and Richerson (1995),

$$a = 1 - ([i][1 - f]/[[1 - i]/f])^{(1/g)}$$

where a is the selective advantage of corn growing, i is initial frequency of corn growing, f is the final frequency of corn growing, and g is number of generations, which are assumed to be 25 years in length.

REFERENCES

Abbo, S. and B. Rubin, 2000. Transgenic Crops: A Cautionary Tale. *Science* 287:1927–38.

Abraham, K. 1997. Flowering deficiencies and sterility preventing natural seed set in *Dioscorea alata* cultivars. *Tropical Agriculture* 74: 272–76.

Abrahams, M. V., and M. C. Healey. 1990. Variation in the competitive abilities of fishermen and its influence on the spatial distribution of the British Columbia Salmon Troll Fleet. *Canadian Journal of Fisheries and Aquatic Sciences* 47:1116–21.

Adams, J. L. 2001. The ground stone assemblage. In *Excavations in the Santa Cruz River Floodplain: The Early Agricultural Period Component at Los Pozos*, ed. by David A. Gregory, pp. 107–34. *Anthropological Papers No. 21*. Tucson, AZ: Center for Desert Archaeology.

Adams, K. R. 1988. The ethnobotany and phenology of plants in and adjacent to two riparian habitats in southeastern Arizona. Unpublished Ph.D. Dissertation, Department of Ecology and Evolutionary Biology, University of Arizona, Tucson, AZ.

———. 1994. A regional synthesis of *Zea mays* in the prehistoric American Southwest. In *Corn and Culture in the Prehistoric New World*, ed. by Sissel Johannesen and Christine A. Hastorf, pp. 273–302. Boulder, CO: Westview Press.

Aikens, C. M. 1966. Fremont-Promontory Plains relationships in northern Utah. *University of Utah Anthropological Papers 82*. Salt Lake City: University of Utah Press.

———. 1970. Hogup Cave. *University of Utah Anthropological Papers 93*. Salt Lake City: University of Utah Press.

Ainslie, P. N., I. T. Campbell, K. N. Frayn, S. M. Humphreys, D. P. M. Maclaren, and T. Reilly. 2002. Physiological and metabolic responses to a hill walk. *Journal of Applied Physiology* 92:179–87.

Aldenderfer, M. 1989. The Archaic Period in the south-central Andes. *Journal of World Prehistory* 3:117–58.

———. 1998. *Montane Foragers: Asana and the South-Central Andean Archaic*. Iowa City: University of Iowa Press.

———. 2002. Explaining changes in settlement dynamics across transformations of modes of production: From hunting to herding in the south-central Andes. In *Beyond Foraging and Collecting: Evolutionary Change in Hunter-Gatherer Settlement Systems*, ed. by B. Fitzhugh and J. Habu, pp. 387–412. New York: Kluwer Academic/Plenum Publishers.

Allee, W. C., A. E. Emerson, O. Park, T. Park, and K. P. Schmidt 1949. *Principles of Animal Ecology*. Philadelphia: W. B. Saunders.

Allen, J. 1991. The role of agriculture in the evolution of the pre-contact Hawaiian state. *Asian Perspectives* 30:117–32.

———. 1993. Notion of the Pleistocene in Greater Australia. In *A Community of Culture: The*

People and Prehistory of the Pacific, ed. by M. Spriggs, D. E. Yen, W. Ambrose, R. Jones, A. Thorne, and A. Andrews, Occasional Papers in Prehistory 21. Canberra: Department of Prehistory, Research School of Pacific Studies, Australian National University.

———. 1994. Radiocarbon determinations, luminescence dating and Australian archaeology. *Antiquity* 68:339–43.

———. 1996. The pre-Austronesian settlement of island Melanesia: Implications for Lapita archaeology. *Transactions of the American Philosophical Society* 86(5):11–27.

Allen, J., and S. Holdaway. 1995. The contamination of Pleistocene radiocarbon determinations in Australia. *Antiquity* 69:101–12.

Allen, J., and J. P. White. 1989. The Lapita homeland: Some new data and an interpretation. *Journal of the Polynesian Society* 98:129–46.

Allen, J., C. Gosden, R. Jones, and J. P. White. 1988. Pleistocene dates for the human occupation of New Ireland, Northern Melanesia. *Nature* 331:707–9.

———. 1989. Human Pleistocene adaptations in the tropical island Pacific: Recent evidence from New Ireland, a Greater Australian Outlier. *Antiquity* 63:548–61.

Alvard, M. S. 1993. Testing the "ecologically noble savage" hypothesis: Interspecific prey choice by Piro hunters of Amazonian Peru. *Human Ecology* 21:355–87.

———. 1998. The evolutionary ecology of resource conservation. *Evolutionary Anthropology* 7:62–74.

Alvard, M. S., and L. Kuznar. 2001. Deferred harvests: The transition from hunting to animal husbandry. *American Anthropologist* 103:295–311.

Alvarez del Torro, M. 1985. *Asi era Chiapas!: 42 Años de Andanzas por Montañas, Selvas y Caminos en el Estado*. Tuxtla Gutiérrez, Chiapas: Universidad Autónoma de Chiapas.

Amblard, S. 1996. Agricultural evidence and its interpretation on the Dhars Tichitt and Oualata, southeastern Mali. In *Aspects of African Archaeology*. ed. by G. Pwiti and R. Soper, pp. 421–8. Harare: University of Zimbabwe Publications.

Ambrose, S. H., and L. Norr 1992. On stable isotopic data and prehistoric subsistence in the Soconusco Region. *Current Anthropology* 33: 401–04.

American Occupational Therapy Association 2002. Backpack strategies for parents and students. American Occupational Therapy Association.

Accessed 3 December, 2002. http://www.aota.org/backpack/index. asp?aud=2.

Amirkhanov, K. A., B. Vogt, A. Sedov, and V. Buffa. 2001. Excavations of a settlement of prehistoric fishermen and mullusk gatherers in the Khor Umayra Lagoon, Gulf of Aden, Republic of Yemen. *Archaeology, Ethnology and Anthropology of Eurasia* 4(8):2–12.

Ammerman, A. J., and L. L. Cavalli-Sforza. 1984. *The Neolithic Transition and the Genetics of Populations in Europe*. Princeton: Princeton University Press.

Anati, E. 1972. *Rock Art in Central Arabia*. Vol. 3. *Corpus of the Rock Engravings, Expédition Philby-Ryckmans-Lippens en Arabie*. Louvain-La-Neuve: Publications de l'Institut Orientaliste de Louvain.

Anderson, A. J. 1981. A model of prehistoric collecting on the rocky shore. *Journal of Archaeological Science* 8:109–20.

———. 1983. Faunal depletion and subsistence change in the early prehistory of southern New Zealand. *Archaeology in Oceania* 18:1–10.

———. 1984. The extinction of moa (Aves: Dinornithidae) in southern New Zealand. In *Quaternary Extinctions*, ed. by P. S. Martin and K. G. Klein, pp. 728–40. Tucson: University of Arizona Press.

———. 1988. Mechanics of overkill in the extinction of New Zealand moas. *Journal of Archaeological Science* 16:137–51.

———. 1989. *Prodigious Birds: Moas and Moahunting in Prehistoric New Zealand*. Cambridge: Cambridge University Press.

———. 1991. The chronology of colonization in New Zealand. *Antiquity* 65:767–95.

———. 1995. Current approaches in East Polynesian colonization research. *Journal of the Polynesian Society* 104:110–32.

———. 1996. Adaptive voyaging and subsistence strategies in the early settlement of East Polynesia. In *Prehistoric Dispersal of Mongoloids*, ed. by T. Akazawa and E. Szathmary, pp. 359–74. Oxford: Oxford University Press.

———. 1997. Te Whenua hou: Prehistoric Polynesian colonisation of New Zealand and its impact on the environment. In *Historical Ecology in the Pacific Islands*, ed. by T. Hunt and P. Kirch, pp. 271–83. New Haven, CT: Yale University Press.

———. 2000a. Slow boats from China: Issues in the prehistory of Indo-Pacific seafaring. In *East of Wallace's Line: Studies of Past and Present Maritime Cultures of the Indo-Pacific Region*, ed. by S. O'Connor and P. Veth, pp. 13–50. Rotterdam: Balkema.

———. 2000b. The advent chronology of south Polynesia. In *Essays in Honour of Arne Skjolsvold 75 years*, ed. by P. Wallin and H. Martinsson-Wallin. Occasional Papers of the Kon-Tiki Musem 5:73–82.

———. 2000c. Defining the period of moa extinction. *Archaeology in New Zealand* 43:195–200.

———. 2001a. Mobility models of Lapita migration. In *The Archaeology of Lapita Dispersal in Oceania: Papers from the Fourth Lapita Conference, June 2000, Canberra, Australia*, ed. by G. R. Clark, A. J. Anderson, and T. Vunidilo. *Terra Australis* 17:15–23.

———. 2001b. No meat on that beautiful shore: The prehistoric abandonment of subtropical Polynesian islands. *International Journal of Osteoarchaeology* 11:14–23.

———. 2001c. Towards the sharp end: The form and performance of prehistoric Polynesian voyaging canoes. In *Pacific 2000: Proceedings of the Fifth International Conference on Easter Island and the Pacific*, ed. by C. M. Stevenson, G. Lee, and F. J. Morin, pp. 29–36. Los Osos, CA: Easter Island Foundation.

———. 2002. Faunal collapse, landscape change and settlement history in Remote Oceania. *World Archaeology* 33:375–90.

———. 2003a. Different mechanisms of Holocene expansion. *Science Debate* 8.5.03.

———. 2003b. Entering uncharted waters: Models of initial colonization in Polynesia. In *Colonization of Unfamiliar Landscapes: The Archaeology of Adaptation*, ed. by M. Rockman and J. Steele, pp. 169–89. London: Routledge.

———. n.d.a. Initial human dispersal in remote Oceania: Pattern and explanation. In *The Prehistory of the Pacific: Assessments of the Archaeological Data*, ed. by C. Sand. Museum of New Caledonia, in press.

———. n.d.b. Taking to the boats: The prehistory of Indo-Pacific colonization. Public Lecture at the National Museum of Australia 18.12.02. National Institute of Asia and the Pacific, in press.

———., and G. Clark. 1999. The age of Lapita settlement in Fiji. *Archaeology in Oceania* 34:31–39.

Anderson, A. J., E. Conte, G. Clark, Y. Sinoto, and F. Petchey. 1999. Renewed excavations at Motu Paeao, Maupiti Island, French Polynesia: Preliminary results. *New Zealand Journal of Archaeology* 21:47–65.

Anderson, A. J., and G. O'Regan. 2000. To the final shore: Prehistoric colonisation of the Subantarctic islands in South Polynesia. In *Australian Archaeologist: Collected Papers in Honour of Jim Allen*, ed. by A. J. Anderson and T. Murray, pp. 440–54. Canberra, Australia: Coombs Academic Publishing, ANU.

Anderson, A. J., S. Bedford, G. R. Clark, I. Lilley, C. Sand, G. Summerhayes, and R. Torrence. 2001a. An inventory of Lapita sites containing dentate-stamped pottery. In *The Archaeology of Lapita Dispersal in Oceania: Papers from the Fourth Lapita Conference, June 2000, Canberra, Australia*, ed. by G. R. Clark, A. J. Anderson, and T. Vunidilo. *Terra Australis* 17:1–13.

Anderson, A. J., L. Ayliffe, D. Questiaux, T. Sorovi-Vunidilo, N. Spooner and T. Worthy. 2001b. The terminal age of the Fijian megafauna. In *Histories of Old Ages: Essays in Honour of Rhys Jones*, ed. by A. J. Anderson, I. Lilley, and S. O'Connor, pp. 251–64. Canberra, Australia: Pandanus Books.

Anderson, A. J., and Y. H. Sinoto. 2002. New radiocarbon ages of colonization sites in East Polynesia. *Asian Perspectives* 41:242–57.

Anderson, A. J., H. Martinsson-Wallin, and P. Wallin. 2002. *The Prehistory of Kiritimati (Christmas) Island, Republic of Kiribati: Excavations and Analyses*. Oslo: Occasional Papers of The Kon-Tiki Museum, Volume 6.

Anderson, A. J., and R. K. Walter. 2002. Landscape and culture change on Niue Island West Polynesia. In *Pacific Landscapes: Archaeological Approaches*, ed. by T. Ladefoged and M. Graves, pp. 153–72. Honolulu: Easter Island Foundation, Bearsville Press.

Anderson, A. J., and J. P. White. 2001 (eds). *The Prehistoric Archaeology of Norfolk Island, Southwest Pacific*. Sydney: Records of The Australian Museum, Supplement 27.

Anson, D. 2000. Excavations at Vunavaung (SDI), Rakival Village, Watom Island, Papua New Guinea. *New Zealand Journal of Archaeology* 20(1998):95–118.

Arnaud, J. M. 1982. Neolithique ancien et processus de neolithisation dans le sud du Portugal. *Archeologie en Languedoc*: 29–48.

Arroyo, B. 1994. The early Formative in Southern Mesoamerica: An explanation for the origins of sedentary villages. Unpublished Ph.D. Dissertation, Department of Anthropology, Vanderbilt University.

———. 1995. Early ceramics of El Salvador. In *The Emergence of Pottery: Technology and Innovation in Ancient Societies*, ed. by W. K. Barnett and J. W. Hoopes, pp. 199–208. Washington, DC: Smithsonian Institution Press.

Asch, D. 1995. Aboriginal specialty-plant propagation: Illinois prehistory and an eastern North American post-contact perspective. Unpublished Ph.D. Dissertation, University of Michigan. University Microfilms.

Asch, D. L., and N. B. Asch. 1985. Prehistoric plant cultivation in west-central Illinois. In *Prehistoric Food Production in North America*, ed. by R. I. Ford, pp. 149–203. Ann Arbor: Museum of Anthropology, Anthropological Papers No. 75.

Asch, N. B., and D. L. Asch. 1978. The economic potential of *Iva Annua* and its prehistoric importance in the lower Illinois Valley. In *The Nature and Status of Ethnobotany*, ed. by R. I. Ford, pp. 301–41. Ann Arbor: Museum of Anthropology, Anthropological Papers No. 67.

Ascher, R. 1961. Analogy in archaeological interpretation. *Southwestern Journal of Anthropology* 17:317–25.

Aswani, S. 1998. Patterns of marine harvest effort in southwestern New Georgia, Solomon Islands: Resource management or optimal foraging? *Ocean and Coastal Management* 40: 207–35.

Athens, J. S., J. V. Ward, H. D. Tuggle, and D. J. Welch. 1999. *Environment, Vegetation Change and Early Human Settlement on the 'Ewa Plain: A Cultural Resource Inventory of Naval Air Station, Barber's Point, O'ahu, Hawai'i. Part III: Paleoenvironmental Investigations*. Honolulu: International Archaeological Research Institute, Inc.

Ayala, F. J., M. E. Gilpin, and J. G. Ehrenfeld. 1973. Competition between species: Theoretical models and experimental tests. *Theoretical Population Biology* 4:331–56.

Badal, E. 1990. *Aportaciones de la Antracología al Estudio del Paisaje Vegetal y su Evolución en el Cuaternario Reciente, en la Costa Mediterránea del País Valenciano y Andalucía (18,000–3,000 BP)*. Tesis doctoral, Universitat de València.

———. 1993. Antracología. In *El III milenio a.C. en el País Valenciano. Los poblados de Jovades (Concentaina, Alacant) y Arenal de la Costa Ontinyent, València*, ed. by J. Bernabeu. *Saguntum* 26:109–15

———. 1994. El antracoanálisis del poblado de Niuet. In *Niuet (L'Alqueria d'Asnar). Poblado del III milenio a*, ed. by J. Bernabeu, J. L. Pascual, T. Orozco, E. Badal, M. P. Fumanal, and O. García. *Recerques del Museu d'Alcoi* 3:67–71.

———. 1999. El potencial pecuario de la vegetacion mediterránea: Las Cuevas Redil. *Saguntum* (Extra-2):69–75.

Badal, E., J. Bernabeu and J. L. Vernet. 1994. Vegetation changes and human action from the Neolithic to the Bronze Age (7000–4000 BP) in Alicante, Spain, based on charcoal analysis. *Vegetation History and Archaeobotany* 3: 155–66.

Badal, E., J. Bernabeu, R. Buxó, M. Dupré, M. P. Fumanal, P. Guillem, R. Martínez, and M. J. Rodrigo. (1991) La Cova de les Cendres (Moraira-Teulada). In *Guia de las Excursiones de la VIII Reunión Nacional sobre Cuaternario*, pp. 21–78. València: Universitat de València.

Bailey, R. C., and T. N. Headland. 1991. The tropical rain forest: Is it a productive environment for human foragers? *Human Ecology* 19:261–85.

Bailey, R. C., and N. R. Peacock. 1993. Efe Pygmies of northeast Zaire: Subsistence strategies in the Ituri Forest. In *Peoples of the Ituri*, ed. by M. H. Pulford, pp. 102–29. Fort Worth: Harcourt Brace.

Bailey, R. C., G. Head, M. Jenike, B. Owen, R. Rechtman, and E. Zechenter. 1989. Hunting and gathering in tropical rain forest: Is it possible? *American Anthropologist* 91:59–82.

Bakels, C. C. 1982. Zum wirtschaftlichen Nutzungsraum einer bandkeramischen Siedlung. In *Siedlungen der Kultur mit Linearkeramik in Europa*, ed. by J. Pavuk, pp. 9–16. Nitra: Institut der Slowakischen Akademie der Wissenschaften.

Baker, P., G. Seltzer, S. Fritz, R. Dunbar, M. Grove, P. Tapia, S. Cross, H. Rowe, and J. Broda. 2001. The history of South American precipitation for the past 25,000 years. *Science* 291:640–3.

Bala, B. K. 1997. *Drying and Storage of Cereal Grains*. Enfield, NH: Science Publishers, Inc.

Balean, C. E. 1989. *Caves as Refuge Sites: An Analysis of Shell Material from Buang Merabak, New Ireland*. Unpublished B. A. Honours Thesis, Australian National University, Canberra.

Balée, W., and A. Gély. 1989. Managed forest succession in Amazonia: The Ka'apor case. In *Resource Management in Amazonia: Indigenous and Folk Strategies*. Advances in Economic Botany, Vol. 7, ed. by D. A. Posey, and W. Balée. pp. 129–58. New York: The New York Botanical Garden.

Balescu, S., J.-F. Breton, B. Coque-Delhuille, and M. Lamothe. 1998. La datation par luminescence des limons de crue: Une nouvelle approche de l'etude chrnologique des perimetres d'irrigation antiques du Sud-Yemen. *C. R. Acad. Sci. Paris, Sciences de la Terre et des Planetes* 327:31–37.

Ballard, C. 1995. *The Death of a Great Land: Ritual, History and Subsistence Revolution in the Southern Highlands of Papua New Guinea.* Unpublished Ph.D. thesis, Australian National University.

Balouet, J. C. 1987. Extinctions des vertébrés terrestres de Nouvelle-Calédonie. *Memoires de la Société Geologique de France* 150:177–83.

Balouet, J. C., and S. L. Olson. 1989. *Fossil Birds from Late Quaternary Deposits in New Caledonia.* Smithsonian Contributions to Zoology 469. Washington DC: Smithsonian Institution.

Bamforth, D. 2002. Evidence and metaphor in evolutionary archaeology. *American Antiquity* 67:435–52.

Barakat, H., and A. G. el-Din Fahmy. 1999. Wild grasses as "Neolithic" food resources in the eastern Saharah: A review of the evidence from Egypt. In *The Evolution of Plant Resources in Ancient Africa,* ed. by M. van der Veen, pp. 33–46. New York: Kluwer Academic/Plenum Publishers.

Barlow, K. R. 1997. Foragers that farm: A behavioral ecology approach to the economics of corn farming for the Fremont case. Unpublished Ph.D. dissertation, University of Utah, Salt Lake City. Ann Arbor: University Microfilms.

———. 2002. Predicting maize agriculture among the Fremont: An economic comparison of farming and foraging in the American Southwest. *American Antiquity* 67:65–88.

Barlow, K., and M. Heck. 2002. More on acorn eating during the Natufian. In Hunter-Gatherer Archaeobotany, ed. by S. R. Mason and J. G. Hather, pp. 128–45. London: Institute of Archaeology.

Barlow, K. R., P. R. Henriksen, and M. D. Metcalfe. 1993. Estimating load size in the Great Basin: Data from conical burden baskets. *Utah Archaeology* 1993:27–37.

Barlow, K. R., and D. Metcalfe. 1996. Plant utility indices: Two Great Basin examples. *Journal of Archaeological Science* 23:351–71.

Barlow, K. R., D. Metcalfe, and S. Arnold. 2002. *Preliminary Report of the 2001 Excavations at the Bead Tree Site: 42Wn2401.* Salt Lake City: Manuscript on file at the Utah Museum of Natural History.

Bar-Matthews, M., and A. Ayalon. 1997. Late Quaternary paleoclimate in the Eastern Mediterranean region from stable isotope analysis of speleothems at Soreq Cave, Israel. *Quaternary Research* 47:155–68.

Bar-Yosef, O. 1986. The walls of Jericho: An alternative interpretation. *Current Anthropology* 27:157–62.

Bar-Yosef, O., and R. H. Meadow. 1995. The origins of agriculture in the Near East. In *Last Hunters-First Farmers: New Perspectives on the Prehistoric Transition to Agriculture,* ed. by T. D. Price and A. B. Gebauer, pp. 39–94. Santa Fe: School of American Research Press.

Bar-Yosef, O. and A. Belfer-Cohen. 1992. From foraging to farming in the Mediterranean Levant. In *Transitions to Agriculture in Prehistory,* ed. by A. B. Gebauer and T. D. Price, pp. 21–48. Madison, WI: Prehistory Press.

Barnett, W. K. 1995. Putting the pot before the horse: Earliest ceramics and the Neolithic transition in the western Mediterranean. In *The Emergence of Pottery: Technology and Innovation in Ancient Societies,* ed. by W. K. Barnett and J. W. Hoopes, pp. 79–88. Washington, DC: Smithsonian Institution Press.

———. 2000. Cardial pottery and the agricultural transition in Mediterranean Europe. In *Europe's First Farmers,* ed. by T. D. Price, pp. 93–116. Cambridge: Cambridge University Press.

Barnola, J. M., D. Raynaud, Y. S. Korotkevich, and C. Lorius. 1987. Vostoc ice core provides 160,000-year record of atmospheric CO_2. *Nature* 329:408–14.

Bartlein, P. J., M. E. Edwards, S. L. Shafer, and E. D. Barker, Jr. 1995. Calibration of radiocarbon ages and the interpretation of paleoenvironmental records. *Quaternary Research* 44:417–24.

Barton, C. M., J. Bernabeu, J. E. Aura, and O. García. 1999. Land-use dynamics and socioeconomic change: An example from the Polop Alto Valley. *American Antiquity* 64:609–34.

Barton, C. M., J. Bernabeu, J. E. Aura, O. García, and N. LaRoca. 2002. Dynamic landscapes, artifact taphonomy, and landuse modeling in the western Mediterranean. *Geoarchaeology* 17(2): 155–90.

Barton, C. M., J. Bernabeu, J. E. Aura, O. García, S. Schmich, and Ll. Molina. 2004. Long-term socioecology and contingent landscapes. *Journal of Archaeological Method and Theory* 11(3): (in press).

Barton, H., and J. P. White. 1993. Use of stone and shell artefacts at Balof 2, New Ireland, Papua New Guinea. *Asian Perspectives* 32(2):169–81.

Barton, H., R. Torrence, and R. Fullagar. 1998. Clues to stone tool function re-examined: Comparing starch grain frequencies on used and unused obsidian artefacts. *Journal of Archaeological Science* 25:1231–38.

Bateson, M., and A. Kacelnik. 1995. Preferences for fixed and variable food sources: Variability in amount and delay. *Journal of the Experimental Analysis of Behavior* 63:313–29.

Bayham, F. E., and P. Hatch. 1985. Hohokam and Salado animal utilization in the Tonto Basin. In *Studies in the Hohokam and Salado of the Tonto Basin*, ed. by G. Rice, pp. 191–210. *Report No. 63*. Tempe: Office of Cultural Resource Management, Arizona State University.

Bayliss-Smith, T. 1985. Pre-Ipomoean agriculture in the New Guinea Highlands above 2000 metres: Some experimental data on taro cultivation. In *Prehistoric Intensive Agriculture in the Tropics*, ed. by I. Farrington, pp. 285–320. Oxford: British Archaeological Reports, International Series 232, Part I.

———. 1996. People-plant interactions in the New Guinea highlands: Agricultural hearthland or horticultural backwater? In *The Origins and Spread of Agriculture and Pastoralism in Eurasia*, ed. by D. R. Harris, pp. 499–52. London: UCL Press.

Beadle, G. W. 1972. The mystery of maize. *Field Museum Natural History Bulletin* 43(10):2–11.

———. 1977. The origins of *Zea mays*. In *Origins of Agriculture*, ed. by C. A. Reed, pp. 615–36. Mouton: The Hague.

———. 1980. The ancestry of corn. *Scientific American* 242:112–19.

Beck, C. 1999 (ed.). *Models for the Millennium: Great Basin Archaeology Today*. Salt Lake City, UT: University of Utah Press.

Becker, G. S., and C. B. Mulligan. 1997. The endogenous determination of time preference. *The Quarterly Journal of Economics* 112:729–58.

Bedegian, D. 2004. Sesame in Africa: Origins and dispersals. In *Food, Fuel, and Fields: Progress in African Archaeobotany*, pp. 17–36. ed by K. Neumann, A. Butler, and S. Kahlheber. Koln: Heinrich Barth Institute.

Bedford, S., M. Spriggs, M. Wilson, and R. Regenvanu. 1998. The Australian National University-National Museum of Vanuatu archaeology project: A preliminary report on the establishment of culture sequences and rock art research. *Asian Perspectives* 37(2):165–93.

Bedford, S., M. Spriggs, M. Wilson, and R. Regenvanu. 1999. The Australian National University-Vanuatu Culture Centre archaeology project, 1994–1997: Aims and results. *Oceania* 70(1):16–24.

Beech, M., and E. Shepherd. 2001. Archaeobotanical evidence for early date consumption on Dalma Island, United Arab Emirates. *Antiquity* 75:83–89.

Behling, H., H. W. Arz, J. Patzold, and G. Wefer. 2000. Late Quaternary vegetational and climate dynamics in Northeastern Brazil: Inferences from marine core GeoB 3104-1. *Quaternary Science Reviews* 19:981–94.

Bellwood, P. S. 1975. *Man's Conquest of the Pacific*. London: Collins.

———. 1978. The Great Pacific Migration. In *Yearbook of Science and the Future for 1984*, pp. 80–93. Encyclopedia Britannica.

———. 1985. *Prehistory of the Indo-Malaysian Archipelago*. Sydney: Academic Press.

———. 1996. The origins and spread of agriculture in the Indo-Pacific region: Gradualism and diffusion or revolution and colonisation? In *The Origins and Spread of Agriculture and Pastoralism in Eurasia*, ed. by D. R. Harris, pp. 465–98. London: UCL Press.

———. 2001. Early agriculturalist population diasporas? Farming, languages, and genes. *Annual Review of Anthropology* 30:181–207.

Belovsky, G. E. 1988. An optimal foraging-based model of hunter-gatherer population dynamics. *Journal of Anthropological Archaeology* 7:329–72.

Bender, B. 1978. Gatherer-hunter to farmer: A social perspective. *World Archaeology* 10:204–22.

Benson, K. E., and D. W. Stephens. 1996. Interruptions, tradeoffs, and temporal discounting. *American Zoologist* 36:506–17.

Benz, B. F. 1994. Reconstructing the racial phylogeny of Mexican maize: Where do we stand? In *Corn and Culture in the Prehistoric New World*, ed. by S. Johannessen and C. A. Hastrof, pp. 156–179. Boulder, CO: Westview Press.

———. 1999. On the origin, evolution, and dispersal of maize. In *Pacific Latin America in Prehistory: The Evolution of Archaeic and Formative Cultures*, ed. by M. Blake, pp. 25–38. Pullman, WA: Washington State University Press.

———. 2001. Archaeological evidence of teosinte domestication from Guila Naquitz, Oaxaca. *Proceedings of the National Academy of Sciences of the United States of America* 98(4):2104–06.

Benz, B. F., and H. Iltis. 1990. Studies in archaeological maize: The 'wild' maize from San Marcos cave reexamined. *American Antiquity* 55: 284–318.

Benz, B. F. and A. Long. 2000. Prehistoric maize evolution in the Tehuacan Valley. *Current Anthropology* 41(3):459–65.

Berkovitch, F. B. 1991. Social stratification, social hierarchies and reproductive success in primates. *Ethnology and Sociobiology* 12:315–33.

Bernabeu, J. 1989. *La Tradición Cultural de las Cerámicas Impresas en la Zona Oriental de la Península Ibérica*. Valencia: Servicio de Investigación Prehistorica.

———. 1993. El IIIr. Milenio a. C. en el País Valenciano. Los poblados de Jovades (Concentaina, Alacant) y Arenal de la Costa (Ontinyent, Valencia). *Saguntum* 26:11–179.

———. 1995. Origen y consolidación de las sociedades agrícolas. El País Valenciano entre el Neolítico y la Edad del Bronce. *Actes de les Segones Jornades d'Arqueologia*:37–60.

———. 1996. Indigenismo y migracionismo. Aspectos de la neolitización en la fachada oriental de la península Ibérica. *Trabajos de Prehistoria* 53:37–54.

Bernabeu, J. and J. L. Pascual. 1998. *La Expansión de la Agricultura. El Valle del Serpis Hace 5000 Anos*. Valencia: Museu de Prehistoria.

Bernabeu, J., E. Aura, and E. Badal. 1993. *Al Oeste del Eden*. Valencia: Editorial Sintesis.

Bernabeu, J., and E. Badal. 1990. Imagen de la vegetación y utilización económica del bosque en los asentamientos neolíticos de Jovades y Niuet (Alicante). *Archivo de Prehistoria Levantina* XX:143–66.

Bernabeu, J., C. M. Barton, and M. Pérez Ripoll. 2001. A taphonomic perspective on Neolithic beginnings: Theory, interpretation, and empirical data in the Western Mediterranean. *Journal of Archaeological Science* 28(6):597–612.

Bernabeu, J., T. Orozco Köhler, and A. Díez Castillo. 2002. El poblamiento neolítico: Desarrollo del paisaje agrario en Les Valls de l'Alcoi. In *La Sarga. Arte Rupestre y Territorio*, ed. by M. S. Hernández Pérez and J. M. Segura Martí, pp. 171–84. Alcoi: Ayuntamiento de Alcoy y Caja de Ahorros del Mediterráneo.

Bernabeu, J., C. M. Barton, O. García, and N. La Roca. 1999. Prospecciónes sistemáticas en el Valle del Alcoi (Alicante, España): Primeros resultados. *Arqueología Espacial* 21:29–64.

Bernabeu, J., T. Orozco Köhler, A. Díez Castillo, M. Gómez Puche, and F. J. Molina Hernández. 2003. Mas d'Is (Penàguila, Alicante): Aldeas y recintos monumentales del neolítico inicial en el valle del Serpis. *Trabajos de Prehistoria* 60(2): 39–59.

Bernabeu, J., J. L. Pascual, T. Orozco, E. Badal, M. P. Fumanal, and O. García. 1994. Niuet (L'Alqueria d'Asnar). Poblado del IIIr milenio a. C. *Recerques del Museu d'Alcoi* 3:9–74.

Bernard-Shaw, M. 1989 (ed.). *Archaeological Investigations of the Redtail Site, AA:12:149 (ASM), in the Northern Tucson Basin. Technical Report No. 89-8*. Tucson, AZ: Center for Desert Archaeology.

———. 1990 (ed.). *Archaeological Investigations at the Lonetree Site, AZ AA:12:120 (ASM), in the Northern Tucson Basin. Technical Report No. 90-1*. Tucson, AZ: Center for Desert Archaeology.

Berry, M. S. 1974. The Evans Mound: Cultural adaptation in southwestern Utah. Unpublished M. A. thesis, Department of Anthropology, Salt Lake City: University of Utah.

Best, S. 1993. At the halls of the mountain kings. Fijian and Samoan fortifications: Comparison and analysis. *The Journal of the Polynesian Society* 102(4):385–447.

Betancourt, J. L. 1990. Late Quaternary biogeography of the Colorado Plateau. In *Packrat Middens: The Last 40,000 Years of Biotic Change*, ed. by J. L. Betancourt, T. R. Van Devender, and P. S. Martin, pp. 259–92. Tucson: University of Arizona Press.

Bettinger, R. L. 1991a. Aboriginal occupation at high altitude: Alpine villages in the White Mountains of California. *American Anthropologist* 93:656–79.

———. 1991b. *Hunter-Gatherers: Archaeological and Evolutionary Theory*. New York: Plenum Press.

———. 1999a. From traveler to processor: Regional trajectories of hunter-gatherer sedentism in the Inyo-Mono region, California. In *Settlement Pattern Studies in the Americas: Fifty Years Since Viru*, ed. by B. R. Billman and G. M. Feinman, pp. 39–55. Washington, DC: Smithsonian Institution Press.

———. 1999b. What happened in the Medithermal? In *Models for the Millennium: Great Basin Anthropology Today*, ed. by C. Beck, pp. 62–74. Salt Lake City: University of Utah Press.

———. 2001. Holocene hunter-gatherers. In *Archaeology at the Millennium*, ed. by G. Feinman and T. D. Price, pp. 137–95. New York: Kluwer/Plenum.

Bettinger, R. L., and M. A. Baumhoff. 1982. The Numic Spread: Great Basin cultures in competition. *American Antiquity* 47:485–503.

Bettinger, R. L., and J. Eerkens. 1999. Point typologies, cultural transmission, and the spread of bow and arrow technology in the prehistoric Great Basin. *American Antiquity* 64(2): 231–42.

Bettinger, R. L., R. Malhi, and H. McCarthy. 1997. Central place models of acorn and mussel processing. *Journal of Archaeological Science* 24: 887–99.

Betts, A., K. van der Borg, A. de Jong, C. McClintock, and M. van Strydonck. 1994. Early cotton in north Arabia. *Journal of Archaeological Science* 21:489–99.

Biagi, P., and R. Nisbet. 1992. Environmental history and plant exploitation at the aceramic sites of RH5 and RH6 near the mangrove swamp of Qurm (Muscat, Oman). *Bulletin de la Société Botanique de France* 139:575.

Binder, D. 2000. Mesolithic and Neolithic interaction in southern France and northern Italy: New data and current hypotheses. In *Europe's First Farmers*, ed. by T. D. Price, pp. 117–43. Cambridge: Cambridge University Press.

Binford, L. R. 1968. Post-Pleistocene adaptations. In *New Perspectives in Archaeology*, ed. by S. R. Binford and L. R. Binford, pp. 313–41. Chicago: Aldine Publishing Co.

———. 1971. Post-Pleistocene adaptations. In *Prehistoric Agriculture*, ed. by S. Struever, pp. 22–49. Garden City: Natural History Press.

———. 1980. Willow smoke and dog's tails: Hunter-gatherer settlement systems and archaeological site formation. *American Antiquity* 45:4–20.

———. 1983. *In Pursuit of the Past: Decoding the Archaeological Record*. New York: Thames and Hudson.

———. 1990. Mobility, housing and environment: A comparative study. *Journal of Anthropological Research* 46:119–52.

Bird, D. W. 1997. Behavioral ecology and the archeological consequences of central place foraging among the Meriam. In *Rediscovering Darwin: Evolutionary Theory and Archeological Explanations*, ed. by C. M. Barton and G. A. Clark, pp. 291–308. Archeological Papers of the American Anthropological Association (7).

Arlington, VA: American Anthropological Association.

———. 2002. Explaining shellfish variability in middens on the Meriam Islands, Torres Strait, Australia. *Journal of Archaeological Science* 29: 457–69.

Bird, D. W., and J. F. O'Connell. 2003. Behavioral ecology and archaeology. *Journal of Archaeological Research*. In press.

Bird, D. W., and R. Bliege Bird. 1997. Contemporary shellfishing strategies among the Meriam of the Torres Straits Islands, Australia: Testing predictions of a central place foraging model. *Journal of Archaeological Science* 24:39–63.

———. 2000. The ethnoarchaeology of juvenile foragers: Shellfishing strategies among Meriam children. *Journal of Anthropological Archaeology* 19:461–76.

Blackburn, F. R., and R. A. Williamson. 1997. *Cowboys & Cave Dwellers: Basketmaker Archaeology in Utah's Grand Gulch*. Santa Fe: School of American Research Press.

Blackman, J., and S. Méry. 1999. Les importations de céramiques harappéennes en Arabie orientale: État de la question. *Proceedings of the Seminar for Arabian Studies* 29:7–28.

Blackman, J., S. Méry, and R. P. Wright. 1989. Production and exchange of ceramics on the Oman Peninsula from the perspective of Hili. *Journal of Field Archaeology* 16:61–85.

Blake, M. 1991. An emerging Early Formative chiefdom at Paso de la Amada, Chiapas, Mexico. In *The Formation of Complex Society in Southeastern Mesoamerica*, ed. by W. R. Fowler, Jr., pp. 27–46. Boca Raton: CRC Press.

Blake, M., and J. E. Clark. 1999. The emergence of herditary inequality: The case of Pacific coastal Chiapas, Mexico. In *Pacific Latin America in Prehistory*, ed. by M. Blake, pp. 55–73. Pullman, WA: Washington State University Press.

Blake, M., B. S. Chisholm, J. E. Clark and K. Mudar. 1992a. Non-agricultural staples and agricultural supplements: Early Formative subsistence in the Soconusco Region, Mexico. In *Transitions to Agriculture in Prehistory*, ed. by A. B. Gebauer and T. D. Price, pp. 133–51. Madison: Prehistory Press.

Blake, M., B. S. Chisholm, J. E. Clark, B. Voorhies, and M. W. Love. 1992b. Prehistoric subsistence in the Soconusco Region. *Current Anthropology* 33(1):83–94.

Blake, M., J. E. Clark, G. Michaels, M. W. Love, M. E. Pye, A. A. Demarest and B. Arroyo. 1995.

Radiocarbon chronology for the Late Archaic and Formative Periods on the Pacific coast of southeastern Mesoamerica. *Ancient Mesoamerica* 6:161–83.

Blanchet, G., P. Sanlaville, and M. Traboulsi. 1997. Le moyen-orient de 20,000 ans BP à 6000 ans BP. Essai de reconstitution paléoclimatique. *Paléorient* 23(2):187–96.

Bliege Bird, R. 1999. Cooperation and conflict: The behavioral ecology of the sexual division of labor. *Evolutionary Anthropology* 8:65–75.

Bliege Bird, R., and E. A. Smith, 2005. Signaling theory, strategic interaction, and symbolic capital. *Current Anthropology* 46:221–48.

Bliege Bird, R., E. A. Smith, and D. W. Bird. 2001. The hunting handicap: Costly signaling in human foraging strategies. *Behavioral Ecology and Sociology* 50:9–19.

Blumler, M. A. 1996. Ecology, evolutionary theory and agricultural origins. In *The Origins and Spread of Agriculture and Pastoralism in Eurasia*, ed. by D. R. Harris, pp. 25–50. Washington, DC: Smithsonian Institution Press.

———. 2002. Changing paradigms, wild cereal ecology, and agricultural origins. In *The Dawn of Farming in the Near East*, ed. by T. J. René, C. Bottema and S. Bottema, pp. 95–111. *Studies in Near Eastern Production, Subsistence, and Environment* 6. Berlin: ex oriente.

Blumler, M. A., R. Byrne, A. Belfer-Cohen, et al. 1991. The ecological genetics of domestication and the origins of agriculture. *Current Anthropology* 32:23–54.

Blurton Jones, N. G. 1987. Tolerated theft, suggestions about the ecology and evolution of sharing, hoarding and scrounging. *Social Science Information* 26:31–54.

Blust, R. 1997. Subgrouping, circularity and extinction: Some issues in Austronesian comparative linguistics. In *Papers for the Eighth International Conference on Austronesian Linguistics*, pp. 1–54. Taipei: Academia Sinica.

Boehm, C. 1992. Segmentary "warfare" and the management of conflict: Comparison of East African chimpanzees and patrlineal-patrilocal humans. In *Coalitions and Alliances in Humans and Other Animals*, ed. by A. Harcourt and F. de Waal, pp. 4137–73. New York: Oxford Science Publications.

———. 2000. Forager hierarchies, innate dispositions, and the behavioral reconstruction of prehistory. In *Hierarchies in Actino: Cui Bono?* ed. by M. W. Diehl, pp. 31–58. *Occasional Papers No. 27*. Carbondale, IL: The Center for Archaeological Investigations, Southern Illinois University.

Bogaard, A., G. Jones, and M. Charles. 2001. On the archaeobotanical inference of crop sowing time using the FIBS Method. *Journal of Archaeological Science* 28: 1171–83.

Bogucki, P. 1982. *Early Neolithic Subsistence and Settlement in the Polish Lowlands*. Oxford: Oxford University Press.

———. 2000. How agriculture came to north-central Europe. In *Europe's First Farmers*, ed. by T. D. Price, pp. 197–218. Cambridge: Cambridge University Press.

Bogucki, P., and R. Grygiel. 1993. The first farmers of central Europe: A survey article. *Journal of Field Archaeology* 20:399–426.

von Böhm-Bawerk, E. 1970. (1889). *Capital and Interest*. South Holland: Libertarian Press.

Boone, J. L. 1992. Competition, conflict, and the development of social hierarchies. In *Evolutionary Ecology and Human Behavior*, ed. by E. A. Smith and B. Winterhalder, pp. 301–37. New York: Aldine de Gruyter.

———. 2000. Status signaling, social power, and lineage survival. In *Hierarchies in Action: Cui Bono?* ed. by M. W. Diehl, pp. 84–110. *Occasional Papers No. 27*. Carbondale, IL: The Center for Archaeological Investigations, Southern Illinois University.

Boone, J. L., and E. A. Smith. 1998. Is it evolution yet? A critique of evolutionary archaeology. *Current Anthropology*, Supplement to Volume 39:141–73.

Borgerhoff Mulder, M. 1991. Human behavioural ecology. In *Behavioural Ecology: An Evolutionary Approach*, 3rd ed., ed. by J. R. Krebs and N. B. Davies, pp. 69–98. Oxford: Blackwell.

Bosch, A., J. Chinchilla, and J. Tarrús. 2002 (eds). *El Poblat Lacustre Neolitíc de la Draga. Excavacions de 1990 a 1998*. Girona: Museu d'Arqueologia de Catalunya.

Boserup, E. 1965. *The Conditions of Agricultural Growth*. New York: Aldine.

Bourke, R. M. 1996. Edible indigenous nuts in Papua New Guinea. *South Pacific Indigenous Nuts* 69:45–55.

Bourke, R. M. n.d. Altitudinal limits of 220 economic crop species in Papua New Guinea. Unpublished manuscript.

Bowles, S., and J.-K. Choi n.d. The first property rights revolution. In *Sante Fe Institute Working Paper 2002*.

Boxall, R. A, and D. J. B. Calverly. 1986. Grain quality considerations in relation to aeration and in-store drying. In *Preserving Grain Quality by Aeration and In-store Drying*, ed. by B. Champ, R., and E. Highley, pp. 17–23. *Proceedings No. 15*. Canberra, Australia: Australian Centre for International Agricultural Research.

Boyd, R., and P. J. Richerson. 1985. *Culture and the Evolutionary Process*. Chicago: University of Chicago Press.

———. 1988. The evolution of reciprocity in sizable groups. *Journal of Theoretical Biology* 132: 337–56.

Boyer, P. 1995. Ceteris paribus (All else being equal). In *How Things Are: A Science Tool-Kit for the Mind*, ed. by J. Brockman and K. Matson, pp. 169–75. New York: William Morrow and Company.

Braconnot P., S. Joussaume, N. de Noblet, and G. Ramstein. 2000. Mid-Holocene and Last Glacial Maximum African monsoon changes as simulated with the Paleoclimate Modelling Intercomparison Project. *Global and Planetary Change* 26:51–66.

Bradley, D. G., and R. Loftus. 2000. Two eves for taurus? Bovine mitochondrial DNA and African cattle domestication. In *The Origins and Development of African Livestock: Archaeology, Genetics, Linguistics and Ethnography*, ed. by R. M. Blench and K. C. Macdonald, pp. 244–50. London: UCL Press.

Braemer, F., T. Steimer-Herbet, L. Buchet, J.-F. Saliège, and H. Guy. 2001. Le Bronze Ancien du Ramlat as-Sabatayn (Yémen). Deux nécropoles de la première moitié du IIIe millénaire à la bordure du désert: Jebel Jidran et Jebel Ruwaiq. *Paléorient* 27(1):21–44.

Braidwood, R. J., and B. Howe. 1960. *Prehistoric Investigations in Iraqi Kurdistan*. Chicago: University of Chicago Press.

Brandt, S. A. 1984. New perspectives on the origins of food production in Ethiopia. In *From Hunters to Farmers*, ed. by J. D. Clark and S. A. Brandt, pp. 173–90. Los Angeles: University of California Press.

Brantingham, P. J. 2003. A neutral model of stone raw material procurement. *American Antiquity* 68:487–509.

Braun, L. 1950. *Deciduous Forests of Eastern North America*. New York: Hafner.

Bray, W. 2000. Ancient food for thought. *Nature* 408:145–6.

Breton, J.-F. 2000. The Wadi Surban (District of Bayhan, Yemen). *Proceedings of the Seminar for Arabian Studies* 30:49–60.

Brinkman, R. 1996a. Pedological characteristics of anthrosols in the al-Jadidah Basin of Wadi al-Jubah, and native sediments in Wadi al-Ajwirah, Yemen Arab Republic. In *The Wadi al-Jubah archaeological project, volume V. Environmental research in support of archaeological investigations in the Yemen Arab Republic 1982–1987*, ed. by M. Grolier, R. Brinkman, and J. Blakeley, pp. 45–211. Washington DC: American Foundation for the Study of Man.

Brinkman, R. 1996b. Thermoluminescence analysis of anthrosol from the Wadi al-Jubah Area, Yemen Arab Republic. In *The Wadi al-Jubah archaeological project, volume V. Environmental research in support of archaeological investigations in the Yemen Arab Republic 1982–1987*, ed. by M. Grolier, R. Brinkman, and J. Blakeley, pp. 213–14. Washington DC: American Foundation for the Study of Man.

Bronson, B. 1977. The earliest farming: Demography as cause and consequence. In *Origins of Agriculture*, ed. by C. A. Reed, pp. 23–48. The Hague: Mouton Publishing Company.

Brookfield, H. 1989. Frost and drought through time and space, part III: What were conditions like when the high valleys were first settled? *Mountain Research and Development* 9: 306–21.

Broughton, J. M. 1984. Late Holocene resource intensification in the Sacramento Valley, California: The vertebrate evidence. *Journal of Archaeological Science* 21(4):501–14.

———. 1997. Widening diet breadth, declining foraging efficiency, and prehistoric harvest pressure: Icthyofaunal evidence from the Emeryville Shell Mound, California. *Antiquity* 71:845–62.

———. 1999. *Resource Depression and Intensification During the Late Holocene, San Francisco Bay*. Berkeley, CA: University of California Press.

———. 2001. Resource intensification and Late Holocene human impacts on Pacific coast bird populations: Evidence from the Emeryville Shellmound avifauna. In *Posing Questions for a Scientific Archaeology*, ed. by T. D. Hunt, C. P. Lipo, and S. L. Sterling. Westport, CT: Bergin and Garvey.

———. 2002. Prey spatial structure and behavior affect archaeological tests of optimal foraging models: Examples from the Emeryville

Shellmound vertebrate fauna. *World Archaeology* 34:60–83.

Broughton, J. M., and F. E. Bayham. 2003. Showing off, foraging models, and the ascendance of large-game hunting in the California Middle Archaic. *American Antiquity* 68:783–89.

Broughton, J. M., and J. F. O'Connell. 1999. On evolutionary ecology, selectionist archaeology, and behavioral archaeology. *American Antiquity* 64:153–65.

Brown, D. 2000. *Aroids: Plants of the Arum Family.* Portland, Oregon: Timber Press.

Brown, J. L. 1969. The buffer effect and productivity in tit populations. *American Naturalist* 103: 347–54.

———. 1980. A brief report on Paleoindian-Archaic occupation in the Quiche Basin, Guatemala. *American Antiquity* 45:313–24.

Brown, T. A., R. G. Allaby, R. Sallares, and G. Jones. 1998. Ancient DNA in charred wheats: Taxonomic identification of mixed and single grains. *Ancient Biomolecules* 2:185–93.

Brunner, U. 1997. Geography and human settlement in ancient Southern Arabia. *Arabian Archaeology and Epigraphy* 8:190–202.

Brunner, U., and H. Haefner. 1986. The successful floodwater farming system of the Sabeans, Yemen Arab Republic. *Applied Geography* 6:77–86.

Bulmer, S. 1966. The prehistory of the Australian New Guinea Highlands: A discussion of archaeological field survey and excavations, 1959–60. Unpublished MA thesis, University of Auckland.

———. 1973. *Notes on 1972 Excavations at Wañelek, An Open settlement Site in the Kaironk Valley, Papua New Guinea.* Auckland: University of Auckland, Department of Anthropology Working Paper 29.

———. 1975. Settlement and economy in prehistoric Papua New Guinea: a review of the archaeological evidence. *Journal de la Société des Océanistes* 31(46):7–75.

———. 1977. Between the mountain and the plain: Prehistoric settlement and environment in the Kaironk Valley. In *The Melanesian Environment*, ed. by J. H. Winslow, pp. 61–73. Canberra: ANU Press.

———. 1991. Variation and change in stone tools in the highlands of Papua New Guinea: The witness of Wanelek. In *Man and a Half: Essays in Pacific Anthropology and Ethnobiology in Honour of Ralph Bulmer*, ed. by A. Pawley, pp. 470–78. Auckland: The Polynesian Society.

Burkill, I. H. 1935. *A Dictionary of the Economic Products of the Malay Peninsula.* London: Crown Agents.

Burley, D. V. 1998. Tongan archaeology and the Tongan past, 2850–150 BP. *Journal of World Prehistory* 12:337–92.

Burley, D. V., and W. R. Dickinson. 2001. Origin and significance of a founding settlement in Polynesia. *Proceedings of the National Academy of Sciences* 98:11829–31.

Burley, D. V., W. R. Dickinson, A. Barton, and R. Shutler Jr. 2001. Lapita on the periphery: New data on old problems in the Kingdom of Tonga. *Archaeology in Oceania* 36:89–104.

Burns, B. T. 1983. Simulated Anasazi storage behavior using crop yields reconstructed from tree rings: A D 652–1968. Unpublished Ph.D. Dissertation, University of Arizona Department of Anthropology. Ann Arbor: University Microfilms.

Burns, S. J., A. Matter, N. Frank, and A. Mangini. 1998. Speleothem-based paleoclimate record from northern Oman. *Geology* 26:499–502.

Butler, V. L. 2000. Resource depression on the Northwest coast of North America. *Antiquity* 74:649–61.

Butz, W. P., and J. Habicht. 1976. The effects of nutrition and health on fertility: Hypothesis, evidence and interventions. In *Population and Development: The Search for Selective Interventions.* Baltimore: Johns Hopkins Unviersity Press.

Butzer, K. W. 1976. *Early Hydraulic Civilization in Egypt.* Chicago: University of Chicago Press.

Byrd, B. 1992. The dispersal of food production across the Levant. In *Transitions to Agriculture in Prehistory*, ed. by A. B. Gebauer and T. D. Price, pp. 49–62. Madison: Prehistory Press.

Callen, E. O. 1967a. Analysis of the Tehuacán coprolites. In *The Prehistory of the Tehuacán Valley* (Vol 1): *Environment and Subsistence*, ed. by D. S. Byers, pp. 261–89. Austin: University of Texas Press.

———. 1967b. The first New World cereal. *American Antiquity* 32:535–38.

Camerer, C. F., and R. M. Hogarth. 1999. The effects of financial incentives on experiments: A review and capital-labor production framework. *Journal of Risk and Uncertainty* 19:7–42.

Cancián, F. 1965. *Economics and Prestige in a Maya Community: The Religious Cargo System in Zinacantan.* Stanford: Stanford University Press.

Cane, S. 1989. Australian aboriginal seed grinding and its archaeological record: A case study from the western desert. In *Foraging and Farming: The Evolution of Plant Exploitation*, ed. by D. R. Harris and G. C. Hillman, pp. 99–119. London: Unwin Hyman.

Cannon, M. D. 2003. A model of central place forager prey choice and an application to faunal remains from the Mimbres Valley, New Mexico. *Journal of Anthropological Archaeology* 22:1–25.

Caraco, T., S. Martindale, and T. S. Whittam. 1980. An empirical demonstration of risk-sensitive foraging preferences. *Animal Behaviour* 28: 820–30.

Carneiro, R. L. 1970. A theory of the origin of the state. *Science* 169:733–38.

———. 1978. Political expansion as an expression of the principle of competitive exclusion. In *Origins of the State: The Anthropology of Political Evolution*, ed. by R. Cohen and E. R. Service, pp. 205–33. Philadelphia: Institution for the Study of Human Issues.

———. 1987. Further reflections on resource concentration and its role in the rise of the state. In *Studies in the Neolithic and Urban Revolutions*, ed. by L. Manzanilla, pp. 245–60. Oxford: BAR International Series 349.

———. 1988. The circumscription theory: Challenge and response. *American Behavioral Scientist* 31(4):497–511.

Carter, W. 1969. *New Lands and Old Traditions: Kekchi Cultivators in the Guatemalan Lowlands*. Gainesville, FL: University of Florida Press.

Cartwright, C. 1998. Seasonal aspects of Bronze and Iron Age communities at Ra's al-Hadd, Oman. *Environmental Archaeology* 3:97–102.

Cashdan, E. 1990 (ed.). *Risk and Uncertainty in Tribal and Peasant Economies*. Boulder, CO: Westview Press.

Castro, V., and M. Tarrago. 1992. Los inicios de la producción de alimentos en el Cono Sur de America. *Revista de Arqueología Americana* 6: 92–124.

Cattani, M., and S. Bökönyi. 2002. Ash-Shumah, an early Holocene settlement of desert hunters and mangrove foragers in the Yemeni Tihamah. In *Essays on the Late Prehistory of the Arabian Peninsula*, ed. by S. Cleuziou, M. Tosi, and J. Zarins, pp. 31–53. Serie Orientale Roma 93. Roma: Istituto Italiano per L'Africa e L'Oriente.

Cavalli-Sforza, L. L. 1996. The spread of agriculture and nomadic pastoralism: Insights from genetics, linguisitics and archaeology. In *The Origins and Spread of Agriculture and Pastoralism in Eurasia*, ed. by D. R. Harris, pp. 51–69. Washington, DC: Smithsonian Institution Press.

Chamberlain, T. 1965. The method of multiple working hypotheses. *Science* 148: 754–9.

Chamberlain, T. 1972. *Introduction to Logic*. Fourth Edition. New York: Macmillan.

Chappell, J. A. C. 2001. Climate before agriculture. In *Histories of Old Ages: Essays in Honour of Rhys Jones*, ed. by A. Anderson, I. Lilley, and S. O'Connor, pp. 171–83. Canberra: Pandanus Books, RSPAS, ANU.

Charles, M., A. Bogaard, G. Jones, J. Hodgson, and P. Halstead. 2002. Toward the archaeobotanical identification of intensive cereal cultivation: Present-day ecological investigation in the mountains of Asturias, northwest Spain. *Vegetation History and Archaeobotany* 11:133–42.

Charnov, E. L. 1976. Optimal foraging, the marginal value theorem. *Theoretical Population Biology* 9(2):129–36.

Charnov, E. L., G. H. Orians, and K. Hyatt. 1976. Ecological implications of resource depression. *The American Naturalist* 110(972):247–59.

Charpentier, V. 1994. A specialized production at a regional scale in Bronze Age Arabia: Shell rings from R's al-Junayz Area (Sultanate of Oman). In *South Asian Archaeology*, ed. by A. Parpola and P. Koskikallio, pp. 157–70. Helsinki: Annales Academiae Scientarium Fennicae. Series B, 271.

———. 1996. Entre sables du Rub' al-Khali et mer d'Arabie, Préhistoire récente du Dhofar et d' Oman: Les industries à pointes de "Fasad." *Proceedings of the Seminar for Arabian Studies* 26:1–12.

———. 2001. Les industrie lithiques de Ra's al-Hadd. *Proceedings of the Seminar for Arabian Studies* 31:31–45.

Charpentier, V., D. E. Angelucci, S. Méry, and J.-F. Saliège. 2000. Autour de la mangrove morte de Suwayh, l'habitat VIᵉ-Vᵉ millénaires de Suwayh SWY-11, Sultanat d'Oman. *Proceedings of the Seminar for Arabian Stuides* 30:69–85.

Chikwendu, V. E., and C. E. A. Okezie. 1989. Factors responsible for the ennoblement of African yams: Inferences from experiments in yam domestication. In *Foraging and Farming: The Evolution of Plant Exploitation*, ed. by D. R. Harris and G. C. Hillman, pp. 344–57. London: Unwin Hyman.

Childe, V. G. 1928. *The Most Ancient East*. London: Trubner and Co.

———. 1951. *Social Evolution*. London: Watts.

———. 1965. *Man Makes Himself*. London: Watts & Co.

Christensen, C.M., and R.A. Meronuck. 1986. *Quality Maintenance in Stored Grains and Seeds*. Minneapolis, MN: University of Minnesota Press.

Christensen, O.A. 1975. Hunters and horticulturalists: A preliminary report of the 1972–4 excavations in the Manim Valley, Papua New Guinea. *Mankind* 10(1):24–36.

Ciolek-Torrello, R. 1998 (ed.). *Early Farmers of the Sonoran Desert: Archaeological Investigations at the Houghton Road Site, Tucson, Arizona. Technical Series No. 72*. Tucson, AZ: Statistical Research, Inc.

Ciolek-Torrello, R., E.K. Huber, and R.B. Neily. 1999 (eds.). *Investigations at Sunset Mesa Ruin: Archaeology at the Confluence of the Santa Cruz and Rillito Rivers, Tucson, Arizona. Technical Series No. 66*. Tucson, AZ: Statistical Research, Inc.

Clark, G.R. 1999. Post-Lapita Fiji: Cultural transformation in the mid-sequence. Unpublished Ph.D. Thesis, Department of Archaeology and Natural History, Research School of Pacific and Asian Studies, Australian National University, Canberra, Australia.

Clark G.R., and A.J. Anderson. 2001. The pattern of Lapita settlement in Fiji. *Archaeology in Oceania* 36:77–88.

Clark, J.E. 1991. The beginnings of Mesoamerica: Apologia for the Soconusco Early Formative. In *The Formation of Complex Society in Southeastern Mesoamerica*, ed. by W.R. Fowler, Jr., pp. 13–26. Boca Raton: CRC Press.

———. 1994. The development of early formative rank societies in the Soconusco, Chiapas, Mexico. Unpublished Ph.D. dissertation, Department of Anthropology, University of Michigan, Ann Arbor.

Clark, J.E., and M. Blake. 1994. Power of prestige: Competitive generosity and the emergence of rank in lowland Mesoamerica. In *Factional Competition and Political Development in the New World*, ed. by E.M. Brumfiel and J.W. Fox, pp. 17–30. Cambridge: Cambridge University Press.

Clark, J.T. 1991. Early settlement of the Indo-Pacific. *Journal of Anthropological Archaeology* 10:27–53.

Clark, J.T., and K.M. Kelly. 1993. Human genetics, paleoenvironments, and malaria: Relationships and implications for the settlement of Oceania. *American Anthropologist* 95: 612–30.

Clark, J.T., and J.E. Terrell. 1978. Archaeology in Oceania. *Annual Review of Anthropology* 7: 293–319.

Clark, R. 1990. The beginnings of agriculture in sub-alpine Italy: Some theoretical considerations. *Neolithisation of the Alpine Region* 13: 123–37.

Cleuziou, S. 1992. The Oman peninsula and the Indus civilization: A reassessment. *Man and Environment* 17:93–103.

Cleuziou, S. 1997. Construire et proteger son terroir: les oasis d'Oman a l'age du bronze. In *La Dynamique des Paysages Protohistoriques, Antigues, Medievaux et Modernes*, ed. by J.P. Bravard, T. Bernouf and C. Chouquer, pp. 389–412. Antibes: ADPCA.

Cleuziou, S., and L. Costantini. 1982. A l'origine des oasis. *La Recherche* 137:1180–82.

Cleuziou, S., and M. Tosi. 1994. Black boats of Magan: some thoughts on Bronze Age water transport in Oman and beyond from the impressed bitumen slabs of Ra's al-Junayz. In *South Asian Archaeology 1993*, Vol. II, ed. by A. Parpola and P. Koskilkallio, pp. 745–61. Helsinki: Soumalainen Tiedeakatemia.

———. 1997. Hommes, climats, et environnements de la Péninsule arabique à l'Holocène. *Paléorient* 23(2):121–36.

Cleuziou, S., and B. Vogt. 1985. Tomb A at Hili North (United Arab Emirates) and its Materila connections to southeast Iran and the Greater Indus Valley. In *South Asian Archaeology 1983*, ed. by J. Schotsmans and M. Taddei, pp. 249–77. Naples: IUO Series XXIII.

Cleuziou, S., M.-L. Inizan, and B. Marcolongo. 1992. Le peuplement pré- et protohistorique du systéme fluviatile fossile du Jawf-Hadramawt au Yémen. *Paléorient* 18(2):5–29.

Close, A., and F. Wendorf. 1992. The beginnings of food production in the eastern Sahara, In *Transitions to Agriculture in Prehistory*, ed. by A.B. Gebauer and T.D. Price, pp. 63–72. Madison, Wisconsin: Prehistory Press.

Clutton-Brock, T.H., and P.H. Harvey. 1978. Mammals, resources and reproductive strategies. *Nature* 273:191–5.

Coe, M.D. 1961. *La Victoria: An Early Site on the Pacific Coast of Guatemala*. Archaeological and Ethnological Papers 53. Cambridge, Massachussetts: Peabody Museum and Harvard University.

Coe, M.D., and K.V. Flannery. 1967. *Early Cultures and Human Ecology in South Coastal Guatemala*.

Smithsonian Contributions to Anthropology 3. Washington DC: Smithsonian Institution.

Cohen, M. N. 1977. *The Food Crisis in Prehistory: Overpopulation and the Origins of Agriculture.* New Haven: Yale University Press.

Colledge, S. 2001. *Plant Exploitation on Epi-Palaeolithic and Early Neolithic Sites in the Levant.* British Archaeological Reports International Series 986. Oxford: John and Erica Hedges and Archaeopress.

Coltrain, J. B. 1993. Fremont corn agriculture: A pilot stable carbon isotope study. *Utah Archaeology* 1993:49–55.

Coltrain, J. B., and S. W. Leavitt. 2002. Climate and diet in Fremont prehistory: Economic variability and abandonment of maize agriculture in the Great Salt Lake Basin. *American Antiquity* 67:453–85.

Coltrain, J. B., and J. T. W. Stafford. 1999. Stable carbon isotopes and Great Salt Lake wetlands diet: Toward an understanding of the Great Basin Formative. In *Prehistoric Lifeways in the Great Basin Wetlands,* ed. by B. E. Hemphill and C. S. Larsen, pp. 55–83. Salt Lake City: University of Utah Press.

CONAF. 1983. Bases para el manejo de la vicuña en la Provincia de Parinacota: Región I, Chile. *Documento de Trabajo* 3. Arica.

Cooke, R. G. 1998. Human settlement of Central America and northernmost South America (14000–8000 BP). *Quaternary International* 49/50:177–90.

Cooke, R. G., and A. J. Ranere. 1992. Prehistoric human adaptations to the seasonally dry forests of Panama. *World Archaeology* 24:114–33.

———. 1997. *The Relation of Fish Resources to the Location, Diet Breadth, and Procurement Technology of Preceramic and Ceramic Sites in an Estuarine Embayment on the Pacific Coast of Panama.* Olympia: Washington State University Press.

Cooke, R. G., L. Norr, and D. R. Piperno. 1996. Native Americans and the Panamanian landscape. In *Case Studies in Environmental Archaeology,* ed. by E. J. Reitz, L. A. Newsome, and S. J. Scudder, pp. 103–26. New York: Plenum Press.

Cooke, R. G., M. Jiménez, C. Tapia, and B. Voorhies. 2004. A closer look at the Late Archaic fish fauna. In *Coastal Collectors in the Holocene: The Chantuto People of Southwest Mexico,* ed. by B. Voorhies. Gainesville, FL: University Press of Florida.

Copi, I. M. 1972. *Introduction to Logic* (Fourth Edition). New York: Macmillian Publishing Co.

Coque-Delhuille, B. and P. Gentille. 1998. Controlee des perimetres d'irrigation antiques. In *Une Vallée Aride du Yémen Antique: Le Wadi Bayhan,* ed. by J.-F. Breton, J.-C. Arramond, B. Coque-Delhuille, and P. Gentille, pp. 87–94. Paris: Editions Recherches sur les Civilisations.

Cordell, L. S. 1984. *Prehistory of the Southwest.* New York: Academic Press.

———. 1997. *Archaeology of the Southwest.* (2d ed.). New York: Academic Press.

Coronel, R. E. 1992. *Canarium ovatum* Engl. In *Plant resources of South-East Asia 2: Edible Fruits and Nuts,* ed. by E. W. M. Verheij and R. E. Coronel, pp. 105–08. Indonesia: Prosea.

Costantini, L. 1984 The beginnings of agriculture in the Kachi plain: The evidence of Mehrgahr. In *South Asian Archaeology 1981,* ed. by B. Allchin, pp. 29–33. Cambridge: Cambridge University Press.

———. 1990a. Ecology and farming of the proto-historic communities in the central Yemeni highlands. In *The Bronze Age Culture of Hawlan at-Tiyal and al-Hada (Republic of Yemen),* ed. by A. de Maigret, pp. 187–204. Roma: Istituto Italiano per il Medio ed Estremo Oriente.

———. 1990b. Harappan agriculture in Pakistan: The evidence of Nausharo. In *South Asian Archaeology 1987.* ed. by M. Taddei, pp. 321–32. Roma: Istituto Italiano per il Medio ed Estremo Oriente.

Costantini, L., and P. Audisio. 2000. Plant and insect remains from the Bronze Age site of Ra's al Jinz (RJ-2), Sultanate of Oman. *Paleorient* 26(1):143–56.

Cowan, C. W. 1975. *An Archaeological Survey and Assessment of the Proposed Red River Reservoir in Powell, Wolfe, and Menifee Counties, Kentucky.* University of Kentucky Museum of Anthropology. Submitted to National Park Service, Interagency Archaeological Services.

———. 1976. *Test Excavations in the Proposed Red River Lake, Kentucky: 1974 Season.* University of Kentucky Museum of Anthropology. Submitted to National Park Service, Interagency Archaeological Service.

———. 1985a. From foraging to incipient food production: Subsistence change and continuity on the Cumberland Plateau of Eastern Kentucky. Unpublished Ph.D. dissertation, University of Michigan, Ann Arbor.

————. 1985b. Understanding the evolution of plant husbandry in eastern North America: Lessons from botany, ethnography, and archaeology. In *Prehistoric Food Production in North America*, ed. by R. I. Ford, pp. 205–43. Anthropological Papers No. 75. Ann Arbor: Museum of Anthropology, University of Michigan.

Cowan, C. W., and P. J. Watson. 1992 (ed.). *The Origins of Agriculture: An International Perspective.* Washington, DC: Smithsonian Institution Press.

Cowan, C. W., and F. T. Wilson. 1977. *An Archaeological Survey of the Red River Gorge Area in Menifee, Powell, and Wolfe Counties, Kentucky.* Frankfort: Kentucky Heritage Commission.

Cowan, C. W., E. E. Jackson, K. Moore, A. Nickelhoff, and T. Smart. 1981. The Cloudsplitter Rockshelter, Menifee County, Kentucky: A preliminary report. *Southeastern Archaeological Conference Bulletin* 24:60–75.

Cowling, S. A., and M. T. Sykes. 1999. Physiological significance of low atmospheric CO_2 for plant-climate interactions. *Quaternary Research* 52:237–42.

Crawford, G. 1992. Prehistoric plant domestication in East Asia. In *The Origins of Agriculture: An International Perspective*, ed. by C. W. Cowan and P. J. Watson, pp. 7–38. Washington DC: Smithsonian Institution Press.

Cronk, L. 1991. Human behavioral ecology. *Annual Review of Anthropology* 20:25–53.

Crosswhite, F. S. 1980. The annual saguaro harvest and crop cycle of the Papago, with reference to ecology and symbolism. *Desert Plants* 2:3–61.

Crown, P. L., and W. H. Wills. 1995. Economic intensification and the origins of ceramic containers in the American Southwest. In *The Emergence of Pottery: Technology and Innovation in Ancient Societies*, ed. by W. K. Barnett and J. W. Hoopes, pp. 241–54. Washington, DC: Smithsonian Institution Press.

Cullen, H. M., P. B. DeMenocal, S. Hemming, G. Hemming, F. H. Brown, T. Guilderson, and F. Sirocko. 2000. Climate change and the collapse of the Akkadian empire: Evidence from the deep sea. *Geology* 28:379–82.

Currey, D. R., and S. R. James. 1982. Paleoenvironments of the northeastern Great Basin and northeastern basin rim region: A review of geological and biological evidence. In *Man and Environment in the Great Basin, SAA Papers No. 2*, ed. by D. B. Madsen and J. F. O'Connell, pp. 27–52. Washington, DC: Society for American Archaeology.

Custred, G. 1979. Hunting technologies in Andean cultures. *Journal de Societe des Americanistes* 66:7–19.

Cutler, H. C., and T. W. Whitaker. 1967. Cucurbits from the Tehuacán caves. In *The Prehistory of the Tehuacán Valley, Vol. I., Environment and Subsistence*, ed. by D. Byers, pp. 212–19. Austin: University of Texas Press.

Czaplicki, J. S., and J. C. Ravesloot. 1988 (eds). *Hohokam Archaeology along Phase B of the Tucson Aqueduct, Central Arizona Project*: Vol. 2. Excavations at Fastimes (AZ AA:12:384), a Rillito Phase Site in the Avra Valley. Archaeological Series No. 178. Tucson, AZ: Arizona State Museum, University of Arizona.

Czaplicki, J. S., and J. C. Ravesloot. 1989 (eds). *Hohokam Archaeology along Phase B of the Tucson Aqueduct, Central Arizona Project*: Vol. 3. Excavations at Water World (AZ AA:16:94), a Rillito Phase Ballcourt Village in the Avra Valley. Archaeological Series No. 178. Tucson, AZ: Arizona State Museum, University of Arizona.

Dalton, G. 1971. Introduction. In *Studies in Economic Anthropology*, ed. by G. Dalton, pp. 1–15. Anthropological Studies. vol. 7. Washington DC: American Anthropological Association.

D'Andrea, A. C., M. Klee, and J. Casey. 2001. Archaeobotanical evidence for pearl millet (*Pennisetum glaucum*) in sub-Saharan West Africa. *Antiquity* 75:341–48.

D'Andrea, A. C., D. Lyons, M. Haile, and A. Butler. 1999. Ethnoarchaeological approaches to the study of prehistoric agriculture in the highlands of Ethiopia. In *The Exploitation of Plant Resources in Ancient Africa*, ed. by M. van der Veen, pp. 101–22. New York: Kluwer Academic/Plenum Press.

Daniels, J., and C. Daniels. 1993. Sugarcane in prehistory. *Archaeology in Oceania* 28:1–8.

Darwin, C. 1874. *The Descent of Man and Selection in Relation to Sex.* New York: Thomas Y. Crowell and Co.

David, H. 1996. Styles and evolution: Soft stone vessels during the Bronze Age in the Oman Peninsula. *Proceedings of the Seminar for Arabian Studies* 26:31–46.

Davidson, J., and F. Leach. 2001. The Strandlooper concept and economic naivety. *The Archaeology of Lapita Dispersal in Oceania* 17:115–23.

Davies, M. S., and G. C. Hillman. 1988. Effects of soil flooding on growth and grain yield of populations of tetraploid and hexaploid species of wheat. *Annals of Botany* 62:597–604.

Davis, W. G. 1973. *Social Relations in a Phillipine Market*. Berkeley: University of California Press.

Decker, K. W., and L. L. Tieszen. 1989. Isotopic reconstruction of Mesa Verde diet from Basketmaker III to Pueblo III. *The Kiva* 55:33–47.

Delcourt, P. A., H. Delcourt, C. R. Ison, W. Sharp, and K. J. Gremillion. 1998. Prehistoric human use of fire, the eastern agricultural complex, and Appalachian oak-chestnut forests: Paleoecology of Cliff Palace Pond, Kentucky. *American Antiquity* 63:263–78.

de Maigret, A. 1996. New evidence from the Yemenite "Turret Graves" for the problem of the emergence of the South Arabian States. In *The Indian Ocean in Antiquity*, ed. by J. Reade, pp. 321–37. London: Kegan Paul International.

de Menocal, P., and J. Bloemendal. 1995. Plio-Pleistocene climatic variability in subtropical Africa and the paleoenvironment of homonid evolution: A combined data-model approach. In *Paleoclimate and Evolution with Emphasis on Human Origins*, ed. by E. S. Vrba, G. H. Denton, T. C. Partridge, and L. H Burckle, pp. 262–88. New Haven: Yale University Press.

de Moulins, D., C. Phillips, and N. Durrani. 2003. The archaeobotanical record of Yemen and the question of Afro-Asian contacts. In *Food, Fuel, and Fields: Progress in African Archaeobotany*. ed. by K. Neumann, A. Butler, and S. Kahlheber, pp. 213–28. Koln: Heinrich Barth Institute.

Denham, T. 2003a. The Kuk morass: Multidisciplinary investigations of early agriculture (phases 1, 2 and 3 at Kuk Swamp) in the Highlands of New Guinea. Unpublished Ph.D. Dissertation, Australian National University.

———. 2003b. Archaeological evidence for mid-Holocene agriculture in the interior of Papua New Guinea: A critical review. In *Perspectives on Prehistoric Agriculture in New Guinea*, ed. by T. P. Denham and C. Ballard. *Archaeology in Oceania*, Special Issue 38(3):159–76.

———. 2004. Early agriculture in the Highlands of New Guinea? An assessment of Phase 1 at Kuk Swamp. In *A Pacific Odyssey: Archaeology and Anthropology in the Western Pacific. Papers in Honour of Jim Specht*, ed. by V. Attenbrow and R. Fullagar. Records of the Australian Museum, Supplement 29:47–57.

———. in press a. Agricultural origins and the emergence of rectilinear ditch networks in the Highlands of New Guinea. In *Papuan Pasts: Studies in the Cultural, Linguistic, and Biological History of the Papuan Speaking People*, ed. by A. Pawley, R. Attenborough, J. Golson, and R. Hide. Canberra: Pandanus Books.

Dennell, R. W. 1985. The hunter-gatherer/agricultural frontier in prehistoric Europe. In *The Archaeology of Frontiers and Boundaries*, ed. by S. Green and S. Perlman, pp. 113–40. New York: Academic Press.

———. 1992. The origins of crop agriculture in Europe. In *The Origins of Agriculture*, ed. by C. W. Cowan and P. J. Watson, pp. 71–100 Washington DC: Smithsonian Institution Press.

Deotare, B. C., and M. D. Kajale. 1996. Quaternary pollen analysis and palaeoenvinronmental studies on the salt basins at Pachpadra and Thob, Western Rajasthan, India: Preliminary observations. *Man and Environment* 21(1): 24–31.

De Wet, J. M. J. 1977. Domestication of African cereals. *African Economic History* 3:15–32.

Diamond, J. 1977. Colonization cycles in man and beast. *World Archaeology* 8:249–61.

———. 1997. *Guns, Germs, and Steel: The Fates of Human Societies*. New York: W. W. Norton and Company.

———. 2002. Evolution, consequences and future of plant and animal domestication. *Nature* 418:700–07.

Diamond, J., and P. Bellwood. 2003. Farmers and their languages: The first expansions. *Science* 300:597–603.

Dickens, C. 1853. The noble savage. *Household Words* N.S. I:337–39.

Diehl, M. W. 1992. Architecture as a material correlate of mobility strategies: Some implications for archaeological interpretation. *Behavior Science Research* 26:1–35.

———. 1996a. The intensity of maize processing and production in upland Mogollon pithouse villages, AD 200–1000. *American Antiquity* 61:102–15.

———. 1996b (ed.). *Archaeological Investigations of the Early Agricultural Period Settlement at the Base of A-Mountain, Tucson, Arizona. Technical Report No. 96–21.* Tucson, AZ: Center for Desert Archaeology.

———. 1997. Rational behavior, the adoption of agriculture, and the organization of subsistence during the Late Archaic Period in the Greater Tucson Basin. In *Rediscovering Darwin: Evolutionary Theory and Archaeological Explanation*, ed. by C. M. Barton and G. A.

Clark, pp. 251–66. Archaeological Papers No. 7. Arlington, VA: American Anthropological Association.

———. 2000. Some thoughts on the study of hierarchies. In *Hierarchies in Action: Cui Bono?*, ed. by M. W. Diehl, pp. 11–30. Occasional Papers No. 27. Carbondale, IL: The Center for Archaeological Investigations, Southern Illinois University.

———. 2001. Flotation samples: Methods, procedures, and identified taxa. In *Excavations in the Santa Cruz River Floodplain: The Early Agricultural Period Component at Los Pozos*, ed. by D. A. Gregory, pp. 305–32. Anthropological Papers No. 21. Tucson, AZ: Center for Desert Archaeology.

———. 2005. Morphological observations on recently recovered early agricultural period maize cob fragments from southern Arizona. *American Antiquity* 70:361–75.

Dillehay, T. D. 1997. *Monte Verde: A Late Pleistocene Settlement in Chile. Volume 2: The Archaeological Context and Interpretation*. Washington DC: Smithsonian Institution Press.

Dillehay, T. D., G. A. Calderón, G. Politis, and M. da C. Coutinho Beltrâo. 1992. Earliest hunters and gatherers of South America. *Journal of World Prehistory* 6:145–204.

Dincauze, D. F. 2000. *Environmental Archaeology: Principles and Practice*. Cambridge: Cambridge University Press.

Dodd, W. A, Jr. 1982. *Final year excavations at the Evans Mound Site. University of Utah Anthropological Papers* 106. Salt Lake City: University of Utah Press.

Doebley, J. 1990. Molecular evidence and the evolution of maize. *Economic Botany* 44(3 supplement):6–27.

Doelle, W. H. 1976. *Desert Resources and Hohokam Subsistence: The Conoco Florence Project. Archaeological Series No. 103*. Tucson, AZ: Arizona State Museum.

———. 1978. Hohokam use of nonriverine resources. In *Discovering Past Behavior*, ed. by P. Grebinger, pp. 245–74. New York: Gordon and Breach.

———. 1980. Past adaptive patterns in western Papagueria: An archaeological study of a nonriverine resource use. Unpublished Ph.D. Dissertation, Department of Anthropology, Tucson, AZ: University of Arizona.

———. 1985. *Excavations at the Valencia Site, a Preclassic Hohokam Village in the Southern Tucson Basin. Anthropological Papers No. 3*. Tucson, AZ: Institute for American Research.

Donahue, R. E. 1992. Desperately seeking Ceres: A critical examination of current models for the transition to agriculture in Mediterranean Europe. In *Transitions to Agriculture in Prehistory*, ed. by A. B. Gebauer and T. D. Price, pp. 73–80. Madison: Prehistory Press.

Donoghue, D. 1988. Pandanus and changing site use: A study from Manim Valley, Papua New Guinea. Unpublished B.A thesis (Hons.), University of Queensland.

Donald, C. M., and J. Hamblin. 1983. The convergent evolution of annual seed crops in agriculture. *Advances in Agronomy* 36:97–143.

Doolittle, W. E. 1990. *Canal Irrigation in Prehistoric Mexico: The Sequence of Technological Change*. First edition. Austin: University of Texas Press.

———. 2000. *Cultivated Landscapes of Native North America*. New York: Oxford University Press.

Dorweiler, J. E., and J. Doebley. 1997. Developmental analysis of *Teosinte Glume Architecture 1*: A key locus in the evolution of maize (Poaceae). *American Journal of Botany* 84: 1313–22.

Dounais, E. 1996. Perception and use of wild yams by the Baka hunter-gatherers in South Cameroon. In *Tropical Forests, People and Food*, ed. by C. M. Hladik, A. Hladik, O. F. Linares, H. Pagezy, A. Semple, and M. Hadley, pp. 621–32. Paris: Unesco and The Parthenon Publishing Group.

Drucker, P. 1948. Preliminary notes on an archaeological survey of the Chiapas coast. *Middle American Research Records* 1:151–69.

Drury, R. 1826 [1729]. *The Pleasant and Surprising Adventures of Robert Drury During his Fifteen Years' Captivity on the Island of Madagascar*. London: Hunt and Clarke.

Duke, J. A. 2002. Dr. Duke's Phytochemical and Ethnobotanical Databases. Agricultural Research Service, USDA. Accessed 6/13, 2002. http://www. ars-grin.gov/duke/

Dumont, R., and P. Vernier. 2000. Domestication of yams (*Dioscorea cayenensis-rotundata*) within the Bariba ethnic group in Benin. *Outlook on Agriculture* 29:137–42.

Dupré, M. 1988. *Palinologia y Paleoambiente. Nuevos Datos Españoles. Referencias*. Valencia: Diputación Provincial de Valencia.

Dwyer, P. D. 1983. Etolo hunting performance and energetics. *Human Ecology* 11:145–74.

————. 1985. The contribution of non-domesticated animals to the diet of the Etolo, Southern Highlands Province, Papua New Guinea. *Ecology of Food and Nutrition* 17:101–15.

Dwyer, P., and M. Minnegal. 1993. Are Kubo hunters 'show offs'? *Ethology and Sociobiology* 14:53–70.

Dye, T. 1992. The South Point radiocarbon dates thirty years later. *New Zealand Journal of Archaeology* 14:89–97.

Dyson-Hudson, R., and N. Dyson-Hudson. 1970. The food production system of a semi-nomadic society: The Karimojong, Uganda. In *African Food Production Systems*, ed. by P. McLoughlin, pp. 91–123. Baltimore: Johns Hopkins Press.

Edens, C. 1994. On the complexity of complex societies: Structure, power, and legitimation. In *Chiefdoms and Early States in the Near East*, ed. by K. Babylonia, G. Stein, and M. S. Rothman, pp. 209–23. Madison, Wisconsin: Prehistory Press.

————. 1999a. Khor Ile-Sud Qatar: The archaeology of Late Bronze Age purple dye production in the Arabian Gulf. *Iraq* 61:71–88.

————. 1999b. The Bronze Age of highland Yemen: Chronological and spatial variability of pottery and settlement. *Paléorient* 25(2):105–28.

————. (forthcoming). Exploring early agriculture in the highlands of Yemen.

Edens, C., T. J. Wilkinson, and G. Barratt. 2000. Hammat al-Qa and the roots of urbanism in southwest Asia. *Antiquity* 74:854–62.

Eder, J. 1978. The caloric returns to food collecting: Disruption and change among the Batak of the Philippine tropical forest. *Human Ecology* 6:55–69.

Ekstrom, H., and C. Edens. 2003. Prehistoric agriculture in highland Yemen: New results from Dhamar. *Bulletin of the American Institute for Yemeni Studies* 45:23–35.

El Mahi, A. T. 2000. Traditional fish preservation in Oman: The seasonality of a subsistence strategy. *Proceedings of the Seminar for Arabian Studies* 30:99–113.

————. 2001. The traditional pastoral groups of Dhofar, Oman: A parallel for ancient cultural ecology. *Proceedings of the Seminar for Arabian Studies* 31:131–43.

El-Moslimany, A. P. 1983. *History of climate and vegetation in the Eastern Mediterranean and the Middle East from the Pleniglacial to the Mid-Holocene.* Unpublished Ph.D. dissertation, University of Washingon. Ann Arbor: University Microfilms International.

Elson, M. D. 1986 (ed.). *Archaeological Investigations at the Tanque Verde Wash Site: A Middle Rincon Settlement in the Eastern Tucson Basin.* Anthropological Papers No. 7. Tucson, AZ: Institute for American Research.

Elster, J. 1986. Introduction. In *Rational Choice*, ed. by J. Elster, pp. 1–33. New York: New York University Press.

Elston, R. G., and D. W. Zeanah. 2002. Thinking outside the box: A new perspective on diet breadth and sexual division of labor in the prearchaic Great Basin. *World Archaeology* 34:103–130.

Enard, W., M. Przeworski, S. E. Fisher, C. S. L. Lai, V. Wiebe, T. Kitano, A. P. Monaco, and S. Pääbo. 2002. Molecular evolution of *FOXP2*, a gene involved in speech and language. *Nature* Online, August 14, 2002, pp. 1–4.

Endicott, K., and P. Bellwood. 1991. The possibility of independent foraging in the rain forest of peninsular Malaysia. *Human Ecology* 19:151–85.

Enloe, J. G., and F. David. 1992. Food sharing in the Paleolithic: Carcass refitting at Pincevent. In *Piecing Together the Past: Applications of Refitting Studies in Archaeology*, ed. by J. L. Hofman and J. G. Enloe, pp. 296–315. Oxford: Tempvs Reparatvm.

Ensminger, A. H., M. E. Ensminger, J. E. Konlande, and J. R. K. Robson. 1994. *Foods and Nutrition Encyclopedia*, 2nd ed. Boca Raton, FL: CRC Press.

Erlandson, J. M. 2001. The archaeology of aquatic adaptations: Paradigms for a new millennium. *Journal of Archaeological Research* 9(4):287–350.

Estrada Belli, F. 1998. The evolution of complex societies in Southeastern Pacific Coastal Guatemala: *A regional GIS archaeological approach.* Unpublished Ph.D. Dissertation, Department of Archaeology, Boston University.

Evans, L. T. 1993. *Crop Evolution, Adaptation and Yield.* Cambridge: Cambridge University Press.

Fairbanks, R. G. 1989. A 17,000-year glacio-eustatic sea level record: Influence of glacial melting rates on the Younger Dryas event and deep-ocean circulation. *Nature* 342:637–41.

Fanony, F. 1986. A propos des Mikea. In *Madagascar: Society and History*, ed. by C. P. Kottak, J-A. Rakotoarisoa, A. Southall, and P. Vérin, pp. 133–42. Durhan, NC: Carolina Academic Press.

Fedele, F. G. 1988. North Yemen: The neolithic. In *Yemen: 3000 Years of Art and Civilization in Arabia Felix.* ed. by W. Daum, pp. 34–37. Frankfurt: Pinguin.

———. 1990. Man, land, and climate: Emerging interactions from the Holocene of the Yemen Highlands. In *Man's Role in the Shaping of the Eastern Mediterranean Landscape,* ed. by S. Bottema, G. Entjes-Nieborg, and W. Van Zeist, pp. 31–42. Rotterdam: A.A. Balkema.

Feddema, V. L. 1993. Early formative subsistence and agriculture in southeastern Mesoamerica. Unpublished Master's Thesis, Department of Anthropology and Sociology, The University of British Columbia, Vancouver, Canada.

Fedick, S. 1996 (ed.). *The Managed Mosaic: Ancient Maya Agriculture and Resource Use.* Salt Lake City: University of Utah Press.

FEIS (2004). Fire Effects Information Service. www.fs.fed.us/database/feis/plants/forb/despin/management_considerations.html, (last reviewed 14 March 2004).

Field, J. S. 2004. Environmental and climatic considerations: a hypothesis for conflict and the emergence of social complexity in Fijian prehistory. *Journal of Anthropological Archaeology* 23:79–99.

Finney, B. R. 1979. *Hokule'a: The Way to Tahiti.* New York: Dodd, Mead and Co.

Fish, S. K., P. R. Fish, and J. H. Madsen. 1992 (eds). The Marana community in the Hohokam world. *Anthropological Papers of the University of Arizona, Number 56.* Tucson, AZ: The University of Arizona Press.

Fisher, I. 1930. *The Theory of Interest.* New York: MacMillan.

Fitzpatrick, S. 2004. *Voyages of Discovery: The Archaeology of Islands.* Westport, CT: Praeger Publishers/Greenwood Press.

Flannery, K. V. 1968. Archeological systems theory and early Mesoamerica. In *Anthropological Archeology in the Americas,* ed. by B. J. Meggers, pp. 67–87. Washington, DC: Anthropological Society of Washington.

———. 1969. Origins and ecological effects of early domestication in Iran and the Near East. In *The Domestication and Exploitation of Plants and Animals.* ed. by P. J. Ucko and G. W. Dimbleby, pp. 73–100. London: Duckworth.

———. 1971. Origins and ecological effects of early domestication in Iran and the Near East. In *Prehistoric Agriculture,* ed. by S. Struever, pp. 50–79. Garden City, NJ: Natural History Press.

———. 1973. The origins of agriculture. *Annual Review of Anthropology* 2:271–310.

———. 1986a. *Guilà Naquitz: Archaic Foraging and Early Agriculture in Oaxaca, Mexico.* Orlando: Academic Press.

———. 1986b. Adaptation, evolution, and archaeological phases: Some implications of Reynolds' simulation. In *Guilà Naquitz: Archaic Foraging and Early Agriculture in Oaxaca, Mexico,* ed. by K. V. Flannery, pp. 501–7, Orlando, FL: Academic Press.

———. 1986c. The research problem. In *Guila Naquitz: Archaic Foraging and Early Agriculture in Oaxaca, Mexico,* ed. by K. V. Flannery, pp. 3–18. Orlando, FL: Academic Press.

Flannery, K. V., J. Marcus, and R. Reynolds. 1989. *Flocks of the Wamani.* San Diego: Academic Press.

Flannery, T. F. 1995. *Mammals of the South West Pacific and Moluccan Islands.* Sydney: Australian Museum and Reed Books.

Flannery, T. F., and J. P. White. 1991. Animal translocation. *National Geographic Research and Exploration* 7(1):96–113.

Flenley, J. R. 1979. *The Equatorial Rainforest: A geological history.* London: Butterworths.

———. 1996. The palaeoecology of Easter Island, and its ecological disaster. In *Easter Island Studies: Contributions to the History of Rapanui in Memory of William T. Mulloy.* ed. by S. R. Fischer. pp. 27–45. Oxford: Oxbow Books.

Foley, R. L. 1985. Optimality theory in anthropology. *Man* 20:222–42.

———. 1987. Hominids, humans and hunter-gatherers: An evolutionary perspective, in *Hunters and Gatherers 1: History, Evolution and Social Change,* ed. by T. Ingold, D. Riches, and J. Woodburn, pp. 207–221. Oxford: Berg.

Fontugne, M. R., and J. C. Duplessy. 1986. Variations of the monsoon regime during the upper Quaternary: Evidence from carbon isotopic record of organic matter in north Indian Ocean sediment cores. *Palaeogeography, Palaeoclimatology, Palaeoecology* 56:69–88.

Ford, R. I. 1981. Gardening and farming before AD 1000: Patterns of prehistoric cultivation north of Mexico. *Journal of Ethnobiology* 1: 6–27.

———. 1985. The processes of plant food production in prehistoric North America. In *Prehistoric Food Production in North America,* ed. by R. I. Ford, pp. 1–18. Ann Arbor, MI: Museum of Anthropology, University of Michigan.

Francaviglia, V. M. 2000. Dating the ancient dam of Ma'rib (Yemen). *Journal of Archaeological Science* 27:645–53.

Franklin, W. 1975. Guanacos in Peru. *Oryx* 13: 191–202.

———. 1982. Biology, ecology, and relationship to man of the South American Camelids. In *Mammalian Biology in South America,* ed. by M.A. Mares and H.H. Genoways, pp. 457–89. Special Publications Series Pymatuning Laboratory of Ecology, University of Pittsburgh.

Frederick, S., G. Loewenstein, and T. O'Donoghue. 2002. Time discounting and time preference: A critical review. *Journal of Development Economics* 40:351–401.

Fredericksen, C., M. Spriggs, and W. Ambrose. 1993. Pamwak Rockshelter: A Pleistocene rockshelter on Manus Island, PNG. In *Sahul in Review: Pleistocene Archaeology in Australia, New Guinea and Island Melanesia,* ed. by M. Smith, M. Spriggs, and B. Fankhauser. Occasional Papers in Prehistory 24, Department of Prehistory, Research School of Pacific Studies, Australian National University, Canberra.

Freeman, A. K. L. 1997 (ed.). Archaeological Investigations at the Wetlands Site, AZ AA:12:90 (ASM). *Technical Report No. 97–5.* Tucson, AZ: Center for Desert Archaeology.

Fretwell, S. D. 1970. On territorial behavior and other factors influencing habitat distribution in birds. III. Breeding success in a local population of field sparrows (*Spizella pusilla* Wils.). *Acta Biotheoretica* 19:45–52.

Fretwell, S. D., and H. L. Lucas Jr. 1970. On territorial behavior and other factors influencing habitat distribution in birds. *Acta Biotheoretica* 19:16–36.

Fritz, G. J. 1990. Multiple pathways to farming in precontact eastern North America. *Journal of World Prehistory* 4:387–435.

———. 1994a. Are the first American farmers getting younger? *Current Anthropology* 35(3): 305–9.

———. 1994b. Precolumbian *Cucurbita argyrosperma* (Cucurbitaceae) in the Eastern Woodlands of North America. *Economic Botany* 48: 280–92.

———. 1997. A three-thousand year old cache of crop seeds from Marble Bluff, Arkansas. In *People, Plants, and Landscapes: Studies in Paleoethnobotany,* ed. by K. J. Gremillion, pp. 42–62. Tuscaloosa: University of Alabama Press.

Fritz, G., and T. Kidder. 1993. Recent Investigations into Prehistoric Agriculture in the Lower Mississippi Valley. *Southeastern Archaeology* 12:1–14.

Frumkin, A., M. Magaritz, I. Carmi and I. Zak. 1991. The Holocene climatic record of the salt caves of Mount Sedom, Israel. *The Holocene* 1:191–200.

Fullagar, R., 1992. Lithically Lapita: Functional analysis of flaked stone assemblages from West New Britain Province, Papua New Guinea. In *Poterie Lapita et peuplement,* ed. by J-C. Galipaud, pp. 135–43. Noumea: ORSTROM.

———. 1993. Flaked stone tools and plant food production: A preliminary report on obsidian tools from Talasea, West New Britain, Papua New Guinea. In *Traces et fonction: les gestes retrouvés,* ed. by P. Anderson, S. Beyries, M. Otte and H. Plisson, pp. 331–37. Liège: Colloque Internationale de Liège.

Fullagar, R., M. Therin, C. Lentfer, and J. Field. 2002. Tool-use and plant processing: Stone artefacts and sediments from Kuk, Papua New Guinea. Talk at SAA meeting, Denver.

Fuller, D. Q. 2002. Fifty years of archaeobotanical studies in India: Laying a solid foundation. In *Indian Archaeology in Retrospect, volume 3, Protohistory: Archaeology of the Harappan civilization,* ed. by S. Settar and R. Korisettar, pp. 247–364. Manohar: Indian Council of Historical Research.

Fuller, D. Q., and M. Madella. 2002. Issues in Harappan Archaeobotany: Retrospect and prospect. In *Indian Archaeology in Retrospect, volume 2, Protohistory: Archaeology of the Harappan civilization,* ed. by S. Settar and R. Korisettar, pp. 317–90. Manohar: Indian Council of Historical Research.

Fumanal, M. P. 1986. *Sedimentologia y Clima en el País Valenciano. Las Cuevas Habitadas en el Cuaternario Reciente.* Valencia: Diputación Provincial de Valencia.

Fumanal, M. P., and M. Dupré. 1986. Aportaciones de la sedimentología y de la palinología al conocimiento del paleoambiente valenciano durante el Holoceno, in *Quaternary Climate in the Western Mediterranean,* ed. by F. Lopéz-Vera, pp. 325–43. Madrid: Universidad Autónoma de Madrid.

Funkhouser, W. D., and W. S. Webb. 1929. *The So-Called "Ash Caves" in Lee County, Kentucky.* Reports in Archaeology and Anthropology 1(2). University of Kentucky, Lexington.

———. 1930. *Rock Shelters of Wolfe and Powell Counties, Kentucky*. Reports in Archaeology and Anthropology 1(4). University of Kentucky, Lexington.

Galinat, W. C. 1975. The evolutionary emergence of maize. Bulletin of the Torrey Botany Club 102:313–24.

———. 1988. The origins of maiz de ocho. *American Anthropologist* 90:682–83.

———. 1992. Evolution of corn. *Advances in Agronomy* 47:203–31.

———. 1995. El origen del maiz. El grano de la humanidad; The origin of maize: Grain of humanity. *Economic Botany* 49:3–12.

Galipaud, J-C. 1988. La poterie préhistorique néocalédonienne et ses implications dans l'étude du processus de peuplement du Pacifique occidental. *Unpublished Thèse de Doctorat*, Paris I University, Paris.

———. 1996. New Caledonia: some recent archaeological perspectives. In *Oceanic Culture History: Essays in Honour of Roger Green*, ed. by J. M. Davidson, G. Irwin, B. F. Leach, A. Pawley and D. Brown, pp. 297–305. *New Zealand Journal of Archaeology*, Special Publication.

Garcia, M. A., and M. Rachad. 1997. *L'Art des origines au Yemen*. Paris: Editions du Seuil.

Garcia, M. A., M. Rachad, D. Hadjouis, M.-L. Inizan, and M. Fontugnes. 1991. Découvertes préhistorique de l'art rupestre de la région de Saada. *Comptes Rendus de l'Académie des Sciences de Paris*. 313 série II:1201–06.

Gardner, P. S. 1992. Diet optimization models and prehistoric subsistence change in the eastern Woodlands. Unpublished Ph.D. Dissertation, University of North Carolina, Chapel Hill.

Garrard, A. 1999. Charting the emergence of cereal and pulse domestication in south-west Asia. *Environmental Archaeology* 4:67–86.

Garrett-Jones, S. 1979. Evidence for changes in Holocene vegetation and lake sedimentation in the Markham Valley, Papua New Guinea. Unpublished Ph.D. Dissertation, Australian National University.

Gasco, J., and B. Voorhies. 1989. The ultimate tribute: The role of the Soconusco as an Aztec tributary. In *Ancient Trade and Tribute: Economies of the Soconosco Region of Mesoamerica*, ed. by B. Voorhies, pp. 48–94. Salt Lake City: University of Utah Press.

Gasser, R. E. 1982. Hohokam use of desert food plants. *Desert Plants* 3:216–34.

Gebauer, A. B., and T. D. Price. 1992a. *Transitions to Agriculture in Prehistory*. Monographs in World Archaeology, No. 4. Madison, WI: Prehistory Press.

———. 1992b. Foragers to farmers: An introduction. In *Transitions to Agriculture in Prehistory*, ed. by A. B. Gebauer and T. D. Price, pp. 1–10. Madison, WI: Prehistory Press.

Ghazanfar, S. A. 1994. *Handbook of Arabian Medicinal Plants*. Boca Raton, FL: CRC Press.

Gibbons, A. 2000. Europeans trace ancestry to Paleolithic people. *Science* 290:1080–81.

Gieb, P. R. 1993. New evidence for the antiquity of Fremont occupation in Glen Canyon, south-central Utah. In *Proceedings of the First Biennial Conference on Research in Colorado Plateau National Parks*, ed. by P. G. Rowlands, C. van Riper III, and M. K. Sogge, pp. 154–65. Denver: National Park Services Natural Resources Publication Office.

Gieb, P. R., and P. W. Bungart. 1989. Implications of early bow use in Glen Canyon. *Utah Archaeology* 1989:32–47.

Gillieson, D., P. Gorecki, and G. S. Hope. 1985. Prehistoric agricultural systems in a lowland swamp, Papua New Guinea. *Archaeology in Oceania* 20:32–7.

Gillin, J. 1938. Archaeological investigations in Nine Mile Canyon, Utah, during the year 1936. University of Utah Bulletin 28, No. 11. Salt Lake City: University of Utah Press.

Gintis, H., E. A. Smith, and S. Bowles. 2001. Costly signaling and cooperation. *Journal of Theoretical Biology* 213:103–19.

Glass, M. 1991. *Animal Production Systems in Neolithic Central Europe*. Oxford: British Archaeological Reports International Series 572.

Glassow, M. A. 1978. The concept of carrying capacity in the study of culture process. In *Advances in Archaeological Method and Theory*, ed. by M. B. Schiffer, pp. 31–48. New York: Academic Press.

Glennie, K. W. 1998. The desert of southeast Arabia: A product of Quaternary climatic change. In *Quaternary Deserts and Climatic Change*, ed. by A. S. Al Sharhan, K. W. Glennie, G. L. Whittle, and C. G. St. C. Kendall, pp. 279–91. Rotterdam: Balkema.

Gnecco, V. C., and H. S. López. 1989. Adaptaciones precerámicas en el suroccidente de Colombia. *Museo de Oro Boletín* 24:35–53.

Godoy, R., K. Kirby, and D. Wilkie. 2001. Tenure security, private time preference, and use of natural resources among lowland Bolivian Amerindians. *Ecological Economics*, 38:105–18.

Godoy, R., E. Byron, V. Reyes-Garcia, W. R. Leonard, K. Patel, L. Apaza, E. Pérez, V. Vadez, and D. Wilkie. 2004. Patience in a foraging-horticultural society: A test of competing hypotheses. *Journal of Anthropological Research*, 60:179–202.

Goland, C. 1991. The ecological context of hunter-gatherer storage: Environmental predictability and environmental risk. *Michigan Discussions in Anthropology* 10:107–25.

———. 1993a. Agricultural risk management through diversity: Field scattering in Cuyo Cuyo, Peru. *Culture and Agriculture* 45–46:8–13.

———. 1993b. Field scattering as agricultural risk management: A case study from Cuyo Cuyo, Department of Puno, Peru. *Mountain Research and Development* 13:317–38.

Golson, J. 1977a. No room at the top: Agricultural intensification in the New Guinea Highlands. In *Sunda and Sahul: prehistoric studies in southeast Asia, Melanesia and Australia*, ed. by J. Allen, J. Golson, and R. Jones, pp. 601–38. London: Academic Press.

———. 1977b. The making of the New Guinea Highlands. In *The Melanesian Environment*, ed. by J. H. Winslow, pp. 45–56. Canberra: Australian National University Press.

———. 1981. New Guinea agricultural history: A case study. In *A Time to Plant and a Time to Uproot*, ed. by D. Denoon and C. Snowden, pp. 55–64. Port Moresby: Institute of Papua New Guinea Studies.

———. 1982. The Ipomoean revolution revisited: Society and sweet potato in the upper Wahgi Valley. In *Inequality in New Guinea Highland Societies*, ed. by A. Strathern, pp. 109–36. Cambridge: Cambridge University Press.

———. 1990. Kuk and the development of agriculture in New Guinea: Retrospection and introspection. In *Pacific Production Systems: Approaches to Economic Prehistory*, D.E. Yen and J. M. J. Mummery, pp. 139–47. Canberra: Australian National University.

———. 1991a. Bulmer Phase II: Early agriculture in the New Guinea Highlands. In *Man and a Half: Essays in Pacific Anthropology and Ethnobiology in Honour of Ralph Bulmer*, ed. by A. Pawley, pp. 484–91. Auckland: The Polynesian Society.

———. 1991b. The New Guinea Highlands on the eve of agriculture. *Bulletin of the Indo-Pacific Prehistory Association* 11:48–53.

———. 1992. The ceramic sequence from Lasigi. In *Poterie Lapita et Peuplement*, ed. by J-C Galipaud, Noumea: ORSTOM.

———. 1997. The Tambul spade. In *Work in Progress: Essays in New Guinea Highlands Ethnography in Honour of Paula Brown Glick*, ed. by H. Levine and A. Ploeg, pp. 142–71. Frankfurt: Peter Lang.

———. 2000. A stone bowl fragment from the Early Middle Holocene of the Upper Wahgi Valley, Western Highlands Province, Papua New Guinea. In *Australian Archaeologist: Collected Papers in Honour of Jim Allen*, ed. by A. Anderson and T. Murray, pp. 231–48. Canberra: Coombs Academic Publishing, ANU.

———. 2002. Gourds in New Guinea, Asia and the Pacific. In *Fifty years in the Field. Essays in Honour and Celebration of Richard Shutler Jr.'s Archaeological Career*, ed. by S. Bedford, C. Sand, and D. Burley, pp. 69–78. Auckland: New Zealand Archaeological Association (Monograph 25).

Golson, J., and P. J. Hughes. 1980. The appearance of plant and animal domestication in New Guinea. *Journal de la Société des Océanistes* 36:294–303.

Golson, J., R. J. Lampert, J. M. Wheeler, and W. R. Ambrose. 1967. A note on carbon dates for horticulture in the New Guinea Highlands. *Journal of the Polynesian Society* 76(3):369–71.

Gonzales, F. G., G. A. Slafer, and D. J. Miralles. 2002. Vernalization and photoperiod responses in wheat pre-flowering reproductive phases. *Field Crops Research* 74:183–95.

Gonzalez, J. J. S. 1994. Modern variability and patterns of maize movement in Mesoamerica. In *Corn and Culture in the Prehistoric New World*, ed. by S. Johannessen and C. A. Hastorf, pp. 135–56. Boulder, CO: Westview Press.

Gorecki, P. 1992. A Lapita smoke screen? In *Poterie Lapita et peuplement*, ed. by J-C. Galipaud, pp. 27–47. Noumea: ORSTOM.

Gorecki, P. 1993. The Sepik river people of Papua New Guinea: Culture and catastrophes. In *People of the Stone Age: Hunter-gatherers and Early Farmers*, pp. 154–55. San Francisco: Harper.

Gororo, N. N., R. G. Flood, R. F. Eastwood, and H. A. Eagles. 2001. Photoperiod and vernalization responses in *Triticum turgidum* x *T. tauschii* synthetic hexaploid wheats. *Annals of Botany* 88:947–52.

Gosden, C. 1989. Prehistoric social landscapes of the Arawe Islands, West New Britain Province, Papua New Guinea. *Archaeology in Oceania* 24(1):45–58.

———. 1992. Production systems and the colonization of the Western Pacific. *World Archaeology* 24:55–69.

———. 1995. Arboriculture and Agriculture in Coastal Papua New Guinea. In *Transitions: Pleistocene to Holocene in Australia and Papua New Guinea*, ed. by J. Allen and J. F. O'Connell. *Antiquity* 69:807–17.

Gosden, C., and N. Robertson. 1991. Models for Matenkupkum: Interpreting a Late Pleistocene site from Southern New Ireland, Papua New Guinea. In *Report of the Lapita Homeland Project*, ed. by J. Allen and C. Gosden, Occasional Papers in Prehistory 20, Department of Prehistory, Research School of Pacific Studies, Australian National University, Canberra.

Gosden, C., and J. Specht. 1991. Diversity, continuity and change in the Bismark Archipelago, Papua New Guinea. In *Indo-Pacific Prehistory 1990*, ed. by P. S. Bellwood, *Bulletin of the Indo-Pacific Prehistory Association* 11:276–80.

Gosden, C., and J. Webb. 1994. The creation of a Papua New Guinea landscape: Archaeological and geomorphological evidence. *Journal of Field Archaeology* 21(1):29–51.

Gotelli, N. J. 1998. *A Primer of Ecology*. Sunderland, MA: Sinauer Associates, Inc.

Gould, S. J. 1980. The promise of paleobiology as a nomothetic evolutionary discipline. *Paleobiology* 6(1):96–118.

Gragson, T. L. 1993. Human foraging in lowland South America: Pattern and process of resource procurement. *Research in Economic Anthropology* 14:107–38.

Graham, C., and R. Douglas. 1990. Geology. In *Archaeological Site Distributions on the Cumberland Plateau of Eastern Kentucky*, ed. by T. Sussenbach, pp. 13–24. Archaeological Report 218. Program for Cultural Resource Assessment, University of Kentucky, Lexington.

Graham, M. 1994. Mobile farmers: An ethnoarchaeological approach to settlement organization among the Rarámuri of northwestern Mexico. *Ethnoarchaeological Series No. 3*. Ann Arbor, MI: International Monographs in Prehistory.

Grayson, D. K. 2001. Explaining the development of dietary dominance by a single ungulate taxon at Grotte Xvi, Dordogne, France. *Journal of Archaeological Science* 28:115–25.

Grayson, D. K., and M. D. Cannon. 1999. Human paleoecology and foraging theory in the Great Basin. In *Models for the Millennium: Great Basin Anthropology Today*, ed. by C. Beck, pp. 141–51. Salt Lake City: University of Utah Press.

Grayson, D. K., and F. Delpech. 1998. Changing diet breadth in the early Upper Palaeolithic of Southwestern France. *Journal of Archaeological Science* 25:1119–30.

Grayson, D. K., and D. J. Meltzer. 2003. A requiem for North American overkill. *Journal of Archaeological Science* 30:585–93.

Grayson, D. K., F. Delpech, J. P. Rigaud, and J. F. Simek. 2001. Explaining the development of dietary dominance by a single ungulate taxon at Grotte XVI, Dordogne, France. *Journal of Archaeological Science* 28:115–25.

Green, L., and J. Myerson. 1996. Exponential versus hyperbolic discounting of delayed outcomes: Risk and waiting time. *American Zoologist* 36:496–505.

Green, L., N. Fristoe, J. Myerson. 1994a. Temporal discounting and preference reversals in choice between delayed outcomes. *Psychonomic Bulletin and Review* 1:383–9.

Green, L., A. F. Fry, and J. Myerson. 1994b. Discounting of delayed rewards: A life-span comparison. *Psychological Science* 5:33–36.

Green, L., E. B. Fisher, S. Perlow, and L. Sherman. 1981. Preference reversal and self-control: Choice as a function of reward amount and delay. *Behaviour Analysis Letters* 1:43–51.

Green, R. C. 1976. Lapita sites in the Santa Cruz Group. In *Southeast Solomon Islands Cultural History: A Preliminary Survey*, ed. by R. C. Green and M. Cresswell, Royal Society of New Zealand Bulletin 11, Wellington, pp. 245–65.

———. 1979. Lapita. In *The Prehistory of Polynesia*, ed. by J. D. Jennings. Canberra: Australian National University Press.

———. 1991. A reappraisal of the dating for some Lapita sites in the Reef-Santa Cruz group of the South-east Solomons. *Journal of the Polynesian Society* 100:197–207.

Green, R. C., and D. Anson. 2000. Excavations at Kainapirina (SAC), Watom Island, Papua New Guinea. *New Zealand Journal of Archaeology* 20(1998):29–94.

Green, R. C., and R. V. Kirch. 1997. Lapita exchange systems and their Polynesian transformations: Seeking explanatory models. In *Prehistoric Long-Distance Interaction in Oceania: An Interdisciplinary Approach*. New Zealand Archaeological Association Monograph 21.

Green, W. 1994 (ed.) *Agricultural Origins and Development in the Midcontinent.* Report 19, Office of the State Archaeologist, Iowa City, Iowa.

Gregg, S. A. 1988. *Foragers and Farmers. Population Interaction and Agricultural Expansion in Prehistoric Europe.* Chicago: The University of Chicago Press.

Gregory, D. A. 2001. Architectural features and their characteristics. In *Excavations in the Santa Cruz River Floodplain: The Early Agricultural Period Component at Los Pozos,* ed. by David A. Gregory, pp. 29–70. *Anthropological Papers No. 21.* Tucson: Center for Desert Archaeology.

————. 2001 (ed.). Excavations in the Santa Cruz River floodplain: The Early Agricultural Period Component at Los Pozos. *Anthropological Papers No. 21.* Tucson: Center for Desert Archaeology.

Gregory, D. A., and M. W. Diehl. 2002. Duration, Continuity, and the Intensity of Occupation at a Late Cienega Phase Settlement in the Santa Cruz River Floodplain. In *Traditions, Transitions, and Technologies: Themes in Southwestern Archaeology,* ed. by Sarah H. Schlanger, pp. 200–23. Boulder, CO: University of Colorado Press.

Gremillion, K. J. 1993a. Crop and weed in prehistoric eastern North America: The *Chenopodium* example. *American Antiquity* 58:496–509.

————. 1993b. The evolution of seed morphology in domesticated *Chenopodium*: An archaeological case study. *Journal of Ethnobiology* 13: 149–69.

————. 1993c. Plant husbandry at the Archaic/Woodland transition: Evidence from the Cold Oak Shelter, Kentucky. *Midcontinental Journal of Archaeology* 18:161–89.

————. 1994. Evidence of plant domestication from Kentucky caves and rockshelters. In *Agricultural Origins and Development in the Midcontinent,* ed. by William Green, pp. 87–104. Report (19). Office of the State Archaeologist, University of Iowa, Iowa City.

————. 1995. *Archaeological and Paleoethnobotanical Investigations at the Cold Oak Shelter, Kentucky.* The Ohio State University. Submitted to National Geographic Society. Grant Number 5226–94.

————. 1996a. Diffusion and adoption of crops in evolutionary perspective. *Journal of Anthropological Archaeology* 15:183–204.

————. 1996b. Early agricultural diet in eastern North America: Evidence from two Kentucky rockshelters. *American Antiquity* 61:520–36.

————. 1997a (ed.) *People, Plants and Landscapes: Studies in Paleoethnobotany.* Tuscaloosa: University of Alabama Press.

————. 1997b. New perspectives on the paleoethnobotany of the Newt Kash Shelter. In *People, Plants, and Landscapes: Studies in Paleoethnobotany,* pp. 23–41, ed. by K. J. Gremillion. Tuscaloosa: University of Alabama Press.

————. 1998. Changing roles of wild and cultivated plant resources among early farmers of eastern Kentucky. *Southeastern Archaeology* 17: 140–57.

————. 1999. National Register Evaluation of the Courthouse Rock Shelter (15po322), Powell County, Kentucky. The Ohio State University. Submitted to USDA Forest Service.

————. 2002. Foraging theory and hypothesis testing in archaeology: An exploration of methodological problems and solutions. *Journal of Anthropological Archaeology* 21:142–64.

Gremillion, K. J., and K. R. Mickelson. 1996. *National Register Evaluation of the Mounded Talus Shelter (15le77), Lee County, Kentucky.* The Ohio State University. Submitted to USDA Forest Service, Winchester, Kentucky.

Gremillion, K. J., and K. D. Sobolik. 1996. Dietary variability among prehistoric forager-farmers of eastern North America. *Current Anthropology* 37:529–39.

Gremillion, K. J., K. Jakes, and V. Wimberley. 2001. The research potential of prehistoric textiles from Kentucky: An example from Carter county. In *Current Archaeological Research in Kentucky,* Vol. 6, ed. by D. Pollack and K. J. Gremillion. Kentucky Heritage Council, Frankfort, Kentucky.

Greubel, R. A. 1996. Archaeological investigations of 11 sites along Interstate 70: Castle Valley to Rattlesnake Bench. UDOT Project No. I-IR-70-2(19)87. Salt Lake City: CRM report prepared for the Utah Department of Transportation.

Grigson, C. 1982. Sex and age determinations of some bones and teeth of domestic cattle: A review of the literature. In *Aging and Sexing Animal Bones from Archaeological Sites,* ed. by B. Wilson, C. Grigson, and S. Payne, pp. 7–23. Oxford: British Archaeological Reports International Series 109.

————. 1996. Early cattle around the Indian Ocean. In *The Indian Ocean in Antiquity,* ed. by J. Reade, pp. 41–74. London: Kegan Paul International.

Groube, L. 1989. The taming of the rainforests: A model for Late Pleistocene forest exploitation in New Guinea. In *Foraging and Farming: The Evolution of Plant Exploitation*, ed. by D. R. Harris and G. C. Hillman, pp. 292–304. London: Unwin Hyman.

Groube, L., J. Chappell, J. Muke, and D. Price. 1986. A 40,000 year-old human occupation site at Huon Peninsula, Papua New Guinea. *Nature* 324(4):453–5.

Gunnerson, J. H. 1969. *The Fremont Culture: A Study in Culture Dynamics on the Northern Anasazi Frontier*. Cambridge: Peabody Museum.

Gurven, M. 2004. To give and to give not: The behavioral ecology of human food transfers. *Behavioral and Brain Sciences* 27:543–83.

Guthrie, E., and L. Lincoln-Babb. 1997. Human remains from the wetlands site. In *Archaeological Investigations at the Wetlands Site, AZ AA:12:90 (ASM)*, ed. by A. K. L. Freeman, pp. 129–45. *Technical Report No. 97–5*. Tucson, AZ: Center for Desert Archaeology.

Haaland, R. 1995. Sedentism, cultivation and plant domestication in the Holocene middle Nile region. *Journal of Field Archaeology* 22:157–74.

Haberle, S. G. 1993. Late Quaternary environmental history of the Tari Basin, Papua New Guinea. Unpublished PhD thesis, Australian National University.

———. 1994. Anthropogenic indicators in pollen diagrams: Problems and prospects for late Quaternary palynology in New Guinea. In *Tropical Archaeobotany: Applications and New Developments*, ed. by J. G. Hather, pp. 172–201. London: Routledge.

———. 1995. Identification of cultivated *Pandanus* and *Colocasia* in pollen records and the implications for the study of early agriculture in New Guinea. *Vegetation History and Archaeobotany* 4:195–210.

———. 1998. Late Quaternary change in the Tari Basin, Papua New Guinea. *Palaeogeography, Palaeoclimatology, Palaeoecology* 137:1–24.

———. 2002. The emergence of an agricultural landscape in the Highlands of New Guinea: The palynological record from Kuk Swamp. Talk at SAA meeting, Denver.

———. 2003. The emergence of an agricultural landscape in the Highlands of New Guinea. In *Perspectives on Prehistoric Agriculture in New Guinea*, ed. by T. P. Denham and C. Ballard. *Archaeology in Oceania, Special Issue* 38(3): 149–58.

Haberle, S. G., G. S. Hope, and Y. de Fretes. 1991. Environmental change in the Baliem Valley, Montane Irian Jaya, Republic of Indonesia. *Journal of Biogeography* 18:25–40.

Haberle, S., G. S. Hope, S. van der Kaars. 2001. Biomass burning in Indonesia and Papua New Guinea: Natural and human induced fire events in the fossil record. *Palaeogeography, Palaeoclimatology, Palaeoecology* 171:259–68.

Halbirt, C. D., and T. K. Henderson. 1993 (eds). *Archaic Occupations on the Santa Cruz Flats: The Tator Hills Archaeological Project*. Flagstaff, AZ: Northland Research, Inc.

Halstead, P. 1981. Counting sheep in Neolithic and Bronze Age Greece. In *Pattern of the Past*, ed. by I. Hodder, G. Isaac, and N. Hammond, pp. 307–39. Cambridge: Cambridge University Press.

———. 1996. The development of agriculture and pastoralism in Greece: When, how, who and what? In *The Origins and Spread of Agriculture and Pastoralism in Eurasia*, ed. by D. R. Harris, pp. 296–309. Washington DC: Smithsonian Institution Press.

Halstead, P., and J. M. O'Shea. 1989. *Bad Year Economics: Cultural Responses to Risk and Uncertainty*. Cambridge: Cambridge University Press.

Hames, R. 1990. Sharing among the Yanomamo: Part I, the effects of risk. In *Risk and Uncertainty in Tribal and Peasant Economies*, ed. by E. Cashdan, pp. 89–106, Boulder: Westview Press.

Hames, R. B., and W. T. Vickers. 1982. Optimal diet breadth as a model to explain variability in Amazonian hunting. *American Ethnologist* 9:358–78.

Hanotte, O., D. Bradley, J. W. Ochieng, Y. Verjee, E. W. Hill, J. Edward, and O. Rege. 2002. African pastoralism: Genetic imprints of origins and migrations. *Science* 296:336.

Hardin, G. 1968. Tragedy of the commons. *Science* 162:1243–48.

Hard, R. J. 1986. Ecological relationships affecting the rise of farming economies: A test for the American Southwest. Unpublished Ph.D. Dissertation, Department of Anthropology, University of New Mexico, Albuquerque.

Harlan, J. R. 1992a. *Crops and Man* (2d ed.) Madison: American Society of Agronomy and Crop Science Society of America.

———. 1992b. Indigenous African agriculture. In *The Origins of Agriculture: An International Perspective*, ed. by C. W. Cowan and P. J. Watson, pp. 59–70. Washington, DC: Smithsonian Institution Press.

———. 1992c. Wild grass seed harvesting and implications for domestication. In *Préhistoire de L'Agriculture: Nouvelles Approches Expérimentales et Ethnographiques*, ed. by P. C. Anderson, pp. 21–27. Paris: Editions du CNRS (Centre National de la Recherche Scientifique).

———. 1999. Harvesting of wild grass seeds and implications for domestication. In *Prehistory of Agriculture: New Experimental and Ethnographic Approaches*, ed. by P. C. Anderson, pp. 1–5. Los Angeles: Monograph 40, Institute of Archaeology, University of California, Los Angeles.

Harlan, J. R., J. M. J. DeWet, and G. E. Price. 1973. Comparative Evolution of Cereals. *Evolution* 27: 311–25.

Harris, D. R. 1977. Alternate pathways toward agriculture. In *Origins of Agriculture*, ed. by C. A. Reed, pp. 173–249. The Hague: Mouton.

———. 1989. An evolutionary continuum of people-plant interaction. In *Foraging and Farming: The Evolution of Plant Exploitation*, ed. by D. R. Harris and G. Hillman, pp. 11–26. London: Unwin Hyman.

———. 1995. Early agriculture in New Guinea and the Torres Strait divide. *Antiquity* 69(Special Number 265):848–59.

———. 1996a. Introduction: themes and concepts in the study of early agriculture. In *The Origins and Spread of Agriculture and Pastoralism in Eurasia*, ed. by D. R. Harris, pp. 1–11. Washington DC: Smithsonian Institution Press.

———. 1996b. The origins and spread of agriculture and pastoralism in Eurasia: An overview. In *The Origins and Spread of Agriculture and Pastoralism in Eurasia*, ed. by D. R. Harris, pp. 552–73. Washington DC: Smithsonian Institution Press.

———. 1998. The origins of agriculture in southwest Asia. *The Review of Archaeology* 19:5–11.

Harris, D. R., and C. Gosden. 1996. The beginnings of agriculture in west-central Asia. In *The Origins and Spread of Agriculture and Pastoralism in Eurasia*, ed. by D. R. Harris, pp. 370–89. Washington DC: Smithsonian Institution Press.

Harris, D. R., and G. C. Hillman. 1989 (ed.) *Foraging and Farming: The Evolution of Plant Exploitation*. London: Unwin Hyman.

Harris, D. R., V. M. Masson, Y. E. Berezkin, M. P. Charles, C. Gosden, G. C. Hillman, A. K. Kasparov, G. F. Karobkova, K. Kurbansakhatov, A. J. Legge, S. Limbrey. 1993. Investigating early agriculture in Central Asia: New research at Jeitun, Turkmenistan. *Antiquity* 67:324–38.

Harris, E. C., and P. J. Hughes. 1978. An early agricultural system at Mugumamp Ridge, Western Highlands Province, Papua New Guinea. *Mankind* 11(4):437–45.

Harris, Marvin. 1978. *Cultural Materialism*. New York: Random House.

Hart, J. 1999 (ed.). *Current Northeast Paleoethnobotany*. New York State Museum Bulletin No. 494. Albany, New York.

Hart, J., and M. Scarry. 1999. The age of common beans *(Phaseolus vulgaris)* in the northeastern United States. *American Antiquity* 64:653–58.

Hart, T., and J. Hart. 1986. The ecological basis of hunter-gatherer subsistence in African rain forests: the Mbuti of Eastern Zaire. *Human Ecology* 14:29–55.

Hassan, F. A. 1977. The dynamics of agricultural origins in Palestine: A theoretical model. In *Origin of Agriculture*, ed. by C. A. Reed, pp. 589–609. The Hague: Mouton.

———. 1984. Environment and subsistence in predynastic Egypt. In *From Hunters to Farmers*, ed. by J. D. Clark and S. A. Brandt, pp. 57–64. Los Angeles: University of California Press.

———. 2000. Holocene environmental change and the origins and spread of food production in the Middle East. *Adumatu* 1:7–28.

Hastorf, C. A. 1993. *Agriculture and the Onset of Political Inequality Before the Inka*. Cambridge: Cambridge University Press.

———. 1999. Cultural implications of crop introductions in Andean prehistory. In *The Prehistory of Food: Appetites for Change*, ed. by C. Gosden and J. Hather, pp. 35–58, New York: Routledge.

Hather, J. G. 1992. The archaeobotany of subsistence in the Pacific. *World Archaeology* 24(1): 70–81.

———. 1996. The origins of tropical vegeculture: Zingiberaceae, Araceae and Dioscoreaceae in Southeast Asia. In *The Origins and Spread of Agriculture and Pastoralism in Eurasia*, ed. by D. R. Harris, pp. 538–50. London: UCL Press.

Hather, J. G., and P. V. Kirch. 1991. Prehistoric sweet potato *(Ipomoea batatas)* from Mangaia Island, central Polynesia. *Antiquity* 65:887–93.

Haury, E. W. 1962. The Greater American Southwest. In *Courses toward Urban Life: A Worldwide Survey of Man's History from the Late Stone Age to the Threshold of Urban Civilizations,* ed. by R. J. Braidwood and G. R. Willey, pp. 106–31. New York: Aldine.

Hawkes, J. G. 1989. The domestication of roots and tubers in the American tropics. In *Foraging and Farming: The Evolution of Plant Exploitation,* ed. by D. Harris and G. Hillman, pp. 481–503. London: Unwin Hyman.

———. 1990. *The Potato: Evolution, Biodiversity, and Genetic Resources.* Washington DC: Smithsonian Institution Press.

Hawkes, K. 1987. How much food do foragers need? In *Food and Evolution,* ed. by M. Harris and E. B. Ross, pp. 341–55. Philadelphia: Temple University Press.

———. 1990. Why do men hunt? Some benefits for risky strategies. In *Risk and Uncertainty in Tribal and Peasant Economies,* ed. by E. Cashdan, pp. 145–66. Boulder: Westview Press.

———. 1991. Showing off: tests of another hypothesis about men's foraging goals. *Ethology and Sociobiology* 12:29–54.

———. 1992. Sharing and collective action. In *Evolutionary Ecology and Human Behavior,* ed. by E. A. Smith and B. Winterhalder, pp. 269–300. Hawthorne, NY: Aldine de Gruyter.

———. 1996. Foraging differences between men and women: Behavioral ecology of the sexual division of labor. In *The Archaeology of Human Ancestry: Power, Sex, and Tradition,* ed. by J. Steele and S. Shennan, pp. 283–305. London: Routledge.

———. 2000. Hunting and the evolution of egalitarian societies: Lessons from the Hadza. In *Hierarchies in Action: Cui Bono?* ed. by Michael W. Diehl, pp. 59–83. *Occasional Papers No. 27.* The Center for Archaeological Investigations, Carbondale, IL: Southern Illinois University.

Hawkes, K., and R. L. Bliege Bird. 2002. Showing off, handicap signaling, and the evolution of men's work. *Evolutionary Anthropology* 11:58–67.

Hawkes, K., and J. F. O'Connell. 1981. Affluent hunters? Some comments in light of the Alywara case. *American Anthropologist* 83:622–26.

———. 1992. On optimal foraging models and subsistence transitions. *Current Anthropology* 33:63–6.

Hawkes, K., K. Hill, and J. F. O'Connell. 1982. Why hunters gather: Optimal foraging and the Aché of eastern Paraguay. *American Ethnologist* 9:379–98.

Hawkes, K., J. F. O'Connell, and N. G. Blurton-Jones. 1991. Hunting income patterns among the Hadza: Big game, common goods, foraging goals and the evolution of the human diet. *Philosophical Transactions of the Royal Society of London B* 334:243–51.

Hawkes, K., J. F. O'Connell, and L. Rogers. 1997. The behavioral ecology of modern hunter-gatherers and human evolution. *Trends in Ecology and Evolution* 12:29–32.

Hawkes, K., H. Kaplan, K. Hill, and A. M. Hurtado. 1987. Ache at the settlement: Contrasts between farming and foraging. *Human Ecology* 15:133–61.

Hayden, B. 1990. Nimrods, piscators, pluckers, and planters: The emergence of food production. *Journal of Anthropological Archaeology* 9:31–69.

———. 1992. Models of domestication. In *Transitions to Agriculture in Prehistory,* ed. by A. B. Gebauer and T. D. Price, pp. 11–19. Madison: Prehistory Press.

———. 1995a. A new overview of domestication. In *Last Hunters-First Farmers: New Perspectives on the Prehistoric Transition to Agriculture,* ed. by T. D. Price and A. B. Gebauer, pp. 273–99. Santa Fe, NM: School of American Research Press.

———. 1995b. Pathways to power: Principles for creating socioeconomic inequalities. In *Foundations of Social Inequality,* ed. by T. D. Price and G. M. Feinman, pp. 15–85. New York: Plenum Press.

———. 2001. Fabulous feasts: A prolegomenon to the importance of feasting. In *Feasts: Archaeological and Ethnographic Perspectives on Food, Politics and Power,* ed. by M. Dietler and B. Hayden, Washington, DC: Smithsonian Institution Press.

Hayes, L. T. 1992. Plant macroremains from archaeological sites in the Arawe Islands, Papua New Guinea: A study of tree exploitation and the interpretation of archaeobotanical remains in Melanesian prehistory. Unpublished B. A. Honours thesis, La Trobe University, Bundoora.

Hayes, R. A. 1993. *Soil Survey of Powell and Wolfe Counties, Kentucky.* Soil Conservation Service, United States Department of Agriculture.

Hayes, T. L. 1992. Plant macrofossils from archaeological sites in the Arawe Islands, Papua New Guinea. Unpublished Honours thesis, Department of Archaeology, La Trobe University.

Haynes Jr., C. V. 2001. Geochronology and climate change of the Pleistocene-Holocene transition in the Darb el Arba'in Desert, Eastern Sahara. *Geoarchaeology* 16:119–41.

Headland, T. N. 1987. The wild yam question: How well could independent hunter-gatherers live in a tropical rain forest ecosystem? *Human Ecology* 15:463–91.

Heffley, S. 1981. The relationship between Northern Athapaskan settlement patterns and resource distribution: An application of Horn's Model. In *Ethnographic and Archaeological Analyses*, ed. by B. Winterhalder and E. A. Smith, 139–88. Chicago: The University of Chicago Press.

Hegmon, M. A. 1991. The risks of sharing and sharing as risk reduction: Interhousehold food sharing in egalitarian societies. In *Between Bands and States*, ed. by Susan A. Gregg, pp. 309–32. *Occasional Papers No. 9*. The Center for Archaeological Investigations, Carbondale, IL: Southern Illinois University.

Hehmeyer, I. 1989 Irrigation farming in the ancient oasis of Marib. *Proceedings of the Seminar for Arabian Studies* 19:33–44.

Heidke, J. M. 1999. Cienega Phase incipient plain ware from Southeastern Arizona. *Kiva* 64:311–38.

Heidke, J. M., and J. A. Habicht-Mauche. 1998. The first occurrences and early distribution of pottery in the North American Southwest. *Revista de Arqueologia Americana* 14:65–99.

Heidke, J. M., E. Miksa, and M. K. Wiley. 1998. Ceramic artifacts. In *Archaeological Investigations of Early Village Sites in the Middle Santa Cruz Valley: Analyses and Synthesis, Part II*, ed. by J. B. Mabry, pp. 471–544. *Anthropological Papers No. 19*. Tucson, AZ: Center for Desert Archaeology.

Helbig, C. 1964. *El Soconusco y su Zona Cafetalera en Chiapas*. Tuxtla Gutiérrez, Chiapas: Instituto de Ciencias y Artes de Chiapas.

Hemphill, B. E., and C. S. Larsen. 1999 (eds). *Prehistoric Lifeways in the Great Basin Wetlands: Bioarchaeological Reconstruction and Interpretation*. Salt Lake City, UT: University of Utah Press.

Henrich, J. 2004. Demography and cultural evolution: Why adaptive cultural processes produced maladaptive losses in Tasmania. *American Antiquity* 69:197–214.

Henry, D. O. 1989. *From Foraging to Agriculture: The Levant at the End of the Ice Age*. Philadelphia, PA: University of Pennsylvania Press.

Henry, D. O., J. J. White, J. E. Beaver, S. Kadowaki, A. Nowell, C. Cordova, R. M. Dean, H. Ekstrom, J. McCorriston, and L. Scott-Cummings. 2003. The early Neolithic site of Ayn Abu Nukhayla, Southern Jordan. *Bulletin of the American Schools of Oriental Research* 330:1–30.

Hernández J., and J. León. 1994. *Neglected Crops: 1492 from a Different Perspective*. FAO Plant Production and Protection Series 26. Cordoba, Spain: Botanical Garden of Cordoba.

Herrera, L., W. Bray, M. Cardale de Schrimpff, and P. Botero. 1992. Nuevas fechas de radiocarbono para el Preceramico en la cordillera occidental de Colombia. In *Archaeology and Environment in Latin America*, ed. by O. R. Ortiz-Troncoso and T. Van Der Hammen, pp. 145–64. Amsterdam: Universiteit van Amsterdam.

Hertwig, R., and A. Ortmann. 2001. Experimental practices in economics: A methodological challenge for psychologists? *Behavioral and Brain Sciences* 24:383–451.

Hesse, B. 1982a. Animal domestication and oscillating climates. *Journal of Ethnobiology* 2:1–15.

———. 1982b. Archaeological evidence for camelid exploitation in the Chilean Andes. *Säugetierekunde Mitteilungen* 30:201–11.

Higgs, E. S. 1972. The origins of animal and plant husbandry. In *Papers in Economic Prehistory*, ed. by E. S. Higgs, pp. 3–15. Cambridge: Cambridge University Press.

Higgins, P. D. 1970. A preliminary survey of the vascular flora of the Red River Gorge of Kentucky. Unpublished Master's thesis, University of Louisville, Louisville, Kentucky.

Higham, T. G. F., A. J. Anderson, C. Jacomb. 1999. Dating the first New Zealanders: The chronology of Wairau Bar. *Antiquity* 73:420–27.

Hildebrandt, W. R., and K. R. McGuire. 2002. The ascendance of hunting during the California Middle Archaic: An evolutionary perspective. *American Antiquity* 67:231–56.

———. 2003. Large-game hunting, gender-differentiated work organization, and the role of evolutionary ecology in California and Great Basin prehistory: A reply to Broughton and Bayham. *American Antiquity* 68:790–92.

Hill, J. B. 2000. Decision making at the margins: Settlement trends, temporal scale, and ecology in the Wadi al Hasa, West-Central Jordan. *Journal of Anthropological Archaeology* 19:221–41.

Hill, K. 1988. Macronutrient modifications of optimal foraging theory. *Human Ecology* 16: 157–97.

———. 1993. Life history theory and evolutionary anthropology. *Evolutionary Anthropology* 2: 78–88.

Hill, K., and K. Hawkes. 1983. Neotropical hunting among the Ache of eastern Paraguay. In *Adaptive Responses of Native Amazonians*, ed. by R. Hames and W. Vickers, pp. 139–88. New York: Academic Press.

Hill, K. R., and A. M. Hurtado. 1996. *Ache Life History: The Ecology and Demography of a Foraging People*. New York: Aldine de Gruyter.

Hill, K., and H. Kaplan. 1992. The evolutionary ecology of food acquisition. In *Evolutionary Ecology and Human Behavior*, ed. by E. Smith and B. Winterhalder, pp. 167–202. New York: Aldine.

Hill, K., H. Kaplan, K. Hawkes, and A. M. Hurtado. 1987. Foraging decisions among Aché hunter-gatherers: New data and implications for optimal foraging models. *Ethology and Sociobiology* 8:1–36.

Hillman, G. C. 1996. Late Pleistocene changes in wild plant-foods available to hunter-gatherers of the northern Fertile Crescent: Possible preludes to cereal cultivation. In *The Origins and Spread of Agriculture and Pastoralism in Eurasia*, ed. by D. R. Harris, pp. 159–203. London: University College London Press.

———. 2000. Abu Hureyra I: The epipalaeolithic. In *Village on the Euphrates*, ed. A. M. T. Moore, G. C. Hillman & A. J. Legge, pp. 327–98. Oxford: Oxford University Press.

———. 2001. New evidence of Late glacial cereal cultivation at Abu Hureyra on the Euphrates. *The Holocene* 11:383–93.

Hillman, G. C., and M. S. Davies. 1990a. Domestication rates in wild-type wheats and barely under primitive cultivation. *Biological Journal of the Linnean Society* 39:39–78.

———. 1990b. Measured domestication rates in wild wheats and barley under primitive cultivation, and their archaeological implications. *Journal of World Prehistory* 4:157–222.

———. 1992. Domestication rate in wild wheats and barley under primitive cultivation: Preliminary results and archaeological implications of field measurements of selection coefficient. In *Préhistoire de L'Agriculture: Nouvelles Approches Expérimentales et Ethnographiques*, ed. by P. C. Anderson, pp. 113–58. Paris: Editions du CNRS (Centre National de la Recherche Scientifique).

Hitchcock, R. K., and J. I. Ebert. 1984. Foraging and food production among Kalahari hunter/gatherers. In *From Hunters to Farmers: the Causes and Consequences of Food Production in Africa*, ed. by J. Clarke and S. Brandt, pp. 328–48. Berkeley: University of California Press.

Hladik, A., and E. Dounias. 1993. Wild yams of the African rain forest as potential food resources. In *Tropical Forests People and Food*, ed. by C. M. Hladik, A. Hladik, O. F. Linares, H. Pagezy, A. Semple, and M. Hadley, pp. 163–76. Paris: UNESCO and The Parthenon Publishing Group.

Hobbes, T. 1952. *Leviathan, or Matter, Form, and Power of Commonwealth Ecclesiastical and Civil*. Chicago, IL: University of Chicago Press.

Hodell, D. A., J. H. Curtis, and M. Brenner. 1995. Possible role of climate in the collapse of Classic Maya civilization. *Nature* 375:391–94.

Holdaway, R. N., and C. Jacomb. 2000. Rapid extinction of the moas (Aves: Dinornithiformes): model, test and implications. *Science* 287:2250–54.

Hole, F. 1984. A two-part, two stage model of domestication. In *The Walking Larder*, ed. by J. Clutton-Brock, pp. 97–104. London: Unwin Hyman.

Hoopes, J. W. 1995. Interaction in hunting and gathering societites as a context for the emergence of pottery in the Central American Isthmus. In *The Emergence of Pottery: Technology and Innovation in Ancient Societies*, ed. by W. K. Barnett and J. W. Hoopes, pp. 185–98. Washington, DC: Smithsonian Institution Press.

Hope, G. S. 1976. Vegetation. In *The Equatorial Glaciers of New Guinea*, ed. by G. S. Hope, J. A. Peterson, U. Radok, and I. Allison, pp. 113–72. Rotterdam: AA Balkena.

———. 1982. Pollen from archaeological sites: a comparison of swamp and open site pollen spectra at Kosipe Mission, Papua New Guinea, in *Archaeometry: an Australasian perspective*, ed. by W. Ambrose and P. Duerden, pp. 211–19. Canberra: RSPAS, ANU.

———. 1983. The vegetational changes of the last 20,000 years at Telefomin, Papua New Guinea. *Singapore Journal of Tropical Geography* 4:25–33.

———. 1996. Quaternary change and historical biogeography of Pacific Islands. In *The Origin and Evolution of Pacific Island Biotas, New*

Guinea to Eastern Polynesia: Patterns and Process, ed. by A. Keast and S. E. Miller, pp. 165–90. Amsterdam: SPB Publishing.

———. 1998. Early fire and forest change in the Baliem Valley, Irian Jaya, Indonesia. *Journal of Biogeography* 25:453–61.

Hope, G. S., and J. Golson. 1995. Late Quaternary change in the mountains of New Guinea. *Antiquity* 69(Special Number 265):818–30.

Hope, G. S., and J. A. Peterson. 1976. Palaeoenvironments. In *The Equatorial Glaciers of New Guinea*, ed. by G. S. Hope, J. A. Peterson, U. Radok and I. Allison, pp. 173–205. Rotterdam: AA Balkena.

Hope, G. S., and J. Tulip. 1994. A long vegetation history from lowland Irian Jaya, Indonesia. *Palaeogeography, Palaeoclimatology, Palaeoecology* 109:385–98.

Hope, G. S., D. Gillieson, and J. Head. 1988. A comparison of sedimentation and environmental change in New Guinea shallow lakes. *Journal of Biogeography* 15:603–18.

Hopf, M. 1991. South and Southwest Europe. In *Progress in Old World Palaeoethnobotany*, ed. by W. Van Zeist, R. Wasylikowa and K. Behre, pp. 241–76. Rotterdam: Balkema.

Horn, H. S. 1968. The adaptive significance of colonial nesting in the Brewer's Blackbird (*Euphagus Cyanocephalus*). *Ecology* 49:682–94.

Horowitz, L. K. (with a contribution by O. Lernau) 2003. Temporal and spatial variation in Neolithic Caprine exploitation strategies: A case study of fauna from the site of Yiftah'el (Israel). *Paléorient* 29(1):19–58.

Horridge, G. A. 1987. The evolution of Pacific canoe rigs. *Journal of Pacific History* 21:83–99.

Hostetler, S. W., and A. C. Mix. 1999. Reassessment of ice-age cooling of the tropical ocean and atmosphere. *Nature* 399:673–76.

Huang, Y., F. A. Street-Perrott, S. E. Metcalfe, M. Brenner, M. Moreland, and K. H. Freeman. 2001. Climate change as the dominate control on glacial-interglacial variations in C_3 and C_4 plant abundance. *Science* 293:1647–51.

Huckell, B. B. 1990. Late preceramic farmer-foragers in Southeastern Arizona: A cultural and ecological consideration of the spread of agriculture into the arid southwestern United States. Unpublished Ph.D. dissertation. Department of Anthropology, University of Arizona, Tucson.

———. 1995. Of marshes and maize: Preceramic agricultural settlements in the Cienega Valley, Southeastern Arizona. *Anthropological Papers No. 59.* Tucson, AZ: University of Arizona Press.

Huckell, B. B., L. W. Huckell, and S. K. Fish. 1994. Investigations at Milagro, a late preceramic site in the Eastern Tucson Basin. *Technical Report No. 94-5.* Tucson, AZ: Center for Desert Archaeology.

Huckell, B. B., M. D. Tagg, and L. W. Huckell. 1987 (eds). The Corona de Tucson Project: Prehistoric Use of a Bajada Environment. *Archaeological Series 174.* Tucson, AZ: Cultural Resource Management Division, Arizona State Museum.

Huckell, L. W. 1995. Farming and foraging in the Cienega Valley: Early agricultural period paleoethonobotany. In *Of Marshes and Maize: Preceramic Agricultural Settlements in the Cienega Valley, Southeastern Arizona*, by Bruce D. Huckell, pp. 74–97. *Anthropological Papers No. 59.* Tucson, AZ: University of Arizona Press.

Hughes, I. 1977. *New Guinea Stone Age Trade.* Canberra: RSPAS, ANU.

Hughes, P. J., M. E. Sullivan and D. Yok. 1991. Human induced erosion in a Highlands catchment in Papua New Guinea: The prehistoric and contemporary records. *Zeitschrift für Geomorphologie Suppl.* 83:227–39.

Hunt, T. L. 1987. Patterns of human interaction and evolutionary divergence in the Fiji Islands. *Journal of the Polynesian Society* 96:299–334.

Huntington, F. W. 1986 (ed.). Archaeological investigations at the west branch, Early and Middle Rincon Occupation in the Southern Tucson Basin. *Anthropological Papers No. 5.* Tucson, AZ: Institute for American Research.

Hurtado, A. M., and K. R. Hill. 1987. Early dry season subsistence ecology of Cuiva (Hiwi) foragers of Venezuela. *Human Ecology* 15:163–87.

Hutchinson, J. 1976. India: Local and introduced crops. In *Early History of Agriculture.* ed. by J. Hutchinson, pp. 129–41. London: Philosophical Transactions of the Royal Society London (Botany) 275.

Hyndman, D. C. 1979. Wopkaimin subsistence: Cultural ecology in the New Guinea Highland fringe. Unpublished PhD Dissertation, University of Queensland.

Iltis, H. H., and B. F. Benz. 2000. *Zea nicaraguensis* (Poaceae), a new teosinte from Pacific coastal Nicaragua. *Novon* 10(4):382–90.

Ingold, T. 1976. *Hunters. Pastoralists, and Ranchers: Reindeer Economies and Their Transformations.* Cambridge: Cambridge University Press.

———. 1996. Growing plants and raising animals: An anthropological perspective on domestication. In *The Origins and Spread of Agriculture and Pastoralism in Eurasia*, ed. by D. R. Harris, pp. 12–24. London: University College London Press.

Inizan, M. L. 1988. *Préhistoire à Qatar*. Paris: Editions Recherche sur les Civilisations.

———. 2000. Some reflections on the Neolithic in the Central Desert of Yemen. *Neolithics* 2-3/00:10–12.

Inizan M.-L., A. M. Lezine, B. Marcolongo, J. F. Saliege, C. Robert and F. Werth. 1997. Paléolacs et peuplements holocènes du Yémen: le Ramlat As-Sab'atayn. *Paléorient* 23(2):137–50.

Irwin, G. 1992. *The Prehistoric Exploration and Colonization of the Pacific*. Cambridge: Cambridge University Press.

Ison, C. R. 1991. Prehistoric upland farming along the Cumberland Plateau. In *Studies in Kentucky Archaeology*, ed. by Charles D. Hockensmith, pp. 1–10. Kentucky Heritage Council, Frankfort.

Jacomet, S., and J. Schibler. 1985. Die Nahrungsversorgung eines jungsteinzeitlichen Pfynerdorfes am unteren Zürichsee. *Archäologie der Schweiz* 8:125–41.

Janetski, J. C. 1993. The Archaic to Formative transition north of the Anasazi: A Basketmaker perspective. In *Anasazi Basketmaker: Papers from the 1990 Wetherill-Grand Gulch Symposium*, ed. by V. M. Atkins, pp. 223–41. Salt Lake City: BLM Cultural Resource Series No. 24.

———. 1997. Fremont hunting and resource intensification in the eastern Great Basin. *Journal of Archaeological Science* 24:1075–88.

Janetski, J. C., G. Timican, D. Timican, R. Pikyavit, and R. Pikyavit. 1999. Cooperative research between native Americans and Archaeologists: The Fish Lake archaeological project. In *Models for the Millennium: Great Basin Anthropology Today*, ed. by C. Beck, pp. 223–37. Salt Lake City, UT: University of Utah Press.

Jennings, J. D. 1978. Prehistory of Utah and the Eastern Great Basin. *University of Utah Anthropological Papers* 98. Salt Lake City, UT: University of Utah Press.

Jennings, J. D., and E. Norbeck. 1955. Great Basin prehistory: A review. *American Antiquity* 21:1–10.

Jochim, M. A. 2000. The origins of agriculture in south-central Europe. In *Europe's First Farmers*, ed. by T. D. Price, pp. 183–96. Cambridge: Cambridge University Press.

Johnson, A. 1983. Machiguenga gardens. In *Adaptive Responses of Native Amazonians*, ed. by R. B. Hames and W. T. Vickers, pp. 29–63. New York: Academic Press.

Johnson, A., and C. A. Behrens. 1982. Nutritional criteria in Machiguenga food production decisions: A linear programming analysis. *Human Ecology* 10:167–89.

Johnson, L. 1995. *In the Midst of a Prodigious Ocean: Archaeological Investigations of Polynesian Settlement of the Kermadec Islands*. Department of Conservation, Resource Series 11, Auckland, New Zealand.

Jones, J. G., and B. Voorhies. 2004. Human-plant interactions. In *Coastal Collectors in the Holocene: The Chantuto People of Southwest Mexico*. Gainesville, FL: University Press of Florida.

Jones, K. T., and D. B. Madsen. 1989. Calculating the cost of resource transportation: A Great Basin example. *Current Anthropology* 30:529–34.

———. 1991. Further experiments in native food procurement. *Utah Archaeology* 1991:68–77.

Jones, M., T. Brown, and R. Allaby. 1996. Tracking early crops and early farmers: The potential of biomolecular archaeology. In *The Origins and Spread of Agriculture and Pastoralism in Eurasia*, ed. by D. R. Harris, pp. 93–100. London: University College London Press.

Jones, M., and S. Colledge. 2001. Archaeobotany and the transition to agriculture. In *Handbook of Archaeological Sciences*, ed. by D. R. Brothwell and A. M. Pollard, pp. 393–401. Chichester: John Wiley and Sons.

Jones, R. 1980. Hunters in the Australian coastal savanna. In *Human Ecology in Savanna Environments*, ed. by D. R. Harris, pp. 107–46. London: Academic Press.

Jones, R., and B. Meehan. 1989. Plant foods of the Gidjingali: Ethnographic and archaeological perspectives from northern Australia on tuber and seed exploitation. In *Foraging and Farming: The Evolution of Plant Exploitation*, ed. by D. R. Harris and G. C. Hillman, pp. 120–35. London: Unwin Hyman.

Jones, R., and M. Spriggs. 2002. Theatrum Oceani: Themes and arguments concerning the prehistory of Australia and the Pacific. In *Archaeology: The Widening Debate*, ed. by B. Cunliffe, W. Davies, and C. Renfrew, pp. 245–94. London: British Academy.

Jones, T. L. and J. R. Richman. 1995. On mussels: *Mytilus californianus* as a prehistoric resource. *North American Archaeologist* 16:33–58.

Jones, V. 1936. The vegetal remains of Newt Kash Hollow Shelter. In *Rock Shelters in Menifee County, Kentucky*, ed. by W. S. Webb and W. D. Funkhouser, pp. 147–65. Reports in Archaeology and Anthropology 3(4). University of Kentucky, Lexington.

Jouzel, J. 1999. Calibrating the isotopic paleothermometer. *Science* 286:910–12.

Judd, N. M. 1926. Archaeological observations north of the Rio Colorado. *Bureau of American Ethnology Bulletin 82*. Washington: Smithsonian Institution.

Juyal, N., A. K. Singhvi, and K. W. Glennie. 1998. Chronology and paleoenvironmental significances of Quaternary desert sediment in southeastern Arabia. In *Quaternary Deserts and Climatic Change*, in A. S. Al Sharhan, K. W. Glennie, G. L. Whittle and C. G. St. C. Kendall, pp. 315–25. Rotterdam: Balkema.

Kajale, M. D. 1991. Current status of Indian palaeoethnobotany: Introduced and indigenous food plants with a discussion of the historical and evolutionary development of Indian agriculture and agricultural systems in general. In *New Light on Early Farming*, ed. by J. M. Renfrew pp. 155–89. Edinburgh: Edinburgh University Press.

Kallweit, H. 1997. New lithic sites in Wadi Dhahr, Republic of Yemen. *NeoLithics* 1/97:7–8.

Kantner, J. 1999. Survival cannibalism or sociopolitical intimidation? Explaining perimortem mutilation in the American Southwest. *Human Nature: An Interdisciplinary Biosocial Perspective* 10(1):1–50.

Kaplan, D. 2000. The darker side of the "original affluent society". *Journal of Anthropological Research* 56:301–24.

Kaplan, H., and K. Hill. 1992. The evolutionary ecology of food acquisition. In *Evolutionary Ecology and Human Behavior*, ed. by Eric Alden Smith and Bruce Winterhalder, pp. 167–202. New York: Aldine de Gruyter.

Keall, E. J. 1998. Encountering megaliths on the Tihamah coastal plain of Yemen. *Proceedings of the Seminar for Arabian Studies* 28:139–47.

Kealhofer, L. R., R. Torrence, and R. Fullagar. 1999. Integrating phytoliths within use-wear/residue studies of stone tools. *Journal of Archaeological Science* 26:527–46.

Kearney, T. H., and R. H. Peebles. 1973. *Arizona Flora*. Berkeley, CA: University of California Press.

Keefer, D. K., S. D. de France, M. E. Moseley, J. B. Richardson III, D. R. Satterlee, and A. Day-Lewis. 1998. Early maritime economy and El Niño events at Quebrada Tacahuay, Peru. *Science* 281:1833–35.

Keegan, W. F. 1986. The optimal foraging analysis of horticultural production. *American Anthropologist* 88:92–107.

———. 1987 (ed.). *Emergent Horticultural Economies of the Eastern Woodlands*. Center for Archaeological Investigations, Occasional Paper No. 7. Carbondale, IL: Southern Illinois University.

Keegan, W. F., and J. M. Diamond. 1987. Colonization of the islands by humans: A biogeographical perspective. In *Advances in Archaeological Method and Theory*, Vol. 10, ed. by M. B. Schiffer, pp. 49–92. New York: Academic Press.

Keeley, L. H. 1995. Protoagricultural practices among hunter-gatherers: A cross-cultural survey. In *Last Hunters—First Farmers: New Perspectives on the Prehistoric Transition to Agriculture*, ed. by T. D. Price and A. B. Gebauer, pp. 243–72. Santa Fe, NM: School of American Research Press.

———. 1996. *War Before Civilization*. Oxford: Oxford University Press.

Kelly, K. M. 1999. Malaria and immunoglobulins in Pacific prehistory. *American Anthropologist* 101(4):806–9.

Kelly, I. T. 1976. Southern Paiute Ethnography. In *Paiute Indians II*, Garland American Indian Ethnohistory Series, pp. 3–224. New York: Garland Publishing Inc.

Kelly, R. L. 1992. Mobility/sedentism: Concepts, archaeological measures, and effects. *Annual Review of Anthropology* 21:43–66.

———. 1995. *The Foraging Spectrum: Diversity in Hunter-Gatherer Lifeways*. Washington, DC: Smithsonian Institution Press.

———. 2000. Elements of a behavioral ecological paradigm for the study of prehistoric hunter-gatherers. In *Social Theory in Archaeology*, ed. by M. B. Schiffer, pp. 63–78. Salt Lake City: University of Utah Press.

Kennett, D. J. 1998. Behavioral ecology and the evolution of hunter-gatherer societies on the Northern Channel Islands, California. Unpublished Ph.D. Dissertation. University of California, Santa Barbara.

Kennett, D. J., and J. P. Kennett. 2000. Competitive and cooperative responses to climatic instability in coastal southern California. *American Antiquity* 65:379–95.

Kennett, D. J., and B. Voorhies. 1995. Middle Holocene periodicities in rainfall inferred from oxygen and carbon isotopic fluctuations in prehistoric tropical estuarine mollusk shells. *Archaeometry* 37(1):157–70.

———. 1996. Oxygen isotopic analysis of archaeological shells to detect seasonal use of wetlands on the southern Pacific Coast of Mexico. *Journal of Archaeological Science* 23: 689–704.

———. 2001. Informe de Campo: Proyecto Costero Arcaico-Formativo, Chiapas. Submitted to the Consejo de Arqueología, I. N. A. H.

Kennett, D. J., B. Voorhies, and S. B. McClure. 2002. Los Cerritos: an early fishing-farming community on the Pacific Coast of Mexico. *Antiquity* 76:631–32.

Kennett, D. J., A. Anderson, M. Prebble, and E. Conte. 2003. Research Report-National Geographic Society: The Colonization and Fortification of Rapa, French Polynesia.

Kenoyer, J. M. 1986. The Indus bead industry: Contributions in bead technology. *Ornaments* 10(1):18–23.

Kihara, H., and M. Tanaka. 1958. Morphological and physiological variation among *Aegilops squarrosa* strains collected in Pakistan, Afghanistan and Iran. *Preslia* 30:241–51.

Kirby, K. N., and R. J. Hernnstein. 1995. Preference reversals due to myopic discounting of delayed reward. *Psychological Science* 6:83–89.

Kirby, K. N., and N. N. Maracovic. 1996. Delay-discounting probabilistic rewards: Rates decrease as amounts increase. *Psychonomic Bulletin & Review* 3:100–04.

Kirby, K. N., R. Godoy, V. Reyes-García, E. Byron, L. Apaza, W. Leonard, E. Pérez, V. Vadez, and D. Wilkie. 2002. Correlates of delay-discount rates: Evidence from Tsimane' Amerindians of the Bolivian rain forest. *Journal of Economic Psychology* 23:291–316.

Kirch, P. V. 1984. *The Evolution of Polynesian Chiefdoms*. Cambridge: Cambridge University Press.

———. 1988. *Niuatoputapu: the prehistory of a Polynesian chiefdom*. Thomas Burke Memorial Washington State Museum Monograph No. 5. Seattle: The Burke Museum.

———. 1989. Second millennium B.C. arboriculture in Melanesia: Archaeological evidence from the Mussau Islands. *Economic Botany* 43(2):225–40.

———. 1996. Late Holocene human-induced modifications to a central Polynesian island ecosystem. *Proceedings of the National Academy of Sciences* 93:5296–5300.

———. 1997. *The Lapita Peoples: Ancestors of the Oceanic World*. Oxford: Blackwell.

———. 2000. *On the Road of the Winds: An Archaeological History of the Pacific Islands before European Contact*. Berkeley, CA: University of California Press.

Kirch, P. V., and R. C. Green. 2001. *Hawaiki, Ancestral Polynesia: an essay in historical Anthropology*. Cambridge: Cambridge University Press.

Kirch, P. V., and T. L. Hunt. 1988. *Archaeology of the Lapita Cultural Complex: A Critical Review*. Thomas Burke Memorial Washington State Museum Research Report No. 5. Seattle: Burke Museum.

Kirch, P. V., T. L. Hunt, M. Weisler, V. Butler, and M. S. Allen. 1991. Mussau Islands prehistory: results of the 1985–1986 excavations. In *Report of the Lapita Homeland Project*, ed. by J. Allen and C. Gosden, pp. 144–63. *Occasional Papers in Prehistory* 20. Canberra: Department of Prehistory, Research School of Pacific Studies, Australian National University.

Kirch, P. V., D. W. Steadman, V. L. Butler, Jon Hather, and M. I. Weisler. 1995. Prehistory and human ecology in eastern Polynesia: Excavations at Tangatatau rockshelter, Mangaia, Cook Islands. *Archaeology and Oceania* 30(2): 47–65.

Kirkby, A. V. T. 1973. *The Use of Land and Water Resources in the Past and Present Valley of Oaxaca*. Memoirs No. 5. Museum of Anthropology, Ann Arbor: University of Michigan.

Kislev, M. E. 1997. Early agriculture and paleoecology of Netiv Hagdud. In *An Early Neolithic Village in the Jordan Valley, Part I: The Archaeology of Netiv Hagdud*, ed. by O. Bar-Yosef and A. Q. Gopher, pp. 209–36. Cambridge, MA: Harvard University.

Klein, R. G. 1999. *The Human Career: Human Biological and Cultural Origins* (2d ed.). Chicago: University of Chicago Press.

———. 2001. Southern Africa and modern human origins. *Journal of Anthropological Research* 57:1–16.

Koford, C. 1957. The vicuña and the puna. *Ecological Monographs* 27:153–219.

Kohler, T. A. 2000. Putting social sciences together again: An introduction to the volume. In *Dynamics in Human and Primate Societies: Agent-based Modeling of Social and Spatial Processes*, ed. by T. A. Kohler and G. J. Gumerman, pp. 1–18. Oxford: Oxford University Press.

Kohler, T. A., and G. J. Gumerman. 2000 (ed). *Dynamics in Human and Primate Societies: Agent-based Modeling of Social and Spatial Processes.* Oxford: Oxford University Press.

Kohler, T. A., and C. R. Van West. 1996. The calculus of self-interest in the development of cooperation: Sociopolitical development and risk among the Northern Anasazi. In *Evolving Complexity and Environmental Risk in the Prehistoric Southwest*, ed. by J. Tainter and B. B. Tainter, pp. 169–96. Reading, MA: Addison-Wesley.

Koziol, M. J. 1993. Quinoa: A potential new oil crop. In *New Crops*, ed. by J. Janick and J. E. Simon, pp. 328–36. New York: Wiley.

Krebs, J. R, and N. B. Davies. 1991. *Behavioral Ecology: An Evolutionary Approach.* Oxford, England: Blackwell Scientific.

Krebs, J. R., and N. B. Davies. 1997. *Behavioural Ecology: An Evolutionary Approach.* Cambridge, MA: Blackwell Science.

Krebs, J. R., and A. Kacelnik. 1991. Decision-making. In *Behavioral Ecology: An Evolutionary Approach* (3rd ed.), ed. by J. R. Krebs and N. B. Davies, pp. 105–36. Oxford: Blackwell Scientific Publications.

Kuchikura, Y. 1993. Wild yams in the tropical rainforest: Abundance and dependence among the Semaq Beri in Peninsular Malaysia. *Man and Culture in Oceania* 9:81–102.

Kuhn, S. L., and M. C. Stiner. 2001. The antiquity of hunter-gatherers, in *Hunter-gatherers: An interdisciplinary perspective*, ed. by C. Panter-Brick, R. H. Layton, and P. Rowley-Conwy, pp. 99–142. Cambridge: Cambridge University Press.

Kuhn, T. S. 1962. *The Structure of Scientific Revolutions.* Chicago: University of Chicago Press.

———. 1977. Objectivity, value judgment, and theory choice. In *The Essential Tension: Selected Studies in Scientific Tradition and Change*, ed. by T. S. Kuhn, pp. 320–39. Chicago, IL: University of Chicago Press.

Kutzbach, J. E. 1981. Monsoon climate of the early Holocene: Climatic experiment using the earth's orbital parameters for 9,000 years ago. *Science* 214:59–61.

Kutzbach J. E., G. Bonan, J. Foley and S. P. Harrison. 1996. Vegetation and soil feedbacks on the response of the African monsoon to orbital forcing in the early to middle Holocene. *Nature* 384:623–26.

Kuznar, L. 1990. Economic models, ethnoarchaeology, and early pastoralism in the high sierra of the south central Andes. Unpublished Ph.D. dissertation, Department of Anthropology, Northwestern University.

———. 1993. Mutualism between *Chenopodium*, herd animals, and herders in the south-central Andes. *Mountain Research and Development* 13(3):257–65.

Laland, K. N. and G. R. Brown. 2002. *Sense and Nonsense: Evolutionary Perspectives on Human Behavior.* Oxford: Oxford University Press.

Lampert, R. J. 1967. Horticulture in the New Guinea Highlands-C14 dating. *Antiquity* 41: 307–9.

———. 1970. Archaeological report of the Minjigina site (Appendix 5). In The impact of man on the vegetation of the Mount Hagen Region, *New Guinea*. by J. M. Powell, Unpublished Ph.D. Dissertation, Australian National University.

Lancaster, J. 1984. Groundstone artifacts. In *The Galaz Ruin: A Prehistoric Mimbres Village in Southwestern New Mexico*, edited by R. Anyon and S. A. LeBlanc, pp. 247–62. Albuquerque, NM: University of New Mexico Press and the Maxwell Museum of Anthropology.

Lancaster, W., and F. Lancaster. 1999. *People, Land and Water in the Arab Middle East.* Amsterdam: Harwood Academic Publishers.

Lawler, A. 2002. Report of oldest boat hints at early trade routes. *Science* 296:1791–92.

Layton, R. H., and R. A. Foley. 1992. On subsistence transitions: Response to Hawkes and O'Connell. *Current Anthropology* 33:218–19.

Layton, R., R. Foley, and E. Williams. 1991. The transition between hunting and gathering and the specialized husbandry of resources. *Current Anthropology* 32:255–74.

Lebot, V. 1999. Biomolecular evidence for plant domestication in Sahul. *Genetic Resources and Crop Evolution* 46:619–28.

Lee, R. B., and R. Daly. 1999 (ed.). *The Cambridge Encyclopedia of Hunters and Gatherers.* Cambridge: Cambridge University Press.

Lentfer, C. 2002. Phytolith analysis of sediments from the Kundil's sections at Kuk, Papua New Guinea, and evidence for early Holocene banana cultivation. Paper presented at the 67th annual meeting of the Society for American Archaeology, Denver.

Levi-Strauss, C. 1964. *Totemism*. Translated by R. Needham. London: Merlin Press.

Levkovskaya, G. M., and A. A. Filatenko. 1992. Palaeobotanical and palynological studies in South Arabia. *Review of Palaeobotany and Palynology* 73:241–57.

Lewis, D. 1994. *We, the Navigators. The Ancient Art of Landfinding in the Pacific*. Honolulu: University of Hawaii Press.

Lézine, A.-M., J.-F. Saliège, C. Robert, F. Wertz, and M.-L. Inizan. 1998. Holocene lakes from ramlat as-Sab'atayn (Yemen) illustrate the impact of monsoon activity in southern Arabia. *Quaternary Research* 50:290–99.

Lilley, I., 1995. Lapita and post-Lapita developments in the Vitiaz Straits-West New Britain Area. *Indo-Pacific Prehistory Association Bulletin* 11:313–22.

Lindeman, M. W. 2000 (ed.). Excavations at Sunset Mesa ruin. *Technical Report 2000–02*. Tucson, AZ: Desert Archaeology, Inc.

Lindsay, L. M. W. 1986. Fremont fragmentation. In *Anthropology of the Desert West, Essays in Honor of Jesse D. Jennings*, University of Utah Anthropological Papers 110, ed. by C. J. Condie and D. D. Fowler, pp. 229–51. Salt Lake City: University of Utah Press.

Lindström, S. 1996. Great Basin fisherfolk: Optimal diet breadth modeling the Truckee River subsistence aboriginal fishery. In *Prehistoric Hunter-Gatherer Fishing Strategies*, ed. by M. Plew, pp. 114–79. Boise, Idaho: Boise State University Press.

Lipe, W. D. 1983. The Southwest. In *Ancient North Americans*, ed. by J. D. Jennings, pp. 421–93. San Francisco, CA: W. H. Freeman.

Lipe, W. D. 1993. The Basketmaker II Period in the Four Corners Area. In *Anasazi Basketmaker: Papers from the 1990 Wetherill-Grand Gulch Symposium*. Salt Lake City: BLM Cultural Resource Series No. 24.

Lister, A. M., and A. V. Sher. 1995. Ice cores and mammoth extinction. *Nature* 378:23–24.

Loewenstein, G. 1987. Anticipation and the valuation of delayed consumption. *The Economic Journal* 97:666–84.

———. 1992. The rise and fall of psychological explanations in the economics of intertemporal choice. In *Choice Over Time,* ed. by G. Loewenstein and J. Elster, pp. 3–32. New York: Russell-Sage Foundation.

Loewenstein, G., and D. Prelec. 1992. Anomalies in intertemporal choice: Evidence and an interpretation. *The Quarterly Journal of Economics* 107:573–97.

Logue, A. W., A. Chavarro, H. Rachlin, R. W. Reeder. 1988. Impulsiveness in pigeons living in the experimental chamber. *Animal Learning & Behavior* 16:31–39.

Logue, A. W., M. Rodriguez, T. E. Pena-Correal, B. C. Mauro. 1987. Quantification of individual differences in self-control. In *Quantitative Analyses of Behavior, Vol 5: The Effect of Delay and Intervening Events on Reinforcement Value*, M. L. Commons, J. E. Mazur, J. A. Nevin, and H. Rachlin, pp. 245–65. Hillside, NJ: Erlbaum.

Lombard, P. 1981. Poignards en Bronze de la péninsule d'Oman. *Iranica Antiqua* 16:87–93.

Long, A., B. F. Benz, D. J. Donahue, A. J. T. Jull, and L. J. Toolin. 1989. First direct AMS dates on early Maize From Tehuacán, Mexico. *Radiocarbon* 31(3):1035–40.

Long, A., L. A. Warneke, J. L. Betancourt, and R. S. Thompson. 1990. Deuterium variations in plant cellulose from fossil packrat middens. In *Packrat Middens: The Last 40,000 Years of Biotic Change*, ed. by J. L. Betancourt, T. R. Van Devender and P. S. Martin, pp. 380–96. Tucson: University of Arizona Press.

Lorenzo, J. L. 1955. Los concheros de la costa de Chiapas. *Anales del Instituto Nacional de Antropología*, Bol. 7:41–50. México.

Love, M. W. 1989. Early settlements and chronology of the Río Naranjo, Guatemala. Unpublished Ph.D. Dissertation, University of California, Berkeley.

———. 1993. Ceramic chronology and chronometric dating: Stratigraphy and seriation at La Blanca, Guatemala. *Ancient Mesoamerica* 44:17–29.

Lowe, G. W. 1975. *The Early Preclassic Barra Phase of Altamira, Chiapas: A Review of the New Data*. Papers of the New World Archaeological Foundation, No. 38. Provo, Utah.

———. 1982. *Izapa, an Introduction to the Ruins and Monuments*, ed. by G. W. Lowe, T. A. Lee, Jr., and E. M. Espinosa. Provo, UT: New World Archaeological Foundation, Brigham Young University.

Loy, T., M. Spriggs, and S. Wickler. 1992. Direct evidence for human use of plants 28,000 years ago: starch residues on stone artefacts from northern Solomon Islands. *Antiquity* 66:898–912.

Lyman, R. L. 2003. The influence of time averaging and space averaging on the application of foraging theory in zooarchaeology. *Journal of Archaeological Science* 30:595–610.

Mabry, J. D. 1998. Conclusion. In *Archaeological Investigations of Early Village Sites in the Middle Santa Cruz Valley: Analyses and Syntheses,* Part II, ed. by J. B. Mabry, pp. 757–92. *Anthropological Papers No. 19.* Tucson, AZ: Center for Desert Archaeology.

———. 2000. The Role of Irrigation in the Transition to Agriculture and Sedentism in the Southwest. Paper Presented at the Southwest Symposium, January 13–15, Santa Fe, New Mexico.

———. 1998 (ed.). Archaeological Investigations of Early Village Sites in the Middle Santa Cruz Valley: Analyses and Syntheses, Part I. *Anthropological Papers No. 19.* Tucson, AZ: Center for Desert Archaeology.

MacArthur, R. H., and E. R. Pianka. 1966. On optimal use of a patchy environment. *The American Naturalist* 100:603–9.

MacArthur, R. H. and E. O. Wilson. 1967. *The theory of island biogeography.* Princeton, N.J.: Princeton University Press.

Mace, R. 1990. Pastoralist herd compositions in unpredictable environments: a comparison of model predictions and data from camel-keeping groups. *Agricultural Systems* 33:1–11.

———. 1993a. Nomadic pastoralists adopt subsistence strategies that maximise long-term household survival. *Behavioral Ecology and Sociobiology* 33:329–34.

———. 1993b. Transitions between cultivation and pastoralism in sub-Saharan Africa. *Current Anthropology* 34(4):363–82.

Mace, R., and A. Houston. 1989. Pastoralist strategies for survival in unpredictable environments: A model of herd composition that maximises household viability. *Agricultural Systems* 31: 184–204.

Mackay, E. J. H. 1943. Chanhu-daro Excavations 1935–36. *American Oriental Series* 20. New Haven, CT: American Oriental Society.

Madsen, D. B. 1979. The Fremont and the Sevier: Defining prehistoric agriculturalists north of the Anasazi. *American Antiquity* 44:711–22.

———. 1982. Get it where the gettin's good: a variable model of Great Basin subsistence and settlement based on data from the eastern Great Basin. In *Man and Environment in the Great Basin, SAA Papers No. 2,* ed. by D. B. Madsen and J. F. O'Connell, pp. 207–26. Washington: Society for American Archaeology.

———. 1989. *Exploring the Fremont.* Salt Lake City: Utah Museum of Natural History.

———. 1993. Testing diet breadth models: Examining adaptive change in the late prehistoric Great Basin. *Journal of Archaeological Science* 20:321–30.

Madsen, D. B., and D. N. Schmitt. 1998. Mass collecting and the diet breadth model: A Great Basin example. *Journal of Archaeological Science* 25:445–56.

Madsen, D. B., L. Eschler, and T. Eschler. 1997. Winter cattail collecting experiments. *Utah Archaeology* 1997:1–19.

Madsen, D. B., and J. E. Kirkman. 1988. Hunting hoppers. *American Antiquity* 53:593–604.

Madsen, D. B., and S. R. Simms. 1998. The Fremont complex: A behavioral perspective. *Journal of World Prehistory* 12:255–336.

MAG (Ministerio Agricultura y Ganadería). 1985. *Estimación de la Superficie Cosechada y de la Producción Agrícola del Ecuador.* Ministerio Agricultura y Ganadería, Quito, Ecuador.

Majnep, I. S., and R. N. H. Bulmer. 1990. *Kalam hunting traditions* (10 volumes). Auckland: University of Auckland.

Mangelsdorf, P. C. 1974. *Corn: Its Origins, Evolution, and Improvement.* Cambridge, MA: Harvard University Press.

———. 1986. The origin of corn. *Scientific American* 254:80–86.

Mangelsdorf, P. C., and R. G. Reeves. 1939. The origin of Indian corn and its relatives. *Texas Agricultural Experiment Station Bulletin 574.*

Mangelsdorf, P. C., R. S. MacNeish, and W. C. Galinat. 1967. Prehistoric wild and cultivated maize. In *The Prehistory of the Tehuacan Valley, Vol. I: Environment and Subsistence,* ed. by D. S. Byers, pp. 178–200. Austin, TX: University of Texas Press.

Marcolongo, B., and A. M. Palmieri. 1990. Paleoenvironmental history of western Al-A'Rus. In *The Bronze Age culture of Hawlan at-Tiyal and al-Hada (Republic of Yemen).* ed. by A. de Maigret, pp. 137–43. Roma: Istituto Italiano per il Medio ed Estremo Oriente.

Marshall, B., and J. Allen. 1991. Excavations at Panakiwuk Cave, New Ireland. In *Report of the Lapita Homeland Project,* ed. by J. Allen and C. Gosden, Occasional Papers in Prehistory 20. Department of Prehistory, Research School of Pacific Studies, Australian National University, Canberra.

Marshall, F., and E. Hildebrand. 2002. Cattle before crops: The beginnings of food production in Africa. *Journal of World Prehistory* 16: 99–142.

Martí, B. 1998. El Neolítico, in *Prehistoria de la Península Ibérica*, ed. by I. Barandiaran, B. Martí, M. A. del Rincon and J. L. Maya, pp. 121–96. Barcelona: Editorial Ariel, S.A.

Martí, B., and J. Juan-Cabanilles. 1987. *El Neolitíc València. Els Primers Agricultors i Ramaders.* València: Servei d'Investigació Prehistorica de la Diputació Provincial de València.

———. 1997. Epipaleolíticos y neolíticos: Población y territorio en el proceso de neolitización de la Península Ibérica. *Espacio, Tiempo y Forma, Serie I, Prehistoria y Arqueología* 10: 215–64.

Martin, L. A. 1999. Mammal remains from the eastern Jordanian Neolithic and the nature of caprine herding in the steppe. *Paléorient* 25(2):87–104.

Martin, P. S., and F. Plog. 1973. *The Archaeology of Arizona: A Study of the Southwest Region.* Garden City, NY: Doubleday/American Museum of Natural History Press.

Martínez-Soriano, J. P. R., and D. S. Keal-Klevezas 2000. Transgenic maize in Mexico: No need for concern. *Science* 286:1399.

Marwitt, J. P. 1968. Pharo Village. *University of Utah Anthropological Papers* 91. Salt Lake City, UT: University of Utah Press.

———. 1970. Median Village and Fremont culture regional variation. *University of Utah Anthropological Papers* 95. Salt Lake City, UT: University of Utah Press.

———. 1986. Fremont Cultures. In *Handbook of North American Indians Vol. 11, The Great Basin*, ed. by W. L. D'Azevedo, pp. 161–72. Washington, DC: Smithsonian Institution.

Massimino, J., and D. Metcalfe. 1999. New form for the formative. *Utah Archaeology* 1999:1–16.

Matson, R. G. 1994. Anomalous Basketmaker II sites on Cedar Mesa: Not so anomalous after all. *Kiva* 60:219–37.

Matson, R. G., and B. Chisolm. 1991. Basketmaker II subsistence: Carbon isotopes and other dietary indicators from Cedar Mesa, Utah. *American Antiquity* 56:444–59.

Matsuoka, Y., Vigouroux, Y., Goodman, M. M., Sanchez, J., Buckler, E., and J. Doebley. 2002. A single domestication for maize shown by multilocus microsatellite genotyping. *Proceedings of the National Academy of Sciences USA* 99: 6080–84.

Matthews, P. J. 1991. A possible wildtype taro: *Colocasia esculenta* var. *aquatilis*. *IPPA Bulletin* 11:69–81.

———. 1995. Aroids and the Austronesians. *Tropics* 4(2):105–26.

Matthews, P. J. and Gosden C. 1997. Plant remains from waterlogged sites in the Arawe Islands, West New Guinea Province, Papua New Guinea: Implications for the history of plant use. *Economic Botany* 51:121–33.

Matthews, R. 2002. Zebu: hargingers of doom in Bronze Age western Asia? *Antiquity* 76:438–46.

Mauldin, R. 1993. The Relationship between ground stone and agricultural dependence in western New Mexico. *Kiva* 58:317–44.

Mazur, J. E. 1984. Test of an equivalence rule for fixed and variable reinforcer delays. *Journal of Experimental Psychology: Animal Behavior Processes* 10:426–36.

———. 1987. An adjusting procedure for studying delayed reinforcement. In *Quantitative Analyses of Behavior: Vol 5: The Effect of Delay and Intervening Events on Reinforcement Value*, ed. by M. L. Commons, J. E. Mazur, J. A. Nevin, and H. Rachlin, pp. 55–73. Hillside, NJ: Erlbaum.

McBryde, F. W. 1947. *Cultural and Historical Geography of Southwest Guatemala*. Smithsonian Institution Institute of Social Anthropology 4, Washington, DC: Smithsonian Institution.

McCarthy, H. 1993. A political economy of western mono acorn production. Unpublished Ph.D. Dissertation, University of California, Davis.

McClure, H. A. 1976. Radiocarbon chronology of late Quaternary lakes in the Arabian desert. *Nature* 263:755–56.

———. 1984. Late Quaternary palaeoenvironments of the Rub'al Khali. Unpublished Ph.D. Dissertation, University of London.

———. 1988. Late Quaternary palaeogeography and landscape evolution if the Rub'al Khali, In *Araby the Blest*, ed. by D. T. Potts, pp. 9–13. Copenhagen: Carston Niebuhr Institute Publication 7, Tusculanum Press.

McClure, H. A., and N. Y. al-Shaikh. 1993. Palaeogeography of an 'Ubaid archaeological site, Saudi Arabia. *Arabian Archaeology and Epigraphy* 4:107–25.

McCorriston, J. 2000. Early settlement in Hadramawt: Preliminary report on prehistoric occupation at Shi'b Munayder. *Arabian Archaeology and Epigraphy* 11:129–53.

McCorriston, J., and F. Hole. 1991. The ecology of seasonal stress and the origins of agriculture in the Near East. *American Anthropologist* 93: 46–69.

McCorriston, J., and Z. Johnson. 1998. Agriculture and animal husbandry at Ziyadid Zabid, Yemen. *Proceedings of the Seminar for Arabian Studies* 28:175–88.

McCorriston, J., and E. A. Oches. 2001. Two early Holocene check dams from Southern Arabia. *Antiquity* 75:675–76.

McCorriston, J., E. A. Oches, D. E. Walter, and K. Cole. 2003. Holocene paleoecology and prehistory in Highland Southern Arabia. *Paléorient* 28(1):61–88.

McCorriston, J., M. Harrower, E. Oches, and A. Bin 'Aqil (with contributions by C. Heyne, A. Noman, R. Crassard, K. BaDhofary, and J. Anderson). 2005. Foraging Economies and Population in the Middle Holocene Highlands of Southern Yemen. *Proceedings of the Seminar for Arabian Studies* 35:143–54.

McCracken, R. D. 1971. Lactose deficiency: an example of dietary evolution. *Current Anthropology* 12:479–517.

McDonald, E. K. 1994. A spatial and temporal examination of prehistoric interaction in the Eastern Great Basin and on the Northern Colorado Plateau. Unpublished Ph.D. dissertation. Boulder: University of Colorado.

McElreath, R., R. Boyd and P. Richerson. 2003. Shared Norms and the Evolution of Ethnic Markers. *Current Anthropology* 44:122–29.

McGlone, M. S., and J. M. Wilmshurst. 1999. Dating initial Maori environmental impact in New Zealand. *Quaternary International* 59: 5–16.

McGrain, P., and J. Currens. 1978. *Topography of Kentucky.* Special Publication 25. Kentucky Geological Survey, Lexington.

McGrail, S. 2003. *Boats of South Asia.* New York: Routledge.

McMullin, E. 1983. Values in science. *Philosophy of Science Association* 2:3–28.

Meadow, R. H. 1987. Faunal exploitation patterns in eastern Iran and Baluchistan: A review of recent investigations, In *Orientalia Iosephi Tucci memoriae dicta, volume 2,* ed. by G. Gnoli, pp. 881–916. Roma Istituto Italiano per il Medio ed Estremo Oriente, *Serie Orientale Roma* 46.

———. 1996. The origins and spread of agriculture and pastoralism in northwestern South Asia. In *The Origins and Spread of Agriculture and Pastoralism in Eurasia,* ed. by D. R. Harris, pp. 390–412. Washington DC: Smithsonian Institution Press.

Meehan, B. 1982. *Shell Bed to Shell Midden.* Canberra: Australian Institute for Aboriginal Studies.

Meire, P., and E. Kuyken. 1984. Relations between the distribution of waders and the intertidal benthic fauna of the Oosterschelde, Netherlands. In *Coastal Waders and Wildfowl in Winter,* ed. by P. R. Evans, J. D. Goss-Custard, and W. G. Hale, pp. 57–68. Cambridge: Cambridge University Press.

Mellers, P. 1996. *The Neanderthal Legacy: An Archaeological Perspective from Western Europe.* Princeton, NJ: Princeton University Press.

Meltzer, D. J., J. M. Adovasio, and T. D. Dillehay. 1994. On a Pleistocene human occupation at Pedra Furada, Brazil. *Antiquity* 68:695–714.

Menger, C. 1951. *Principles of Economics.* Translated by J. D. a. B. F. Hoselitz. Glencoe, Ill: Free Press.

Mengoni, G. L. 1986. Viscacha (*Lagidium viscacia*) and taruca (*Hippocamelus* sp.) in early south Andean economies. *Archaeozoología* 63–71.

Merkt, J. 1987. Reproductive seasonality and grouping patterns of the north Andean deer or taruca (*Hippocamelus antisensis*) in southern Peru. In *Biology and Management of the Cervidae,* ed. by C. M. Wemmer, pp. 388–401. Washington, DC: Smithsonian Institution Press.

Méry, S., and G. Schneider. 1996. Mesopotamian pottery wares in Eastern Arabia from the 5th to the 2nd millennium BC: A contribution of archaeometry to economic history. *Proceedings of the Seminar for Arabian Studies*: 79–96.

Metcalfe, D., and K. R. Barlow. 1992. A model for exploring the optimal trade-off between field processing and transport. *American Anthropologist* 94:340–56.

Metcalfe, D., and K. M. Heath. 1990. Microrefuse and site structure: The hearths and floors of the Heartbreak Hotel. *American Antiquity* 55: 781–96.

Metcalfe, D., and L. V. Larrabee. 1985. Archaeological evidence for Fremont irrigation. *Journal of California and Great Basin Anthropology* 7: 244–54.

Michaels, G. H., and B. Voorhies. 1999. Late Archaic Period coastal collectors in southern Mesoamerica: The Chantuto People revisited. In *Pacific Latin America in Prehistory: The Evolution of Archaic and Formative Cultures,* ed. by M. Blake, pp. 39–54. Pullman, WA: Washington State University Press.

Mickelson, K. R. 2002. Environmental factors affecting the preservation of botanical remains at the Mounded Talus Shelter (15le77), Kentucky. Unpublished Unpublished Ph.D. dissertation, Ohio State University, Columbus.

Miksicek, C. H. 1987. Formation processes of the archaeobotanical record. In *Advances in Archaeological Method and Theory, Vol. 10*, ed. by M. B. Schiffer, pp. 211–47. New York: Academic Press.

Milton, K. 1984. Protein and carbohydrate resources of the Maku indians of northwestern Amazonia. *American Anthropologist* 86:7–27.

Minnis, P. E. 1981. Seeds in archaeological sites: Sources and some interpretive problems. *American Antiquity* 46:143–51.

———. 1985. *Social Adaptation to Food Stress: A Prehistoric Southwestern Example*. Chicago, IL: University of Chicago Press.

Minturn, P. D., L. Lincoln-Babb, and J. B. Mabry. 1998. Human Osteology. In *Archaeological Investigations of Early Village Sites in the Middle Santa Cruz Valley: Analyses and Synthesis , Part II*, ed. by Jonathan B. Mabry, pp. 739–55. *Anthropological Papers No. 19*. Tucson, AZ: Center for Desert Archaeology.

Miranda, F. 1975. *La Vegetación de Chiapas*. Tuxtla Gutiérrez, Chiapas: Ediciones del Gobierno del Estado.

Moerman, D. E. 1998. *Native American Ethnobotany*. Eugene, OR: Timber Press.

Molet, L. 1958. Aperçu sur un groupe nomade de la forêt epineuse des Mikea. *Bulletin de l'Academie Malgache* 36:241–43.

Molnar, R. E., T. Worthy, and P. M. A. Willis. 2002. An extinct Pleistocene mekosuchine crocodylian from Fiji. *Journal of Vertebrate Paleontology* 22:612–28.

Moore, K. 1989. Hunting and the origins of herding in Peru. Unpublished Ph.D. Dissertation, Department of Anthropology, University of Michigan.

Moorey, P. and S. Roger. 1974. *Ancient Persian Bronzes in the Adam Collection*. London: Faber & Faber.

Morrison, F. B. 1954. *Feeds and Feeding*. Ithaca, New York: Morrison Publishing Co.

Morss, N. 1931. The Ancient Culture of the Fremont River in Utah: Report on the Explorations Under the Claflin-Emerson Fund, 1928–29. *Papers of the Peabody Museum, Vol. XII, No. 3*. Harvard University: Peabody Museum of American Archaeology and Ethnology.

Moser, M. E. 1988. Limits to the numbers of grey plovers *Pluvialis squatarola* wintering on British Estuaries: An analysis of long-term trends. *Journal of Applied Ecology* 25:475–86.

Mosley, W. H. and L. C. Chen. 1984. *Child Survival: Strategies for Research*. New York: Cambridge University Press.

Mountain, M. J. 1991. Highland New Guinea hunter-gatherers: The evidence of Nombe Rockshelter, Simbu, with emphasis on the Pleistocene. Unpublished Ph.D. Dissertation, Australian National University.

Muhs, D. R., H. R. Simmons, and B. Steinke. 2001. Timing and warmth of the last Interglacial period: New U-series evidence from Hawaii and Bermuda and a new fossil compilation for North America. *Quaternary Science Reviews*.

Mujica, E. 1994. Andean grains and legumes. In *Neglected Crops: 1492 from a Different Perspective*, ed. by J. Bermejo and J. León, pp. 131–48. Rome: FAO.

Muke, J., and H. Mandui. 2003. Shadows of Kuk: Evidence for wetland agriculture at Kana, Wahgi Valley, Papua New Guinea. In *Perspectives on Prehistoric Agriculture in New Guinea*, ed. by T. P. Denham and C. Ballard. *Archaeology in Oceania, Special Issue* 38(3):177–85.

Müller, H. H. 1985. Tierreste aus Siedlungsgruben der Bernburger Kultur von der Schaldenburg bei Quenstedt, Kr. Hettstedt. *Jahresschrift für Mitteldeutsche Vorgeschichte* 68:179–220.

Muzzolini, A. 1986. *L'art rupestre préhistorique des massif centraux sahariens*. Oxford: British Archaeological Reports International Series 318.

Myerson, J., and L. Green. 1995. Discounting of delayed rewards: Models of individual choice. *Journal of the Experimental Analysis of Behavior* 64:263–76.

Nagaoka, L. 2001. Using diversity indices to measure changes in prey choice at the Shag River Mouth Site, Southern New Zealand. *International Journal of Osteoarchaeology* 11:101–11.

———. 2002. The effects of resource depression on foraging efficiency, diet breadth, and patch use in southern New Zealand. *Journal of Anthropological Archaeology* 21:419–42.

Naqvi, W. A., and R. G. Fairbanks. 1996. A 27,000 year record of Red Sea Outflow: Implication for timing of post-glacial monsoon intensification. *Geophysical Research Letters* 23(12):1501–04.

Nash, M. J. 1985. *Crop Conservation and Storage in Cool Temperate Climates* (2nd ed.). New York: Pergamon Press.

Nations, J. D. and R. B. Nigh. 1980. The evolutionary potential of Lacandon Maya sustained-yield tropical forest agriculture. *Journal of Anthropological Research* 36(1):1–30.

Navarrete, C. n.d. Resumen de las exploraciones del reconocimiento arqueológico de la costa de Chiapas en la temporada de. 1969. Ms. New World Archaeological Foundation, San Cristóbal de las Casas, México.

Nayar, N. M., and K. L. Mehra. 1970. Sesame: its uses, botany, cytogenetics and origin. *Economic Botany* 24:20–31.

Neff, H., B. Arroyo, J. G. Jones, D. M. Pearsall, and D. E. Freidel 2003. Nueva evidencia pertinente a la ocupación temprana del sur de Mesoamérica. In *Proceedings of the XII Encuentro Internacional: "Los Investigadores de la Cultura Maya," 11, TOMO 1, Universidad Autonoma de Campeche*, pp 20–31.

Neff, U., S. J. Burns, A. Mangini, M. Mudelsee, D. Fleitmann, and A. Matter. 2001. Strong coherence between solar variability and the monsoon in Oman between 9 and 6 kyr ago. *Nature* 411:290–93.

Nesbitt, M., and D. Samuel. 1996. From staple crop to extinction? The archaeology and history of the hulled wheats. In *Hulled Wheats: Proceedings of the first International Workshop on Hulled Wheats* (21–22 July 1995), ed. by S. Padulosi, K. Hammer and J. Heller, pp. 41–100. Roma: IPGRI.

Newton, L., and J. Zarins. 2000. Aspects of Bronze Age art in southern Arabia: The pictorial landscape and its relation to aspects of economic and socio-political status. *Arabian Archaeology and Epigraphy* 11:154–79.

Nguyen, T., and T. Bunch. 1980. Blood groups and evolutionary relationships among domestic sheep (*Ovis aries*), domestic goat (*Capra hircus*), aoudad (*Ammortragus lervia*) and European mouflon (*Ovis musimon*). *Annales de Genetique et de la Selection Animale* 12:169–80.

Nichols, D. L., and T. H. Carlton. 1997 (eds.). *The Archaeology of City-States: Cross-Cultural Approaches*. Washington DC: Smithsonian Institution Press.

Niewoehner, W. 2001. Behavioral inferences from the Skhul/Qafzeh early modern human hand remains. *Proceedings of the National Academy of Sciences USA* 98:2979–84.

Nisbet, R. 1985. Evidence of sorghum at site RH5, Qurm, Muscat. *East and West* 35(4):415–17.

Norton, C. J. 2000. Subsistence change at Konam-Ri: Implications for the advent of rice agriculture in Korea. *Journal of Archaeological Research* 56:325–48.

Nuñez, L. 1981. Asentamiento de cazadores tardios de la puna de Atacama: Hacia el sedentarismo. *Chungará* 8:137–68.

Oates, J., T. E. Davidson, D. Kamilli, and H. McKerrell. 1977. Seafaring Merchants of Ur. *Antiquity* 51:221–34.

O'Brian, M. J., and H. C. Wilson. 1988. A paradigmatic shift in the search for the origin of agriculture. *American Anthropologist* 90:958–65.

O'Connell, J. F. 1995. Ethnoarchaeology needs a general theory of behavior. *Journal of Archaeological Research* 3:205–55.

O'Connell, J. K., and K. Hawkes. 1981. Alyawara plant use and optimal foraging theory, in *Hunter-Gatherer Foraging Strategies*, ed. by B. Winterhalder and E. A. Smith, pp. 99–125. Chicago: University of Chicago Press.

———. 1984. Food choice and foraging sites among the Alyawarra. *Journal of Anthropological Research* 40:504–35.

Olivera, D., and D. Elkin. 1994. De cazadores y pastores: el proceso de domesticación de camélidos en la puna meridional de Argentina. *Zooarqueología de Camélidos* 1:95–124.

Olsen, K. M., and B. A. Schaal. 1999. Evidence on the origin of cassava: Phylogeography of *Manihot esculenta*. *Proceedings of the National Academy of Science USA* 96:5586–91.

O'Shea, J. 1989. The role of wild resources in small-scale agricultural systems: Tales from the lakes and plains. In *Bad Year Economics: Cultural Responses to Risk and Uncertainty*, ed. by P. Halstead and J. O'Shea, pp. 57–67. Cambridge: Cambridge University Press.

Oregon State University. 2000. Average Annual Precipitation Utah. Map of annual precipitation using PRISM digital data, supported by the NRCS Water and Climate Center, copyright 2000 by Spatial Climate Analysis Service, Oregon State University: www.ocs.orst.edu.

Orians, G. H., and N. E. Pearson. 1979. On the theory of central place foraging. In *Analysis of Ecological Systems*, ed. by D. J. Horn, B. R. Stairs and R. D. Mitchell, pp. 155–77. Columbus, OH: Ohio State University Press.

Overpeck, J., D. Anderson, S. Trumbore, and W. Prell. 1996. The southwest Indian Monsoon over the last 18,000 years. *Climate Dynamics* 12:213–25.

Paillés, H. M. 1980. *Pampa E. Pajón: An Early Middle Preclassic Site on the Coast of Chiapas, Mexico*. Papers of the New World Archaeological Foundation no. 44. Brigham Young University, Provo.

Paine, R. 1971. Animals as capital: Comparisons among northern nomadic herders and hunters. *Anthropological Quarterly* 44(3):157–72.

Palacios Rios, F. 1977. Pastizales de regadio para alpacas. In *Pastores de Puna*, ed. by F. Palacios Rios, pp. 155–70. Lima: Instituto de Estudios Peruanos.

Panchur H. J., and P. Hoezlmann. 1991. Paleoclimatic implications of late Quaternary lacustrine sediments in western Nubia, Sudan. *Quaternary Research* 36:257–76.

Parkes, A. 1997. Environmental change and the impact of Polynesian colonization: Sedimentary records from central Polynesia. In *Historical Ecology in the Pacific Islands: Prehistoric Environmental Change*, ed. by P. V. Kirch and T. L. Hunt, pp. 166–99. New Haven, CT: Yale University Press.

Parkes, A., and J. R. Flenley. 1990. *Final Report of the Hull University Moorea Expedition*. University of Hull, School of Geography and Earth Resources, Miscellaneous Series No. 37.

Pascual, J. L. 1989. Les Jovades (Concentaina, Alacant), habitat del Neolitic final amb estructures excavades: sitges i fosses. *Alberri* 2:9–54.

Patton, M. 1996. *Islands in Time: Island Sociogeography and Mediterranean Prehistory*. New York: Routledge.

Pavlides, C. 1993. New Archaeological Research at Yombon, West New Britain, Papua New Guinea. *Archaeology in Oceania* 28:55–59.

Pavlides, C., and C. Gosden. 1994. 35,000 year old sites in the rainforests of New Britain, Papua New Guinea. *Antiquity* 68:604–10.

Pawley, A. 1998. The Trans New Guinea Phylum Hypothesis: A reassessment. In *Perspectives on the Bird's Head of Irian Jaya, Indonesia*, ed. by J. Miedema, C. Odé and R. A. C. Dam, pp. 665–90. Amsterdam and Atlanta: Editions Rodopi.

Pearsall, D. 1989. Adaptation of prehistoric hunter-gatherers to the high Andes: The changing role of plant resources. In *Foraging and Farming: The Evolution of Plant Exploitation*, ed. by D. Harris and G. Hillman, pp. 318–22. London: Unwin Hyman.

———. 1992. The origins of plant cultivation in South America. In *Origins of Agriculture: An International Perspective*, ed. by C. Cowens and P. Watson, pp. 173–205. Washington, DC: Smithsonian Institution Press.

———. 1995. Domestication and agriculture in the New World tropics. In *Last Hunters-First Farmers: New Perspectives on the Prehistoric Transition To Agriculture*, ed. by T. D. Price and A. Gebauer, pp. 157–92. Santa Fe: School for American Research Press.

Pender, J. L. 1996. Discount rates and credit markets: Theory and evidence from rural India. *Journal of Development Economics* 50:257–96.

Pérez, M. 1999. La explotación ganadera durante el III milenio a.C. en la Península Ibérica. *Saguntum* (Extra-2):95–106.

———. 2002. Extinción de la fauna endémica y colonización humana de las grandes islas del Mediterráneo. *Saguntum* (Extra-5):147–63.

Perlman, S. M. 1980. An optimum diet model, coastal variability, and hunter-gatherer behavior. In *Advances in Archaeological Method and Theory*, volume 3, ed. by M. B. Schiffer, pp. 257–310. New York: Academic Press.

Piperno, D. R. 1998. Paleoethnobotany in the Neotropics from microfossils: New insights into ancient plant use in the New World tropical forest. *Journal of World Prehistory* 12:393–449.

———. 2001a. The occurrence of genetically-controlled phytoliths from maize cobs and starch grains from maize kernels on archaeological stone tools and human teeth, and in archaeological sediments from southern Central America and northern South America. *The Phytolitharien* 13:1–7.

———. 2001b. On maize and the sunflower. *Science* 292:2260.

———. in press. Identifying manioc (*Manihot esculenta* Crantz) and other crops in Pre-Columbian tropical America through starch grain analysis: A case study from Panama. In *Documenting Domestication: New Genetic and Archaeological Paradigms*, ed. by Melinda Zeder, Eve Emschwiller, and Bruce Smith. University of California Press.

Piperno, D. R., and K. V. Flannery. 2001. The earliest archaeological maize (*Zea mays* L.) from highland Mexico: New accelerator mass spectrometry dates and their implications. *Proceedings of the National Academy of Sciences USA* 98:2101–03.

Piperno. D. R., and J. Jones. 2003. Paleoecological and archaeological implications of a Late Pleistocene/Early Holocene record of vegetation and climate from the Pacific coastal plain of Panama. *Quaternary Research* 59:79–87.

Piperno, D. R., and D. M. Pearsall. 1998. *The Origins of Agriculture in the Lowland Neotropics*. San Diego: Academic Press.

Piperno, D. R., and K. E. Stothert. 2003. Phytolith evidence for early Holocene *Cucurbita* domestication in Southwest Ecuador. *Science* 299: 1054–57.

Piperno, D. R., A. J. Ranere, I. Holst, and P. Hansell. 2000a. Starch grains reveal early root crop horticulture in the Panamanian tropical forest. *Nature* 407:894–97.

Piperno, D. R., I. Holst, T. C. Andres, and K. E. Stothert. 2000b. Phytoliths in *Cucurbita* and other Neotropical Cucurbitaceae and their occurrence in early archaeological sites from the lowland American tropics. *Journal of Archaeological Science* 27:193–208.

Piperno, D. R., K. Husum Clary, R. F. Cooke, A. J. Ranere, and D. W. Weiland. 1985. Preceramic maize from central Panama: Evidence from phytoliths and pollen. *American Anthropology* 87:871–78.

Pohl, M. D., K. O. Pope, J. G. Jones, J. S. Jacob, D. R. Piperno, S. D. deFrance, D. L. Lentz, J. A. Gifford, M. E. Danforth, and J. K. Josserand. 1996. Early agriculture in the Maya lowlands. *Latin American Antiquity* 7(4):355–72.

Pope, K. O., M. E. D. Pohl, J. G. Jones, D. L. Lentz, C. von Nagy, F. J. Vega, and I. R. Quitmyer. 2001. Origin and environmental setting of ancient agriculture in the lowlands of Mesoamerica. *Science* 292:1370–73.

Possehl, G. L. 1987. Africa millets in South Asian prehistory. In *Studies in archaeology of India and Pakistan*, ed. by J. Jacobsen, pp. 237–56. Delhi: Oxford and IBH Publishing and American Institute for Indian Studies.

Potts, D. T. 1997. *Mesopotamian Civilization: The Material Foundations*. Ithaca NY: Cornell University Press.

Poulsen, J. 1987. Early Tongan prehistory. *Terra Australis* 12. Department of Prehistory, Research School of Pacific Studies, Australian National University.

Powell, J. M. 1970a. The history of agriculture in the New Guinea Highlands. *Search* 1(5):199–200.

Powell, J. M. 1970b. The impact of man on the vegetation of the Mount Hagen region, New Guinea. Unpublished Ph.D. Dissertation, Australian National University.

———. 1976. Vegetation. In *New Guinea Vegetation*, ed. by K. Paijmans, pp. 23–105. Canberra: CSIRO and ANU Press.

———. 1982a. The history of plant use and man's impact on the vegetation. In *Biogeography and Ecology of New Guinea*. Volume 1, ed. by J. L. Gressitt, pp. 207–27. The Hague: Junk.

———. 1982b. Plant resources and palaeobotanical evidence for plant use in the Papua New Guinea Highlands. *Archaeology in Oceania* 17:28–37.

———. 1984. Ecological and palaeoecological studies at Kuk I: Below the grey clay. Unpublished manuscript.

Powell, J. M., and S. Harrison. 1982. *Haiyapugua: Aspects of Huli Subsistence and Swamp Cultivation*. Port Moresby: Department of Geography, UPNG (Occasional Paper No. 1[New Series]).

Powell, J. M., A. Kulunga, R. Moge, C. Pono, F. Zimike, and J. Golson. 1975. *Agricultural Traditions in the Mount Hagen area*. Port Moresby: Department of Geography, UPNG (Occasional Paper No. 12).

Powell, J. W. 1885. From savagery to barbarism. *Transactions of the Anthropological Society of Washington* 3:173–96.

Pregill, G., and T. Dye. 1989. Prehistoric extinction of giant iguanas in Tonga. *Copeia* 1989:505–08.

Prell, W. L., and J. E. Kutzbach. 1987. Monsoon variability over the past 150,000 years. *Journal of Geophysical Research* 82:8411–25.

Prell, W. L., and E. Van Campo. 1986. Coherent response of Arabian Sea upwelling and pollen transport to late Quaternary monsoonal winds. *Nature* 323:526–28.

Price, T. D. 1995. Social inequality at the origins of agriculture. In *Foundations of Social Inequality*, ed. by T. D. Price and G. M. Feinman, pp. 129–51. New York: Plenum Press.

———. 1996. The first farmers of southern Scandinavia, in *The Origins and Spread of Agriculture and Pastoralism in Eurasia*, ed. by D. R. Harris, pp. 346–62. London: University College Press.

———. 2000a (ed.). *Europe's First Farmers*. Cambridge: Cambridge University Press.

———. 2000b. Europe's first farmers: An introduction. In *Europe's First Farmers*, ed. by T. D. Price, pp. 1–18. Cambridge: Cambridge University Press.

———. 2000c. Lessons in the transition to agriculture. In *Europe's First Farmers*, ed. by T. D. Price, pp. 301–18. Cambridge: Cambridge University Press.

Price, T. D., and J. Brown. 1985. *Prehistoric Hunter-Gatherers: the Emergence of Cultural Complexity*. Orlando: Academic Press.

Price, T. D., and G. M. Feinman. 2001. *Images of the Past*. Mountain View, CA: Mayfield.

Price, T. D., and A. B. Gebauer. 1995a (ed.). *Last Hunters-First Farmers: New Perspectives on the Prehistoric Transition to Agriculture*. Santa Fe, NM: School of American Research Press.

———. 1995b. New perspectives on the transition to agriculture. In *Last Hunters-First Farmers: New Perspectives on the Prehistoric Transition to Agriculture*. ed. by T. D. Price and A. B. Gebauer, pp. 3–19, Santa Fe: School of American Research Press.

Price, T. D., A. B. Gebauer, and L. Keeley. 1995. The spread of farming in Europe north of the Alps. In *Last Hunters-First Farmers*, ed. by T. D. Price and A. B. Gebauer, pp. 95–126. Santa Fe: School of American Research Press.

Protestant Episcopal Church. 1945. *The Book of Common Prayer*. New York: Church Pension Fund.

Pyke, G. H., H. R. Pulliam, and E. L. Charnov. 1977. Optimal foraging: A selective review of theory and tests. *The Quarterly Review of Biology* 52:137–54.

Rachlin, H., A. Raineri, and D. Cross. 1991. Subjective probability and delay. *Journal of the Experimental Analysis of Behavior* 55:233–44.

Rae, J. 1834. *The Sociological Theory of Capital*. London: Macmillan.

Rafferty, J. E. 1985. The archaeological record on sedentariness: recognition, development and implications. In *Advances in Archaeological Method and Theory*, Vol. 8, ed. by M. B. Schiffer, pp. 113–56. New York: Academic Press.

Rands, S. A., A. I. Houston, and C. E. Gasson. 2000. Prey processing in central place foragers. *Journal of Theoretical Biology* 202:161–74.

Ranere, A. J. 1992. Implements of change in the Holocene environment of Panama. In *Archaeology and Environment in Latin America*, ed. by O. R. Ortiz-Troncoso and T. Van der Hammen, pp. 25–44. Amsterdam: Universiteit van Amsterdam.

Ranere, A. J. and R. G. Cooke. 1991. Paleoindian occupation in the Central American tropics. In *Clovis: Origins and Adaptations*, ed. by R. Bonnichsen and K. L. Turnmire, pp. 237–53. Corvallis, OR: Center for the Study of the First Americans, Oregon State University.

———. 2003. Late glacial and early Holocene occupation of Central American tropical forests. In *Under the Canopy: The Archaeology of Tropical Rain Forests*, ed. by J. Mercader, pp. 201–48. New Brunswick: Rutgers University Press.

Ratnagar, S. 2001. Harappan trade in its 'world' context. In *Trade in Early India*, ed. by R. Chakravarti, pp. 102–27. Oxford: Oxford University Press.

Raven, C., and R. G. Elston. 1989. *Prehistoric Human Geography in the Carson Desert, Pt. I, A Predictive Model of Land-Use in the Stillwater Wildlife Management Area*. Portland: U. S. Fish and Wildlife Service Cultural Resource Series No. 3.

Read, J., G. S. Hope and R. Hill. 1990. The dynamics of some Nothofagus-dominated rain forests in Papua New Guinea. *Journal of Biogeography* 17:185–204.

Reboreda, J. C., and A. Kacelnik. 1991. Risk sensitivity in starlings: Variability in food amount and food delay. *Behavioral Ecology* 2:301–08.

Redding, R. W. 1981. *Decision Making in Subsistence Herding of Sheep and Goats in the Middle East*. Ann Arbor: University Microfilms International.

———. 1982. Theoretical determinants of a herder's decisions: Modeling variation in the sheep/goat ratio. *Animals and Archaeology. Vol. 3: Early Herders and Their Flocks*, ed. by J. Clutton-Brock and C. Grigson. Oxford: BAR International Series. 202:223–41.

———. 1988. A general explanation of subsistence change: From hunting and gathering to food production. *Journal of Anthropological Archaeology* 7:56–97.

Redman, C. L. 1999. *Human Impacts on Ancient Environments*. Tucson: University of Arizona Press.

Reed, C. A. 1977. Origins of agriculture: Discussion and some conclusions. In *Origins of Agriculture*, ed. by C. A. Reed, pp. 879–953. The Hague: Mouton.

Reidhead, V. A. 1976. Optimization and food procurement at the prehistoric Leonard Haag Site, Southeast Indiana: A linear programming analysis. Unpublished Ph.D. Dissertation, Indiana University, Bloomington.

———. 1980. The economics of subsistence change: Test of an optimization model. In *Modeling Change in Prehistoric Subsistence Economies*, ed. by T. K. Earle and A. L. Christenson, pp. 141–86. New York: Academic Press.

Renfrew, C., and K. Boyle. 2000 (eds.). *Archaeogenetics: DNA and the Population Prehistory of Europe*. Cambridge: McDonald Institute for Archaeological Research.

Reynolds, R. G. 1986. An adaptive computer model for the evolution of plant collecting and early agriculture in the Eastern Valley of Oaxaca.

In *Guilà Naquitz: Archaic Foraging and Early Agriculture in Oaxaca, Mexico.* ed. by K. Flannery, pp. 439–500. Orlando, FL: Academic Press.

Rhoads, S. E. 2002. *Marginalism.* The Concise Encyclopedia of Economics.

Rhode, D. 1990. On transportation costs of Great Basin resources: An assessment of the Jones-Madsen model. *Current Anthropology* 31:413–19.

Richards, M. P., P. B. Pettitt, M. C. Stiner, and E. Trinkaus. 2001. Stable Isotope evidence for increasing dietary breadth in the European mid-Upper Paleolithic. *Proceedings of the National Academy of Sciences* 98(11):6528–32.

Richards, P. W. 1996. *The Tropical Rainforest.* 2nd ed. Cambridge: Cambridge University Press.

Richerson, P. J., R. Boyd, and R. L. Bettinger. 2001. Was agriculture impossible during the Pleistocene but mandatory during the Holocene? A climate change hypothesis. *American Antiquity* 66:387–411.

Rick, J. W. 1980. *Prehistoric Hunters of the High Andes.* New York: Academic Press.

Rick, J. W., and K. Moore. 2001. Specialized meat-eating in the Holocene: An archaeological case study from the frigid tropics of high-altitude Peru. In *Meat Eating and Human Evolution*, ed. by C. Stanton and H. Bunn, pp. 237–60. New York: Oxford University Press.

Rick, T. C., and J. M. Erlandson. 2000. Early Holocene fishing strategies on the California coast: Evidence from CA-SBA-2057. *Journal of Archaeological Science* 27:621–33.

Rick, T. C., J. M. Erlandson, and R. L. Vellanweth. 2001. Paleocostal marine fishing on the Pacific coast of the Americas: Perspectives from Daisy Cave, California. *American Antiquity* 66: 595–613.

Ridley, B. 2001. *On Science.* New York: Routledge.

Rigsby, C., P. Baker, and M. Aldenderfer. 2003. Fluvial history of the Rio Ilave Valley, Peru, and its relationship to climate and human history. *Palaeogeography, Palaeoclimatology, and Palaeoecology* 3061:1–21.

Riley, T. J. 1987. Ridged-field agriculture and the Mississippian economic pattern. In *Emergent Horticultural Economies of the Eastern Woodlands*, ed. by W. F. Keegan, pp. 295–304. Center for Archaeological Investigations, Occasional Paper No. 7. Carbondale, IL: Southern Illinois University.

Rindos, D. 1980. Symbiosis, instability, and the origins of agriculture: A new model. *Current Anthropology* 21(6):751–72.

———. 1984. *The Origins of Agriculture: An Evolutionary Perspective.* New York: Academic Press.

———. 1985. Darwinian selection, symbolic variation, and the evolution of culture. *Current Anthropology* 26:65–88.

Rittenour, T. M., J. Brigham-Grette, and M. E. Mann. 2000. El Niño-like climate teleconnections in New England during the late Pleistocene. *Science* 288:1039–42.

Roaf, M., and J. Galbraith. 1994. Pottery and p-values: 'Seafaring Merchants of Ur?' Re-examined. *Antiquity* 261:770–83.

Roberts, N. 1998. *The Holocene: An Environmental History.* Oxford: Blackwell Publishers.

Roberts, N., and H. E. Wright, Jr. 1993. Vegetational, lake-level, and climatic history of the Near East and Southwest Asia. In *Global Climates Since the Last Glacial Maximum*, ed. by H. E. Wright, Jr., J. E. Kutzbach, T. Webb III, W. F. Ruddiman, F. A. Street-Perrott, and P. J. Bartlein, pp. 194–220. Minneapolis, MN: University of Minnesota Press.

Roberts, R. G., R. Jones, N. A. Spooner, M. J. Head, A. S. Murray, and M. A. Smith. 1994. The human colonisation of Australia: Optical dates of 53,000 and 60,000 years bracket human arrival at Deaf Adder Gorge, Northern Territory. *Quaternary Science Reviews* 13:575–83.

Roe, N. A., and W. E. Rees. 1976. Preliminary observations of the taruca (*Hippocamelus antisensus:* Cervidae) in southern Peru. *Journal of Mammology* 57:722–30.

Rogers, A. R. 1991. Conserving resources for children. *Human Nature* 2:73–82.

———. 1994. Evolution of time preference by natural selection. *American Economic Review* 84: 460–81.

Rolett, B. V. 1998. *Hanamiai: Prehistoric Colonization and Cultural Change in the Marquesas Islands (East Polynesia).* New Haven, CT: Yale University Publications in Anthropology 81.

Rolett, B. V., and E. Conte. 1995. Renewed investigation of the Ha'atuatua Dune (Nuku Hiva, Marquesas Islands): A key site in Polynesian prehistory. *Journal of Polynesian Society* 104: 195–228.

Rollefson, G. O., and I. Kohler-Rollefson. 1992. Early Neolithic exploitation patterns in the Levant: Cultural impact of the environment. *Population and Environment* 13:243–54.

Roosevelt, A. C. 1989. Resource management in Amazonia before the conquest: Beyond ethnographic projection. In *Resource Management in Amazonia: Indigenous and Folk Strategies. Advances in Economic Botany*, Vol. 7, ed. by D. A. Posey and W. Balée, pp. 30–62. Bronx: New York Botanical Garden.

Roscoe, P. 2002. The hunters and gatherers of New Guinea. *Current Anthropology* 43(1):153–62.

Rosenberg, M. 1990. The mother of invention: Evolutionary theory, territoriality and the origins of agriculture. *American Anthropologist* 92:399–415.

———. 1998. Cheating at musical chairs: Territoriality and sedentism in an evolutionary context. *Current Anthropology* 39:653–82.

Rosenberg, M., and R. Redding. 1998. Hallan Çemi, pig husbandry and the Post-Pleistocene adaptations along the Taurus-Zagros Arc (Turkey) *Paléorient* 24:25–41.

Ross, W. 1941. Present day dietary habits of the Papago Indians. Unpublished M. A. Thesis, Department of Anthropology, Tucson, AZ: University of Arizona.

Roth, B. D. 1992. Sedentary agriculturists or mobile hunter-gatherers? Evidence on the Late Archaic occupation of the northern Tucson Basin. *Kiva* 57:291–314.

———. 1995. Late Archaic occupation of the Upper Bajada: Excavations at AZ AA:12:84 (ASM), Tucson Basin. *Kiva* 61:189–207.

Roucoux, K. H., N. J. Shackleton, and L. de Abreu. 2001. Combined marine proxy and pollen analyses reveal rapid Iberian vegetation response to North Atlantic millennial-scale climate oscillations. *Quaternary Research* 56: 128–32.

Rowley-Conwy, P. 1995. Wild or domestic? On the evidence for the earliest domestic cattle and pigs in south Scandinavia and Iberia. *International Journal of Osteoarchaeology* 5:115–26.

———. 2001. Time, change and the archaeology of hunter-gatherers: How affluent is the "Original Affluent Society"? In *Hunter-gatherers: An Interdisciplinary Perspective*, ed. by C. Panter-Brick, R. H. Layton, and P. Rowley-Conwy, pp. 39–72. Cambridge: Cambridge University Press.

Rowley-Conwy, P., and M. Zvelebil. 1989. Saving it for later: Storage by prehistoric hunter-gatherers in Europe. In *Bad Year Economics: Cultural Responses to Risk and Uncertainty*. ed. by P. Halstead and J. O'Shea, pp. 40–56, Cambridge: Cambridge University Press.

Rowley-Conwy, P., W. Deakin, and C. H. Shaw. 1999. Ancient DNA from sorghum: The evidence

from Qasr Ibrahim, Egyptian Nubia. In *The Exploitation of Plant Resources in Ancient Africa*, ed. by M. van der Veen, pp. 55–62. New York: Kluwer Academic/Plenum Publishers.

Russell, K. W. 1988. *After Eden: Behavioral Ecology of Early Food Production in the Near East and North Africa*. BAR International Series 391. Oxford: British Archaeological Reports.

Rust, W. F., and B. W. Leyden 1994. Evidence of maize use at early and middle Preclassic La Venta Olmec sites. In *Corn and Culture in the Prehistoric New World*, ed. by S. Johannessen and C. A. Hastorf, pp. 181–200. Boulder, Colorado: Westview Press.

Sage, R. F. 1995. Was low atmospheric CO_2 during the Pleistocene a limiting factor for the origin of agriculture? *Global Change Biology* 1: 93–106.

Sahlins, M. 1972. *Stone Age Economics*. Chicago: Aldine.

Salmon, M. H. 1975. Confirmation and explanation in archaeology. *American Antiquity* 40: 459–70.

———. 1976. "Deductive" versus "inductive" archaeology. *American Antiquity* 41:376–80.

———. 1978. What can systems theory do for archaeology? *American Antiquity* 43:174–83.

Salmon, W. 1963. *Logic*. Englewood Cliffs, NJ: Prentice-Hall.

———. 1967. *The Foundations of Scientific Inference*. Pittsburgh, PA: University of Pittsburgh Press.

———. 1973. *Logic* (2nd ed.). Englewood Cliffs, NJ: Prentice-Hall.

Samuelson, P. A. 1937. A note on measurement of utility. *The Review of Economic Studies* 4:155–61.

Sanchez-Velasquez, L. R., R. G. Jimenez, and B. F. Benz. 2001. Population structure and ecology of a tropical rare thizomatous species of teosinte *Zea diploperennis* (Gramineae). *Revista de Biologia Tropical* 49(1):249–58.

Sand, C. 1996a. Recent developments in the study of New Caledonia's prehistory. *Archaeology of Oceania* 31:45–71.

———. 1996b. Structural remains as markers of complex societies in southern Melanesia during prehistory: The case of the monumental forts of Maré Island (New Caledonia). *Indo-Pacific Prehistory Association Bulletin* 15:37–44.

———. 1997. The chronology of Lapita ware in New Caledonia. *Antiquity* 71:539–47.

———. 1998a. Archaeological report on localities WK0013A and WK0013B of the site of Lapita

(Koné, New Caledonia). *Journal of the Polynesian Society* 107:7–33.

———. 1998b. Recent archaeological research in the Loyalty Islands of New Caledonia. *Asian Perspectives* 37(2):194–223.

———. 1999. The beginning of Southern Melanesian Prehistory: The St. Maurice-Vatcha Lapita Site, New Caledonia. *Journal of Field Archaeology* 26:307–23.

———. 2000. The specificities of the 'Southern Melanesian Province': the New Caledonian case. *Archaeology in Oceania* 35:20–33.

Sandweiss, D. H., H. McInnis, R. L. Burger, A. Cano, B. Ojeda, R. Paredes, M. Sandweiss, and M. Glascock. 1998. Quebrada Jaguay: Early maritime adaptations in South America. *Science* 281:1830–32.

Sanjur, O., D. R. Piperno, T. C. Andres, and L. Wessell-Beaver. 2002. Phylogenetic relationships among domesticated and wild species of *Cucurbita* (Cucurbitaceae) inferred from a mitochondrial gene: Implications for crop plant evolution and areas of origin. *Proceedings of the National Academy of Sciences* USA 99:535–40.

Sanlaville, J. 1992. Changements climatiques dans la Pénensule Arabique durant le Pléistocène supérieur et l'Holocène. *Paléorient* 18(1): 5–26.

Santoro, C., and L. Nuñez. 1987. Hunters of the dry puna and the salt puna in northern Chile. *Andean Past* 1:57–110.

Sauer, C.O., 1952. *Agricultural Origins and Dispersals.* New York: American Geographical Society.

Scarry, M. 1993 (ed.). *Foraging and Farming in the Eastern Woodlands.* Gainesville, FL: University Presses of Florida.

Schoener, T. W. 1971. Theory of feeding strategies. *Annual Review of Ecology and Systematics* 2: 369–404.

———. 1974. The compression hypothesis and temporal resource partitioning. *Proceedings of the National Academy of Science USA* 71:4169–72.

Schroedl, A. R. 1992. Culture History. In *The Burr Trail Archeological Project: Small site archeology on the Escalante Plateau and Circle Cliffs, Garfield County, Utah.* Cultural Resources Report 439-01-9132, ed. by B. L. Tipps, pp. 1.5–1.20. Kanab, Utah: submitted to Bureau of Land Management.

Schuiling, D. L., and F. S. Jong. 1996. *Metroxylon sagu* Rottboell. In *Plant Resources of South-East Asia 9: Plants Yielding Non-seed Carbohydrates,* ed. by M. Flach and F. Rumawas. Bogor, Indonesia: PROSEA.

Schuldenrein, J., R. Wright, M. Rafique Mughal, and M. Afzal Khan. 2004. Landscapes, soils, and mound histories of the Upper Indus Valley, Pakistan: New insights on the Holocene environments near ancient Harappa. *Journal of Archaeological Science* 31:777–97.

Schurr, M. R., and D. A. Gregory. 2002. Fluoride dating of faunal materials by ion-selective electrode: High resolution relative dating at an early agricultural period site in the Tucson Basin. *American Antiquity* 67:281–99.

Sharp, N. D. 1989. Redefining Fremont subsistence. *Utah Archaeology* 1989:19–31.

Sheets, P. 2002. Before the volcano erupted: The ancient Cerèn village in Central America, ed. by P. Sheets, Austin, TX: University of Texas Press.

Shennan, S. 2002. *Genes, Memes, and Human History.* London: Thames and Hudson.

Sheppard, C., A. Price, and C. Roberts. 1992. *Marine Ecology of the Arabian region.* London: Academic Press.

Sherratt, A. 1980. Water, soil and seasonality in early cereal cultivation. *World Archaeology* 11: 313–30.

———. A. 1981. Plough and pastoralism: aspects of the secondary products revolution, in *Pattern of the Past,* ed. by I. Hodder, G. Isaac and N. Hammond, pp. 261–306. Cambridge: Cambridge University Press.

Shipek, F. C. 1989. An example of intensive plant husbandry: The Kumeyaay of southern California. In *Foraging and Farming: The Evolution of Plant Exploitation,* ed. by D. R. Harris and G. C. Hillman, pp. 159–70. London: Unwin Hyman.

Shutler, R. J., and J. C. Marck. 1975. On the dispersal of the Austronesian Horticulturalists. *Archaeology and Physical Anthropology in Oceania* 13(2&3):215–28.

Sillitoe, P. 2002. Always been farmer-foragers? Hunting and gathering in the Papua New Guinea Highlands. *Anthropological Forum* 12:45–76.

Simms, S. R. 1986. New evidence for Fremont adaptive diversity. *Journal of California and Great Basin Anthropology* 8:204–16.

———. 1987. *Behavioral Ecology and Hunter-Gatherer Foraging.* Oxford: BAR International Series 381.

———. 2000. Farmers, foragers, and adaptive diversity, the Great Salt Lake Wetlands project. In *Prehistoric Lifeways in the Great Basin Wetlands: Bioarchaeological Reconstruction and Interpretation,* ed. by B. Hemphill, B. Larsen, and C. Larsen. Salt Lake City, UT: University of Utah Press.

Simms, S. R., and K. W. Russell. 1997. Bedouin hand harvesting of wheat and barley: Implications for early cultivation in southwestern Asia. *Current Anthropology* 38:696–702.

Simms, S. R., A. Ugan, and J. R. Bright. 1997. Plain-ware ceramics and residential mobility: A case study from the Great Basin. *Journal of Archaeological Science* 24:779–92.

Sirocko, F., M. Sarnthein, H. Erienkeuzer, H. Lange, M. Arnold, and J. Duplessy. 1993. Century-scale events in monsoonal climate over the past 24,000 years. *Nature* 364:322–24.

Sliva, R. J. 1999. Cienega points and Late Archaic Period chronology in the Southern Southwest. *Kiva* 64:339–67.

Smalley, J., and M. Blake. 2003. Sweet beginnings: Stalk sugar and the domestication of maize. *Current Anthropology* 44:675–703.

Smith, A. 1776. *An Inquiry Into the Nature and Causes of the Wealth of Nations*. London: Strahan and Cadell.

Smith, A. B. 1990. On becoming herders: Khoikhoi and San ethnicity in Southern Africa. *African Studies* 49(2):51–74.

Smith, B. D. 1977. Archaeological inference and inductive confirmation. *American Anthropologist* 79:598–617.

———. 1978. *Prehistoric Patterns of Human Behavior: a Case Studiy in the Mississippi Valley*. New York: Academic Press.

———. 1984. *Chenopodium* as a prehistoric domesticate in eastern North America: Evidence from Russell Cave, Alabama. *Science* 226:165–67.

———. 1985. Mississippian patterns of subsistence and settlement. In *Alabama and the Borderlands: From Prehistory to Statehood*, ed. by R. Reid Badger and Lawrence Clayton, pp. 64–79. Tuscaloosa: University of Alabama Press.

———. 1986. The archaeology of the southeastern United States: From Dalton to De Soto, 10,500–500 B.P. *Advances in World Archaeology*: 1–92.

———. 1987a. The economic potential of *Chenopodium berlandieri* in prehistoric eastern North America. *Journal of Ethnobiology* 7:29–54.

———. 1987b. Independent domestication of indigenous seed-bearing plants in eastern North America. In *Emergent Horticultural Economies of the Eastern Woodlands*, ed. by W. F. Keegan, pp. 3–47. Occasional Paper 7. Center for Archaeological Investigations, Southern Illinois University, Carbondale.

———. 1992. The Economic Potential of *Iva annua* in Eastern North America. In *Rivers of Change: Essays on Early Agriculture in Eastern North America*, ed. by Bruce D. Smith, pp. 185–200. Washington, DC: Smithsonian Institution Press.

———. 1995. The origins of agriculture in the Americas. *Evolutionary Anthropology* 3:174–84.

———. 1997a. Reconsidering the Ocampo Caves and the era of incipient cultivation in Mesoamerica. *Latin American Antiquity* 8(4):342–83.

———. 1997b. The initial domestication of *Cucurbita pepo* in the Americas 10,000 years ago. *Science* 276:932–34.

———. 1998. *The Emergence of Agriculture*. New York: Scientific American Library.

———. 2001a. Low-Level food production. *Journal of Archaeological Research* 9:1–43.

———. 2001b. Documenting plant domestication: The consilience of biological and archaeological approaches. *Proceedings of the National Academy of Sciences* 98:1324–26.

———. 2002. *Rivers of Change* (2d ed.). Washington, DC: Smithsonian Institution Press.

Smith, B. D., and C. W. Cowan. 1987. Domesticated *Chenopodium* in prehistoric eastern North America: New accelerator dates from eastern Kentucky. *American Antiquity* 52: 355–57.

Smith, C. E. Jr. 1967. Plant remains. In *The Prehistory of the Tehuacán Valley, Vol. I. Environment and Subsistence*, ed. by D.S. Byers, pp. 220–255. Austin: University of Texas Press.

———. 1986. Preceramic plant remains from Guila Naquitz. In *Guila Naquitz: Archaic Foraging and Early Agriculture in Archaic Mexico*, ed. by K. V. Flannery, pp. 265–74. Orlando: Academic Press.

Smith, C. S., and W. Martin. 2001. Sego lilies and prehistoric foragers: Return rates, pit ovens, and carbohydrates. *Journal of Archaeological Science* 28:169–83.

Smith, E. A. 1979. Human adaptation and energetic efficiency. *Human Ecology* 7:53–74.

———. 1981. The application of optimal foraging theory to the analysis of hunter-gatherer group size. In *Hunter-Gatherer Foraging Strategies: Ethnographic and Archaeological Analyses*, ed. by B. Winterhalder and E.A. Smith, pp. 36–65. Chicago: The University of Chicago Press.

———. 1983. Anthropological applications of optimal foraging theory: A critical review. *Current Anthropology* 24:625–51.

———. 1985. Inuit foraging groups: Simple models incorporating conflicts of interest, relatedness, and central-place foraging. *Journal of Ethology and Sociobiology* 6:27–47.

———. 1991. *Inujjuamiut Foraging Strategies: Evolutionary Ecology of an Arctic Hunting Economy.* New York: Aldine de Gruyter.

———. 1992a. Human behavioral ecology: I. *Evolutionary Anthropology* 1:20–25.

———. 1992b. Human behavioral ecology: II. *Evolutionary Anthropology* 1:50–55.

Smith, E. A., and R. Bliege Bird. 2000. Turtle hunting and tombstone opening: Public generosity as costly signaling. *Evolution and Human Behavior* 21:245–61.

Smith, E. A., and B. Winterhalder. 1992a (ed.). *Evolutionary Ecology and Human Behavior.* New York: Aldine de Gruyter.

———. 1992b. Natural selection and decision-making: Some fundamental principles. In *Evolutionary Ecology and Human Behavior*, ed. by E. A. Smith and B. Winterhalder, pp. 25–60. New York: Aldine de Gruyter.

Smith, E. A., R. L. Bliege Bird, and D. W. Bird. 2003. The benefits of costly signaling: Meriam turtle hunters. *Behavioral Ecology* 14:116–26.

Smith, P. E. L., and J. T. C. Young. 1972. The evolution of early agriculture and culture in greater Mesopotamia: A trial model. In *Population Growth: Anthropological Implications*, ed. by B. Spooner, pp. 1–59. Cambridge, MA: MIT Press.

———. 1983. The force of numbers: Population pressure in the Central Western Zagros 12,000-4500 B.C. In *The Hilly Flanks and Beyond: Essays on the Prehistory of Southwestern Asia*, ed. by T. C. J. Young et al., pp. 141–61. Chicago, IL: The Oriental Institute of the University of Chicago.

Smith, S. J. 1994. Fremont settlement and subsistence practices in Skull Valley, northeastern Utah. *Utah Archaeology* 1994:51–68.

Snyderman, M. 1983. Optimal prey selection: The effects of food deprevation. *Behaviour Analysis Letters* 3:359–69.

Soderstrom, T. R. 1969. Appendix III Impressions of cereals and other plants in the pottery of Hajar Bin Humeid. In *Hajar Bin Humeid*, ed. by G. W. Van Beek, pp. 399–407. Baltimore: Johns Hopkins Press.

Soltis, J., R. Boyd, and P. J. Richerson. 1995. Can group–functional behaviors evolve by cultural group selection? *Current Anthropology* 36(3): 473–94.

Sonnante, G., T. Stockton, R. O. Nadari, V. L. Becerra Velasquez, and P. Gepts. 1994. Evolution of genetic diversity during the domestication of the common-bean (*Phaseolus vulgaris L.*) *Theoretical and Applied Genetics* 89:629–635.

Sosis, R. 2000. Costly signaling and torch fishing on Ifaluk atoll. *Evolution and Human Behavior* 21:223–44.

Spangler, J. 1993. *Additional Evidence for Cultural Variability among Formative Peoples of the Northern Colorado Plateau.* Jackson: presented at the Rocky Mountain Anthropology Conference.

———. 2000. One-pot pithouses and Fremont paradoxes. In *Intermountain Archaeology*, University of Utah Anthropological Papers No. 122, ed. by D. B. Madsen and M. D. Metcalfe. Salt Lake City, UT: University of Utah Press.

Specht, J., and C. Gosden. 1997. Dating Lapita pottery in the Bismarck Archipelago, Papua New Guinea. *Asian Perspectives* 36:175–89.

Speth, J. D., and S. L. Scott. 1989. Horticulture and large-mammal hunting: The role of resource depletion and the constraints of time and labor. In *Farmers as Hunters: The Implications of Sedentism*, ed. by S. Kent, pp. 71–79. Cambridge: Cambridge University Press.

Spoor, R. H. 1997. Human population groups and the distribution of lithic arrowheads in the Arabian Gulf. *Arabian Archaeology and Epigraphy* 8:143–60.

Spriggs, M. 1990. Why irrigation matters in Pacific prehistory. In *Pacific Production Systems: Approaches to Economic Prehistory*, ed. by D. E. Yen and J. M. J. Mummery, pp. 174–89. Canberra: Department of Prehistory, Research School of Pacific Studies, Australian National University. Occasional Papers in Prehistory 18.

———. 1995. The Lapita culture and Austronesian prehistory in Oceania. In *The Austronesians: Historical and Comparative Perspectives*, ed. by P. Bellwood, J. Fox, and D. Tryon, pp. 112–33. Canberra: RSPAS, ANU.

———. 1996. Early agriculture and what went before in Island Melanesia: Continuity or intrusion? In *The Origins and Spread of Agriculture and Pastoralism in Eurasia*, ed. by D. R. Harris, pp. 524–37. Washington DC: Smithsonian Institution Press.

———. 1997. *The Island Melanesians.* Oxford: Blackwell.

Stadelman, R. 1940. Maize cultivation in northwestern Guatemala. *Contributions to American*

Anthropology and History, Vol. 6. Washington: Carnegie Institution of Washington.

Stanger and J. Orchard. 1994. Third millennium oasis towns and environmental constraints on settlement in the al-Hajar region, part III: Environmental factors affecting early settlement south of the Jabal al-Akhdar, Oman. *Iraq* 56:89–98.

Starfield, A. M., and A. L. Bleloch. 1986. *Building Models for Conservation and Development.* New York: MacMillan Publishing Company.

Steadman, D. W. 1989. Extinction of birds in Eastern Polynesia: A review of the record, and comparisons with other Pacific Island groups. *Journal of Archaeological Science* 16: 177–205.

———. 1993. Biogeography of Tongan birds before and after human impact. *Proceedings of the National Academy of Sciences* 90(3): 818–22.

Steadman, D. W., and P. V. Kirch. 1990. Prehistoric extinction of birds on Mangaia, Cook Islands, Polynesia, *Proceedings of the National Academy of Sciences* 87:9605–09.

Steadman, D. W., A. Plourde, and D. V. Burley. 2002. Prehistoric butchery and consumption of birds in the Kingdom of Tonga, South Pacific. *Journal of Archaeological Science* 29(6): 571–84.

Steadman, D. W., P. Vargas, and C. Cristino. 1994. Stratigraphy, chronology and cultural context of an early assemblage from Easter Island. *Asian Perspectives* 33:79–96.

Stearman, A. L. 1991. Making a living in the tropical forest: Yuqui foragers in the Bolivian Amazon. *Human Ecology* 19:245–60.

Stemler, A. 1990. A scanning electron microscope analysis of plant impressions in pottery from the sites of Kadero, El Zakiab, Um Direwa and el Kadada. *Archaeologie du Nil moyen* 4:87–106.

Stephens, D. W., and E. L. Charnov. 1982. Optimal foraging: Some simple stochastic models. *Behavioral Ecology* 10:251–63.

Stephens, D. W., and J. R. Krebs. 1986. *Foraging Theory.* Princeton, NJ: Princeton University Press.

Stevenson, J. 1999. Human impact from the palaeoenvironmental record on New Caledonia. In *The Pacific from 5000 to 2000 BP: Colonization and Transformations,* ed. by J-C. Galipaud and I. Lilley, pp. 251–58. Paris: Editions de IRD.

Stevenson, J. and J. R. Dodson. 1995. Paleoenvironmental evidence for human settlement of New Caledonia. *Archaeology in Oceania* 30: 36–41.

Steward, J.H. 1930. Irrigation without agriculture. *Papers of the Michigan Academy of Science, Arts, and Letters* 12:149–56.

———. 1933. Early inhabitants of western Utah, *Bulletin of the University of Utah Vol. 23.* Salt Lake City, UT: University of Utah.

———. 1938. *Basin-Plateau Aboriginal Sociopolitical Groups.* Bureau of American Ethnology Bulletin 120. Smithsonian Institution, Washington, DC.

———. 1941. Culture Element Distributions, XIII: Nevada Shoshone. In *University of California Anthropological Records,* pp. 209–59. vol. 4. University of California, Berkeley.

———. 1970. Foundations of Basin-Plateau Society. In *Languages and Cultures of western North America: Essays in honor of Sven Liljeblad,* ed. by E. H. Swanson, Jr., pp. 113–51. Pocatello: Idaho State University Press.

Stiner, M. C. 2001. Thirty years on the "Broad Spectrum Revolution" and paleolithic demography. *Proceedings of the National Academy of Sciences USA* 98:6993–96.

Stiner, M. C., and N. D. Munro. 2002. Approaches to prehistoric diet breadth, demography, and prey ranking systems in time and space. *Journal of Archaeological Method and Theory* 9: 181–214.

Stiner, M. C., N. D. Munro, T. A. Surovell, E. Tchernov, and O. Bar-Yosef. 1999. Paleolithic population growth pulses evidenced by small animal exploitation. *Science* 283:190–94.

Stiner, M. C., N. D. Munro, and T. A. Surovell. 2000. The tortoise and the hare: small-game use, the broad spectrum revolution, and Paleolithic demography. *Current Anthropology* 41:39–73.

Stockstad, E. and G. Vogel. 2003. Mixed message could prove costly for GM crops. *Science* 302: 542–43.

Stone, B. C. 1992. Pandanus Parkinson. In *Plant Resources of South-East Asia 2: Edible Fruits and Nuts,* ed. by E. W. M. Verheij and R. E. Coronel. Bogor, Indonesia: PROSEA.

Storey, G. R. 2000. Cui Bono? An economic cost-benefit analysis of statuses in the Roman Empire. In *Hierarchies in Action: Cui Bono?* ed. by M. W. Diehl, pp. 340–74. *Occasional Papers No. 27.* Carbondale, IL: The Center for Archaeological Investigations, Southern Illinois University.

Stothert, K. E. 1985. The preceramic Las Vegas culture of coastal Ecuador. *American Antiquity* 50:613–37.

Stothert, K. E., D. R. Piperno, and T. C. Andres, in press. Terminal Pleistocene/Early Holocene human adaptation in coastal Ecuador: The Las Vegas evidence. *Quaternary International.*

Summerhayes, G. R. 2000a. *Lapita Interaction.* Terra Australis 15. Canberra: Department of Archaeology and Natural History and the Centre of Archaeological Research, Australian National University.

———. 2000b. Recent archaeological investigations in the Bismarck Archipelago, Anir-New Ireland province, Papua New Guinea. *Bulletin of the Indo-Pacific Prehistory Association* 19: 167–74.

Sutherland, W. J. 1996. *From Individual Behaviour to Population Ecology.* Oxford: Oxford University Press.

Sutton, D. G. 1987. A paradigmatic shift in Polynesian prehistory: Implications for New Zealand. *New Zealand Journal of Archaeology* 9:135–56.

Swadling, P., N. Araho and B. Ivuyo. 1991. Settlements associated with the inland Sepik-Ramu Sea. *Bulletin of the Indo-Pacific Prehistory Association* 11:92–112.

Swartz, D. L. 1991. Archaeological testing at the Romero Ruin. *Technical Report No. 91–2.* Tucson, AZ: Center for Desert Archaeology.

———. 1996. Limited excavation at the eastern margin of the Hodges site. *Technical Report No. 96-6.* Tucson, AZ: Center for Desert Archaeology.

Szuter, C. R., and F. E. Bayham. 1989. Sedentism and animal procurement among desert horticulturalists of the North American Southwest. In *Farmers as Hunters: The Implications of Sedentism,* ed. by S. Kent, pp. 80–95. Cambridge: Cambridge University Press.

Talbot, R. K. 2000. Fremont farmers: the search for context. In *The Archaeology of Regional Interaction: Religion, Warfare and Exchange Across the American Southwest and Beyond,* ed. by M. Hegmon, pp. 275–93. Boulder: University Press of Colorado.

Talbot, R. K., and L. D. Richens. 1996 (eds). Steinaker Gap: An early Fremont farmstead. *Museum of Peoples and Cultures Occasional Papers No. 2,* Provo: Brigham Young University.

Talbot, R. K., and J. D. Wilde. 1989. Giving form to the formative: shifting settlement patterns in the eastern Great Basin and northern Colorado Plateau. *Utah Archaeology* 1989:3–18.

Taylor, D. C. 1957. Two Fremont sites and their position in Southwestern prehistory. *University of Utah Anthropological Papers* 16. Salt Lake City, UT: University of Utah Press.

Tax, S. 1963. *Penny Capitalism: A Guatemalan Indian Economy.* Chicago: University of Chicago Press.

Terrell, J. 1989. Commentary. *Antiquity* 63:623–26.

Terrell, J., and R. Welsch. 1997. Lapita and the temporal geography of prehistory. *Antiquity* 71:548–72.

Therin, M., R. Fullagar, and R. Torrence. 1999. Starch in sediments: A new approach to the study of subsistence and land use in Papua New Guinea. In *The prehistory of Food,* ed. by C. Gosden and J. Hather, pp. 438–62. London: Routledge.

Thiel, B. 1987. Early settlement of the Philippines, Eastern Indonesia, and Australia-New Guinea: A new hypothesis. *Current Anthropology* 28(2): 236–40.

Thomas, D. H. 1986. Contemporary hunter-gatherer archaeology in America: Some cheers, boos, and mixed reviews. In *American archaeology: Past and Future,* ed. by D. J. Meltzer, D. D. Fowler and J. A. Sabloff. Washington, DC: Smithsonian Institution Press.

Thomas, J. 1996. The cultural context of the first use of domesticates in continental central and northwest Europe. In *The Origins and Spread of Agriculture and Pastoralism in Eurasia,* ed. by D. R. Harris, pp. 310–22. Washington, DC: Smithsonian Institution Press.

———. 1999. *Understanding the Neolithic.* London: Routledge.

Thompson, R. S. 1990. Late Quaternary vegetation and climate in the Great Basin. In *Packrat Middens: The Last 40,000 Years of Biotic Change,* ed. by J. L. Betancourt, T. R. Van Devender and P. S. Martin, pp. 200–39. Tucson: University of Arizona Press.

Thorne, A. R. Grun, G. Mortimer, N. A. Spooner, J. J. Simpson, M. McCulloch, L. Taylor, and D. Curnoe. 1999. Australia's oldest human remains: Age of the Lake Mungo 3 skeleton. *Journal of Human Evolution* 36:591–612.

Thorne, A., and R. Raymond. 1989. *Man on the Rim: The Peopling of the Pacific.* Sydney: Angus and Robertson.

Tipps, B. L. 1992. The Burr Trail Archaeological Project: Small site archeology on the Escalante Plateau and Circle Cliffs, Garfield County, Utah. Cultural Resources Report 439–01-9132. Kanab, Utah: Submitted to Bureau of Land Management.

Torrence, R., and C. Stevenson. 2000. Beyond the beach: changing Lapita landscapes on Garua, Papua New Guinea. In *Australian Archaeologist: Collected papers in Honour of Jim Allen*, ed. by A. Anderson and T. Murray, pp. 324–45. Canberra: Coombs Academic Publishing, Australian National University.

Torrence, R., C. Pavlides, P. Jackson, and J. Webb. 2000. Volcanic disasters and cultural discontinuities in the Holocene of West New Britain, Papua New Guinea. In *The Archaeology of Geological, Catastrophes*, ed. by B. McGuire, D. Griffiths, and I. Stewart, Geological Society Special Publications 171: pp. 225–44. London: Geological Society of London.

Tosi, M. 1986. Archaeological activities in the Yemen Arab Republic, 1986. 3B Survey and excavations on the coastal plain (Tihamah) *East and West* 36(4):400–14.

———. 2001. The Harappan civilization beyond the Indian subcontinent. In *Trade in Early India*. ed. by R. Chakravarti, pp. 128–51. Oxford: Oxford University Press.

Trigger, B. G. 1998. *Sociocultural Evolution: Calculation and Contingency*. Oxford: Blackwell.

Tringham, R. 2000. Southeastern Europe in the transition to agriculture in Europe: bridge, buffer, or mosaic, in *Europe's First Farmers*, ed. by T. D. Price, pp. 19–56. Cambridge: Cambridge University Press.

Tschopik, H. 1948. The Aymara. In *Handbook of South American Indians: The Andean Civilizations*, ed. by J. Steward, pp. 501–73. Washington DC: Smithsonian Institution.

Tsunewaki, K. 1968. Origins and phylogenetic differentiation of common wheat revealed by comparative gene analysis. *Proceedings of the Third International Wheat Genetics Symposium*, ed. by K. W. Findlay and K. W. Shepherd, pp. 71–85. Canberra, Australia.

Tucker, B. T. 2001. The behavioral ecology and economics of variation, risk, and diversification among Mikea forager-farmers of Madagascar. Unpublished Ph.D. Dissertation, University of North Carolina at Chapel Hill.

———. (in prep). Do time and risk preferences differ by economic strategy? Choice experiment results in the mixed economy of the Mikea, Madagascar.

———. 2003. Mikea origins: Relicts or refugees? *Michigan Discussions in Anthropology* 14:193–215.

Tucker, B. T., and D. A. Steck (in prep). Experimental evidence for time preference among Mikea foragers and farmers: Implications for subsistence and development.

Tucker, B., and A. G. Young. 2005. Growing up Mikea: Children's time allocation and tuber foraging in southwestern Madagascar. In *Hunter-Gatherer Childhoods*. ed. by B. Hewlett and M. Lamb, pp. 147–71. Somerset, NJ: Transaction Publishers.

Turnbull, C. 1965. *Wayward Servants: The Two Worlds of the African Pygmies*. Garden City, NJ: Natural History Press.

Uerpmann, H.-P. in press. Camel domestication. *Serie Orientale Roma*. Instituto Italiano per il Medio ed Estremo Oriente, Roma.

Uerpmann, H.-P., M. Uerpmann, and S. Jasim. 2000. Stone age nomadism in SE-Arabia—palaeo-economic considerations on the neolithic site of Al-Buhais 18 in the Emirate of Sharjah, U.A.E. *Proceedings of the Seminar for Arabian Studies* 30:229–34.

Uerpmann, M., and H.-P. Uerpman. 1996. 'Ubaid Pottery in the eastern Gulf—new evidence from Umm al-Qaiwan (U.A.E.). *Arabian Archaeology and Epigraphy* 7:125–39.

Uerpmann, M., and H.-P. Uerpman. 2000. Faunal remains of Al-Buhais 18: an aceramic Neolithic site in the Emirate of Sharjah (SE-Arabia)—Excavations 1995–1998. In *Archaeozoology of the Near East IVb*, ed. by M. Mashkour, A. M. Choyke, H. Buitenhuis, and F. Poplin, pp. 40–49. Groningen (Netherlands): ARC-Publicatie 32.

Ulijaszek, S. J., and S. P. Paraituk. 1993. Making sago in Papua New Guinea: Is it worth the effort? In *Tropical Forests, People and Food*, ed. by C. M. Hladik, A. Hladik, O. F. Linares, H. Pagezy, A. Semple and M. Hadley, pp. 271–80. Paris: UNESCO.

United States Department of Agriculture. 2000. USDA Nutrient Database for Standard Reference, Release 13, Agricultural Research Service, Nutrient Data Laboratory. Accessed December, 2000. http://www.nal.usda.gov/fnic/foodcomp/Data/index.html.

Upham, S. 1994. Nomads of the desert west: A shifting continuum in prehistory. *Journal of World Prehistory* 8:113–67.

———. 2000. Scale, innovation, and change in the desert west: a macroregional approach. In *The Archaeology of Regional Interaction: Religion, Warfare and Exchange Across the American Southwest and Beyond*, ed. by M. Hegmon, pp. 235–56. Boulder: University Press of Colorado.

Upham, S., R. S. MacNeish, W. C. Galinat, and C. M. Stevenson. 1987. Evidence concerning the origin of maiz de ocho. *American Anthropologist* 89:410–18.

Upham, S., R. S. MacNeish, and C. M. Stevenson. 1988. The age and evolutionary significance of southwestern maiz de ocho. *American Anthropologist* 90:683–84.

Valmayor, R. V., and M. E. Wagih. 1996. *Musa L.* (plantain and cooking banana). In *Plant Resources of South-East Asia 9: Plants Yielding Non-seed Carbohydrates*, ed. by M. Flach and F. Rumawas. Bogor, Indonesia: PROSEA.

van Balgooy, M. M. J. 1971. *Plant Geography of the Pacific*. Blumea Supplement, vol. 6, Leyden: J. J. Groen.

Van Campo, E., J.-C. Duplessy, and M. Rossignol-Strick. 1982. Climatic conditions deduced from a 150-kyr oxygen isotope-pollen record from the Arabian Sea. *Nature* 296:56–59.

van der Veen, M. 1999. Introduction. In *The Exploitation of Plant Resources in Ancient Africa*. ed. by M. van der Veen, pp. 1–10. New York: Kluwer Academic/Plenum Publishers.

Van West, C. R. 1994. Modeling prehistoric agricultural productivity in southwestern Colorado: a GIS approach, *Washington State University Department of Anthropology Reports of Investigation* 67. Pullman and Cortez: Washington State University Department of Anthropology and the Crow Canyon Archaeological Center.

van Zeist, W. 1988. Some aspects of early neolithic plant husbandry in the Near East. *Anatolica* 15:49–67.

Varisco, D. M. 1994. *Medieval agriculture and Islamic science*. Seattle: University of Washington Press.

Vavilov, N. I. 1951. The origins, variation, immunity and breeding of cultivated plants: selected writings of N. I. Vavilov. (trans. K. Starr Chester) *Chronica Botanica* 13. Waltham, MA.

———. 1992. *Origin and Geography of Cultivated Plants* (ed. and trans. D. Löve). Cambridge: Cambridge University Press.

Vilá, B. L., and V. G. Roig. 1992. Diurnal movements, family groups and alertness of vicuña (*Vicugna vicugna*) during the late dry season in the Laguna Blanca Reserve (*Catamarca Argentina*). *Small Ruminant Research* 7: 289–97.

Vincent, A. 1985. Plant foods in savanna environments: A preliminary report of tubers eaten by the Hadza of northern Tanzania. *World Archaeology* 17:131–48.

Vivó Escoto, J. A. 1964. Weather and climate of Mexico and Central America. In *Natural Environment and Early Cultures*, ed. by Rober West, pp. 187–215. Handbook of Middle American Indians Vol. 1, Wauchope, general editor. Austin: University of Texas Press.

Vogt, B., and A. Sedov. 1998. The Sabir culture and coastal Yemen during the second millennium BC—the present state of discussion. *Proceedings of the Seminar for Arabian Studies* 28:261–70.

von Neumann, J. and O. Morgenstern 1944. *Theory of Games and Economic Behavior*.

Voorhies, B. 1976. *The Chantuto People: An Archaic Period Society of the Chiapas Littoral, Mexico*. Papers of the New World Archaeological Foundation, No. 41. Provo, UT: Brigham Young University.

———. 1989a. An introduction to the Soconusco and its prehistory. In *Ancient Trade and Tribute: Economies of the Soconosco Region of Mesoamerica*. Salt Lake City, UT: University of Utah Press.

———. 1989b. Settlement patterns in the western Soconusco: Methods of site recovery and dating results. In *New Frontiers in the Archaeology of the Pacific Coast of Mesoamerica*, ed. by F. J. Bové and L. Heller. Arizona Research Papers 39:329–69.

———. 1996. The transformation from foraging to farming in the tropical lowlands of Mesoamerica. In *The Managed Mosaic: Ancient Maya Agriculture and Resource Use*, ed. by S. L. Fedick, pp. 17–29. Salt Lake City, UT: University of Utah Press.

———. 2000a. Informe Final de las Investigaciones en Cerro de las Conchas, Municipio de Huixtla, Chiapas. Submitted to the Consejo de Arquelogía, I. N. A. H.

———. 2000b. Reconstructing Mobility Patterns of Late Hunter-Gatherers in Coastal Chiapas, Mexico: The View from the Shellmounds. Anais do IX Congresso da Sociedade de Arqueologia Brasiliera. Compact Disk.

———. 2004. *Coastal Collectors in the Holocene: The Chantuto People of Southwest Mexico*. Gainesville, FL: University Press of Florida.

Voorhies, B., and D. J. Kennett. 1995. Buried Sites on the Soconusco Coastal Plain, Chiapas, Mexico. *Journal of Field Archaeology* 22(3):65–79.

Voorhies, B., and S. Metcalfe n.d. Culture and climate in western middle America during the Middle Holocene. In *Climate and Culture Change,* ed. by D. Sandweiss and K. A. Maasch. New York: Academic Press.

Voorhies, B., G. H. Michaels, and G. M. Riser. 1991. Ancient Shrimp Fishery. *National Geographic Research and Exploration* 7:20–35.

Voorhies, B., D. Kennett, J. Jones, T. Wake. 2002. Middle Archaic archaeoogical site on the west coast of Mexico. *Latin American Antiquity* 13(2): 179–200.

Waezolt, H. 1985. Ölpflanzen und Pflanzenöle im 3. Jartausend. *Bulletin on Sumerian Agriculture* 2:77–96.

Wagner, P. L. 1977. The concept of environmental determinism in cultural evolution. In *Origins of Agriculture*, ed. by C. A. Reed, pp. 49–74. The Hague: Mouton.

Waguespack, N. M. 2002. Caribou sharing and storage: Refitting the Palangana site. *Journal of Anthropological Archaeology* 21:396–417.

Waguespack, N. M. and T. A. Surovell. 2003. Clovis hunting strategies, or how to make out on plentiful resources. *American Antiquity* 68: 333–52.

Wake, T. A., B. Voorhies, and N. Anikouchine. 2004. Food Procurement and Processing: Fish and Game Remains at the Shellmound Sites. In *Coastal Collectors in the Holocene: The Chantuto People of Southwest Mexico*. Gainesville, FL: University Press of Florida.

Walker, D., and J. R. Flenley. 1979. Late Quaternary vegetational history of the Enga Province of upland Papua New Guinea. *Philosophical Transactions of the Royal Society of London* 286:265–344.

Walczak, J. 2001. Le peuplement de la Polynésia orientale: Une tentative d'approche historique par les exemples de Tahiti et de Rapa (Polynésia Française), Unpublished Ph.D. Dissertation, Department of Ethnology and Anthropology, University of Paris, Sorbonne.

Wallace, H. D. 1995 (ed.). Archaeological Investigations at Los Morteros, a Prehistoric Settlement in the Northern Tucson Basin. *Anthropological Papers No. 17.* Tucson, AZ: Center for Desert Archaeology.

———. 2002 (ed.). Roots of Sedentism: Archaeological Excavations at Valencia Vieja, a Founding Village in the Tucson Basin of Southern Arizona. *Anthropological Papers No. 29*, Tucson, AZ: Center for Desert Archaeology.

Wang, R-L., A. Stec, J. Hey, L. Lukens, and J. Doebley. 1999. The limits of selection during maize domestication. *Nature* 398:236–39.

Wasson, R. J., G. I. Smith, and D. P. Agrawal. 1984. Late Quaternary sediments, minerals, and inferred geochemical history of Didwana Lake, Thar Desert, India. *Palaeogeography, Palaeoclimatology, Palaeoecology* 46:345–72.

Wasylikowa, K. and J. Dahlberg. 1999. Sorghum in the economy of the early Neolithic nomadic tribes at Nabta Playa, southern Egypt. In *The Exploitation of Plant Resources in Ancient Africa.* ed. by in M. van der Veen, pp. 11–32. New York: Kluwer Academic and Plenum Publishers.

Wasylikowa, K., J. Mitka, F. Wendorf, and R. Schild. 1997. Exploitations of wild plants by the early Neolithic hunter-gatherers of the Western Desert, Egypt: Nabta Playa as a case study. *Antiquity* 71:932–41.

Waterman, T. T., and A. L. Kroeber. 1938. The Kepel Fish Dam. *University of California Publications in American Archaeology and Ethnology* 35:49–80.

Watson, P. J. 1989. Early plant cultivation in the eastern woodlands of North America. In *Foraging and Farming. The Evolution of Plant Exploitation,* ed. by D. R. Harris and G. C. Hillman, pp. 555–71. London: Unwin Hyman.

———. 1995. Explaining the transition to agriculture. In *Last Hunters-First Farmers: New Perspectives on the Prehistoric Transition to Agriculture,* ed. by T. D. Price and A. B. Gebauer, pp. 21–37. Sante Fe, NM: School of American Research Press.

Watson, V. D., and J. D. Cole. 1977. *Prehistory of the eastern Highlands of New Guinea.* Seattle: University of Washington Press.

Weber, S. 1998. Out of Africa: The Initial Impact of Millets in South Asia. *Current Anthropology* 39:267–74.

Webb, R. S, R. D. Rind, S. J. Lehman, R. J. Healy, and D. Sigman. 1997. Influence of ocean heat transport on the climate of the Last Glacial Maximum. *Nature* 385:695–99.

Webb, W. S., and W. D. Funkhouser. 1936. *Rock Shelters in Menifee County, Kentucky.* Reports in Anthropology and Archaeology 3(4). Lexington: University of Kentucky.

Webster, D. 2002. *The Fall of the Ancient Maya.* London: Thames and Hudson.

Weeks, L. 1999. Lead isotope analyses from Tell Abraq, United Arab Emirates: New data regarding the "tin problem" in Western Asia. *Antiquity* 73:49–64.

Weir, G. W., and P. W. Richards. 1974. Geological Map of the Pomeroyton Quadrangle,

East-Central Kentucky. United States Geological Survey, Reston, Virginia.

Weisgerber, G. 1987. Copper production during the third millennium BC in Oman and the question of Makan. *Journal of Oman Studies* 6:269–76.

Weisler, M. I. 1995. Henderson Island prehistory: Colonization and extinction on a remote Polynesian island. *Biological Journal of the Linnean Society* 56(1–2):377–404.

Weisler, M. I., and P. V. Kirch. 1996. Interisland and interarchipelago transport of stone tools in prehistoric Polynesia. *Proceedings of the National Academy of Sciences* 93:1381–85.

Weisler, M. I., and J. D. Woodhead. 1995. Basalt Pb isotope analysis and the prehistoric settlement of Polynesia. *Proceedings of the National Academy of Sciences* 92:1881–85.

Weissburg, M. 1991. Mean-variance sets for dietary choice models: Simplicity in a complex world. *Evolutionary Ecology* 5:1–11.

Wellman, K. D. 2000 (ed.). Farming through the Ages: 3400 Years of Agriculture at the Valley Farms Site in the Northern Tucson Basin. *Cultural Resource Report No. 98–226.* Tucson, AZ: SWCA, Inc.

Wetterstrom, W. 1993. Foraging and farming in Egypt: The transition from hunting and gathering to horticulture in the Nile valley. In *The Archaeology of Africa*, ed. by T. Shaw, P. Sinclair, B. Andah and A. Okpoko, pp. 165–226. London: Routledge.

Wheeler, J. C. 1995. Evolution and present situation of the South American Camelidae. *Biological Journal of the Linnean Society* 54:271–95.

Whitaker, T. W., and H. C. Cutler. 1986. Cucurbits from preceramic levels at Guilá Naquitz. In *Guilá Naquitz: Archaic Foraging and Early Agriculture in Oaxaca, Mexico*, ed. by K. V. Flannery, pp. 275–80. New York: Academic Press.

White, J. P. 1972. *Ol Tumbuna: Archaeological Excavations in the Eastern Central Highlands, Papua New Guinea.* Canberra: RSPAS, ANU (Terra Australis 2).

———. 1996. Paleolithic colonisation in Sahul Land. In *Prehistoric Mongoloid Dispersals*, ed. by T. Akazawa and E. J. E. Szathmary, pp. 303–8. Oxford: Oxford University Press.

———. 2004. Where the wild things are: Prehistoric animal translocations in the Circum New Guinea Archipelago. In *Voyages of Discovery: The Archaeology of Islands*, ed. by S. Fitzpatrick.

Westport, CT: Praeger Publishers/Greenwood Press.

White, J. P., and M. N. Harris. 1997. Changing sources: Early Lapita period obsidian in the Bismarck Archipelago. *Archaeology in Oceania* 32:97–107.

White, J. P., J. Allen, and J. Specht. 1988. Peopling the Pacific: the Lapita Homeland Project. *Australian Natural History* 22:410–16.

White, J. P., K. A. W. Crook, and B. P. Ruxton. 1970. Kosipe: a late Pleistocene site in the Papua Highlands. *Proceedings of the Prehistoric Society* 36:152–70.

White, J. P., T. F. Flannery, R. O'Brien, R. V. Hancock, and L. Pavlish. 1991. The Balof Shelters, New Ireland. In *Report of the Lapita Homeland Project*. ed. by J. Allen and C. Gosden. Occasional Papers in Prehistory 20, Department of Prehistory, Research School of Pacific Studies, Australian National University.

Whitehead, H., and P. L. Hope. 1991. Sperm whalers off the Galapagos Islands and in the western North Pacific, 1830–1850. Ideal Free Whalers? *Ethnology and Sociobiology* 12:147–61.

Whiting, J. W., and B. Ayers. 1968. Inferences from the shape of dwellings. In *Settlement Archaeology*, ed. by K. C. Chang, pp. 117–33. Palo Alto, CA: National Press.

Whitlock, C. 1992. Vegetational and climate history of the Pacific Northwest during the last 20,000 years: Implications for understanding present-day biodiversity. *Northwest Environmental Journal* 8:5–28.

Whitney, J. W., D. J. Faulkender, and M. Rubin. 1963. Erosional History and Surficial Geology of Western Saudi Arabia. *Technical record* 04-1. Washington, DC: U.S. Geological Survey.

Whittle, A. 1996. *Europe in the Neolithic. The Creation of New Worlds.* Cambridge: Cambridge University Press.

Wickler, S., and M. Spriggs. 1988. Pleistocene human occupation of the Solomon Islands, Melanesia. *Antiquity* 62:703–06.

Wiens, J. A. 1976. Population responses to patchy environments. *Annual Review of Ecology and Systematics* 7:81–120.

Wiessner, P. 2002. Hunting, healing, and *hxaro* exchange: A long-term perspective on! Kung (Ju/'hoansi) large-game hunting. *Evolution and Human Behavior* 23:407–36.

Wigboldis, J. S. 1996. Early presence of African millets near the Indian Ocean. In *The Indian*

Ocean in Antiquity, ed. by J. Reade, pp. 75–86. London: Kegan Paul International.

Wilde, J. D., D. E. Newman, and A. E. Godfrey. 1986. The late Archaic/early Formative transition in central Utah: Pre-Fremont corn from the Elsinore Burial Site 42Sv2111, Sevier County, Utah. *Brigham Young University Museum of Peoples and Cultures Technical Series* 86-20. Provo: Museum of Peoples and Cultures.

Wilkinson, G. S. 1990. Food sharing in vampire bats. *Scientific American* 262:76–82.

Wilkinson, T. J. 1997. Holocene environments of the high plateau, Yemen. Recent geoarchaeological investigations. *Geoarchaeology* 12:833–64.

———. 1999. Settlement, soil erosion and terraced agriculture in highland Yemen: A preliminary statement. *Proceedings of the Seminar for Arabian Studies* 29:183–91.

Willcox, G. H. 1994. Archaeobotanical finds. In *Qala'at al-Bahrain volume 1: The Northern City Wall and the Islamic Fortress*, ed. by F. Højlund and H.H. Andersen, pp. 459–62. Jutland Archaeological Society Publications 30(1). Aarhus: Aarhus University Press.

———. 1996. Evidence for plant exploitation and vegetation history from three early Neolithic pre-pottery sites on the Euphrates (Syria). *Vegetation history and archaeobotany* 5:143–52.

Williams, J.T., and D. Brenner. 1995. Grain Amaranth (*Amaranthus* species). In *Cereals and Pseudocereals*, ed. by J. T. Williams, pp. 129–86. New York: Chapman and Hall.

Williamson, G., and W. J. A. Payne. 1965. *An Introduction to Animal Husbandry in the Tropics*. New York: Longmans.

Wills, W. H. 1992. Plant cultivation and the evolution of risk-prone economies in the prehistoric American Southwest. In *Transitions to Agriculture in Prehistory*, ed. by A. B. Gebauer and T. D. Price, pp. 153–76. *Monographs in World Archaeology No. 4*. Ann Arbor, MI: Prehistory Press.

———. 1995. Archaic Period foraging and the beginning of food production in the American Southwest. In *Last Hunters-First Farmers: New Perspectives on the Prehistoric Transition to Agriculture*, ed. by T. D. Price and A. B. Gebauer, Santa Fe, NM: School of American Research Press.

Wilson, H. D. 1981. Domesticated *Chenopodium* of the Ozark Bluff Dwellers. *Economic Botany* 35: 233–39.

Wilson, L. A., L. D. Wickham, and T. Ferguson. 1998. Alternative manifestations in origin, form, and function of the primary nodal complex of yams (*Dioscorea* spp.): A review. *Tropical Agriculture* 75:77–83.

Wilson, S. M. 1985. Phytolith evidence from Kuk, an early agricultural site in New Guinea. *Archaeology in Oceania* 20:90–97.

Wintch, K. W., and C. Springer. 2001. *Archaeological re-inventory and testing at the Teasdale OBA parcels in Wayne County, Utah*. Salt Lake City: State Institutional and Trust Lands Administration.

Winter, J. C., and H. G. Wylie. 1974. Paleoecology and diet at Clydes Cavern. *American Antiquity* 39:303–15.

Winterhalder, B. 1977. Foraging strategy adaptations of the boreal forest Cree: an evaluation of theory and models from evolutionary ecology. Unpublished Ph.D. Dissertation, Department of Anthropology, Cornell University.

———. 1981a. Optimal foraging strategies and hunter gatherer research in anthropology: Theory and models. In *Hunter-Gatherer Foraging Strategies: Ethnographic and Archaeological Analyses*, ed. by B. Winterhalder and E. A. Smith, pp. 13–35. Chicago: University of Chicago Press.

———. 1981b. Foraging strategies in the boreal forest: An analysis of Cree hunting and gathering, in *Hunter-Gatherer Foraging Strategies: Ethnographic and Archaeological Analyses*, ed. by B. Winterhalder and E.A. Smith, pp. 66–98. Chicago: University of Chicago Press.

———. 1983. Opportunity-cost foraging models for stationary and mobile predators. *American Naturalist* 122:73–84.

———. 1986. Diet choice, risk, and food sharing in a stochastic environment. *Journal of Anthropological Archaeology* 5:369–92.

———. 1987. The analysis of hunter-gatherer diets: Stalking an optimal foraging model. In *Food and Evolution: Toward a Theory of Human Food Habits*, ed. by M. Harris and E. B. Ross, pp. 311–39. Philadelphia: Temple University Press.

———. 1990. Open field, common pot: Harvest variability and risk avoidance in agricultural and foraging societies. In *Risk and Uncertainty in Tribal and Peasant Economies*, ed. by E. Cashdan, pp. 67–87, Boulder, CO: Westview Press.

———. 1993. Work, resources and population in foraging societies. *Man* 28:321–40.

———. 1996. A marginal model of tolerated theft. *Ethology and Sociobiology* 17:37–53.

———. 1997. Gifts given, gifts taken: The behavioral ecology of nonmarket, intragroup exchange. *Journal of Archaeological Research* 5: 121–68.

———. 2001. Recent work on the behavioral ecology of hunter-gatherers. In *Hunter-Gatherers: An Interdisciplinary Perspective,* ed. by C. Panter-Brick, R. H. Layton, and P. Rowley-Conwy, pp. 12–38. Cambridge: Cambridge University Press.

———. 2002a. Models. In *Darwin and Archaeology: A Handbook of Key Concepts,* ed. by J. Hart and J. Terrell, pp. 201–23. Westport, Connecticut: Bergin and Garvey.

———. 2002b. The behavioral ecology of hunter-gatherers. In *Hunter-Gatherers: An Interdisciplinary Perspective,* ed. by C. Brick, R. Layton, and P. Rowley-Conwy, pp. 12–38. Cambridge, England: Cambridge University Press.

Winterhalder, B., and C. Goland. 1993. On population, foraging efficiency, and plant domestication. *Current Anthropology* 34:710–15.

———. 1997. An evolutionary ecology perspective on diet choice, risk and plant domestication. In *People, Plants and Landscapes: Studies in Paleoethnobotany,* ed. by K. J. Gremillion, pp. 123–60. Tuscaloosa: University of Alabama Press.

Winterhalder, B., and F. Lu. 1997. A forager-resource population ecology model and implications for indigenous conservation. *Conservation Biology* 11(6):1354–62.

Winterhalder, B., and E. A. Smith. 1981 (eds). *Hunter-Gatherer Foraging Strategies*: Ethnographic and Archaeological Analyses. Chicago: University of Chicago Press.

———. 1992. Evolutionary ecology and the social sciences. In *Evolutionary Ecology and Human Behavior,* ed. by E. A. Smith and B. Winterhalder, pp. 3–23. New York: Aldine De Gruyter.

———. 2000. Analyzing adaptive strategies: Human behavioral ecology at twenty five. *Evolutionary Anthropology* 9:51–72.

Winterhalder, B., F. Lu, and B. Tucker. 1999. Risk-sensitive adaptive tactics: Models and evidence from subsistence studies in biology and anthropology. *Journal of Archaeological Researcy* 7:301–48.

Winterhalder, B., W. Baillargeon, F. Cappelletto, I. R. Daniel Jr., and C. Prescott. 1988. The population ecology of hunter-gatherers and their prey. *Journal of Anthropological Archaeology* 7: 289–328.

Wobst, H. M. 1978. The archaeo-ethnology of hunter gatherers or the tyranny of the ethnographic record in archaeology. *American Antiquity* 43:303–09.

Woodburn, J. 1980. Hunters and gatherers today and reconstruction of the past. In *Soviet and Western Anthropology,* ed. by E. Gellner, pp. 95–117. New York: Columbia University Press.

———. 1982. Egalitarian societies. *Man* 17:431–51.

Woodhouse, C. A., and J. T. Overpeck. 1998. 2000 years of drought variability in the central United States. *Bulletin of the American Meteorological Society* 79:2693–2714.

Woods, W. 1992 (ed.). *Late Prehistoric Agriculture.* Studies in Illinois Archaeology No.8. Springfield, IL: Illinois Historic Preservation Agency.

Wormington, H. M. 1955. *A Reappraisal of the Fremont Culture.* Denver: Denver Museum of Natural History Proceedings No. 1.

Worthy, T. H. 1997. What was on the menu? Avian extinction in New Zealand. *Archaeology in New Zealand* 19:125–60.

———. 2000. The fossil megapodes (Aves: Megapodiidae) of Fiji with descriptions of a new genus and two new species. *Journal of the Royal Society of New Zealand* 30:337–64.

Worthy, T. H., A. J. Anderson, and R. E. Molnar. 1999. Megafaunal expression in a land without mammals: The first fossil faunas from terrestrial deposits in Fiji (Vertebrata: Amphibia, Reptilia, Aves) *Senckenbergiana biologica* 79:237–42.

Wright, H. E., Jr. 1968. Natural environment of early food production north of Mesopotamia. *Science* 161:334–39.

———. 1993. Environmental determinism in Near Eastern Prehistory. *Current Anthropology* 34: 458–69.

Wright, K. I. 1994. Ground-stone tools and hunter-gatherer subsistence in southwest Asia: Implications for the transition to farming. *American Antiquity* 59(2):238–63.

Wright, M. K. 1993. Simulated use of experimental maize grinding tools from Southwestern Colorado. *Kiva* 58:345–55.

Wu Leung, W.-T. 1968. *Food Composition Table for Use in Africa.* Rome: Food and Agriculture Organization of the United Nations.

Wylie, A. 1992. The interplay of evidential constraints and political interests: Recent archaeological research on gender. *American Antiquity* 57:15–36.

Yarnell, R. A. 1972. *Iva annua* Var. *Macrocarpa:* Extinct American cultigen? *American Anthropologist* 74:335–41.

———. 1974a. Intestinal contents of the Salts Cave Mummy and analysis of the initial Salts Cave flotation series. In *Archaeology of the Mammoth Cave Area*, ed. by Patty Jo Watson, pp. 109–112. New York: Academic Press.

———. 1974b. Plant foods and cultivation of the Salts Cavers. In *Archaeology of the Mammoth Cave Area*, ed. by Patty Jo Watson, pp. 113–122. New York: Academic Press.

———. 1978. Domestication of sunflower and sumpweed in eastern North America. In *The Nature and Status of Ethnobotany*, ed. by Richard I. Ford, pp. 289–300. Anthropological Papers 67. Museum of Anthropology, Ann Arbor: University of Michigan.

Yen, D. E. 1973. The origins of Oceanic agriculture. *Archaeology and Physical Anthropology in Oceania* 8(1):68–85.

———. 1985. Wild plants and domestication in Pacific islands. In *Recent Advances in Indo-Pacific Prehistory*, ed. V. N. Misra and P. Bellwood, pp. 315–26. New Dehli: Oxford and IBH Publishing.

———. 1989. The domestication of environment. In *Foraging and Farming*, ed. by D. R. Harris and G. C. Hillman, pp. 55–75. London: Unwin Hyman.

———. 1990. Environment, agriculture and the colonisation of the Pacific. In *Pacific Production Systems: Approaches to Economic Prehistory*, ed. by D. E. Yen and J. M. J. Mummery, pp. 258–77. Canberra: RSPAS, ANU.

———. 1991. Domestication: The lessons from New Guinea. In *Man and a Half: Essays in Pacific Anthropology and Ethnobiology in Honour of Ralph Bulmer*, ed. by A. Pawley, pp. 558–69. Auckland: The Polynesian Society.

———. 1995. The development of Sahul agriculture with Australia as bystander. *Antiquity* 69 (Special Number 265):831–47.

———. 1996. Melanesian aboriculture: Historical perspectives with emphasis on the Genus *Canarium. South Pacific Indigenous Nuts* 69: 36–44.

———. 1998. Subsistence to commerce in Pacific agriculture: Some four thousand years of plant exchange. In *Plants for Food and Medicine*, ed. by H. D. V. Pendergast, N. L. Etkin, D. R. Harris, and P. J. Houghton, pp. 161–83. Kew: Royal Botanic Gardens.

Yesner, D. R. 1987. Life in the "Garden of Eden": Causes and consequences of the adoption of marine diets by human societies. In *Food and Evolution*, ed. by M. Harris and E. B. Ross, pp. 285–309. Philadelphia: Temple University Press.

Yount, J. W., Tsiazonera, B. Tucker. 2001. Constructing Mikea identity: Past or present links to forest and foraging. *Ethnohistory* 48:257–91.

Zarins, J. A. 2001. *The Land of Incense. Archaeological work in the Governate of Dhofar, Sultanate of Oman 1990–1995*. Sultan Qaboos University Publications Archaeology and Cultural Heritage Series Vol. 1. Sultanate of Oman: The Project of the National Committee for the supervision of Archaeological survey in the Sultanate, Ministry of Information.

Zeanah, D. W. 2000. Transport costs, central place foraging, and hunter-gatherer alpine land use strategies. In *Intermountain Archaeology: Selected Papers of the Rocky Mountain Anthropological Conference*, ed. by D. B. Madsen and M. D. Metcalf. Salt Lake City, UT: University of Utah Press.

Zeanah, D. W. 2004. Sexual division of labor and central place foraging: A model for the Carson Desert of western Nevada. *Journal of Anthropological Archaeology* 23(1):1–32.

Zeanah, D. W., and S. R. Simms. 1999. Modeling the gastric: Great Basin subsistence studies since 1982 and the evolution of general theory. In *Models for the Millennium: Great Basin Anthropology Today*, ed. by C. Beck, pp. 118–40. Salt Lake City, UT: University of Utah Press.

Zeder, M. A. 1991. *Feeding Cities: Specialized Animal Economy in the Ancient Near East*. Washington, DC: Smithsonian Institution Press.

———. 1995. After the revolution: Post-Neolithic subsistence in northern Mesopotamia. *American Anthropologist* 96:97–126.

———. 1996. The role of pigs in Near Eastern subsistence from the vantage point of the Southern Levant. In *Retrieving the Past: Essays on Archaeological Research and Methodology in Honor of Gus Van Beek*, ed. by J. D. Seger, pp. 297–312. Winona Lake, Indiana: Eisenbrauns/Cobb Institute of Archaeology.

———. 1998. Pigs and emergent complexity in the ancient Near East. *MASCA Research Papers in Science and Archaeology* 15:109–22.

Zeitlin, R. N. 1984. A summary report on three seasons of field investigations into the Archaic Period prehistory of lowland Belize. *American Anthropologist* 86:358–69.

Zeitlin, R. N., and J. F. Zeitlin. 2000. The Paleoindian and Archaic Cultures of Mesoamerica. *The Cambridge History of the Native Peoples* of the America, Vol. II, Mesoamerica, Part 1, ed. by R. E. W. Adams, and M. Macleod, pp. 45–121. Cambridge: Cambridge University Press.

Zhao, Z., and D. R. Piperno. 2000. Late Pleistocene/ Holocene environments in the Middle Yangtze River Valley, China and rice (*Oryza sativa* L.) domestication: The phytolith evidence. *Geoarchaeology* 15:203–22.

Zilhao, J. 1993. The spread of agro-pastoral economies across Mediterranean Europe: A view from the far west. *Journal of Mediterranean Archaeology* 6:5–63.

———. 1998. On logical and empirical aspects of the Mesolithic-Neolithic transition in the Iberian Peninsula. *Current Anthropology* 39:690–98.

———. 2000. From the Mesolithic to the Neolithic in the Iberian Peninsula. In *Europe's First Farmers*, ed. by T. D. Price, pp. 144–82. Cambridge: Cambridge University Press.

Zohary, D., and M. Hopf. 2000. *Domestication of Plants in the Old World: The Origin and Spread of Cultivated Plants in West Asia, Europe and the Nile Valley* (3rd Edition). Oxford: Oxford University Press.

Zvelebil, M. 1986a. Mesolithic societies and the transition to farming: Problems of time, scale and organisation, in *Hunters in Transition: Mesolithic Societies of Temperate Eurasia and Their Transition to Farming*, ed. by M. Zvelebil, pp. 167–88. Cambridge: Cambridge University Press.

———. 1986b (ed.). *Hunters in Transition: Mesolithic Societies of Temperate Eurasia and Their Transition to Farming*. Cambridge: Cambridge University Press.

———. 1993. Hunters or farmers: The Neolithic and Bronze Age societies of north-east Europe. In *Cultural Transformations and Interactions in Eastern Europe*, ed. by J. C. Chapman and P.M. Dolvkhanov, pp. 146–62. Brookfield: Aldershot.

———. 1995. Hunting, gathering, or husbandy? Management of food resources by the late Mesolithic communities of temperate Europe. In *Before Farming: Hunter-Gatherer Society and Subsistence*, ed. by D. V. Campana, pp. 323–45. Philadelphia, PA: University of Pennsylvania Museum of Archaeology and Anthropology.

———. 1996. The agricultural frontier and the transition to farming in the circum-Baltic region. In *The Origins and Spread of Agriculture and Pastoralism in Eurasia*, ed. by D. R. Harris, pp. 323–45. Washington, DC: Smithsonian Institution Press.

Zvelebil, M., and M. Lillie. 2000. Transition to agriculture in eastern Europe. In *Europe's First Farmers*, ed. by T. D. Price, pp. 57–92. Cambridge: Cambridge University Press.

INDEX

acacia *(Acacia gerrardi)*, 227, 234

Acapetahua region (Mexico), 105f, 118–19, 132, 133, 134

accumulation, 29, 30, 316–17, 319. *See also* storage

Aché foragers of Paraguay, 112, 114, 144, 146, 147t, 166n.5, 290, 298; human behavioral ecology and, 309, 310, 311, 320; hunting by, 312f, 314

acorns *(Quercus)*, 9, 47, 98f, 101, 145t, 298

acquisition costs, 301–2; net acquisition rate and, 13, 14, 24, 25

affluence, of foragers, 140, 144

Africa: animal husbandry/pastoralism in, 168, 198, 215, 220; domesticated crops from, 228–29, 230t; rainforest peoples of, 38, 166n.3. *See also specific country*

agent-based modeling, 19

agricultural cycle, 94–95, 96, 313

agricultural intensification, 104, 317–18, 322

agricultural revolution, 165

agriculture: defined, 238; delayed reward in, 25

agriculture, transition to, 1–11, 65, 197; anthropology and, 304–5; climate change and, 3, 5–6, 9, 10; definitions in, 2–4; demographic pressure and, 5; domestication and, 3–4; in eastern Spain, 199–204; environmental change and, 5–6; food scarcity and, 316–17; forces employed in, 4–7; HBE research on, 7–11, 21; research traditions and, 4–5; significance of, 1–2; socioeconomic competition and, 6–7; subsistence strategies compared, 3. *See also* Arizona, early Agricultural period in

Aguadulce rock shelter (Panama), 121, 122, 155

Aldenderfer, M., 167

Allee effect, 16, 205–6, 214; in colonization of Oceania, 271–73, 283, 287, 288

alluvial soils, 49, 107. *See also* flood-plain farming

Alocasia macrorrhiza (giant taro), 245, 246, 259

alpaca *(Lama pacos)*, 168

Alvard, M. S., 168–69, 188–89, 192

Amaranthus spp. (pigweed), 75, 77, 86n.5, 244t, 246, 260t; Fremont and, 92, 93

Amazon foragers, 146, 149, 152, 159, 166nn.3–4

Ambrosia trifida (giant ragweed), 50

American tropics. *See* neotropics, plant domestication in

Andean highlands. *See* Asana valley (Peru)

Anderson, A., 265, 277, 281, 318

Andrevola kings (Madagascar), 23

animal domestication/husbandry, 3, 4; in Andean highlands, 167, 168, 193 (*See also* Asana valley (Peru); costs of, 211–12; discount rate in, 33; foraging theory and, 198; meat production and, 208, 211, 212–13, 214; in Neolithic Spain, 202–3, 206–12; secondary products from, 168–69, 203, 204, 207, 208–11, 212; in south Arabia, 218–19. *See also* pastoralism/herding; *specific domesticates*

animal translocation, 265, 277

anthropogenic disturbance, 246, 248–50, 253–54, 257, 261; plant translocation, 250, 258. *See also* burning

anthropology, 304–5, 321

anticipated value, 29–30, 35

Apodanthera (wild melon), 161

Arabia. *See* South Arabia, agriculture in; Yemen

Araceae (aroids), 259, 263. *See also* taro

arboriculture, 245, 261, 277, 278, 283. *See also* tree crops; *specific species*

archaeological record, 5, 10, 295, 297, 298, 302; HBE and, 19, 305–6, 308, 311–12, 320–21, 322

Arenal de la Costa (Spain), 200f, 201, 202f, 203

Argentina, 195

Linearbandkeramik (LBK) culture group, 199
Lithocarpus spp., 247, 248
littoral zone. *See* coastal plain
llama *(Lama glama)*, 168. *See also* guanaco; taruca; vicuña
Los Posos (Arizona), 67f, 68f
Lotka-Volterra model, 106, 128–31, 134–35
low-level food production, 4, 54, 64, 83, 131, 299; HBE and, 308, 310, 313, 318–20; in Oceania, 281, 284, 286–87; in south Arabia, 218, 220, 223, 225, 228, 235

maca *(Lepidium meyenii)*, 168
MacArthur, R. H., 267, 306
McClure, S. B., 197, 319
McCorriston, J., 217
Mace, R., 33, 198, 215
McGuire, K., 194
Machiguenga of Peru, 7–8, 146, 147t, 166n.5
Madagascar. *See* Mikea of Madagascar
Madsen, D. B., 43–44, 54, 62, 86n.5, 117
maize-beans-squash economy, 77, 92, 104–5, 124, 134, 292–93
maize *(Zea mays)* horticulture, 9, 152, 154f, 155–56, 159, 198; ceramic technology and, 63, 64, 81–82, 88t, 90, 91, 93, 319; in early Agricultural period Arizona, 63–66, 68–69, 71t, 74, 77, 78, 80, 81, 84n.2; in Fremont culture (Utah), 87–88, 90, 92, 93, 94–99, 100t, 101, 310; manioc and, 146; of Mikea in Madagascar, 23, 24, 30, 33–34, 36, 134, 135, 313–14; time and labor investment for, 54. *See also* teosinte (wild maize)
maize *(Zea mays)* horticulture in Soconusco (Mexico), 103–6, 111, 113, 121–35; adoption of, 131–33; ceramic technology and, 124, 135; domestication and dispersal, 121–23; Lotka-Volterra model and, 106, 128–31, 134–35; return rates for, 123–28. *See also* Soconusco (Mexico)
malaria, 283, 284
Malaysia, 143t, 145t
Mangaia rock shelters (Cook Islands), 276
manioc *(Manihot esculenta)*, 23, 34, 159; in neotropics, 146, 153, 154f, 155, 157, 159
Man the Hunter conference (1966), 140
Maranta arundinacea (arrowroot), 153, 154f, 155, 157
marginal value, 11, 12, 13, 31; rate of substitution and, 28; theorem of, 15–16, 18, 241, 256, 264
marine resources, 156, 283, 286–87. *See also* clams; fishing; mollusks; shellfish
maritime technology, 272, 274, 284, 285, 286
market economy, 38. *See also* trade
marsh clams *(Polymesoda radiata)*, 109t, 115, 119, 120, 132, 134
marsupials, translocation of, 250, 277, 283
Martorama, D., 103

mashua *(Tropaeolum tuberosum)*, 168
Masikoro (Madagascar), 23, 24, 38
maximum sustainable yield (MSY), 187, 188, 189
maximum transport distance (MTD), 44, 62, 117. *See also* travel/transport costs
Maya, 112–14, 124, 125, 125t, 126
maygrass *(Phalaris caroliniana)*, 47, 52, 58, 293
Mazama americana (brocket), 113, 113t, 114t, 143t, 144
Mazatán region, Mexico, 105f, 132, 133, 134
Mazur, J. E., 27, 28
Mbuti pygmies (Zaire), 166n.3
meat production, 208, 211, 212–13, 214. *See also* animal domestication
Mediterranean climate, 231, 233
Melanesia, 143t, 237, 242; Austronesian influence in, 240, 245–46, 247; Lapita cultural complex in, 239, 275, 279–80. *See also* New Guinea, agriculture in; Oceania, colonization of
Meleagris gallopavo (turkey), 47
men, hunting and, 195; costly signaling and, 190, 192, 193, 194; fitness of, 188; status competition by, 167, 169, 171–72, 183, 190, 192, 193. *See also* labor, sexual division of
Menger, C., 306
Mesoamerica, 161, 319; maize horticulture in, 104, 106, 124, 127. *See also* Mexico
mesquite *(Prosopis juliflora)*, 71t, 75, 85n.4
Metroxylon sagu (sago), 243, 247, 256, 258, 262, 263; colonization of Oceania and, 276; return rate for, 259, 260t, 261
Mexico, 38, 161, 293; Acapetahua region, 105f, 118–19, 132, 133, 134; maize horticulture in, 54, 155, 156. *See also* Soconusco (Mexico)
microclimates, 45. *See also* climate change
microeconomics, 11–12, 20, 42, 135, 218
migration, 199, 318; of Andean camelids, 174; despotic behavior and, 269. *See also* mobility; Oceania, colonization of
Mikea of Madagascar, 22–40, 281, 311, 317, 319; delayed rewards and, 24, 29–30, 31, 33t, 36; discounting and, 24, 34–35, 36, 313–14, 316; foraging/farming model, 4, 34–37, 104; hunger penalty and, 34, 36, 37–38; maize and, 23, 24, 29, 33–34, 36, 134, 135, 313–14; Masikoro compared, 23, 24, 38
milk production, 210, 211t. *See also* animal domestication, secondary products from
millet *(Pennisetum* spp.), 160, 220, 228, 229, 230t, 233, 234
Moa extinction, 282
mobility, 17, 116, 144, 180, 283, 322; in New Guinea highlands, 241, 243, 255, 256, 257, 261–63; residential, 83, 92, 225, 227; seasonal, 226. *See also* migration
modern humans *(Homo sapiens)*, 158–59, 163, 266, 274
molle trees *(Schinus molle)*, 172